YOUR QUESTIONS ANSWERED

THE

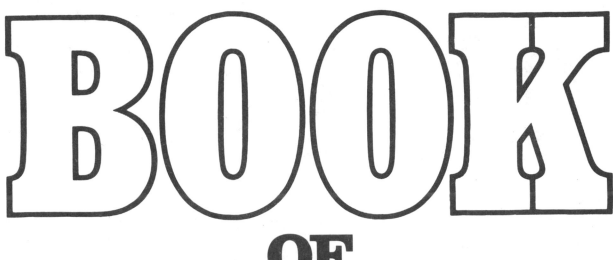

BOOK

OF
KNOWLEDGE

DEAN

Contents

Our Mysterious Earth

How old is

THE idea that the Earth is round was first suggested by the Greek thinker Pythagoras in the 6th century B.C., but it was not until a very few years ago that man was able to look down from space and see his round, cloud-covered planet for himself.

The Earth really is round — or nearly round. It is, in fact, almost an oblate spheroid — a sphere slightly flattened at the poles.

But we mustn't exaggerate this flattening. If the Earth was the size of a football, lying on a table before you, you would be quite unable to see any flattening at the top and bottom; it would appear to be a perfect sphere. And on the same scale, the highest land masses such as the Himalayas would be no higher than a coat of paint on our football;

the deepest ocean trenches would be almost invisible scratches in the paint.

The Earth's structure is made up of three basic layers. The outer layer, the *crust*, is very thin; it varies in thickness between 31 km. (20 miles) under the continents to a mere 5 km. (3 miles) under the oceans. Beneath the continents, the crust is made up of two layers of rock.

The top layer, called the *sial*, consists of rocks like granite. The sial layer rests on a denser layer of rocks such as basalt — the *sima*. This denser rock layer extends under the oceans, but there is no sial layer under the Earth's oceans, and this is why the crust is thinner there. Geologists think of the sial layer as floating on the denser sima. Temperatures deep in the crust may be as high as 870°C.

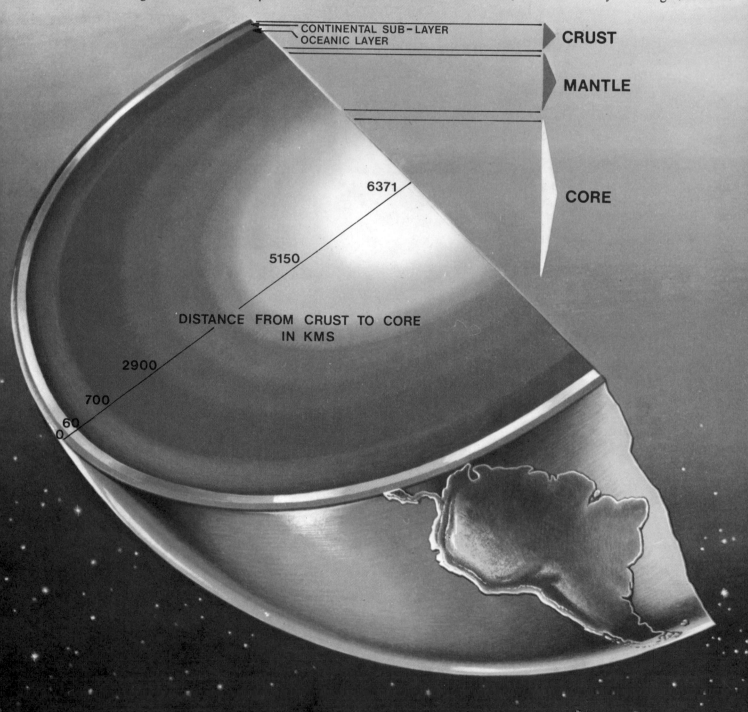

CONTINENTAL SUB-LAYER
OCEANIC LAYER

CRUST

MANTLE

CORE

6371

5150

DISTANCE FROM CRUST TO CORE
IN KMS

2900

700

60
0

the Earth?

Beneath the Earth's crust lies a much thicker layer called the *mantle*, a layer which man has never reached, even in his deepest drilling. Boreholes have been sunk to depths of nearly 8 km. (5 miles) in the search for oil. The mantle is about 2,800 km. (1750 miles) thick and forms about three-quarters of the whole Earth. It consists of solid rock at temperatures which vary from about 870°C (1600°F) near the crust to over 2200°C (4000°F) at its greatest depths.

Beneath the mantle lies the Earth's *core*, a great ball which may consist of molten iron under enormous pressure — perhaps 20,000 tons per square inch. It is this central core that is the source of the Earth's magnetic field since the liquid iron in it generates its own electricity.

THE CREATION OF OUR PLANET

Even today, no one can say for certain how the Earth began. Since the dawn of history, men have put forward theories about its creation. But in the light of recent knowledge, the probability is that the Earth formed over billions of years from a whirling cloud of gas and dust, circling around the Sun, which was then a new star. The effects of static electricity, then of gravity, probably caused the dust particles to lump together, gradually forming a larger and larger body. The heat generated by its formation created a crust around the Earth, roughly 3,900,000,000 years ago — the date taken as the beginning of our planet's geological history.

SANDSTONE
SHALE
SANDSTONE
COAL
SANDSTONE
SHALE
LIMESTONE

A section of the upper layer of the Earth's crust, typical of Northern Europe.

The fertile top soil contains life — from insects to plant roots — but the sub-soil has no organic matter, dead or alive.

Sandstone, made of compressed sand, is referred to as a 'sedimentary' rock because the sand of which it was made was deposited as sediment by wind or water, millions of years ago.

Shale is made up of fine mud particles compressed, the deposit of an ancient river emptying into a sea nearby. Coal is plant matter — including ancient forests — turned to carbon after millions of years of compression.

Limestone is a rock composed mainly of calcium carbonate, or chalk, a sediment produced from the skeletons of long-dead sea creatures.

The vast limestone bed at the bottom of this section shows that this stratum, or layer, was under the sea for millions of years and fossils found in the limestone would back this up. The alternate layers of shale, sandstone and coal suggest that the area became a river delta, followed by a drier, desert-like environment as indicated by the thicker layer of sandstone at the top.

Very little is known about the mysterious core, as the only way scientists can obtain any information about the Earth's centre is by studying earthquake waves which travel through our planet.

THE EARTH'S LAYERS

The Earth's history is recorded in the rocks beneath our feet. For millions upon millions of years the rocks that make up the Earth's crust have been forming and re-forming. This constant change has resulted in layers of rock called *strata*, which we can often see in cliff faces — layers of rock of different ages, with the oldest at the bottom and the most recent at the top.

Rock strata hold many clues which tell geologists about the Earth's past in the area being studied — clues such as the chemicals that make up the rocks in each layer, fossils found in the layers, and the thickness of the layers

themselves. No two slices of the Earth's layer-cake are the same.

By studying successive rock layers geologists have found that life began with tiny, simple forms that gave rise to larger and more complex plants and animals. But the first simple forms of life occurred quite late in the Earth's history. Scientists believe the Earth to be about 4,600 million years old, and about half that time had passed before the first animals appeared in the seas.

During the 70 million years of the Carboniferous period, which began about 300 million years ago, vast seams of coal were produced from the rotted and compressed remains of plants. But when our coal was being formed, even the dinosaurs had not appeared on Earth. They did not evolve until Triassic times, about 225 million years ago, and they died out long, long before man's apelike ancestors appeared on the scene.

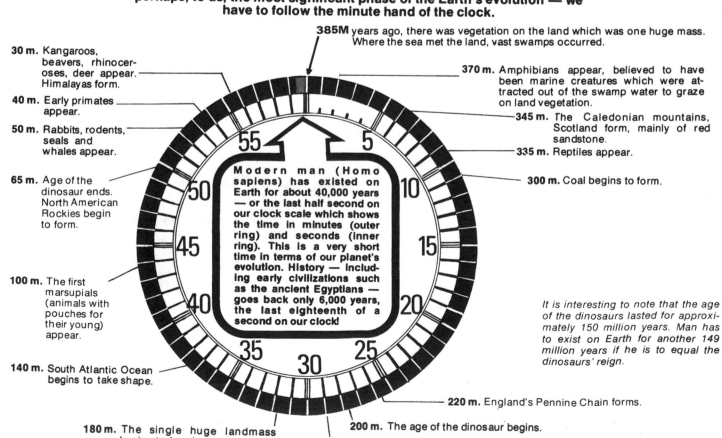

STOP-WATCH ON THE WORLD

If the period of the Earth's existence is condensed into twelve hours on a clock, it shows that most of the events which have contributed to its present-day appearance have occurred in the last 500 million years, or the final hour on the clock. The figures given are, of course, approximate ones.

435 m. Sharks and rays appear.

470 m. First fish.

570 m. Earth's atmosphere similar to today.

690 m. Sponges, jellyfish and corals form.

4,600 Million years ago, many scientists believe the Earth was formed.

3,900 m. The oldest rocks to be found on the Earth's surface today, formed at this time. *At this period, the Earth's atmosphere was still being formed.*

3,300 m. First elementary single-cell plant life forms.

3,000 m. Rocks in the Outer Hebrides, Scotland, form. Known as 'Lewisian' rock.

1,600-1,800 m. Rocks in the Grand Canyon, Colorado form.

2,500 m. Single-cell animal life appears in the sea.

To examine in greater detail the developments during this final hour — perhaps, to us, the most significant phase of the Earth's evolution — we have to follow the minute hand of the clock.

385M years ago, there was vegetation on the land which was one huge mass. Where the sea met the land, vast swamps occurred.

30 m. Kangaroos, beavers, rhinoceroses, deer appear. Himalayas form.

40 m. Early primates appear.

50 m. Rabbits, rodents, seals and whales appear.

65 m. Age of the dinosaur ends. North American Rockies begin to form.

100 m. The first marsupials (animals with pouches for their young) appear.

140 m. South Atlantic Ocean begins to take shape.

370 m. Amphibians appear, believed to have been marine creatures which were attracted out of the swamp water to graze on land vegetation.

345 m. The Caledonian mountains, Scotland form, mainly of red sandstone.

335 m. Reptiles appear.

300 m. Coal begins to form.

Modern man (Homo sapiens) has existed on Earth for about 40,000 years — or the last half second on our clock scale which shows the time in minutes (outer ring) and seconds (inner ring). This is a very short time in terms of our planet's evolution. History — including early civilizations such as the ancient Egyptians — goes back only 6,000 years, the last eighteenth of a second on our clock!

It is interesting to note that the age of the dinosaurs lasted for approximately 150 million years. Man has to exist on Earth for another 149 million years if he is to equal the dinosaurs' reign.

220 m. England's Pennine Chain forms.

200 m. The age of the dinosaur begins.

195 m. The first mammals and birds appear, existing side by side with the dinosaurs.

180 m. The single huge landmass begins to break up into continents.

How the Continents were formed

MOST of the Earth's land area lies north of the Equator — but it was not always so. Over 200 million years ago, when the earliest forms of dinosaur were beginning to roam the world, all the Earth's land was joined together in one huge mass that stretched from Pole to Pole. Since then, this vast super-continent has been breaking apart into the continents as we know them today.

In 1912, the German geologist Alfred Wegener suggested that the continents were originally a single vast continent which he called 'Pangaea', Greek for 'all-land'. He produced evidence to show that around 200 million years ago Pangaea began breaking apart. Wegener knew that the Earth's crust is made up of two main types of rock — great blocks of granite-type rock (the continents) that are embedded in heavier basalt.

He pictured the granite continents as rafts floating on the basalt crust, and he argued that they were slowly drifting. In fact, we now know that the movement of the continents is very slow indeed — between a centimetre and 12 centimetres per year.

For over 20 years Wegener's ideas were looked upon with disbelief, but as time passed, more and more evidence came to light in support of continental drift. If we compare the shapes of the coasts of western Africa and eastern South America it is seen that they would fit together rather well. And if the continents are matched, not at the shore lines, but at the centre of their undersea continental shelves, the fit is better still. America and Africa were once joined together.

It has also been found that rock formations in parts of eastern South America match exactly formations in western Africa. The theory of continental drift also helped to explain how closely related species of animals were found in lands now separated by sea.

In the course of time the continents have travelled enormous distances. By examining fossils in the rocks, and by other means, scientists are able to plot the history of a place's climate.

They know, for instance, that Antarctica was at one time in the tropics and that North America was on the Equator. By measuring magnetic field directions fixed in rocks of different ages experts have been able to plot the drift of Britain's Dogger Bank from the time when it was south of the Equator 400 million years ago.

Although the continental plates move very slowly, they move with tremendous force because of their enormous masses. Wegener showed that the advancing edge of a continent moving through the basalt crust would buckle up to form mountain chains. The Alps were formed when Europe collided with Africa, the Himalayas when Asia ran into India.

Wegener put forward another interesting suggestion in support of his theories. He studied the enormously long journey made by European eels to mate in the Caribbean, and the equally long return journey to European waters made by the young eels.

The only explanation Wegener could find for these journeys was that the eels had an inherited instinct dating back to the time when Europe and America were close together.

As geologists have found more and more clues to the history of our Earth it has become apparent that the globe on which we stand is not nearly as solid as it seems to be. Indeed, the land under our feet is constantly on the move and by studying this move-

All continents were once joined in a single land mass called Pangaea which began breaking up in late Carboniferous times (about 200 million years ago). The Tethys was a deep broad sea, of which the modern Mediterranean is the only surviving vestige, extending east-west and eventually dividing the 'supercontinents' of Laurasia and Gondwanaland. The positions of the poles gave rise to very different climatic conditions in certain areas from those today. Britain, for example, once supported tropical life.

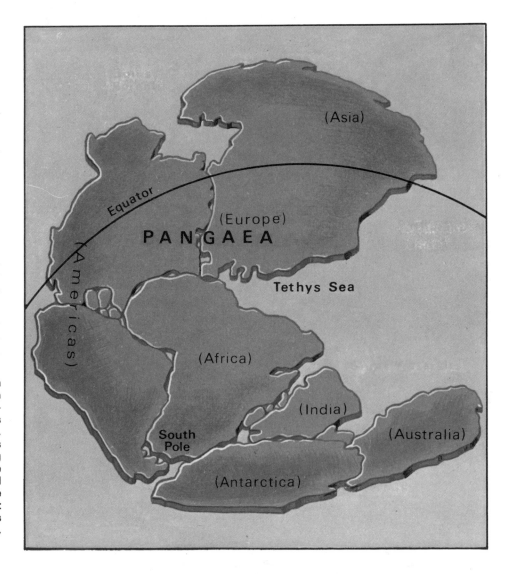

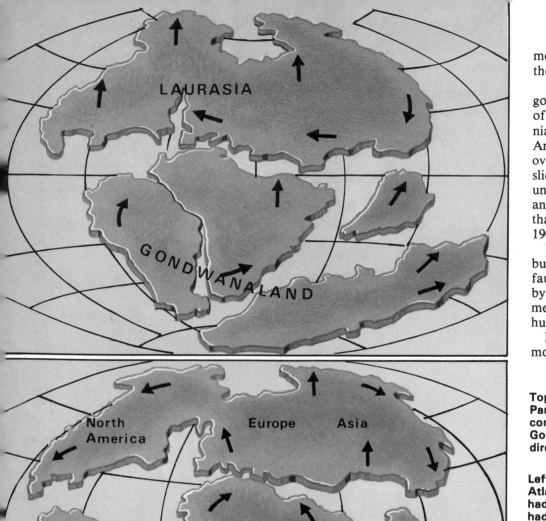

LAURASIA

GONDWANALAND

North America

Europe   Asia

South America

Africa

India

Australia

Antarctica

ment we will be able to work out what the future holds for our planet Earth.

Much research, for example, is going on into likely Earth movements of the San Andreas fault in California. At this fault the great North American continental plate is sliding over the Pacific plate. But it doesn't slide easily; huge resistance is built up until, suddenly, the rock gives way and there is an earthquake such as that which shook San Francisco in 1906.

No doubt the strain is again building up along the San Andreas fault, and this strain will be relieved by an Earth movement of only a few metres some time within the next hundred years.

Man is still helpless against the moving continents.

Top left: About 125 million years ago Pangaea had split apart into two main continental masses, Laurasia and Gondwanaland. (The arrows show the direction of movement.)

Left: About 65 million years ago the Atlantic Ocean had opened up; India had not joined up with Asia; Australia had still to separate from Antarctica; and North America and Europe were still joined.

Below: Scientists can now tell with some accuracy the likely future movement of the continents. Africa will drift north, almost closing the Mediterranean; a part of Africa will break away; and Australia will continue on its journey northward. But that's 50 million years into the future. The Oceanic trenches are deep indentations in the crust.

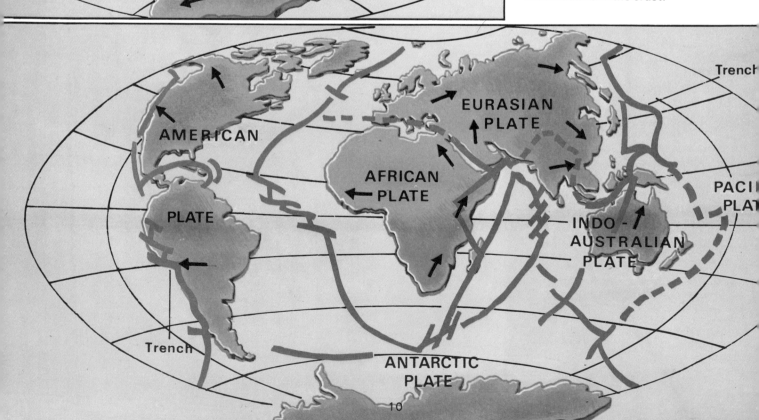

AMERICAN

PLATE

Trench

EURASIAN PLATE

AFRICAN PLATE

INDO-AUSTRALIAN PLATE

PACIFIC PLATE

Trench

ANTARCTIC PLATE

Fast-flowing streams and rivers erode deep, steep-sided V-shaped valleys, particularly if the terrain over which they flow is of soft material. These valleys become progressively steeper upstream.

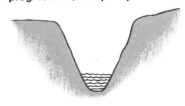

If the river reaches flatter ground, the speed of the flow lessens, the river bed becomes shallower and wider, and the river begins to wind as it seeks the easiest path to the sea. This slowing of the flow affects the way the water behaves and causes deposits to be left behind.

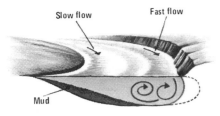

Slow flow   Fast flow

Mud

Mud carried from other parts is deposited on the inside bank of the river, building it up. Eddies on the outer edge of bends, where the water flows fastest, will eventually undercut the bank, which then falls away into the river.

How an 'ox-bow' lake forms

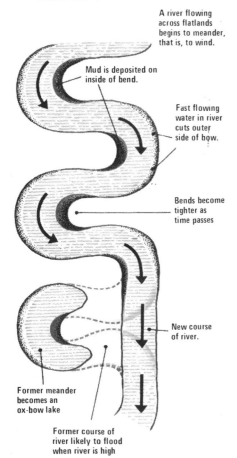

A river flowing across flatlands begins to meander, that is, to wind.

Mud is deposited on inside of bend.

Fast flowing water in river cuts outer side of bow.

Bends become tighter as time passes

New course of river.

Former meander becomes an ox-bow lake

Former course of river likely to flood when river is high

How rivers begin

Rivers and streams change the Earth's surface. Running water has the power to carve out and mould the landscape, tunnelling gorges, widening valleys, forming deltas or crashing hundreds of metres in magnificent waterfalls. The friction of the water on its bed and banks erodes the surface earth, which is carried downstream and later deposited as silt in the river's lower reaches.

Rivers start as mountain streams which have their source in underground springs, marshes, melting glaciers or rivulets caused by falling rain. As they flow downhill they are joined by other streams and rivers, known as tributaries, which add to the strength and volume of the main river. The river and its tributaries together form a river system, and the area drained by the river and its tributaries is called the river basin.

In its upper course, the river rushes down the steep mountain sides in a fast torrent, cutting a deep V-shaped valley and littering its bed with the rocks and boulders which are too heavy for it to carry downstream. Rapids and waterfalls form where it encounters a barrier of hard rock, which resists erosion, or a sudden steep slope.

Plunging Congo

The 50 metres high Niagara Falls in North America occur where a layer of hard limestone overlies softer rocks. In Africa, the Congo plunges 270 metres in a series of 32 rapids at the rim of a high plateau to form the Livingstone Falls.

In areas where there were once great glaciers or sheets of ice, such as Wales, the Lake District and Scotland, there are many waterfalls where a hanging valley meets the main valley. Glacial movement has caused the dramatic Yosemite Falls in California, which descend 700 metres in three cascades.

Falls also occur when a stream flows over cliffs into the sea, as for example, on the coast of Devon or the Isle of Skye.

Sometimes the action of a waterfall creates a tunnel as it erodes the underlying softer rock. Eventually, the roof caves in, leaving a steep-sided gorge. Where the River Axe has tunnelled its way through the Mendip Hills in Somerset, large caves such as Wookey Hole have

been formed and nearby, where the caves have collapsed, is the famous Cheddar Gorge.

The longest and deepest gorge in the world is the 480 km. long Grand Canyon of the Colorado River in the United States which reaches a depth of 1.6 km.

As the slope of the land becomes gentler the river broadens and its valley becomes wider and shallower. The river erodes the outside of its curves and deposits material on the inside. These curves, which become more and more pronounced, are called meanders. In its lower course, as it approaches its mouth, the river flows over a broad, almost level, valley in sweeping meanders. Eventually, through further erosion and deposition, some of the meanders get cut off from the main river and are left behind as crescent-shaped lagoons, called ox-bow lakes.

Fine Silt

The river is now so sluggish that it barely erodes and instead leaves behind fine silt or alluvium, which in times of flood is deposited on its banks and the surrounding plain.

Over the years some rivers, such as the Mississippi in the United States, build up their embankments, or levées, raising the level of the water above that of the adjoining land. In Holland, where the rivers Rhine, Meuse and Scheldt reach the sea, much of the land is below sea-level, and is subject to constant flooding. The Dutch have built canals, dykes and windmills to contain flooding.

The flood-plains of rivers such as the Nile and the Tigris-Euphrates, with their rich deposits of alluvium, are highly fertile and have supported populations for thousands of years.

But while flooding rivers enrich the soil, in full spate they can cause devastation. In recent years, the Po in Northern Italy, the Mississippi and the Hwang-Ho, known as 'China's sorrow', have flooded causing loss of life and extensive damage. In England, in 1952, the seaside resort of Lynmouth in Devon was ravaged by the flooding of the East and West Lyn rivers.

Flooding occurs when rivers become swollen with water at particular times of year. This seasonal variation in volume of water is

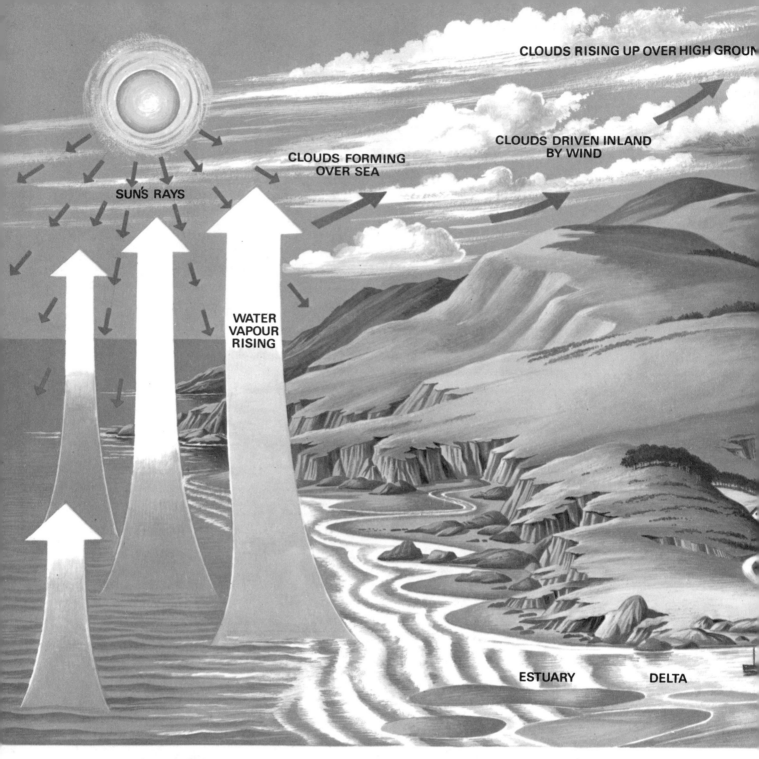

CLOUDS RISING UP OVER HIGH GROUN[D]

CLOUDS DRIVEN INLAND
BY WIND

CLOUDS FORMING
OVER SEA

SUN'S RAYS

WATER
VAPOUR
RISING

ESTUARY   DELTA

The Sun's heat beating down on the sea causes evaporation, and water vapour is drawn up into the atmosphere where it condenses to form clouds. Active volcanoes also produce water vapour.

Clouds move over the land as they are driven by wind currents in the upper atmosphere. The clouds release the water as snow or rain which falls on the hills and mountains.

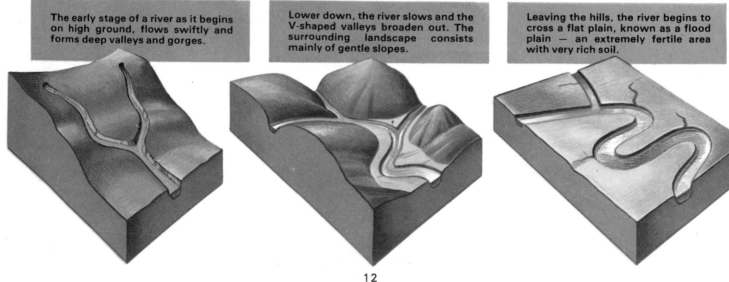

The early stage of a river as it begins on high ground, flows swiftly and forms deep valleys and gorges.

Lower down, the river slows and the V-shaped valleys broaden out. The surrounding landscape consists mainly of gentle slopes.

Leaving the hills, the river begins to cross a flat plain, known as a flood plain — an extremely fertile area with very rich soil.

RAIN CLOUDS FORMING

AIN SHEETS ON HILLS

WATER RUNNING DOWNHILL AFTER RAINFALL

LAKE

FLOOD PLAIN

FLOOD PLAIN

TIDAL BANKS

FLOW OF RIVER TO SEA

SAND BANKS

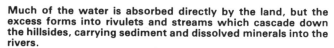

Much of the water is absorbed directly by the land, but the excess forms into rivulets and streams which cascade down the hillsides, carrying sediment and dissolved minerals into the rivers.

FEED RIVER FROM HIGHER GROUND

LAKE

RAPIDS   RAVINE

HIGH DROP WATERFALL

WATERFALL

Glaciers, or frozen rivers, move or 'flow' extremely slowly, on average only a few metres a day, sometimes only centimetres. The water which has fallen as snow becomes compacted as an ice field. When it reaches a certain thickness it begins to move downhill, and may be joined by other glaciers. When they reach lower and warmer levels, they melt and form whole river systems.

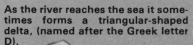

As the river reaches the sea it sometimes forms a triangular-shaped delta, (named after the Greek letter D).

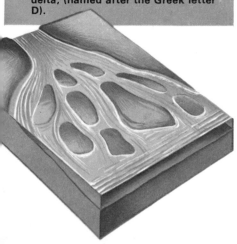

known as the river's regime, and has become very important both in flood control and in the production of hydro-electricity. The Alpine rivers, which are fed by melting snow and ice, are at their lowest during the cold winter months and at their highest in early summer when the snows are melting. But rivers which are fed mostly by rain, such as the River Seine, tend to have low water in summer when rainfall is lowest. In the tropics, rivers such as the Irrawaddy and the Yangtse flood after the monsoon.

Rivers have played a key role in Man's history from the earliest civilisations to the present day. They have been vital to the development of agriculture, and they have supplied power to meet the needs of modern industry. Today, hydro-electric power provides an essential source of energy.

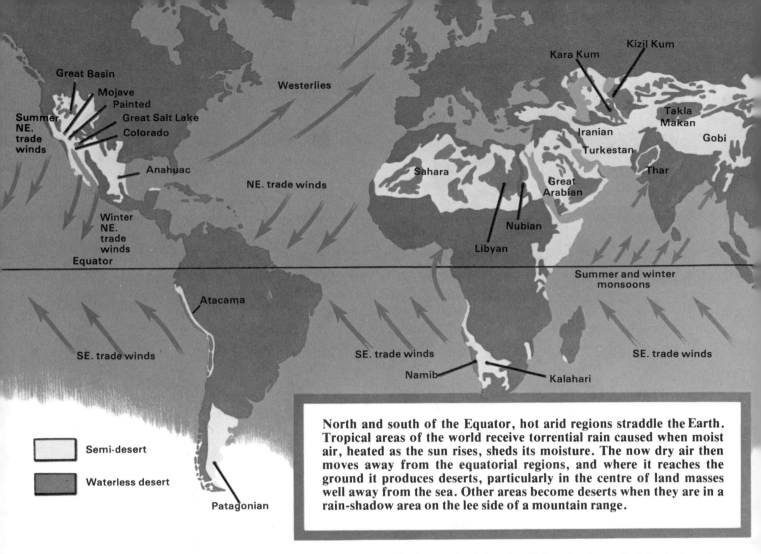

North and south of the Equator, hot arid regions straddle the Earth. Tropical areas of the world receive torrential rain caused when moist air, heated as the sun rises, sheds its moisture. The now dry air then moves away from the equatorial regions, and where it reaches the ground it produces deserts, particularly in the centre of land masses well away from the sea. Other areas become deserts when they are in a rain-shadow area on the lee side of a mountain range.

The Desolate Deserts

ABOUT a third of the world's land surface is desert or semi-desert. Deserts are dry areas, experiencing very high temperatures and little or no rainfall, with very sparse vegetation.

The great deserts of the world, including the Sahara and the Kalahari in Africa, and the deserts of Arabia and India, are found within the tropics in the interior or western sides of continents. They are sometimes called the 'Trade Wind' deserts because the trade winds, which blow either from the north-east or the south-east, have long since lost their moisture by the time they reach the centre and west of the continental land mass.

Another group of deserts, including the Gobi and

Turkestan in Asia, the Colorado desert in North America, and the Atacama in South America, lie in the rain shadow of the surrounding mountain ranges. The winds blowing in from the sea bring heavy rainfall to the high peaks, which shelter the areas immediately beyond. Many of these deserts are at high altitudes and are known as desert basins, such as the Tarim Basin in Western China and the Great Basin of North America. These desert basins have a very extreme climate, with high summer temperatures, and temperatures well below freezing in winter.

The highest temperatures in the world are found in the deserts in the interior of continents. The sun heats the dry surface soil very rapidly, which in turn warms the air above it. At night, the soil loses heat very quickly and temperatures can fall by 17 degrees Centigrade within a couple of hours of sunset.

A day-time temperature of 52°C has been recorded at Azizia in Tripoli, with a night-time temperature during the same 24 hours of —3°C, the widest temperature range ever recorded in the same place in one day.

The intense heat of the desert can cause an optical effect known as a mirage. As the sun's rays strike the layer of hot expanding air above the surface of the desert, they bend, reflecting the sky, and giving the thirsty traveller the impression of a silvery, shimmering pool of water.

The action of the wind on the bare surface of the desert reduces any loose top soil or pebbles to fine particles of sand. In some areas, the desert is covered with rocks and boulders, which are polished, smooth and chiselled by the wind-borne sand. Desert rocks are often sculpted into fantastic mushroom shapes, as the wind erodes with greatest force about a foot or two above the ground.

Where the wind encounters layers of softer rock alternating with harder rock, it eats into the softer rock causing the tiered effect typical of the valleys and canyons of Arizona and Utah in the United States.

In sandy deserts, the surface is blown into ridges and

This illustration shows the effect of wind on sandy deserts. The rises and escarpments are caused by wind pushing up particles of sand. The slopes are gentle on the side facing the wind, and steeper on the sheltered side. Ripples in the sand are also caused by the wind. Always shifting, never still, the dunes travel along, often enveloping rocks, houses and historic monuments.

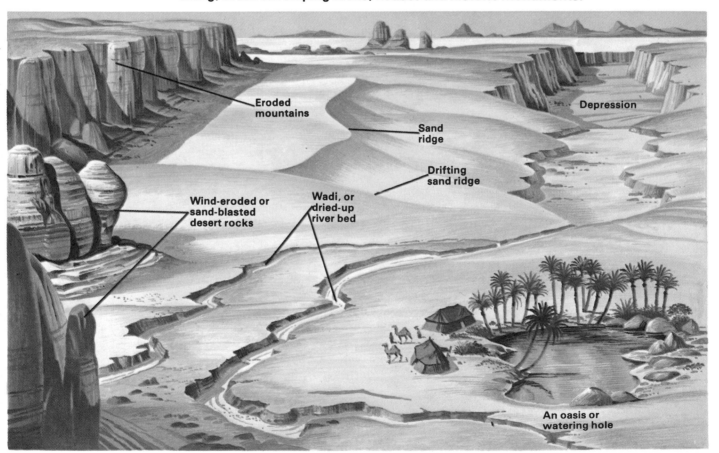

Eroded mountains

Depression

Sand ridge

Drifting sand ridge

Wind-eroded or sand-blasted desert rocks

Wadi, or dried-up river bed

An oasis or watering hole

This picture shows the various types of scenery typical in a desert region. Most erosion takes place close to the ground, and where the wind encounters layers of soft rock alternating with layers of hard rock it eats into the soft rock causing natural sculptures of great beauty. This action produces the tiered effects seen in the great canyons of Arizona and Utah in the United States of America. In the right foreground is a small oasis, and beyond it a dry river bed, a wadi, as it is called, which is often followed by travellers wanting to shelter from the wind.

15

waves by the wind. In the Sahara, there are crescent-shaped dunes, up to 30 metres in height, known as 'barkhans'. They lie at right angles to the wind's direction, with a long gentle slope facing the wind, and a steeper slope on the leeward side, away from the wind. The horns of the crescent point in the direction the wind is blowing.

These dunes are gradually moving forward like waves as the wind blows the sand up and over the sides in a steady trickle. In countries such as Libya, Egypt and Israel, belts of trees have been planted to prevent the shifting dunes from encroaching on the oases and the irrigated land.

The intense heat, the lack of fixed land-marks, and the desert sand-storms which throw up whirling clouds of dust, obscuring the view and stinging the eyes, make day-time travel in the desert hazardous and uncomfortable. In the past, caravans — strings of camels bearing spices, salt and other trading goods — used to cross the desert by night, navigating by the stars. Sometimes the route followed a wadi, a steep-sided, dry river bed, which offered some shelter from the wind. The wadis could also be treacherous, as sudden rainfall can cause a 'flash-flood', filling the river bed and engulfing travellers without warning.

Although rain is rare in the desert, it is not unknown, usually falling in brief but torrential downpours.

The desert traveller relies for water and other supplies on the oases, often found in well-defined chains, not far from the bases of mountains, as in the Sahara and the Tarim Basin. An oasis is a fertile area where water comes to the surface in a spring or from a well. Some oases are large enough to support an agricultural community, growing date-palms, maize, millet and other crops, since the desert soil, when irrigated, can be highly fertile.

Apart from oasis-dwellers, the only inhabitants of the desert are the nomadic tribes, such as the Bedouin and Tuareg, who roam the desert for pasture for their camels, sheep and goats.

Vegetation is very scanty in the desert. Plants have to

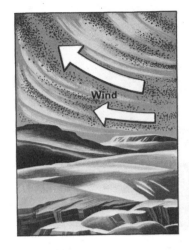

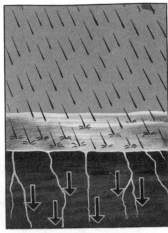

Winds blow away the last of the top soil because there are no trees, grass or other plants to hold it in place. Desert rocks are often polished smooth by the action of wind-borne sand.

As there is little plant life in the desert, any rain which may fall on the area soaks away immediately. If it can be irrigated some desert soil is fertile and many crops can be grown.

adapt to the lack of water, and have few leaves, from which they would lose moisture, and long, wide-ranging roots. The cactus family, for example, has a fleshy stem, covered with ribs, bulges and prickly spines. Some plants may lie dormant for a year or more until moisture reaches them, and they bloom again for a brief moment.

The animals which survive in the desert must also be adapted to the arid conditions and able to cover large distances without drinking. The camel stores water in its stomach and food in its hump. Its feet are padded to enable it to walk on sand and its nostrils are shaped to keep out sand and dust.

Some deserts contain valuable mineral deposits, such as gold in the Australian desert, oil in Eastern Arabia and the Sahara and nitrates in Chile.

Some deserts in areas bordering the sea have constant hot air blowing out to sea over them. This prevents any clouds from floating inland where they might produce some rain.

Rain clouds forced up to high altitudes by mountains give off rain because of the drop in temperature. As a result, no rain reaches the region behind the high ground and deserts are formed.

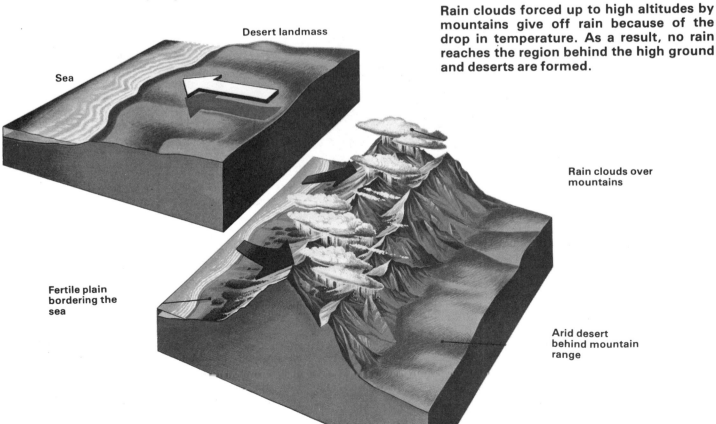

Desert landmass

Sea

Fertile plain bordering the sea

Rain clouds over mountains

Arid desert behind mountain range

Some 90 per cent of the world's snow and ice lies in Antarctica. It is a larger continent than Europe or Australia and is by far the coldest, with an average temperature of –50° Centigrade. Antarctica is covered by an ice-sheet, average two kilometres thick, formed by the accumulation of snow over thousands of years. The great weight of this ice causes the bottom layers to change in form so that they flow like syrup.

In places the ice-sheet extends beyond the coast as a floating ice-shelf. Inland, ice moving in different directions forms huge domes, terraced steps and deep crevasses or fissures. The ice-hills or ridges seen here are pressure ridges pushed up when glaciers move against the mass of the ice-sheet causing great stresses and upsurges. In isolated areas ice-free peaks protrude through the ice.

Ice on the move

C an you imagine a mountain made of ice? This is what the name *iceberg* means, and although these masses of ice floating in the sea sometimes look as big as mountains, only a small proportion of the iceberg can be seen above the water.

Icebergs form in the polar regions of Greenland and Antarctica, where it is too cold for snow to melt, even in summer. As the weight of snow increases, air is squeezed out and compact ice remains. Over thousands of years, sheets of thick ice have formed, spreading out to cover these large areas. They are called *continental glaciers* or ice sheets, and it is from the edge of these glaciers that icebergs break away to drift in the sea on ocean currents.

Four-fifths of Greenland is covered by a continental glacier. This moves over mountains and breaks up into individual smaller glaciers that reach down to the sea. But the glaciers do not stop there. They are pushed out into the sea by more ice continually moving from behind. Eventually there is no land to support the front edge which begins to float. When it becomes too heavy the ice breaks away as tall, irregular icebergs or glacier bergs.

In Antarctica, the ice-sheet is even bigger and because of this great volume the ice-sheet extends from the land in places and covers the sea as a thick ice-shelf. Stresses at the edge of the shelf cause huge, flat-topped chunks to crack

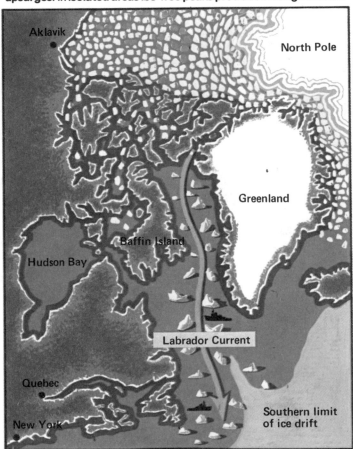

Icebergs form in the North Atlantic Ocean off Greenland and in the seas around Antarctica. In the North Atlantic, some drift south on the cold Labrador Current towards the shipping lanes connecting Europe and North America. Here they meet the warm Gulf Stream and melt. In the summer, when more icebergs form, ships have to sail further south to avoid them.

off. These icebergs, called tabular bergs, are larger and more regular in shape than glacier bergs, but not as high.

Icebergs can last for two years drifting on cold ocean currents but melt quite quickly as they pass into warmer waters, although some have been sighted within 3,000 kilometres of the Equator. Since by far the largest part of an iceberg is hidden underwater, a drifting iceberg can be a treacherous hazard to shipping. In the North Atlantic ocean especially, they often drift across the important sea routes between Europe and North America.

The most famous collision occurred in 1912 when the S.S. *Titanic* collided with a huge iceberg in mid-North Atlantic. She quickly sank with over 1,500 passengers and crew lost. After this disaster an International Ice Patrol was set up to locate and report icebergs.

However, icebergs have their merits too. They return water to the oceans from where water first comes and, as they melt, they cool the water heated by the Sun. If the oceans were not cooled much of the world would be too hot to live in.

Above: Franz Josef Glacier, Mount Cook National Park, New Zealand.

Left: Svartisen Glacier, Norway.

Below: Rhone Glacier, Furka Pass, Switzerland.
Photographs: J. Allan Cash Ltd.

Recently scientists have been investigating the possibility that icebergs could help to increase supplies of drinking water, especially in our coastal cities. Icebergs are composed of fresh water, not salt water, and if they could be towed closer to the shore floating tanks could be placed around them. The ice would melt, and because fresh water is less dense it would float on top of the salt water. We could then pump this water into our reservoirs.

The ice-sheets of the North and South Poles are areas of permanent snow, where temperatures are too low to melt the ice. But permanent snow is found at high altitudes in countries with much warmer climates. It forms the mountain glaciers found in many of the world's great mountain ranges. Glaciers form above the snow-line, where the supply of snow is greater than the rate at which it melts.

A glacier descends at an imperceptible speed until it reaches a level where the temperature is warm enough to melt it. The speed of movement was first investigated in the 19th century. In 1820, on the Glacier des Bosson on Mònt Blanc in France, three climbers fell into a deep crevasse and were buried by an avalanche. As scientists predicted, their bodies emerged at the end of the glacier, 3.2 kilometres downhill, 40 years later.

It has also been shown that the speed of a glacier is faster at the centre, where the ice is thickest, than at the sides. This difference in speed causes tension within the glacier which cracks without warning, forming deep crevasses.

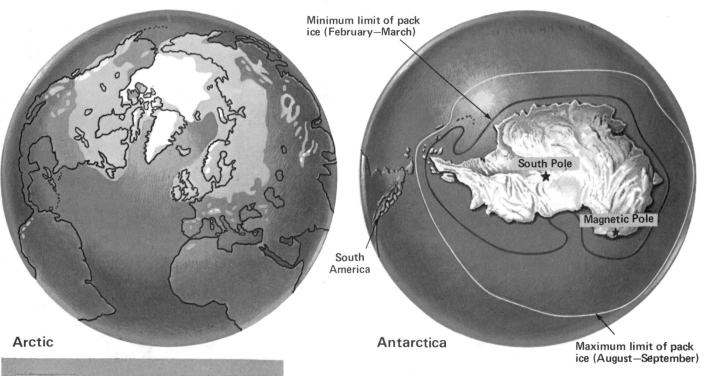

Arctic

Antarctica

Minimum limit of pack ice (February—March)

South Pole

Magnetic Pole

South America

Maximum limit of pack ice (August—September)

The ice-cap limit of the last great Ice Age

Present ice-cap limit

The polar ice-caps were much more extensive than they are now. About 10,000 years ago, during the last Ice Age, the Northern ice-cap covered much of Europe and North America. Today one-tenth of the Earth's land surface is covered by polar ice. If this melted completely it would raise the general sea level by about 60m. which would cover many major cities, including New York and London. Antarctica is an ice-covered land mass but the North Pole area includes the Arctic Ocean which is permanently covered by a floating mass of ice. Pack-ice or drift-ice is frozen sea-water which forms at the ends of the polar regions. It is not as thick or massive as the ice-sheet, and varies with the time of year.

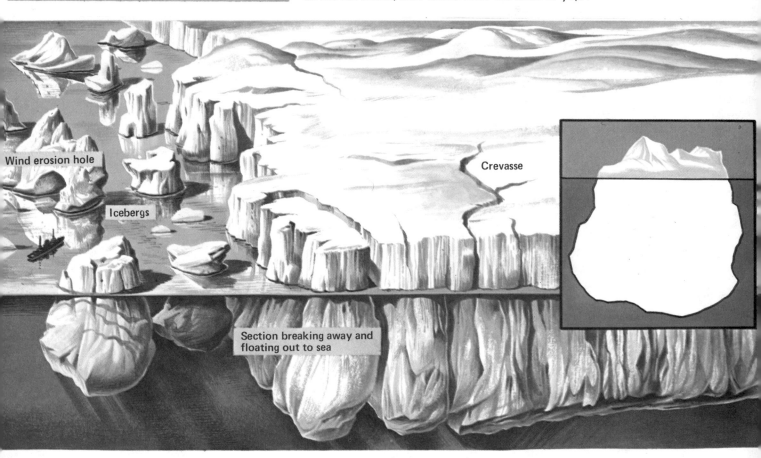

Wind erosion hole

Icebergs

Crevasse

Section breaking away and floating out to sea

A glacier or ice-sheet does not stop when it reaches the sea. The front edge is continually pushed by more ice behind it and begins to float in the water. When this ice becomes too heavy great chunks break away into the sea. These are called icebergs and the process of forming them is called *calving*.

Ice floats because it is slightly lighter than water, but only about one-eighth of an iceberg sticks up above the surface. The rest is hidden and this can make an iceberg dangerous to shipping. If a ship comes too close it may ram the hidden part while the visible part still seems a safe distance away.

Changing Patterns of the Skies

We all think of clouds in different ways. The meteorologist sees them as a means of forecasting the weather. The artist paints them in all their endless variety. The poet sees castles and other fantastic shapes in them. We all blame them for obscuring our holiday sunshine or raining on sister Agatha's wedding.

Clouds are many things to many people. But what are they?

They are masses of cooled water vapour floating in the atmosphere. All air holds some water vapour. (The *humidity* of air is a measure of the amount of water vapour in it.) When the sun warms the earth, the air next to the ground is heated. Warm air rises and, as the warm moist air rises, it expands and cools. Cool air cannot hold as much water vapour as warm air, and, after a while, rising air cools to a temperature at which it can no longer hold all its moisture.

Water crystals

The water vapour is deposited on small particles that are always floating in the air — particles of dust, pollen grains, salt crystals, etc. It forms tiny drops of water or ice crystals that clump together to make a cloud. If the temperature of the air falls even more, the cloud becomes so heavy with moisture that it rains or snows.

On a clear day we also see man-made clouds — the trails left behind by high-flying aircraft. They are made up of ice crystals. Hot moisture from the aircraft exhausts condenses and freezes when it hits the cold upper air, causing the trails.

Clouds are grouped into classes according to their height above the ground. The highest clouds, the *cirrus*, lie about 6-8 km above the Earth. Cirrus means 'curl', and these clouds are delicate wispy formations made of ice crystals.

There are seldom any clouds higher than 10,000 metres, which is why long-haul aircraft fly at altitudes greater than this.

Sometimes cirrus clouds cover a large part of the sky with a hazy layer, making the Sun look pale. This cloud formation is called *cirrostratus*, and it is often a sign of rain within a few days.

A 'mackerel' sky, rounded small masses of cloud in a ripple pattern, is *cirrocumulus*. Mackerel skies are often followed by strong winds. All these clouds are made up of ice crystals.

Low clouds

At lower levels, clouds consist of water droplets. Those at heights between 2000 and 6000 metres are called *altostratus* and *altocumulus*. Altostratus clouds form smooth grey sheets across the sky, with the sun sometimes shining through as a pale light. These clouds often produce the 'watery' sky seen before rain. Altocumulus are roundish puffs of cloud floating across the sky in groups, often merged together.

Low clouds are called *stratus, nimbostratus* and *stratocumulus*. Stratus cloud is rarely more than 300 metres high. It is usually an unbroken grey sheet, similar to fog. Higher, thicker and darker is the nimbostratus, often blurred by falling rain or snow. Stratocumulus is a greyish-white sheet of low cloud made up of rounded masses, often merged together.

Cumulus and *cumulonimbus*

Right: Clouds are classified according to their height above the ground. Heavy rainclouds (*nimbostratus*) **are lowest, cirrus highest. Thunderclouds** (*cumulonimbus*), **although they have their bases relatively near the ground, reach up to 6000 m. The top of a thundercloud is often flattened out to form an 'anvil'.**

Up to 12,000 metres

Cirrostratus

6000 metres

Altostratus

3000 metres

Cumulus

Nimbostratus

Cirrus

Cirrocumulus

Altocumulus

'Anvil'

Cumulonimbus

Cumulus

Nimbostratus

Stratus

Ice crystals form

Snow

Cold downdraft

Warm updraft

Rain droplets

Hot, rising moist air

Above: Thunderstorms are caused by violent air currents inside cumulus clouds. Water vapour carried in hot, rising air condenses out into water and then freezes into ice. When it condenses, and again when it freezes, it gives up energy called *latent heat,* **and this energy makes the air rush up even faster. It only stops many kilometres above the ground, when the heavy ice crystals fall earthwards as snow, melting to form rain. The ice crystals rub violently against the uprushing water droplets causing static electricity — which is discharged as lightning.**

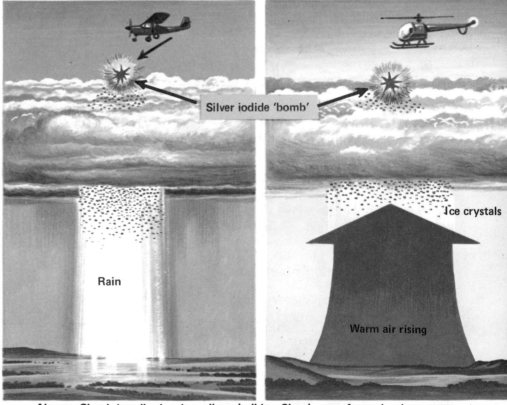

Silver iodide 'bomb'

Rain

Ice crystals

Warm air rising

Above: Cloud 'seeding' using silver iodide. Clouds are formed when water vapour crystallises, either as ice crystals or as water droplets, on to particles of dust in the atmosphere. When the crystals or droplets become too heavy, they fall as rain. Man has tried to copy Nature and produce rain by 'seeding' small clouds with silver iodide particles on which the water vapour can crystallise. But despite much research, seeding is only successful 5 to 10 per cent of the time. The diagram on the right shows one of the reasons why it often fails. On a hot, dry day, rising warm air may evaporate rain before it reaches the ground.

clouds may rise to great heights even though their bases are near the ground. Cumulus clouds are heaped up in piles, brilliant white when lit by the sun. They often float lazily across the sky. But they can soon change into the most spectacular of all clouds, the cumulonimbus. This is the dense thundercloud. Its upper portion is usually flattened out in an anvil shape, and may be 6000 metres high, with its base only a few hundred metres from the ground. In equatorial regions, cumulonimbus clouds may be as much as 12 to 14 kilometres thick from top to bottom. Aircraft pilots avoid them at all costs because of the fierce winds they can contain. On rare occasions a cumulonimbus cloud can produce a deadly tornado.

Thunder and lightning

Thunderstorms are caused by a build-up of opposite electric charges in different parts of a tall cumulonimbus cloud. When these charges become too great, a lightning spark occurs, and thunder is caused by the sudden heating of the air by the lightning. This sudden heating makes the air expand with explosive violence, the noise of the explosion and its reverberations being called *thunder*.

We see the lightning simultaneously as the flash occurs, but we hear the thunder later because of the much slower speed of sound. The interval between seeing the lightning and hearing the thunder can be used to estimate the distance of the flash, calculating 3 seconds per kilometre.

On average 45,000 thunderstorms occur every day somewhere in the world. They are among the most powerful and devastating of all natural occurrences. It has been estimated that there are 50,000 amperes of electricity in a flash of lightning. In a split second the flash can travel from 3 kilometres high to the ground, or it may flash between clouds as much as 16 kilometres apart.

But don't worry. Your chances of being struck by lightning are very small indeed. In Britain, only about 10 people are killed by lightning every year. And some unusual escapes have been reported. Among the strangest is that of a man whose gold pocket-watch was completely melted by the heat of the flash, while he was himself, quite unharmed.

Tomorrow in the clouds

They may not be always right — but more often than not weathermen are able to forecast the weather fairly accurately. They are able to do this because weather usually follows predictable patterns. Clouds are probably the most useful clue the weathermen have.

In temperate areas (countries of middle latitudes — including Britain, Europe and most of North America) rain is most often associated with a *depression*. This is an area of low atmospheric pressure around which winds travel anti-clockwise in the Northern Hemisphere, clockwise in the Southern Hemisphere.

Depressions particularly tend to occur when a band of warm air moving from the tropics meets colder polar air. Because the atmosphere is always spinning (as the Earth spins beneath it) the result is a huge eddy with the cold air flowing behind and in front of a band of warmer air. The weather we then experience is a warm 'front' followed by a cold 'front'.

Depressions are between 800 and 4000 km across and take about two to five days to pass. Because cold air is heavier than warm air, the warm air rises above the cold. As it rises, clouds are formed, producing rain. Certain cloud types are associated with

particular stages of the depression, so you can predict what the weather will be like in the next day or so.

The first clouds of a depression are the high cirrus. Then, in four to five hours, as the atmospheric pressure falls, they are followed by cirrostratus covering the whole sky. Later the cirrostratus imperceptibly merges into lower and blacker nimbostratus and rain begins to fall. The wind freshens and soon the rain is falling heavily.

This is the centre of the storm. But after several hours, the pressure stops falling and it stops raining. The nimbostratus thins to reveal ragged drizzly stratus.

Now the depression is passing the pressure begins to rise. The wind freshens and there is often a short, sharp burst of heavy rain as the rain clouds break up. There is a little cirrus and then clear sky.

The only clouds now are cumulus, white fluffy fine-weather clouds. But some of them may develop into large cumulonimbus thunder clouds bringing heavy showers of rain.

Throughout this time, the pressure rises and the wind lessens. Eventually even the cumulus clouds pass over. The whole of the storm system has now gone — until the next time!

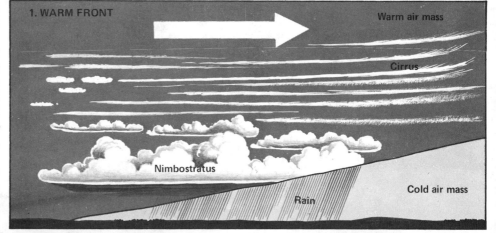

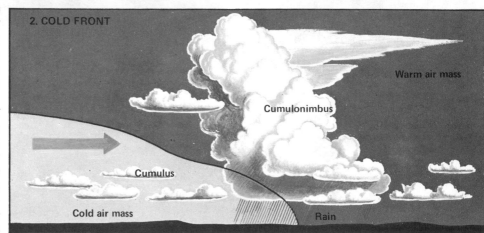

These two diagrams show a section through a depression. In (1) warm air rises above a cold air mass along a gradient of about 1 in 1000. The rising warm air produces clouds and rain along the front's edge. In (2) cold air pushes beneath the band of warm air. Cumulonimbus clouds associated with the end of the warm air are replaced by cumulus clouds and clear skies as the cold air moves in.

The Ever - Moving Atmosphere

The air around us is never still. It can produce anything from a cooling breeze to a hurricane with power equivalent to several hundred H-bombs.

The atmosphere of the Earth acts as a protective layer screening us from the harmful radiation of the Sun and insulating us against its excessive heat.

The layer of air surrounding our planet also prevents the Earth cooling too rapidly at night — as the atmosphereless Moon does, for example — and is a life-saving barrier that burns up meteors before they can hit the Earth's surface. And without it, of course, we could not breathe. But compared to the size of the Earth, the envelope of atmosphere surrounding it is quite shallow.

The densest layer, which lies nearest the Earth's surface, is only 5.5 km high. Above that the atmosphere becomes thinner and thinner until, at a height of 40 km, it becomes difficult to detect.

Nearest the Earth, however, these great layers of air shift and sweep around the planet in almost constant movement.

The basic force which produces these winds is the difference in temperature between the poles and the equator. Hot air is less dense than cold air and hence rises, (this is the principle that hot air balloons work on) and cold air sweeps in to replace it. Thus equatorial air rises and cold polar air moves in to take its place.

But these air movements are made more complicated by the fact that the Earth is spinning. As the Earth spins, it tends to leave the atmosphere behind, so that air moving north swings to the right, air moving south swings to the left.

A further complication is the difference between land and sea. Land tends to warm up quickly and cool quickly; sea warms slowly and cools slowly. The result is that in summer air over the continents is warmed and colder air moves in from the oceans; in winter ocean air is warmer and air moves from the continents to the oceans. (The same effect also occurs daily, with sea breezes coming off the sea during the day, land breezes heading out to sea at night.)

In addition to the effects of the Earth's spin and the different heating and cooling of the continents and oceans, the seasons and the Earth's topography (mountain ranges, hills and plains) also have an effect. So the circulation of the atmosphere is always changing to produce what we call 'weather'.

The most important aspect of the weather is the formation of depressions (cyclones) and anti-cyclones. Depressions are areas of low pressure caused by warm air rising and expanding. The surrounding air spirals in — anti-clockwise in the Northern Hemisphere, clockwise in the Southern Hemisphere — to fill the area of low pressure. Anti-cyclones are areas of high pressure caused by cooling air sinking. Air spirals away from an anticyclone clockwise in the north, anti-clockwise in the south, to fill surrounding depressions.

Violent storms

The most violent movements of air tend to occur in the western Atlantic Ocean and then sweep over the Gulf of Mexico on to the east coast of the United States. They are called hurricanes, cyclones or typhoons (and sometimes willy-willies!) depending on the part of the world in which they occur.

These revolving tropical storms are mainly very deep depressions in the atmosphere. They can be up to 320 km across and 9,100 metres in depth.

Air spirals downwards and is whirled round at speeds up to 320 kph while torrential rain falls from the circling storm clouds. At the centre, or 'eye', of the hurricane is an eerie area of calm 30 to 35 km in diameter, and the whole storm usually moves along its track at about 30 kph.

Another extremely dangerous disturbance of the atmosphere is the whirlwind or tornado. Unlike hurricanes, these whirling storms usually start over land.

Although there are one or two theories, meteorologists are still not yet quite sure how these intense disturbances of our atmosphere originate, but at least they are now able to give ample warning to ships or people in the path of a hurricane.

Weather satellites circling 160 km above the Earth's surface take a steady stream of photographs of the cloud formations below and transmit these to ground stations where the weathermen keep close watch for any significant changes in the vast ocean of our ever-moving atmosphere.

THE BEAUFORT WIND SCALE

The force of the wind is measured by an *anemometer,* an instrument with three cups mounted on the arms of a revolving post. The wind makes the cups spin round, and the rate at which they spin measures the velocity of the wind, normally in miles per hour. Weather stations use the Beaufort Scale to record the force of the wind. The scale was devised by the English Admiral Sir Francis Beaufort in the 19th century.

Force	Wind speed in mph (kph in brackets)	Type of wind (as given in weather forecasts)
0	Less than 1 (less than 2)	Calm
1	1 - 3 (2 - 5)	Light air
2	4 - 7 (6 - 11)	Light breeze
3	8 - 12 (12 - 19)	Gentle breeze
4	13 - 18 (20 - 29)	Moderate breeze
5	19 - 24 (30 - 39)	Fresh breeze
6	25 - 31 (40 - 50)	Strong breeze
7	32 - 38 (51 - 61)	Moderate gale
8	39 - 46 (62 - 74)	Fresh gale
9	47 - 54 (75 - 87)	Strong gale
10	55 - 63 (88 - 101)	Whole gale
11	64 - 75 (102 - 121)	Storm
12	Above 75 (Above 121)	Hurricane

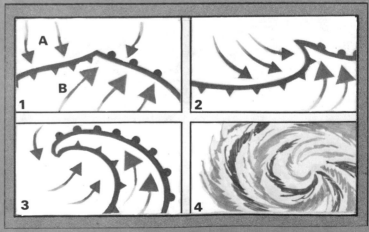

HOW A DEPRESSION DEVELOPS

Depressions form when a cold mass of air (A) meets a mass of warm air (B). A kink develops between them and becomes deeper as the 'cold front' or leading edge of the cold air continues to overtake the warm air (Picture 2). Finally the cold air overtakes the 'warm front' (Pic 3). The cold air pushes beneath the warm air making it move higher into the atmosphere. As it rises, it forms rain clouds (Pic 4), shown here as a weather satellite might see them.

HURRICANES

A very deep depression is known as a hurricane. These wind storms can be up to 300 km across and 9 km high. At their centre is a small area of calm, usually 15-30 km in diameter, called an 'eye'. Here all is relatively still, but outside winds may spiral round the eye at as much as 300 kph.

The word 'hurricane' is used only in the southern United States and in the West Indies. In the China Sea these tropical storms are called 'typhoons', and in the Indian Ocean they are called 'cyclones'. Those that develop off the coast of Australia are known as 'willy-willies'. But whatever they are called, such storms can be devastating. Hurricane David swept across the West Indies and Florida in August and September 1979 killing hundreds of people and destroying houses and crops. In the Dominican Republic 400 people died in one incident alone when the church in which they were sheltering was carried away by flood water, caused by the ferocity of the hurricane.

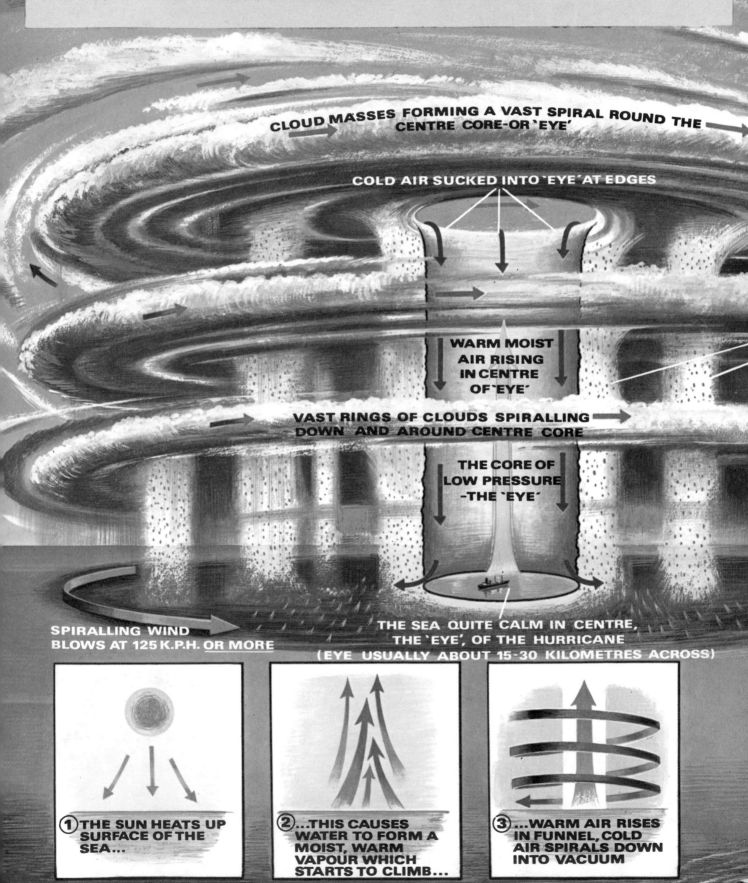

CLOUD MASSES FORMING A VAST SPIRAL ROUND THE CENTRE CORE-OR 'EYE'

COLD AIR SUCKED INTO 'EYE' AT EDGES

WARM MOIST AIR RISING IN CENTRE OF 'EYE'

VAST RINGS OF CLOUDS SPIRALLING DOWN AND AROUND CENTRE CORE

THE CORE OF LOW PRESSURE –THE 'EYE'

SPIRALLING WIND BLOWS AT 125 K.P.H. OR MORE

THE SEA QUITE CALM IN CENTRE, THE 'EYE', OF THE HURRICANE (EYE USUALLY ABOUT 15-30 KILOMETRES ACROSS)

① THE SUN HEATS UP SURFACE OF THE SEA...

② ...THIS CAUSES WATER TO FORM A MOIST, WARM VAPOUR WHICH STARTS TO CLIMB...

③ ...WARM AIR RISES IN FUNNEL, COLD AIR SPIRALS DOWN INTO VACUUM

THE FORMATION OF A HURRICANE, STAGE BY STAGE

TORNADOES

A tornado is the most violent of storms. It is like a hurricane but much smaller, being only a few hundred metres across. The air moves round the central core very fast — sometimes as fast as 315 kph. These fast rising winds are able to uproot trees, demolish houses, and even pick up cars and fling them several hundred metres. The storm may move along its path at 50 kph and is usually accompanied by lightning, thunder and torrential rain. Tornadoes are particularly destructive when they occur in groups, moving across country together and leaving a trail of destruction behind them.

When tornadoes occur over water, they are known as 'waterspouts.' In these a column of water leads from the sea (or lake) at the spout's base up into a large black thunder cloud perhaps several hundred metres in the air. However, despite popular opinion, the spouts are not formed of water sucked up from the bottom — except at the very base — but from water which has condensed out from the damp air lifted from near the sea.

Despite the destructive importance of tornadoes, and despite much study of them, scientists are still not sure how tornadoes form. One theory is that when the layers of the atmosphere are unstable, producing strong upcurrents, the small eddies which occur commonly near the ground can become magnified, growing ever stronger as they become larger. Strangely enough, right in the centre of the tornado, air is probably moving *downwards*, which is why there is very little debris or dust in the centre of a torndado.

Few natural phenomena can compare with tornadoes for sheer destructive power. In one case a school with 85 pupils inside was demolished and the pupils carried 137 metres before being safely returned to the ground. In another case, five railway coaches, each weighing 70 tonnes, were lifted from their track, one being carried 24 metres. In 1965, 371 people were killed, and more than 3,000 injured, when a series of 37 tornadoes moved across the states of Iowa, Wisconsin, Illinois, Indiana, Michigan and Ohio in the United States.

AREAS OF HEAVY RAINFALL (RAIN CAUSED BY INTERPLAY OF COLD AIR MEETING WARM MOIST VAPOUR, WATER DROPLETS FORMED)

A 'TORNADO' TRAVELLING OVER LAND

A 'TORNADO' OVER WATER IS KNOWN AS A 'WATERSPOUT'

The Cliff-Destroying Waves

The sea never tires. It is continually moving, continually washing against the land. And when rocky headlands stand out, the relentless waves eat away the cliffs to produce some spectacular formations

D AY in, day out, waves wash against the land. Little by little they shape the coastline by their continual action.

The energy needed to knock down cliffs and build up beaches comes from the wind. As the wind blows over the sea, the layer of air near the sea surface is slowed down by friction.

The nearer the air is to the sea, the more it is slowed. So the layer a few centimetres above the water moves faster than the layer only millimetres from the sea. As it overtakes the lower layer, it tumbles forwards, pushing the sea down and forming the troughs of waves. Further back, the water is pushed up to form the crests of waves.

Although waves move, the water in them actually stays in the same place. Each molecule of water follows a circular path which brings it back to where it started. This circular journey uses up very little energy, so large waves can continue long after the storm winds that produced them have gone.

Along the shore, however, waves break down. Here the land has the same sort of effect on the bottom of the sea as the wind had on the surface when the wave was formed. The friction of the land slows down the bottom of the wave more than the top, so that the faster moving top layer is thrown forward as a breaker.

These breakers can have great force, pounding cliffs and breaking off large boulders. As bits of cliff are broken away the following waves throw them against the cliff, so that the rock is being constantly bombarded with stones and water.

Gradual erosion

As the forward breaker smashes the cliff, the backwash of the waves removes the debris. Normally the forward wash is stronger than the backwash, but when waves are frequent (more than twelve a minute) the forward surge of the wave collides with the backwash of the preceding wave. This weakens the forward wash. As a result, more material is removed from the coast than is added to it, and the land slowly retreats from the sea.

When a coastline is made up of headlands and bays, the waves do not strike it equally all the way along. Rolling in from the sea, they strike the headlands first, wearing them away. But the waves are spread out before they reach the shore of the bay, usually striking about ten times a minute. In such waves, the forward breakers are stronger than the backwash, so material is washed up on the shore. This material forms a beach, which gradually gets bigger while the headland gets smaller.

If this went on for millions of years, the result would be a boring, straight coastline with the headlands eroded away and the bays filled in. But usually, before the process is completed, the sea level either rises or falls, either flooding new valleys or revealing new cliffs. And the relentless action of the waves starts anew.

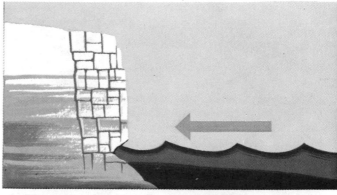

1. These diagrams show how a cliff is slowly eaten away by waves. Starting at the cliff's base, the waves compress air trapped in cracks and joints in the rock. The continual action of the air in the cracks enlarges them.

2. Eventually the cracks become so large that bits of the cliff break off and fall into the sea below. The cliff may become *undercut* as most erosion occurs at its base. The rocks on the sea floor are also pounded.

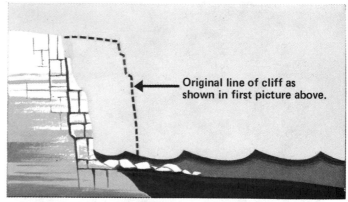

Original line of cliff as shown in first picture above.

3. Rocks at the cliff's base protect it to some extent from the waves. Nevertheless the cliff still retreats slowly from the sea. Where it has been cut away, a *wave-cut platform* is formed, littered with rock fragments.

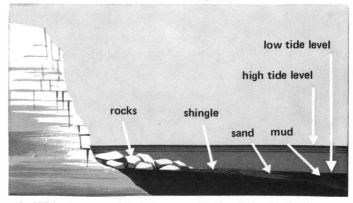

low tide level

high tide level

rocks   shingle

sand   mud

4. With time, the waves wear the fragments down into small particles. These form a *beach* and are carried out to sea by the backwash of the waves, finer particles being carried the farthest.

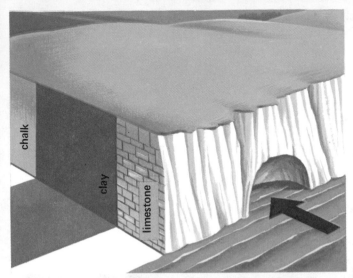

5. Coves are often formed when a soft rock, such as clay, lies behind a harder rock, such as limestone. In the first stage, the sea attacks the limestone. If there is a local weakness in the cliff, the sea may hollow away part to form a cave.

6. Whether a cave is formed or not, the waves eventually break through the outer limestone. The softer rock behind is eaten away faster than the limestone, so, although the cove entrance is slowly widened, it is soon narrower than the bay behind it.

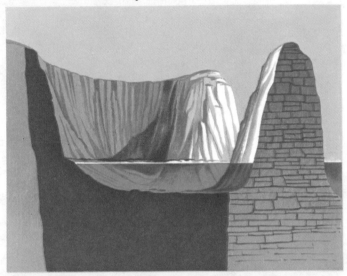

7. The sea swirls around inside the cove making it roughly circular in shape. After a while the clay is eroded sufficiently to reveal the next layer of rock, perhaps chalk. If this layer is harder than the clay, it will prevent further erosion inland.

8. This cross-section shows how the different rocks — which can be identified by their colour — are revealed. A very fine example is Lulworth Cove in Dorset. Nearby, at Mupe Rocks, can be seen a newly-formed cove just beginning to develop.

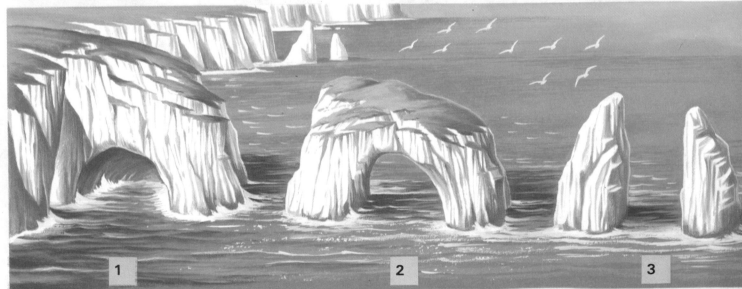

Sea stacks start as two caves, one on each side of a headland (1). After a while these caves meet, forming a natural arch (2). Then, as the sea continues to pound, the roof of the arch collapses leaving one or two rocky pillars (3). Eventually these too are reduced by the waves as the headland is steadily eroded by the sea.

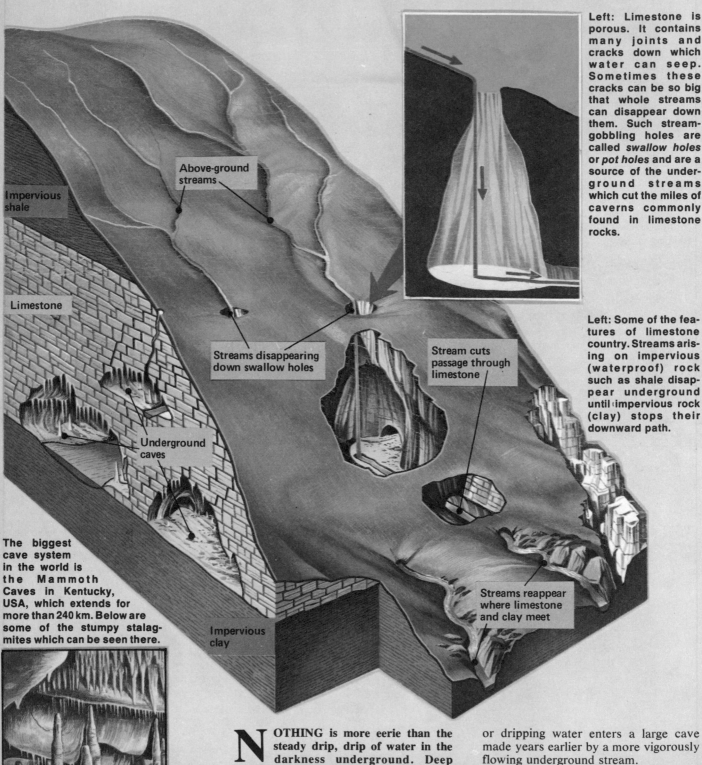

Left: Limestone is porous. It contains many joints and cracks down which water can seep. Sometimes these cracks can be so big that whole streams can disappear down them. Such stream-gobbling holes are called *swallow holes* or *pot holes* and are a source of the underground streams which cut the miles of caverns commonly found in limestone rocks.

Left: Some of the features of limestone country. Streams arising on impervious (waterproof) rock such as shale disappear underground until impervious rock (clay) stops their downward path.

Impervious shale

Above-ground streams

Limestone

Streams disappearing down swallow holes

Stream cuts passage through limestone

Underground caves

The biggest cave system in the world is the Mammoth Caves in Kentucky, USA, which extends for more than 240 km. Below are some of the stumpy stalagmites which can be seen there.

Impervious clay

Streams reappear where limestone and clay meet

NOTHING is more eerie than the steady drip, drip of water in the darkness underground. Deep beneath the earth, this steady trickle builds spectacular shapes of stone that may take hundreds or thousands of years to form.

Underground caves are usually formed in rocks — particularly limestone — which dissolve in water. Obviously these rocks do not dissolve quickly, but over the years large underground spaces can be formed if there is flowing water — especially if the water contains dissolved carbon dioxide which makes it slightly acid. Stalactites, stalagmites and other cave formations develop when trickling or dripping water enters a large cave made years earlier by a more vigorously flowing underground stream.

Seeping out of small cracks in the roof, the water is saturated with dissolved limestone. But within a large cavern some of the water may evaporate away or some of the carbon dioxide in the water may escape into the air. In either case, the water can now hold less dissolved limestone, which therefore *precipitates* out — often forming beautifully delicate rock structures.

The diagram on the next page shows how the two best-known cave formations, *stalactites* (which grow down from

Nature's Needles

the ceiling) and *stalagmites* (which grow up from the ground) are formed. Each drop of water deposits a little limestone before dripping down. There it splatters, depositing even more limestone. Thus icicle-like fingers grow down from the cave roof and up from the cave floor.

The simplest stalactites are just 6 mm thick — the thickness of a water drop. They have a narrow central channel down which the water flows. But as a stalactite grows, water usually runs down the outside of it as well, turning the stalactite into an elongated cone.

Stalagmites, formed by drips from above, have no central core and are usually thicker than stalactites. Over many years, a stalactite and a stalagmite may meet in the middle to form a rock column.

Above: Part of the Cheddar Caves in Somerset, England. This cavern is called the 'Ladye Chapel' and contains many stalactites and stalagmites which have joined together.

Below: A spectacular curtain of stalactites in the Augusta Caves, Western Australia. Upward-growing stalagmites can be seen on the right.

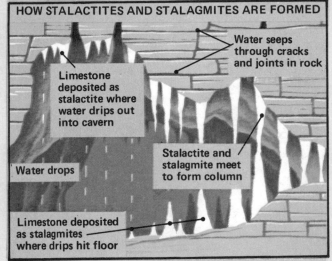

HOW STALACTITES AND STALAGMITES ARE FORMED

Water seeps through cracks and joints in rock

Limestone deposited as stalactite where water drips out into cavern

Water drops

Stalactite and stalagmite meet to form column

Limestone deposited as stalagmites where drips hit floor

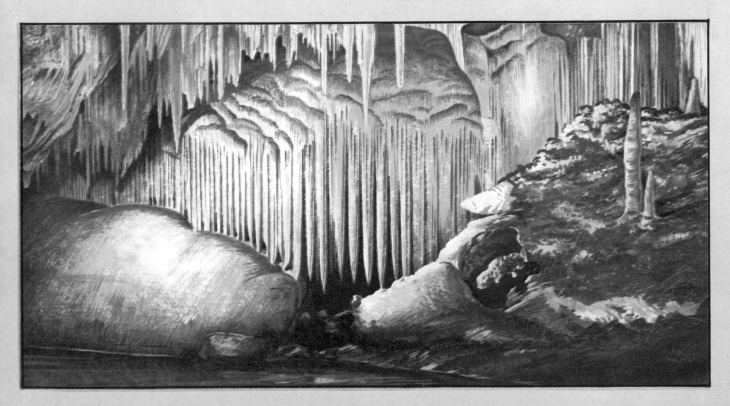

How an Earthquake

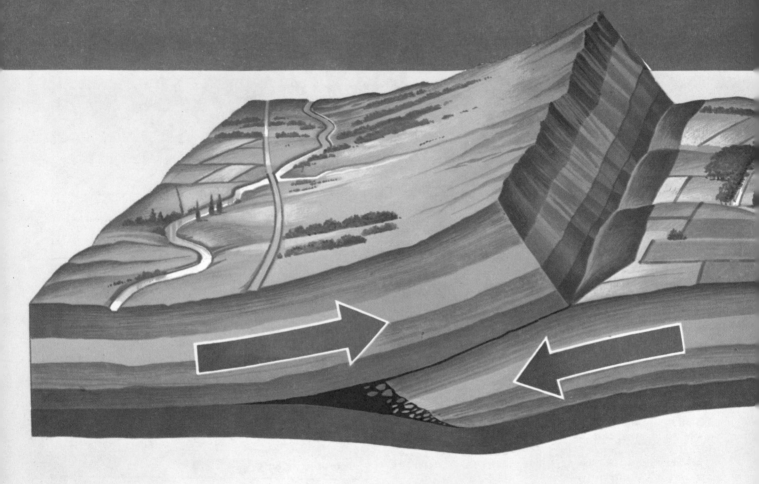

Hopefully, most of us will go through our lives without ever experiencing an earthquake. We will never know that awesome shaking of the solid ground beneath our feet, the crash of falling buildings.

Nevertheless it has been calculated that every day some 250 earthquakes take place in various parts of the world. Most of them occur beneath the sea and, of those that happen on land, comparatively few cause any damage.

Large earthquakes, however, are the most destructive of all natural phenomena. Although they seldom last for more than a few seconds, the energy released can be equal to 200 million tonnes of T.N.T (trinitrotoluene, a very powerful explosive) — 10,000 times more than the energy of the first atomic bomb. And about 14,000 lives are lost because of earthquakes every year.

The rocks that make up the earth's crust, deep under our feet, are continually moving, so the strains and stresses build up until suddenly great masses or 'plates' of rock split apart along a line of weakness, known as a *fault*. The masses slide along the fault line, shaking the ground above and often opening up great cracks in the earth.

Most faults lie deep beneath the surface of the earth, but some can be seen on the surface. One famous surface scar is the San Andreas Fault which can be seen in California, U.S.A. It is a lateral fault, one of sideways movement, and can be seen as a definite offsetting of river valleys and, in some places, even of pavements.

It can be noticed particularly in satellite photographs but is also obvious to anyone going along it for some distance with nose to the ground. The total length of the fault is some 1200 km. (800 miles) but only certain bits move at one time.

It was this fault that caused the disastrous San Francisco earthquake in 1906 as the two sides of the huge crack moved side by side a distance of more than six metres (21 feet). The fault still exists and there is no doubt that the strain is once more building up and that it will trigger off another earthquake some time within the next hundred years.

Although earthquakes can occur at great depths, some over 600 km. (400 miles) below the surface, most are comparatively shallow — about 60 km. (40 miles) down.

Unfortunately, it is the shallow ones that cause most damage to man for they are by far the most frequent. In between — in terms of frequency, depth and damage — are those between 60 and 600 km. deep, the intermediate earthquakes.

Above is a sectional diagram, showing the movement of one plate over another. Where plates meet, great strains build up. The plates slide past each other at the margins and it is at these margins that earthquakes occur. The crust is unable to withstand the strain, so it cracks and breaks. The actual reason for the movement is not yet fully understood but observation may enable earthquakes to be forecast sufficiently accurately to stop such great loss of life in the future.

The diagram on the right shows a fault like the San Andreas Fault in California. The fault there is known as a 'right lateral fault'. It appears that the plates are moving in opposite directions. In fact, though, one is merely moving faster than the other in the same direction. As you can see, the line of the road is actually broken, so that the movement itself can be observed clearly.

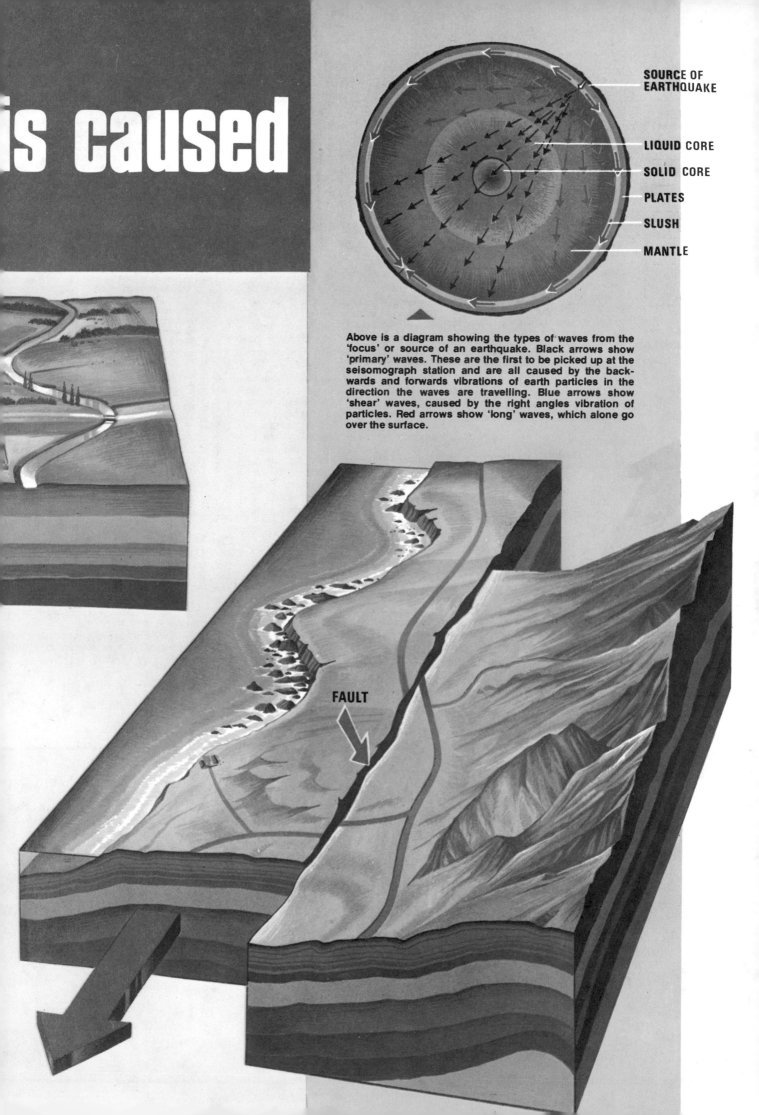

is caused

SOURCE OF EARTHQUAKE

LIQUID CORE

SOLID CORE

PLATES

SLUSH

MANTLE

Above is a diagram showing the types of waves from the 'focus' or source of an earthquake. Black arrows show 'primary' waves. These are the first to be picked up at the seisomograph station and are all caused by the backwards and forwards vibrations of earth particles in the direction the waves are travelling. Blue arrows show 'shear' waves, caused by the right angles vibration of particles. Red arrows show 'long' waves, which alone go over the surface.

FAULT

The point at which an earthquake starts is called its *focus* and the point on the surface of the earth directly above its focus is known as its *epicentre*.

The energy released by an earthquake travels out from the focus in all directions as *seismic waves*. Some waves travel down through the earth and other waves travel over the surface of the ground. The surface waves travel faster than the interior waves. The waves from a large earthquake can be recorded on instruments on the opposite side of the world, having taken about 21 minutes to pass right through the earth.

Most earthquakes take place in two great belts where volcanoes and new mountains are still being formed. One narrow belt circles the Pacific Ocean along the coasts of North and South America and runs through the islands of Asia to New Zealand. The second belt runs from Burma to southern Europe, passing through the mountains of the Himalayas, the Caucasus and the Alps. More 'quakes take place in the Pacific than in the other belt — about 80 per cent of all damaging earthquakes occur there.

Japan lies directly in the line of the greatest earthquake activity and there an average of six heavy shocks take place every year, with two or three smaller shocks every day. One of the most disastrous earthquakes of all time occurred in Tokyo in 1923 when over 100,000 died in the 'quake itself and, in the fires that followed it, some 700,000 houses were burned to the ground.

We know very little about the most catastrophic earthquake in history. It took place in Shensi Province, China, in 1556 when some 830,000 people are said to have died.

Sometimes the earth splits open during a severe earthquake. In the Quetta shock of 1935 in Pakistan, the town was completely destroyed and great cracks opened in the streets, swallowing animals and people.

It is seldom the actual force of the earthquake that is the greatest danger to life. Earthquakes affecting cities are liable to smash water, electric and gas mains, creating serious fire hazards. There is also

grave danger of disease caused by the pollution of the water supplies.

Steel and concrete buildings with deep foundations withstand shocks well and, in countries such as Japan, a great deal of effort is going into the construction of shock-proof houses and offices.

Seismic sea waves, called *tsunami* by the Japanese, often miscalled 'tidal waves', are another hazard caused by earthquakes. An underwater or coastal earthquake sets up waves which may be only a metre high in the open ocean, although the distance from wave crest to wave crest may be as much as 150 kilometres (100 miles). As these waves approach the shore, their height increases and may rise to 30 metres (100 feet), causing great destruction and loss of life when they strike an inhabited area.

Tsunami travel over vast distances at very high speeds. Those caused by an earthquake in the Aleutian islands in 1946 were 16 metres (54 feet) high in Hawaii and even 4 metres (13 feet) high on the distant Californian coast. The waves reached a speed of 720 kph (450 mph).

Earthquakes are recorded and measured by an instrument called a seismograph. The early seismographs consisted of a heavy pendulum suspended by a long wire. On the ground beneath the pendulum was a dish containing a layer of sand. When an earthquake shook the ground, the heavy pendulum tended to remain still because of its inertia and a stylus attached to the end of the pendulum traced a record of the earthquake in the moving sand. Later, in more accurate seismographs, a fine stylus traced a record on a roll of smoked paper wound on a drum and worked by clockwork. Seismographs now use beams of light and record on photographic paper.

Although most shocks take place in the two great earthquake belts, no part of the world is entirely free. Even Britain has suffered over a thousand 'quakes since the Norman Conquest, the worst being that at Colchester in 1884 when over a thousand buildings were destroyed and a number of people were killed.

EARTHQUAKE INTENSITY

This is judged by what is felt by a human being at the time of an earthquake and by how much damage is caused at that time.

1. Not felt at all as a rule.
2. A pendulum at rest may swing.
3. Most people indoors feel it and cars may rock slightly.
4. Felt by everyone indoors. People awakened. Things rattle.
5. Nearly everyone feels it — inside and out. Things may be broken, like china or glass.
6. Felt by everyone — inside and out. Objects moved.
7. Some general damage. Felt by people travelling in vehicles.
8. Statues fall down. General alarm.
9. People panic-stricken. Holes appear in ground. Buildings damaged.
10. Panic. Only very strong buildings remain standing.
11. Panic. Most buildings destroyed. Damage to underground pipes.
12. Complete pandemonium and nothing left standing.

John Wesley, the famous preacher and founder of Methodism, described a shock he experienced in 1750. He said, "There were three distinct shakes, or wavings to and fro, attended with a hoarse rumbling like thunder." This earthquake is said to have demolished many houses in the City of London and stones were shaken from Westminster Abbey.

The worst earthquake recorded in Britain this century was one in the Midlands on February 11, 1957.

Below is a map of the 'plates', 'trenches' and 'faults' of the world. The arrows show the direction of the movements. Ocean Ridges form where plates separate. Trenches occur when one plate dips below another as shown by the dotted lines.

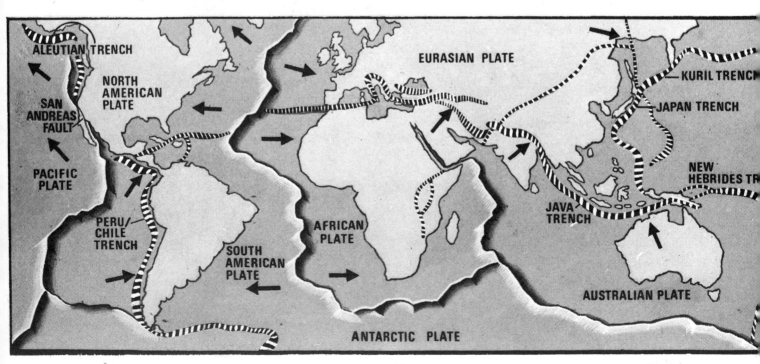

History for all to see

The Grand Canyon is one of the world's scenic marvels. It is also a chart recording the passing of millions of years.

"IN the Grand Canyon, Arizona has a natural wonder which, so far as I know, is unparalleled throughout the rest of the world."

So spoke Theodore Roosevelt, America's President, after he had visited this wonderland in 1903. His words have been echoed by millions of people since then.

On page 11 you can read how a river can cut a path through the land, wearing away the rocks and soil beneath. The Grand Canyon is a perfect example of this type of erosion. Nowhere else in the world is it easier to see how running water can change the face of the Earth.

The river that brought about this change is the Colorado, which for millions of years has been cutting, tearing and eating its way through the countryside until it and its tributaries, aided by wind and frost, have carved countless numbers of canyons for thousands of kilometres. The greatest of these is the Grand Canyon.

Some 350 kilometres long and varying from six to 30 kilometres in width, the Grand Canyon is well over a kilometre and a half deep. From the rim the river far below looks a mere trickle yet it is over 90 metres wide and 9 metres deep, plunging and leaping over boulders and rocks, churning the water into a white froth.

Indians have long lived in the area, but the first Europeans to see the canyon were a band of Spanish soldiers led by Don Garcia Lopez de Cardenas. That was in 1540. Realising that the canyon was an impassable barrier and discovering no gold in the area, he moved on, and for more than three centuries this inaccessible area remained virtually unknown and unexplored.

It was not until little over 100 years ago that a full exploration was carried out, the American geologist John Wesley Powell, leading a team in rowing boats.

"All these canyons unite to form one canyon," he wrote, "the most sublime spectacle on Earth."

Since then the Grand Canyon has been a magnet to millions. Today over three million people visit the canyon every year. Some come to trek through the wild countryside with its bizarre shapes and sculptured mountains; some come to make the hazardous trip to the bottom along the narrow Bright Angel Trail — either on mules or on foot; some come to challenge the river's power in canoes; and some come simply to take in its awesome grandeur.

And here too come scientists and students for, in the mile-high sides of the gorge, layers of different multi-coloured rocks, changing hue according to the time of day or degree of sunshine, reveal the whole pattern of the Earth's changes in a period covering hundreds of millions of years.

By examining the various rock layers clearly visible, by studying the fossil remains of prehistoric plants, fish and tiny animals, scientists can unravel the story of the Earth's crust as surely as a detective story writer revealing the details of a 'who-done-it' mystery story.

They can show how millions of years ago great mountains were formed by movements of the Earth's crust or volcanic upheavals, how these were worn down by erosion into plains, how the plains were entirely covered by vast seas — the pattern of movement and flooding and erosion being repeated many times.

At the very bottom of the canyon the rock is granite, formed perhaps 2,000 million years ago from hot liquid rock like the lava that pours out of volcanoes. Then come layers of limestone and shale, formed when the seas deposited their sediment on the land, and sandstone formed from grains of sand piled high and compacted.

In the same way as the rings of a felled tree tell the story of its life, so too do the rock layers in the canyon tell the story of Arizona. It is all there for the trained eye to see, a chart recording history as plainly as a teacher might draw it on a blackboard.

The Mighty VOLCANO

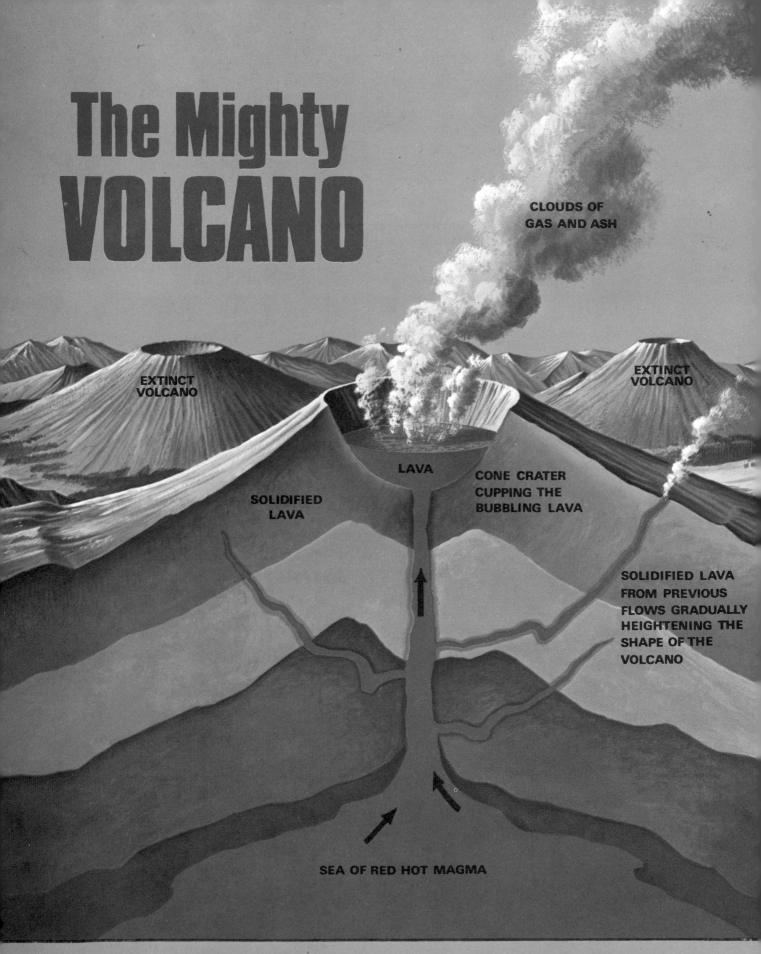

CLOUDS OF GAS AND ASH

EXTINCT VOLCANO

EXTINCT VOLCANO

LAVA

SOLIDIFIED LAVA

CONE CRATER CUPPING THE BUBBLING LAVA

SOLIDIFIED LAVA FROM PREVIOUS FLOWS GRADUALLY HEIGHTENING THE SHAPE OF THE VOLCANO

SEA OF RED HOT MAGMA

ON August 27, 1883, Mount Krakatoa in the Sundra Strait between the islands of Sumatra and Java exploded, throwing out almost 20 cubic km. of rock and dust to a height of 30 km.

Above Krakatoa, the sky turned black as a heavy rain of ash fell over a wide area, covering the ground at a rate of a metre an hour. The explosion created a tidal wave that killed 36,000 people, and the sound of it was heard almost 5,000 km. away in Australia.

The power of this awful volcanic eruption was many times greater than that of any man-made hydrogen bomb explosion.

Fortunately, very few such catastrophic volcanic explosions occur in a lifetime. But there is always some volcanic action taking place somewhere on Earth.

What is a volcano? At its simplest, it is an opening in the Earth's crust through which hot gases and molten rock are erupted or blown out. The

34

1. Stromboli-types erupt rarely but persistently, exploding and giving off ash, rock fragments and gas.

2. Vulcano-types are more explosive than 1. and produce volcanic 'bombs'. These are formed by fragments of lava being flung high into the air and then solidifying before falling back to the ground.

3. Pelean-types give off suffocating clouds of white-hot gas and dust, known as 'glowing clouds'. The dome bursts and solid spines arise, still incredibly hot.

4. Hawaiian-types, like Mauna Loa, a 'shield' volcano, are non-violent but produce more lava in all directions than any other.

molten rock, called 'lava', comes from 30 to 60 km. below the surface.

In many cases the lava flows out quietly, the speed at which it flows determining the steepness of the sides of the volcanic mountain that is formed. The more liquid the lava, the faster it flows and the gentler the mountain slopes. Explosive volcanoes, with nearly solid lava, make steep-sided cones. In highly explosive volcanoes such as Krakatoa, the material thrown out is largely gas, ash and pumice, with little lava.

Another famous example of an explosive volcano is Mount Pelée on the Caribbean island of Martinique. In 1902, the town of St. Pierre nestled peacefully at the mountain's base. Then, on the morning of May 8 of that year a great crack opened up in the side of the mountain. A fiery blast of steam and ash shot out of the vent with a crashing roar and, in less than a minute, St. Pierre was a vast pile of smoking rubble. By repute, all but one of its 30,000 inhabitants were

dead. He was saved by being imprisoned at the bottom of a well.

It was a disaster similar to that at St. Pierre which wiped out the Roman town of Pompeii, when Vesuvius erupted on August 24, A.D. 79. Pompeii and its inhabitants were suddenly buried beneath a deep layer of volcanic ash and dust, preserving for the archaeologist this prosperous market town, exactly as it was at the peak of its prosperity. It was rediscovered in 1748 and has since been painstakingly excavated.

Just as the inhabitants of Pompeii were taken by surprise on that fatal day, present-day scientists find it difficult to tell very much in advance when a volcano is going to erupt. We still cannot tell when a volcano is quite 'dead'. Since that day in A.D. 79, Vesuvius has had many minor eruptions and more than a dozen major ones, the latest in 1944. No one is quite sure when it will happen again.

Scientists do, however, know more about the quieter kind of volcano,

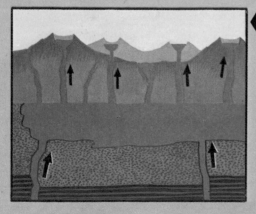

Fissure eruptions occur in Iceland. A sea of magma, or molten rock, rises through vents to form a line of craters which seem like numerous volcanoes. The vents appear at faults in the rocks, caused by movement there.

Sometimes, a sea of magma rises to just below the surface. There it solidifies and is revealed much later, when the soil is worn away by natural erosion. Magmas, though, vary in chemical composition.

volcanoes which give out vast quantities of liquid basaltic lava and build up into more gently-sloping mountains. Such a mountain is Mauna Loa in the Hawaiian islands. It is over 9000 metres in height, the highest mountain on Earth, but nearly 5000 metres is below the ocean.

The rare and spectacular formation of a volcano came under scientific observation for the first time in history when Paricutin, 320 km. west of Mexico City, erupted in 1943.

One afternoon, a farmer was ploughing his cornfield when he was surprised to see a jet of steam issue from a small depression. By next morning, after a night of rumbling explosions, and the throwing out of showers of rock, the volcano had a cone 15 metres high. After two weeks it had risen to a height of 135 metres and was still throwing out great red-hot lumps of rock hundreds of metres into the air. Paricutin stopped erupting in 1952, by which time it was 425 metres high, and lava had spread as much as 10 km. from the centre of the mountain.

Some volcanoes, like Stromboli in the Mediterranean Lipari Islands, erupt with great regularity. Others erupt faily regularly, the length of their erupting cycle being governed by the time it takes for enough heat to be generated in the magma (the liquid rocks and gases) deep down below the Earth's surface. Mount Etna is this kind of volcano. Volcanoes that have shown no sign of activity for many years are called dormant. Those that are thought to be 'dead' are called extinct.

> Lava may flow at a speed of 80 kph, but speeds of less than 16 kph are more usual.
>
> There are some 500 active volcanoes in the world today.
>
> There are no active volcanoes in the Himalayas or in the Alps.
>
> More than three-quarters of all active volcanoes are in the Pacific 'Ring of Fire'.
>
> The highest inactive volcanic mountain on the American continent is Aconcagua in Argentina — 7,023 metres.
>
> The word 'volcano' comes from Vulcan, the Roman god of fire. The god was thought to live on an island, also called Vulcano, in the Lipari group in the Mediterranean.
>
> It has been calculated that since the birth of Christ about a million people have died as a result of volcanic activity.
>
> On November 14, 1963, Icelandic fishermen were trawling, when, quite close by, the sea began to boil. There arose a great cloud of steam and slowly the cone of a volcanic island rose above the surface. Within a few weeks, as the lava continued to flow, the new island was over 150 metres high and over two kilometres long. It was named Surtsey. Now flowers grow on Surtsey.

Nearly all volcanoes are found close to mountain chains in areas where there are weaknesses or faults in the Earth's crust. The great majority of the Earth's active volcanoes lie around the border of the Pacific Ocean in a so-called 'Ring of Fire'. There is another volcanic belt across the Mediterranean Sea into western Asia. A lesser string runs down the middle of the Atlantic Ocean from Iceland in the north, through the Azores, Ascension, St. Helena to the small island of Tristan da Cunha in the south.

Why volcanoes exist is not fully understood, but they are certainly the most spectacular natural phenomena on Earth. We have a graphic eye-witness account of the eruption of Vesuvius that engulfed Pompeii and adjacent towns, giving us some idea of the forces released.

It is written in a letter to the historian Tacitus from Pliny the Younger, '. . . Some lifted their hands to the gods; others thought there were no gods at all — they believed that the final endless night of which we have heard had come upon the world.'

Four diagrams are shown on the right, illustrating the variations in volcanic eruptions.

1. Quiet, with some cloud floating down the side.

2. Magma rising and boiling up violently in cone as lava. Small fragments, cloud and gas erupting into sky.

3. Fragments in expanding gases, rushing down from crater.

4. Boiling lava pouring down from crater, giving off poisonous fumes.

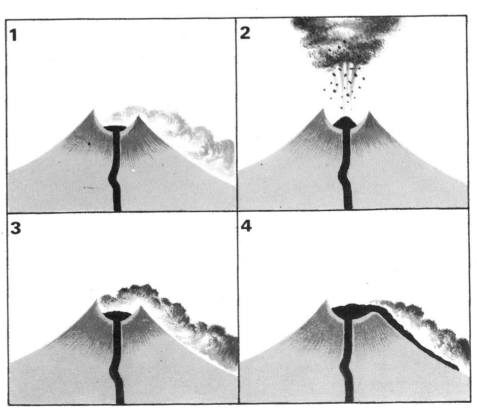

The Moon is more than just a romantic light in the night sky. The colossal forces that bind — and at the same time repel — the Earth's nearest neighbour also pull the oceans ceaselessly back and forth. As the Moon spins round it drives

The Ever-turning Tides

ONE winter's morning in 1953, the people of Holland woke to scenes of devastation. Large areas of the picturesque Dutch countryside were totally under water. The wide, flat fields, in which millions of spring flowers would normally grow, lay desolate — the victims of powerful storm winds and an unusual spring tide that had raised the level of the North Sea by 3 metres above normal. There was the power of the sea and its turning tides at their worst.

Yet tides are useful, too. They act almost like a clock to fishermen around the world, who need high water to leave or enter harbour. Many great seaports depend on the rise and fall of the waters to sweep out the main shipping channels and keep them deep enough for big ships to come in and out. They need them as well to pick up waste materials floating near the shoreline and carry them out to deeper waters where they will sink harmlessly to the sea-bed.

Twice a day the seas advance and retreat on ocean shores, leaving a thin line of flotsam at high tide, and a line of rich green seaweed at low tide.

Day in, day out, the rise and fall goes on, predictable yet at the same time mysterious. At one time in the day the sea is a long, long way out, leaving a huge expanse of bare beach. But return to that scene a few hours later and the waters are crashing at your feet at high tide.

What drives this ceaseless motion?

The answer lies in the gravitational attraction between the Earth, the Moon, and the Sun.

Although these forces act on everything in the world, their effect on solid objects is hardly noticeable. But the waters of the oceans are free to move and are considerably affected. The effects are known as tides.

The Moon is smaller than the Sun, but because it is nearer, it has a much greater effect on the Earth than the Sun does. On the side of the Earth nearer the Moon, the waters of oceans (and large lakes) are pulled by the Moon's gravity towards the Moon. There is thus a bulge of water — a high tide — facing the Moon, and it moves round the Earth as the Moon revolves round the Earth.

But strangely, a high tide also occurs at the same time on the *opposite* side of the Earth. It occurs just where you would expect it to be lowest if the only force affecting tides were the gravitational pull of the Moon.

Yet gravity is not the only force acting between the Earth and the Moon. If it were, the Earth and Moon would fall together with one final, catastrophic smash. Another force keeps the two apart.

This is *centrifugal force*. It is the force which makes a rope swing out when you swing it round your head, or which pushes

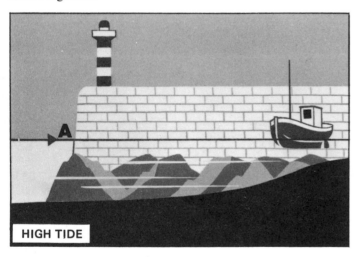

HIGH TIDE

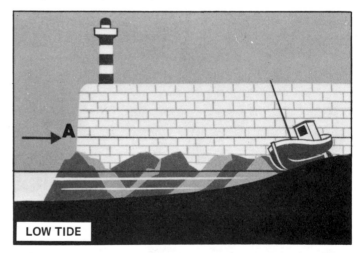

LOW TIDE

Many million tonnes of water are moved between a high tide (above) and the following low tide (above, right). But tides aren't always the same size. In our diagrams, line A is the high water mark of a normal high tide. A spring tide (below, left) is higher than a normal tide. A neap tide (below) is lower.

HIGH SPRING TIDE

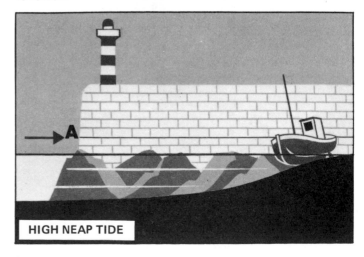

HIGH NEAP TIDE

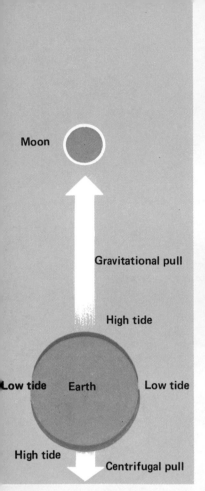

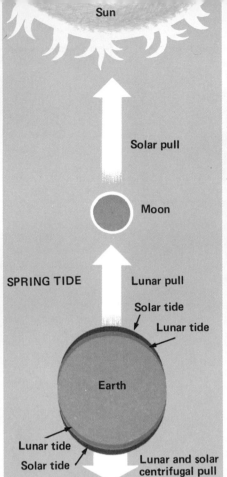

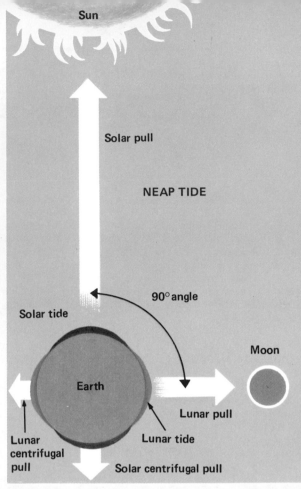

Above: The Moon causes two tides — one facing it, and one directly opposite. Low tides occur at right angles to the Moon.

Above: The Sun causes tides in just the same way as the Moon — only because the Sun is farther away, its tides are smaller. However, they are noticeable. When the Sun and Moon are pulling in the same direction (and when they are directly opposite), the result is an extra-large tide called a *spring tide*. When they are pulling at right angles, there is an extra-small tide called a *neap tide*.

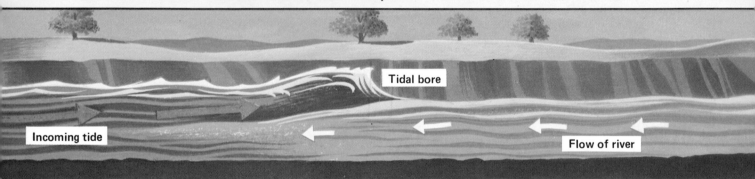

Below: Extra large tides can be caused by an incoming tide being channelled up a bay which becomes progressively narrower. In the Bay of Fundy, this effect causes a difference between high and low tide of 16 metres.

Above: When a tide flows into a river, it pushes water against the river's flow. In a shallow, strongly flowing river, such as the Severn, this advancing tidal water may travel up river as a wall of water or *bore*.

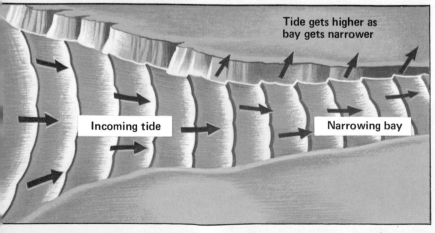

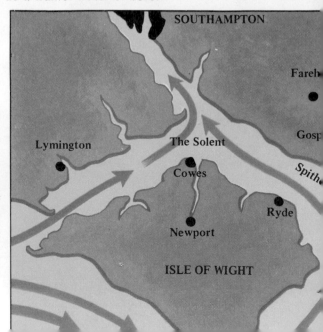

Right: Southampton has a *double* high tide. The first tide comes up from the Atlantic via the western Solent. The second tide occurs two hours later and comes round the Isle of Wight and up through Spithead.

38

you outwards when you hold hands with a friend and spin round and round. The Earth and Moon spin round each other in much the same way — although, of course, it is more like spinning round with your little brother because the Moon is much smaller than the Earth.

As we know, the Moon doesn't come tumbling down from the sky. This is because the centrifugal force exactly balances the gravitational attraction between the Earth and Moon. And so the high tide on the side of the Earth opposite the Moon is just as high as the high tide on the side facing it. This tide is water thrown out by centrifugal force.

Low tides occur at parts of the Earth at right angles to the direction of the Moon. It is from here that water is pulled to make the high tides opposite and facing the Moon.

The Moon goes round the Earth once every 24 hours and 50 minutes, pulling the tides with it. So high tides generally occur once every 12 hours and 25 minutes — or roughly twice a day.

Sun-caused tides

The Sun's tidal effect is about half that of the Moon. Nevertheless, it does pull oceans in exactly the same way. When the Sun and Moon are both pulling in the same direction, the result is a particularly high high tide — and a particularly low low tide. These extra large tides are called *spring tides*. They have nothing whatsoever to do with spring, but occur twice in every lunar month (roughly 27½ days, the time it takes the Moon to complete one revolution of the Earth).

When the Sun and Moon are pulling at right angles to each other, the result is unusually small tides. These are called *neap tides*. Of course, they too occur twice in a lunar month — exactly halfway between successive spring tides.

If the world were smooth like a billiard ball, with no land and completely covered in sea, then tides would occur regularly and be the same size all over the planet. But in fact tides vary greatly from place to place. The Atlantic Ocean has a regular twice-daily ebb and flow, whereas some islands in the Pacific have two high tides daily, with very little ebb (or retreat) between them, and then just one very low tide. At Saint Michael, in Alaska, only one daily tide occurs, a slow rise and fall every 24 hours.

In other seas tidal action is hardly noticeable. When Julius Caesar came to Britain, he was astonished to see the tides that were considered commonplace. The Mediterranean, into which Italy juts, is practically tide-free.

The reason for all this variation is the shape, size and depth of the oceans. Although the Moon and Sun are the primary forces that set the tides in action, once moving the water slops around in the seas rather like water in some giant bath-tub. Each sea or ocean has a *natural* frequency at which the water would slop about if left to its own devices — just as a drum vibrates at its natural frequency when it is struck. When the natural frequency roughly corresponds with the pull of the Moon, there are large regular twice-daily tides. When the natural frequency is different, the tides come at different periods and are generally smaller.

Imagine a swinging swing. If you push it in the direction it is swinging, it swings higher. If you push it in the opposite direction, it swings lower. The tides work is much the same way.

Dramatic effects occur when a tide is chanelled up a narrowing bay or river mouth as it comes in from the open sea. In the Bay of Fundy, off Nova Scotia, for example, the difference between high and low tide is a remarkable 16 metres. A strong Atlantic tide churns into the deep trough of the Bay, getting higher and higher as the Bay gets narrower. So powerful is this drive into the River St John that the sea waters form a spectacular 'Reversible Waterfall' as they are thrown up on to the rocks.

Another vivid spectacle produced by tidal action can be seen off the Lofoten Islands of Norway. Here the channels between the islands turn the fast-moving tides into violently whirling streams called the Maelstrom or whirlpool.

Tidal bores

In Britain perhaps the most spectacular tidal effect occurs at the estuary of the River Severn. Here an incoming tide meets the shallow waters of the river in the confined space of the estuary to form a 'bore' — a high wall-like front of water surging up the river. Bores also occur in the River Trent, where they are called 'eagres', and in the Seine in France, with its 'mascarets' and the Amazon with its 'pororocas'.

The most exciting — and dangerous — 'tidal' effect of all is not, strictly speaking, tidal, even though its name suggests that it is. 'Tidal waves' (also known by their Japanese name — *tsunami* — are really caused by undersea earthquakes ('seaquakes') or hurricanes raging far out to sea.

In the future, tides promise to be of use in solving the world's energy shortage. Harnessing the power of the sea is not easy, but at suitable sites, high tides can be held back behind dams and the water then let out through turbines to generate electricity. "Time and tide wait for no man," says the old proverb. But perhaps Man will one day learn to benefit from tidal power, the ceaseless, abundant energy that every day rolls up on to the shores of the world.

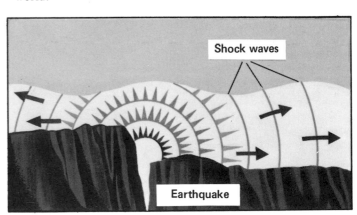

Shock waves

Erupting volcano

Shock waves

Earthquake

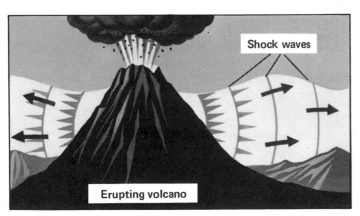

Wave gets higher as it approaches land

TIDAL WAVES

Tidal waves — often known by their Japanese name *tsunami* — are not strictly tidal at all. Instead, they are huge shock waves caused by earthquakes, volcanic eruptions, or hurricanes far out to sea. As these waves reach land, the friction of the water on the sea-bed slows them down; but at the same time they become higher and can destroy everything in their path. One hundred and seventy-three people died when a tidal wave, caused by an earthquake 3,220 km away, struck the delightful island of Honolulu in 1946.

Visitors from Space

If only a fraction of the number of meteors that bombard us daily were to hit the Earth there would be utter devastation. Fortunately, they are vaporized more quickly than you can say "Star Wars."

EVERY day of our lives about 8,000 million meteors, enter the Earth's atmosphere and, captured by the gravity of our planet, hurtle down at speeds of up to 40 km per second. Fortunately for us, very few of them ever reach the ground, thanks to our protective blanket of the atmosphere. Nearly all of these visitors from space are vaporized some 80 km above our heads.

What is a meteor? Strictly speaking, it is any piece of solid matter, not large enough to be called an asteroid (minor planet), that travels around the Sun. Meteors do not come from outer space; they are part of our solar system and follow regular elliptical orbits around the Sun.

We may think of space as being empty outside the Earth's atmosphere, but it is never completely so. It has been calculated that in 'empty' space there are about 1000 particles in every cubic kilometre. Most of these particles are very small — from an invisible hundred-thousandth of a centimetre to a millimetre across.

But even a particle a millimetre across can produce that sudden streak of light in the night sky we call a 'shooting star' as it plunges into our atmosphere and becomes white-hot through friction with the air. Particles this size are burned up before they reach the Earth. A few meteors are bigger — some a centimetre across that are brighter than the brightest stars as they flash towards us; still fewer are bigger still, and some of these large ones, or parts of them, reach the Earth as *meteorites*.

It has been estimated that something like 400 tonnes of meteoric matter lands on Earth every day, chiefly in tiny particles that arrive completely unnoticed.

Large meteorites are very rare. The polar explorer Robert Peary brought back from Greenland one weighing 36 tonnes,

A meteorite crater nearly 1,300 m wide and at least 20,000 years old, near Winslow, Arizona.

The craters of the Moon are the result of meteors. The Moon has no atmosphere, so there is nothing to stop the space rock from smashing into its surface.

Shooting stars aren't stars at all. They are meteors — glowing white-hot as the friction of the atmosphere burns them up. Some may be only a millimetre in diameter.

while the biggest complete specimen was found near Hoba in Namibia (South-west Africa). This weighs about 60 tonnes.

But we know that much larger meteorites have hit the Earth in the past. About 20,000 years ago, a huge lump of metal about 20 metres across, consisting mainly of iron and nickel, plunged into the Arizona Desert. This giant meteorite must have weighed about a million tonnes as it ploughed its way into the earth, to leave a crater some 200 metres deep and 1,200 metres in diameter. Scientists have calculated that the explosion at impact shifted about 300 million tonnes of rock.

Such falls are few and far between but this century has seen two comparatively major falls. Strangely both occurred in uninhabited wasteland in Siberia, Russia. One took place in 1947, but the other, nearly 40 years earlier, still has no real explanation.

On June 30, 1908, a huge explosion took place in the bleak wilderness near the River Tunguska. The ball of fire was seen, and windows blown in, as much as 150 km away, with a terrific roaring noise like thunder. The pressure of the blast was even registered on barometers in England.

Strange find

Due to the inaccessibility of the region, a scientific expedition took several years to organise and a huge meteorite seemed the most feasible explanation. But when scientists finally reached the site they found an extraordinary scene: a forest, 1.5 km wide and over 30 km long, had been completely flattened and an intense heat had scorched the whole area.

If the cause was a meteorite then it had been a giant (over 50,000 tonnes) which had approached at a low angle. However, no impact crater was found and no definite meteor fragments.

A possible explanation could be that the meteorite exploded above the ground, vaporizing as it did so. But radioactivity levels were high in the area and mutated vegetation nearby suggested atomic fall-out. It may well be that an actual comet nucleus caused this cataclysmic explosion. If this had taken place on a built-up area like Moscow the devastation and death toll would have been greater than that caused by a hydrogen bomb.

On any clear night an occasional meteor can be seen flashing across the sky. But sometimes there are meteor showers which astronomers believe come from the debris in the tails of comets. These showers also travel in elliptical orbits around the Sun. When such a shower enters the atmosphere, the night sky seems to be filled with flying sparks.

In 1966, for example, what is called the Leonid shower produced a spectacular 2000 meteors a minute. (This shower is so named because the meteors appear to come from the region of the constellation Leo, and it appears to re-occur in 33-year cycles.) The best-known annual shower seen in the Northern Hemisphere is called the Perseids. This shower occurs between 10 and 13 August every year, its meteors coming in parallel paths from the direction of the constellation Perseus.

Even though there are millions of meteors whizzing through our atmosphere, it is highly unlikely that you will ever be hit by one; in fact, there is no authenticated case of anyone ever being killed by a meteorite. In 1955 at Sylacuaga, Alabama, in the United States, a woman, while asleep, was hit a glancing blow by a meteorite that crashed through her house. This is the 'closest shave' documented.

There are three types of meteorite: those made entirely of stone — mostly silicates; those made of metal — mostly iron alloyed with nickel and other metals; and those consisting of a mixture of the first two types. Most meteors are of the stony kind, and very few are a mixture of stone and iron.

Meteorites are valuable to science because they are the only objects that come to us from outside the Earth. They are especially valuable if they are found and analysed before they have had a chance to be contaminated by substances found normally on Earth. These meteoric visitors from space may date back to a time when the solar system itself was being formed. They are therefore giving astronomers more and more information on the age of the Sun and its orbiting planets, and also on the chemical make-up of the universe itself.

Although it is very unlikely that you will see a meteorite fall, you can certainly see many 'shooting stars' if you observe the night sky at the right times. But if possible, it is worth going to a museum and looking at some of these 'stones from the sky'.

THE SHADOW OF THE MOON.

Are you afraid of the daytime darkness? Then you won't look forward to ...

Eclipses-Night for Day

THERE'S something very frightening about darkness in the middle of the day. So dependent is the Earth on the life-giving Sun that to lose it somehow is probably the worst disaster Man can imagine — far, far worse than total nuclear war.

Yet every year or so somewhere in the world the Sun does disappear quite naturally. This happens when the Moon passes between the Earth and the Sun obscuring it from view. Such an event is called an *eclipse*.

Nowadays, when we understand what is happening, eclipses hold no great fear. But in the past people were extremely afraid of them. They were first regularly recorded in about 747 B.C., in Babylon, and here, as elsewhere, they were regarded as portents of disaster. In fact, in Ancient Chinese legend, the Emperor Yao appointed two officials to prevent eclipses, and punished them severely when they failed to do so.

Sun-worshippers

The Incas of Peru, who were Sun-worshippers, believed that the eclipse itself was a disaster: they thought that a monster puma or serpent was trying to gobble up the life-giving Sun. The only solution was to make a deafening din — shouting, shrieking, blowing trumpets or conch shells and even beating dogs to make them howl — in order to frighten the monster away.

Today, such superstitious behaviour seems primitive and unintelligent. However, witnessing an eclipse is an eerie experience. It can turn from daylight into darkness in an instant. In place of the brilliantly shining Sun, there is only a black disc — the intervening Moon — with a sparkling circle of pearl-white light around it. This circle is the Sun's corona.

It may seem strange that so small a heavenly body as the Earth's Moon, (diameter 3,473 km), can completely obscure a colossal star like the Sun (diameter over 1,392,000 km). The explanation lies in distance, and the fact that the farther away an object is, the smaller it looks.

Total eclipse

So, although the Sun's diameter is a little over 400 times the diameter of the Moon, it can appear to be much the same size because it is between 367 and 419 times farther from Earth than the Moon is. The figure is not constant because neither the orbit of the Earth round the Sun nor that of the Moon round the Earth is completely regular. At its closest to Earth, the Moon actually looks a bit larger than the Sun and that is when it can obscure the Sun completely and so cause a *total* eclipse.

Precisely what observers see during an eclipse depends where they are on Earth. An eclipse appears total only in

PENUMBRA

UMBRA

These diagrams show how the Moon is eclipsed by the Earth's shadow (top), and the Earth by the Moon's shadow (below). The area of total darkness in which the Sun is completely obscured is called the *umbra;* the area in which only part of the Sun is obscured is called the *penumbra.*

PENUMBRA

UMBRA

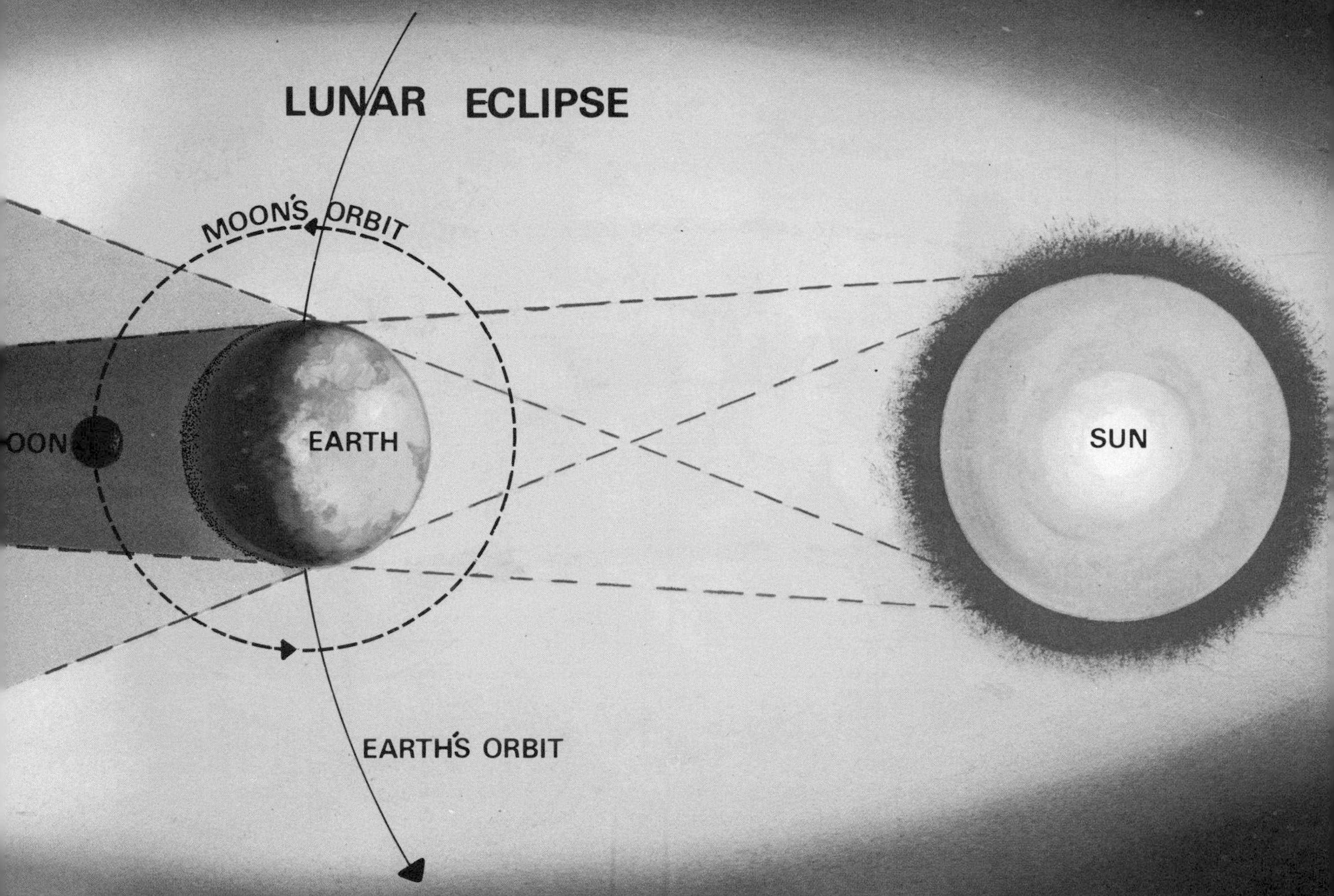

LUNAR ECLIPSE

MOON'S ORBIT

MOON

EARTH

SUN

EARTH'S ORBIT

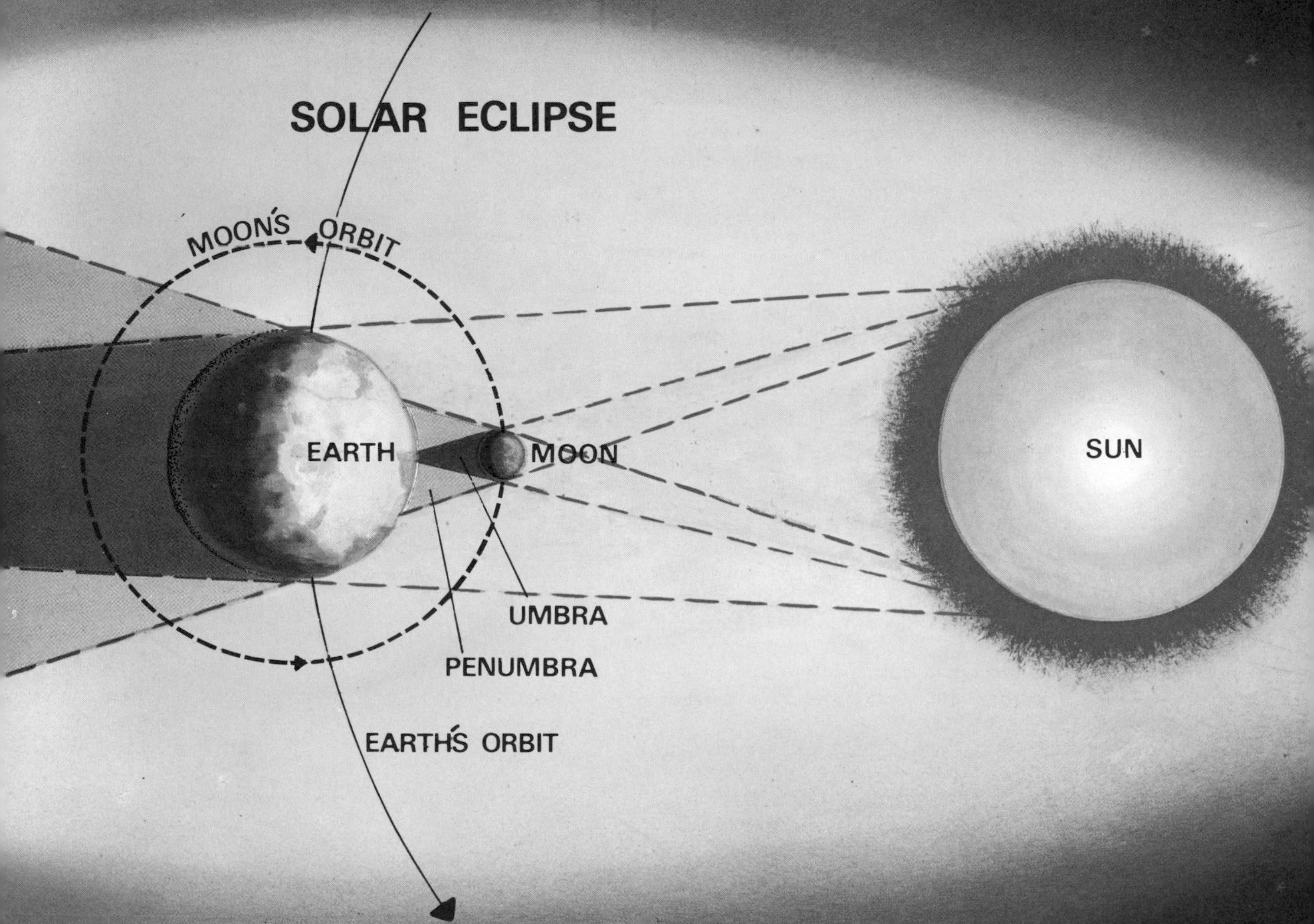

SOLAR ECLIPSE

MOON'S ORBIT

EARTH

MOON

SUN

UMBRA

PENUMBRA

EARTH'S ORBIT

43

Even during a total eclipse like this, some light — the Sun's *corona* — can be seen round the edge of the Moon.

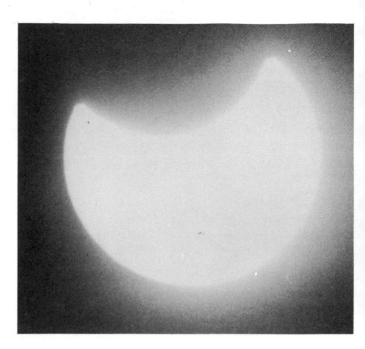

The solar eclipse seen in London in 1976. The next one visible in Britain does not occur until 1999.

places which are directly in line with the Sun and Moon. Here, the Moon's 'umbra', the totally dark part of its shadow, touches the Earth, creating a limited area, about 241 km wide in which the Sun is completely obscured.

Partial eclipse

Elsewhere, the eclipse is *partial,* with one edge of the Sun hidden by the Moon and the other edge visible. In this area, about 6,437 km wide, the Moon's 'penumbra', the lighter part of its shadow, falls on the Earth. The penumbra is lighter because it contains some sunlight, whereas the umbra contains none.

Of course, the effects are not nearly so spectacular or dramatic when the Moon itself goes into eclipse. This happens when it moves through the shadow of the Earth. At this time, the Moon almost disappears, leaving only the faintest outline. As no sunlight reaches it, we see it only by faint reflected 'Earthlight'.

The four moons or satellites of Jupiter, the largest planet in our solar system, go into eclipse in the same way, by passing through Jupiter's shadow. When observed from Earth, each satellite disappears behind Jupiter and is not seen again until it comes out on the other side: then, the satellite appears as a small dark spot, moving across Jupiter's face.

Astronomy aid

All this makes eclipse-time especially precious for astronomers. For only then can they make certain observations. Eclipses make it possible to study the outer parts of the Sun and its chromosphere (atmosphere). Studies can also be made of the corona, and in fact during the eclipse of 1968, the corona was found to contain the gas helium. Eclipses also make it easier to photograph the stars, and some, near the Sun, can only be successfully photographed during these times.

Since 1931, when the French astronomer, Bernard Lyot, first used his invention, the coronagraph, it has been possible to study the Sun's corona at times other than eclipse-time. The other observations, however, must have the Moon to create a screen over the Sun as it does during an eclipse. Otherwise, the Sun is far too bright, and the glare in the sky far too great.

So whereas their ancestors dreaded the blackness of an eclipse, nowadays men actually look forward to those few minutes of darkness in the daytime sky.

This time-lapse photograph clearly shows the stages of this lunar eclipse over Tokyo in 1960. From left to right the Moon is shown at 6.35, 6.45, 7.05 and 7.15 p.m.

Our Changing Climate

YOU might not think your teacher has anything to do with climate, but we can use her to help us distinguish between weather and climate. Although they are naturally closely linked, it is important to make the distinction because many factors that influence our lives are themselves affected by the climates in which we live.

Consider this statement: "My teacher, Mrs. Brown, was in a very bad mood this morning (the *weather*), but she's really a nice person most of the time (the *climate*). In other words, *weather* refers to the atmospheric conditions found at a place at a specified time (the weather forecast tells us what the weather will probably be like the next day). *Climate* is the average weather conditions of a place usually taken over all the days throughout the year.

For any particular place, this means that several measurements have to be made. These include the average daily temperature and the average daily maximum and minimum temperature, the average humidity (amount of water vapour in the atmosphere), amounts of cloud and sunshine and rainfall, and direction and speed of winds. All are taken for each month and for the year to indicate the particular type of climate.

Climatic clues

But there is much more to climate than just everyday measurements. Droughts that parch the land and floods that devastate it are frightening examples of the effects of a change in climate. Scientists dream of someday preventing these by harnessing the climate and perhaps even bringing life-giving water to regions like the Sahara desert.

However, much work remains to be done if we are to unravel the complexity of our climate and discover the reasons for such changes. And, strange as it may seem, scientists are using evidence of the Earth's climate as it has been in the past to help provide a basis for our long-term prospects in the future.

It was during the last century that geologists and scientists found evidence that, thousands of years ago, much of Britain had lain under a massive ice-sheet while at another period in the past the Sahara desert had once been grassy and fertile. Such conditions contrasted sharply with those found today and had been caused by climatic changes.

Since these discoveries, more evidence has been found to tell us how climate varied in the past. Each climatic period leaves evidence of its presence so we have been able to build up a historical pattern of climatic change.

In terms of Man's record of climate change, we can only account for a period of about 3,000 years. Even the more developed nations of the world have kept official records of temperature, rainfall and other features for little more than a century. To go back further, using direct written evidence, researchers have depended on the diaries of people who took a keen interest in the weather and climate after thermometers and barometers first became available in the middle of the 17th century.

From these we have a good record of the so-called 'Little Ice Age' at the end of the 17th century. This was a period when it was very cold; glaciers advanced again and the River Thames in London often froze over.

Old records

To get an idea of climatic conditions before this, we have to infer the evidence from sources like old farm records. For example, many details are found in the records of English farms and manor houses from the 12th and 13th centuries. The number of lambs that died at lambing time gives us a clue as to whether the spring was severe or not; the yield of crops as to how wet it was; and orders of horseshoes how dry it was, as horseshoes wore out more easily on hard, dry soil.

Strangely-marked oracle, or prophecy bones, found in China during the 19th century, take us back even further. These are around 3,000 years old and inscriptions referring to rain seem to indicate that winters in North China were much milder then than now.

From now on, though, we must look to the evidence in Nature to tell us how climate has changed throughout the history of the Earth.

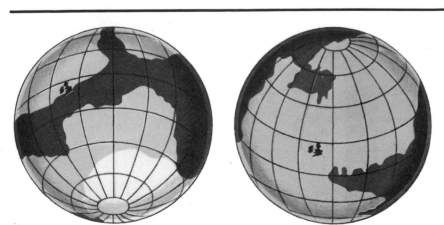

Far left: 300 million years ago. According to rock samples studied, Britain lay near the Equator and had a moist tropical climate. In the Southern Hemisphere South America and South Africa formed part of a large continent much of which was covered by a thick ice sheet, including the South Pole. Conditions were much colder in this region. (The lighter areas show the land masses).

Left: 200 million years ago. The supercontinent of Pangaea had formed (see pages 9 and 10). Britain lay in the interior of this vast area which was out of reach of rain-bearing winds from the sea, giving rise to widespread desert conditions. Measurements of fossil magnetism have helped to show the effects continental drift had on global climate over the last 250 million years. Rock deposits also give us clues to the environment.

Of all Nature's records, the most accurate dating yet developed for past climate comes from tree rings. Their width, density and other features tell us how the local climate changed with each year. For instance, a year of low temperature or rainfall causes a narrow ring. Of course, most trees live for no more than a few hundred years, and even the oldest living things on Earth, the bristlecone pines of California and the American West, are no older than 4,500 years. However, nearby dead trees may be much older. By cross-matching the rings of a living tree with those of a dead tree, it is possible to determine exactly when the dead tree died. The early rings of this dead tree can then be used to determine climate patterns up to 8,000 years ago.

Grains of pollen do not record yearly changes in climate, but they can survive for many centuries. In undisturbed ground, the older pollen grains tend to be buried deepest and in this way the pollen grains give a record of the successive types of vegetation that grew in an area. Different European pollens have been studied that date from the end of the last Great Ice Age, about 10,000 years ago. They indicate that this was followed by a much warmer period in Europe when average temperatures were more than 1°C above those of today. They even tell us that much of Northern Europe was covered by oak forests during this time.

But to go back even further into the past for evidence of climate, we must look not above the Earth, but in it: in the sea, in the ice and in the rocks.

Fossil evidence

Seas and oceans are very important factors in the climates found on Earth, today as in the past. They absorb the heat of the Sun and their currents carry heat from the Equator towards the Poles. But it is in the fossil debris of the ocean floor that we find a record of climate above the surface. Billions of tiny shelled animals and plants live in the upper layers of the oceans. In shallower waters, their shells do not dissolve when they die but drift to the bottom. They collect very slowly, taking thousands of years to form narrow layers.

By drilling cores from the sea-bed we can get a record of the temperature changes over millions of years. Different species can only live in warm waters while others can tolerate much colder conditions. Some cores drilled in the Atlantic Ocean have given us a temperature chart going

Below: A probable scene in the North of England during the last Ice Age, about 18,000 years ago. The glacial landscape was scarred and barren with rock debris thrown up from other regions. These signs of the past presence of large glaciers and ice-sheets in countries like Britain that now have a mild, temperate climate, provide conclusive evidence of great changes in temperature. At the height of the last Ice Age, temperatures in Britain must have been at least 10°C below those of today. Ice cores have been drilled in the great caps of Antarctica and Greenland to measure the oxygen present since this varies according to the temperature in which snow fell to form the ice-sheet. Such measurements can give us a climate record going back over 100,000 years.

back over 100 million years. Also, by checking the amount of oxygen in the shells we can discover how icy conditions were because there is a greater proportion of oxygen present when there is a large volume of ice.

And it is ice itself that has given us a lot of climate information. We know that much of the Earth has been covered in the past by massive ice-sheets because in many cases their action shaped the landscape. The advance and retreat of glaciers (as our drawings show) also tells us whether it is getting warmer or colder.

It is the Polar ice-caps that especially tell us a great deal. These have accumulated over thousands of years rather like the fossils in the sea. It has been discovered that oxygen in glacial ice varies according to the temperature in which the snow fell to form the ice-cap. The lower the temperature, the lower the proportion of oxygen in the snow.

Ice cores that have been drilled in Greenland show detailed changes in climate over the past 100,000 years. We now know that 90,000 years ago there was a sharp drop in temperatures around the world. For the next 80,000 years the Polar ice-caps expanded over different Ice Ages until around 10,000 years ago when a period of relative warmth began.

For climates on the longest time scales we must look at rocks in the Earth's crust. Layers of rock were laid down when the continents looked very different from today. Coal seams were laid down about 300 million years ago. Since coal consists of plants that have broken down and become a rock layer this suggests that much of the Northern Hemisphere was covered by tropical swamps.

Surface changes

But as the continents came together to form the 'supercontinent' of Pangaea (see pages 9 and 10) 200 million years ago, much sandier rock layers tell us that much of this area was very hot and desert-like. The pictures on these pages show how the surface of the Earth changes as the climate changed over millions of years.

From all these records Man has built up a fairly detailed picture of how climate has changed over many millions of years. But in terms of Man himself, climate has given us a curious historical feature. The civilisation of Man has only grown up over the last 10,000 years, that is, since the end of the last Ice Age. And within that short Earthly time the Romans, from 300 B.C. to A.D. 400, built a great empire in what we know was a warm, dry period. This was followed by the 'Dark Ages' and a cooler period of climate.

One thing is certain; Man is affected by climate and we must continue researching to see what changes there may be in store in the future. But we have now reached a stage where Man can influence his climate and that needs careful study, too.

Left: This picture gives an impression of the plant and animal life of 50 million years ago in what is, today, the London area. About 100 million years ago the supercontinent of Pangaea had begun to break up and wide seas formed between the new continents. This allowed moisture-bearing winds to penetrate far inland and consequently such tropical rain-forests sprang up over much of the Earth. Studying sediment cores from the ocean floor gives us some idea of the temperature changes of these prehistoric times. As the continents kept moving, Polar ice-sheets formed and there was world-wide cooling.

Above: The retreat of glaciers. An engraving made in the 1850s (above) of a village in the French Alps shows that the valley glacier was then very close to the village down in the valley. However, by 1966 (right) the glacier had retreated back up the mountain and was almost out of sight. The study of the advance and retreat of mountain glaciers is often a sensitive guide to changes in temperature and snowfall in an area over several years. In fact, the last 100 years has been a period of comparative warmth compared to the previous 400 years, known in Europe as the 'Little Ice Age', when the River Thames in London was often completely frozen over.

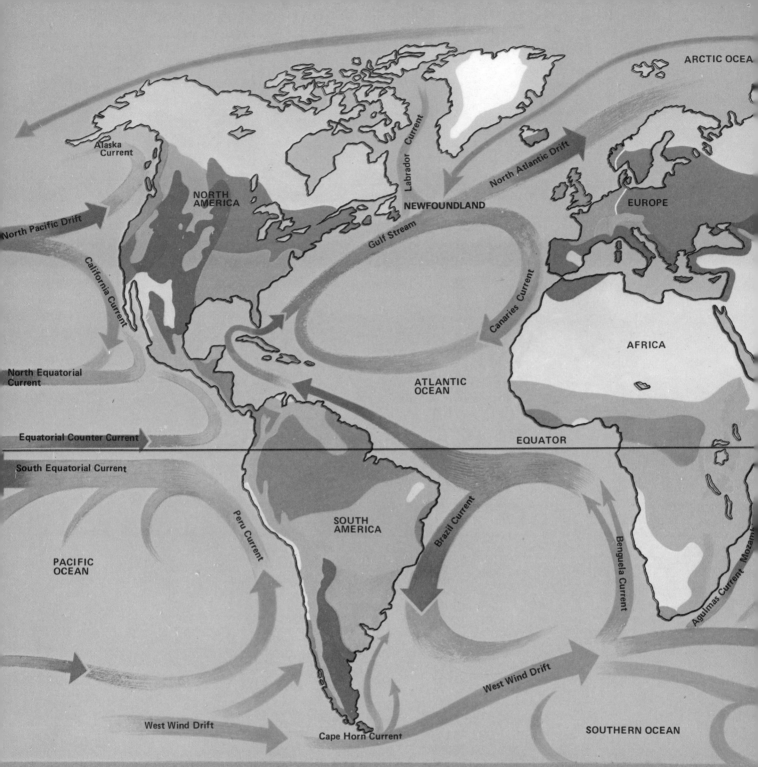

PRESENT-DAY WORLD CLIMATES

	Rain forest: continuously hot; heavy rainfall in all seasons.
	Savanna: hot summers; warm winters; moderate to heavy rainfall.
	Low Latitude Desert and Steppe: continuously hot; little or light rain.
	Sub-Tropical Dry: hot summers; mild winters; light to moderate rain.
	Sub-Tropical Moist: warm summers; cool winters; moderate rainfall.
	Marine Temperate: warm summers; cool winters; mod.-heavy rainfall.
	Continental Moist: warm summers; cold winters; moderate rainfall.
	Continental Steppe: warm summers; cool to cold winters; little rain.
	Continental Desert: warm summers; cold winters; light rainfall.
	Sub-Arctic and Tundra: short summers; long winters; rainfall varies.
	Highland: colder than lowlands in same latitude; rainfall varies.

Our Changing Climate

Part 2: Present and Future

NUMBERS and photographs — these are what Man is using to explore his present-day climate.

On the previous pages you will have read how climates of the recent and distant past have been studied using very different techniques: from old farm records and tree rings to drilled ocean cores and rock layers. There were very few specific written records, and certainly no photographs!

But today, this has all changed. The study of climate now involves a whole series of measurements taken on a world-wide scale. This mass of information is then analysed by powerful com-puters. Similarly, the use of weath- satellites orbiting the Earth gives scie-tists information and photographs climatic features like ocean surfa- temperature, cloud cover and heat th land reflects.

In some ways, the Earth's climate sy- tem can be compared to a vast machin- with the Earth's atmosphere, oceans, a- icecaps as the major components.

The fuel supply is the continuous sol- energy from the Sun, which keeps the- components in constant motion, interac- ing to produce our daily weather a- overall climate.

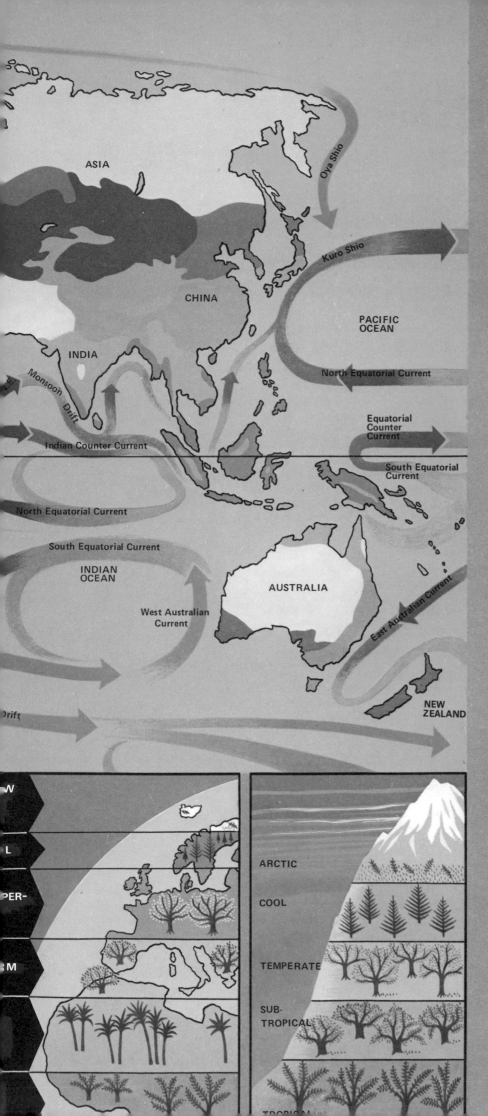

ASIA

CHINA

INDIA

Monsoon Drift

Indian Counter Current

North Equatorial Current

South Equatorial Current

INDIAN
OCEAN

West Australian
Current

AUSTRALIA

Oya Shio

Kuro Shio

PACIFIC
OCEAN

North Equatorial Current

Equatorial
Counter
Current

South Equatorial
Current

East Australian Current

NEW
ZEALAND

Drift

ARCTIC

COOL

TEMPERATE

SUB-
TROPICAL

But as the Greeks knew over 2,000 years ago, the Earth does not have one constant climate. They knew that the parts of the world near the Equator were hot and those near the Poles were cold. The lands between these points were neither very hot nor very cold — a temperate climate. Climates are more precisely defined today, although in large countries the climate will vary from one part to another. It is the changing gears of the climate machine combined with various features of the place itself that determine any climate in one part of the Earth is different from that in another.

One of the major factors is *latitude*; that is, the distance of a place from the Equator. More sunlight reaches the area close to the Equator than other regions because the Sun's rays strike almost vertically. Their heating power is great, giving us the fairly stable tropical climates that do not change much throughout the year. As one travels away from the Equator the heating power of the Sun gets smaller. For example, Great Britain does not get as much heat as Central Africa, and because the Sun swings across the Equator twice a year, Britain has a seasonal climate. It is warm in summer (July) and cold in winter (January). In the Southern Hemisphere the seasons are switched; New Zealand is cold in July and warm in January.

Because the Sun's heating is greatest at the Equator, it heats up the air which then rises and forms clouds and winds in moving masses of air. These control the general circulation pattern of the atmosphere. The movement is usually directed from the Equator towards the Poles, and the winds are deflected by the rotation of the Earth. They bend to the right in the Northern Hemisphere and to the left in the Southern Hemisphere.

The Polar regions have a cooling effect on the Earth's climate. This is because the great sheets of snow and ice reflect the Sun's rays and lessen the amount of heat retained by the Earth's surface. The cold Polar air whips up into cold, biting winds.

As the different winds sweep across the oceans they create another important climate factor — *ocean currents*. These are great swirls of moving water that 'flow' through the oceans and have a warming or cooling effect depending on the winds that produced them. Our world map shows the major ocean currents; red arrows signify warm currents and blue arrows represent cold currents.

Newfoundland is in the same latitude as Britain but is much cooler. The difference is caused by the Gulf Stream, a warm current which benefits the British

Far left: Latitude affects climate. Each climate has different plant and animal life. This ranges from tropical rain forest near the Equator through desert palm trees, temperate oaks, to Arctic tundra.
Left: Temperature falls as height increases. Tropical forest at sea-level gives way to Arctic vegetation near mountain peaks.

One reason for short-term climate changes may be changes in the Sun itself. Sunspots (patches of cooler gas) are normal features on the Sun. However, very few were seen when the Earth cooled in the Little Ice Age of the 17th century. Such unusual activity may explain cooling trends.

Active volcanos like this one in Hawaii produce great clouds of dust and gas that can reach the upper layers of the atmosphere. This cloud cover reflects the Sun's rays away from Earth and produce a world-wide cooling effect. After Krakatoa exploded in 1883, the next few years were markedly cooler.

Photographs like this, taken by weather satellites orbiting the Earth, have given us more information on climate. They are used to study the distribution and changes in cloud, ice and snow over the Earth. They also give information on the temperature of the atmosphere and oceans. By using satellite pictures we can measure the effect of Man's pollution and overgrazing.

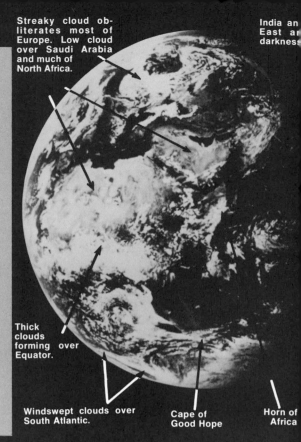

Streaky cloud obliterates most of Europe. Low cloud over Saudi Arabia and much of North Africa.

India an East ar darknes:

Thick clouds forming over Equator.

Windswept clouds over South Atlantic.

Cape of Good Hope

Horn of Africa

climate. The cold Labrador Current affects Newfoundland in the opposite way. Without the Gulf Stream Britain would be about as cold as Greenland. Brrrr!

Since the Earth's oceans can store and transport heat, climates will vary in different places because of their *position* in relation to the ocean.

In summer the land warms up more than the sea, as you may have discovered when you have gone swimming. Cool air from over the sea then blows on to the coast and the temperature falls. At night and in winter the land cools faster than the sea, bringing in warmer air from the sea to raise the temperature.

This means that coastal areas do not have big seasonal and daily temperatures like the centres of continents which are hundreds of kilometres from the sea.

Other important factors affecting climate are local geographical conditions, especially *height*. This usually means the presence of mountains. Although the Sun's rays heat the land surface they have little effect on the air they pass through. So as we go higher it gets colder, and the type of vegetation will change.

High mountain peaks are snow-capped because they reach into very cold upper air layers and are exposed to bitter winds. These upper regions stay cold even when it is summer in the valleys and lowlands below.

Mountains also help in determining how wet a climate is. Moist air rises when winds force it against mountains or over colder air. It then cools and condenses into clouds from which droplets of rain fall.

Air is very moist over the sea and where temperatures are high. This means that there is very heavy rainfall in the rain forests of the tropics when moist air blows in from the oceans.

The future

The driest places on Earth are where winds have blown for long distances over heated land. There is a continuous belt of warm air over the Sahara desert with little cloud formation and very little yearly rainfall.

But even as we become more certain of the characteristics of our present climate, many observers feel that changes are not far away and may be happening now. The frequent droughts of Africa and India and increasing winter sea-ice around Iceland may be the result of gradual alterations.

Some of the possible causes are pictured on these pages. The activity of the Sun is one theory. Increased radiation and sunspots may have climatic effects in the amount of heat our atmosphere absorbs. Volcanic activity has a noticeable effect. The great clouds of ash and dust thrown up form layers that reflect the Sun's rays and consequently cool the Earth.

In terms of longer forecasts, most predictions are bleak. Calculations have been made which indicate that summers in the Northern Hemisphere are getting shorter and colder; the ice-sheet may soon be on the march again.

But any predictions may need to include what effects Man's activities in the 20th century could have on the climate. Atmospheric pollution from cars, aeroplanes and factories means that oxygen is replaced by carbon dioxide. If this formed a 'blanket' around the Earth, the heat that is normally reflected back into Space would be retained and temperatures on Earth would rise. This is known as the 'greenhouse effect'.

Major cities and increasing populations cause local effects (central London is about 2°C warmer than the surrounding countryside), and the removal of vegetation by grazing animals means more heat is reflected away.

Since small changes in climate can have very damaging effects on world food supply and other aspects of our life, Man urgently needs to know more about the natural and man-made changes that may occur. Only then will we know if there is to be a new Ice Age or a major effort to stop pollution and sweltering rises in temperature.

Man's own activities may be starting to affect climates. By burning coal and oil, as in factories like these, we increase the amount of carbon dioxide in the atmosphere at the expense of oxygen. Heat reflected from the Earth's surface is trapped in by these polluted layers producing a warming 'greenhouse effect'.

Blowing hot and cold ... and sometimes wet and dry!

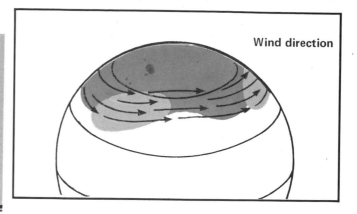

Wind direction

A LL over the world, at some time, Man has been dependent upon winds. Just as the winds shape the sand dunes in the desert so they have helped to shape our lives in whatever part of the world we live.

A particularly striking example is the Netherlands in northern Europe. In the past, the winds have been used to turn the sails of over 10,000 windmills throughout the country. These helped to grind the grain, saw wood for farmers and, very importantly, pump away sea water so that land could be reclaimed. Furthermore, the winds were used by skilful Dutch sailors to propel their ships to many parts of the world, loaded with goods for trade or people who hoped to settle in a different land.

Over the centuries, people have both misunderstood and feared the winds of the world. The ancient Romans had noticed that there were patterns to the winds, and they used these in the spring when ships loaded with grain from Egypt had to cross the Mediterranean Sea quickly if the grain was not to rot.

However, the famous North Atlantic *trade winds* (trade is an old word and here means 'in all directions') frightened the sailors under the command of Christopher Columbus. They blew ceaselessly to the west from North Africa, and Columbus and his crew wondered if they would ever get home. They later discovered that farther to the north, the *westerlies* blew in the opposite direction from the east coast of America.

Ferdinand Magellan, a great Portuguese navigator who was killed during an attempt to find the sea route westwards to the Indies from Spain, also met sets of winds that puzzled him. As he travelled westwards in 1519, he met the trade winds across the Atlantic. Then as he passed Cape Horn, the southernmost tip of South America, he hit the strong *roaring forties*, before sailing up into gentle trade winds in a new ocean that he named the Pacific.

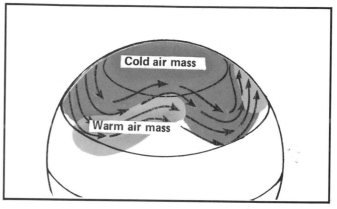

Cold air mass

Warm air mass

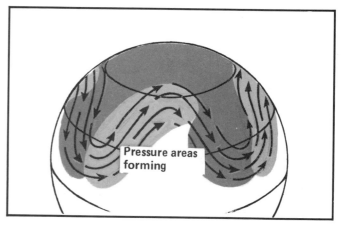

Pressure areas forming

One important factor in wind production is the meeting of warm and cold masses of air. These four diagrams show this occurring in the northern hemisphere. The dark grey areas are cold, dry polar air which slowly disperses outwards from the North Pole. The lighter areas are moist, warm air originating from the tropics and as this moves northwards it produces the westerly winds.

Where the air masses meet is the 'polar front'. This begins to undulate as the cold and warm masses continue their movement, the winds following the flow of these masses or 'cells'. Eventually isolated cells are formed with high-pressure (colder) and low-pressure (warmer) areas. These disturbances contribute to the weather conditions in a particular place.

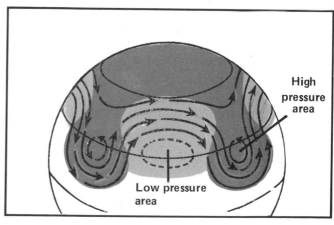

High pressure area

Low pressure area

Right: One of the world's most interesting winds is the *chinook* of the Rocky Mountains in North America. In fact, its mechanism is not yet fully understood. Warm, moist air blows in from the Pacific and has to rise when it meets the Rockies. The air cools and drops moisture as rain on the western slopes. Passing over the mountains it becomes the warm, dry chinook. It is thought that this is due to the air compressing as it descends on the eastern side of the mountains. The chinook can raise the temperature enough to melt snow on these slopes.

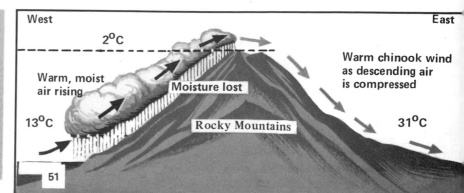

West

East

2°C

Warm, moist air rising

Moisture lost

Warm chinook wind as descending air is compressed

13°C

Rocky Mountains

31°C

It was not until the last century that an American hydrographer (scientist who surveys and maps the seas) called Matthew Fontaine Maury began to study and chart wind patterns throughout the world.

He did this by examining thousands of ships' logbooks, noting the appearance of different winds at specific points in the oceans on certain dates. He was then able to show how ships could use the wind patterns to find a quicker passage between ports.

We have known for a long time that wind is moving air, and the winds were named after the direction *from* which they blow; so a wind blowing from the north is called a north wind. But until recently Man was puzzled as to what forces were the cause of winds.

Wind Factors

Today we know that there are two important factors creating and driving the winds. First there is the rotation of the Earth itself, which 'drags' a mass of air with it. The second factor is the constant interchange between the warm air of the tropics and the cold air of the polar ice-caps. These factors combine to give us regular patterns of wind extending over thousands of kilometres of the Earth's surface.

In many places the wind still plays an absolutely crucial part in peoples' lives. Consider the monsoons of Asia. In summer the central land mass of Asia heats up and the warm air rises forming a low-pressure area. Winds that have passed over the sea picking up moisture rush in to fill this area, and the moisture falls as monsoon rain in India, Japan and much of southern Asia. The farmer planting his crops in these lands each spring is totally dependent on the rainy season so the crops can grow and he can feed his family.

Hills and mountains also cause winds and some of these have been given special names. Warm air over high ground which cools down at night tends to flow down to lower areas; an example is the *mistral* wind which is sucked down the Rhône valley in France towards the Mediterranean.

The *sirocco* wind has another effect. This is a warm wind that forms over the Sahara desert in North Africa then descends northwards over the Mediterranean. Picking up moisture on the way it strikes Italy, Spain and France bringing warm rain.

In fact, the sirocco is an example of a type of wind known as the *Föhn* wind. This is a warm dry wind blowing down the northern slope of the Alps. It starts as moist air over the Mediterranean but drops the moisture as rain as it rises over the Alps. Its warming effect often melts snow on the northern slopes. Föhn wind types are seen in many parts of the world.

Perhaps the most spectacular mountain wind is the *chinook*. This sweeps over the Rocky Mountains in the area around the Canadian border. On the western slopes it drops snow and rain appearing on the eastern slopes as a hot, dry wind. It is named after the Chinook tribe of Red Indians who refer to it as the 'snow eater', and it can cause huge changes in temperature — one February in the Alberta province of Canada it even took the

Local winds of Europe and North Africa. Special local conditions such as desert or mountainous areas give rise to regional winds affecting other areas. These can have different characteristics; the *sirocco* is a warm wind from the Sahara that becomes moist as it passes over the Mediterranean; the *bora* and *mistral* are unpleasantly cold winds that can damage valuable crops; the *Föhn* is a warm mountain wind; while the *helm* is a cold, dry wind that accompanies heavy cloud. These conditions can be repeated in other parts of the world but the winds have their own local names, of course.

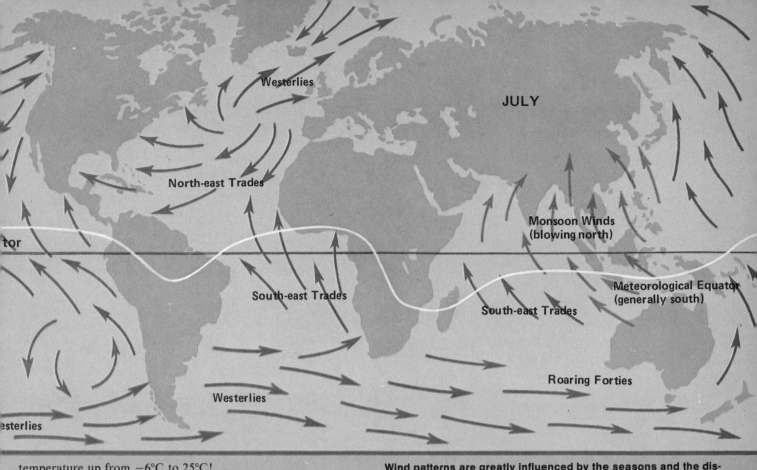

Westerlies

JULY

North-east Trades

Monsoon Winds
(blowing north)

South-east Trades

South-east Trades

Meteorological Equator
(generally south)

Westerlies

Roaring Forties

esterlies

tor

temperature up from −6°C to 25°C!

Hot deserts cause winds to rage. In Iran, winds can carry huge sandstorms with them so that whole villages are almost buried. Other hot winds can dry out vegetation and lead to devastating bush fires.

But we have seen wind's beneficial effects too, and today scientists are experimenting to see if the wind can be used with modern windmills in an alternative energy scheme. So although satellite pictures have told us much about the part wind plays in weather, it could also happen that this ancient source of power will come to Man's aid once more as supplies of natural fuel are reduced.

Wind patterns are greatly influenced by the seasons and the distribution of land and sea. Where the systems of the northern and southern hemispheres meet is called the 'meteorological equator'. This does not lie on the geographical Equator. The diagrams above and below show the major wind directions in January and July respectively.

Below: **Major winds in January. The northern continents are cold forming high-pressure areas. The monsoon winds blow south and the metorological equator is mostly south of the geographical Equator.**

Above: **In July, the summer Sun produces lower pressure over the northern hemisphere and the meteorological equator moves northwards.**

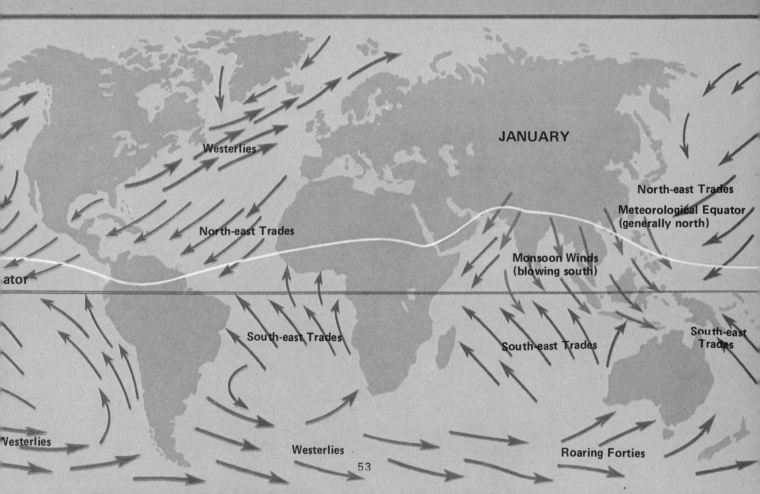

Westerlies

JANUARY

North-east Trades

North-east Trades

Meteorological Equator
(generally north)

Monsoon Winds
(blowing south)

ator

South-east Trades

South-east Trades

South-east Trades

Vesterlies

Westerlies

Roaring Forties

It is a slow process, often taking many thousands of years. But eventually nothing touched by the wind stays the same. Eveything is transfigured by

The Wind of Change

THE great Sphinx that stares calmly out over the Egyptian deserts is today a different statue from the one erected by the Pharaohs. When it was first constructed it was even more impressive than it is today. Over the centuries its once sharp features have been worn away.

But it is not human vandals, or the chemical action of water or acid that have caused this. The agent responsible is the wind.

Yet how can solid rock be shaped by something as insubstantial as the wind?

The process is just the same as that used by a craftsman smoothing and shaping a hand-made violin. Sand particles blown in the wind act in the same way as the craftman's sandpaper.

The gritty wearing-away of sand, year in, year out, can create fantastic shapes and bizarre patterns. In Monument Valley in Utah, U.S.A., for example, millions of years of weathering by the wind have produced unearthly pillars of red sandstone up to 300 metres tall.

Erosion by the wind occurs everywhere — wherever the wind blows. But it is most noticeable in dry desert regions. In other places, erosion by water (see pages 11, 12 and 13) is usually far greater than that by the wind as, of course, you would expect.

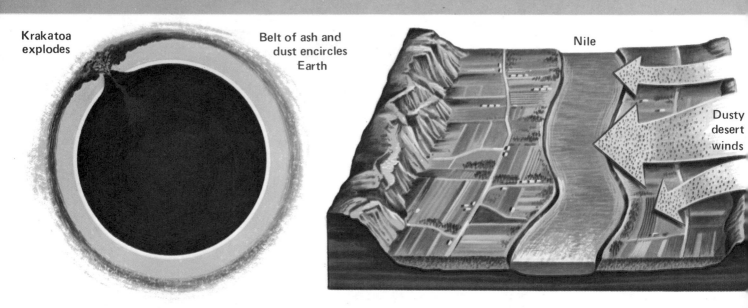

Krakatoa explodes

Belt of ash and dust encircles Earth

Nile

Dusty desert winds

Above: The wind can move mountains! When the island of Krakatoa exploded in 1883, much of it was thrown high into the atmosphere, where it was distributed round the world by the winds.

Erosion in one part of the world often means fertile land in another. The soil of the Nile valley (above) has been improved by fine dust blown in from the surrounding desert. Similarly, each year four million cubic metres of dust — enough to fill 40 daily train-loads of 30 trucks each — are blown on to the Canary Islands from the coast of Africa (below).

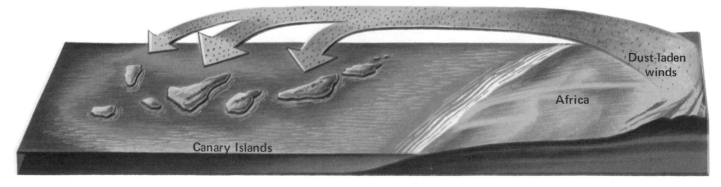

Dust-laden winds

Africa

Canary Islands

Left: The famous lion with a man's head — the Sphinx — of Egypt. Centuries of erosion by the desert wind have worn away its once sharp features.

Below: Some of the most spectacular wind erosion features can be seen in the state of Utah in the U.S.A.
1 Monument Valley, Navajo Tribal Park
2 The 'Delicate Arch', Arches National Park
3 Bryce National Park

The stronger the wind the more wearing away or erosion is likely to take place, and desert regions are often notorious for their powerful, dry and dusty winds. In North Africa, for example, the cold north wind called the *harmattan* can cloak the countryside for hundreds of kilometres in choking dust and even prevent aircraft from landing. Likewise the warm *sirocco* on the coasts of Africa.

Sometimes rapidly rotating colums of air produce particularly violent 'dust devils'. In northern Sudan, travellers are often quite terrified by the sight of these dust storms. But even if a dust devil is not blowing, deserts are constantly being buffeted by winds of some kind.

These winds move sand particles (up to half a millimetre in size) by three processes. First there is sand carried literally in the air by 'suspension' as it is termed. Then some sand is moved along the ground by what is called 'surface creep'. And finally there is 'saltation'.

Saltation has nothing to do with salt. Instead, the word means 'hopping' and this is precisely what happens as the fine particles are jiggled along. Sand is sucked into the air by the action of a strong wind, the grains rising quickly and reaching relatively high speeds — a few metres a second — before falling to the ground. Smaller particles remain airborne for longer, but the bigger grains fall more rapidly. They hit the ground and bounce up a few other grains lying on the ground so that they in turn become pushed on by the wind. So there is constant movement with grains on the ground being helped along by those that are descending from the air.

In desert regions it is easy to see where these sand particles come from. They are swept up from the ground. But that is only part of the answer — where does the sand on the ground come from in the first place?

Much comes from the action of the sand already there

breaking up larger rocks. But initially small particles are produced by the extremes of temperature common in most desert regions. By day it is hot, but at night it often gets very cold. As the temperature changes, the rock alternately expands and contracts, and over the years eventually the rocks crack. In the end — helped by the action of the wind-borne dust — they break up altogether.

By studying the shapes produced and the patterns of winds that blow in dry regions, scientists have been able to discover that wind erosion works in two ways. First there is what is called 'deflation' — the lifting and carrying of sand-sized particles — which will often leave behind a large area strewn with gravel or cobblestones, too big to be lifted by the wind.

Natural sandblast

The second type of erosion is called 'abrasion' and occurs usually within a metre or so of the ground, where sand is lifted from the ground by saltation. The wind-borne sand acts rather like the sandblast used to clean old buildings and is what undercuts rocks and produces patterns and polished surfaces, which look as if they have been shaped by a giant stone mason.

The result of these processes is a landscape such as that of the Bryce National Park in Utah, U.S.A., with its strange sandstone and limestone 'sculptures'. Elsewhere in America, in Texas or Arizona — home of the cowboys — can also be seen towering rock formations moulded by the wind.

Many thousands of years are needed for the wind to erode giant rock outcrops. Yet the wind can shape the scenery far more quickly in sandy regions by blowing the sand into ever-shifting dunes.

In those deserts where the wind usually blows in one direction and the sand does not cover all the ground, the most common shaped dune is a crescent or *barchan*. The gently sloping rippled back faces the wind, the leading edge has a steep slope down which the sand topples after being blown up the back by the wind. As sand continuously falls over the edge, the whole dune moves along. One day it is there, next day it has moved. At their biggest, these barchans can be as much as 400 metres long and 30 metres tall.

When the winds blow in many directions in the desert, they may produce another type of dune that runs in a long straight ridge — the *seif* dune. These are sometimes very narrow but can extend to a few hundred metres wide.

Seif systems are more static than barchan dunes. In the region of Kordofan they are cultivated by local farmers. And they can be of considerable size, literally hundreds of kilometres long and 150 metres high.

Just how the wind forms a seif is not fully understood. Is it through the action of two spiralling gusts acting in concert? Or are seifs formed by winds blowing in a number of directions, the product of a complicated system of cross-winds?

Of course the wind does not only blow in desert regions. Nor is it only there that it carries wind-borne particles. Everywhere minute specks of solid are swept along by the wind, as we all know when we get grit in an eye.

But where there is water, vegetation binds the soil together so that it cannot blow away, and wind erosion does not occur.

Unthinking ploughing of dry grassland, however, can remove the binding vegetation, and soil can just simply blow away. This is what happened in Oklahoma in the U.S.A in the 1930s, resulting in the infamous 'dust bowl' — a desert made from a fertile area. It is never safe to underestimate the eroding power of the wind.

Soft rock eroded most

Hard rock

Hard rock

Wind

Left: Wind erosion is greatest in dry regions where there is a great deal of loose sand and dust. Rather like sandpaper, the wind-blown sand wears away any exposed rocks. If both hard and soft rocks are exposed, the soft rocks are eroded most.

Below: Continual 'sandblasting' by the wind rounds and polishes rock just as a stream polishes the pebbles of its bed. The final result is firstly the sand itself, then fine dust which is blown away by the wind.

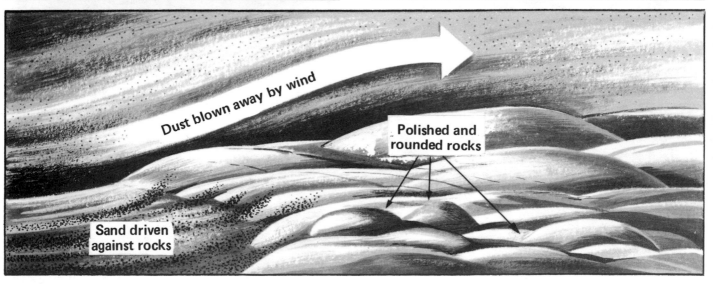

Dust blown away by wind

Polished and rounded rocks

Sand driven against rocks

Nature's Plaster Casts

Thanks to fossils, it is possible for us to have some idea what some forms of life looked like some 600 million years ago . . .

A STUDY of rocks has given scientists a great deal of knowledge about the history of the Earth both before and after the formation of life.

The Earth itself is, in fact, older than the earliest rocks and the earliest rocks are older than the earliest forms of life.

Life forms in any number, however, date back about 600 million years to the first Life Era known as the Palaeozoic Era, since it is in rocks of this era that the earliest fossils have been found.

Nearly all fossils are found in *sedimentary rock*.

Sedimentary rock is formed when rock not covered by the sea is split by the action of wind, rain and ice and the resulting particles in their turn are carried away by wind or water. As the flow of a stream is stopped by some natural hazard, large particles are left behind and smaller ones carried on. Over the centuries, similar-sized particles become welded together and form sedimentary rock.

Variations in the weather or in the water level in which the sedimentary rock has been formed, though, will alter the size and colour of the particles. The result is layering — a phenomenon often seen in cliff faces.

Fossils provide our only means of studying early life forms so it is essential here to give some idea of what fossils are and how they came to be in the rocks in which they are found.

When the world was young it was a dangerous time for all forms of life. Earthquakes, tremendous storms and violent changes in the climate constantly overwhelmed them. Disaster could strike suddenly. Masses of mud, sand and debris buried fish, animals, insects, plants and trees. More and more materials, including rocks, were rapidly piled over the soft watery tomb. The weight exerted such pressure that the debris enclosing the buried objects hardened.

Fossilisation

Inside the natural rock coffin, the once-living matter slowly decayed. Tiny grains of silica seeped into the gap thus left, turning it into a stone-hard replica of the shell-fish, worm, insect, leaf or even large animal. What had happened was that fossilisation had taken place.

There are, however, a number of different sorts of fossil. Some of these will now be described.

Firstly there is the *body fossil*. This is exciting as it

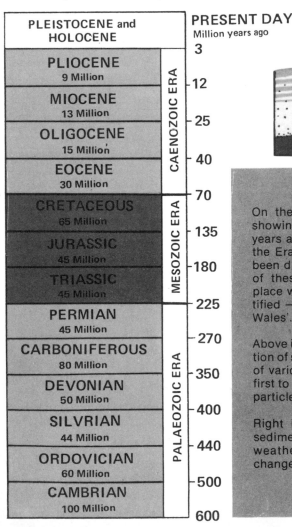

PLEISTOCENE and HOLOCENE		PRESENT DAY	
		Million years ago	
PLIOCENE 9 Million	CAENOZOIC ERA	3	
MIOCENE 13 Million		12	
OLIGOCENE 15 Million		25	
EOCENE 30 Million		40	
CRETACEOUS 65 Million	MESOZOIC ERA	70	
JURASSIC 45 Million		135	
TRIASSIC 45 Million		180	
PERMIAN 45 Million	PALAEOZOIC ERA	225	
CARBONIFEROUS 80 Million		270	
DEVONIAN 50 Million		350	
SILVRIAN 44 Million		400	
ORDOVICIAN 60 Million		440	
CAMBRIAN 100 Million		500	
		600	

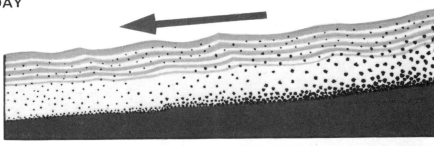

On the left is a time-scale diagram showing the Life Eras from 600 million years ago to the present day. Each of the Eras, except the most recent has been divided into Periods. The names of these Periods often indicate the place where the rocks were first identified — for example, Cambrian is 'of Wales'.

Above is a diagram showing the formation of sedimentary rock by weathering of various kinds. Heavy particles sink first to the bottom of a stream. Lighter particles are carried on further.

Right is seen a diagram of layered sedimentary rock. This is due to weather changes or water level changes.

Far left is shown *Toxodon*, a long extinct South American mammal. Swept downstream, it was covered in silt. Pressure preserved the hard parts and fossilisation took place (see left).
Below are three types of fossil beside a modern Cockle shell. From left to right are a *fossil mould*, a *fossil cast* and an *internal cast*.

shows parts of an animal very little different from what it looked like in real life.

An animal may be drowned or swept downstream by the fast-flowing water. As the water slows its movement, the heavy body of the animal drops to the silt of the bed and more silt settles on top of it, eventually burying it completely. During that time, however, the soft parts of the body are eaten away until only the hard parts remain. When buried, these are safe, as chemical changes occur and fossilisation takes place.

Second there is the *fossil mould*. An object is trapped in silt which solidifies around it. Water drips through cracks in the rock and dissolves the thing which is trapped, leaving just its shape behind it. This shape, used as a mould, will give us the form of the original object in considerable detail.

Third there is the *fossil cast*. This is natural formation of a fossil from a fossil mould.

Fourth there is the *internal cast*. A shell may fill with silt before it disappears. The silt then solidifies and remains as an exact replica of the original shell.

Discovery

Sometimes fossilised animals have been discovered in sedimentary rock which has risen above the water level due to a change in the land level or after change in the water level.

The rock has then been cut into either by water or by Man, excavating a quarry or making a road. One such discovery was of two extinct elephant fossils during quarrying at Aveley in Essex. The particularly fascinating thing about this discovery was that the fossils were found very close to each other but they belong to entirely different times in history. One was of a Woolly Mammoth from the Pleistocene Ice Age and the other was of a Straight-Tusked Elephant of a much warmer time, a number of hundred years later.

Trilobites

Among the earliest fossils are those of the Trilobites. There were a number of different sorts of Trilobite — among them the Strawberry-headed Trilobite, the Spiny Trilobite and the Dolphin-headed Trilobite.

Trilobites lived 500 million years ago, crawling about the sea floor and swimming to the surface to feed on floating weed. Their bodies had two grooves from head to tail, so making them appear to be in three sections. This is why the 'tri' is in their name.

As living creatures, they had numerous legs or feelers. They also had hard heads and armoured bodies. Some, too, had large eyes — although burrowing Trilobites were often blind.

Living relatives of the Trilobites are Crabs but Trilobites as such are no longer to be found.

Many sea creatures of the past, however, as revealed to us in the rocks by their fossils are little changed today. Among these are Jellyfishes and Worms, Starfishes and Sea Cucumbers.

The rocks are indeed of value to modern Man. They show what the world was like, its changes over the centuries and — perhaps most interesting of all — give some indication of what may happen in the future.

Above is shown an excavation that took place quite recently at Aveley in Essex. During quarrying, fossilised bones were noticed. These were removed and examined by scientists and were found to be of two elephants now extinct. The bones were removed and measured and then protected by plaster. After this had been done, they were taken along to a museum and identified more exactly.

Above are three Trilobite fossils. From left to right, they are a Spiny Trilobite, a Dolphin-headed Trilobite and a Strawberry-headed Trilobite. On the right is a reconstruction of animals and plants of seas of the Cambrian Period. In the foreground are shown some Sea Lillies, very common Palaeozoic animals. Beside them is a piece of rock with remains of corals and molluscs.

All About Us

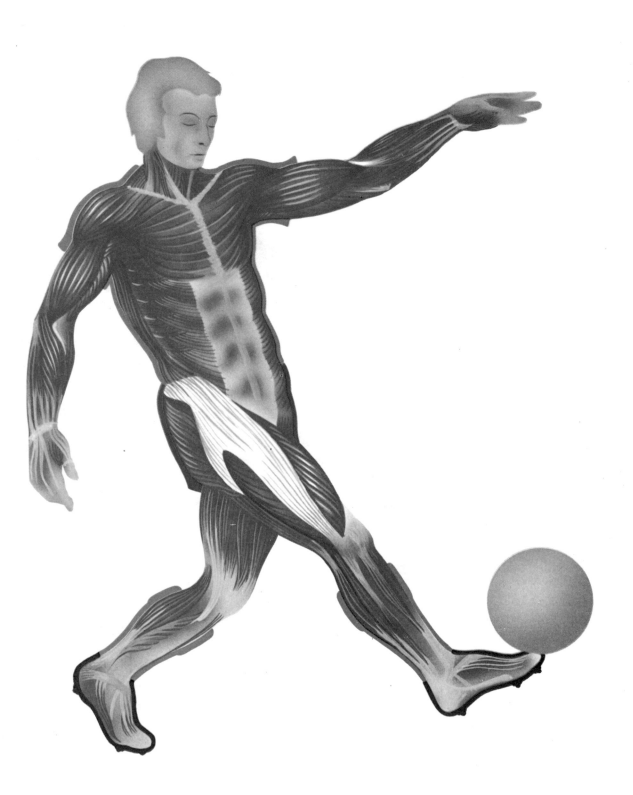

Presenting the bionic man... or the great factory that is inside you

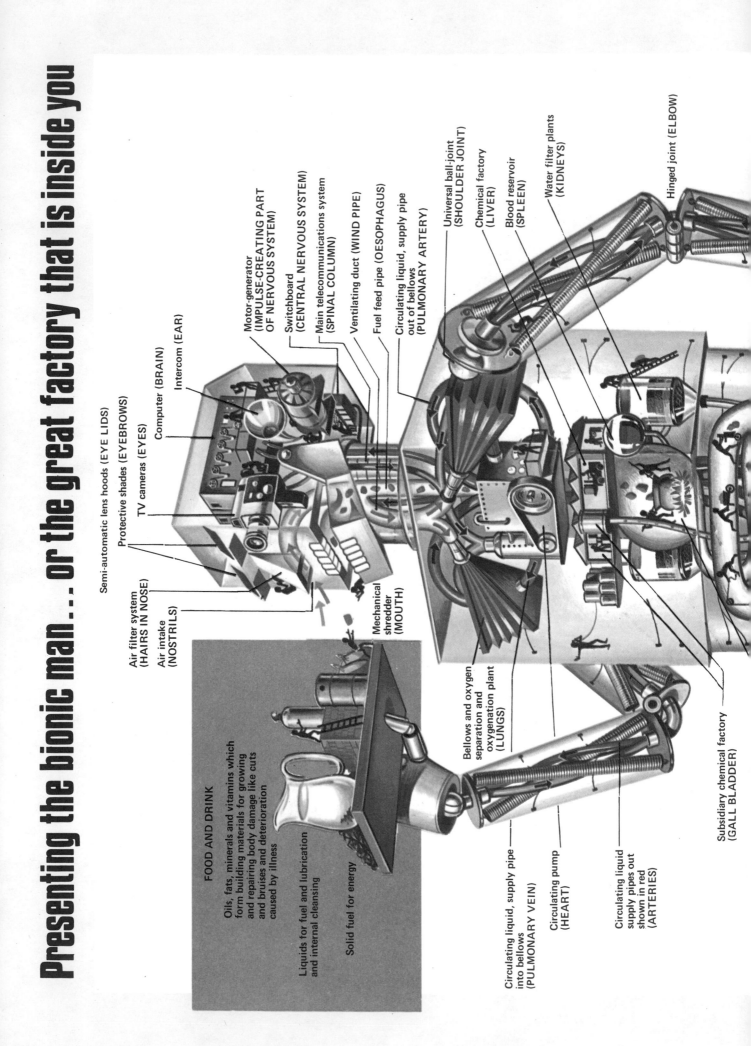

Semi-automatic lens hoods (EYE LIDS)

Protective shades (EYEBROWS)

TV cameras (EYES)

Computer (BRAIN)

Intercom (EAR)

Motor-generator (IMPULSE-CREATING PART OF NERVOUS SYSTEM)

Switchboard (CENTRAL NERVOUS SYSTEM)

Main telecommunications system (SPINAL COLUMN)

Ventilating duct (WIND PIPE)

Fuel feed pipe (OESOPHAGUS)

Circulating liquid, supply pipe out of bellows (PULMONARY ARTERY)

Universal ball-joint (SHOULDER JOINT)

Chemical factory (LIVER)

Blood reservoir (SPLEEN)

Water filter plants (KIDNEYS)

Hinged joint (ELBOW)

Air filter system (HAIRS IN NOSE)

Air intake (NOSTRILS)

Mechanical shredder (MOUTH)

FOOD AND DRINK

Oils, fats, minerals and vitamins which form building materials for growing and repairing body damage like cuts and bruises and deterioration caused by illness

Liquids for fuel and lubrication and internal cleansing

Solid fuel for energy

Circulating liquid, supply pipe into bellows (PULMONARY VEIN)

Circulating pump (HEART)

Circulating liquid supply pipes out shown in red (ARTERIES)

Bellows and oxygen separation and oxygenation plant (LUNGS)

Subsidiary chemical factory (GALL BLADDER)

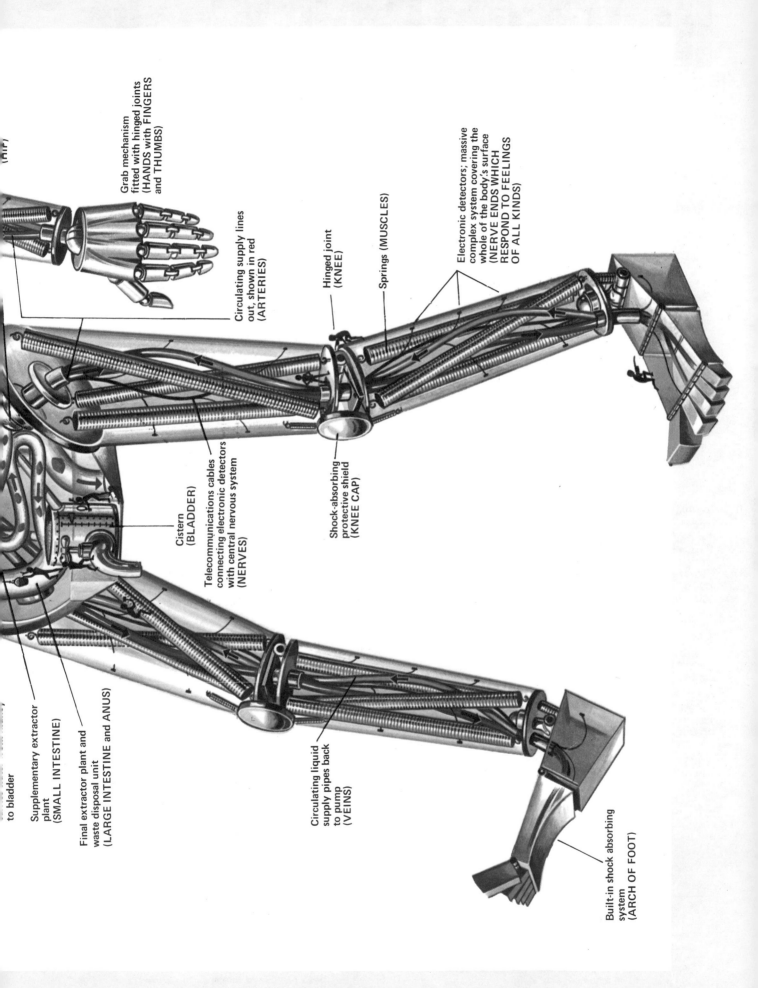

Grab mechanism fitted with hinged joints (HANDS with FINGERS and THUMBS)

Circulating supply lines out, shown in red (ARTERIES)

Hinged joint (KNEE)

Springs (MUSCLES)

Electronic detectors; massive complex system covering the whole of the body's surface (NERVE ENDS WHICH RESPOND TO FEELINGS OF ALL KINDS)

Cistern (BLADDER)

Telecommunications cables connecting electronic detectors with central nervous system (NERVES)

Shock-absorbing protective shield (KNEE CAP)

to bladder

Supplementary extractor plant (SMALL INTESTINE)

Final extractor plant and waste disposal unit (LARGE INTESTINE and ANUS)

Circulating liquid supply pipes back to pump (VEINS)

Built-in shock absorbing system (ARCH OF FOOT)

How Your Body Works

There is no machine more complex than the human body — the most brilliant assembly of scientists and technicians cannot produce anything to match it. Here we look at the fuel it needs.

YOUR body is like a machine in many respects, and, like most machines, it needs fuel. The body gets its fuel from what you eat, drink and breathe, and how well it functions depends to a large extent on all these things.

Oxygen is a vital fuel. It passes into the body through the lungs to energise the blood. Carbon dioxide and other waste gases are breathed out.

Water is also an essential fuel. A healthy adult needs to take in 2.5 litres (5 pints) of water every twenty-four hours, most of it coming from food which contains water and the rest being made up by drinking.

Chemical compounds called *proteins* are needed for bodily health and growth and are found in dairy produce, eggs, meat and vegetables such as peas and beans.

Carbohydrates — compounds of carbon, oxygen and hydrogen — give the body energy and provide power to operate the muscles. Mainly sugars and starches, they come from sweet foodstuffs and starchy foods like cereals, bread, potatoes and pasta. Glucose, the simplest form of sugar, is absorbed quickly into the bloodstream when consumed and people taking part in strenuous activites, such as athletes and mountain-climbers, can give themselves a boost by eating foodstuffs rich in glucose.

Starches have to be broken down into glucose by the body before they can be put to use.

Fats are needed by the human body for warmth and energy. This is why Eskimoes have a fatty diet. Dairy produce, egg yolk, oily fish and nuts are sources of fats.

If you eat too much fatty food and take little exercise to burn it up, your body stores the surplus fat in its tissue and you become overweight.

As well as these fuels, which are consumed in large amounts, the body needs others in smaller quantities.

Minerals like calcium and phosphorus, obtained from milk and fish, promote bone growth. Iron helps to produce red blood cells and is found in spinach. Sodium and potassium maintain the balance of the body's fluids. Other minerals like magnesium, iodine, copper and manganese keep the body working normally.

Vitamins, tiny chemical compounds found in most foods, also perform important functions. From *vita*, Latin for 'life', vitamins are known by letters of the alphabet.

Skin, teeth and bones need Vitamin A: the skin, eyes and the nervous system need Vitamin B; Vitamins C and D are vital for the health of bones, joints and gums; Vitamin E aids the reproduction of new living organs; and Vitamin K helps the blood to clot.

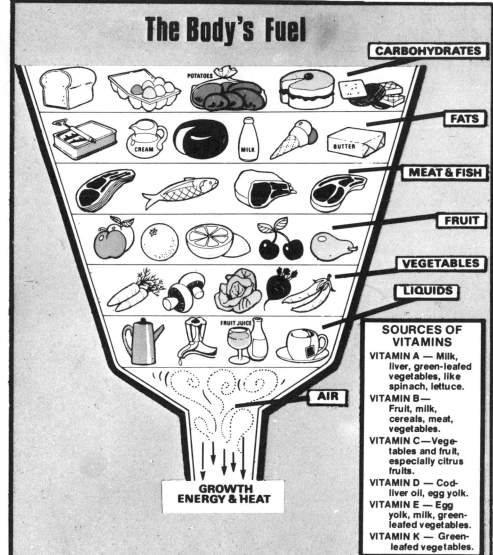

The Body's Fuel

CARBOHYDRATES
POTATOES
FATS
CREAM
MILK
BUTTER
MEAT & FISH
FRUIT
VEGETABLES
LIQUIDS
FRUIT JUICE
AIR
GROWTH ENERGY & HEAT

SOURCES OF VITAMINS

VITAMIN A — Milk, liver, green-leafed vegetables, like spinach, lettuce.

VITAMIN B — Fruit, milk, cereals, meat, vegetables.

VITAMIN C — Vegetables and fruit, especially citrus fruits.

VITAMIN D — Cod-liver oil, egg yolk.

VITAMIN E — Egg yolk, milk, green-leafed vegetables.

VITAMIN K — Green-leafed vegetables.

THE HUMAN MACHINE

The weight of the human body is made up of between 65 and 70 per cent of water.

An adult needs about five pints of water every day. That doesn't mean you have to drink five pints; the solid foods you eat contain a good deal of water.

In the course of a single day the heart of an adult beats a hundred thousand times.

Fair haired people usually have finer hairs and more of them than dark-haired people. A fair haired person has about 150,000 hairs; a dark-haired person about 100,000.

There are more than 600 muscles in the body, varying in length from under 25.4mm. (1 inch) to over half a metre (2ft).

It has been calculated that if all the nerve fibres in the nervous system were tied together, they would go 50 times around the Equator.

The head-to-toe energy of a footballer

Whether you are watching England's Trevor Francis sprinting on to a pass along the wing, or West Germany's Sepp Maier clearing the ball downfield, Argentina's Daniel Passarella surging out of defence into attack or Italy's Roberto Bettega finishing off a move with a headed goal, you are witnessing teamwork in action.

The teamwork which you see on the pitch is the result of players working together to win the match. But within each player, another team is at work and its performance determines how well he plays.

This 'inner team' comprises the systems of the body, organised by the brain and powered by the heart. Just as a footballer is given a specific role to play in his team, each of the body's systems performs a special task.

Masterminding the team's performance is the nervous system, dominated by the brain. In the course of a match, a football player may receive several instructional signals from the trainer's bench or from his team-mates, but the brain receives *100 million* signals *every second* from all parts of the body. Unimportant ones it ignores, but others it has to decide upon in a split second and issue instructions which race along the channels of the nervous system to the points of action.

Some of the body's actions are done instinctively, rather like a footballer trapping a ball. They do not require the brain to think about them. Instead, they are controlled through the spinal cord, a lesser though highly-complex part of the nervous system. The spinal cord assists the brain by taking charge of the many muscular reactions which we perform automatically.

Carrying out the brain's instructions are the muscles which enable parts of the body to move. The heart is, basically, a muscle or muscle-powered pump which does not tire as ordinary muscles do after working hard. It is just as well, since an average person's heart has to beat 42 million times a year for over 70 years.

As muscles need energy in order to work, the body fuels it with *glycogen,* derived from glucose obtained through the digestive system, and oxygen, collected and distributed by the respiratory or breathing system.

The backbone of the body's team, quite literally, is the skeletal system, or system of bones. Its job is to provide support and protection for the softer organs and to give the muscles points to which they can attach themselves.

Driving the team on is the powerhouse, or circulatory system. On instructions from the brain, it distributes the blood to all parts of the body at the rate which is required. At the centre of this system is the heart, or main pump. Vigorous exercise increases the heart's workload dramatically and a person sprinting may need to have 23 litres (40 pints) of blood pumped through his muscles each minute, instead of the normal 4.6 litres (8 pints).

All these systems play their parts in the body's team, a team which is constantly at work within each of us. It is a team without stars — each system is of equal importance for without any single one, you would not survive. And medicine has not yet come up with suitable replacements for the entire bodily systems.

Football team managers can replace players when the need arises, but for the body's team, there are no substitutes waiting to come on.

PHYSICAL FACTS

An athlete's heart has to be able to switch from idling to maximum output in seconds. At rest, it contracts at 70-80 beats per minute. But during vigorous activity, this increases to 140-180 beats per minute.

Sweating helps the body to cool down. Our skin contains 2 million sweat glands. A football player may sweat off 2.5 litres (4.5 pints) of fluid during a 90-minute game, instead of the normal 1-2 pints a day.

Good balance, so admired in any footballer, is maintained by a person's ears. Inside the ears, canals filled with fluid detect any tilting of the head and feed the information to the brain.

Food provides energy for the body in the form of heat. To give his best performance an athlete should choose his diet remembering the temperature as well as his energy output.

Teamwork and energy
Trevor Francis and Trevor Brooking of England combine to beat the Hungarians at Wembley Stadium.

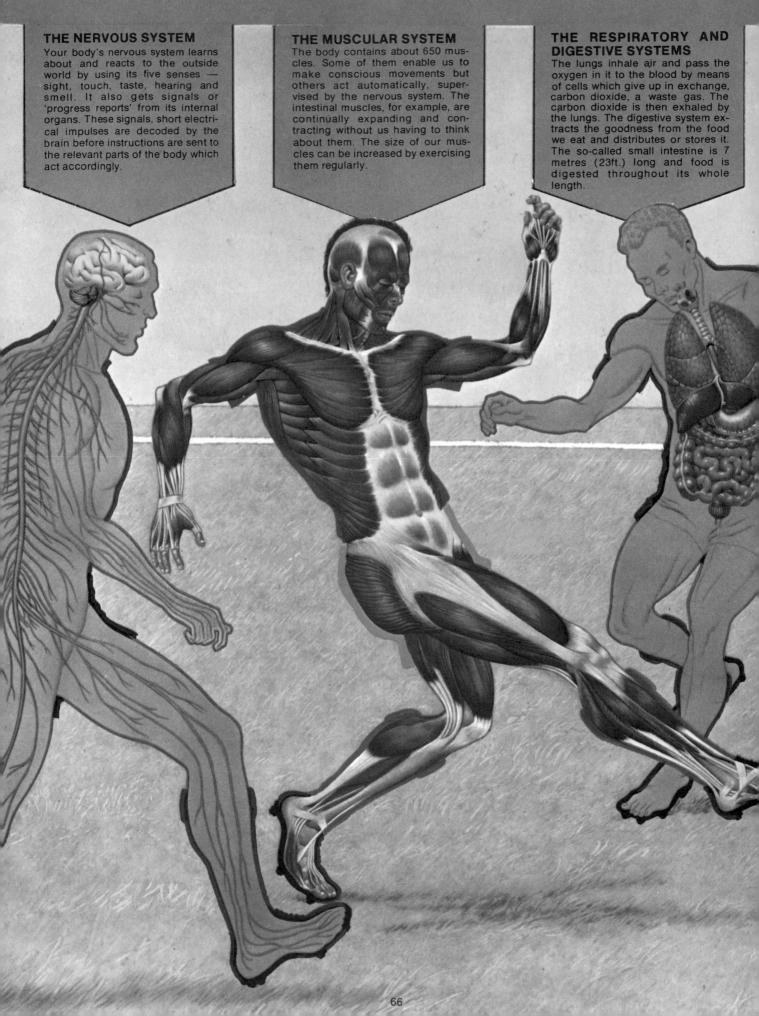

THE NERVOUS SYSTEM
Your body's nervous system learns about and reacts to the outside world by using its five senses — sight, touch, taste, hearing and smell. It also gets signals or 'progress reports' from its internal organs. These signals, short electrical impulses are decoded by the brain before instructions are sent to the relevant parts of the body which act accordingly.

THE MUSCULAR SYSTEM
The body contains about 650 muscles. Some of them enable us to make conscious movements but others act automatically, supervised by the nervous system. The intestinal muscles, for example, are continually expanding and contracting without us having to think about them. The size of our muscles can be increased by exercising them regularly.

THE RESPIRATORY AND DIGESTIVE SYSTEMS
The lungs inhale air and pass the oxygen in it to the blood by means of cells which give up in exchange, carbon dioxide, a waste gas. The carbon dioxide is then exhaled by the lungs. The digestive system extracts the goodness from the food we eat and distributes or stores it. The so-called small intestine is 7 metres (23ft.) long and food is digested throughout its whole length.

THE CIRCULATORY SYSTEM
Your heart, blood and miles of arteries, veins and capillaries (tiny blood vessels) provide a continuous delivery service of vital nourishment to every living cell in your body. The arteries carry the blood from the heart to the cells and the veins take it back again to be recharged. The rate of blood flow through the body increases with exercise.

THE SKELETAL SYSTEM
The skeleton is a framework of bone and cartilage. The body comprises over 200 bones. They are not dry and brittle — each one contains 30 percent of living tissue. Cartilage is a flexible white tissue, rather like unhardened bone. It links bones at the joints, forms pads between spinal vertebrae and stiffens the ears and the tip of the nose.

Bone Hard

THE human skeleton is the result of millions of years of development (or evolution). Man's ancestors left the trees and gradually began to walk upright on two legs, as opposed to creatures like the dog, which found it more convenient to move on four. The result is that Man's bones have developed in a highly specialised way.

The picture on the right shows what happens to Man's bones when he attempts to move on all fours. The skeletal structure of each animal has evolved according to that animal's needs and on the way the animal uses its body, so various different special features evolved. Man's foot developed into a broad flat shape with a complicated group of bones forming the ankle, and five groups of bones forming a platform, with short toes to assist balance. (The feet of apes tend to have much longer toes, more like fingers). A dog's ankle bones have almost vanished, and the heel bone is not used at all to take the weight as it does in a human. The foot bones have fused and almost disappeared. On the other hand, Man has sacrificed his tail. Compare the shoulder, upper arm and elbow of a dog with those of a man and note the differences.

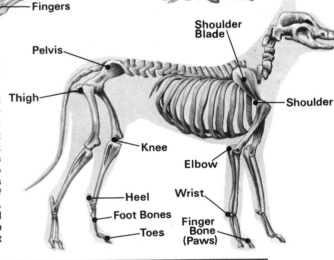

Shoulder Blade · Pelvis · Thigh · Knee · Elbow · Toes · Heel · Wrist · Fingers

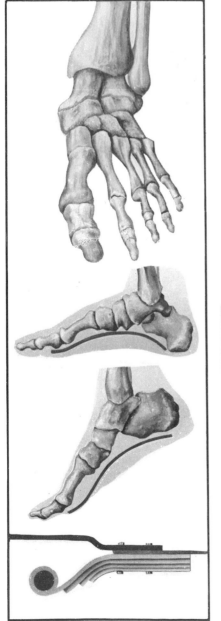

The foot has to adjust quickly to the requirements of standing, walking or running. To enable it to do this, it contains 26 bones and 33 joints held together by over 100 ligaments. Each foot has two main arches which act iike springs or shock absorbers. One arch runs lengthways from the heel to the toes and the other runs across the ball of the foot. If we did not have arches, standing on our feet would be very uncomfortable, like riding a bicycle without tyres.

Pelvis · Thigh · Knee · Heel · Foot Bones · Toes · Shoulder Blade · Shoulder · Elbow · Wrist · Finger Bone (Paws)

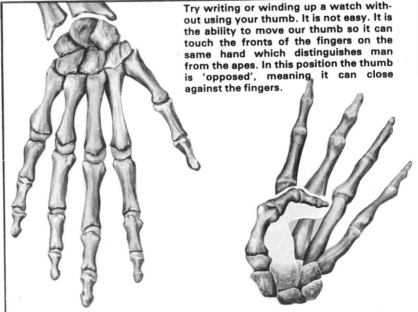

Try writing or winding up a watch without using your thumb. It is not easy. It is the ability to move our thumb so it can touch the fronts of the fingers on the same hand which distinguishes man from the apes. In this position the thumb is 'opposed', meaning it can close against the fingers.

The inside structure of a bone.

Bones are the hardest tissues in the body. They consist of a solid, rigid matrix of cells impregnated with calcium and magnesium salts. We need to take in calcium, phosphorus and Vitamin D in our diet in order to keep our bones strong. Inside the hollow of the bone is a spongy, porous tissue filled with a fatty substance called marrow. Bones of older people contain more mineral substances. They are, therefore, more brittle, and snap in two when they break. Children's bones have more gristle or animal substance. So, instead of snapping, the bone is more likely to bend and split on the outside.

Nature's spring cushions in joints.

The 230 joints in the body all play their parts in allowing the skeleton to maintain its shape and, in some cases, to move. Some of the body's joints do not move at all; for example, the cranial bones of the skull. Others, like the elbow joint, operate like the hinges of a door, allowing movement in one direction only, while the 'ball and socket' joints of the shoulders and hips move in different directions. The ends of bones are covered with cartilage or gristle which forms a rough cushion and prevents two bones jarring upon each other.

THE SKULL

The skull is composed of 22 bones. Eight of these are flat cranial bones which protect the brain and are held together by immovable joints called sutures. The remaining 14 are the facial bones. The spine joins the head underneath and towards the middle of the skull so that the head balances on it.

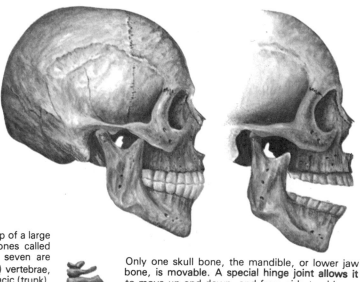

The Spine

The spine is made up of a large number of small bones called vertebrae. The top seven are called cervical (neck) vertebrae, the next twelve thoracic (trunk), and it is to these that the ribs are attached. The bottom five are the lumbar (loin) vertebrae which fit into each other so that they can move freely. Below these are the fused sacral vertebrae (5) and the coccyx (4). Between each of the vertebrae is a cushion similar to those between limb joints. It is when one of these cushions becomes displaced that a person is said to have a slipped disc.

Only one skull bone, the mandible, or lower jaw bone, is movable. A special hinge joint allows it to move up and down, and from side to side, so that we can chew food. The mandible is the heaviest bone in the skull.

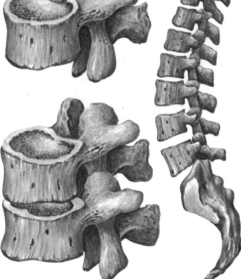

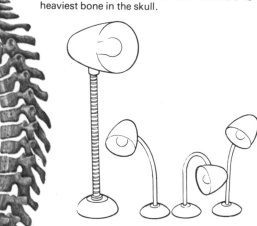

The spine is flexible, rather like the flexible stands of some desk lamps which can be manipulated into a variety of positions.

The body's hinge joints, such as those in the fingers, elbows and knees, move only in a backward and forward direction. Like moving parts of a machine, they need to be lubricated and the body produces its own 'oil', called synovial fluid, from a special membrane around each joint.

The Rib Cage

We have twelve pairs of ribs in our rib-cage (shown above) which has been designed by Nature to have both strength and movement — strength for the protection of vital organs and movement to allow the lungs to expand and contract as we breathe. Elastic cartilage joins 10 of the ribs to the breast bone and to each other as the remaining two are loose and are sometimes called 'floating ribs'.

Whether you are lifting great weights or dancing in a discotheque, playing football or performing somersaults, shaking hands or waving farewell, you are placing demands on the human skeleton, one of the many engineering marvels of Nature. The skeleton is strong and flexible to allow for a wide range of movements and its bones continue to grow until we are in our early 20s. The amount of growth depends on hereditary factors as well as the stresses placed on the various bones.

The skeleton is the body's framework. Without it there would be nothing to keep us upright.   And without this structure of bones, together with the muscles that work them, we would not be able to move either.

The body has 206 bones of different sizes, and as well as supporting us, some of these bones also have an important role in protecting vital organs from injury.

The skeleton is made up of a variety of bones, all designed to do their separate jobs as efficiently as Nature has been able to devise. The long bones of the limbs are tubular, so as to combine lightness with the greatest possible strength. If the bones were solid they would be so heavy that we would become very tired indeed through the effort of moving about!

These long bones of the limbs also act as levers, and through their joints, enable us to bend our arms and legs. The bones are held together by strong bonds of connective tissue, or ligaments. These keep the bones firmly in place.

The shorter bones of the body, those for example in the wrist and the foot, provide great strength. Imagine the weight they have to bear when an acrobat stands on his hands, or a weightlifter groans beneath an enormous load!

The spine is the lynch-pin of the body's bone structure. At the one end, it provides support for the skull, while at the other it allows the weight of our body to be distributed to the pelvis.

It is composed of 33 vertebrae — bony rings separated by discs of gristle called cartilage. The upper seven vertebrae support the skull, and allow us to nod our head.

Twelve thoracic vertebrae support the ribs, while others lower down have less mobility. For example, the five sacral vertebrae attached to the pelvis are all fused together.

Apart from acting as a structural anchor for the body, the spine also encloses the spinal cord, the central mass of nerves that go to the brain, which runs through the hollow canal between the vertebrae.

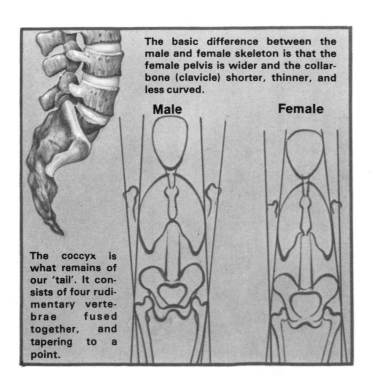

The basic difference between the male and female skeleton is that the female pelvis is wider and the collarbone (clavicle) shorter, thinner, and less curved.

Male   **Female**

The coccyx is what remains of our 'tail'. It consists of four rudimentary vertebrae fused together, and tapering to a point.

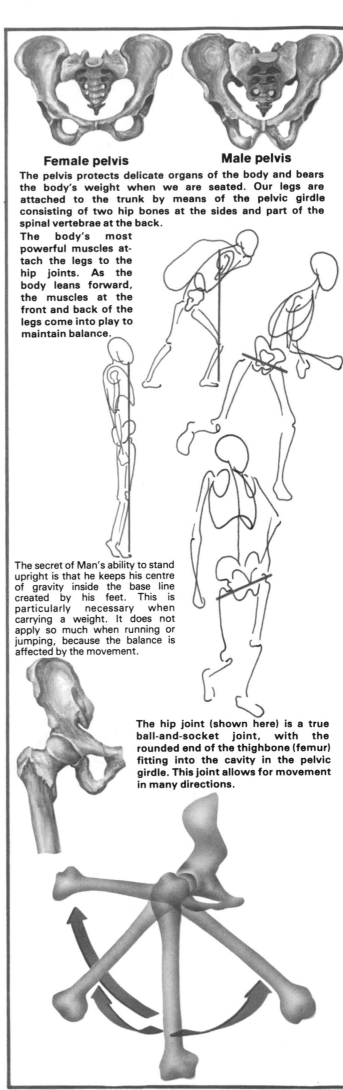

Female pelvis   **Male pelvis**

The pelvis protects delicate organs of the body and bears the body's weight when we are seated. Our legs are attached to the trunk by means of the pelvic girdle consisting of two hip bones at the sides and part of the spinal vertebrae at the back.

The body's most powerful muscles attach the legs to the hip joints. As the body leans forward, the muscles at the front and back of the legs come into play to maintain balance.

The secret of Man's ability to stand upright is that he keeps his centre of gravity inside the base line created by his feet. This is particularly necessary when carrying a weight. It does not apply so much when running or jumping, because the balance is affected by the movement.

The hip joint (shown here) is a true ball-and-socket joint, with the rounded end of the thighbone (femur) fitting into the cavity in the pelvic girdle. This joint allows for movement in many directions.

The Human Camera

Continuing our look at the body, we examine your window on the world.

I f we had no eyes, our world would seem an extremely limited place. We can touch, taste and smell only things which are close to us, but we can see, and so find out, not only about things nearby but also about things which are often a long way away.

However, because most people's eyes work so smoothly and automatically, they rarely think about them. If you pause to consider your eyes, you are confronted by one of the marvels of Nature.

Our eyes are always moving this way and that very rapidly, and are rarely still for more than one-tenth of a second. Our eyelids blink about 20 times each minute to clean away dust and dirt from the surface of the eyes and shut quickly in protection if something flies towards them.

We can glance from one thing to another in a 50th of a second. We can see and recognise a picture flashed on to a screen for a 15th of a second, as well as a bright flash of light that lasts for less than one-thousandth of a second.

In the dark, we can detect a glow of light so faint that it is less than one-thousandth of the brightness of a candle flame, but we are also capable of seeing light which is more brilliant than a billion candles.

From stars to grains of sand

We can see tiny grains of sand, or specks of dust, if they are only a few centimetres away from us, yet we can also see the stars, the nearest of which is 4.2 light years away. (A light year is a measure of astronomical distance, equal to the distance light travels in one year, and is the equivalent of almost 40 million, *million* kilometres). Light is essential for sight. In complete darkness all of us are blind, as our eyes cannot function. However, there is rarely total darkness unless artificially created, and man-made light overcomes the natural darkness that arrives with the setting sun.

But how do these wonderful eyes work?

The eye itself is shaped approximately like a ball but, looking at someone, we only see a small part of it. In the middle of it is a coloured ring called the *iris,* at the centre of which is the *pupil* — an opening through which the light passes, rather like the aperture of a camera. In fact, several structures of the eye have basic equivalents in a camera, but the eye is much more complex and versatile.

The eye is completely surrounded by a tough membrane with a transparent bulge in front, the *cornea.* This acts like a window to allow light rays to pass through to the pupil.

The iris is attached to muscle, and so can expand or contract to vary the size of the pupil according to the power of the light reaching it. In dim light it contracts, making the pupil large or dilated, and in bright light it expands, to make the pupil small. The diaphragm of a camera works like this.

Behind the iris and pupil is the crystalline *lens,* which brings the light rays to focus on a light-sensitive screen at the back of the eyeball called the *retina.* Between the retina and the sclerotic is a layer containing blood vessels, the *choroid.* The lens can alter in shape between flat and circular by the relaxation of the *suspensory ligaments* so the image on the retina is clearly focused. However, because the lens is basically convex, this image is upside down, as the diagram below shows.

Like a film

The retina, which acts something like the film in a camera, is composed of numerous nerve cells of a very specialised nature. These cells are of two types; one called *rods* and the other *cones* (so named because of their shape). Both respond to light stimulation and they can convert light energy into nerve impulses. The rods differentiate between black, shades of grey and white, and are around the outer edge of the retina. The rods detect shape. The cones, more numerous in the middle of the retina, respond to bright and coloured light. Each is sensitive only to one of the three primary colours — red, green or blue, — but by responding in various proportions, all other colours and shades of colours are observed.

Even though the rods and cones are individually very small, each has a connection to a nerve fibre, and at one point on the retina, these fibres join together in a mass to form the optic nerve which conveys the impulses to the brain. At this point there are no light-sensitive cells and, therefore, because no image can form there it is known as the blind spot.

Every minute the visual centre at the back of the brain, to which the optic nerve leads, receives millions of impulses. It is rather like a busy telephone switchboard, where the messages are received and arranged to give us the sensation of vision. Here, the image on the retina is reversed to appear the right way up.

Only the brain can interpret the things our eyes 'see' and so tell us what it is. Our eyes may work perfectly but, if the optic nerve leading to the brain were destroyed, we would see nothing.

Your eyes are your windows on the world, valuable and irreplaceable. Take care of them!

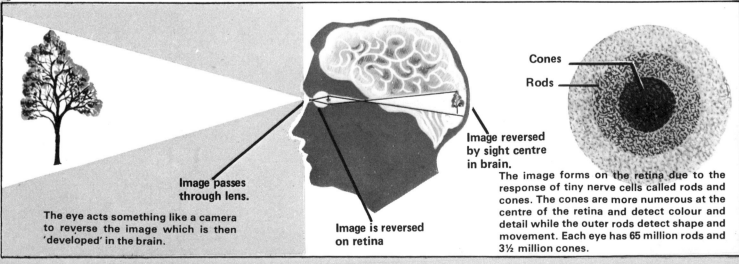

Image passes through lens.

The eye acts something like a camera to reverse the image which is then 'developed' in the brain.

Image is reversed on retina

Image reversed by sight centre in brain.

Cones

Rods

The image forms on the retina due to the response of tiny nerve cells called rods and cones. The cones are more numerous at the centre of the retina and detect colour and detail while the outer rods detect shape and movement. Each eye has 65 million rods and 3½ million cones.

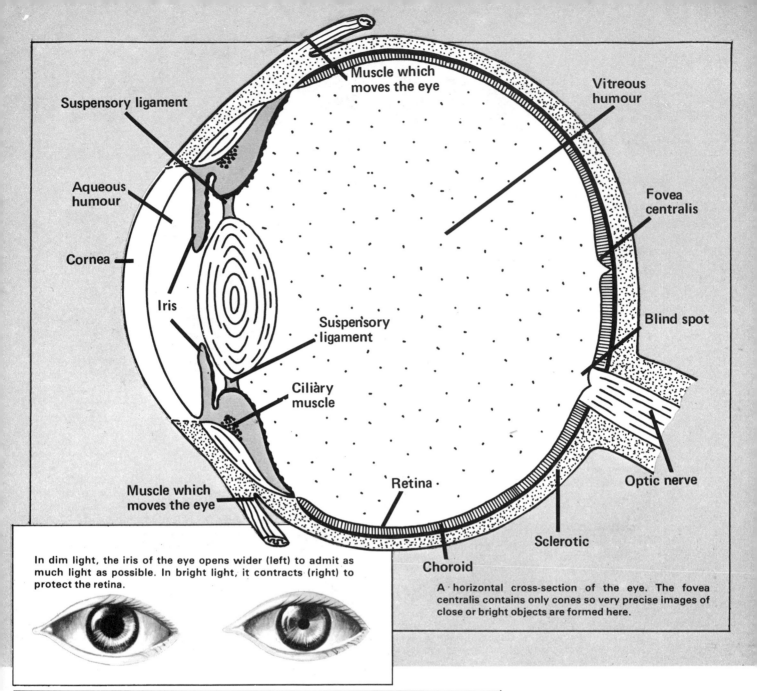

Suspensory ligament

Aqueous humour

Cornea

Iris

Muscle which moves the eye

Suspensory ligament

Ciliary muscle

Muscle which moves the eye

Retina

Vitreous humour

Fovea centralis

Blind spot

Optic nerve

Sclerotic

Choroid

In dim light, the iris of the eye opens wider (left) to admit as much light as possible. In bright light, it contracts (right) to protect the retina.

A horizontal cross-section of the eye. The fovea centralis contains only cones so very precise images of close or bright objects are formed here.

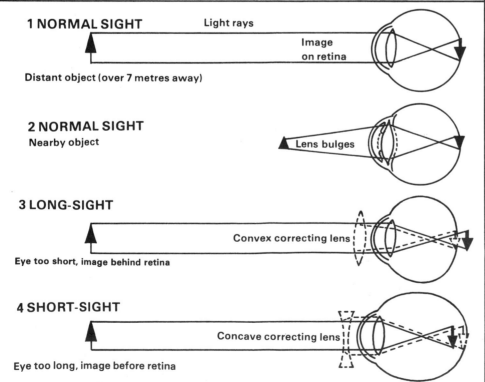

1 NORMAL SIGHT

Light rays

Image on retina

Distant object (over 7 metres away)

2 NORMAL SIGHT

Nearby object

Lens bulges

3 LONG-SIGHT

Convex correcting lens

Eye too short, image behind retina

4 SHORT-SIGHT

Concave correcting lens

Eye too long, image before retina

Why some people need spectacles

The lens of the eye brings light rays to a sharp focus on the retina. The ciliary muscles normally hold this lens flat and this is sufficient to focus on distant objects (diagram 1). If the object is nearby, the lens is made fatter by contracting the ciliary muscles to bend the light rays more sharply (2). However, eyes vary in shape. If the eye is too *short*, the lens has to adjust even for distant objects but these will be clearly focused with the unaided eye. The rays from a nearby object are then focused behind the retina and vision is blurred. The eye has *long-sight* and is corrected by using spectacles with convex lenses (3). If the eye is too *long* the lens can focus on nearby objects but not distant — *short-sight* — and light rays are focused in front of the retina. Spectacles with concave lenses bring the light rays back to focus on the retina (4).

It takes 15 muscles to smile...
so why not make the effort ?

THE human face is capable of more changes of expression than the face of any other member of the animal kingdom. Anger, disappointment, grief, happiness are only a few of the emotions which are reflected in our faces, and all are controlled by **some of our smallest muscles.**

Muscle is the most abundant tissue in the human body. We have more than 500 muscles making up some two-fifths of our bodyweight — muscles that move our legs and arms, pump the blood, churn the food in the digestive system and enable us to smile or frown. They vary in size from the large muscles of the thigh (around sixty centimetres) which help us to walk, run and jump, to a tiny muscle in the middle ear which is only two or three millimetres long.

All muscles are made up of thousands of long slender units called **muscle fibres.** Groups of fibres are wrapped up in bundles by thin connective tissue, and are well supplied with blood vessels and nerves. When nerve impulses reach the fibres they contract powerfully becoming shorter and thicker. With no impulses the muscle relaxes, but never completely. Muscles are kept in a state of slight tension or **tone,** helping to keep the body 'ticking over' normally.

Muscles can act in only one way — they contract and give a pulling force. They usually work in pairs, one pulling one way, the other pulling in the opposite direction. In such muscle pairs, one may be much stronger than the other. For example, the biceps muscle for flexing the arm is stronger than the triceps which straightens it.

There are three types of muscle: striated, smooth, and cardiac. Under the microscope, **striated** muscle fibres have alternating dark and light 'stripes' which take part in muscle contraction. Striated muscle is also known as **voluntary** or **skeletal** muscle because nearly all are under conscious control and they are attached to the skeleton and cause the bones to move. Many voluntary muscles are attached to bones by tough cords of tissue, called **tendons,** but others (as in the face) are attached directly to bones or to the skin.

There are different muscle types which give us a wide range of muscular movements. The simplest muscles, such as the biceps of the arm, consist of parallel straight fibres. Triangular muscles like the deltoid of the shoulder produce a limited but more powerful movement. Orbital muscles like those shown around the eye and mouth have a circular arrangement to control and regulate diameter.

Without the muscles of the face we would have no expression — no frowns, no grimaces, no sniffs. As you can see from this drawing, many muscles are found in the head, and all these help to register our emotions.

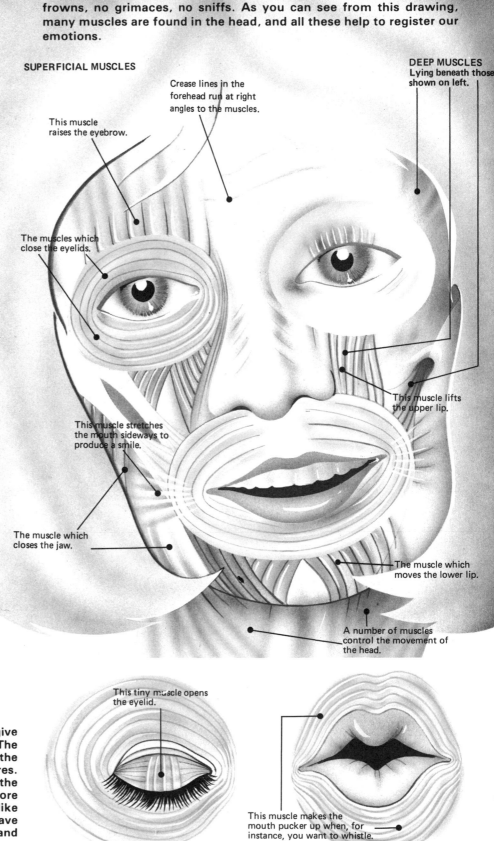

SUPERFICIAL MUSCLES

DEEP MUSCLES
Lying beneath those shown on left.

Crease lines in the forehead run at right angles to the muscles.

This muscle raises the eyebrow.

The muscles which close the eyelids.

This muscle lifts the upper lip.

This muscle stretches the mouth sideways to produce a smile.

The muscle which closes the jaw.

The muscle which moves the lower lip.

A number of muscles control the movement of the head.

This tiny muscle opens the eyelid.

This muscle makes the mouth pucker up when, for instance, you want to whistle.

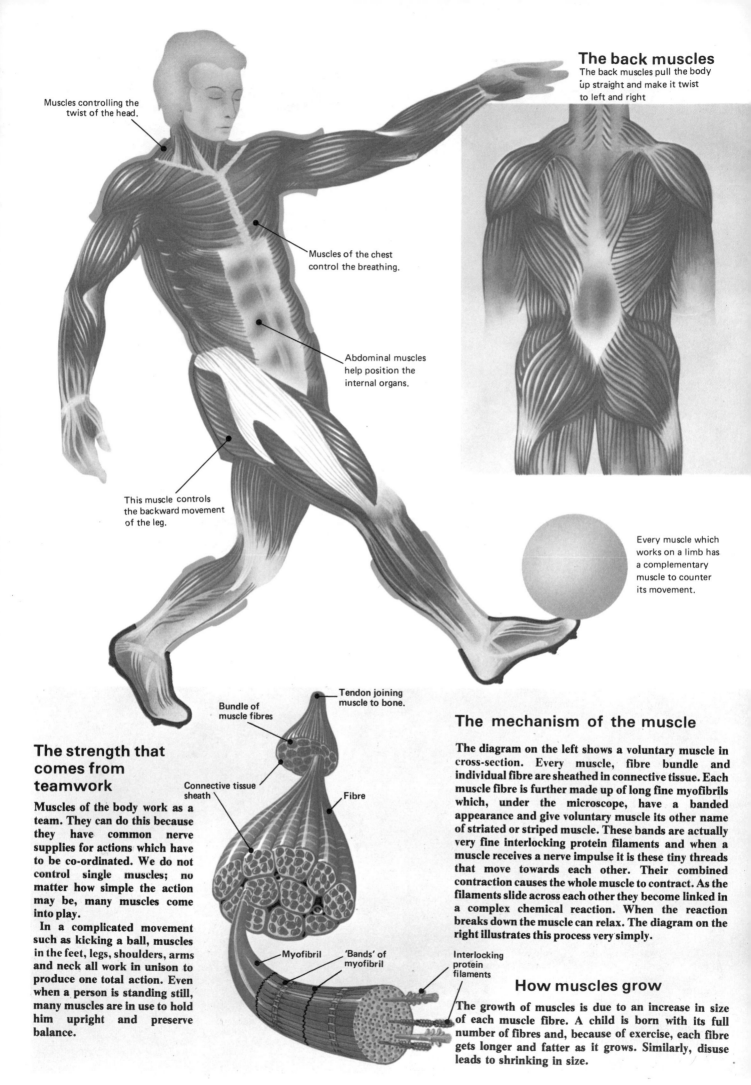

The back muscles
The back muscles pull the body up straight and make it twist to left and right

Muscles controlling the twist of the head.

Muscles of the chest control the breathing.

Abdominal muscles help position the internal organs.

This muscle controls the backward movement of the leg.

Every muscle which works on a limb has a complementary muscle to counter its movement.

The strength that comes from teamwork

Muscles of the body work as a team. They can do this because they have common nerve supplies for actions which have to be co-ordinated. We do not control single muscles; no matter how simple the action may be, many muscles come into play.

In a complicated movement such as kicking a ball, muscles in the feet, legs, shoulders, arms and neck all work in unison to produce one total action. Even when a person is standing still, many muscles are in use to hold him upright and preserve balance.

Tendon joining muscle to bone.

Bundle of muscle fibres

Connective tissue sheath

Fibre

Myofibril

'Bands' of myofibril

Interlocking protein filaments

The mechanism of the muscle

The diagram on the left shows a voluntary muscle in cross-section. Every muscle, fibre bundle and individual fibre are sheathed in connective tissue. Each muscle fibre is further made up of long fine myofibrils which, under the microscope, have a banded appearance and give voluntary muscle its other name of striated or striped muscle. These bands are actually very fine interlocking protein filaments and when a muscle receives a nerve impulse it is these tiny threads that move towards each other. Their combined contraction causes the whole muscle to contract. As the filaments slide across each other they become linked in a complex chemical reaction. When the reaction breaks down the muscle can relax. The diagram on the right illustrates this process very simply.

How muscles grow

The growth of muscles is due to an increase in size of each muscle fibre. A child is born with its full number of fibres and, because of exercise, each fibre gets longer and fatter as it grows. Similarly, disuse leads to shrinking in size.

74

The muscles of the arm and shoulder

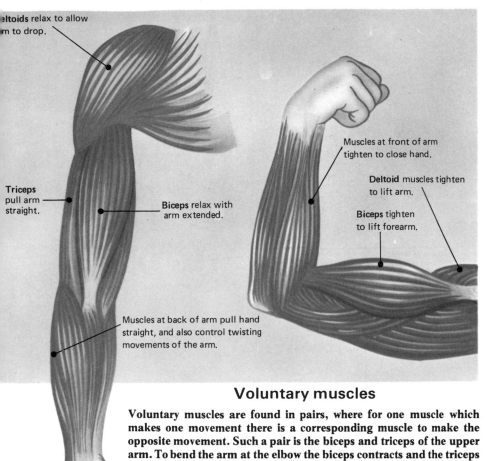

Deltoids relax to allow arm to drop.

Triceps pull arm straight.

Biceps relax with arm extended.

Muscles at back of arm pull hand straight, and also control twisting movements of the arm.

Muscles at front of arm tighten to close hand.

Deltoid muscles tighten to lift arm.

Biceps tighten to lift forearm.

...sors control the fingers.

Muscles of the hand

The hand is controlled by tendons from the arm muscles as well as its own small muscles to each finger.

Voluntary muscles

Voluntary muscles are found in pairs, where for one muscle which makes one movement there is a corresponding muscle to make the opposite movement. Such a pair is the biceps and triceps of the upper arm. To bend the arm at the elbow the biceps contracts and the triceps relaxes. When the arm is straightened the triceps contracts and the biceps relaxes.

Muscles of the leg

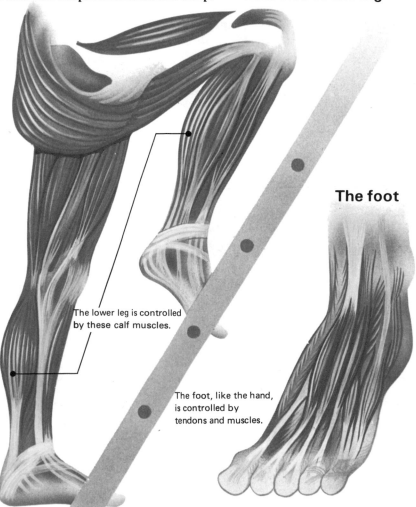

The lower leg is controlled by these calf muscles.

The foot

The foot, like the hand, is controlled by tendons and muscles.

How muscles pull

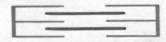

In contraction the filaments are drawn into each other...

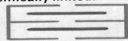

eventually sliding across each other to become chemically linked.

The protein filaments are the fundamental components of muscle contraction . . .

and this movement is multiplied throughout each fibre causing the whole muscle to contract.

The beginning of a hair. Epidermal cells — which form the skin — grow inwards to produce the hair follicle. At the base of the follicle a small 'bulb' — the papilla — develops. This is the 'seed' from which the hair grows.

Horny layer of dead epidermal cells

papilla

Living epidermal cells

Hairs grow inside holes called follicles. The hair grows from a tiny 'bulb' (1) which, when the hair is actively growing, is well supplied with blood and nutrients. The hair does not grow straight up but at an angle. The erector muscle (2) can pull the follicle — and hence the hair — upright, making the hair stand on end. If an animal does this, it will make its coat thicker and warmer. Contracting the erector muscles also puckers up the skin, which is why you get goose pimples when you are cold — as you try to thicken that ancestral coat of hair you no longer have. The sebaceous glands (3) produce oil which keeps the hair healthy.

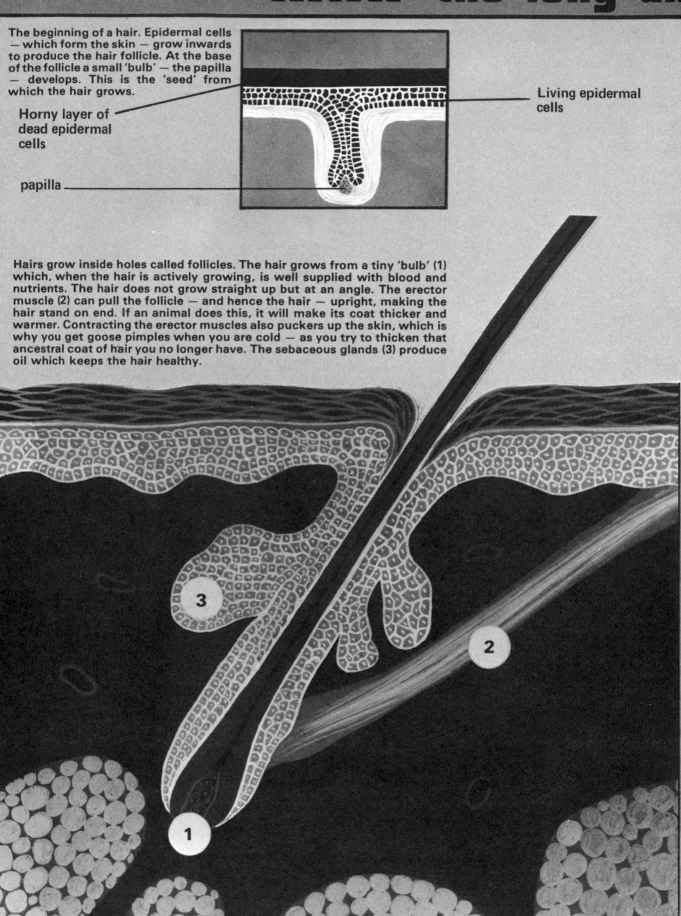

he short of it

Although he has been called 'the naked ape', Man is remarkably hairy. There are something like a million or so hairs on the average person's body, with 120,000 on the head alone. But do they have any use or are they just decorative?

They say that looking for hairs on the palm of your hand is a sign of madness — which is not surprising because hair doesn't grow there. But if you look virtually anywhere else (except the soles of your feet) you will find hairs. Yet surprisingly enough most of these thousands of hairs don't seem to have any value other than decoration and sexual attraction.

Probably human hair — except that on the head, which provides protection from the sun — is a relic from man's ancestors, which were much hairier than we are. Their hair, like the fur of most mammals, probably kept them warm — and cool, for hair acts as an insulation layer both to keep heat out and to keep it in.

All hairs begin as a tiny ingrowth, called a follicle, of the surface layer of the skin. At the bottom of this is a minute 'bulb' called a papilla from which the hair grows.

The hair is made up of two, or sometimes three layers of cells. The outer cells are horny and overlap each other. Although the cells of the bottom of the follicle are always alive, as the hair grows, the older cells near the tip die before the hair projects above the surface of the skin — which is just as well otherwise your hair would hurt when you cut it!

Hairs grow about ⅓ mm a day, but apart from the hairs on your head, they don't keep growing. Most grow for a period and then stop, producing the short hairs on most of your body. The follicle then rests for a period of six months to several years, until a new papilla forms at the follicle's base. As this new papilla grows, it loosens the old hair, which falls out.

The hair on your head, which keeps growing, will grow to about 55-70cm before it falls out. In other words, starting with a bald head, it would take you six or seven years to grow hair long enough to sit on.

The amount of hair on a person's body varies a great deal. Babies are sometimes very hairy, with hair on their faces as well as on their scalps. As they grow older, however, this hair is lost, so that children only have longish hair on their scalps and on their eyebrows and lashes.

At puberty, however, this all changes. Both boys and girls grow hair in the armpits and groin, and boys also grow it on their chin, moustache and chest. (Strangely enough they may also go bald on top in later years.) All of this hair is produced by sexual hormones (chemicals) in the body.

But even so, people are less hairy than most mammals — except for whales, elephants, hippopotamuses and rhinoceroses. The main reason for this is probably that man has evolved a very sophisticated way of keeping cool — that of sweating. Imagine the horrible wet fur that would result if you were both furry and sweaty! Which means that if you don't live in the middle of Africa, where Man evolved, you have to wear clothes to keep warm.

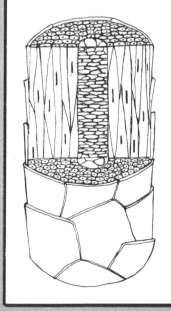

A section through the hair. The flat cells on the outside overlap, rather like the tiles on a house, with their uncovered edges positioned towards the tip. Beneath the outer layer of cells orientated along the hair. In coarser hairs there is often also a thin layer of cells — the medulla — right in the centre of the hair.

Hair is a distinctive characteristic of the different races of the world, and is determined by the genes inherited at birth. Straight hair is round in cross-section, wavy hair is oval, and tightly twisted negroid hair is almost flat. Hair colour is also genetically determined. The colour comes from the amount of a dark pigment, called melanin, in the hair cells. When the cells stop producing pigment, the hair goes grey. But this can only happen as old hair falls out and new hair replaces it; hair does not change colour after it has grown. So however much you worry, you cannot go grey overnight.

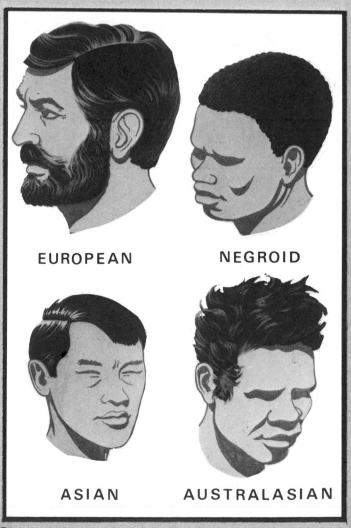

EUROPEAN   NEGROID

ASIAN   AUSTRALASIAN

How the blood circulates

Continuing our look at the human body

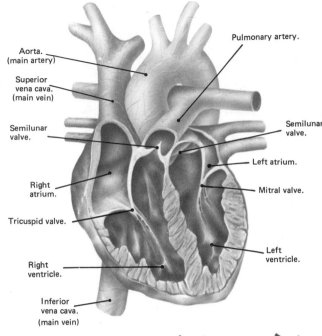

Aorta. (main artery)
Pulmonary artery.
Superior vena cava. (main vein)
Semilunar valve.
Semilunar valve.
Left atrium.
Right atrium.
Mitral valve.
Tricuspid valve.
Left ventricle.
Right ventricle.
Inferior vena cava. (main vein)

THE heart is a hollow cone-shaped muscular organ. The average adult heart weighs about 284 grams and is really a double pump. One side of it takes blood from the veins and pumps it back into the lungs. The other side takes blood from the lungs and pumps it around the body through the arteries.

The left-hand side of the heart pumps the blood to the body, the right-hand side to the lungs. On each side there are two chambers, the atrium for receiving blood, and the ventricle which pumps blood to the body tissue or the lungs.

The rhythmic contraction of the heart is called the heartbeat. Heart muscle is specialised as it has to contract and relax rapidly. The 'signal' to contract comes from the heart's pacemarker which is a special group of cells in the right atrium. The signal passes like a wave across the heart muscle and is carried by special conducting tissue as shown in our diagram.

Pacemaker. (regulates heartbeat)

A   B   C   D

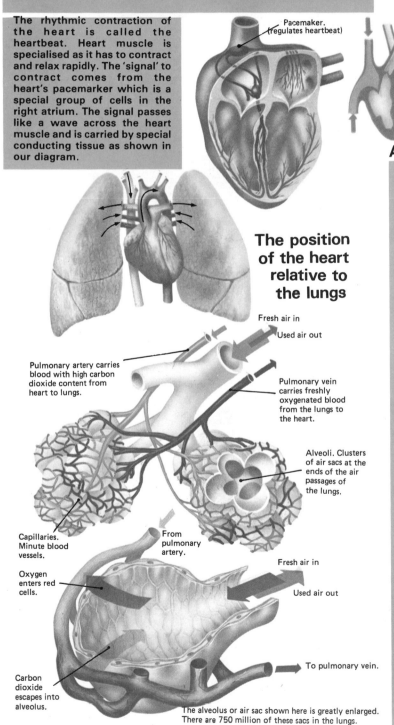

The position of the heart relative to the lungs

Fresh air in
Used air out

Pulmonary artery carries blood with high carbon dioxide content from heart to lungs.

Pulmonary vein carries freshly oxygenated blood from the lungs to the heart.

Alveoli. Clusters of air sacs at the ends of the air passages of the lungs.

Capillaries. Minute blood vessels.

From pulmonary artery.

Fresh air in

Used air out

Oxygen enters red cells.

Carbon dioxide escapes into alveolus.

To pulmonary vein.

The alveolus or air sac shown here is greatly enlarged. There are 750 million of these sacs in the lungs.

Like most pumps, the heart has valves which prevent the blood flowing back. The right-side is called the tricuspid valve, which consists of three fibrous flaps. On the left side is the mitral or bicuspid valve with two fibrous flaps.

Illustrated above is the sequence of events during one heartbeat. (A) Blood returning in the veins fills the atriums. (B) As the atriums fill, they contract and the valves between the atriums and ventricles open. The blood flows into the ventricles. (C) The ventricles now contract forcing open two *semi lunar valves,* one protecting the aorta (the artery carrying the blood from the left ventricle to the body) and one protecting the pulmonary artery to the lungs. The blood is sent through these valves and on its way to the lungs and body. (D) The whole sequence (which takes 0.8 seconds when the heart is beating a normal 75 times a minute) is ready to start again.

The body really breathes in two ways. There is external respiration or breathing fresh air, which is the exchange of oxygen and carbon dioxide between the body and the external environment, and there is internal respiration, which is concerned with the 'processing' of these gases inside the body.

The task of the lungs is to allow oxygen to enter the blood and to extract the carbon dioxide so that the body's cells are not poisoned.

Blood flows to the lungs along the pulmonary artery and is distributed to thin-walled tiny blood vessels or capillaries which are in contact with the alveoli or air sacs, the 'respiratory surfaces' of the lungs.

So how does the oxygen from the air in our lungs get into the blood? And how does the carbon dioxide get out? The answer lies in the tension (pressure) of the gases in the lungs and in the blood. Gases always move from a region of high tension to one of low tension. The oxygen in the lungs is at a higher, the carbon dioxide at a lower tension than that in the blood. When we breathe in, the lungs are filled with gases from the atmosphere - mainly oxygen, carbon di-oxide, nitrogen and water vapour.

The tissues of the lungs are constructed to ensure efficient gas exchange. Oxygen is absorbed and carbon dioxide removed from the blood at the same time. The carbon dioxide is breathed out together with all the other unwanted gases.

Blood for work

Blood is distributed to the body's muscles through the aorta, which is the chief blood vessel of the body. It is an artery about 45 centimetres long and the thickness of a garden hose. From it run a great many branches which divide and sub-divide into further arteries.

Muscles use energy as they work, and require oxygen to convert the fuel which is obtained from food we eat into energy. Both the oxygen and the fuel are brought to the muscles by the blood.

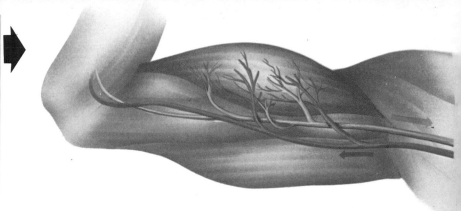

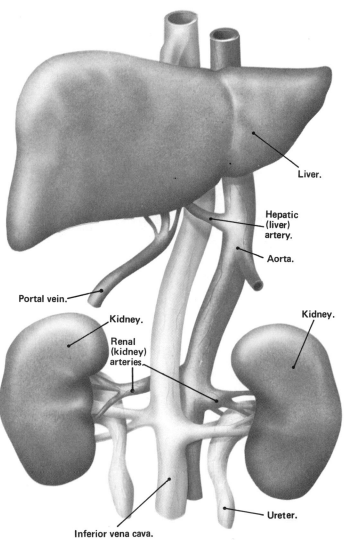

Liver.

Hepatic (liver) artery.

Aorta.

Portal vein.

Kidney.

Renal (kidney) arteries.

Kidney.

Inferior vena cava.

Ureter.

The body's internal cleansing system

Together with the respiratory system and the skin, the kidneys are the excretory organs of the body. The blood is supplied to them by the renal arteries which are branches of the aorta.

The function of the kidneys is to filter and excrete the waste products of the body from the blood. They require a constant supply of blood to their special cell structure to carry out this task. They also help to keep our body fluids relatively constant.

The liver is the 'factory' of the body with many vital functions. Among these are the regulation of red blood cells and the conversion of foodstuffs into suitable substances for storing or into waste products which may be subsequently excreted by the kidneys.

Failure of either kidneys or liver will result in death, although kidney failure can be off-set by a machine to which the patient is connected through tubes so that the blood can be washed clear of impurities. Kidney transplants can be 100 per cent effective in many cases, although sufferers have to wait for a suitable donor to become available. The liver has great powers of recovery and damaged liver cells can often regenerate.

In our diagrams, arteries and veins containing blood carrying oxygen are shown as red, those carrying blood without oxygen are blue. The portal vein is special. It carries blood from the intestines and spleen to the liver. Its blood has lost some of its oxygen but not all so it is coloured mauve.

The blood supply to the brain

Our blood circulating system has to work against gravity to send blood to the brain. If we suddenly stand up after lying down, the supply to the brain is temporarily lessened and we become dizzy.

However, a special centre in the brain, the vasomotor centre, immediately sets everything right by constricting the blood vessels in the abdomen, so diverting more blood to the brain.

If the supply to the brain were to be cut off, we would soon lose consciousness. The brain needs blood to function. Its cells require certain salts brought by the blood, and the nerve fibres must have a plentiful supply of oxygen.

When they have too little of one or too much of the other we get tired. Sleeps gives the nervous system a rest and enables the products of overwork to be washed away and removed by blood.

The blood supply to the brain also maintains the chemical balance of a special fluid in the brain called cerebrospinal fluid which bathes the delicate brain tissues.

Our diagram shows just the arteries to the brain. The two main veins from the brain (the jugular veins) run next to the carotid arteries.

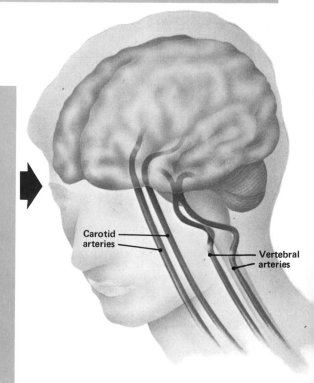

Carotid arteries

Vertebral arteries

How the blood fights disease

WHY blood? Simply because our bodies would not work without it. It would be like trying to run an engine without oil — the entire machinery would seize up.

Blood transports vital substances to all parts of the body, and also carries away the waste. It contains food materials for the cells, respiratory gases, and chemical substances which protect the body and regulate its complicated chemistry.

Blood in the arteries, which carry it **from** the heart, is bright red due to the presence of oxygen. In the veins it is dark red (shown blue in the diagram), and instead of oxygen contains carbon dioxide, which will eventually be expelled through the lungs.

An adult has about 5 litres of blood, and the body is constantly manufacturing blood cells to maintain its 'quality'. These cells are divided into white corpuscles and red corpuscles. Most red blood cells are produced in the bone marrow. The white corpuscles of which there are 5,000-10,000 per cubic millimetre are the body's 'army'. They attack bacteria, and produce chemicals called antibodies which neutralize the invading bacteria.

For example, if you have measles, certain of your white corpuscles, the ones called lymphocytes, will manufacture antibodies, so it is very unlikely that you will get the disease again.

There are around 4-6 million red blood corpuscles per cubic millimetre and these transport the oxygen and carbon dioxide already mentioned.

The blood also contains cells called platelets which are important in helping the blood to clot. This clotting 'ability' of the blood is very important; cuts would not heal without it.

All this very complex mixture is pumped at an average rate of 5 litres a minute.

Blood groups

The Nationwide Blood Transfusion Service receives blood from volunteer donors, but before any is taken from a donor a simple test is carried out to determine the Group or type of blood in his body.

The discovery that humans had varying types of blood was made in 1900 by an Austrian-born American pathologist named Karl Landsteiner. He found that before blood could be safely transfused from one person to another it was important to check that their groups were compatible.

Every day of your life your heart will pump blood around your body. All vital organs — lungs, kidneys, liver and brain — must have blood for you to survive. The picture of the footballer seen below shows the circulation of the blood around the body — the arteries carrying oxygenated blood from the heart and the veins waste-carrying blood to the heart.

The only veins that carry oxygenated blood are those from the lungs to the heart. Salts, vitamins and other nutrients are also carried to all parts of the body in the blood. It is, in truth, a life-giving fluid!

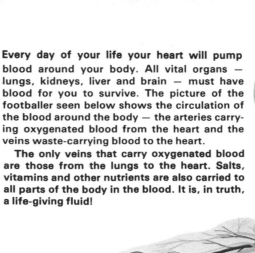

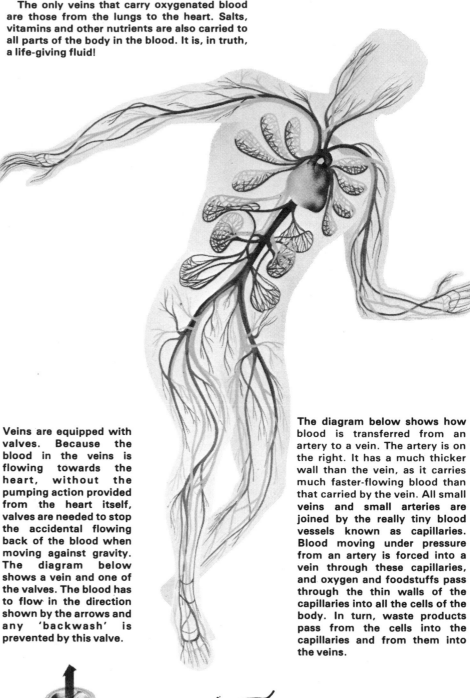

Veins are equipped with valves. Because the blood in the veins is flowing towards the heart, without the pumping action provided from the heart itself, valves are needed to stop the accidental flowing back of the blood when moving against gravity. The diagram below shows a vein and one of the valves. The blood has to flow in the direction shown by the arrows and any 'backwash' is prevented by this valve.

The diagram below shows how blood is transferred from an artery to a vein. The artery is on the right. It has a much thicker wall than the vein, as it carries much faster-flowing blood than that carried by the vein. All small veins and small arteries are joined by the really tiny blood vessels known as capillaries. Blood moving under pressure from an artery is forced into a vein through these capillaries, and oxygen and foodstuffs pass through the thin walls of the capillaries into all the cells of the body. In turn, waste products pass from the cells into the capillaries and from them into the veins.

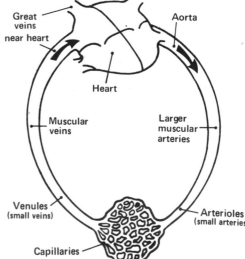

Great veins near heart

Aorta

Heart

Muscular veins

Larger muscular arteries

Venules (small veins)

Arterioles (small arteries)

Capillaries

ARTERY

Thick-walled, elastic sided

VEIN

Thin-walled bundles of muscle fibre, not elastic

Heredity Have you ever wondered why you are the way you are?

THE TALE OF TWO MARRIAGES

Judy Garland

Vincente Minnelli

Liza Minnelli

Judy Garland

Sid Luft

Lorna Luft

We can see some of the effects of heredity in these two marriages. Both Liza Minnelli and Lorna Luft had the same mother — Judy Garland. But just by looking at them it is obvious that Liza is Vincente Minnelli's daughter and Lorna is Sid Luft's.

WHAT would you get if you crossed a kangaroo with a sheep? Why, a woolly jumper of course. And if you crossed a snake with a building set? Yes, you've guessed it, a boa constructor.

These are just jokes, of course, but they show a surprisingly good understanding of what is called *heredity*. Heredity explains how characteristics are passed on from one generation to another.

The children of a black mother and a white father are usually a light brown; the children of a short mother and a tall father are usually of medium height; the children of a stout mother and skinny father are usually of medium build. What is happening is that when the child is conceived it gets instructions from both parents and the result is usually — but not always — a mixture of the two.

Genes

The instructions are carried on *genes*, which are located on tiny coiled threads called chromosomes found inside the cells of all living things, and which are the fundamental units of heredity. The threads contain a very special molecule, called deoxyribonucleic acid (DNA), which if it could be seen would look like a twisted ladder. The 'rungs' of the ladder make up the genes which carry the genetic instructions.

As an animal or plant grows, its cells are continuously dividing — each cell becoming two new cells. Even in an adult, damaged cells die and are replaced by neighbouring cells dividing. Each of these new cells always contains a complete set of genetic instructions because the chromosomes double up before the cell splits. Genetically, therefore, all the cells are identical and contain a full number of chromosomes. In humans this number is 46.

Something special happens, however, when a baby is formed. To make a baby, two cells fuse together to make just one cell. The cells that fuse are called *sex cells*. They are the *sperm* of the father and the *egg* of the

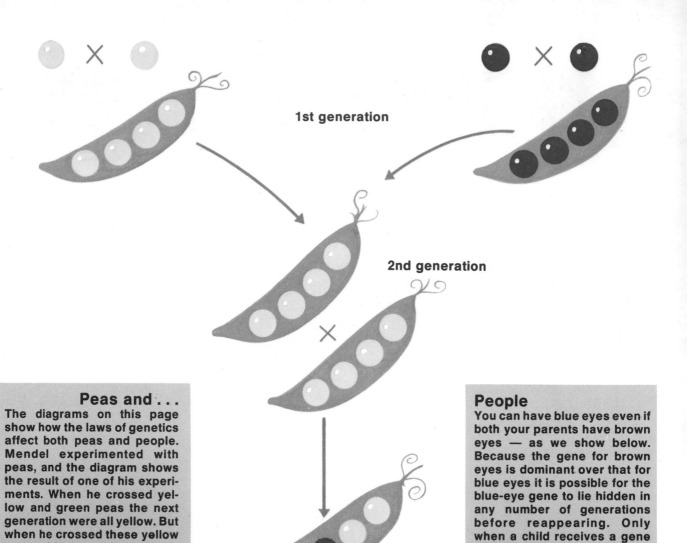

1st generation

2nd generation

3rd generation

Peas and . . .

The diagrams on this page show how the laws of genetics affect both peas and people. Mendel experimented with peas, and the diagram shows the result of one of his experiments. When he crossed yellow and green peas the next generation were all yellow. But when he crossed these yellow peas with themselves he got pods which contained on average three yellow peas to each green pea. This result is to be expected if the gene for yellow is dominant over the gene for green.

People

You can have blue eyes even if both your parents have brown eyes — as we show below. Because the gene for brown eyes is dominant over that for blue eyes it is possible for the blue-eye gene to lie hidden in any number of generations before reappearing. Only when a child receives a gene for blue eyes from *both* parents will it grow up to have blue eyes. The children of two blue-eyed parents should all be blue-eyed — because their parents each contain only genes for blue eyes.

grandparents

parents

child

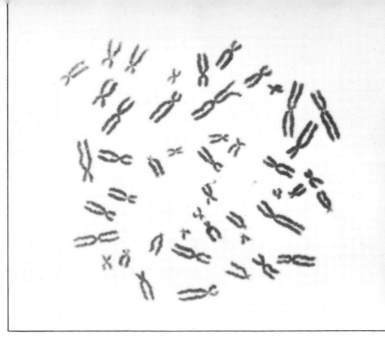

Left: Gregor Mendel, the first to discover the laws of heredity.

Right: The 46 (count them!) chromosomes of a woman, about 2,000 times life size. In the picture each chromosome has a similar partner in shape and size — that is there are 23 pairs. A man, however, has 22 pairs plus an odd pair — the X chromosome and the Y chromosome. (A woman has two Xs). Children always receive an X chromosome from their mother, but either a Y or an X from their father. If they receive a Y, they grow up as boys, if they receive an X, they grow up as girls.

mother, and they contain only *half* the normal number of chromosomes. Obviously, if this were not the case, when they fused the baby would end up with double the normal number of chromosomes. The child therefore receives 23 chromosomes from its father, 23 from its mother — a total of 46, or 23 pairs.

The fact that the chromosomes are in pairs is important. Each set of 23 received from just one parent contains most of the information in itself to control all the aspects of the baby's growth, development and future life. So the baby has two different sets of instructions — one from each parent. The way these two sets interact governs the appearance and character of the child.

Gregor Mendel

The earliest work on the interaction of genes was done in the middle of the nineteenth century by the Abbot of the monastery of Brno in Czechoslovakia. Abbot Mendel experimented with peas.

Mendel found that if he crossed green peas with green peas, he always got green peas, and when he crossed yellow peas with yellow peas he got yellow peas.

But when he crossed the green peas with the yellow peas something strange happened.

The diagram shows the results of Mendel's experiments. The second generation of peas was entirely yellow, but the third generation — produced by crossing the second generation with themselves — contained both yellow and green. To be precise, there were three yellow peas to each green pea. The factor which caused

green peas had been forgotten in the second generation, but had reappeared in the third generation.

Mendel didn't know that genes were responsible for these effects, but he did realize that there must be a factor passed on from generation to generation for both green and yellow peas. More remarkably, he realized that if the factor for yellow peas was *dominant* over the factor for green peas, and if each pea contained two factors — one from each parent — the result would come out as in his experiments.

In the first generation, both the yellow peas and the green peas were *pure bred,* that is they contained only genes for yellow or green respectively. In the next generation, the offspring would have received a gene for yellow from one parent, a gene for green from the other. But because yellow is dominant over green, they would all be yellow.

In the third generation, the plants would receive *either* a gene for yellow *or* a gene for green from each parent. So they could receive either a yellow and a yellow, a yellow and a green, a green and a yellow, or a

green and a green. Because yellow is dominant over green, that makes three yellows and one green.

In-between characters

But the children of a mixed black-and-white marriage are not always black, or the children's children three-quarters black and one quarter white. Instead the children are nearly always a light brown *in-between* colour. Obviously there is more to heredity than the simple dominant genes of Mendel.

In fact, Mendel was extremely lucky in choosing a character which was determined by just one gene. (The nearest equivalent in people is eye colour, where brown is dominant over blue). Most characteristics are determined by many genes, all of which interact with each other and which are also affected by the environment in which the animal or plant is brought up. The result of many genes affecting a character is that there is a wide band of variation, with most people in the middle. So a few people are very tall, a few people very short — but most are of medium height.

Right: The twisted ladder that is DNA. Four chemicals — (A) adenine, (T) thymine, (C) cytosine and (G) guanine — make up DNA 'rungs', and each rung consists of two of them joined together in one of four ways (T-A, A-T, G-C and C-G).

THE LADDER OF LIFE

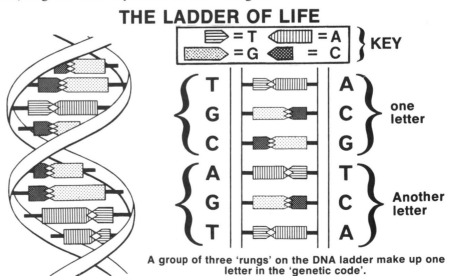

A group of three 'rungs' on the DNA ladder make up one letter in the 'genetic code'.

How your body

The spinal cord is the continuation of the brain below the skull. From it the main lines of nerves pass down the body and out along the limbs. To kick a football, the brain becomes conscious of the decision to do so and a message in the form of an electrical impulse is sent from the part of the brain which controls muscle movements. The message travels with amazing speed (up to 100 metres per second) along a system of nerves to the relevant muscles.

WE have nerves in every part of our body. There are so many that it is impossible to count them. Together with the brain and spinal cord they make up the *nervous system* which passes on messages to our muscles and sense organs so we can receive information from the outside world and adjust when necessary.

In the 3rd century B.C. a Greek named Erasistratus taught that nerves were hollow and contained a 'vital

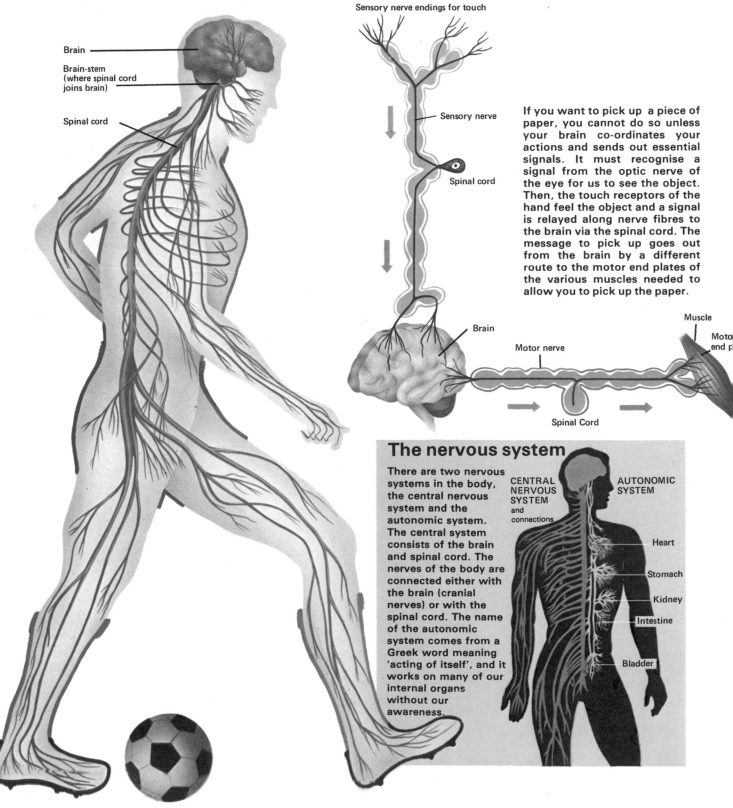

Brain

Brain-stem (where spinal cord joins brain)

Spinal cord

Sensory nerve endings for touch

Sensory nerve

Spinal cord

If you want to pick up a piece of paper, you cannot do so unless your brain co-ordinates your actions and sends out essential signals. It must recognise a signal from the optic nerve of the eye for us to see the object. Then, the touch receptors of the hand feel the object and a signal is relayed along nerve fibres to the brain via the spinal cord. The message to pick up goes out from the brain by a different route to the motor end plates of the various muscles needed to allow you to pick up the paper.

Brain

Motor nerve

Muscle

Motor end p

Spinal Cord

The nervous system

There are two nervous systems in the body, the central nervous system and the autonomic system. The central system consists of the brain and spinal cord. The nerves of the body are connected either with the brain (cranial nerves) or with the spinal cord. The name of the autonomic system comes from a Greek word meaning 'acting of itself', and it works on many of our internal organs without our awareness.

CENTRAL NERVOUS SYSTEM and connections

AUTONOMIC SYSTEM

Heart

Stomach

Kidney

Intestine

Bladder

gets the message

spirit' which flowed through the nerves into the muscles causing them to contract. It was only 200 years ago that this idea was disproved when nerves were found to be solid.

Serious scientific research on the nervous system began during the last century. Just over 100 years ago, during the Franco-Prussian war, a German doctor named Fritsch was operating on the head of wounded solider. He accidentally passed an electric current through the patient's head and was astonished to see that some of the soldier's muscles twitched. In 1871, Fritsch and a colleague, Hitzig, began experiments to discover why this should be so.

Using chloroformed animals, the men found that if they passed the current to a certain part of the brain on the right-hand side of the head, the muscles of the left foreleg were stimulated; applying the current to the corresponding brain area on the left, the right foreleg would twitch as the muscles contracted.

Soon other researchers took up the work and, in the years since then, it has gradually been established which areas of the brain control which muscles.

We now know that the brain does not merely control the muscles, but both receives and sends messages to all parts of the body. These messages are actually electrical impulses conveyed by the nervous system to tell the brain what is going on and send appropriate instructions to our organs.

It is rather like a telephone system with two main exchanges, one in the brain and the other in the spinal chord. Like a telephone system there are two kinds of message; those that get passed automatically — and of which we are not conscious — and those involving the operator which, to some degree, are sent with our awareness.

Our overall nervous system has two parts, the *central* nervous system and the *autonomic* nervous system. The central system takes care of all the actions which are done deliberately (like walking or writing) and of which we are aware. Through the central system the body responds to outside influences and without it we would have no thought, action or feeling. Even the simple act of picking up a piece of paper involves the co-ordinated action of the eyes, their nerves, and the 'operator' in the brain which sends out the impulses needed to bring the various muscles into play.

But much goes on in the body that has to be carried out without conscious thought, and this is done in the autonomic nervous system which deals with 'automatic' messages. Possibly you may have had a doctor 'test' your nervous system by giving the patellar tendon of the knee a smart tap. This stretches the thigh muscle which stimulates a receiving station to send a message to the spinal cord exchange which deals with the automatic reflex. Back comes another message — which you can't prevent — commanding the muscle to contract. Up jerks your leg.

Similarly, our breathing and digestive mechanisms are kept ticking over automatically. The autonomic system links many of our internal organs like the heart and liver.

Adrenalin

This system also helps to mobilise our bodies for

Continued on the next page

THE BODY'S REFLEXES

The nervous system has two main 'telephone exchanges', one in the brain and the other in the spinal column. Nervous reflexes (involuntary responses) are controlled by a nerve complex in the spinal column. For example, if your hand accidentally comes in contact with something hot, like an open flame, it is the spinal column complex which commands the arm muscles to move the hand away. Also, a message is immediately sent to the brain about what is happening and you feel pain.

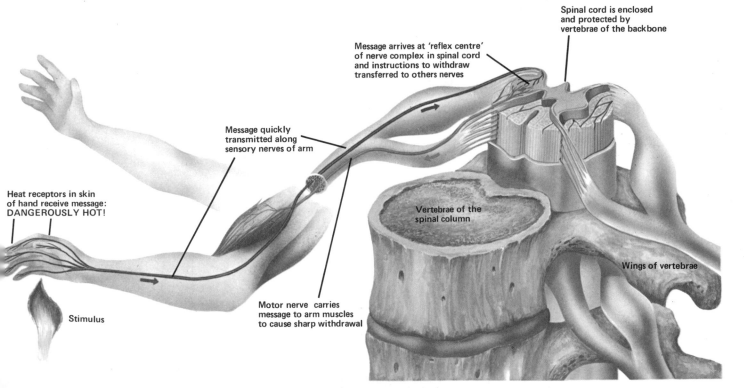

Spinal cord is enclosed and protected by vertebrae of the backbone

Message arrives at 'reflex centre' of nerve complex in spinal cord and instructions to withdraw transferred to others nerves

Message quickly transmitted along sensory nerves of arm

Heat receptors in skin of hand receive message: DANGEROUSLY HOT!

Vertebrae of the spinal column

Wings of vertebrae

Stimulus

Motor nerve carries message to arm muscles to cause sharp withdrawal emergency action, causing changes over which, like the knee reflex, we have no conscious control. The nerves stimulate the release of a chemical called adrenalin which has many effects as our diagram shows. Very much a case of 'all systems go!'

The messages of the nervous system are conveyed through nerves which reach out from the brain and spinal cord. These have sensory fibres to take messages from receptors *to* the brain and spinal cord, and other fibres which conduct impulses *from* the brain to all parts of the body via the spinal cord.

These nerve fibres require plenty of oxygen and must be kept free of carbon dioxide, or we begin to feel tired. Plenty of sleep is important too, so that our nervous system can take a rest (slow down at least) and stay efficient.

It is an incredible system, marvellous in its action and staggering in its complexity. Even today, scientists still work to discover more of its many secrets.

Competition also stimulates the body's nervous systems to make an all-out effort

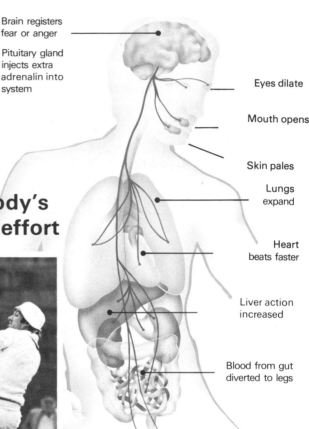

EMERGENCY ACTION - IT'S ALL SYSTEMS GO!

Brain registers fear or anger

Pituitary gland injects extra adrenalin into system

Eyes dilate

Mouth opens

Skin pales

Lungs expand

Heart beats faster

Liver action increased

Blood from gut diverted to legs

Here the batsman is acting with conscious aggression. The fieldsmen are reacting defensively and to some degree automatically. All three, though, are keyed up for instantaneous reaction with adrenalin release.

Heather Hunte sprints to victory — her body primed for maximum effort and reacting accordingly.

In an emergency, maybe a sudden attack by a dog or a strange noise at night, you body mobilises itself for action. The *sympathetic* division of your autonomic nervous system stimulates the release of a chemical called adrenalin into the bloodstream. This works on certain cells around your body to cause changes that switch you into top gear.

Hairs stand on end and you come out in 'goose pimples.'

The pupils of the eyes dilate to admit the maximum light.

Breathing is stimulated and the mouth widens to take in more air.

The heart pumps faster and stronger, pushing more blood to the muscles so they can work harder. The blood supply to the gut is reduced and is diverted to limb muscles.

The liver releases stored food to provide more fuel for the energy-consuming muscles.

This 'fight or flight' reaction cannot be consciously controlled. In an emergency, you make a *sympathetic* nervous reaction without thinking about it. This allows you to respond to the threat in the best possible physical condition. Of course, you would not wish to stay in an emergency state any longer than necessary and, when the danger or excitement has passed, a parallel system, the *parasympathetic* nerves, reacts to restore the body to normal balance.

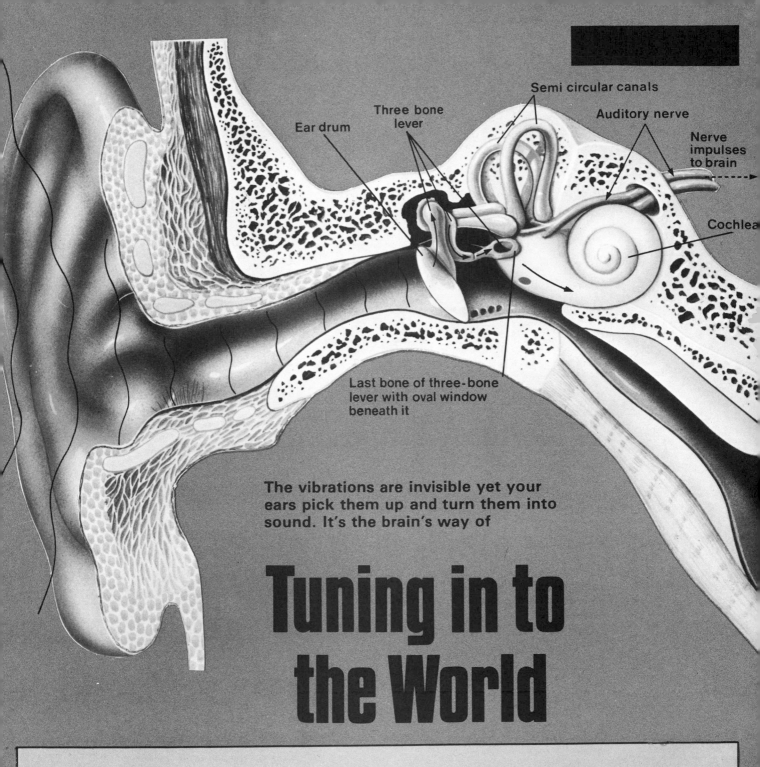

Ear drum

Three bone lever

Semi circular canals

Auditory nerve

Nerve impulses to brain

Cochlea

Last bone of three-bone lever with oval window beneath it

The vibrations are invisible yet your ears pick them up and turn them into sound. It's the brain's way of

Tuning in to the World

Y OU are about to step off the kerb of a busy street. You look left and right but don't see any cars. Then just as you are about to step into the road you hear the blare of a horn. Back you jump, saved by your ears.

You can see only what's in front of you, but your ears obtain information from every side. They continuously keep you in touch with the world around you.

The sounds you hear are vibrations in the air. Everything that moves vibrates — even if it vibrates so quickly and over such small distances that you cannot see the vibrations. These vibrations set up shock waves in the air much the same way as waves are set up in the bath if you wiggle your toes. The shock waves radiate out in all directions — getting weaker the farther they go — and if they reach your ear, your brain registers them as sound.

But it is not the ears on the side of your head which do the hearing. There is much

more to the ear than this outer fleshy part. All this does is channel the air waves down to the two other parts, the middle and inner ears, deep inside the head. It is here that the real hearing takes place.

From the outer ear a channel leads down to the middle ear. At the end of the channel is a membrane — a thin skin stretched taut like a drum. Not surprisingly, this membrane is called the *ear drum*.

Vibrations amplified

Sound waves make the drum vibrate. These vibrations are then amplified by a lever made of three tiny bones (called the *hammer, anvil* and *stirrup*).

The vibrations have to be amplified because the next part of the ear, the inner ear, is filled not with air but with a watery liquid. This would damp down the vibrations too much if they were not magnified.

From the stirrup bone, the vibrations pass on to a similar, but smaller, membrane called the *oval window*. On the other side of this is a snail-shaped organ called the *cochlea*.

The cochlea is the real organ of hearing. It is a coiled-up tube filled with liquid. Although it is coiled like a snail, it is easier to understand if you imagine it unravelled into a long tube. Then imagine this tube split into three parts, like the layers of a cake, by two thin membranes. When the oval window vibrates it makes the liquid and the membranes inside the tube vibrate.

On one of the membranes, called the *basilar membrane* there is a structure called the *organ of Corti*. This organ turns the vibrations into nerve impulses which go to the brain. The brain registers these impulses as sound. The harder the basilar membrane vibrates, the stronger the impulses, and the louder the noise 'heard'

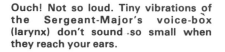

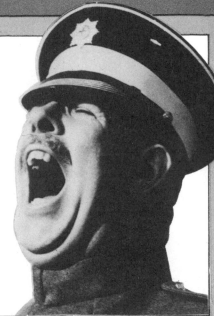

Left: This diagrammatic picture of the ear shows how vibrations striking the ear drum are transmitted via the three-bone lever and the oval window to the cochlea (see below) which sends signals along the auditory nerve to the brain. The brain interprets these signals as sound. The semi-circular canals are not directly related to hearing but control balance.

Ouch! Not so loud. Tiny vibrations of the Sergeant-Major's voice-box (larynx) don't sound so small when they reach your ears.

by the brain.

But when you listen to a sound, you can tell more about it than just how loud it is. You can also tell how high or low it is — that is, its pitch. The cochlea is shaped like a long tube so it can determine pitch. (It is coiled up so that it takes up less space.)

To understand how the ear hears pitch, once again imagine the cochlea unravelled into a long tube with the oval window at one end. At this end the basilar membrane is fairly thin, but at the end farther from the oval window the membrane is thicker. High pitched sounds use up their energy before they have travelled far up the tube as they find it easier to vibrate the thinner part of the membrane. But low pitched sounds can travel nearly to the end of the tube. The lower they are, the farther they travel.

So the brain is able to work out the pitch of the sound by knowing from what part of the membrane the message it receives comes.

Wide range

A normal human ear can detect sounds as low as 40 and as high as 30,000 Hz (cycles per second. Hertz was a German physicist). Some animals, such as dogs, have an even wider range.

However, in older people the membranes of the ear become thicker and less sensitive. In particular, many old people find it difficult to hear high-pitched sounds. As speech, for example, is made up of a mixture of high and low sounds, even though a partially deaf person can hear someone speaking he may be unable to determine what they are saying.

Deafness in younger people can be caused by too loud a noise or, more commonly, from prolonged exposure to loud noise — as produced by too much amplification in a disco or by machinery in a factory.

Try to avoid such exposure; those vibrations in the air are what keep you in touch with the world — whether they mean the danger of an approaching car when you step off the kerb or just understanding what someone says. Deaf aids are a poor substitute for the brain's own sensitive microphones.

Placing a sound

Shut your eyes and get a friend to move a radio around the room you are in. You can still work out where the sound comes from. You can decide whether it is coming from in front or behind, from the left or the right, from up or down. Only if your friend places the radio the same distance exactly in front or behind you will you have trouble deciding where it is.

Just as you need two eyes to work out where things are in relation to each other — to put things in perspective — so you need two ears to put sounds in perspective. If, for example, a sound is on your left, then the sound waves reach your left ear just before they reach your right. In addition your head is between your right ear and the sound and partly shields it. Your brain is able to detect these slight differences and work out where the sound comes from.

But when the radio is either exactly behind or in front, the sound reaches both ears at the same time — and you have trouble in working out whether the sound is coming from in front or behind.

Neither the fleshy outer ear nor the three-bone lever of the middle ear are the real organs of hearing. It is, in fact, minute hairs inside the snail-like cochlea of the inner ear that actually turn vibrations into the nerve impulses which the brain registers as sound. Sound waves transmitted to the cochlea from the middle ear make the basilar membrane vibrate, and when it does the hairs are pushed back and forth against the tectorial membrane. This stimulates nerves in the hair cells which then send impulses on to the brain. Our diagram is about 60 times life size.

Hair cells produce signals

Tectorial membrane

Hairs

Supporting cells

Nerves carry signal to brain

Nucleus

Basilar membrane

The making of Modern Man

IT all started in 1871 when Charles Darwin published a book called *The Descent of Man*. This book stated that Man had evolved from apes; human beings had not suddenly appeared on Earth, they had developed slowly over millions of years.

In mid-Victorian Britain this seemed a shocking idea, quite contrary to what was written in the Bible. How could civilized Man be descended from a bunch of hairy apes?

But now the idea that Man, like every other creature, is the product of evolution is widely accepted, and it is difficult to imagine what all the fuss was about.

Part of the problem in Darwin's time was the lack of actual evidence for the stages in the evolution of Man, the 'missing links' as they were called. Since then, scientists have discovered many fossil bones, skulls and other remains of human-like creatures, and have pieced together quite a large part of the story of Man.

But much still remains to be discovered. Experts are still searching for the missing links in Man's history.

Man belongs to a group of animals called the primates. The first primates appeared about the time that the dinosaurs were dying out. They were small, insect-eating creatures like shrews and lived in trees. It was these small, furry animals that over the centuries developed into the monkeys and apes and much later into Man.

We know that a primate *(Dryopithecus)* with a skull and teeth very similar to a modern ape's lived in East Africa some 20 million years ago. Later, around 12 million years ago, a man-like primate known as *Ramapithecus* existed. But these creatures were still nothing like Man.

The first important fossil 'ape-man' was found in

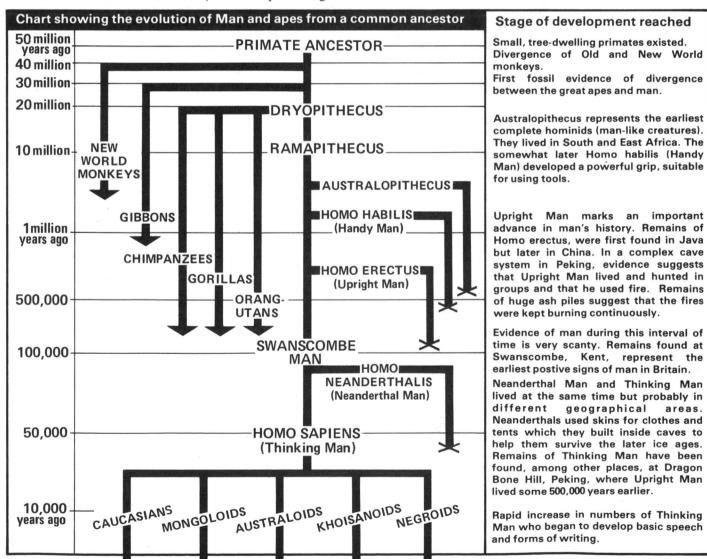

Chart showing the evolution of Man and apes from a common ancestor

Time	Chart	Stage of development reached
50 million years ago	PRIMATE ANCESTOR	Small, tree-dwelling primates existed. Divergence of Old and New World monkeys. First fossil evidence of divergence between the great apes and man.
40 million		
30 million		
20 million	DRYOPITHECUS	Australopithecus represents the earliest complete hominids (man-like creatures). They lived in South and East Africa. The somewhat later Homo habilis (Handy Man) developed a powerful grip, suitable for using tools.
10 million	NEW WORLD MONKEYS — RAMAPITHECUS — AUSTRALOPITHECUS	
1 million years ago	GIBBONS — HOMO HABILIS (Handy Man)	Upright Man marks an important advance in man's history. Remains of Homo erectus, were first found in Java but later in China. In a complex cave system in Peking, evidence suggests that Upright Man lived and hunted in groups and that he used fire. Remains of huge ash piles suggest that the fires were kept burning continuously.
	CHIMPANZEES — GORILLAS — ORANG-UTANS — HOMO ERECTUS (Upright Man)	
500,000		
100,000	SWANSCOMBE MAN	Evidence of man during this interval of time is very scanty. Remains found at Swanscombe, Kent, represent the earliest postive signs of man in Britain.
	HOMO NEANDERTHALIS (Neanderthal Man)	Neanderthal Man and Thinking Man lived at the same time but probably in different geographical areas. Neanderthals used skins for clothes and tents which they built inside caves to help them survive the later ice ages. Remains of Thinking Man have been found, among other places, at Dragon Bone Hill, Peking, where Upright Man lived some 500,000 years earlier.
50,000	HOMO SAPIENS (Thinking Man)	
10,000 years ago	CAUCASIANS MONGOLOIDS AUSTRALOIDS KHOISANOIDS NEGROIDS	Rapid increase in numbers of Thinking Man who began to develop basic speech and forms of writing.

Today, the human race is classified into five major groups — *Caucasians* ('white' or light skinned. Origin — Europe, North Africa, Middle East); *Mongoloids* (straight black hair, broad cheekbones and dark, slanted eyes. Examples - Tibetans, Mongolians, American Indians); *Australoids* (dark skin, wavy hair, large teeth. Origin — South East Asia. Examples — Fijians, Australian Aborigines); *Khoisanoids* (short build, yellowish-brown skin, sparse body hair. Origin — southern Africa. Examples — Bushman, Hottentots); *Negroids* (brown to black skin, broad nose, fleshy lips, tight curly hair. Origin — Africa.)

South and East Africa. He was called *Australopithecus africanus* and he walked upright on two feet, but not as well as we do. He probably hunted in groups for animals, ate berries and fruit, and was less than five feet tall. It is unlikely that he could talk, but he may have communicated to his fellows by grunts and other sounds. Most people think that *Australopithecus* was Man's cousin, rather than his direct ancestor.

In the 1880s a young Dutchman called Dubois decided to search for Man's early ancestors in the island of Java. Dubois was much more successful than he expected; he found the fossil remains of a man-like creature which was called *Homo erectus (Homo* — man, *erectus* — upright).

Then, other fossils of *Homo erectus* were found, both in Java and in China. As the pieces were put together it became apparent that these early men were truly upright, and they had a completely human arrangement of the teeth and jaw, although still didn't have a chin. Their brains were smaller than ours, but among their fossil remains were signs of hearths where they had cooked their food. They had discovered fire.

In 1856 a fossil skeleton was discovered by workmen in a cave near Dusseldorf in Germany, in the Neander valley.

Physical differences between Man and Apes

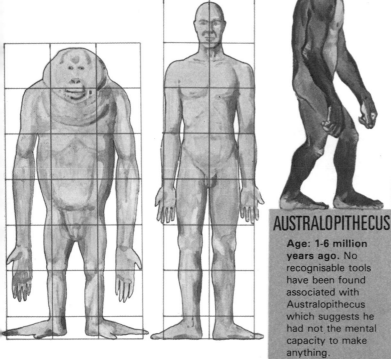

Of the many differences between man and apes, the following are among the most obvious:

Man walks with an upright stance while apes walk on their back legs, balancing on the knuckles of their hands while so doing.

The hands of a man can grip an implement precisely, because he has opposable thumbs (thumbs which can cross the palm and touch the fingers face to face). Apes can grasp food or implements but they have no opposable thumbs and precise movements are impossible.

The feet of a man form a stable platform on which he can walk or balance. An ape's feet are capable of grasping, like a hand, and balance is achieved on all fours.

The skull of a man has a chin, a small face and incisor teeth (cutting teeth at the front of the mouth) of the same size as canine teeth (larger, pointed teeth behind the incisors). Apes have projecting faces, no chins and their canines are much larger than their incisors.

The brain capacity of a man is 1,400c.c. on average while that of a gorilla, for example, is 500c.c.

AUSTRALOPITHECUS
Age: 1-6 million years ago. No recognisable tools have been found associated with Australopithecus which suggests he had not the mental capacity to make anything.

HOMO HABILIS
Age: 1¾ million years ago. Used pebble choppers, made by flaking a pebble on both sides to form a cutting edge. Found in north-east Africa.

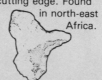

HOMO ERECTUS
Age: ½ — ¾ million years ago. As well as using pebble choppers, he made stone hand axes. These were large, efficient tools used for cutting and scraping. Homo erectus was the first to have used fire.

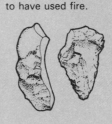

SWANSCOMBE MAN
Age: 375,000 years ago. Swanscombe Man used sophisticated flint hand axes and the flakes formed during the manufacture of these axes were used as knives or scrapers. Concave scrapers were used to shape wooden spea[r]

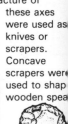

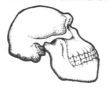
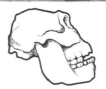
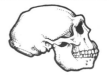

HOMO ANDERTHALIS

e: 100,000-
,000 years ago.
anderthal Man
d flint hand axes,
.es (for cutting
d skinning
mals) flint or bone
ils, wooden
ars and throwing
nes.

Neanderthal Man was subject to a harsh climate and lived through the last great Ice Age. In Europe especially, he gave way (but did not give rise) to another sub-species, which was first recorded as Cro-Magnon Man, more intelligent and adaptable. Other Neanderthal types occurred in different regions of the world but the line disappeared around 25,000 years ago, leaving our ancestors, *Homo sapiens,* as the dominant sub-species.

HOMO SAPIENS (CRO-MAGNON)

Age: 40,000-10,000 years ago. These men used a wide range of tools including stone flakes and parallel-sided knives and chisels. The latter were used for working bone and wood. The earliest art is associated with Homo sapiens.

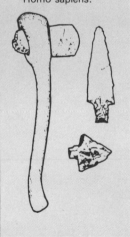

This famous skeleton came to be called Neanderthal Man, and since that first skeleton was found, many more have been dug up. Neanderthal Man had a brain as big as ours, probably wore some kind of clothes, and made sophisticated tools and weapons. Neanderthal men, disappeared about 25,000 years ago, leaving another different group of creatures who lived at the same time.

These creatures, we know, were our true ancestors, *Homo sapiens* (Thinking Man), and the first records we have of them date back about 40,000 years.

They were called Cro-Magnons after the French site which produced some early important discoveries.

The Cro-Magnon people probably looked very much like modern Man. They were a little shorter than today's average European. And they were probably the first human beings capable of talking to each other.

These early men lived in rock shelters, often with inner tents of skins. Their clothes were made from skins, roughly sewn together, and they used tools of bone and stone. They carved ornaments, and their paintings were usually executed deep inside caves. Charcoal and coloured earths were mixed with oil and used as paints; sticks, feathers and fingers were used as brushes.

Burial sites

Both Neanderthal and Cro-Magnon men ceremonially decorated and buried their dead. Cro-Magnon burial places dating from 35,000 to 10,000 B.C. have been found in more than 25 sites across Europe and Siberia.

Bone tubes with equally-spaced holes tell us that Cro-Magnon men made music. These flutes date from 30,000 to 20,000 B.C. It also appears that they invented the bow and arrow about 12,000 to 11,000 B.C.

We have proof that Cro-Magnon Man was quite sophisticated in his use of fire. From a cave site in Belgium has come a beautifully-rounded piece of a mineral called iron pyrites. This substance is one of the few natural minerals, that will produce sparks when struck by flint — sparks hot enough to set dry tinder on fire. And, more important, this piece of pyrites has a groove across it showing where it has been struck again and again with pieces of flint.

Archaeologists fail to agree when these early men started to farm the land, but it probably took place some time between 10,000 and 8,000 B.C. It was the domestication of plants and animals, leading to the beginning of a settled way of life that brought to an end the nomadic existence of Stone Age Man.

These first modern men began to dominate nature in ways that their ancestors could never have dreamed of. In the wake of agriculture would come all the complex forms of social life that we know today.

Skulls

Australopithecus — Brain capacity 500c.c. Ape-like brow ridges. Man-like teeth (incisors and canines similar).

Homo habilis — Brain capacity 680c.c.

Homo erectus — Brain capacity 860c.c. Large brow ridges. Low forehead and flattened brain case.

Swanscombe Man — Brain capacity 1,300c.c. Rounded brain case.

Homo neanderthalis — Brain capacity 1,500c.c. Brain case has an odd protruding "bun" at the back. Cheek bones are swept back. Large brow ridges.

Homo sapiens — Brain capacity 1,400c.c. High forehead with small brow ridges. Small face. Jaw has distinct chin.

Historical Events

About 2900 B.C. the Pharaoh Khufu built the Great Pyramid at Gizeh. It is said to have taken 100,000 men twenty years to build. Near it stands the Great Sphinx. A riddle no longer, it is now known to be the portrait head of the pharaoh Khafra, attached to the body of a lion.

The step-pyramid of King Zoser is the oldest surviving masonry building in the world. It was erected around 3000 B.C. near the site of the royal city of Memphis.

This is a mural painting 4000 years old found in a rock tomb at Beni Hassan. The hot drifting sands and rainless atmosphere of Egypt have helped to preserve these ancient treasures, and enabled archaeologists to discover many of the secrets of this ancient civilisation and its mighty pharaohs.

Above: Is a reconstruction of the sanctuary of the great temple at Tell el-Amarna, built by Amenhotep IV north of Thebes.

The tomb of King Tutankhamen, the pharaoh who died when he was about 18, was discovered almost intact by archaeologist Howard Carter in 1922. The gold-plated wood carving, right, is from his coffin.

These are the ruins of the temple of Rameses II. Its pillars had drawings of the king depicted as a god.

In the shadow of the mighty cliffs at Deir el-Bahri rises the mortuary temple of Queen Hatshepsut. A complex of colonnaded shrines ascend in terraces, making a magnificent memorial to a Queen whose right to the throne was challenged but who ruled in male clothes.

At Karnak, near the modern town of Luxor, is the greatest colonnaded hall ever erected, covering as much space as Notre Dame cathedral in Paris. The figures are 24 metres high.

Secrets of Ancient Egypt

SAILING southwards on the River Nile in Egypt is like taking a time machine back through the ages, through thousands of years of history when the pharaohs ruled that desert land. The impressive ruins of pyramids, temples and tombs are more complete there than in most places in the ancient world.

A whole learning, called Egypt-ology, is devoted to the study of the records and remains of ancient Egypt. Thanks to the diligence of these ancient people in writing down most things — household accounts, letters,

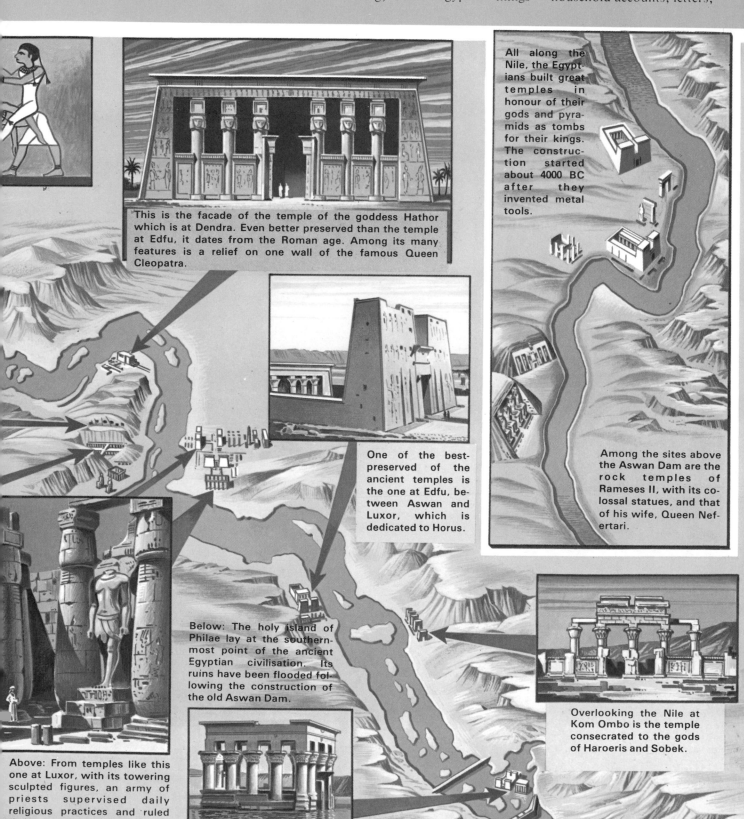

This is the facade of the temple of the goddess Hathor which is at Dendra. Even better preserved than the temple at Edfu, it dates from the Roman age. Among its many features is a relief on one wall of the famous Queen Cleopatra.

All along the Nile, the Egyptians built great temples in honour of their gods and pyramids as tombs for their kings. The construction started about 4000 BC after they invented metal tools.

One of the best-preserved of the ancient temples is the one at Edfu, between Aswan and Luxor, which is dedicated to Horus.

Among the sites above the Aswan Dam are the rock temples of Rameses II, with its colossal statues, and that of his wife, Queen Nefertari.

Below: The holy island of Philae lay at the southern-most point of the ancient Egyptian civilisation. Its ruins have been flooded following the construction of the old Aswan Dam.

Overlooking the Nile at Kom Ombo is the temple consecrated to the gods of Haroeris and Sobek.

Above: From temples like this one at Luxor, with its towering sculpted figures, an army of priests supervised daily religious practices and ruled the people.

poems, excuses for absence from work — we know a good deal about the way they lived.

The hot, drifting sands and rainless atmosphere which preserved these records have preserved much more: the burial pits and rock tombs, the pots and pans, jewellery and furniture, tools and weapons which they used. Even dresses worn by noble ladies 4,000 years ago, the flower garlands they wove, and the meals prepared for their tables have sometimes survived intact. Paintings on

Above: An aerial view of the Pyramid of Chepren at Gizeh, near Cairo. The outer casing, once covering it, remains at the top.

the walls of tombs show the owner supervising the activities of his farm labourers or craftsmen, feasting and listening to music, or fowling, hunting or fishing in the papyrus reed swamps alongside the Nile.

Why did the Egyptians take such pains to preserve their bodies, their records, and the objects of their everyday life? The answer lies in their religion.

"The Egyptians," wrote the Greek historian Herodotus, "are the most religious of all men." They believed that the soul lived on after death and that after it had been judged by the great god Osiris, if the good deeds outweighed the bad, it could return to the body and eat the food and drink prepared for it and read the sacred texts. It would then continue to enjoy in after-life the pursuits and pastimes it had loved on earth.

When about 4000 B.C., or earlier, the people of the Nile Valley invented metal tools, and learned to work large blocks of stone, they built temples in honour of their gods and pyramids to protect the bodies of their pharaohs.

Their pyramids, vast edifices of masonry, extend for more than 96 kilometres along the Nile. Each one marks the last resting place of one of the pharaohs of the Pyramid Age, which was from 3000 to 2500 B.C.

At Sakkara, near the site of the royal city of Memphis, traditionally founded by Menes, called the first Pharoah, about 3400 B.C., stands the oldest surviving masonry building, the step-pyramid (with six steps) of King Zoser, erected not much after 3000 B.C. This first pyramid was

Below: The Great Sphinx at Gizeh. Large compared with a man, tiny compared with a pyramid.

really a series of flat tomb structures built one on top of the other.

Not more than a century later (about 2900 B.C.) the Pharaoh Khufu (sometimes called Cheops) built the Great Pyramid at Gizeh, near Cairo. It covers more than 5 hectares, each side being originally 230 metres long, and is 147 metres tall. It contains 2,300,000 blocks of limestone and Herodotus the Greek tells us that it took 100,000 men twenty years to build.

Near it stands another giant, the pyramid of Pharaoh Khafra (Chepren). In front of it is the Great Sphinx.

The age of the pyramids — or the Old Kingdom as it is called — lasted about 500 years. In about 2500 B.C. the great nobles became powerful enough to take considerable privileges from the pharaohs, each ruling great estates much as the barons did in Europe during the Middle Ages. These feudal lords were buried in rock-cut cliff tombs in Middle Egypt, about 320 kilometres south of Memphis, while the royal pyramids were built in Fayum, which had become Egypt's new capital.

The shepherd kings

The Middle Kingdom was at its height from 2000 to 1800 B.C. Afterwards, Egypt seems to have been ruled by a line of foreigners, the Hyksos, or shepherd kings. Little is known of them, for their memory was hated and all traces of their rule was blotted out by a later age.

About 640 kilometres south of Cairo the Nile Valley suddenly widens and on the west bank are two huge statues known as the Colossi of Memnon. They are figures of the Pharaoh Amenhotep the Third.

The statues stand on the plain of Thebes, the site of the greatest period of Egyptian history — from the sixteenth to the twelfth century B.C. — when the pharaohs no longer ruled a single river valley nation but an empire stretching from the River Euphrates in Asia to the fifth cataract of the Nile.

The modern centre of this plain is the luxury town of Luxor. Near it, at Karnak, where the ancient city of Thebes once stood, is a tangle of vast ancient temples approached from the Nile by a broad avenue of ram-headed sphinxes.

Army of priests

An army of priests once supervised daily religious practices from the Karnak temples, and they dominated the peoples' lives. They were powerful because it was believed they worked magic, and all learning was from them alone.

On the other bank of the Nile from Thebes, the western bank, is the Valley of the Kings. Here, in this secret valley, the pharaohs of the Middle and New Kingdoms were buried in rock tombs, almost all of which were subsequently plundered by robbers. Here, too, in 1922, one of the most sensational discoveries in the story of archaeology was made with the finding of the tomb of Tutankhamen (sometimes spelt Tutankhamun), the pharaoh who died when he was 18 about the year 1350 B.C. In it was found the most magnificent collection of Egyptian antiquities ever, for the tomb had remained untouched by thieves.

The first great conqueror of the New Kingdom, Thotmes the First, led his armies into Asia and laid the foundations of Egypt's overseas empire. One of his successors was Queen Hatshepsut, who reigned in male clothes as pharaoh, since the Egyptians would not have accepted

Above: An imaginative, composite picture, showing an Egyptian stone-mason at work and part of the Temples of Abu Simbel, which were carved by the slow laborious method. The marvel and artistry of this achievement are clearly seen and the grandeur of the size is obvious.

being ruled by a woman. She built a mortuary temple facing Thebes which still rises terrace upon terrace.

All the principal towns and cities of ancient Egypt had their own great gods. They were usually worshipped under the form of some animal, and in some places sacred animals were mummified after death. Vast cemeteries of mummified cats have been found, and crocodiles, lizards, bulls, ibises and other animals were similarly treated. A Nile traveller can still see some of them — looking

almost as alive as they were 4,000 years ago.

Another New Kingdom pharaoh, Akhnaton, decided to sweep away the prodigious collection of Egyptian gods and to supplant them by a new one, that of the universal power of the Sun. A poet and dreamer — some said he was in fact quite mad — Akhnaton moved his capital to Amarna, where he built a new city with fine avenues flanked by public buildings. But after he died, the old order quickly returned.

Final glory

The Egyptian empire in its decline enjoyed one final blaze of glory under Pharaoh Seti the First and his son, Rameses the Second, or Rameses the Great. Rameses was the pharaoh responsible for the great rock temples of Abu Simbel, where colossal statues of him look down from the cliff.

After the pharaohs, Egypt was ruled by the Ptolemies — descendants of a Macedonian general who took Egypt as his share of Alexander the Great's territories after Alexander's death. The Ptolemies left many fine temples, new or remodelled, along the Nile. They built the temple of the sun-god Horus at Edfu and another fine temple at Dendera.

The last of the Ptolemies was Cleopatra. After her, Egypt became a province of the Roman Empire, and was later ruled by the Byzantines. That put the Egyptians in a mood to welcome the Saracen conquest in A.D. 641 and since that time the creed of Islam has always prevailed in the land of the pharaohs.

Far left: The columns of the Great Hall at the Temple of Karnak. It is really a complex of temples, with statues, obelisks and numerous hieroglyphic inscriptions.

Left: The innermost coffin showing the gold mask of Tutankhamen. This tomb is the only one found virtually intact — one of the great splendours of ancient Egypt.

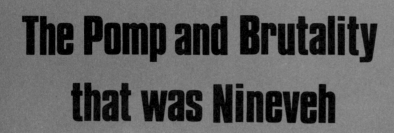

The Pomp and Brutality that was Nineveh

A thousand years before the birth of Christ no country's name struck greater terror into the hearts of men than that of Assyria.

Torture, burning and slavery were the weapons the Assyrians used to subject their conquered foes. They were a fearsome sight in battle, with their bushy black beards and curly hair.

There was no peace for a city which resisted the Assyrians. And when they had forced it to capitulate, they would celebrate their triumph by riding their chariots, built with wheels of iron, the new material of war, through the beaten defenders, impaling them on their spears and transfixing them with arrows as they knelt begging for mercy. Such was the spread of their imfamy that whole city-kingdoms decided to surrender, as soon as they heard of their coming.

The Assyrians came from the north of Babylonia, where modern Iraq is today. About the year 704 B.C. a new terrorist king named Sennacherib came to the Assyrian throne and set up his capital at Nineveh — pictured at the height of its glory on these pages. Beautiful though the city may look to us, it was from here that Sennacherib dictated wars fought with such horrifying brutality that men shuddered even at the name of Nineveh.

Wealthiest in the world

The city was already a vast and splendid place when Sennacherib came to the Assyrian throne. The new king then set about making it the wealthiest and most resplendent capital in the known world, greatly extending its size and bringing in all the looted treasures from the towns of Syria and Palestine.

Sennacherib surrounded his capital with an inner and outer wall, variously computed as from five to ten metres high and wide enough, it was said, for four chariots to be driven abreast on the ramparts. One side of the walled city flanked the left bank of the River Tigris.

At intervals, the walls were pierced by huge gateways flanked by winged bulls or lions and closed by doors of cedar wood embossed with bronze.

Sennacherib's palace was probably designed by architects brought captive to Nineveh. "It was the soul of the East miraculously expressed in stone," we are told.

Its lower facade, rising from a stone platform inlaid with tiles, was sculptured with figures from mythology and carved with records of Assyrian battle glories.

From it rose lines of light and slender columns, holding beautiful upper storeys. Their towers were connected by colonnades which enclosed a courtyard that caught the cool evening airs of the east.

Inside, the palace was decorated with brilliant paintings and sculptures that provided a vivid panorama of Assyrian life and customs.

Sennacherib scrapped a number of decayed buildings in the old Nineveh to create broad avenues flanked by white buildings with sculptured, painted facades — all the work of prisoners taken by the king's armies in battle.

For two centuries before Sennacherib, the 'Bible kingdoms' of Israel and Judah had been among the nations oppressed by the Assyrians, until Israel in the north was obliterated.

When Sennacherib arrived, the Hebrew kingdom of Judah, which was not to last as a separate kingdom for much longer, was a vassal state of Assyria, but the peace was an uneasy one, and when Sennacherib's reign was only three years old the King of Judah, Hezekiah, joined with the Egyptians in a revolt against the Assyrians.

What happened next has been dramatically caught in a poem by Lord Byron:

The Assyrians came down like the wolf
on the fold,
And his cohorts were gleaming in
purple and gold;
And the sheen of their spears was like
stars on the sea,
When the blue wave rolls nightly on
deep Galilee.

Dramatically, the angry Sennacherib swept through Judah, burning and looting. Then, still with his eye on his name in history, he wrote:

"I attacked Hezekiah of Judah, who did not to me. I took forty-six of his cities and forts and other small places around them. I shut up Hezekiah like a bird in a cage in Jerusalem. I raised forts about the

Nineveh as it may have looked: this is an artist's impression of the Assyrian capital viewed from the right bank of the River Tigris. It must indeed have been a splendid sight, its magnificent sculptures and graceful columns giving it a fairy-tail quality, far removed from the fiery brutality within.

city and barred its main gate.

Two and half thousand years after that war report was written, you can still see it, inscribed in stone, in the British Museum in London.

Sennacherib found a new enemy in the city-state of Babylon. Down came the Assyrians again like a wolf on the fold, causing complete devastation.

Babylon was taken and burned to the ground, and its citizens were massacred in what must have been one of the most savage destructions in ancient times. And when all the fine buildings and beautiful temples that had taken centuries to build were flattened, Sennacherib triumphantly opened the flood gates and turned the life-giving water into a torrent of death, flooding the city and completely obliterating it from the map.

But one day, the Assyrian king went into his temple to pray to his god and, while he knelt, two of his sons crept up behind him and plunged a sword into him.

By 624 B.C. Babylon had risen again from its ashes and its new king was a strongly determined man named Nabopolassar, upon whom was to fall the history-making role of overthrowing the Assyrians.

"*Woe to the bloody city*," wrote the Hebrew prophet Nahum about the Assyrian capital of Nineveh, "*it is full of lies and robbery; the prey departeth not.*"

Towards that bloody city, Nabopolassar and his allies now went like the wind, scything their way through Assyria. For three months in 611 B.C., they laid siege to the citadel of terror. Then, it is said, the Tigris river burst its banks and the flood water swept away some of the city's fortifications. At once the besiegers roared in through the walls of Nineveh — and lit the place from end to end in a huge fire that melted the great statues and boiled the river waters. Into the furnace the last king of Assyria, Sin-shar-ishkun, plunged to his death.

One thing the victors made certain of as they triumphantly went about their grim work of fire, plunder and pillage was that Nineveh would never again rise to terrorise the world.

After its destruction, the very situation of Nineveh vanished so utterly from human recollection that when Xenophon and his army passed its ruins two hundred years later, they concluded that they must represent the remains of a Parthian city.

Today Nineveh is a series of hummocks, carved and tunnelled by excavators. No 'ruins' are visible, for the unbaked Assyrian brick, which was mostly dug from the soil to build the city, once more became part of that soil, and it needed great skill for nineteenth century archaeologists to separate one from the other. And the magnificent bas-reliefs and sculptures have now all been removed to museums in the capitals of Europe.

The golden age of Greece

The Erechtheum

Curtain walls designed to be defended

FOUR and a half centuries before the birth of Christ a poor Greek villager found a ram with a single horn growing from the centre of its forehead. The villager decided to take the strange animal to Pericles, an intellectual politician in Athens.

Pericles turned to his friend Lampon and asked his opinion of the ram.

"It is an omen, noble Pericles," declared Lampon. "Today there are two men struggling for leadership in Athens, yourself and Thucydides. The one-horned ram has been brought to you as a sign that there will soon be only one leader in our city — Pericles!"

Pericles was flattered, but frowned when he heard a growl of dissent.

"Anaxagoras," he said, "I see you don't agree, so how do you explain this strange beast?"

Anaxagoras said nothing but took a knife and slew the one-horned ram. Carefully he opened the animal's head, then he said to Pericles, "Here is the reason for this animal's single horn. It has a malformation of the skull. It is all quite natural, though I admit rather unusual."

Anaxagoras was just one of many brilliant thinkers and artists who lived during the 5th and 4th centuries B.C., in the greatest age of Greek civilisation. There were poets like Sophocles and Euripides, philosophers like Socrates, Plato and Aristotle, historians like Herodotus and scientists like Hippocrates.

Birth of democracy

It was in Athens during this period that democracy — government by the people — had its first stirrings. Although it was quite different from our own democracy of today, at least it gave the Athenians a chance to discuss their political ideas freely.

Pericles, a democrat, did become the leader of Athens, and under his rule Athens became by far the most brilliant of all the Greek city-states.

Before Pericles came to power, 10,000 Athenian soldiers had routed a Persian army that invaded Greece. Ten years later the Persians tried again and this time they burned Athens to the ground.

The Athenians fled to the island of Aegina, but they would not give in. They lured the huge Persian fleet into the narrow Bay of Salamis and then pounced on it and destroyed it.

Then, under the leadership of Pericles the democrat, the Athenians returned to their smoke-blackened city and rebuilt it. Its Acropolis — the steep rocky citadel overlooking the city-state — looked like the illustration on these pages when they had finished. Even today, in ruins, it is a sight so beautiful as to make you catch your breath in wonder.

The Acropolis was crowned by the Parthenon — a perfect temple building created for a perfect age. Built entirely of marble, it took nearly ten years to complete. It had seventeen columns at each side and eight at each end and above them was a frieze or band of magnificent sculptures below a gently sloping roof of marble tiles.

The columns taper gradually to the top but are slightly convex (swelling) in the centre. The Greek sculptors did this deliberately because they knew that the effect would be to make the columns graceful as well as strong.

The frieze, a continuous decorative border 157 metres long, depicted the great Panathenic Procession held every four years in honour of Athena, the goddess of wisdom, after whom the city-state was named. Part of that frieze is now in the British Museum.

Inside the Parthenon stood a huge figure of the goddess Athena, sculpted in gold and ivory by the renowned Greek sculptor Phidias, the Michelangelo of the Golden Age of Greece.

Outside the Parthenon stood a colossal statue of Athena, reputed to have been 10 metres high. Sailors fifteen miles out at sea could get their bearings from the glint of the sun on the crest of its helmet.

On the other side of the flat platform that tops the Acropolis the Athenians built a small temple, called the Erechtheum, in honour of Erectheus, who was supposed to have been a king of Athens in days long past.

Looking down from here, the Athenians could see the superb Propylaea, or Entrance Gate. Today, far below, framed within its columns, gleam the white walls of the modern city and, beyond them, a straight road leads to Piraeus, the port of

Two thousand years ago, on a hill above Athens which came to be called the Acropolis, the ancient Greeks erected temples and statues in glittering white marble, to the glory of their gods. Among the most majestic was the great temple to the goddess Athena, the Parthenon, with the majestic columns which still survive today.

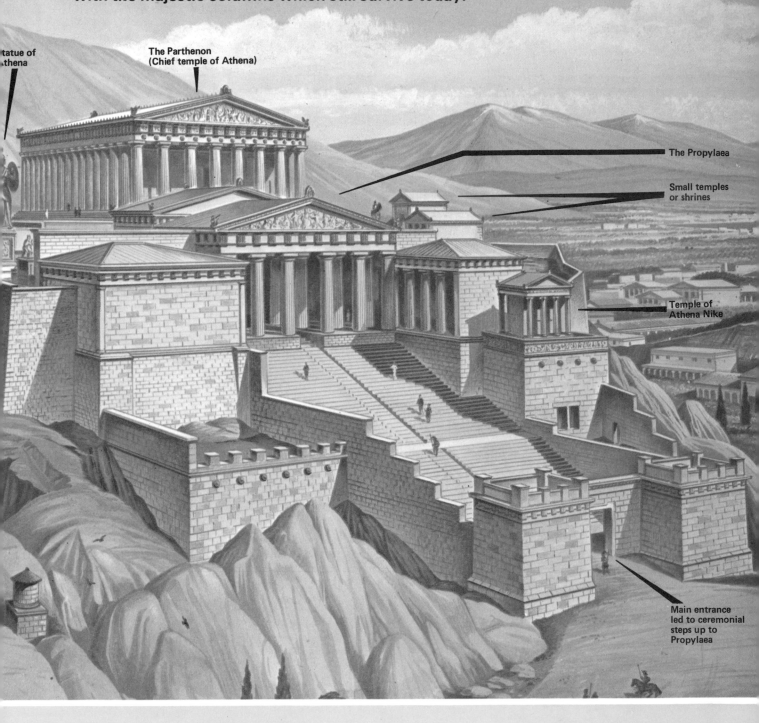

Statue of Athena

The Parthenon (Chief temple of Athena)

The Propylaea

Small temples or shrines

Temple of Athena Nike

Main entrance led to ceremonial steps up to Propylaea

ancient and modern Athens. If, from the ruins of the ancient *agora,* or market-place, you look up to the rocky crag that is the Acropolis, you will see a monument to the suffering the Athenians endured when, almost alone, they successfully defended their freedom against the invading Persians. Into the wall of the Acropolis they built the ruined columns thrown down by the

Persians — as a reminder that the fight for freedom sometimes involves sacrifice.

While all this building was going on, Pericles made Athens the champion of democratic rule — rule by the people — in the face of the old-fashioned aristocratic rule — rule dictated by noblemen — which was championed by Sparta in southern Greece.

While the great thinkers and artists of the Golden Age have inspired much of modern European civilisation, so Athenian democracy was the foundation of modern democracy. Once again, however, it would be wrong to imagine Classical Athens as a democracy in anything like the sense we know today. Far from it. Athens was a slave-owning society where the privileges of citizenship were restricted to a favoured few.

Apart from being the cultural centre of Greece, Athens soon became a ruthless exploiter of other Greek city-states. In fact, Athenian democracy was strictly for Athenians only.

As so often happens in history, Athenian aggression eventually brought disaster to Athens herself. When Alcibiades, the young friend and successor of Pericles, sent a powerful Athenian fleet to conquer the Greek city of Syracuse in 415 B.C., he doomed Athenian supremacy in the eastern Mediterranean. Athens' power was destroyed, along with thousands of her bravest sons, in the unsuccessful siege of Syracuse.

Few at that time can have been sorry to see Athens humbled, for Athenian arrogance had become intolerable. Even a philosopher like Anaxagoras must take some responsibility for this. He, and others like him, had undermined the old religious ideas of good and evil, putting in their place the Laws of Nature, where the strong preyed upon the weak. This concept of "might being right" became something of a driving force behind Athenian imperialism.

Few tears were shed, therefore, when the brilliant, arrogant city of Athens ceased to dominate Greece. But less than 80 years were to pass before a far greater imperial power, Macedonia, crushed Greece itself and brought the Golden Age to an end.

As for the magnificent Parthenon, it lasted almost intact for 2,000 years. Then, in 1687, during a war between the Turks (who were occupying Athens) and the Venetians, the Turks used the beautiful temple as an ammunition store. An explosion set fire to the store and more than half the building was destroyed. A tragedy indeed for future generations!

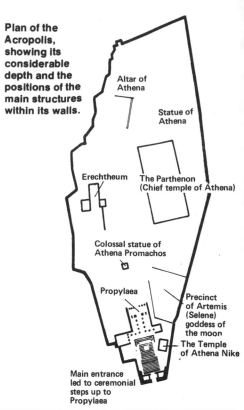

Plan of the Acropolis, showing its considerable depth and the positions of the main structures within its walls.

- Altar of Athena
- Statue of Athena
- Erechtheum
- The Parthenon (Chief temple of Athena)
- Colossal statue of Athena Promachos
- Propylaea
- Precinct of Artemis (Selene) goddess of the moon
- The Temple of Athena Nike
- Main entrance led to ceremonial steps up to Propylaea

The Elgin Marbles

At the beginning of the 19th century, a British peer, Lord Elgin brought some marbles from the Acropolis to Britain. These marvellous figures and scenes from Greek life and mythology, mainly taken from the Parthenon, are in the British Museum.

Left. Panel from the Parthenon, showing the struggle between a legendary hero and a mythical centaur. Right. Part of frieze from inside the Parthenon, showing a procession held in honour of the Greek goddess, Athena. (Both from the Elgin Marbles).

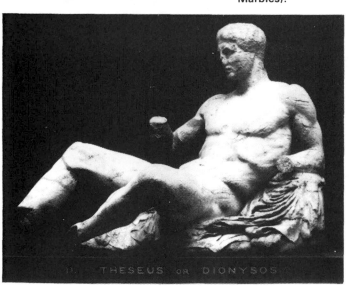

The figure on the left is either Theseus or Dionysos. Its exact identity is unknown. It is from the pediment shown below and is part of the Elgin Marbles. Below is a drawing of the east pediment of the Parthenon. A pediment is the triangular frontispiece over the door of a Grecian-style building. When it was complete, the one below showed the birth of Athena. The figures depicted were Greek gods or heroes. Helios, the sun god, was supposed to drive his chariot across the sky; Theseus was the heroic son of Aegeus, who was once king of Athens; Dionysos was the god of wine; Persephone was queen of the realms of the dead and Demeter was the goddess of agriculture; Iris was the goddess of the rainbow; The Three Fates determined the destiny and lifespan of each newborn child; and Selene was the Greek moon goddess.

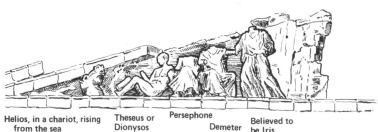

Helios, in a chariot, rising from the sea | Theseus or Dionysos | Persephone Demeter | Believed to be Iris

The Three Fates | Horse drawing the chariot of Selene descending below the horizon

Seven wonders of the world PART 1

TIME has been unkind to the seven great buildings which ancient people called the Seven Wonders of the World. Today just one of them — the Pyramids near Cairo — remains. So what we know about the other six comes only from what eye-witnesses wrote of them, and drawings have to be built up from that sometimes conflicting information.

On the following pages you can see how two of the seven ancient wonders, the Colossus of Rhodes and the Mausoleum at Halicarnassus, possibly looked. Of all the Seven Wonders, the Colossus probably suffered the most; even its exact site is now forgotten.

From ancient writers, though, we know that it stood somewhere near the entrance to the harbour of the Greek island of Rhodes; that it was made of bronze in sections, strengthened inside with masonry.

The Colossus was an immense statue of Helios, or Apollo, the Sun god and protecting god of Rhodes. It took its designer, Chares of Lindus, 12 years to build and it stood awesomely above the harbour for 56 years.

Then, in 224 B.C., the Colossus was thrown down by an earthquake. For centuries its shattered pieces lay upon the ground, where they were seen, in the first century A.D., by Pliny, a Roman writer travelling in the Greek islands.

"Even as the statue lies there it excites our wonder and imagination," declared Pliny. "Few men can clasp a thumb in their arms and the fingers are larger than most statues. Where the limbs have been broken apart, vast caverns are seen yawning in the interior. Inside, too, are masses of rocks, by the aid of which the artist steadied it while erecting it."

Why was it, in fact, erected? The answer is buried deep in the island's past. While Athens was a splendid city of ancient Greece, Rhodes rivalled it and the Rhodians, who were seafarers and merchants, were the richest people in the Aegean Sea.

In 312 B.C. Ptolemy, king of Egypt, became involved in a struggle with Antigonus, ruler of Macedon. The people of Rhodes decided to rally to the side of Ptolemy and their contribution undoubtedly helped Ptolemy to defeat the Macedonians.

Antigonus, however, decided to have his revenge on Rhodes and, in 307 B.C., he sent a great expedition against the island, under the command of his son, Demetrius. With 370 ships, 40,000 men and a powerful and awe-inspiring siege-artillery, Demetrius looked invincible. His soldiers outnumbered the entire population of Rhodes. How could the islanders hope to repel that huge armada?

Nonetheless, for twelve months they put up a desperate resistance. Women worked night and day making weapons and gave their hair as bow strings. Temples were pulled down so that the stones could be used to strengthen and repair the walls.

Demetrius, meanwhile, delivered attack after attack. When at last he seemed certain to break through the grim resistance, Ptolemy of Egypt, remembering the services which the Rhodians had rendered him, arrived off the island with a fleet and forced the Macedonians to withdraw. To commemorate their deliverance, the Rhodians raised the Colossus in honour of their protecting deity, the Sun god.

They made it wholly of metal taken from the engines of war left by Demetrius and chose Chares to design it because, besides his fame as a sculptor, he had fought gallantly in defence of Rhodes.

Chares put a spiral staircase within the statue, ascending to its head. In the eyes, according to some accounts, the Rhodians kept burning a beacon light to serve as a guide to ships.

After the earthquake overturned it, numerous attempts were made to restore the dismembered giant to its place. But no means could be found of raising it. In A.D. 672 the Arabs, who then occupied Rhodes, sold what remained as waste metal to a merchant. That merchant, it is said, carried away 900 camel-loads — over 300 tonnes — of bronze.

OUR second wonder of the world, the Mausoleum at Halicarnassus (which is now the Turkish town of Bodrum) was erected for an entirely different reason, although, except for a few pieces now in the British Museum, it, too, has vanished.

Mausolus, a Persian, about the year 380 B.C. became the satrap, or ruler, of the important town and district of Halicarnassus, on the south-west coast of Asia Minor.

Mausolus was married to Artemisia, who appears to have been completely devoted to him and was therefore consumed by grief when he died.

She resolved to perpetuate his memory by building for him the most splendid tomb ever seen and she sent to Greece for the world's best artists to plan it for her.

There were Satyros and Pythos, the architects; Scopas, the greatest sculptor of that time; and Timetheos, Bryaxis and Leochares, other famed workers in stone. They set to work with a will, but less than two years later Queen Artemisia herself died.

What to do with the unfinished tomb? The artists had a meeting and resolved to complete it as a labour of love "for their own fame and a record of their skill." The result was so spectacular that its name, the Mausoleum, has passed down into our language as a word meaning any elaborate tomb.

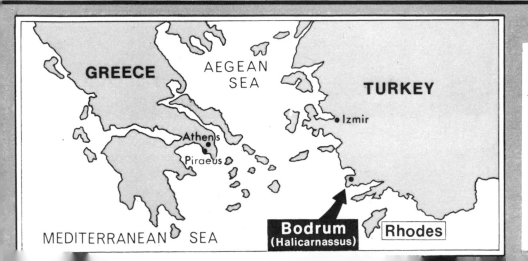

This map shows the position of the Colossus of Rhodes and the Mausoleum at Halicarnassus when they towered in all their glory. Old Halicarnassus is now no longer known by that name. It is the present-day Bodrum. While it was Halicarnassus, however, it was the birthplace of the ancient historian, Herodotus.

The Colossus of Rhodes!

As with the Colossus, we have only a general idea from the writings of the ancients what the Mausoleum looked like. We know that the tomb chamber, containing the bodies of Mausolus and Artemisia, was the solid lower storey; that bands of sculpture ran round all four sides.

Above this was a colonnade of 36 columns of rich, golden-white marble, surmounted by a pyramid of 24 steps and on the top of the pyramid was a chariot with four horses. Its total height was around 13 metres.

But what appeared to ancient sightseers as the most remarkable feature of the building was the impression of lightness. The massive pyramid, poised on top of the slender colonnade, appeared to float in air.

Probably the building survived virtually undamaged right down to the twelfth century. Then, in 1402, the Knights of St. John moved into Halicarnassus and began to build a castle.

To obtain the necessary building materials they pulled down the remains of the ancient city and probably about this time the superstructure of the Mausoleum was destroyed. In 1472 the building was in ruins and the last of these ruins was destroyed fifty years later, just before the Knights were driven out of Asia Minor and Rhodes. Their leader, realising the importance of the

The Mausoleum at Halicarnassus!

castle in the impending Turkish attack they would have to face, ordered its walls to be repaired. For this purpose the Knights broke up the base of the Mausoleum and burnt the marble blocks for lime.

While doing so, the story goes, they broke into the inner chamber containing a sarcophagus (stone coffin). At nightfall they returned to their castle and in the morning when they went back they found that the tomb had been robbed during the night.

Then, in the nineteenth century, British archaeologists laboriously collected scattered fragments from the excavation they made and brought them back to the British Museum. The most

striking of the sculptures they recovered are the fragments of the chariot group which stood on top of the pyramid. Big pieces of the huge bodies of the marble horses still remain and it is thought that the two portrait statues of Mausolus and Queen Artemisia stood in the chariot, crowning the whole building.

We know that the male statue is of Mausolus because he can be identified from his coins. He appears as a bearded man, richly robed and with an expression of quiet dignity.

Thus the memory of Mausolus, who would hardly merit a marginal note in the world's story, lives on today, known probably by more people than he was in his own lifetime.

Seven wonders of the world

PART 2

T HE ancient world was full of temples built to honour the gods. They were huge, magnificent buildings, brilliantly carved and decorated and intended to last for eternity.

But two of these temples, declared the ancients, were more spectacular and more beautiful than all the others. They were the temple of Artemis at Ephesus now part of Western Turkey and the temple at Olympia which housed a statue of Zeus, the supreme god according to the Greeks.

The temple of Artemis and the statue of Zeus were rated so wonderful to gaze upon that they were included among the seven wonders of the world. And we have to accept the few eye-witnesses' accounts for that, because unfortunately neither of them lasted for eternity.

Lost glory

Even the insect life seems to have left the deserted site of the once fabulous temple of Artemis. Visitors to Ephesus are taken to see the ancient city's splendid theatre, library, streets and homes. A mile down a narrow road, the temple site rarely figures on a guide list.

Yet this temple was often assigned first place in the list of ancient wonders. One writer said of it: "I have seen the hanging gardens of old Babylon, the statue of Olympian Zeus, the Colossus of Rhodes, the great labour of the lofty pyramids, and the tomb of Mausolus, but when I beheld the temple at Ephesus towering to the clouds, all these other marvels were eclipsed."

In fact, the writer was talking about the fifth temple built on the site — the first four had all been destroyed. The very first was constructed about 700 B.C.; the fourth must have been spectacular, for one of the principal subscribers to it was Croesus, King of Lydia, whose wealth was famed throughout the ancient world.

In the year 356 B.C., this fourth temple was wantonly burned down by a man named Herostratus and it was decided to construct a new, fifth temple on a scale of even greater magnificence.

The ladies of Ephesus sold their jewels to provide funds; kings, in emulation of Croesus, presented columns sculptured by the greatest artists of the age. Alexander the Great, passing through Ephesus on the way to the conquest of Asia, offered to pay for the whole building if the Ephesians would allow him to inscribe his name upon it as the dedicator. They refused, diplomatically suggesting that it was not for one god to make dedications to another.

Completion

By about 323 B.C. the new temple, dedicated to the goddess of hunting and wild animals, was finished. It was 150 metres long with 127 columns 20 metres high.

In due time the temple became a sort of treasure house for the ancient world. "All nations," said a Greek author, "deposit their riches in the temple." Besides all that wealth, it was filled with wonderful works of art. The Roman writer Pliny tells us that the statues alone would need many columns to describe: "It is full of sculpture, almost all by Praxiteles."

Among the great paintings that hung there was a famous portrait of Alexander the Great on horseback, for which the artist, Apelles, was paid twenty talents of gold. It was said that Alexander did not praise this painting as much as it deserved when he first saw it. But his horse began to neigh at the horse in the painting as if it were alive, too, believing it to be real.

"King," said Apelles sourly, "your horse is a better judge of painting than you are."

The temple was several times partly damaged by earthquakes but it does not seem to have needed extensive repairs until the reign of the Roman Emperor Gallienus (A.D. 260-268), when it was plundered and burnt by the Goths.

Rediscovery

It is doubtful whether it was ever restored after that catastrophe, for the worship of Artemis was beginning to go out of fashion. A hundred years later it was certainly in ruins and local people were using its stones for building material. Later still, a church was built on the ruins, but this was destroyed by a change in the course of the nearby river. Its waters covered the scanty remains of the temple with a layer of ooze, obliterating all traces of the site until it was rediscovered in the last century.

Some time during the last hundred years enthusiasts piled some of the column drums one upon the other to make a solitary complete column on the marshy field where the temple stood. A few years ago a heron built its nest on the top of this column but now that, too, has gone.

Statue of Zeus

THE statue of Zeus at Olympia was the work of a sculptor named Pheidias (or Phidias), the designer too of the Parthenon temple that crowns the Acropolis in Athens.

The god-statue was said to be of gold and ivory and to be seated on a throne. In his right hand was a figure of the goddess of Victory, also of ivory and gold.

In Zeus's left hand was a sceptre, decorated with many different metals and providing a perch for an eagle. The god's sandals were made of gold and so, too, were the drapes.

We know most of this from the writings of a traveller named Pausanias, who visited Greece in the latter half of the second century A.D.

How big though was this brilliant statue, which was constructed about 440 B.C.? With Pausanias's description and the painstaking putting together of the pedestal slabs to a height of one metre (all that is left of mighty Zeus) the enthroned figure is calculated to have been seven or eight times life size.

The temple in which it reposed had an inner chamber 32 metres by 15 metres. The god sat at one end of this chamber, flanked by columns.

Outside the temple, the bustling city of Olympia (where the Greeks held the Olympic Games) thrived on the tourist trade which the temple bought it all the year round. People burned human victims, as offerings to the god outside the temple and the pile of ashes thus caused became so high that steps had to be made to reach the top of it.

The later history of the great statue of Zeus is uncertain. The Roman Emperor Caligula, it is said, had a plan to transport it to the Capitol in Rome, where he intended to substitute a representation of his own head for that of the god.

But when his workmen moved in they were quickly driven away by terrifying peals of supernatural laughter which broke out when they laid hands on the throne, and the ship sent to carry the statue was struck by lightning and wrecked.

What happened after that is unknown. Perhaps the statue fell in one of the many earthquakes that troubled Olympia, or perhaps it was destroyed by raiders.

Today the temple is a pathetic pile of broken masonry and pillars. Grasshoppers jump over the broken white stones and lizards bask on them.

Seven wonders of the world

PART 3

The Hanging Gardens of Babylon and The Pharos Lighthouse

WHAT bothered the Queen of Babylon as she rode around the city that her husband was fast turning into the most glittering one in the ancient world, was the flatness of the place. She missed the hills of her native Persia. "If only there were a few here," she sighed to King Nebuchadnezzar.

The King, ever anxious to please, consulted his architects and out of their deliberations, so the old Greek story goes, came the Hanging Gardens of Babylon.

Reputedly, the gardens were laid out on terraces, forming an artificial hill fit to please the Queen. Steps three metres wide connected these terraces, which were built in tiers held up by large arches, raised upon other arches, one above the other to a height of more than 100 metres, and strengthened by a wall seven metres thick surrounding the entire gardens.

On top of the arches were laid huge flat stones covered with lead, and on this lead was the earth on which the plants were grown. Elaborate building techniques prevented the earth's moisture from reaching the arches and undermining them, and the entire gardens were watered by a pump built on the top tier, which drew water from the River Euphrates which flowed below. On these lead-based flower beds were planted the finest flowers and trees (probably very large) that Nebuchadnezzar's empire could produce.

Nebuchadnezzar II was the dynamic young son of a Babylonian king who, around 606 B.C., utterly destroyed the Assyrian city of

Nineveh, which had ruled the Bible lands with a rod of iron. For their allies in this work of destruction the Babylonians had a tribe called the Medes, who came from west Persia — modern Iran, and it was a princess of the Medes who married Nebuchadnezzar and inspired the idea of the Hanging Gardens when she came to live in Babylon.

In the days of its splendour, Nineveh had been a vast and wonderful city. Nebuchadnezzar decided to build a Babylon which would be greater and more wonderful still.

The Hanging Gardens are thought to have been the only Babylonian structure in which hewn stone was used to any considerable extent, because there was hardly any stone in the basin of the Tigris and Euphrates rivers, where the city was built. This in itself made the gardens wonderful, because stone was much prized. Because the gardens were built in tiers, the word "hanging" is inaccurate. Balcony Gardens might be a better description.

After the death of Nebuchadnezzar, the Persians conquered Babylon and the city fell into decline.

Two thousand years later, early in our own century, archaeologists — particularly the German R. Koldewey — uncovered what is possibly the site of the Hanging Gardens. They found a vaulted crypt, or cellar and the foundations of a building in whose construction a great deal of stone had been used. Inscriptions on tablets on the stairway leading to the crypt suggested that this once served as a place for preserving foods.

And of course it doesn't need much imagination to realise that under all those beautiful flowers and trees, under all that lead and stone and cascading water, there would indeed be a very cool place in a city that knew little respite from the sun.

The ruins of the old Babylon are near the town of Al-Hillah in modern Iraq, and can still be seen.

Unlike most of the seven wonders of the ancient world the Lighthouse on what was the island of Pharos near Alexandria stood for more than a thousand years. It was completed around the year 279 B.C. by the architect Sostratus of Cnidus, a man who took great care over his work.

It is said that Sostratus decided to test various materials to see which could best withstand the sea and the humidity common in the area. His method was simply to throw samples of stones, bricks, granite, gold, silver, lead and glass into the water and leave them for months.

The glass stood up best to the test, with the result that the father of all lighthouses was made from glass, in blocks and mixed with stones.

Built by thousands of slaves, the tower itself must have been between 125 and 150 metres high. It had three floors on a square base and the main part of its structure and the top storey were cylindrical in shape. Beneath the lighthouse were rooms for keepers and attendants.

Its light came from fires of resinous wood and great torches, or was provided by burning oil in vast containers on the top floor of the tower, and was said to have been reinforced by concave metal mirrors which reflected the light. These mirrors were supposedly designed and built by Archimedes, the Greek mathematician.

It is said that the light could be seen over 48 km away, although this is probably an exaggerated claim.

The idea of building it had come originally from Ptolemy I, Emperor of Egypt, who had once served as a general under Alexander the Great. Remembering Alexander's belief that men needed to build huge buildings to perpetuate their names and recall their feats, he decided to build the lighthouse at Alexandria.

Foolish Caliph

If self-promotion was the reason for its construction, greed has been said to be the reason for its destruction. This came about, so we are told, in the ninth century A.D., when a very foolish caliph was defender of the Moslem faith in Africa.

One day a silver-tongued merchant named Chrysostom (actually, his name meant "golden mouth") inveigled his way into the caliph's confidence and told him an incredible story. Under the Pharos, said Chrysostom, was buried a fabulous treasure, put there more than a thousand years ago by Sostratus.

Even more incredibly, the caliph believed the story and ordered that the Pharos should be demolished in order to reveal the treasure.

More slaves were brought in and stone by stone one of the world's most wonderful buildings was taken down. When no treasure was found Chrysostom, the merchant, fled for his life.

By then the foolish caliph had lost all interest in the Pharos. Sadly for the world, the stones were left in their piles and gradually fell into the sea.

A more common story, however, is that the lighthouse was destroyed by an earthquake around the end of the 13th century.

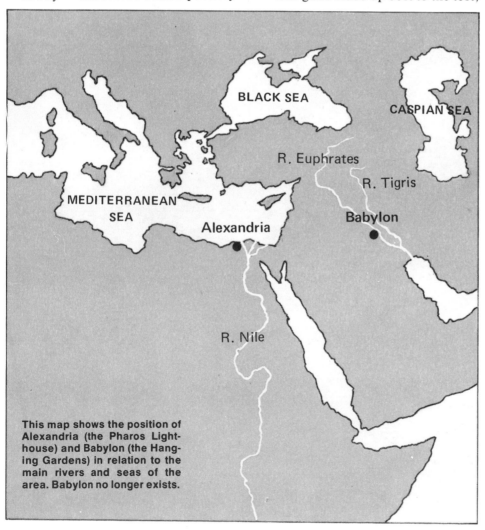

This map shows the position of Alexandria (the Pharos Lighthouse) and Babylon (the Hanging Gardens) in relation to the main rivers and seas of the area. Babylon no longer exists.

BLACK SEA

CASPIAN SEA

R. Euphrates

R. Tigris

MEDITERRANEAN SEA

Alexandria

Babylon

R. Nile

Seven wonders of the world

Part 4

The Pyramids

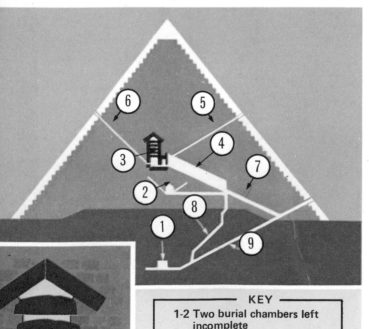

KEY
1-2 Two burial chambers left incomplete
3 Final chamber
4 Grand gallery to final chamber
5 Narrow ventilator airshaft
6 Narrow ventilator airshaft
7 Descending corridor
8 Escape shaft
9 Ascending corridor

FIVE thousand years ago the ancient Egyptians had organised themselves into a powerful, unified and civilised state under one ruler. They were able to measure accurately the rise and fall of the flooding river Nile, build irrigation canals to conserve the water in the dry season, grow enough food to support not only the labouring masses but a class of intellectual leaders who had invented a writing system, developed arithmetic and geometry, and were able to plan and erect enormous buildings.

All this had been achieved by a people who had begun as simple hunter-farmers living in small settlements besides the Nile — and at a time when Britain was still a wild country of barbaric tribesmen.

Yet so much of all that colossal effort of the ancient Egyptians was directed towards ends which today seem strange, even futile. The evidence is still in Egypt today — triangles of golden stone piercing the blue sky on the desert horizon; the pyramids.

About eighty of these vast stone structures appear to have been built between 2800 and 2000 B.C. At a distance they are impressive; at close quarters they are overpower-

The pictures on the left and on the right on the opposite page show diagrammatically the interior of a pyramid generally and the Pyramid of Cheops in particular. The small diagram below left shows the final burial chamber with the relative size of a man. The key for the picture on the right is: 1, 2 and 3 stone sealing blocks, 4 scaffolding of restraining crossbeams, 5 escape shaft and 6 ascending corridor.

The picture above shows one ancient Wonder of the World still standing. It is an artist's impression with the facing blocks intact (which now they are not), so the picture indicates what they may have looked like when first built. They are from left to right: the Pyramid of Mycerinus with three mini step pyramids in front; the Pyramids of Chephren; and the Pyramid of Cheops. The Pyramid of Cheops is, in fact, the largest but perspective makes it smaller.

ing. The most famous of them are the Pyramids at Giza, near Cairo, and the only one of the seven wonders of the world that still stands.

The largest of these, the Great Pyramid of Cheops is over 230 metres along each side and nearly 150 metres high, about the height of St. Paul's Cathedral, London. Apart from the entrance gallery and burial chambers it is a sold mass of masonry consisting of 2,300,000 accurately cut blocks of stone, each weighing about two and a half tonnes. The total weight is 6,840,000 tonnes.

When the building was completed, five thousand years ago, it was covered from top to bottom with casing-blocks of limestone. A few of these remain at the top. The rest were removed centuries ago for building materials.

After the mummified body of the pharaoh had been conveyed to the final burial chamber, the pyramid was sealed. Blocks had already been stored and scaffolding (4) built to support them in the Grand gallery. When the work was finished, the scaffolding was removed and the blocks (1, 2 & 3) slid down the descending corridor and sealed it. The workmen escaped by sliding down the escape shaft (5) and coming up the ascending corridor (6) to the exit. If robbers entered the tomb down (6), it was hoped that they would notice the blockage of the descending corridor but would continue on to incomplete burial chamber 1. If by any chance they managed to find the descending corridor, they could still be misled and enter incomplete burial chamber 2. Unfortunately, in spite of this, all the Pyramids were plundered.

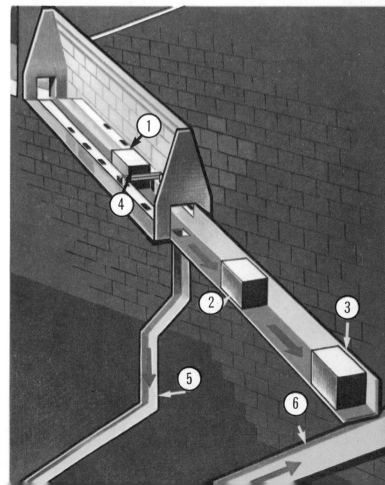

Despite its colossal size and grandeur, the Great Pyramid, and all the other pyramids of Egypt, were built by men who had no draught animals, and no mechanical equipment. Every block of stone had to be moved by muscle power. One hundred thousand slaves toiled for 20 years to build this tomb of the Pharaoh (Cheops) Khufu, about 2700 B.C.

Near the Great Pyramid stands another almost as large, the Pyramid of Chepten, and behind that, a third, the Pyramid of Mycenius.

Preservation

Each of these pyramids was a tomb of a Pharaoh —that and nothing more. For generations the effort and labour, skill, craftsmanship and wealth of a great kingdom had been directed to one end — the preservation of one body under millions of tonnes of masonry.

Why did the Egyptians do this? To answer this question we must grasp two essential facts. The first is the sacredness of the King, who was not only a ruler but a god. The Egyptians believed that the Pharaoh was the son of Re, the Sun-god, and it has been suggested that the pyramid-shape was copied from that made by the rays of the sun shining down through cloud.

The second fact is the Egyptians' belief that the royal *ka* — the spirit or soul of the Pharaoh — could not survive unless his body was preserved and protected from violation, unless it was accompanied by his furniture, clothing, ornaments and other objects which were suitable to his rank, and unless offerings of food were made regularly in a funeral temple adjoining the pyramid. Such a temple can still be seen near the Pyramid of Chephren, near the Sphinx, which is a 62-metre long representation of that king in the form of a human-headed lion.

The first Pharaoh to build a stone pyramid was Djoser (2800 B.C.) at Sakkara. It was the first large stone monument in the world.

Its construction shows us how the builders were feeling their way towards the best use of this new building material. For instance the stones are relatively small, almost like mud-bricks, and the buildings surroundings the pyramid are imitations in stone of the wooden doors, palm-log ceilings and mud-and-plaster walls of the palace in which the Pharaohs had lived. Yet only a hundred years later the Egyptians were building straight-sided pyramids, twice as high, and with accurately cut blocks each weighing two-and-a-half tonnes.

They had discovered how to cut these great blocks of stone, to drag them on rollers from the quarry many miles away, and then to haul them up ramps as the 'storeys' rose.

Djoser's burial chamber is at the bottom of a huge pit, nearly thirty metres beneath the pyramid; that of Cheops who built the Great Pyramid, is inside the structure itself.

Most of the pyramid tombs were robbed thousands of years ago, but occasionally achaeologists have found a few fragments which the robbers overlooked. At Dashur, Sir Flinders Petrie found the jewellery of a princess, Sit-Hathor-Unet, buried under her own miniature pyramid which stood beside that of her father, the Pharaoh Amenemhat III.

There were golden diadems, golden bracelets, and necklaces set with semi-precious stones, all of exquisite beauty and craftsmanship. Yet these represented only one tiny particle of the wealth which a Pharaoh's pyramid must once have contained.

Robbers

The Pharaohs knew all about tomb robbers and, dreading them, took elaborate precautions to foil their entry into the tomb-pyramids. Inside some pyramids there are false doors in the corridors which open on to a huge and frightening drop into space — a death trap calculated to put a swift end to any robber who got inside the pyramid.

When, after a four-month embalming process, the Pharaoh Cheops was laid to rest within his Great Pyramid, a rope attached to the last block of stone was pulled; the stone slid down a ramp, and the pyramid was sealed.

The architect, the builders and the Pharaoh hoped, of course, that this would be for all time, and that no one would ever find a way into the pyramid, let alone find the secret chamber inside which the King's body lay. All such hopes were proved futile.

No doubt because someone somewhere had the plans, or had kept notes of the construction, the Great Pyramid was soon pillaged. All the jewellery, gold, furniture and other effects were stolen, and when modern archaeologists found their way to the King's room, even the Pharaoh's body was missing.

The sarcophagus in which it lay was empty, and it is still in the death room today. Visitors can see it by crawling up a steep ramp into the very heart of the pyramid — a back-breaking journey that takes you back to the very beginning of civilisation.

About 1450 B.C. the Egyptians gave up building pyramids and hollowed out tombs in the Theban hills. Here, in the Valley of the Kings up the Nile, the tomb of Tutankhamen was discovered — the only Pharaoh still to be surrounded by most of his golden treasure. Fortunately the colossal size of the Great Pyramid defeated even the efforts of medieval looters to destroy its stones, and it stands today almost intact as the world's greatest monument to the work of early civilised man.

The Giza Pyramids are thought to have been constructed as shown in the diagram below. While a pyramid rose, four ramps, made of mud and rubble, were built alongside. The giant blocks were then dragged on sleds up three of these ramps. When the top was reached, this was capped and empty sleds were brought down the fourth ramp. Friction may have been reduced by pouring water or oil over the skids of the sleds. No draught animals appear to have been used at any time.

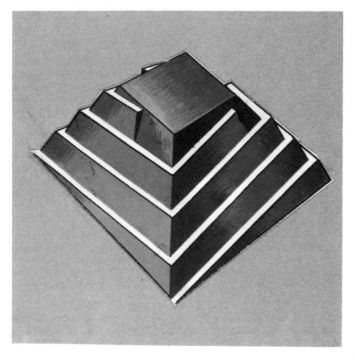

How Stonehenge was built

A remarkable achievement of prehistoric engineering, Stonehenge still puzzles modern archaeologists.

NO one can say for certain where the story of Britain begins. The name of the country is Celtic and comes from tribesmen who invaded our islands in the Iron Age. That was 2,500 years ago, but people lived in Britain far back beyond this.

So where to begin? As well as anywhere, it is a good idea to start with a landmark. And since at Stonehenge, on Salisbury Plain, Britain has the largest pre-historic monument in all Europe, let's start there.

Like so much of what happened in Britain before Julius Caesar and his Romans came over 2,000 years ago, Stonehenge is a mystery.

When modern scientists study Stonehenge to try to solve its riddle, they are not helped by the fact that its builders seemed to have no permanent plan. The ancient Britons just didn't seem to be able to make up their minds from the moment that they laid out the first circle about 1800 B.C. until about 200 years later, when they put in place their double circle of 80 or more huge boulders, called bluestones, each weighing up to four tonnes.

Then, it seems, there came still more second thoughts. A few centuries later the Britons took out the bluestones and put them aside for later erection, replacing them with eighty huge blocks of natural sandstone which they brought from Marlborough Downs, about 19 miles away. They then had a far larger monument, made of uprights weighing 25 tonnes each and capped by lintels weighing seven tonnes.

This entire structure is surrounded by a mysterious outer circle of holes called the Aubrey Holes. They were named after a seventeenth-century writer who had made all sorts of speculations about them.

These holes — there are 56 of them — are intriguing because they are just holes, or pits; they never held upright posts. Each hole is about a metre deep and a little more than a metre wide. Many of them contain the remains of burned human bones, but they were not meant to be graves.

The building of Stonehenge undoubtedly presented the early Britons with a daunting task. At least 550 men would have been needed, it has been calculated, to drag one of the huge 25-tonne sandstone blocks up the hill between Marlborough Downs and Stonehenge.

On the site, it would have taken 200 men to get the larger stones upright. Then there was the problem of raising the lintel stones — seven tonnes of solid rock. Quite apart from the muscle-power needed, all this building required organisation, team-work and discipline — attributes which suggest that the builders must have had considerable intelligence and will-power.

What was it all for? What made these ancient people toil so mightily to erect this monumental conundrum?

Well, people have been wondering about the purpose of Stonehenge for a very long time. In the twelfth century Geoffrey of Monmouth declared that the monument commemorated British warriors treacherously slain by Hengist and Horsa, leaders of the Anglo-Saxon invasion of Britain. This is a tale which, however, does not bear a second glance.

About that time, too, lots of people believed that the giant stones had been magicked over from Ireland and placed on Salisbury Plain by Merlin the wizard, a story whose probability ranks with that of Geoffrey of Monmouth's.

Gradually the idea grew up that it was a solar temple built by a people who worshipped the Sun. This belief stemmed from the fact that on Midsummer Day the rising sun shines almost straight down the central avenue of the structure — the slight angular deviation today leading scientists to calculate an approximate date of 1680 B.C. for its erection.

In our century a spectacular idea has been put forward by British-born Professor Gerald Hawkins, working from Boston University in America.

Taking the well-documented fact that the main axis of the structure is aligned to sunrise on Midsummer Day, Professor Hawkins pointed out that only two marker-stones would be needed to achieve that simple result.

Using a calculator, he reasoned that Stonehenge was in

The mortice and tenon joints of Stonehenge

Despite having only primitive tools, the early Britons made tenon joints and mortice holes to hold the uprights and lintels together.

Raising the sarsens

First, the foundation hole would have been dug with a sloping edge on one side to help guide the sarsen into position once it had been levered to the pit on rollers.

The sarsen would have been levered up slowly. Each time a few degrees of height was gained, the timber platform would be built up and used as a higher leverage point.

The lintels would have been dragged to the foot of the sarsens, probably on rollers and a sledge, then packed up with small timbers. As it was levered up, the packing was increased. To keep the structure steady, a large platform would have been needed to support it.

On the log platform, the lintel would have been raised until it was level with the top of the sarsens.

How the Stonehenge site developed over

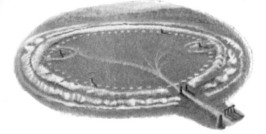

The site of Stonehenge was used about 3,000 B.C. for some unknown ritual meeting, but the structure was quite simple.

About 2,100 B.C. the structure was made more important by the introduction of the bluestones.

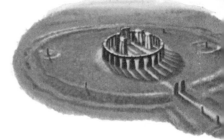

The sarsen stones replaced the blue stones about 2,000 B.C. but their position ing was somewhat different.

fact one of the world's earliest computers, a late Stone Age-early Bronze Age device for predicting, by the way in which the stones are aligned, positions of the Sun and Moon and eclipses up to 300 years ahead.

Stonehenge was thus used as a calendar and in a pre-writing era this was useful for telling when to plant crops. It was also used in a religious connection by the priests, whose powers were greatly enhanced when they were able to predict with spell-binding accuracy spectacular risings and settings of the Sun and Moon.

Modern scientists know for sure that the actual cycle of the Moon in relation to Earth, from beginning to end, is a total of 18.61 years. Every 19 years the eclipse of the Moon takes place not only in the same season but on the same date.

The first recorded instance of these calculations occurs

more than a thousand years after Stonehenge was built. Yet the positioning of the Aubrey Holes and the great stones of Stonehenge, say some scientists, makes them an efficient protractor of the movement of the Sun and the Moon — more accurate than we had before modern science devised the system we now use.

In fact the whole arrangement made Stonehenge a reliable calendar based on the lunar month of 28 days.

If all this is true, if this really was the purpose of Stonehenge, our ancestors must have been excellent at maths, engineering and geometry, in order to have been able to pick this site and plan it as a basic computer.

It would put their civilisation among the most advanced of its time in the world — a far cry from the popular picture of men dressed in skins, grunting and beating each other over the head with clubs.

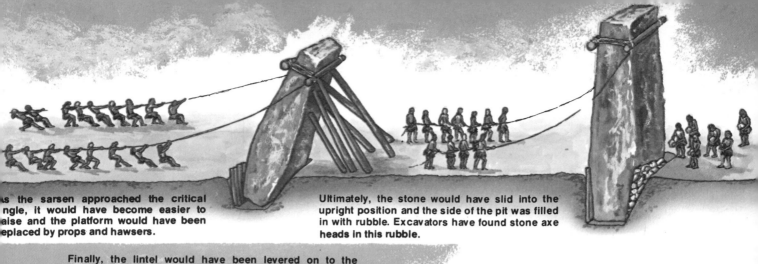

As the sarsen approached the critical angle, it would have become easier to raise and the platform would have been replaced by props and hawsers.

Ultimately, the stone would have slid into the upright position and the side of the pit was filled in with rubble. Excavators have found stone axe heads in this rubble.

Finally, the lintel would have been levered on to the tenons. The timber platform would have then been dismantled for use elsewhere.

Facts about Stonehenge

The main circle of sarsen stones (also known as megaliths) is about 30m. (100ft.) in diameter.

The uprights of this circle average about 4.11m. (13½ft.) above the ground and weigh about 25 tonnes each.

The lintels (the crosspieces set on top of the uprights) weigh about 7 tonnes each.

The sarsen stone uprights forming the inner horseshoe are about 6.70m. (22ft.) above the ground and weigh about 45 tonnes each.

The sarsen stones — 'sarsen' being sandstone — came from the Marlborough Downs in Wiltshire, a distance of about 30km. (19 miles) from Stonehenge.

The bluestones, so called because of their faintly bluish colour, originally formed a circle of 60 stones and a horseshoe shape of 19 stones. These came from the Preseli Mountains in S.W. Wales, about 208km. (130 miles) away by land, but 385km. (240 miles) away by land and sea, the route most probably taken to transport them.

eriod of fifteen hundred years

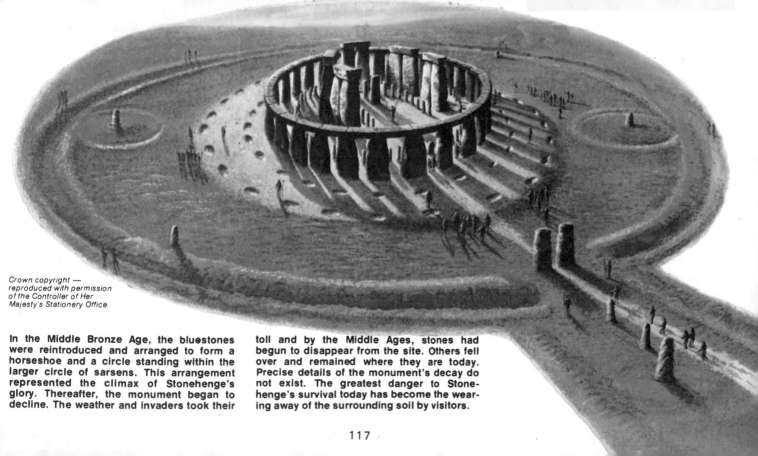

Crown copyright — reproduced with permission of the Controller of Her Majesty's Stationery Office.

In the Middle Bronze Age, the bluestones were reintroduced and arranged to form a horseshoe and a circle standing within the larger circle of sarsens. This arrangement represented the climax of Stonehenge's glory. Thereafter, the monument began to decline. The weather and invaders took their toll and by the Middle Ages, stones had begun to disappear from the site. Others fell over and remained where they are today. Precise details of the monument's decay do not exist. The greatest danger to Stonehenge's survival today has become the wearing away of the surrounding soil by visitors.

T wasn't the first time that an army had gathered on the coast of Northern France to invade the islands on the other side of the Channel, and it wouldn't be the last. But the soldiers who filed into the 80 invasion ships were unusually apprehensive. Very little was known about the place where they were going — indeed, for the common soldiers, it was beyond the rim of the world.

One bright thought, however, comforted the 10,000 Roman legionaries. That was that their beloved commander, Gaius Julius Caesar, the greatest general in the world was coming to Britain with them.

A Roman army cohort consisting of six centuries. Nine cohorts made up a legion, although one of these cohorts was of double strength. On his first expedition to Britain Julius Caesar brought two legions of infantry, or rather more than twenty times the number of men shown here.

From left to right: a legion commander, a tribune, a centurion and an aquilifer. The commander was like a modern general, and the tribune either commanded a cohort or acted as an aide-de-camp. The centurion commanded a century (80-120 men) and the aquilifer was the non-commissioned officer who carried the Eagle standard.

The Britons were far from a collection o savages. They knew they would have problem defending themselves against the most sophisticat ed army in the world. Those Gauls fleeing t Britain from the Roman terror had told th Britons all about Caesar and his army.

They probably knew that the invading force wa formed by two legions — the Tenth and th Seventh. Each Roman legion was formed of nin cohorts. One special cohort was 1,000 strong, th others were each about 500-600 strong.

A cohort was made up of three maniples or si centuries — each about 80 to 120 strong. Th century was the backbone of the Roman army. I was commanded by a centurion, whose duties an status varied from legion to legion, so he could b the equivalent in rank in the modern British arm to anything between a sergeant-major and lieutenant-colonel.

The centurion was junior enough to lead h men into battle and important enough to sway th result. He was generally a professional soldier. H

repares to invade

Their job, Caesar, had told them, was to teach the British natives a lesson. The Britons had been sheltering men of Gaul (France) who were wanted by the Romans. They had to be taught that Rome ruled the world. But Rome, at least in this year 55B.C., wasn't interested in ruling Britain.

GALEA
Helmet

BALTEUS
Belt

LORICA
Cuirass

GLADIUS
Sword

SCUTUM
Shield

BRACAE
Breeches

PILUM
Lance

CALIGA
Marching boot

Caligatus — the "Tommy" or private soldier of the Roman army — derived his nickname from his marching boots.

en carried a vine branch, his baton of office.

n the ranks the non-commissioned soldiers re closer in organisation to a modern army. We d private soldiers "Tommy Atkins" and the mans had a nickname for their lowesr rankers ligati, "the booted ones". The Emperor Caligu- was so called because as a small boy he liked to lk around in army boots.

The Immunes (immune from rough duties) were e corporals, and Tesserarius and Optio were like geants. A Signifer was a standard-bearer — iilar in rank and duties to the old British army sign. An Aquilifer carried the legion emblem, or gle. He is not to be confused with the standard- arers — one for each maniple and one for each hort. These standards were the rallying points the battlefield.

A Caligateus fought with a long spear, the um, and after he had thrown it, with a short ord, the gladius. He carried a cylindrical shield d his uniform was a metal helmet and a tunic surmounted by a cuirass, usually of leather, and later of metal, strips.

There was one fact that distinguished the Roman army from all others — one that gave them a considerable advantage over their enemies. They were nearly all professional soldiers; the army was their career. Many of them were Roman citizens — a status that was important in the ancient world.

Those who were not, the "auxiliaries" or foreigners, knew that they were likely to be rewarded with Roman citizenship after 25 years on active service — so they had something worth fighting for.

The Roman Army also used cavalry — Caesar brought them to Britain in 18 special ships, in addition to the 80 invasion craft that brought the *Caligati.*

The infantry ships sailed from Boulogne about midnight on the 24th August, 55B.C., but a harsh wind, blowing up the Channel, scattered the cavalry ships. Caesar himself arrived off Deal in Kent, where the Britons, amply informed by their Gaulish spies, had gathered in force on the cliffs, to prevent any landing. It was then about 9 a.m.

What was known about the British Isles was that they were cold and cheerless, and covered with swamps and dark forests. There were no British people as such — the natives lived in tribes constantly at war with each other. Their crops were quick to grow and slow to ripen, because the climate was always damp.

It was the climate as much as anything that made the sunny Roman soldiers shudder. They hated the rains of northern Europe after the blue skies of Italy.

ARTILLERY PIECES OF THE FINEST ARMY IN THE ANCIENT WORLD

Before the introduction of gunpowder, missiles were hurled at the enemy by various forms of catapult. The Romans were fine engineers and devised some very effective machines to do this.

They were all made mainly of wood and army engineers would chop down local trees and construct the catapults on the spot, thus avoiding having to carry heavy equipment everywhere.

Right: A catapult, or ballista, which hurled javelins. The power was provided by a large metal bow. The "string" was made of twisted ox sinews or human hair, kept taut by the two ratchets on the front. The weapon was a light field piece which had the advantage of greater range than a thrown javelin.

Left: The trebuchet was a siege weapon. It was first pushed against the wall of a fortification. Then the arm was wound back and released so that the heavy weight in the sling smashed against the enemy's stonework. The same principle of using a heavy weight to knock down walls is still used today by demolition workers.

Right: A catapult, another siege weapon, powered by a large wooden bow. It could be wheeled to the front line. The released sling projected the missile, a large and heavy stone, with great force on to the enemy. This early artillery piece was the forerunner of the medieval cannon.

The Romans invade

The Aquilifer of the 10th Legion wears the traditional leopard skin head dress. The letters S.P.Q.R. below the eagle stand for *Senatus Populusque Romanus* — Roman Senate and People.

Roman warships were modelled on the galleys of ancient Greece and Phoenicia (now part of Lebanon and Syria). Galleys were powered by sails and oars. the 'castle' construction on board a Roman galley is shown on Roman paintings and pottery but its origin is a mystery. Below, we show part of a Roman galley, from a painting found at the site of Praeneste, an ancient city east of Rome.

Galleys with three banks of oars were called triremes. This one has the top row of oars pulled in.

Roman war galleys could be up to 45 metres long with an overall width of 5.5 metres.

There are no records showing how the rowers were seated but this arrangement was suggested, after much research by the naval historian, Björn Landström.

The Aquilifer bearing the eagle emblem (above) is wearing a 'lorica squamata' — a type of waistcoat made of small plates of armour stitched to each other and on to an undershirt.

JULIUS CAESAR, the first foreign general ever to record British fighting methods, considered carefully the battle he had just witnessed and then set about writing up his notes.

"Their method of fighting with their chariots," he wrote, "is this. First, they drive about in all directions and throw their weapons and generally break the ranks of the enemy with the very dread of their horses and the noise of their wheels.

"When they have worked themselves in between the troops of horse, they leap from their chariots and engage on foot. The charioteers, in the meantime, withdraw some little distance from the battle and so place themselves with the chariots that if their masters are overpowered by the number of the enemy they may have a ready retreat to their own troops."

No better witness could have commented upon the British warriors. For when Caesar, the greatest general in the world, came with his Roman army to the Kent coast in 55 B.C., the Battle of Deal, which he had to win in order to establish a landing in Britain, was unquestionably one of the most difficult fights he ever had.

"There was great difficulty," he says, "because the ships on account of their size could only be kept in deep water. The soldiers, oppressed with the weight of their arms, ignorant of the ground and with their hands encumbered, were obliged to leap from the ships and to engage the enemy while standing in the water."

When finally the Romans gained their foothold, they put the Britons to flight. But Caesar's first victory in Britain was to be short-lived. A fearful storm blew up, scattering the Roman ships that were bringing their cavalry, and wrecking their infantry invasion ships.

The British were quick to recognise the invaders' plight. They reaped all the corn in every district around the Roman camp except in one place, and when the men of the Roman Seventh Legion went there to get the corn, a powerful British ambush was sprung, killing many of them and putting the rest to flight.

Caesar managed to hold off the raiding Britons while his ships were repaired. He wasted no more time in Britain and as soon as there was a spell of good sailing weather he and his men were gone.

The Roman Senate, believing that their ruler had gained an important victory, decreed a thanksgiving of twenty days in his honour. But some Senators called the

121

expedition to Britain a failure and a disgrace, and charged Caesar with ''turning his back upon the victorious Britons.''

Notwithstanding that, Caesar led his Romans back to Britain the following year for a second invasion. This time he brought between 25,000 and 30,000 infantry and 2,000 cavalry — more than twice as many men as the year before. Clearly he had acquired some respect for his British enemies.

Caesar in his own account tells us that this time he was unopposed. Great bands of Britons had assembled to meet the invaders but, fearful of their numbers, withdrew to higher ground.

The Romans advanced immediately towards Canterbury. At Barham Downs there was a battle in which the Britons were finally driven into the woods.

Then, as in the year before, the Roman advance was checked by the awful British weather. News was brought to Caesar that another storm had wrecked his invasion ships on the coast, and wearily he went back to supervise the repairs.

Continued on next page

Roman soldiers were trained to use their shields as weapons to buffet opponents and throw them off balance so that the short sword or 'gladius' could be jabbed under their opponents' shields.

This legionary is wearing a 'lorica segmentata' (segmented shirt) the type of armour in use by Claudius's troops

THE CELTS OF BRITAIN

THE ancient Britons were an industrious people. A couple of thousand years before Christ, their islands were inhabited by a short, dark race called the Iberians — the same race that was found in Spain.

Later, there were other invasions by Celtic peoples, who drove the Iberians into Wales and Cornwall.

The descendants of these Celts cultivated wheat and oats and ground their grain into flour for bread and cakes. Pytheas, a Greek traveller who visited Britain in the time of Alexander the Great — that is, in the 4th century B.C. — tells us that he saw fine fields of grain in Kent.

The people, highly skilled in metal-work, made shields, helmets, brooches, rings and bracelets. They wove cloth on looms and built their ships with high prows and sterns. Metal nails were used to fasten the planks together.

They were a religious people and their priests, the Druids, formed a special class. They taught that their gods lived in the darkest parts of the forests and they used to go to pray to these gods under the oak trees.

The Druids were also teachers of history and poetry and were the doctors of the day, making medicines from herbs collected in the woods. The medicine was greatly mixed up with magic. Mistletoe, which was always cut down with a golden knife, was regarded as particularly sacred. The Druids were the judges and the magistrates of the ancient Britons.

There were no British people as such — the natives lived in tribes which were constantly at war with each other.

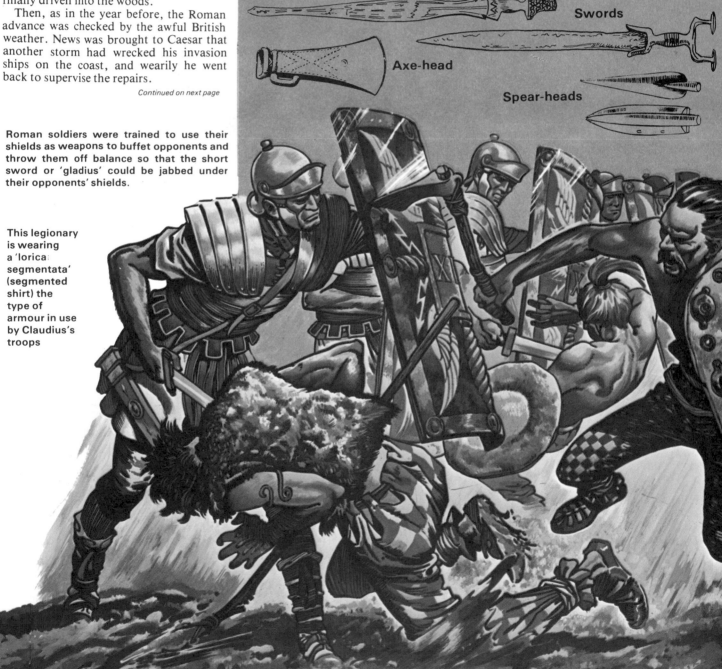

Celtic weapons

Swords

Axe-head

Spear-heads

Meanwhile, the Britons made one of their chieftains, Caswallon (called Cassivellaunus by Caesar) their commander-in-chief. The new commander reorganised his troops and when Caesar again began to advance inland his progress was resisted at every stage.

However, there were a few British chiefs who saw an opportunity to increase their own power if they aided the Romans. These chiefs joined Caesar's army.

Because of these defections, the southern Britons sued for peace. After fixing terms, Caesar returned to the coast and set sail for Gaul (France) in 54 B.C.

Caesar never returned to Britain after that. Indeed, the Britons did not see the Romans again for nearly a century. But when at last the invaders did come back it was to stay — and to change the character of the country in ways which have left their mark on our lives to this day.

THE ROMAN ARMY ON THE MARCH

No matter how far the Roman legions travelled, their infantrymen had to get there on foot (except, of course, when crossing seas). Many of the countries which they passed through had not had the benefit of well-made Roman roads and, to make things worse, the soldiers had to carry a load of heavy equipment. A march of more than twenty miles in five hours was quite common and at the end of it they had to be ready, perhaps, to fight a battle against fresh opponents.

A Roman legionary (shown left) also carried his possessions with him, parcelled up in bags and hitched on to a forked stick which was carried on his shoulder. As well as his weapons and armour, he had his entrenching tool (a sort of spade for digging defences), a cloak (rolled up in warm weather), a water bottle or jar, his cooking utensils and his food rations.

Most soldiers were tradesmen or specialists of some kind and carried the tools of their trade. In theory, tools and personal possessions could be put in the baggage wagons which followed the army columns but these wagons moved slowly and frequently lost contact with the men. Sometimes they were lost or ambushed, so soldiers were reluctant to put anything which they considered important in the wagons.

The Roman soldiers did have one privilege, however. In occupied countries they were entitled to call upon any fit men and order them to carry their loads for one mile. Needless to say, this was a very unpopular practice with the native inhabitants of those countries.

Below is a Roman helmet made of iron in the 1st Century A.D., a water bottle made of New Forest pottery, a bronze razor (now in the British Museum) and a Roman sword, unearthed in London.

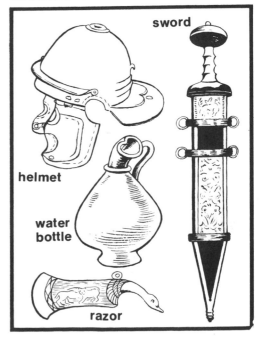

sword

helmet

water bottle

razor

Boudicca sets London ablaze

WHEN the Romans ruled Britain, the King of the Iceni, a tribe occupying the area which now forms the counties of Norfolk and Suffolk, was a rich man. Believing that if he made the Roman emperor joint heir to his property with his wife and daughters (a custom of those times) he would preserve a share of his property for his relatives, he made a will to this effect.

But as soon as the King died, the Roman officials seized the whole of his property. When his widow Boudicca (or Boadicea) protested, they flogged her cruelly and brutally ill-treated her daughters.

Infuriated with shame and indignation, Boudicca urged her Iceni tribesmen to rise against their oppressors, especially as the Roman governor, Suetonius Paulinus, was far away in Anglesey with the bulk of his army.

The Britons rose, but they laid their plans with cunning. They persuaded another powerful tribe, the Trinobantes, who occupied what are now Essex and Middlesex, to join them. While they were gathering their forces they lulled the Roman colony at Colchester into a false sense of security. Then they suddenly swept down and destroyed the city.

The Roman garrison shut itself up in the temple of Claudius but the Britons took the temple after two days' bitter fighting and slaughtered the garrison. Then with her great rabble army, Queen Boudicca set off for London.

Meanwhile Suetonius hurried back from Anglesey, collecting troops as he marched. Arriving in London, he reeled back in astonishment at the sight of the 200,000-strong British army, complete with chariots and horsemen.

"London will have to be left to its fate," Suetonius said simply.

It was a fate never equalled since, not even during the Second World War bombing. The city, overrun by a furious mob, was burned to the ground. Almost all its inhabitants, men, women and children, died.

Tacitus, the great Roman historian, tells us that 70,000 Romans were massacred in the rising of that year, A.D. 60, none at all being spared, not even to be sold as slaves.

St. Albans, too, shared the same fate, but by this time Suetonius had collected enough troops to strike back.

He chose his ground well. The British method of fighting was to make a frontal attack while vast numbers outflanked the foe on both sides. With only 10,000 men, Suetonius held a position in a narrow valley where it was

When the Romans invaded Britain, the South was quickly subdued but the tribes of the North and West refused to submit to Roman rule. Indeed, the Picts and Scots were never completely conquered by the Romans. In Wales, there were frequent rebellions. The tombstone shown above, from the legionary fortress of Glevum (Gloucester) depicts a first-century cavalryman called Rufus Sita running down a Western Briton.

The Roman silver coin (below) shows a Celtic chieftain with shaved cheeks, drooping moustache and stiffened hair in readiness for battle. Prisoners (left) were taken as hostages or sold as slaves.

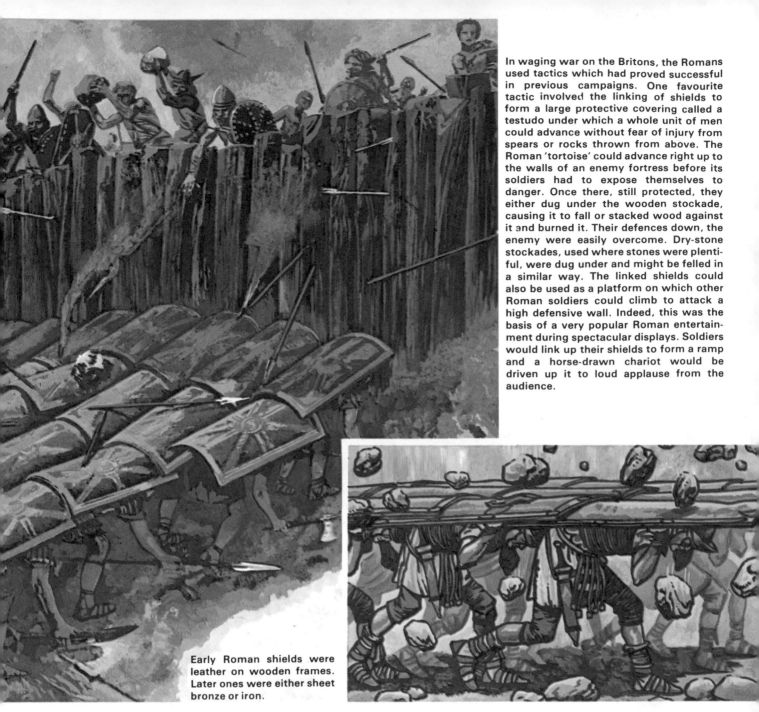

In waging war on the Britons, the Romans used tactics which had proved successful in previous campaigns. One favourite tactic involved the linking of shields to form a large protective covering called a testudo under which a whole unit of men could advance without fear of injury from spears or rocks thrown from above. The Roman 'tortoise' could advance right up to the walls of an enemy fortress before its soldiers had to expose themselves to danger. Once there, still protected, they either dug under the wooden stockade, causing it to fall or stacked wood against it and burned it. Their defences down, the enemy were easily overcome. Dry-stone stockades, used where stones were plentiful, were dug under and might be felled in a similar way. The linked shields could also be used as a platform on which other Roman soldiers could climb to attack a high defensive wall. Indeed, this was the basis of a very popular Roman entertainment during spectacular displays. Soldiers would link up their shields to form a ramp and a horse-drawn chariot would be driven up it to loud applause from the audience.

Early Roman shields were leather on wooden frames. Later ones were either sheet bronze or iron.

impossible for the Britons to employ their usual outflanking tactics.

The Britons were brave. Boudicca, who was accompanied in her chariot by her daughters, drove up and down the lines of her army, shrieking out the story of their brutal treatment at the hands of their oppressors and urging the warriors to avenge the insults which she and the princesses had received.

In the result, Roman discipline again told. The Britons were overwhelmingly defeated and according to the historian, 80,000 of them were killed, while the Romans lost only 400. Probably these figures are exaggerated, but the slaughter was undoubtedly very great.

Boudicca had determined that she would never fall into the hands of the enemy and, finding all was lost, she poisoned herself.

The name Boudicca is connected with the Welsh word "budd", meaning "victory", and so it is curious to think that this early queen really had the same name as a much later British queen, Victoria.

The battle after which Boudicca took her life was the end of the British revolt, and from that moment of tragedy and grief for the British tribes, the Roman power was definitely established in Britain. But the Romans learned from the revolt that it was wiser for them to treat their brave British subjects with reasonable justice.

Agricola, the governor who followed Suetonius, at once realised this. He was the first really good governor that the islands had. He lessened as far as possible the tribute levied on the vanquished Britons, encouraged trade and spread education and a taste for art among the people. He gained the good opinion of the Britons by his bravery and his strict justice and under him the Roman province of Britannia flourished.

Agricola also extended the Roman power as far north as the Grampian Mountains in Scotland. In order to protect his conquests he built a line of forts from the Forth to the Clyde and then circumnavigated Great Britain to prove that it was an island.

The tribes in the north of Scotland, however, were not subdued and later, when the Emperor Hadrian came to Britain, he abandoned Agricola's line of forts and built a double rampart — Hadrian's Wall — between the Tyne and the Solway Firth.

Later Agricola's old forts from the Forth to the Clyde were connected by Antonine's Wall, which was named after another emperor.

Still the northern tribes were troublesome, and in A.D. 208 the Emperor Severus found it necessary to strengthen Agricola's lines and Hadrian's Wall.

Solway Firth

Bowness

Advanced fort
beyond the line
of the Wall

Birdoswald fort
(Camboglanna)

River Irthing

Willowford
Bridge

Military road

The Vallum

The fortified Willowford Bridge

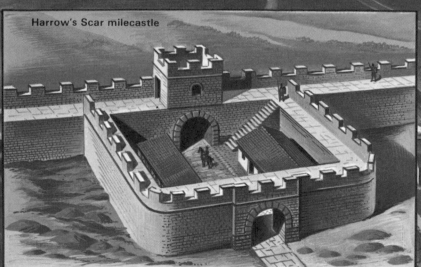

Harrow's Scar milecastle

DAN ESCOTT

SITUATED on the cold, bleak northernmost frontier of the Roman Empire, Hadrian's Wall was a grim posting for Roman soldiers used to the sunshine of Italy. Built by legionary craftsmen and masons, the Wall was at first manned by 15,000 soldiers recruited from all parts of the Roman Empire. Before long, however, recruits to man the Wall were found locally. These native Northumbrians were just as keen as the Romans to protect their land from the raiding tribesmen of the North. The Wall itself stood about 4.6 metres high with a parapet of 1.8 metres on top. Large portions of it still stand, a tribute to the skill of the Roman builders.

The large forts incorporated in the Wall housed 500 to 1,000 men. The most exciting of them for the modern visitor is the fort of Housesteads (shown below). Its Roman name can only be guessed at but it may have been Vercovicium. The ramparts and gateways of Housesteads are well preserved. The granaries, headquarters, latrines, barracks and some civilian settlement buildings outside the fort have been excavated to show what they looked like. The garrison of 1,000 men was housed in 12 long barracks, each divided into 12 rooms. There were 8 to 10 men to a room. Centurions and non-commissioned officers lived in larger rooms at the ends of the blocks.

The smaller Wall forts, or milecastles, vary in design, probably because they were built by different legions. Below (bottom left hand corner) is an example of a milecastle, housing 25 to 50 men.

Along its course, the Wall had to cross many obstacles such as the River Irthing, spanned by the fortified Willowford Bridge (below, left). Because of its enormous length, look-outs had to be posted at frequent intervals along the Wall, between the forts. The look-out turrets were small constructions with an upper floor reached by means of a ladder.

Where to find the remains of Hadrian's Wall today.

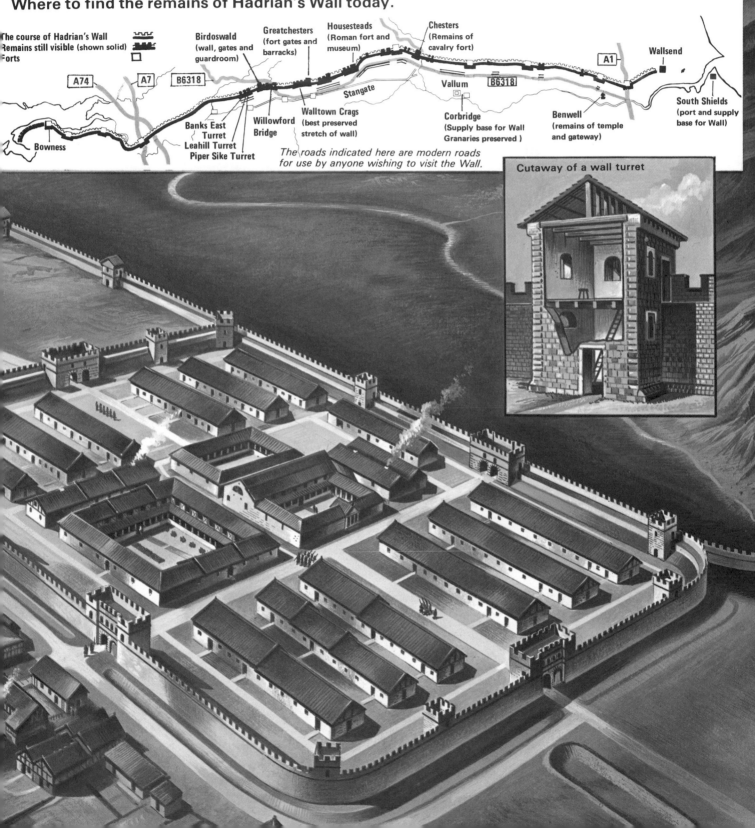

The course of Hadrian's Wall
Remains still visible (shown solid)
Forts

A74   A7   B6318

Bowness

Banks East Turret
Leahill Turret
Piper Sike Turret

Birdoswald (wall, gates and guardroom)

Willowford Bridge

Greatchesters (fort gates and barracks)

Walltown Crags (best preserved stretch of wall)

Housesteads (Roman fort and museum)

Stangate

Chesters (Remains of cavalry fort)

Vallum

Corbridge (Supply base for Wall Granaries preserved)

B6318

Benwell (remains of temple and gateway)

A1   Wallsend

South Shields (port and supply base for Wall)

The roads indicated here are modern roads for use by anyone wishing to visit the Wall.

Cutaway of a wall turret

Britain finds a hero-and a traitor

IN the early days of their control of Britain the Romans behaved like tyrants. It was only after Agricola became Governor of Britain in the year A.D. 78 that the conquered people received justice.

After the departure of Julius Caesar in 54 B.C. the islands of Britain were left alone for nearly a century. Then in A.D. 43, the Romans determined not merely to invade but to conquer the islands. Aulus Plautius, a famous Roman general, was sent to carry out this task.

Plautius succeeded only partially. He advanced as far as the Humber in the north and the Severn in the west, and then his conquests were carried farther by his successor, Ostorius Scapula.

In the west Ostorius came up against a formidable foe - the legendary Caractacus, a British nobleman described by a Roman writer as having "superior cunning". Caractacus held up the Roman war machine only temporarily but his courage and determination make him the first great hero of our islands' story.

For years, Caractacus had been craftily pulling back his British warriors into Wales, avoiding battle with the stronger foe, and settling for guerilla tactics. He wanted to fight the big battle in a place of his own choosing. When he found it he was reported to have told his men that "this was the day, this the battle, which would either win back their freedom or enslave them for ever".

But face-to-face with the Romans, the Britons had more than they bargained for. Their bravery and enthusiasm not equal to the Romans' discipline and experience and they were outfought. When the Romans lined up their prisoners, however, Caractacus was not among them. He had escaped and was heading north to hoped-for sanctuary with the Brigantia tribe.

If Caractacus was Britain's first hero, Queen Cartimandua of the Brigantes emerges as the country's first traitor. She was in league with the Romans and promptly handed over Caractacus to the invaders. The British hero was taken to Rome as a chained captive by Ostorius to celebrate his triumph.

However, on being told of the brave exploits of Caractacus, the Emperor Claudius reprieved him and his family, granting them their lives instead of comdemning them to death - the usual sentence for adversaries of Rome.

The next Roman general sent to Britain as governor was Suetonius Paulinus, a determined and ruthless man. Suetonius was particularly concerned about the powerful sway of the Druids over the Britons. These Druids were the priests and instructors of the people, and they taught not only religion but astronomy and other sciences. They were also the doctors of the day, using herbs as medicine.

Julius Caesar tells us that they were cruel even by ancient standards. He wrote that they made huge wicker-work images and after filling them with living men, set them on fire as human sacrifices to the gods. Usually they burned people guilty of some crime, but if there were not enough they added innocent people.

As the Roman war machine marched across England the Druids had retired to the island of Mona, now called Anglesey. Resolved to crush them, Suetonius marched to the shore opposite the island and built a fleet of flat-bottomed ships on which he conveyed his infantry across the sea. The cavalry followed, partly by fording and partly by swimming beside their horses in deep water.

The Druids and their British supporters stood on the shore, a wild-looking rabble. Women dressed in black and worked up to a frenzy rushed among the armed warriors with their hair flying in the breeze and, waving firebrands, urged them to fight fiercely.

The Druid priests lifted up their hands to heaven and poured dreadful curses upon the Romans.

But Suetonius urged his men forward, told them not to quail before a troop of frenzied women, and quickly inflicted a crushing defeat on the Britons. There was a cruel scene of slaughter, and the sacred tree groves of the Druids were all destroyed and burned.

How Hadrian built his wall

P. Aelius Hadrianus - the Emperor Hadrian as he is better known - was a great traveller. He believed the best way to rule his Roman Empire was to go out and get first hand knowledge of it, and he travelled the length and breadth of the known world doing just that.

In the year A.D. 122 Hadrian arrived in the Roman province of Britannia and was soon given some grave news. One of Rome's finest legions, the Ninth, a crack corps of veterans stationed in the north of Britain for many years, had simply vanished.

Although today no one really knows what happened to the Ninth Legion, we do know that at about the time Hadrian became Emperor there was an uprising in Britain which coincided with a grave disaster to the Roman army. Almost certainly we can say that a great raid by the British tribesmen wiped out the elite Ninth.

Arriving in the north, Hadrian got the full story from his officers - how tribes like the Picts swarmed down from what is now Scotland and retreated with their plunder before the legionaries could get into position. It was then that Hadrian decided to build his wall.

The wall, with its forts, milecastles, turrets, outer and inner "stations", and communicating roadways was to be more than 112 kms long, stretching from the River Tyne in the east to the Solway Firth in the west. With many modifications during building, it took eight years to construct - just under 16 kilometres a year. It had a deep ditch on the northern side, and, on the south side, a second wall made of earth, called the *vallum*.

When the wall was finished, milecastles housing the troops who patrolled it were built at regular intervals of one Roman mile (1,620 metres) apart. Between the milecastles, 540 metres apart, were two big turrets, used for giving smoke signals. A minimum of 1,300 troops were needed to man the parapeted walks along the wall, although probably far more were often stationed there.

A pirate becomes Emperor of Britain

THE first man to declare himself the sole ruler of Britain was probably born in the land which is now Belgium. His name was Carausius; he was born in obscurity and carved out a name for himself in the Roman occupation of Europe that still lives today.

Besides the Scottish tribesmen raiding Roman Britain over its northern boundary, the country was increasingly under attack from Saxon pirates, who came from North Germany to raid its coasts.

To counteract this threat, the Romans built a chain of forts all the way from the Wash to the Solent and put them in the charge of an official they called 'The Count of Saxon Shore'. He was, in fact, an admiral, and had charge of a fleet which used to watch out for raiders and, if possible, drive them back before they could land.

Carausius was the first Count of the Saxon Shore. He began his working life as a sea pilot, but he was soon in action and getting himself commended for valour, fighting with the Roman legionaries against hostile tribesmen rebelling against their Roman masters.

Stealing the spoils

But when he was given his lordly title and the task of fighting off the Saxons, another side of Carausius's character was revealed. It seems he would let the pirates get past his fleet, allow them to plunder the coasts of Holland, Gaul and Britain, and then, when they were returning loaded with plunder he would steal the spoils and keep them for his own use rather than return them to their rightful owners.

Two Roman Emperors, Diocletian and Maximian, ruled jointly at that time and, realising what Carausius was doing, Maximian decided that the 'Count' must die. Carausius, however, was too quick. Hearing what was afoot, he took off, taking the Roman fleet with him, and sailed for Britain.

Smouldering with resentment, Maximian collected a new fleet. It took him some time, and while he was bringing the ships together, Carausius

was ruling the waves. He bought his men's loyalty with rich booty plundered from the European coastline and sailed triumphantly from the Mediterranean to the Channel like some early Blackbeard.

Carausius was big and bold. The Roman troops in Britain were quickly won over to him. Who, indeed, was there to oppose him? "I am henceforth the Emperor of

Defending the coasts against the invaders.

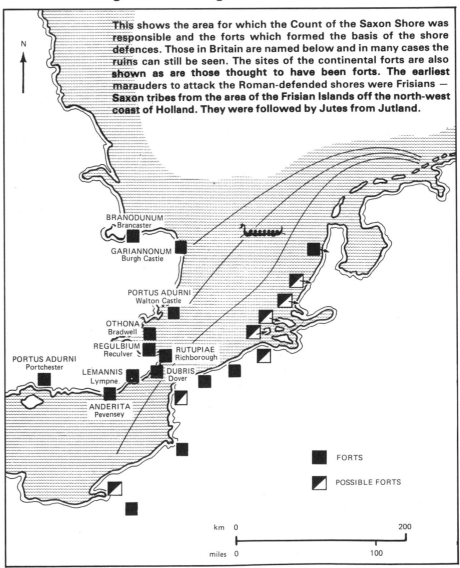

This shows the area for which the Count of the Saxon Shore was responsible and the forts which formed the basis of the shore defences. Those in Britain are named below and in many cases the ruins can still be seen. The sites of the continental forts are also shown as are those thought to have been forts. The earliest marauders to attack the Roman-defended shores were Frisians — Saxon tribes from the area of the Frisian Islands off the north-west coast of Holland. They were followed by Jutes from Jutland.

BRANODUNUM Brancaster
GARIANNONUM Burgh Castle
PORTUS ADURNI Walton Castle
OTHONA Bradwell
REGULBIUM Reculver
RUTUPIAE Richborough
PORTUS ADURNI Portchester
LEMANNIS Lympne
DUBRIS Dover
ANDERITA Pevensey

FORTS
POSSIBLE FORTS

km 0 — 200
miles 0 — 100

For over 100 years, the people of Britain and the Northern coasts of France and Belgium depended on the Count of the Saxon Shore for their defence. Vegetius, a Roman chronicler, writing about A.D.365, described the sea patrols in the North Sea. He recorded that they used light craft, their hulls and rigging painted green, crewed by 20 rowers in green uniforms. The patrol's task was to seek out and report the movements of Saxon raiders who, at that time, still rowed across the North Sea, as they had not developed sailing vessels.

Britain," he declared, and even the Roman Emperors were obliged to accept that declaration.

And so, says a writer, "Under his command, Britain, destined in a future age to obtain the empire of the sea, already assumed its natural and respectable station of a maritime power."

Unable to crush the usurper, Diocletian and Maximian decided to acknowledge him as their colleague and a medal was struck in his honour. This was typical Roman treachery, for the two Roman Emperors were only waiting for the right moment to strike at their 'colleague'.

Carausius, who had styled himself Emperor of Britain in the year A.D.287, made a man named Allectus his chief minister, and for a time all went well. This was perhaps because the two Roman Emperors had other problems on their hands; their Empire was in a bad way and was being assailed on all sides by barbarian hordes.

But in the year A.D.292 two additional Roman Emperors were proclaimed and one of these, Constantius, was made responsible for Britain, Gaul and Spain.

Constantius was determined that his title would be no empty one and that he actually would rule over his territory. While he was gathering a fleet and an army to sail to Britain and deal with the 'Emperor' there, he heard that Carausius had been murdered by his minister, Allectus, who had proclaimed himself Emperor.

Allectus 'reigned' for three years, for it was three years before Constantius was ready to sail for Britain. In A.D.296 Allectus was defeated and Britain was once more brought under the control of the Roman Emperors.

When Constantius arrived in Britain he was accompanied by his son, Constantine, who later became the first Christian Emperor of Rome. Constantine's mother was named Helena, and it is generally agreed that she was a British woman, although we know nothing about her parents.

Helena herself was, early in her life, converted to Christianity and went to Palestine where, according to an old story, she discovered the Holy Sepulchre and the true cross on which Jesus was crucified. She has now been honoured as a saint.

Remains to be seen

SAXON SHORE FORTS
The remains of six of the British coastal forts on page 169 can still been seen today. They are at: Burgh Castle, Suffolk; Pevensey Castle, Sussex; Portchester Castle, Hampshire; Richborough, Kent; Stutfall Castle, Lympne, Kent; Reculver, Kent.

ROMAN VILLAS AND BATHS
Anyone interested in Roman baths should visit the city of Bath in Avon where the most important Roman architectural remains in Britain are to be found. For those intested in Roman villas, the following are well worth visiting: Bignor, Sussex, (mosaics); Brading, Isle of Wight (mosaics); Chedworth, Gloucestershire (best-preserved Roman villa in Britain); Dicket Mead, Hertfordshire (bath-house); Fishbourne, Sussex (largest Roman residence known in Britain); King's Weston, Avon (hypocaust or heating system, mosaics and bath suite); Lullingstone, Kent (chapel, bath-house and mosaics); North Leigh, Oxfordshire (courtyard villa, mosaics, hypocausts); Rockbourne, Hampshire (courtyard villa, bath suites, mosaics); Shide, Isle of Wight (tiled floors, fireplace, bath suite); Woodchester, Gloucestershire (largest Roman mosaic in Britain, on display every ten years.)

The Romans stamp their style on Britain

BEFORE the Romans came to Britain to begin their colonisation in the latter half of the first century A.D., the standards of housing and personal hygiene in Britain were not very high. The early British farmers and their families lived in crudely-built circular wood-framed buildings, with roofs of thatch, or turves, or wattle and daub (interlaced rods and twigs plastered with mud.)

Heating would come from a wood fire in the centre of the structure, with the smoke escaping haphazardly through a hole in the centre of the roof.

The Romans, however, were accustomed to much better housing, and their great civilising influence on Britain also included the introduction of such things as bathrooms, and even a form of central heating.

From remains left behind it has been possible to reconstruct with considerable accuracy what these Romano-British houses or villas looked like. Their size varied according to the importance and financial circumstances of the owner, but a well-appointed bathroom, and even a swimming pool, was considered essential by middle and upper-class citizens, while the less affluent made use of communal washing facilities.

If possible, villas were sited near a steady water supply which was used not only for cooking purposes, but also supplied bath houses and often toilets.

Every Roman home, whether rich or poor, had its own shrine and altar dedicated to chosen gods. The family worshipped and made offerings before them each day.

A visit to the public baths was one of life's greatest pleasures for most Romans. They spent hours there each day, for the baths were popular meeting places. The largest ones were really recreation centres. They included libraries, gardens and gymnasiums.

The Romans introduced underfloor central heating to their villas which often had chilly marble floors. A furnace provided the heat and warm air flowed beneath the floors and along ducts in the walls, as we see in our artist's impression below.

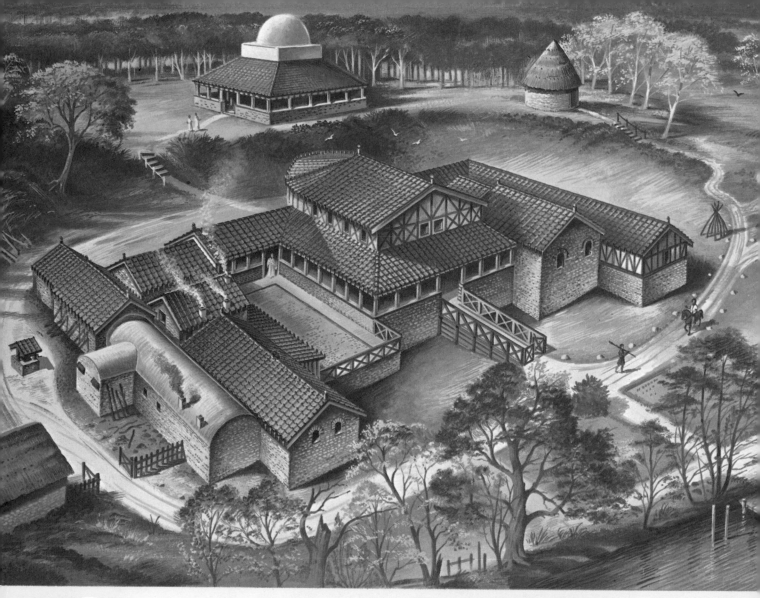

LULLINGSTONE ROMAN VILLA

Some of the most interesting Roman villa ruins in Britain are those of Lullingstone in Kent. They were found in the 18th century when parts of a mosaic floor were seen in the holes made for the reception of wooden posts.

No excavation was done until 1949, when reclamation began.

The picture above shows an imaginative view of the whole site as it probably looked in its heyday; the garden reaching down to the River Darent and the house, a largish

sort of bungalow, set behind and above it.

From the uncovered ruins, it has also been established that there was a small, circular, pagan temple and a larger, grand temple-mausaleum.

The villa was probably occupied for around three hundred years and, during that time, was in the centre of extensive farmlands, all highly organised and productive, the river almost certainly being used for transport of both men and goods.

Typical bronze stool, used as a seat. never just as a foot-rest.

Small table with metal legs, struts and marble top. (Wooden furniture was also made but most has rotted away).

Bronze lamp standard with hanging lamps which burned oil and were made from metal, clay or stone. The light given out was not very bright but probably rather more than that given by a modern candle. The bronze couch was for reclining. To recline was a sign of freedom, indulged in by wealthy Romans, even when eating.

Close-up of lamp

Artist's impression of 3rd to 4th century Roman London

It is now usually accepted that London was not an old Celtic village, enlarged by the Romans, but a town founded entirely by them in about A.D. 42. The Romans called it Londinium and, in A.D. 60, it was virtually destroyed by Boudicca (Boadicea), Queen of the East Anglian Iceni tribe.

It was rebuilt and became the chief city and capital of Britain. A strong defensive wall was built around it which, at first, had five gates and later, six. This wall was probably built between A.D. 190 and 225, when there must have been a considerable threat to the city's safety. Exactly what that threat was is not known.

Parts of the wall are still on view to the public and can be seen beside the Tower of London and at a site near the new Museum of London. Another portion has been preserved under the Central Post Office.

1. **Fort:** A.D. 125. Probably used as a barracks not defence. Found 1949.

2. **Temple of Mithras:** built A.D. 200. Found 1954. Many fine sculptures, now in Museum of London. Parts reconstructed, Noble Street.

3. **Public baths.** Excavated 1964 and 1969. Nothing now to be seen. Originally it had 3 heated rooms.

4. **Governor's Palace:** built A.D. 90. Found 1964-5. Originally number of buildings. Nothi now visible.

5. **Basilica:** built A.D. 90. Found 1881. Once 152 m long by 43 m. wide. Among largest in Empir Nothing now visible.

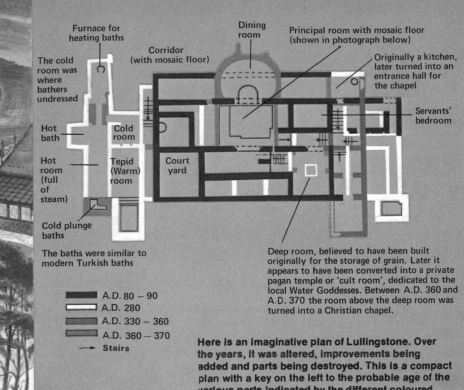

Furnace for heating baths

The cold room was where bathers undressed

Corridor (with mosaic floor)

Dining room

Principal room with mosaic floor (shown in photograph below)

Originally a kitchen, later turned into an entrance hall for the chapel

Hot bath

Cold room

Hot room (full of steam)

Tepid (Warm) room

Court yard

Servants' bedroom

Cold plunge baths

The baths were similar to modern Turkish baths

Deep room, believed to have been built originally for the storage of grain. Later it appears to have been converted into a private pagan temple or 'cult room', dedicated to the local Water Goddesses. Between A.D. 360 and A.D. 370 the room above the deep room was turned into a Christian chapel.

■	A.D. 80 – 90
□	A.D. 280
■	A.D. 330 – 360
■	A.D. 360 – 370
→	Stairs

Here is an imaginative plan of Lullingstone. Over the years, it was altered, improvements being added and parts being destroyed. This is a compact plan with a key on the left to the probable age of the various parts indicated by the different coloured lines.

Above is a typical kitchen. All cooking was done by heat from a wood furnace and the utensils used were of metal — bronze, copper or possibly iron. A wooden stand holds an oil pot, known as an amphora. This would have been made of clay, as would the nearby jug or flagon. Glass bottles (not shown) were also made, although the glass was not the clear glass of later ages.

Left is a photograph of a detail of the mosaic floor of the principal room at Lullingstone. The top part shows the mythical killing of the Chimaera (a fire-breathing goat) by the hero, Bellerophon, riding the winged horse, Pegasus. Bellerophon (a Greek hero and dressed as a Greek hero) was condemned to several such contests for offending Proteus, the King of Argus. The dolphins around Bellerophon may symbolise his journey across the sea to take part in these contests. There is also a humanised portrayal of one of the seasons in each corner of the mosaic. The lower part shows the kidnapping of Europa by the god, Jupiter, in the form of a bull. The inscription is in Latin.

ivate baths
ouse.
vated 1968-9.
n view now.

gates of six
n. Other two
cture —
ate and
ate.

rook: stream
y, deep and
ow, which
ed between
hill and
gate Hill. Filled
0-400 years
and now
ed through a
.

Newgate

Aldersgate

Cripplegate

Bishopsgate

Walbrook

Betrayed at the Feast of Treachery

Soon after the last Roman soldier was recalled from Britain, about A.D. 410, to defend his own home-land, the position of the Britons, faced with invasions on all sides, was desperate.

The Angles, Saxons and Jutes were swarming across the North Sea from Germany. And over the wall built by the Emperor Hadrian in the north came small armies of plundering, looting Picts and Scots.

Vortigern, a British king of Kent, and his chieftains were assembled in council discussing what steps they could take to defeat the northern invaders, when three Jutish ships appeared off the coast, carrying about 300 warriors under two of their chiefs, Hengist and Horsa, who were brothers.

Vortigern thought it would be a good idea to hire these sea wolves, as they have been called, to fight the Picts and Scots. No doubt it seemed clever to set one group of invaders against the other. But it is a plan that never works. No sooner had the Jutes thrashed the Picts and Scot than they turned on the Britons and demanded the money which they had been promised and land as well.

"These barbarians," says the British historian Gidas, "being thus introduced as soldiers into the island to defend their hosts from danger, obtain an allowance of provisions which, for some time, stop their doggish mouths. Then they complain that their monthly supplies are not sufficient and they use this complaint to start a quarrel, saying that unless more liberality is shown them they will break the treaty and plunder the whole island. In a short time they follow up their threats with deeds."

Jutes gain Kent

Soon other Jutish ships began to arrive and we are told that Vortigern became the villain of the piece. The king fell madly in love with Hengist's daughter, a blue-eyed beauty named Rowena. In order to win her hand, he gave the Jutes the kingdom of Kent.

But not all the British chieftains thought like Vortigern, and bitter warfare broke out between them and the Jutish newcomers.

The Jutes, under Hengist and Horsa, then formed an alliance with the Picts and the Scots and the results must have been terrible for the Britons. From bits of stories that have come down to us from old songs, we know something of the dreadful battles that took place.

At one, at Aylesford — which means 'the Ford of the Eagles' — in Kent, Horsa was killed by Vortimer, one of Vortigern's sons by a former marriage.

Another son of Vortigern was killed at the battle, for the

Continued on page 136

The coast of Suffolk in East Anglia is indented with creeks and inlets. One of these is the River Deben, and about 16 kilometres inland along this river is a small village called Sutton Hoo. In the summer of 1939, just before the outbreak of World War II, one of Britain's most important archaeological discoveries was made on a sandy wasteland outside the village.

Excavating one of a group of medieval barrows, Mr. B. J. Brown of Ipswich Museum unearthed the remains of a Saxon ship, complete with a treasure of Saxon jewellery, bowls, weapons and coins.

Over 30 metres above the level of the river, the ship could not have been driven or pulled ashore and then accidently preserved. The finery found inside confirmed that it must have been a grave ship. Although a Saxon commoner was lucky if he was buried with a small mound to mark the spot, Viking and Saxon kings and noblemen were often buried in the longships that were their pride

Above: One of nine silver bowls, each 23 cm in diameter, probably made in the fourth century and looted later by the Saxons.

THE TREASURE TROVE OF SUTTON HOO
Beneath the sand lay a burial ship — without a body

and joy. Sometimes these ships were pushed out to sea or burnt; quite often, as at Sutton Hoo, they were buried.

Although its planks had long since rotted, from the position of the iron bolts that remained it was easy to build up a picture of what the shop looked like. It was about 25 metres long, with pointed prow and stern, and about four metres wide amidships. As there was no support for a mast, it was almost certainly a rowing galley. It was probably built about A.D. 600.

The great treasure of Anglo-Saxon and other goods found inside came from as far away as Byzantium (Istanbul). Some of the finds

are shown on this page. No other Saxon excavation has produced such a valuable collection. But one thing the excavators expected to find was missing. There was no body.

No one knows for sure who was buried at Sutton Hoo, or why the body is missing. But the burial was certainly fit for a king and the most likely candidate is Raedwald, King of East Anglia, who died in 624 or 625.

Whichever king it was, it seems at first strange that he should be buried in this way, as most kings of this time were nominally Christian. But in those early times, Christian and pagan customs went hand in hand — often with the concealed blessing of the Church, which considered it too dangerous to stamp out all pagan traditions too quickly. It is also possible that although the Sutton Hoo ship was set up as a monument to the king, the body itself was given a Christian burial — which is one explanation of the riddle of the missing corpse.

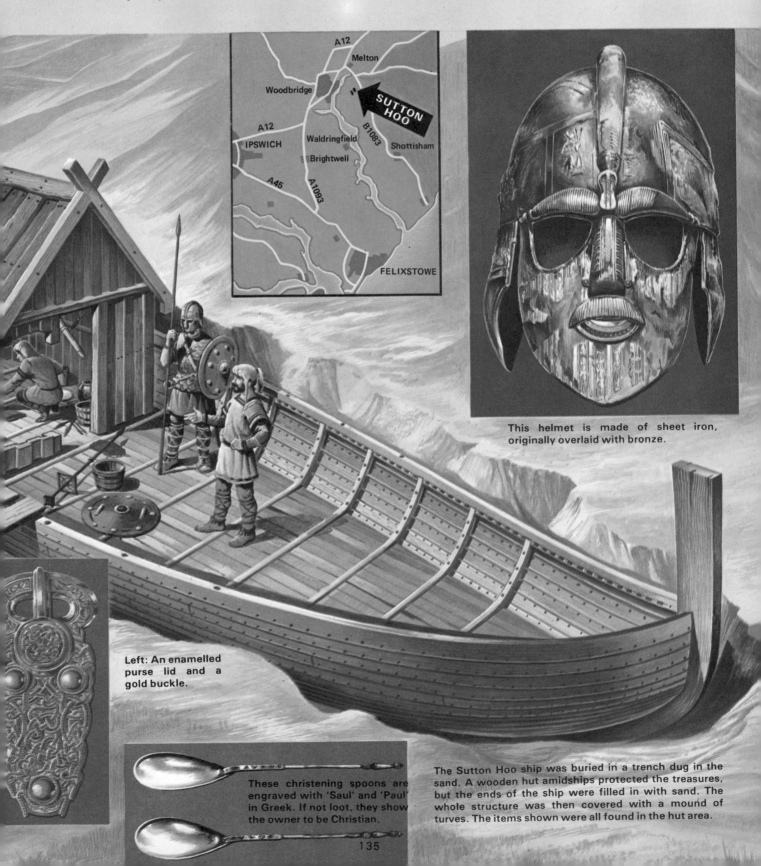

This helmet is made of sheet iron, originally overlaid with bronze.

Left: An enamelled purse lid and a gold buckle.

These christening spoons are engraved with 'Saul' and 'Paul' in Greek. If not loot, they show the owner to be Christian.

The Sutton Hoo ship was buried in a trench dug in the sand. A wooden hut amidships protected the treasures, but the ends of the ship were filled in with sand. The whole structure was then covered with a mound of turves. The items shown were all found in the hut area.

British king's sons were fighting against the Jutes while their father dallied with his Jutish bride.

Vortimer was undoubtedly the leader and inspiration of the British defences and finally the Jutes were driven back.

But one of the old chronicles tells us that Rowena then stepped in to avenge the death of her uncle Horsa by bribing a servant to poison her stepson. As soon as Vortimer lay dead, back came the Jutes, including Hengist, father of Rowena.

Hengist made an offer of peace to the Britons and invited their chiefs to a feast. It was agreed that both Britons and Jutes were to come without arms, but Hengist treacherously instructed his Jutes to ignore that agreement. Thus the Jutes came to the the tables with daggers concealed under their cloaks.

"Unsheathe your swords!"

The feast began and the wine cup circulated. Jutes and British chiefs sat at the board side by side. The Britons never dreamed of treachery and the loving cup was going round when suddenly the Jutish chief gave the order: "Unsheathe your swords!" In a few moments every one of the 300 British chiefs lay dead on the ground.

It is said that Princess Rowena, who was present at the banquet, looked on all this bloodshed unmoved. The place where it happened is supposed to have been near Stonehenge, even perhaps within its circles of stones.

No doubt the Jutes looked upon the massacre of the Christian Britons as pleasing to their bloodthirsty gods, led by their great god Odin.

Had the Britons been united, they might possibly have been able to drive back both the Picts and the Scots in the north and the Jutes in the east. But their divided counsels and continual arguments weakened them and in another great battle fought at Crayford in Kent they were defeated with great slaughter.

According to the Anglo-Saxon Chronicle — an account of early English history, written by monks and others — the Britons lost 4,000 killed and they had to flee from Kent in terror and make for the comparative safety of London.

Despite his success, though, Hengist was unable to keep possession of very much more territory than the area covered by the present county of Kent. Even then he could probably not have held that much land except for the quarrels that constantly broke out among the British chieftains, thereby preventing them from acting together.

And there is no doubt that if they had acted together they might well have thrown out all the invaders. For it is said that at this very time they were able to send to Gaul (modern France) an army 12,000 strong to make war against the Visigoths.

The problem was that the British Isles were divided under the command of so many petty chieftains or kings that they could not bring their united forces to bear upon the invaders in any one part of the country.

Vortigern, the husband of Rowena and seller of Kent to the Jutes, is said to have fled into Wales from the fury of his own people. There, hated alike "by slave and freeman, monk and layman, strong and weak, small and great", he died with his fair Rowena in the flames which destroyed the fortress where he was sheltering from his enemies.

Fact or fiction

How much of the story of Vortigern is fact and how much is fiction it is impossible to determine. But almost certainly he followed the bad example of the Roman emperors when they were attacked by barbarians from the East, by inviting the 'sea pirates' to help him against other invaders.

No doubt without invitation the Angles, Saxons and Jutes would have come and stayed in Britain sooner or later. But the example of those earliest invaders was quickly followed, and soon more pirates swarmed across the North Sea and drove the Britons into the west, burning and destroying most of the fruits of civilisation which had resulted from the Roman occupation. In the wilds of Cornwall and Wales the Britons managed to survive and even today their language is being kept alive in Wales.

It is from the barbarian invaders who came from the tribes of Germany that the English people and the southern Scots of today are mostly descended. There is, of course, a considerable admixture of many other races, like the Celts, the Danes and their kinsmen the Normans, or Northmen, who had settled in France.

VORTIGERN'S ALLIANCE STILL AFFECTS THE COUNTY OF KENT

Fifteen hundred years after their alliance with Vortigern, the influence of Hengist and Horsa can still be felt in Kent. Now just a county, it was for long a kingdom in its own right — the Kingdom of Kent.

It had its own laws, customs and kings, separate both from Essex to the north and Wessex and Sussex to the west.

Even when it was successfully invaded by the Essex king Sigehere in A.D. 687, or when it was later merged into the enlarged Kingdom of Wessex around 825, it was still treated as a separate realm and entrusted to a member of the ruling royal family.

For example, around 890, during the last years of Alfred the Great's reign, Alfred's son Edward was given Kent to rule.

Throughout this time, the Kentish people retained their links with their Jutish past. Indeed, the memory of Hengist and Horsa is kept alive even to this day in the emblem of Kent. This is a prancing white horse. Both 'hengist' and 'horsa' are words for horse in the Jutish language.

The emblem of Kent

Arthur... hero of a howling wilderness

One day early in the fifth century A.D., shortly after the Roman troops had left Britain, some Britons sent an urgent letter to the Emperor of Rome. "Send us back our troops!" it urged. "We are being raided from all sides. We cannot properly defend ourselves."

The Emperor, who had troubles enough of his own, replied tersely. "I have no more troops left to send," he said. "They are all needed to defend Rome herself against the barbarian invaders. Therefore you Britons should take steps to defend yourselves."

The letter from Britain, which was described by the ancients as "The groans of the Britons", signalled the end of Roman power in northern Europe. Faced with rebellions among her own soldiers and with attacks by wild tribes seeking new lands for themselves, Rome pulled back the

KING ARTHUR'S ENGLAND

The invading Angles, Saxons and Jutes occupied much of the British mainland, driving the Celtic population back to the areas indicated on the map below. The Bernicians, Deirans and Rheghed were Saxon tribes. Also shown are the places associated with the legends of King Arthur.

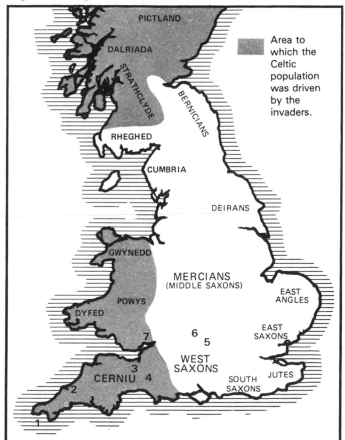

1. **St. Michael's Mount**, reputed to be one of King Arthur's strongholds.
2. **Tintagel**, traditionally King Arthur's birthplace.
3. **Glastonbury**, possible site of Camelot and lake where Arthur found his sword, Excalibur. May be Arthur's burial place, too.
4. **South Cadbury**
5. **Uffington** } possible sites of the Battle of
6. **Badbury Hill** } Badon (see text).
7. **Caerleon**, another contender for the site of Camelot

frontiers of her Empire, leaving those on the edge of it, such as the Britons, to their own fate.

Even as the legionaries pulled away from the south coast beaches in their painted galleys, the wild Picts and Scots swarmed over the wall that Hadrian had built, leaving it in ruins and attacking the towns and fine country houses which the Romans had deserted.

Still more dangerous enemies came from across the sea. They were the Angles and Saxons from what is now Germany, and the Jutes from Denmark. Initially, their method was to sail along the coast, burning, killing and stealing in surprise attacks. But soon they came looking not just for loot, but land and they brought their families.

Even during the Roman occupation, Saxon settlements had appeared. The Romans ignored them if they caused no trouble — but if they did, they were dealt with harshly.

Sometimes, all the raiders came at once. In one year, the Picts and the Scots raided the north and the Angles and Saxons landed on the south-east coast. The Duke of the Northern Marshes, who was in charge of Britain's northern defences, and the Count of the Saxon Shore, who had the same job in the south, were both killed in battles against the raiders.

Badly frightened

Before long, people who lived in villas, farms and country estates were badly frightened. They had no protection against these surprise attacks. Soon, many of them had moved into the towns. Many magnificent villas — such as that at Mildenhall in Suffolk where the silverware was hidden in the garden by the owners and not unearthed until this century — were deserted and left to the mercy of the raiders. The towns had walls and gateways and the people felt that here, at least, was protection. They soon found that they were wrong, for the invaders sacked and burned Canterbury, London, Silchester and Bath.

In the hundred and fifty years that followed the Roman withdrawal. Britain underwent incredible changes. From a prosperous Empire outpost the country degenerated into a howling wilderness. Yet little is known of those momentous years, the beginning of the Dark Ages in Britain.

This is partly because, unlike the Romans, who were great writers and recorders, the invaders wrote nothing. They were intent only on plunder, and if there was a story to tell about it afterwards, then it was kept for the end of a feast, when the beer flowed freely. It was the same story a man learned from his father, and he from his father, and so on. Probably, it was embellished with each new telling.

Among all these spoken words, weaving fact and legend into an intriguing web of entertainment, one emerged to be told and re-told above all others. About A.D. 500, just after the Romans left Britain, its tribal kings, led by a warrior named Arthur, inflicted a heavy defeat on the Saxons at a place called Mount Badon. Apparently, this Arthur had a number of well-loved comrades, as well as a wife with a name something like Guenevere.

No more is known about him than that, so we are left to wonder whether this was the Arthur of legend, the original Arthur of the Knights of the Round Table, who inspired all men of honour in the Middle Ages.

There is a strong possibility that he was — but only a possibility.

Arthur's castle, the legends said, was at Camelot. Now at South Cadbury, in Somerset, there is an Iron Age hill fort that has always been known locally as Camelot. And legends also say that Arthur and Guenevere were buried at nearby Glastonbury.

A scholar named Gerald of Wales claims that the Glastonbury grave was more than a legend. Writing in the year 1192, he says he saw the tomb and he describes how King Henry the Second ordered it to be opened. He found a lead cross, engraved with the words,

HERE LIES THE RENOWNED KING ARTHUR WITH GUENEVERE HIS SECOND WIFE

There was an oak coffin containing the bones of a man and a woman. A monk apparently jumped down to touch the woman's hair, for it was still golden. But it crumbled to dust.

As real as this story may seem, it was not Arthur's grave that fascinated people so much as the place where he had lived. South Cadbury as the likely location of Camelot has fascinated people since the days of Henry the Eighth. At last, in 1966, a modern scientific investigation of the area began. Remains of a fifth century church were found, and then something that was more than anyone had hoped for.

Exciting discovery

Little by little appeared the remains, not of just a post-Roman settlement, but evidence of a huge hall.

Fragments of Mediterranean wine jars pointed to the fact that whoever had lived there was a person of unusual consequence, civilised enough to import foreign wine. Outside the hall were massive fortifications, clear evidence that here had been a fifth century stronghold of quite unusual magnificence.

Who could have built this great hall? There is no clear proof that it was Arthur, but the period is right for him, as is the evidence of gentle living. It is generally agreed that South Cadbury is as near to Camelot as we are ever likely to get.

If this really was the home of King Arthur and the gathering place of his knights, then what days they must have been for these men defending the honour of their homeland.

SAXON JUSTICE

In Anglo-Saxon times, a man accused of a crime often brought forward 'oath helpers' to swear to his innocence. But it took the testimony of six common men to equal that of one nobleman, as is shown above.

FOR murdering a nobleman — fined £400; for murdering one's own slave — no punishment; for striking out someone's eye — fined sixty-six shillings; and for striking off someone's big toe — fined twenty shillings. These are some of the strange-sounding sentences passed in Anglo-Saxon England when British justice was still in its infancy.

The Witenagemot ('meeting of wise men') or supreme court met twice a year in various cities and consisted of the chief clergymen, nobles and landowners. Its powers extended to choosing the king's successor when he died.

Next in importance came the Shire Moot or county court presided over by the sheriff, appointed by the king. Below that came the Hundred Court attended by the landowners in the hundred (a number of villages), a 'reeve' chosen by the villagers and the four most important men in each village. The 'hundred', as a division of land, still exists today.

Poor people found it hard to get justice in the courts, especially in cases against the rich and powerful who could afford to bribe the judges. A nobleman's word also counted for more in court than a common man's.

Fines were the most usual form of punishment and the amount depended on the severity of the crime.

Murderers were fined according to the ranks of their victims. For killing a king, £1,500 had to be paid; for a prince's murder, it was £750, and so on down through the ranks. The money went to the victims' relatives. The criminal had a year to pay up. If he refused, the relatives were allowed to take the law into their own hands and kill him.

Fines for inflicting wounds were paid to the victims themselves.

Those who failed to appear in court after being summoned were declared outlaws, a terrible punishment which gave them no protection from the law and forbade anyone to supply them with food or shelter.

A person accused of a crime could take sanctuary in a church or monastery and the authorities could not touch him while he remained in the sacred building.

Alfred gives England a Royal Navy

WHEN Alfred the Great and his English inflicted their decisive defeat on Guthrum and his Danes on the Berkshire Downs, the English king brought peace for the first time for years to a land that had been ravaged, exhausted and bled of its menfolk by the savage Viking invaders.

Wisely, Alfred was not content with this victory. He knew he had to build up an army to defend his shores; more importantly, he had to build a navy to meet the Vikings on the seas. For it was at sea that these Danish invaders were second to none.

We know what Viking ships looked like, for when one of their leaders died he was often buried in his ship, with his possessions, gold and jewels and drinking vessels, sometimes even his horses and hounds, around him.

Famous discovery

Several of these buried Viking ships have been dug up. The most famous of them was unearthed in Norway in 1880, almost complete. It even had the cooking pots which the sailors used. Twenty-three metres long and 5 metres wide, the ship was built of solid oak, fastened together with iron bolts and lined with cords of plaited animal hair, to keep out the water. It had a square sail, and held 50 sailors and 30 warriors — or prisoners.

If you had lived in Denmark in those days and wanted to join the Vikings on their voyages, you would have had to prove first that you were strong and an excellent fighter. The leader chose the men for his crew from volunteers. They could be aged between 16 and 60, as long as they were "as good at the helm or oar as they were with the sword."

In due course they sailed to Russia, France, Spain, Iceland, and even America, as well as Britain. When they landed in Ireland, some of them settled and founded the city of Dublin.

Best plunder

They found the best plunder in the monasteries, many of which were built on islands and had no defences.

Once, in mid-winter, when no help could reach the monastery from the mainland, Vikings raided Lindisfarne, or Holy Island. They killed the monks' cattle and roasted them over big fires to eat. They killed many of the monks as well and the younger ones they carried off to be sold in the slave-markets. When they left, the Vikings took with them the rich treasures of the monks, their gold and jewelled vessels and church emblems.

Faced with problems like this, Alfred realised that the most effective way of dealing with the invaders was to prevent them from landing.

Alfred had his men build ships twice the size of those of the Danes. They were propelled by sails and by 60 oars each, and were constructed to a design prepared by Alfred himself. They stood higher out of the water, so that the fighting men on board had an advantage in being able to attack their Viking opponents from above.

Alfred's navy proved highly successful and during the first summer twenty of the formidable Danish ships were sunk.

In the year 893 there was a new invasion of England by the Danes under a chief named Hastings who, incidentally, gave his name to the Sussex town of Hastings. He remained unchallenged for a year, probably because a greater part of Kent, where he camped, was dense forest and difficult to attack.

But when the Danish settlers in Northumbria and East Anglia violated the peace treaty of Wedmore which Alfred had made with them, and joined the Vikings in their raids, the English king decided to act.

Hastings came to terms at once, but then broke his word soon afterwards. Then, for many years, Alfred's armies were harrassed on all sides by Viking invaders and Viking settlers.

The position was a stalemate when Hastings, who had marched right across Wessex to the River Severn, arrived back at Mersea in Essex, where he had left his ships. He sailed his ships up the Thames and then towed them up the River Lea near where the Stort enters that river, and formed a camp about 40 km from London.

Continued on next page

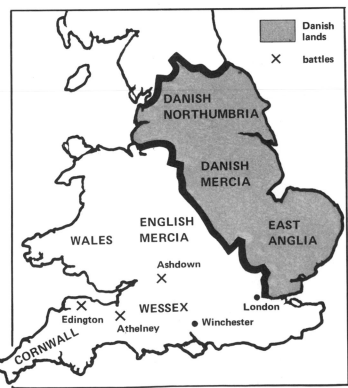

England and Wales, showing the area of Danish settlement and the places where the main battles between the Vikings and Saxons took place.

Alfred followed, and conceived his brilliant plan of building a dam and cutting a fresh channel for the water, so as to divert the river and leave the Danish ships high and dry and unable to return to the sea. The plan was successful. The ships were captured and the Danes had to evacuate their camp, and eventually Hastings had to withdraw to France.

It is interesting to note that one way that we know where the Danes settled in England is by the Danish names of places that have come down to us from those times.

Names ending in *by* indicate places where the settlers lived, for *by* is a Danish word meaning first a home and then a village. Derby, Rugby, Kirby, Netherby, Selby and Ashby are such old Danish settlements.

Thorpe, or *trop*, is another name for a collection of men or houses, and so we get Althorpe, Copmansthorpe, and Wilstrop.

Alfred the Great died at Farringdon in Berkshire in 901 and was buried at Winchester. He had prevented the Danes from getting the upper hand in England, but the country was terribly exhausted by war.

Peace and learning

Yet during the years that followed the Peace of Wedmore, when Alfred was able to devote some of his great powers in the cause of peace and learning, there was something of prosperity in England.

A writer has said of Alfred in these times: "He restored churches; he brought in scholars from other lands; he started schools for the sons of nobles; he collected the old traditional poems, translating good books into English and starting the famous Anglo-Saxon Chronicle. There never was a more enlightened or a nobler king."

Alfred taught himself all he knew, and it seems strange therefore that although he twice visited Rome as a child, he was not taught to read while he was there. Perhaps this was because in those days it was thought that learning was only for priests, and that the right education for princes and nobles was the sword and manly exercises.

The war with the Vikings, however, had broken up all the English schools, and Alfred once said that when he began to reign there were very few priests south of the Humber who could understand the prayer-book. South of the Thames he knew only one priest who could even read.

Alfred's collection and arrangement of the various laws was one of the finest legacies he left to Englishmen. It was his work that set right a situation whereby the poor could not obtain their rights and the rich escaped by bribery.

Great inventiveness

Alfred was also a man of great inventiveness. There were no clocks in England in his day and no way of telling the time except by watching the Sun or a shadow. But in a cloudy, foggy land like England the Sun was not always available.

Alfred therefore, it is said, invented a candle which was divided into sections, and by the time the various sections took to burn away, the passage of time could be marked.

There was, however, a difficulty. In the old Anglo-Saxon houses and churches the windows were unglazed and the wind blew through the rooms at times with great force. This led to unequal burning of the candle and often to the flame being extinguished.

To protect the candle, therefore, Alfred invented a lantern with thin horn sides, through which the light could pass, but which excluded the wind and thus enabled the flame to burn steadily and regularly. Before the days of clocks, this royal invention must have been a considerable boon.

The Vikings – raide

FROM the end of the eighth century until near the end of the tenth, the shores of England were liable to witness such terrifying sights as the one shown on the right. The fast-moving Viking ships would land on a strip of coastline and then the ferocious warriors would go into action.

Quite a lot is known about the Viking boats from archaeological discoveries. Three excavations were particularly interesting; the Tune Ship found in 1867, the Gokstad Ship in 1880 and the Oesberg ship in 1894.

After service on the seas all of these ships were used in ceremonial burial services. They were deposited in burial mounds, where they were embedded in a clay which acted as a preservative for the wood and kept it in good condition.

The Oesberg ship was built around the year 800 while the ships from Gokstad and Tune were constructed some fifty years later.

Up to the middle of the ninth century there had been little difference between ships, whether they were used for trading purposes or for warfare.

Wider ships were then developed for trade and narrow, low boats were adopted for carrying warriors to battle. The war ships were designed for speed and the ease with which they could be landed.

The Danes making a raid from their own country were able to cross the North Sea, attack a village on the East Anglian coast, and be back home with their booty within six days.

These swift-moving raiders caused a monk to write, "Never before has such terror appeared in Britain."

Right: A helmet once worn by a Viking warrior. This fine example was found in a grave at Vendel, Uppland, Sweden. The protection that the helmet gave can quite clearly be seen, with the skull and sides of the face completely covered. The Vikings are often depicted as charging into battle wearing horned, or winged, helmets. There is little evidence that such head-gear was ever worn, and the popular picture owes more to the imagination than to fact.

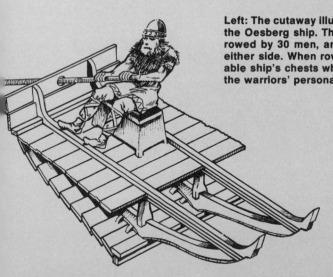

Left: The cutaway illustration shows the design of the Oesberg ship. The ship, 22 metres long, was rowed by 30 men, and had 15 holes for oars on either side. When rowing, the crew sat on moveable ship's chests which were also used to store the warriors' personal belongings.

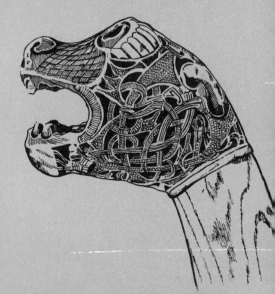

Right: An animal headpost found in the Oesberg ship. The head-post, which was probably made to ward off evil spirits, is very finely carved and shows that the Vikings were quite skilled craftsmen.

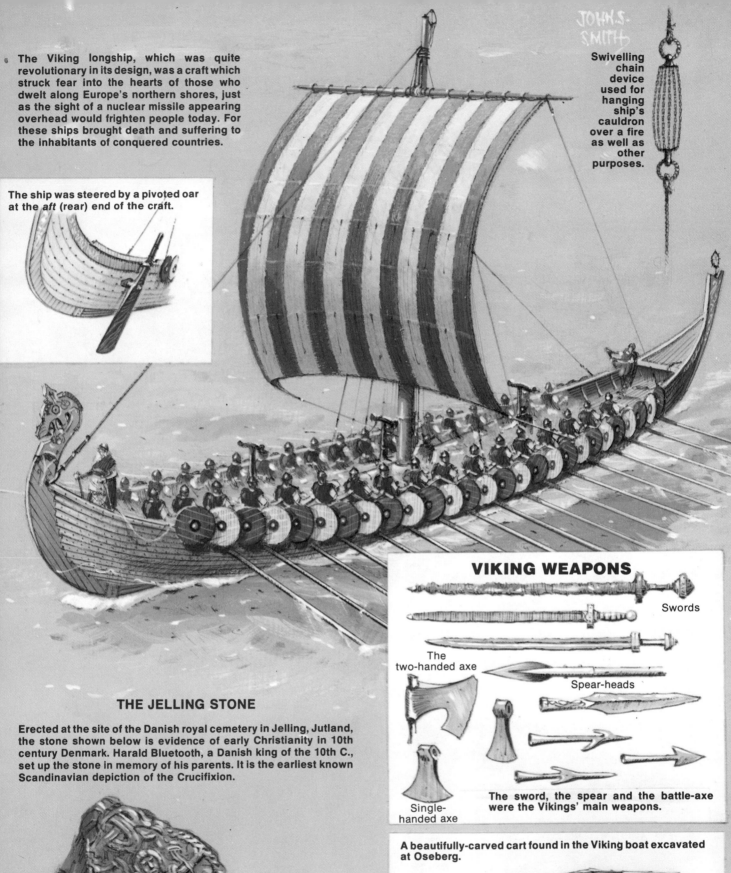

The Viking longship, which was quite revolutionary in its design, was a craft which struck fear into the hearts of those who dwelt along Europe's northern shores, just as the sight of a nuclear missile appearing overhead would frighten people today. For these ships brought death and suffering to the inhabitants of conquered countries.

Swivelling chain device used for hanging ship's cauldron over a fire as well as other purposes.

The ship was steered by a pivoted oar at the *aft* (rear) end of the craft.

VIKING WEAPONS

Swords

The two-handed axe

Spear-heads

Single-handed axe

The sword, the spear and the battle-axe were the Vikings' main weapons.

THE JELLING STONE

Erected at the site of the Danish royal cemetery in Jelling, Jutland, the stone shown below is evidence of early Christianity in 10th century Denmark. Harald Bluetooth, a Danish king of the 10th C., set up the stone in memory of his parents. It is the earliest known Scandinavian depiction of the Crucifixion.

A beautifully-carved cart found in the Viking boat excavated at Oseberg.

Harold sails into disaster

HAROLD, Earl of Wessex, must have rued the day he went sailing in the English Channel about the year 1064. It was a cruise that was destined to change the face of England's story.

As often happens in the Channel, bad weather suddenly closed in. The waves began to beat at Earl Harold's ship and several hours later the wet and exhausted sailors and their noble passenger were thrown upon a part of the French coast that belonged to Count Guy of Ponthieu.

A thousand years ago people believed that if someone were shipwrecked it was because he had been forsaken by God and, therefore, he was legitimate prey. If he were a nobleman he was seized and kept prisoner until a considerable ransom was paid for him.

Count Guy must have rubbed his hands with glee when he learned who had been delivered into his hands for the ransom would be large.

Harold, however, managed to get word of his plight to William, Duke of Normandy, who was Count Guy's overlord.

"Bring him to my court," Duke William said brusquely. And Count Guy had to obey.

Solemn oath

William put a book of the gospels on a table covered with a cloth of gold. "Harold," he said, "before my assembled nobles, bishops and knights, I order you to take an oath to help me obtain the kingdom of England after the death of King Edward the Confessor, to marry my daughter Adela, and to send me your sister so that I can give her as wife to one of my followers."

Harold, it was said, was stunned by this request. But there wasn't much he could do about it, for he was in William's power. Reluctantly, he took the oath.

At a sign from William, servants then took off the cloth of gold. Under it, instead of a table, was a chest filled with bones and relics of the saints.

Harold drew back, shuddering. Without knowing it, he had sworn the oath upon the relics — and he knew that an oath so taken was the most solemn and binding that could be devised.

If that seems fairly trivial to us today — conceived as it was by a piece of blatant trickery — that was far from so in Norman times. For everyone believed that an oath sworn on relics would, if violated, call down upon the offender's head the full vengeance of the Church.

Cheerfully, Duke William heaped presents upon his troubled prisoner and then accompanied him to the coast, where he had a ship prepared to take Earl Harold back to England.

On his return Harold told King Edward the Confessor all that had happened. The old King grew thoughtful. "Your journey will bring calamity on yourself and on the nation," he said finally.

Harold was soon to find out how those words rang with truth.

A long time later Duke William claimed that fourteen years before Harold became Count Guy's prisoner, in the year 1050, he went himself to England and met Edward the Confessor. "The King promised me that I would be his successor on the English throne," he said.

Was the English king perhaps beguiled by the Norman duke, then a strapping, handsome 23-year-old? Did he make this promise in a rash and foolish moment?

For whether William's statement was true or not Edward the Confessor was not in fact entitled to name his successor. That was the duty of the Witenagemot, or council of wise men.

Successor

A year after Earl Harold got back to England after the Normandy shipwreck, Edward the Confessor died. It is said that just before his death he told some of the English nobles that the man best fitted to succeed him was Earl Harold of Wessex.

Harold undoubtedly agreed with this, and so, too, did the Witenagemot. The day after Edward's funeral they elected him King and he was crowned and anointed in the new church at West Minster — built by Edward the Confessor on the site where Westminster Abbey stands today.

The Northumbrians, however, didn't like the idea of Harold as their king, even though he had granted them, like some modern politician, all sorts of favours before his election in order to win their support. He had deposed his own brother Tostig as Earl of Northumbria so that the Northumbrians could make Morcar, their own choice, their earl.

Marriage

Harold showed considerable wisdom when, instead of marching north with an army to meet the truculent Northumbrians, he went alone with the Bishop of Worcester, a churchman beloved by all the English. At a meeting at York the Bishop persuaded the Northumbrians not to resist their King and in gratitude for their agreement Harold married Ealdgyth, the sister of Morcar. That seemed a clever move — but, of course, it did make it impossible for him to marry Duke William's daughter, as he was supposed to have promised.

One night the Saxon English looked in amazement as a brilliant comet appeared in the sky. In their view, a comet was always a sign that some great event was about to happen.

Perhaps, across the Channel in Nor-

NORMAN KNIGHTS

The new line of nobility which William I brought to England

In 1066, William brought to England an army of 2,000 knights and 3,000 archers and squires (young trainee knights). The Norman soldiers were much better equipped than their Saxon counterparts. The long coats of chain mail, called *hauberks,* were especially effective. Both armies were raised by the *feudal system,* a means of governing which developed between the 4th and 10th centuries. The word *feudal* comes from the Latin *feudium,* meaning a *fief* or portion of land given by a king to his supporters in return for loyal service. These landowners or *vassals* retained the loyalty of their own supporters, or *sub-vassals,* by granting them land held *in fief.* William himself was a vassal of the King of France and after his victory at Hastings, he shared the conquered land among his nobles.

mandy, William saw it too. He had already sworn that within a year he would go to England and get the crown he said was his. For him, the comet would have been a special sign indeed.

William called his knights around him and told them he wanted to raise an army.

These Normans who were soon to cross the Channel as invaders of England were the direct descendants of the Northmen, or Viking pirates. As had happened in England, the French people had despaired of ever getting rid of them.

At last, in 911, the French King Charles the Simple gave them the city of Rouen and the lands by the mouth of the River Seine if they would settle down and behave.

Rollo, the Viking leader, agreed. He took the title Duke of the Normans, or Duke of Normandy, and soon his Viking followers had become thoroughly French. Above all, they fought like Frenchmen, on horseback with lance and sword.

This sort of fighting was quite new. It demanded great skill in horsemanship and long training; it demanded also considerable wealth, for the mounted warrior needed expensive armour, good horses and many servants. Only a landowner, or the young son of a landowner, could be a true mounted warrior, what the English called a knight.

In the year 1027 the Normans, now excellent fighters, were ruled by Duke Robert, the great-great-grandson of Rollo, and father of William.

When William was about eight his

father died; at 16, William began to rule his duchy. By this time he was the best horseman and the best warrior in France, although it is not certain that he knew how to read or write.

But for William, enraged by what he thought was the treachery of "King" Harold, pen and book were to be of no consequence in the forthcoming great invasion. Only lance and shield would win him the kingdom of England.

The Saxon village fair

Life in Saxon England was hard and often cruel; disease was rampant and even idyllic scenes such as the one shown above were liable to be interrupted by savage raiders who would butcher the villagers, burn their houses and carry off their wares. But ordinary people had little time to worry about such hazards. For them, scraping a living was hard enough. It took up most of their time.

In a village, the fair (or market) was the highlight of the week. Traders came from far and near to display and sell their goods and wandering entertainers were drawn there in the hope of earning some money from the crowd.

Not all entertainments were harmless fun like juggling or playing musical instruments. Some, like cock-fighting, reflected the cruelty of the times.

A form of entertainment which was free were the stocks — first introduced to England in Saxon times — where petty criminals were displayed for public ridicule.

The Saxon Village

Forest

Common

SECOND ARABLE FIELD

THIRD ARABLE FIELD

FIRST ARABLE FIELD

Elfric
Balda
Gath
Seth
Bede
Swaddy

Hogg
Rigg
Egbert
Het
Gurt
Adam

Herd
Robb
Gilt
Alfred
Nid

Robb
Herd
Gilt
Alfred
Nid
Adam
Gurt

Elfric
Balda
Gath
Seth
Bede
Swaddy
Hogg
Rigg
Egbert
Het

Alfred
Nid
Adam
Gurt

Adam
Seth
Swaddy
Gurt
Hogg
Egbert

Giltham Meadows owned in strips like the arable fields.

Moot Place

Pond

Robb
Herd
Gath
Rigg
Alfred

Lookout

Stable

Thane's barn used by whole village

Palisade and protective ditch

GILT'S HALL
The Thane's home

Grazing for pigs

Track to Bebbanford

Track to Gyldwic

A Saxon village was a tight-knit, self-supporting community. The *thane* (leader) was guided by the *Moot* (village council) in the running of the village. He lived within a fortified area into which the *villeins* (villagers) retreated when the village was attacked.

Agriculture was important for the provision of food so the farming of the surrounding land was highly organised.

Each village had three fields which were divided into strips. Each villein had his own strips which he tended. The thane also had a share of the strips which the villeins farmed for him. The strip system ensured an equal division of the food grown, as seen above where the owners' names have been marked on their respective pieces of land.

The Saxons knew nothing about fertilizers but they realised that to ensure a good return for their efforts, crops had to be grown in different fields over the years. A field would, threfore, grow oats one year, barley the next and lie fallow the following year before the cycle started all over again.

146

1066. The date that everybody remembers

The Battle of Hastings saw the end of the Saxon Kings and the beginning of a new era.

DUKE William of Normandy gave himself a year to capture the realm of England and have himself crowned King. It was a bold ambition. He had to have an army and a fleet of ships to carry it, and he had to raise a lot of money to pay for the undertaking.

At first there wasn't a great deal of enthusiasm among the Normans for an invasion of England. Their duke claimed that England was rightfully his, that he had been promised it. But the Normans were a free people. They would help him to defend Normandy, for that was their duty, but they were under no obligation to conquer a foreign land for their duke. They told William so.

William resorted to cunning. First he gathered a few knights who were his particular friends and persuaded them to provide men and ships. Then, one by one, he talked over all the other knights, until they all agreed. The method he used was to promise them lands and titles in the conquered kingdom, and it was a method which, William knew, would set the Viking blood coursing through their veins in anticipation.

Finally, William gave them all a holy cause. The godless English, he said, were disrespectful to the Pope and a fraud had been created Archbishop of Canterbury. To underline his case, he sent a messenger to the Pope indicating that if he were successful he would make the Church much richer.

The Pope, delighted, at once approved the expedition (without hearing the English side of the argument) and gave William a consecrated banner and a ring with a supposed hair of St. Peter in it. No doubt the Pontiff had been shrewdly advised that his prestige would be greatly enhanced if it were seen that he had the right to dispose of crowns or to judge between claimants to a throne.

The result of all this cunning was that suddenly William's planned invasion of England, spawned from his hatred of King Harold and the grievance he was nurturing against him, was no longer an act of vengeance. It had become a holy war against the enemies of the Faith.

First, a fleet had to be built. All through the early summer of 1066 the shipyards of Normandy rang with the clash of axes on tree-trunks. By August the rough-hewn wood had been fashioned into ships and Normans were flooding in from all over the duchy to fill them, and thus lay their claims to both heavenly and earthly rewards.

Harold knew what was going on, of course. He was busily putting the South of England in a state of defence, assembling the biggest fleet and the biggest army every yet seen in England.

But that summer the weather was bad. The wind blew about and it seemed always to be squally and raining. The Norman ships couldn't get to sea and indeed some of them were actually sunk by the bad weather while they were in port and their sailors were drowned. William's soldiers began to mutter superstitiously. Was God really on their side, they wondered.

Anxiously, William knelt in the Norman church of St. Valery. He had the relics of the local saint carried with great pomp through his camp. His gaze seemed sometimes rivetted on the weathercock on the church steeple.

In England, meanwhile, Harold received a message that sent him hurrying to the north. There Tostig, his brother, had allied himself with the King of Norway and was laying siege to York, in open hostility to Harold. When Harold arrived with his army, battle was joined at once and the fighting was long and hard. At last Tostig and his ally were defeated and killed.

William took a tumble but turned it to his advantage

THE story is told that when William went ashore at Pevensey, he slipped and fell to the ground. His men took this to be a bad omen but William's quick thinking saved the day. Grasping a handful of earth, he got to his feet and declared that he had now taken possession of his English kingdom. Then, just before the Battle of Hastings, the duke's coat of mail was put on back to front, in error. William, however, took this as a good omen. "This day," he said, "the duke will be turned into a king!" Events proved him right.

How The Saxons Lost England

THE armies of Harold of England and Duke William of Normandy finally faced each other on October 14, 1066, a few kilometres from Hastings. The Normans had landed two weeks before in Pevensey Bay and had contented themselves with terrorising the district.

On September 25, the bulk of Harold's army had been busy defeating an invading army led by Harald Hardraada, King of Norway, at the Battle of Stamford Bridge a few miles from York. By early October, the victorious army was summoned south to fight against the Normans.

The two armies were about equal in strength of numbers but Harold had no organised archery corps or cavalry while William's well-armed horsemen were famous for their skills. The 1,000 Norman archers played a big part in the battle by covering the attacks of the knights.

The hard core of Harold's army was a force of 1,300 *housecarls* — regular troops who were well equipped. There was also a large number of part-time soldiers drawn from the local population. These were peasants carrying primitive weapons and without armour. The Saxons countered the archers by throwing stones (many of them had slings to hurl the stones) and little clubs. Worst of all, most

WILLIAM'S ARMY   HAROLD'S ARMY

Archers   Bretons
Infantry   Normans   Soldiers
Cavalry   French

TELHAM HILL

0 100 200 300 400 500 yards

To London

To Hastings

of Harold's men were already exhausted from fighting another invading army in the north of England followed by a forced march of four hundred kilometres, which they completed in less than thirteen days!

As October 14 dawned, the Saxons were positioned behind a ditch which they had dug round a mound on top of a hill which is now the site of Battle Abbey. Harold's men held the best position, waited behind their defences for the enemy to attack. Again and again the Normans failed to pierce the Saxon defence.

Finally William risked victory by having his forces feign terror and turning to flee. The trick worked. The Saxons left their defences to pursue what they took to be a defeated enemy. But suddenly the Normans turned on their pursuers with fury and slaughtered them by the hundred while others rode to the top of the undefended hill and took it.

The luckless Harold, standing close to his standard, is said to have been slain by one of a hail of arrows that struck him in the eye. His death and defeat made William 'the Conqueror' and King of England.

The battle, known as the Battle of Stamford Bridge, was fought on September 25, 1066. Two days later, on September 27, the Channel winds dropped and Duke William's armada embarked for England. Harold and his exhausted army now hurried south.

It has been said that had it not been for the treachery of his brother Tostig in the north, Harold would have won against William with ease. He might even have won had he not rushed south so quickly and allowed himself time to gather more fresh soldiers.

As it was, the Normans landed virtually unmolested, established a bridgehead, and began to harry the countryside in Kent and Sussex while they waited for the English king to come and meet them.

Decisive battle

The decisive battle was fought on October 14, some miles from Hastings. Harold had no archers and no cavalry, and no one from the north or the west had joined his army. He took post on the hill where Battle Abbey now stands and waited to be attacked.

William's army was about equal in numbers, but he had many archers and the famous Norman knights who fought on horseback. First he sent forward his archers to shoot at the Saxons, who replied by throwing stones, little axes and clubs. Then a minstrel named Taillefer rode out by himself, juggling with his sword and singing of the chivalrous deeds of Roland at Roncesvalles. He killed three Saxons before he was cut down. Then the knights charged all together.

On their hillside, the English had positioned themselves behind a ditch and a mound surmounted by a palisade. Harold decided that he would stay behind the palisade and not attack the Normans, but would wait for them to attack him.

This was good tactics, for the English had by far the best position. After the archers had used their arrows, the heavily armed foot soldiers pressed on up the hill to attack the palisade. But any Norman who got too close was quickly felled by a Saxon battleaxe.

Try as they would, the Normans could not break through the palisade. When their horsemen, with Duke William at their head, made a spirited charge up the hillside, they too were beaten back.

William displayed great gallantry. Early in the day he killed Gyrth, Harold's brother, but not before Gyrth had killed William's horse, a present from King Alfonso of Castile. In all, William had three horses killed under him. At one moment the rumour arose that William had been killed, which would have made the whole battle pointless. William countered it by riding along his line bareheaded, among the Saxon missiles.

Norman trick

Unable to break through the English palisade, William decided upon a trick. He told his men to feign flight, as though they had lost the battle. It was a risk, but it worked. The whole Norman army seemed suddenly to be running away and the English, overjoyed, could not restrain themselves. Disobeying their King's orders, they broke lose and ran down the hill, leaving that part where its ascent was easiest open to the invaders.

When the Normans saw that the English had come out from behind their impregnable position, they turned on their pursuers and killed them by the hundreds. Then they rode full speed up that part of the hill which had been left undefended.

The English had lost the supreme advantage of the ground, but they fought on desperately and bravely in a battle that had now become little more than a series of single combats.

Evening was coming on when William ordered his archers to shoot their arrows into the air so that they fell like bolts from heaven on those defending the English standard, near where King Harold was fighting. It is said that one of the arrows pierced the right eye of the English king and he sank to the ground by the side of the standard.

While he still breathed, four Norman horsemen burst through his bodyguards and killed him with a rain of blows and sword thrusts.

The last of the Saxon kings was dead. William the Conqueror was now King of Norman England.

EMBROIDERY is an art form in which material is ornamented by working stitches with a needle and thread. And it has been used by Man — more particularly by woman — for many, many centuries. The oldest piece of English embroidery still in existence is in Durham Cathedral. It is the stole of St. Cuthbert and belongs to the 10th century, A.D.

There are countless forms of embroidery and hundreds of different embroidery stitches. In the past — and still quite often today — some embroidery has been referred to as tapestry. This is particularly true of embroidered pictures and patterns using the stitches known as *petit point* and *gros point*. *Petit point* (sometimes known as 'tent stitch') consists of slanting single stitches, going from left to right over a cross of the canvas. *Gros point* is the same only on a larger scale.

Strictly speaking, however, tapestry is not embroidery at all. It is a hand-woven textile, figured, heavy and reversible. The pattern is woven into the material, not sewn on to it afterwards.

It is not known in which part of the world embroidery originated. It seems to have been — and still is — fairly worldwide. The embroidery of some countries, though,

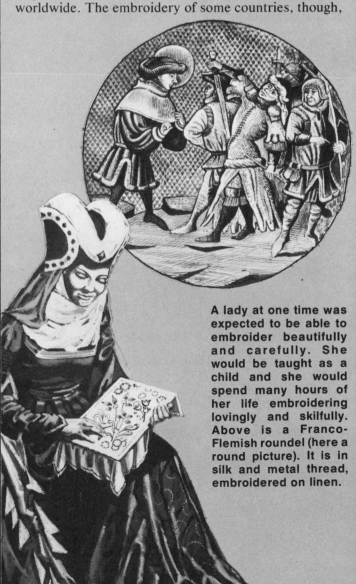

A lady at one time was expected to be able to embroider beautifully and carefully. She would be taught as a child and she would spend many hours of her life embroidering lovingly and skilfully. Above is a Franco-Flemish roundel (here a round picture). It is in silk and metal thread, embroidered on linen.

omen have been
with a needle

is justifiably acclaimed. This applies to the embroidery of ancient Greece, Egypt, Babylon and China. In more modern times, both French and English embroidery has been much admired.

Nowadays, many articles are machine embroidered and this can be and often is very attractive. At one time, though, all little girls of the upper and middle classes were taught embroidery and used to work samplers — examples of stitches — often giving the date of completion and the name of the embroiderer. Old samplers are much sought after by collectors today and may be sold for well over a hundred pounds.

Embroidered articles are varied. That is, they may be clothing, hangings, furniture coverings and the like. And the materials used are also varied. They may be wool, silk, precious metals or mixtures of these.

Needles nowadays are nearly always stainless steel. But at one time, they were bones, twigs, thorns and — later — metal wire.

No doubt delight in personal adornment will remain and so will the wish to create that adornment by hand. But it is unlikely that anything will better the work of the early embroiderers.

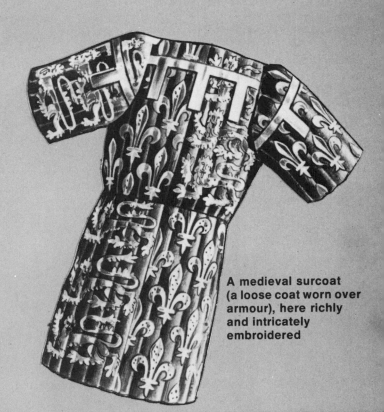

A medieval surcoat (a loose coat worn over armour), here richly and intricately embroidered

The biggest picture-strip of all

THE Bayeux Tapestry is not, in fact, a tapestry at all. It is a crewel-embroidered hanging. That is to say the pictures are not woven into the material but are sewn on to it. But it is, without doubt, a most remarkable and fascinating work of art and an almost 'living' history.

It is not really known who was responsible for the embroidering of the Bayeux Tapestry. Probably a number of people worked on it. After all, it is no small achievement. It is instead a number of small strips, joined together into a long strip, and made up of 72 scenes. Originally, it is thought to have had 76 scenes but the last four scenes have been lost.

At one time, it was believed to have been the work of Queen Matilda, wife of William the Conqueror, but this is no longer accepted. It was almost certainly commissioned and worked for Odo, Bishop of Bayeux, the Conqueror's half-brother, although it is not really known whether by French or English fingers. Certainly, it hung

In this scene from the Bayeux Tapestry, Harold, (second on the left) is shown visiting the aged King Edward the Confessor (centre pic). Both men are attended by henchmen armed with battle-axes.

in the Cathedral at Bayeux for more than 700 years, being removed and exhibited in Paris by Napoleon in 1803-04.

It was returned to Bayeux and stayed there until the beginning of the Second World War, when it was taken to Le Mans for safety. It was, however, removed to Paris by the Germans and was found, at the end of the war, in a cellar under the Louvre.

Now it again hangs at Bayeux, in a special gallery there and a reproduction can be seen in the Victoria and Albert Museum, London.

The total length of the existing 'tapestry' is 21½ metres and it is some 129 centimetres wide. There are decorative borders and a Latin narrative and the 'story' starts with Harold visiting Bosham before proceeding to Normandy and ends with the defeat and flight of the English at the Battle of Hastings.

Eight colours are used on the 'tapestry' and the background material is linen, now brown with age. The colours are not naturalistic. Horses are green, orange or even red and the figures are all highly stylised.

Parts of the Bayeux Tapestry are shown on these two pages. Above, we see the funeral of Edward the Confessor followed — rather strangely, it may seem — by his death. It has been suggested, however, that there is a good reason for the reversal of these episodes.

Placed this way, Edward's death scene, with the translated inscription reading, "Here King Edward addresses his faithful followers in his bed" is next to the scene where Harold is offered the crown. By implication, therefore, Edward was responsible for the crown being offered to Harold although not, of course, for Harold's acceptance of it.

Harold has promised to support William's claim to the throne and his refutation of this promise resulted in his death at the Battle of Hastings and the defeat of the English.

The scene following Harold's coronation (shown above only in part) is the sighting in 1066 of what some people think later came to be known as Halley's Comet.

Since this appears every 76 years and is next due to appear in 1986, the dating, however, is somewhat inaccurate. But a meteor-like object was obviously seen then and afterwards (so we are told) was considered as a portent of Harold's defeat.

Harold's death at the Battle of Hastings is depicted on the Bayeux Tapestry. He is supposed to have been mortally wounded by an arrow in the eye and the 'tapestry' appears to show him attempting to remove the arrow. Whether this was in fact the way he died is now often doubted. As is seen below, a number of men are falling with arrows piercing their eyes while others are being struck down by swords.

It may, therefore, have been a dramatic supposition rather than an actual statement, particularly as the scene showing Harold's death does also show a man being struck down by a sword.

Although Harold was defeated at the Battle of Hastings, having been king for about a year, he and his men fought long and valiantly. They were reputedly outnumbered and also they lacked the horses of the French.

In Harold's defence, it has been maintained that he swore to support William only because he was forced to do so. Even so, he swore on what he later discovered were sacrifical relics and these, at the time, were thought to have tremendous 'religious' power. To break an oath sworn on such relics would have been considered blasphemous so that Harold would, in the opinion of many people, have deserved his defeat and death.

The 'tapestry' ends with the Battle of Hastings but it is thought that the subsequent crowning of William was at one time also shown. This is almost certainly true and it is undoubtedly a pity that a part should now be missing. To have lost only four scenes out of the total of 76, however, is still remarkable when it is considered that it was completed over 900 years ago — and its condition, on the whole, is very good indeed.

However, that may be, as a piece of pictorial history, the Bayeux Tapestry is unsurpassed.

The gentle art of embroidery has given us here, a moving and beautiful portrayal of life as it once was. It is deservedly admired and deservedly protected.

The Conqueror puts England in a book

TWENTY years after his victory at the Battle of Hastings, William the Conqueror called a great gathering of all the principal landowners in England at Sarum, or Salisbury. Mostly they were the Norman barons who had helped their King gain his throne and had received their reward in land.

William's purpose at Sarum was to have all these landowners do homage to him. They were to kneel, place their hands between his and take an oath that they were willing to be faithful to King William, their lord, both within and outside the realm of England.

Feudal System

In this way William, the chief feudal lord in the feudal system, kept the mastery over everyone in his own hands. But at the same time the great barons were all-powerful on their own estates and in their manors, and they took steps to prevent any resistance on the part of their vassals, the poor English villagers. Their chief method was to build strong castles, which dominated not only the people but the landscape.

A vassal had to go through a ceremony of doing homage to his lord as a sign that he accepted the land he occupied on the conditions laid down. The oath required him basically to give military service when asked, and to make three kinds of payments which were called the three "feudal aids."

These were payments of a certain sum towards the dowry of the lord's daughter when she married, another sum when the lord's son became a knight, and yet another sum towards the ransom money if the lord was taken prisoner in war.

The feudal system was a kind of pyramid structure, with the feudal lord, or king, at the top, and each layer below him dependent upon that above. All this could work well only if everyone in the pyramid knew the full sum of his dependents, and if the feudal lord at the top knew everything.

How was this to be achieved? William the Conqueror's novel answer was the celebrated Domesday Book — a book that was to give more detailed information about the country and the people who lived in it and what they owned, than any other statistics that have ever been compiled in any country.

Thorough and Speedy

To conduct the census and write the book, royal commissioners were sent in 1085 to every shire with orders to question upon oath, the sheriffs, barons and people attending the motes or council of the hundred, the priests and reeves or overseers, the bailiffs, and six tenants from every township.

The Anglo-Saxon Chronicle says of William's part in the matter: "So strictly did he cause the survey to be made that there was not a single hide nor a yardland of ground nor — it is shameful to say what he thought no shame to do — was there an ox or cow or a pig passed by, that was not set down in the accounts."

Although it was made thoroughly, the survey was carried out speedily and was completed in 1086. All the information was sorted out and neatly copied on to parchment sheets, the whole being arranged according to shires.

The northernmost counties, Northumberland, Cumberland, Westmorland and Durham, did not appear. Durham and Northumberland had recently been laid waste, and it is probable that they offered so little attraction to the royal commissioners that it was not worth while making a survey there.

Cumberland and Westmorland were not yet under English rule, being still held by the Scottish kings. Lancashire was not yet a separate county.

The whole work — that is, of making the survey and the transcription into a fair copy — was completed in less than eight months, an extraordinary case of hustling worthy of the twentieth century. The English bitterly resented the survey because they believed that it was to be the foundation for the levying of even heavier taxes, and they were not far wrong.

A distinguished modern writer, echoing their resentment, says of the Domesday Book that it "is the surest proof we have of the obedience to which that stark man the Conqueror had reduced Norman, Saxon and Celt from remote Cornish trevs hidden away in woodland creeks of the sea, to the charred townships and wasted dales of Yorkshire."

Norman England

The Domesday Book makes fascinating reading about the state of Norman England. There are, for example, refer-

THE DOMESDAY BOOK

THE Domesday Book is written in Latin, in beautiful handwriting and is in two volumes, of different sizes and appearance. The first volume, 382 pages long, is the larger and records the greater part of England, the smaller containing reports of the three important counties of those days: 'Excessa', 'Norfulk' and 'Sudfulk' recorded on its parchment pages.

The first book measures about 380mm×280mm and the smaller 280mm×200mm. The bindings, however, are modern having been carried out by a member of the staff of the Public Records Office in 1952.

For nearly three hundred years this unique record was housed in an iron bound chest measuring 1010mm×760mm×660mm at Westminster. The volumes and the chest can now be seen by members of the public in the museum of the Public Records Office. (Open 1-4 p.m. weekdays).

The handwriting of the pages has been meticulously done with a quill pen and the photograph of a few paragraphs on the right is about ⅔ actual size. Headings and initial capital letters are executed in red while the rest is in a dark sepia tint.

KEY TO THE CASTLE DEFENCES

Here we illustrate just some of the many defensive measures employed in medieval castles. Similar devices were used to defend walled towns.

ences to Lady Godiva, widow of Leofric, Earl of Mercia, who held lands in Leicester, Warwick and Nottingham. She is the lady who made a famous ride in order to free the people of Coventry from what amounted to slavery. Elsewhere there is the name of Hereward the Wake, who, some say, was Leofric's younger son.

In several places additions have been made in the margins or at the bottom of the page and there are many erasures and alterations. Experts think that the handwriting resembles an Italian script, and it is quite likely that the scribes were Italian. If this is so, then probably Lanfranc, the Italian Archbishop of Canterbury, supervised the book, for with so few scholars in England he was quite likely to use scribes of his own country to do the work.

The name Domesday given to the book is generally regarded as a reference to the Day of Doom or Judgment, the reason being that the survey was noted for its strictness just like that of the Day of Judgment was expected to be.

Some scholars, however, think that Domesday is a corruption of the words *Domus Dei,* the House of God, the name of the building in Winchester where it was kept.

Domesday is the starting point of their history for many English villages and towns and of immeasurable importance to Norman historians.

1. Land surrounding the castle was always cleared of shrubs and trees so no enemy could approach unseen.
2. Guardhouse.
3. Covered walk on top of wall.
4. Stairs to wall walk.
5. Bastion — a tower jutting from wall so defenders could forestall enemy attempts to undermine wall by shooting at them.
6. Outer bailey or courtyard, paved with gutters.
7. Internal stairs to roof of gatehouse.
8. Main gatehouse. Note arrow slits in wall for defenders to shoot through.
9. Portcullis. A huge grill of timber or iron to slide down behind a door to prevent enemy entering.
10. Murder holes. Through these holes above the entrance vestibule missiles or boiling oil could be showered on the heads of the enemy.
11. Barbican or defensive post. This one is also the advanced gatehouse.
12. Main drawbridge for horsemen and carriages.
13. Small drawbridge for pedestrians.
14. Causeway, a totally unprotected approach to the gatehouse.

15. Cutaway, showing counterweight of drawbridge.
16. Gun ports. These were introduced in the fourteenth century after the development of guns in warfare.
17. Outside view of the wooden walk showing timber screen projecting from wall.
18. Diagram showing how balanced drawbridge worked.
19. Waterway connecting outer moat with inner moat.
20. Dungeon. Frequently there was no other entrance than the trap door which prisoners were dropped through.
21. Trap door to dungeon.
22. Machicolations, the slots or firing points are shown by the arrows.
23. Reinforcing buttresses.
24. Garderobe or latrine.
25. Guard room. Cutaway shows an early fireplace.
26. Sally port or postern gate.
27. Over-hung bastion to protect postern gate.
28. Beginning of domestic buildings within castle complex.
29. Cutaway to show rooms in Tower.
30. Machicolations. Masonry version of wooden covered walk with holes in floor to permit boiling oil or missiles to drop on any enemy near foundations.
31. Punishment beam for iron cage to be suspended from holding prisoners, forerunner of the gibbet.
32. Crenellations, sometimes called castellations.
33. Unprotected stairway up to keep entrance.
34. Small drawbridge.
35. Chapel.
36. Keep. The innermost strongpoint. A castle within a castle.
37. Spiral staircase.
38. Well.
39. Inner Bailey.
40. Gatehouse to inner curtain wall protecting inner bailey.
41. Drawbridge.
42. Wooden capped tower — forerunner to machicolations (see 29).
43. Small drawbridge.

Henry, the heavy-strung Monarch

Henry II was determined to rule England fairly but he could not control his own quarrelsome family

FOR centuries the kings of England had found their crowns hard to win and harder still to hold. To be king of England a man had to outwit, outfight and often deceive his rival claimants to the throne, but when Henry II succeeded the troubled Stephen he strode into a reign safe from contenders.

Many of the warring barons who had caused chaos during Stephen's rule, had died; and the rest were sufficiently impressed by their new 21-year-old king who had already inherited the kingdom of Normandy from his brother, and those of Anjou and Maine from his mother, not to contest his royal authority.

Henry was ambitious. He was anxious to extend the power of the crown and to subdue the last traces of rebellion that had so characterised the reign of Stephen. Restless to the point where it was said of him that he made two days march in one and scarcely ever slept, he spent the first months of his rule quelling the rebel strongholds at Scarborough, Hereford and Gloucester.

Yet while some of Henry's predecessors would have had little compunction in putting to death any

Continued on page 158

HENRY II's EMPIRE

ULSTER SCOTLAND

CONNAUGHT

MEATH

LEINSTER

MUNSTER

WALES

ENGLAND

FLANDERS

NORMANDY

ILE DE FRANCE

CHAMPAGNE

BRITTANY

MAINE

BLOIS

ANJOU

BURGUNDY

AQUITAINE

GASCONY

TOULOUSE

HENRY II had already inherited his father's estates before coming to the English throne and marriage to Eleanor in 1152 had brought him all of Aquitaine as her dowry. By 1154 he found himself not only monarch of England but ruler of Normandy, Maine, Anjou and Touraine, virtually half of France. Ruling England gave him an empire that stretched from Scotland to the Pyrenees with complete mastery of the Channel.

Yet even this seems not to have been enough for Henry who spent much of his reign in France scheming and fighting against the French king who, not surprisingly, hated him.

The wonder is that Henry ruled England as well as he did with such vast domains elsewhere. He achieved this by an intelligent use of a civil service he expected to be fair and objective in their administration and in which, with his tremendous energy he took a very personal interest. The French king marvelled at his travels and grumbled that he must fly rather than go by horse or ship.

lands under Henry II's rule

lands acknowledging Henry II as overlord

lands Henry II inherited from his father

lands obtained by Henry II as Eleanor of Aquitaine's dowry

lands belonging to the French king

lands acknowledging the French king as overlord

The King's fatal choice

enemy Henry showed himself shrewder and more statesmanlike. For instance, he spared one of Stephen's friends, William of Ypres, and even allowed him to keep his estates which included the city of Canterbury.

Still Henry's talents for diplomacy and government, greater perhaps than any king's before him, were not enough to endear him to all his subjects. Short and fat, with freckles and ginger hair, he flew easily into rages if crossed. Often, when that happened, he would roll about on the floor, kicking and screaming in fury while his alarmed and terrified henchmen looked on helplessly.

Henry's campaign against the Scots and the Welsh were all successful, and within two years of his accession he was in firm control of his territories in Britain, though the interminable wars in France continued.

Conflict in the Church

What Henry desired, above all, was to restore the full rights of the crown in the administration of the country and it was this that brought him, inevitably, into conflict with the church. Certainly Henry was devout, but his belief in the lay authority of his government was stronger.

This caused the bishops to regard him with an uneasy suspicion, but at first Henry was careful not to provoke any direct confrontation. At issue was whether the church or the crown should be paramount in the dispensation of justice.

Henry's desire to reduce the power of the ecclesiastical courts stemmed largely from reasons of finance. True, he had no wish to see the influence of the church greater than his own, but above all courts could impose fines and confiscate prop-erty; justice was a source of revenue. And Henry's treasury was never large enough.

Henry forced upon the reluctant bishops the appointment of the man who was his Chancellor, his friend, his riding companion and long-time confidante, Thomas Becket, as Archbishop of Canterbury.

Through Becket, believed Henry, he would control the church, but as we shall see in the next part of our story, it was a move doomed to disaster.

Indeed, despite progress in some directions which Henry inspired, his life was touched by restlessness and malevolence that permitted him little personal peace. Through his wife, Eleanor, he was able to control the South-East of France as well as his own territories of Normandy and Anjou but she and his sons all turned against him.

Henry's sons had little time for their over-bearing short-tempered father. He, in turn, ensured that the reins of power remained well beyond their grasp. Titles he bestowed upon them with unstinted generosity, but it was he who continued to decide how the territories over which he 'appointed' them should be governed.

The eldest, and heir to the throne, was known as Henry the Young King; then there was Richard, Duke of Aquitaine, and Geoffrey, Count of Brittany. In 1173 the three of them struck an alliance with the Kings of Scotland and France and went to war against their father.

In an age when it was not unusual for members of ths same family to torture and murder each other, the hand of son was often turned against father and vice versa, but in this case the rebellion soon petered out. The Scots rode into the middle of the English army in a fog and were captured, as was Queen Eleanor who had cast her lot with the rebels.

The young princes made peace with their father, but they were little better than bandits, fighting among themselves and pillaging the country.

Both Geoffrey and the Young King died before they were thirty, the latter of a fever and the former killed by accident in a tournament.

Doubtless Henry took some grim satisfaction in their fate, but his two surviving sons, Richard and John, the youngest remained to haunt Henry to what was to be a sad and far from regal death.

Law reform

Yet before that happened Henry's far-reaching reforms had laid the foundation for many of today's laws and customs. He began to control many of the greedy sheriffs and bailiffs who were lining their pockets at the expense of the poor and strengthened the rights of tenants.

The fact that it is said today that 'possession is nine-tenths of the law' goes back to judgments given by Henry II. And in Henry's time, too, the custom was established of judges being sent around the country to try cases.

This was the beginning of 'professional' judges and clerks, who both represented the crown in the administration of justice and served as Henry's agents for the collection of money.

Henry had the ability to pick the right men to carry out his tasks, though he was despised by his family, he was often admired by those charged to carry out his orders.

Unfortunately in his most important choice — that of Becket as Archbishop of Canterbury, Henry made a dreadful error of judgment. It was to lead him into a battle with the church, and end in murder.

MEDIEVAL MANNERS

THE BIRD CATCHER

THIS picture taken from a decoration on a medieval manuscript serves as a reminder that the fate of small birds in those days was an unenviable one. A few small birds may have been kept in cages for their song, especially by grand ladies, but for most people there was small encouragement to dwell upon the beauties of Nature. More linnets were eaten than were allowed to sing. Larks' tongues were thought a great delicacy on any table. Practically no small bird was safe from the cooking pot at a time when food was hard to come by and monotonous. What the poor did not need to quiet their own hunger could usually be sold to the rich to add variety to their fare. The mechanism of the catcher's net is not too clear but appears to be a sort of butterfly net with a neck able to be closed by a cord which hung down and when pulled would close the opening and so trap unwary birds inside. Obviously the catcher would possess great skill and patience.

Killers in the Cathedral

Henry II had longed for a solution to the struggle between Church and State. But was murder of an old friend the answer?

ONCE they had been firm friends but now King Henry II and his former Chancellor Thomas Becket faced each other as bitter opponents. Dividing them like an unbridgeable moat was the struggle between the Church and the State.

On the one hand Henry wanted to curb the power of the church to try clerics in its own courts for such serious offences as murder, theft and assault. It was a right the Church had exercised since the time of William the Conqueror, but one which Henry now sought to revoke in favour of the State.

In order to achieve that aim Henry had appointed Thomas Archbishop of Canterbury. Surely his friend and companion, the man who owed him his wealth and position, would comply with the King's wishes?

Unfortunately for Henry he made a bad error of judgment, for Thomas fought unswervingly for the rights of the Church. In the face of Henry's arguments Becket responded by emphasising the Church's authority to try its clerics. He ordered one miscreant to be branded for theft and exiled; another, a canon of Lincoln, he ordered to be publicly flogged.

Unable to make any impression on Thomas himself, Henry began to bully and threaten the bishops. He persuaded them to affix their seals to an agreement limiting the authority of the Church, but Becket himself refused to accede to it. Henry sought to enlist the aid of the Pope in his campaign, but the prelate remained studiously neutral.

Quarrels with Becket

Henry's patience, never inexhaustible, began to run out. He felt Becket had betrayed him, and the more his former friend resisted him, the greater became the king's determination to have his way.

In 1164 Henry demanded from Becket the return of money which he claimed he owed from his time as England's Chancellor. Henry had him put on trial and Becket, doubtless feeling that the odds were weighed against him, appealed to the Pope.

This gave Henry the excuse he was looking for. Becket had broken one of the rules which the bishops had agreed — though he himself had not. "Treason," cried Henry.

With the net around Becket closing, the Archbishop left the court and, in disguise, fled to the coast where he embarked to France and exile.

Henry had succeeded in driving his fiercest opponent from the land. Most of the bishops who had little love for their primate and regarded him as an upstart, were not sorry to see him go. They had disliked him as a Chancellor, and they disliked him as Archbishop. He was too showy, too fond of amusement for their taste and they had always resented his appointment.

Yet the absence of the Archbishop, while perhaps solving one problem for Henry, posed another of an equally serious nature. He wanted to have his eldest son crowned at Westminster, but the constitution demanded that the ceremony should be carried out by — the Archbishop of Canterbury.

Henry fretted and schemed. Negotiations between him and the exiled Becket bore fruit, and the Pope forbade anyone other than Becket to carry out the ceremony.

Despite this the Archbishop of York agreed, as much out of hatred for Becket as loyalty to Henry, to perform the ceremony. Henry's triumph however was marred when, having finally patched up his quarrel with Becket, the Archbishop returned to England in 1170.

Not the most tactful or politic of men, Becket's first action on his return was to refuse absolution to the bishops who had taken part in the crowning.

Henry was in his French territory of Normandy when the news reached him. He turned purple with rage, and rising from his chair cried out to his assembled barons:

"Will none of you who sit at this table rid me of this meddlesome priest?"

Four of Henry's knights, hearing his words, took them very much to heart. Reginald FitzUrse, Hugh de Morville, William de Tracey and Richard le Breton rode to the channel and took a boat to England. Swiftly they made the journey to Canterbury and came upon Becket in the cathedral.

Becket was preparing for the evening service as the four armoured knights burst through the doors, drew their swords and struck him down.

MEDIEVAL MANNERS — The Stocks

THE stocks were a popular form of punishment for minor misdeeds from Saxon times and were most widely used during the Middle Ages. They were usually erected in the busiest part of a town or on the village green and consisted of a bench fronted by a long piece of wood, the upper half capable of being raised but when locked to the bottom half providing one of several pairs of holes just wide enough to hold the legs of any victim. No wrongdoer, be they woman, child or churchman could expect to be spared this particular punishment.

Pelting victims with rubbish seems to have been a later refinement, mockery and ridicule being judged humiliation enough in earlier times.

THINKING only to please their master the King, four armoured knights rode post-haste to Canterbury to kill his adversary, Thomas Becket, Archbishop of Canterbury. They arrived three days after Christmas and at first battered at the doors of Becket's house with their battle-axes while monks attending the Archbishop begged him to take sanctuary in the Cathedral. At first he refused but hearing voices singing evening service he said it was his duty to attend. Once inside, his servants wished to bar the doors of the Cathedral but Becket would not allow it saying they were in the house of God and not a fortress. In minutes the knights rushed in crying 'Where is the traitor to his King and country?'. He answered 'I am no traitor but a priest,' and bowed his head in prayer. Roger FitzUrse struck the first blow. Though the monks tried to protect him, one having his arm almost severed, Becket was beaten to the ground and killed.

The whole of Europe was stunned and shocked by the murder, none more so than Henry himself, who maintained that he knew nothing of the intentions of his four men. For three days Henry remained in his room, prostrate with despair and grief.

The murderers were excommunicated by the Pope, and Henry himself was barred from entering a church and ordered to go on a crusade for three years to the Holy Land. While absolved from the crime itself, he submitted to a flogging by monks.

The murder put an end to Henry's ambitions to reform the Church, and he turned to the pacification of Ireland, and to bring the church in Ireland back within the fold of Rome.

He crossed from Milford Haven to Waterford with a large army, and marched on Dublin, forcing the Irish princes to submit

to his rule. By 1175 all his territories were at peace and he was the most powerful king in Europe.

In England he continued to implement reforms in the law, and to dispense justice in the courts, but towards the end of his reign his two surviving sons, Richard and John both rebelled.

By 1189, although Henry was only fifty-six years old, his health had begun to fail, and he was greatly affected by the treachery of his sons.

Richard had made an allegiance with the King of France, and their armies attacked Henry while he was in the town of his birth, Le Mans in the French county of Maine.

Henry galloped through the woods that he knew so well from his childhood, hoping to make his escape. In pursuit, as if chasing a hunted stag, rode his son Richard. Henry was able to reach the castle of Chinon, where he was forced to agree to the demands of the rebels.

When he discovered that his youngest son, John, was also among them he said broken-heartedly: "Let things go as they will. I shall struggle no longer."

Within hours he was dead, leaving his faithless servants to steal everything from the castle, down to the clothes from his corpse. It was a sad end for a king who had achieved much to bring law and order to his lands.

John's rule: recipe for disaster

He was determined to resist all attempts to curb his unlimited power.

IN many ways John was the least attractive of Henry II's sons. Small, dark and not very good-looking, he had also inherited his father's hot temper.

John's elder brother, Richard the Lionheart, did not trust him. When Richard and his other brother Henry had rebelled against their father John had remained loyal.

So when Richard left for the Crusades he made his nephew, Arthur, heir to the throne of England rather than John. But on Richard's death, in 1199, the barons, whose support any future king had to have, preferred John as their monarch.

It was a choice that they were later to regret, and one which was to plunge the nation into civil war. From the start John's rule opened badly.

He made enemies of the Irish princes by making fun of their long beards, and then antagonised the French by marrying Isabella of Angouleme although he was already betrothed to the daughter of a mighty French nobleman, Hugh of Lusignan.

Not surprisingly, his nephew Arthur, frustrated in his claim to the English throne, soon began to make trouble for John, leading a rising in his French territories.

For once John displayed some of the fighting skill and dash of his brother, Richard. He led a 90-mile gallop to the castle of Mirabel, where his 80-year-old grandmother Queen Eleanor was threatened with capture by Arthur's force.

Arthur himself was captured and John had him imprisoned in Rouen castle. The hapless Arthur was never seen alive again, and though his fate is not known for certain, it was widely believed that John had battered him to death with his own hands and thrown his body into the Seine.

Arthur's mysterious fate gave the barons who had originally supported John cause for thought. The one-time claimant to the throne was not the only prisoner to have died in the royal castles, and the barons feared that before long one of their number might also fall victim to the king's cruel power.

John, meanwhile, had as little love for his barons as they for him. He was certain that many were plotting against him — in this he was not far wrong — and he gave instructions to all the commanders of his castles not to obey any order that purported to come from him unless it was accompanied by a secret sign.

The suspicion and mistrust that surrounded John's reign was made worse when the irascible king refused to accept as Archbishop of Canterbury the man whom the Pope himself supported — Stephen Langton.

KING JOHN could not write, so he accepted Magna Carta in 1215 by attaching his seal (shown left) not his signature. At the so-called 'signing' which had been arranged by Archbishop Langton, the knights were eager but John was not. In our picture above are seen the flags of the various knights, held out, as was the custom, by the insertion of staves at the tops. This prevented them drooping and becoming unidentifiable. The effigy on King John's tomb in Worcester Cathedral is shown on the right.

Slowly the quarrel with Rome widened. John himself was not a particularly religious man, but the church was still a powerful influence, and the threat of excommunication was dreaded by rich and poor alike.

Just when it seemed the barons might use the excuse of John's conduct against the church to rebel, John himself suddenly announced that he would accept Langton after all.

Temporarily freed from any threat from that direction John embarked on a long-planned campaign against France, in which Emperor Otto of Germany was his ally.

But the campaign was a disaster, Otto was crushingly defeated and John sailed back to England with nothing to show for all the taxes that had been raised to pay for the war.

What a sad and sorry mess John had made of it all! Suspected of murder; incompetent on the field of battle; disliked by his barons and alienated from the church — it was a catalogue that could lead only to ultimate disaster.

The barons, largely from fear and in part through frustration, decided the time had come to try and curb the king's unlimited powers.

June 15th, 1215, was an historic day in the history of England. At one side of the Thames near Windsor, in a field called Runnymede, waited the bishops and nobles of England.

On the other, looking reluctantly across at that impressive gathering, stood King John and his party. Heralds sounded a fanfare, and the king and his men crossed the river.

Foundation of freedom

He was met by Archbishop Langton and the army commander, Robert Fitzwalter who both stepped forward, bowed and invited the king to be seated at a long table.

Before him they placed a number of parchment documents, and with little good will, the king affixed his seal. Thus was signed Magna Carta, which included in its 63 clauses laws limiting the king's power to raise taxes, the administration of justice in a fairer fashion and the setting up of a court of 25 barons to hear disputes between the king and his subjects.

None of this was to John's liking but, had he refused, his life would doubtless have been in danger. But

even as he affixed the royal seal to the parchment, John had made up his mind not to abide by the charter.

As a result the country was plunged into civil war. The barons sought aid from France, and offered the crown of England to Prince Louis, son of the French king Philip.

Prince Louis landed with a small army in England, but the greater military power lay with John, whose troops included the battle-hardened mercenaries who had fought both in France and on the Crusades.

John was winning the civil war when his forces met with disaster. As they were crossing the river Wash an unusual high tide swept down and engulfed them. In the swirling surf wagons were overturned, soldiers were drowned and all John's baggage as well as much of his treasure, was lost.

It was a set-back from which John himself never recovered. He fell ill, and on October 12th, 1216, died at Newark, not much loved and little mourned.

Another king of England had come and gone, leaving her people little better, and her territories in France lost.

A TOWER OF STRENGTH

KING JOHN was forced to give up the Tower of London in 1215 as a guarantee of observing his Magna Carta promises. When these were broken John's barons invited the French king's son to take up residence while claiming the English crown and there he remained for a whole year. At this time the Tower was more of a residence than the prison it later became but it was a strongly fortified one seen not only as London's defence against foreign invaders but at a bastion against civil rebellion. Only minor repairs and additions were made until Richard I came to the throne and since he went off almost immediately to join a crusade strengthening of the Tower became of first importance. William Longchamp, was appointed to rule in Richard's absence and he planned to extend the Tower's bailey westward and encirle it with a curtain wall, complete with towers and surround it with a wet moat. It was felt such defences would better withstand

New ditch

Bell Tower

Curtain walls protecting west and north of bailey probably built in this position

Extended bailey

Curtain wall known to have been built

White Tower and original bailey

Thames

the improved siege techniques of the day, particularly mining beneath walls and the hurling of huge missiles at them. The Bell Tower was one of the first to be built in England on a circular rather than rectangular plan, for circular walls deflect rather than crumble under a barrage. The new moat was flooded from the Thames which meant only partial effectiveness for it emptied at low tide.

Longchamp was never to complete the refortifications he had undertaken, for Richard's brother Prince John was grabbing more and more power for himself. Longchamp took refuge amid the incomplete defences but finally had to surrender. Once he was king, John himself managed to complete Longchamp's plans before himself being evicted from the Tower of London by his rebellious barons.

War on the borders

EVERYTHING about Edward I smacked of kingship. His appearance alone was imposing. His reddish hair, long hooked nose, gleaming eyes and well-proportioned physique made him look every inch the fine, bold soldier he was.

His father, Henry III, died while Edward was away on the Crusades, but there was never any question of the kind of unseemly squabble over who should inherit the crown of England that had marked the accession of so many of the nation's previous monarchs.

Edward's repute as a warrior and statesman was already established, and England welcomed him back from Palestine warmly as her king.

Justice for all

Soon he was engaged on carrying on the work begun during the reign of his father: strengthening the monarchy and at the same time extending law and justice to all his subjects.

He continued the custom started by de Montfort of summoning 'Parliaments' composed of both nobles and commoners to discuss issues. "What touches all should be approved by all," said Edward, and although these gatherings could hardly be said to represent the advent of democracy they did signal the beginning of the long path that led eventually to the Westminster we know today.

In the interests of resolving some of the injustices that had caused revolt among the monarchy in the past, Edward had agreed to a number of important limitations of the king's powers.

No taxes without consent

One was that no taxes should be raised without the consent of the Lords and Commons. It was an issue that had often provoked unrest, for many a king of England had imposed burdensome taxes in order to fight some foreign war for which his subjects cared little.

Edward also drew up a number of laws governing the administration of law and order in England. Local 'police forces' were set up and it was decreed that hedges and ditches should be at least fifty yards from any main road in order to deprive highway robbers and footpads of places for ambush.

These regulations were enshrined in what was called The Statute of Winchester, and heralded an important step forward. Yet for all Edward's skills in government it was his soldier's instincts that fuelled his greatest ambition.

What he desired, above all, was to see both Wales and Scotland submit to the crown of England. Most of the south and centre of Wales was, in 1276, already ruled by English nobles, but in the north a proud and independent Welsh prince called Llewelyn held sway.

On numerous occasions Edward called upon him to make obeisance to the English crown but Llewelyn stubbornly refused.

So Edward marched into north Wales with a large army, scattering the rebellious Welshmen before him. Many of the Welsh surrendered but Llewelyn escaped and hid in the hills of Snowdonia.

Eventually he too made his peace with Edward, but it was not to last. Six years later Llewelyn invaded England with his forces; Edward lost no time in quelling this impudent incursion. The Welshmen were soon put to flight by the superior numbers ranged against them and Llewelyn himself was surprised by an English patrol and killed.

His brother, David, continued to battle against the English for a time until he, too, was captured and executed.

On the whole, Edward dealt sensibly with the Welsh once the resistance of its fighting men had been crushed. He built mighty castles at such places as Conway, Beaumaris and Caernarvon, and encouraged English people to settle within their shelter.

He imposed English law in Wales, but at the same time he took care to offer a number of the more important administrative posts to Welshmen.

By 1284 all Wales was under Engl-

THE CROW

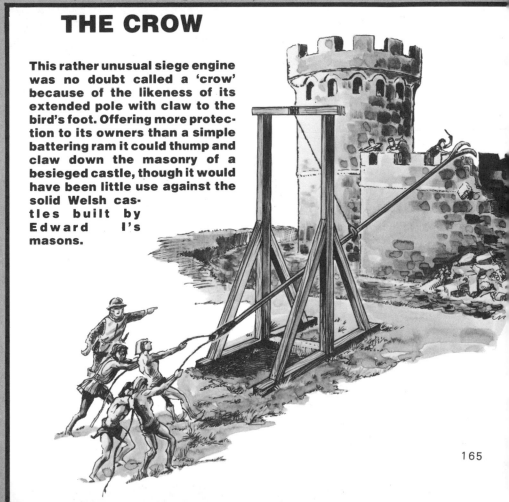

This rather unusual siege engine was no doubt called a 'crow' because of the likeness of its extended pole with claw to the bird's foot. Offering more protection to its owners than a simple battering ram it could thump and claw down the masonry of a besieged castle, though it would have been little use against the solid Welsh castles built by Edward I's masons.

165

ish rule and two years later Edward saw his chance of bringing the Scots to heel as well. The Scottish King, Alexander, died, and soon afterwards so did his granddaughter and only direct heir to the throne.

The Scots Council feared that the rival claimants for the vacant crown would thrust Scotland into civil war, and to avoid that they asked Edward to decide on who should succeed.

John Balliol

Edward agreed, but only on condition that he himself became the overlord of Scotland. The man he picked was John Balliol, but the Scots nobles were soon encouraging Balliol to rebel and make an alliance with England's enemy, France.

Once more Edward went to war and earned himself the title of 'Hammer of the Scots''. At Dunbar, in 1296, he inflicted a heavy defeat upon them; Balliol resigned and Edward took up the title of King of Scotland himself.

But assuming a title and appointing a governor were simply not enough. English government of Scotland was no more than a bubble, and it burst when a tough and ruthless Scots knight, Sir William Wallace, led an army of fanatical followers into Northumberland.

Wallace conducted a ferocious guerilla war until the English King finally managed to defeat him in 1303.

Betrayal

Even then Wallace managed to escape but he was later betrayed and captured. He was shown no mercy; he was hanged, drawn and quartered, yet the Scots were unbowed.

Within three years yet another rebellion erupted, led this time by Robert Bruce. By now Edward was an old man of nearly seventy; he was tired and he knew that his ambition to unite Britain must remain, for him, a dream.

Wearily he led his troops into what was his last battle, and he died on the way to putting down a rebellion. His body was carried back from the north to Westminster without final victory won.

But in sound government and justice, he left a lasting triumph.

Once Edward I had repulsed the Welsh incursions he set about making sure there would be no repetition by ringing in the Welsh with castles so sturdy that many of them still stand today. But Edward was clever enough to ensure that many of his administrators who lived in the castles were Welsh and not English.

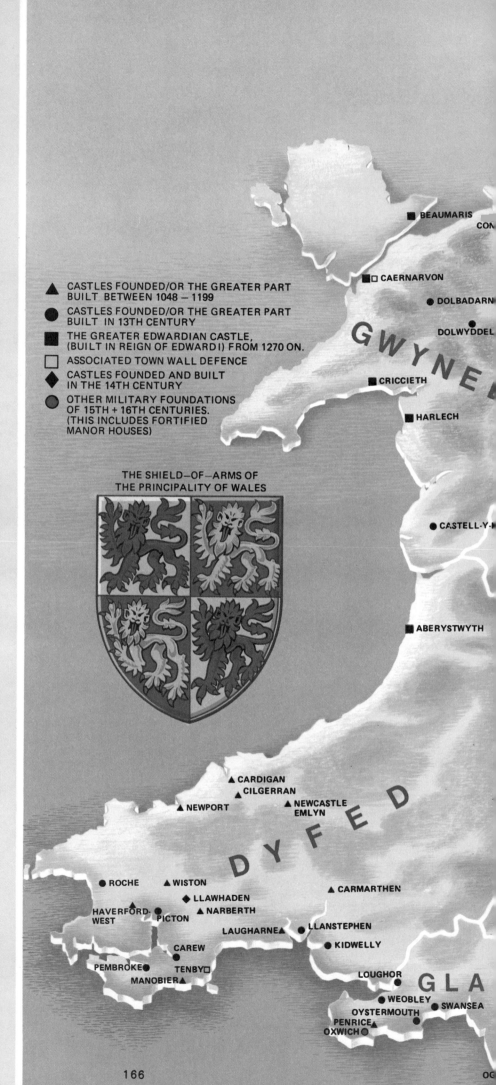

CASTLES FOUNDED/OR THE GREATER PART BUILT BETWEEN 1048 – 1199

CASTLES FOUNDED/OR THE GREATER PART BUILT IN 13TH CENTURY

THE GREATER EDWARDIAN CASTLE, (BUILT IN REIGN OF EDWARD I) FROM 1270 ON.

ASSOCIATED TOWN WALL DEFENCE

CASTLES FOUNDED AND BUILT IN THE 14TH CENTURY

OTHER MILITARY FOUNDATIONS OF 15TH + 16TH CENTURIES. (THIS INCLUDES FORTIFIED MANOR HOUSES)

THE SHIELD—OF—ARMS OF THE PRINCIPALITY OF WALES

BEAUMARIS
CON
CAERNARVON
DOLBADARN
GWYNE
DOLWYDDEL
CRICCIETH
HARLECH
CASTELL-Y-
ABERYSTWYTH

CARDIGAN
CILGERRAN
NEWPORT
NEWCASTLE EMLYN
DYFED
ROCHE
WISTON
CARMARTHEN
LLAWHADEN
HAVERFORD-WEST
PICTON
NARBERTH
LAUGHARNE
LLANSTEPHEN
CAREW
KIDWELLY
PEMBROKE
TENBY
LOUGHOR
MANOBIER
GLA
WEOBLEY
SWANSEA
OYSTERMOUTH
PENRICE
OXWICH

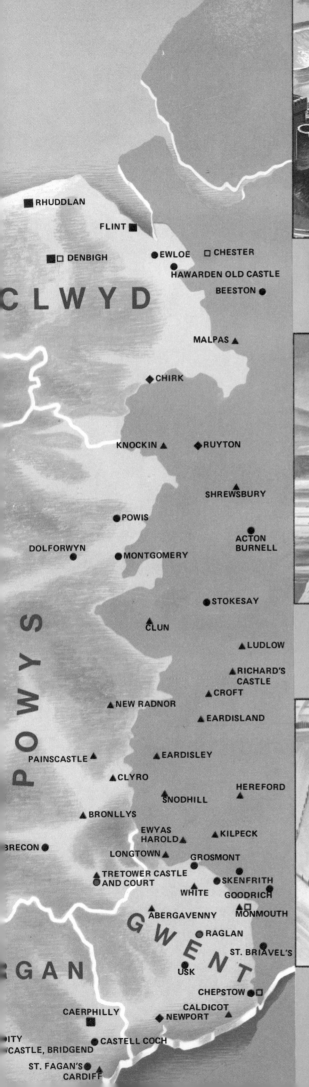

RHUDDLAN

FLINT

DENBIGH

EWLOE

CHESTER

HAWARDEN OLD CASTLE

BEESTON

C L W Y D

MALPAS

CHIRK

KNOCKIN

RUYTON

SHREWSBURY

POWIS

ACTON BURNELL

DOLFORWYN

MONTGOMERY

P O W Y S

STOKESAY

CLUN

LUDLOW

RICHARD'S CASTLE

CROFT

NEW RADNOR

EARDISLAND

PAINSCASTLE

EARDISLEY

CLYRO

HEREFORD

SNODHILL

BRONLLYS

EWYAS HAROLD

KILPECK

BRECON

LONGTOWN

GROSMONT

TRETOWER CASTLE AND COURT

SKENFRITH

WHITE

GOODRICH

ABERGAVENNY

MONMOUTH

G W E N T

RAGLAN

ST. BRIAVEL'S

USK

CHEPSTOW

CALDICOT

CAERPHILLY

NEWPORT

CASTELL COCH

...ITY

CASTLE, BRIDGEND

ST. FAGAN'S

CARDIFF

...EGAN

CONWAY CASTLE

Though Conway Castle covers only a small area and has a simple plan, it presents the most impressive sight of all Edward I's castles in North Wales. This is achieved by the massive round towers, four on the north and four on the south. The castle was built on the most impregnable site in the area, previously occupied by monks, and dominating the river.

HARLECH CASTLE

Scarcely less imposing than Conway is Harlech Castle, built on an imposing crag overlooking the coast and one of the finest existing examples of concentric defences with two complete circular walls one inside the other surrounding a compact mass of a building with four great towers and a gatehouse. It was besieged unsuccessfully by Welsh rebels in 1294.

BEAUMARIS CASTLE

The year after the fruitless siege of Harlech, work began on Beaumaris, the last castle Edward I was to build in North Wales. It stands on the Menai Strait where it could protect landings, and was again built on a concentric plan with six huge towers and two gatehouses. This is the Welsh castle with the most peaceful history and the building was never completed.

Sar•
BAHAMAS
12 Octob
SAN
CUBA
HISPAN
Caribbea

Pacific Ocean

Journey to a New Land

L and ho!'' came the excited cry. It was a cry that some of the sailors had never expected to hear again. Everyone stopped work and peered in the direction indicated by the lookout. Yes, there it was. Land.

Christopher Columbus, who was in charge of the expedition, ordered the ships to lay at anchor whilst he took a party ashore. As he stepped onto the beach he sank to his knees to thank God for a safe voyage and the realisation of his dreams.

Columbus was one of the few people of the time who believed that the world was round. ''It should be possible,'' he said, ''to sail west to China.''

Many laughed at this ludicrous suggestion. ''Everyone knows the Earth is flat,'' they cried, ''If you sail too far west you will topple over the edge into unseen realms where hideous monsters will tear you limb from limb.''

But Columbus was sure he was right. All the learning he had gained at the high school at Pavia, near Genoa where he was born in 1451, convinced him. He had listened to the stories of seamen and their travels to distant lands. He had possibly heard of Leif Ericcson the Viking and his voyage to a strange new land in the west nearly 500 years earlier.

King John II of Portugal, whom Columbus first approached for money for the great adventure, turned down the idea as being too expensive.

But the crafty king had some ideas of his own. He managed to obtain details of the intended voyage and he dispatched his own vessel on the journey. His sailors ventured well beyond the Cape Verde Islands but when a storm arose they scuttled back to Portugal.

Columbus was so disgusted by the king's intrigue that he left Lisbon and went to Spain for help. Eventually his story reached the ears of Mendoza, Archbishop of Toledo, who was so impressed by the young man's idea that he arranged for Columbus to be granted an audience before King Ferdinand and Queen Isabella.

King Ferdinand referred the problem to a special council of the leading scholars, geographers, and scientists of the day which turned the idea down.

Columbus decided to try elsewhere. He sent his brother Bartholomew to England to seek Henry VII's assistance. Unfortunately, Bartholomew was captured by pirates and he never completed his journey until several years later. By this time the Spanish King and Queen had decided to sponsor Columbus's trip.

On 3rd August, 1492 three wooden vessels, the *Santa Maria,* the *Pinta,* and the *Nina,* with a total of about 90 men on board set sail from Palos at the start of their epic voyage. Nine days later they dropped anchor in the

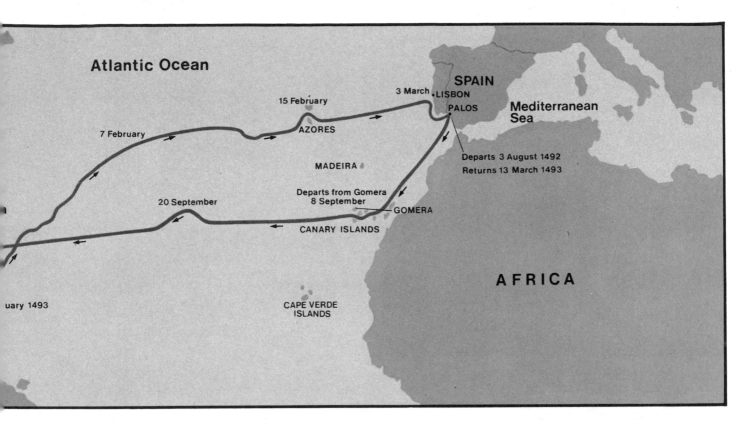

Atlantic Ocean

SPAIN

3 March · LISBON
PALOS

Mediterranean Sea

15 February

AZORES

7 February

MADEIRA

Departs 3 August 1492
Returns 13 March 1493

20 September

Departs from Gomera
8 September

GOMERA

CANARY ISLANDS

AFRICA

uary 1493

CAPE VERDE ISLANDS

Above: An engraving of Columbus.

Right: Columbus carried bells, brass basins, scissors, coins, knives, beads, needles, pins, mirrors, bonnets and coloured cloth to trade with the tribes he expected to find. But the natives had no gold to barter in exchange.

Canary Islands, where they stayed for almost a month refitting the vessels for their long voyage. Much had to be done before the ships were suitable for the journey that Columbus envisaged.

On 6th September they set sail from the Canaries. After sailing westwards for several weeks there was no sign of land and the men became restless. No-one had dared sail this far from land before and they were frightened for their lives.

Feelings eventually reached such a pitch that Columbus was forced to appeal to the men. "If we have not sighted land within three days I promise that we shall turn around and sail back home," he said. Although they did not like the idea the men agreed. Two days later they still had not sighted land and everyone was about to prepare for the return voyage when, five weeks after they had left the Canaries, there came the cry of "Land ho" from the lookout.

When Columbus landed the natives were so in awe of this strange white man with silvery-white hair that they

Left: The first pictorial representation of Columbus's expedition. The original is a woodcut made in Spain the year after Columbus returned from his first voyage.
(Photo: Mansell Collection)

Gold, God and Cathay

COLUMBUS did not set off on his dangerous voyage to prove that the world was round. Although most common people of this time still probably believed in a flat Earth, most mariners and geographers realized that the world was probably a sphere.

Marco Polo had told of the wealth, power and sheer size of the East, of the magnificence of the court of Kublai Khan, the Mongol Emperor. Columbus realized that if the world were truly a sphere, the magical lands of Cathay (China) could be reached by sailing west, as easily as by the long overland journey eastwards.

Different world

It is difficult now, with modern maps, to appreciate how different and how small the world looked to medieval Europeans.

No one knew how far Africa stretched to the south, or how far Asia extended to the east. China and India were thought to be more or less the same place. And, of course, America and Australia were entirely unknown. To the west stretched untold miles of sea. The farthest known place was the Azores. This was the mariners' last land.

As well as the new-found belief that the world was round, one other

thought he and his men were gods. Columbus took possession of the island and named it San Salvador.

After exploring the area, he sailed farther south-west, first to what is now called Cuba, and then to Hispaniola, where he established a small colony. So certain was he that Cuba was mainland China and Hispaniola was Japan that he stuck to this belief throughout his life despite mounting evidence to the contrary.

Columbus returned to Spain in March, 1493 to acclaim and honours. He was made Admiral of the 'Ocean Seas' and Viceroy of the new lands. Six months later he set sail again, this time with a much larger fleet, and reached Puerto Rico and Jamaica.

Still convinced that he could find the fabled Cathay of Marco Polo, Columbus made two more voyages, in 1498 and 1502, touching the mainland of South America on the second.

Without knowing it, Columbus discovered a whole new continent whose existence had not even been suspected. How ironic that the New World he discovered was not named after him but after Amerigo Vespucci, a Florentine navigator who described his travels to Central America in 1499 and 1501.

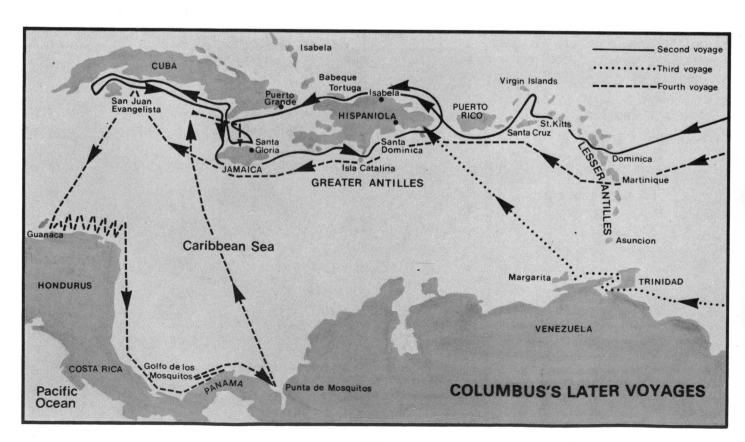

COLUMBUS'S LATER VOYAGES

new thing made Columbus's voyage possible. This was the rediscovery of the compass in the fourteenth century. Before this, to venture out of sight of land was to risk death, because there was then no knowing where you were or which way to navigate. But with the magical needle pointing ever northwards, deep-sea voyages became that little less daunting.

So it was the compass and the new geography that made Columbus's voyage possible.

But it was gold and religion that were the real driving forces behind the expedition. It was these that made Columbus and hard-headed sailors like the brothers Pinzon, who captained the *Pinta* and *Nina* to set out on the seemingly mad-cap scheme.

We do not know why Columbus should imagine that the heirs to Kublai Khan — described by Marco Polo as 'the greatest Lord that is now in the world or who has ever been' — should hand over their gold and their lands for the worthless beads and trinkets that Columbus carried, but this seems not to have worried either Columbus or the King and Queen of Spain who were footing the bill.

And Columbus — or at least those that followed him — was also going to convert the peoples of the New World to Christianity; he would save the millions of Asians from eternal damnation.

Moreover, he was going to use untold quantities of gold he would find to finance an army to recapture Jerusalem from the Saracens — something that centuries of Crusades had failed to do.

Above: Columbus was brought back to Spain in fetters in 1500 to answer charges of mismanagement.

Left: Raising the Cross on San Salvador. Columbus claimed all the lands he discovered in the names of the King and Queen of Spain.
(Photo: Mansell Collection)

Admiral of the Ocean Seas brought home in fetters

It took the Santa Maria, Pinta **and** Nina **just 33 days to sail from the Canaries to San Salvador. They met no storms and had favourable winds for most of the journey. Columbus and his captains were at one time afraid that they would stick fast in the vast seaweed beds of the Sargasso Sea — then much bigger than they are now — but the three small ships floated over the yellowish mass without difficulty.**

Columbus had calculated that Japan was 2,400 nautical miles from the Canaries, China 3,550 miles. He had travelled 3,066 miles when he reached San Salvador. Although he was in reality still 8,000 miles from Japan, it seemed that his calculations were right. Hispaniola was **Japan, Cuba** was **mainland China, even though there was no sign of Marco Polo's Quinsay — a city built of gold — and the natives went naked and lived in poor thatched huts.**

In all of his four trips to the New World, Columbus never found the gold he was looking for. He took to enslaving the natives to provide some revenue to compensate for the lack of gold. But his brutality and the Spaniards' lust of gold led to his being twice charged with mismanagement. On the second occasion he was brought back to Spain in irons.

But his eloquent pleas moved the King and Queen to pity. Queen Isabella wept. Columbus returned to the New World.

Throughout his life, Columbus remained convinced that he had found Cathay. On his second voyage, he turned back just before he reached the western tip of Cuba — which would have shown it to be an island — convinced it was mainland China. On his third voyage he sailed to Venezuela but thought South America to be an island. On his fourth voyage, he sailed for months up and down the coast of Central America looking in vain for the Strait of Malacca (between Malaysia and Indonesia) which lead from the China Sea to India and which were described by Marco Polo.

Of course, he never found them. He realized he had found a whole new continent.

When his worm-ridden ships finally fell to pieces in Jamaica, Columbus was a broken man. He waited a year before a ship came to take him back to Spain in 1504. On May 19, 1506 he died — still believing he had found Cathay.

SOME 20,000 years ago, the ancestors of today's American Indians began to migrate from Asia across the Bering Strait which is now a narrow stretch of sea but was then virtually a land bridge. These wandering bands of nomads peopled North, Central and South America down the centuries, giving rise to many widely differing civilisations.

The most advanced of these civilisations flourished in Central and South America. The mighty monuments of the Toltecs and the Mayas which now lie decaying in jungles and on plains are memorials to the greatness of these Central American peoples. Yet we know far more about the Aztecs who came after them because they — like the Incas of Peru — had the misfortune to come up against and be conquered by the invading Spanish. That thrilling, tragic, murderous story will be told on later pages. But now the spotlight is on the Aztecs' history and their way of life.

The Rise of the Aztecs

A poor, backward people entered the beautiful Valley of Mexico in the thirteenth century. They had called themselves *Azteca*, but by now they had restyled themselves *Mexica*, as they tried to settle down in a land where more powerful and advanced tribes persecuted them. In 1325 (it is thought), the Mexica settled on a wretched group of islands in Lake Texcoco, founding the twin towns of Mexico-Tenochtitlan and Mexico-Tlatelolco. The first of these was destined to become one of the greatest cities on Earth, as grand as any European capital, and later to be destroyed by the Spaniards who built Mexico City on its ruins.

In a single century from the founding of the twin cities, the Aztecs, once despised, became all-powerful, so much so that they dominated most of central and southern Mexico. They did it by brilliance in war, by ruthlessness, and by clever alliances. The other city states of the lake succumbed one by one to the interlopers, as Tenochtitlan soared upwards and expanded swiftly and grandly.

In the short space of 300 years, a great civilisation developed, flourished and died in Central America. Yet it has left its mark on modern-day Mexico, the land of

The Mighty Aztecs

Now the Mexica, remembering their legendary home of Aztlan, began calling themselves Aztecs again. And they invented a heroic past history (as the Romans did) to fit their new-found greatness. Unfortunately, they also trapped themselves with a terrifying religion.

Most Aztecs lived simple peasant lives, the men working on the fields, the women grinding corn and making clothing. All enjoyed three things whose Aztec names are still used by us: tomatoes, chilli and chocolate, the last being drunk not eaten.

Above: The partly-overgrown ruins of a pyramid at the Toltec-Maya city of Chichen Itza in Yucatan.
Photo: Mansell Collection.

Aztec society was not so very different from a European one at the time, with a king, nobility and merchants, skilled craftsmen, ordinary workers and slaves, who, of course, had fewer rights even than European serfs. Clans of workers owned communal land.

Canals

Every Aztec must have tried to visit the capital at least once in his life. Built on the swampy shallows on the south-west of the lake, the swampland was soon reclaimed and the island made bigger. There was an aquaduct 5 kilometres long bringing in fresh water, and, as in Venice, there were canals everywhere. Three causeways connected the city with the mainland, all having drawbridges in case of attack.

The city centre was breathtaking, a huge plaza, with pyramids crowned by

Left: a map of Central America indicating the extent of the Mayan empire which was at its peak from about A.D. 300-900, and the Aztec empire which reached its zenith in the 15th and early 16th centuries.

GULF OF MEXICO

Mexico City (Tenochtitlan)

AZTEC

MAYA

PACIFIC OCEAN

Above: An exquisite turquoise mosaic pendant, probably owned by an Aztec nobleman.

Right: An Aztec warrior's feather-trimmed shield. The mosaic shows a prairie wolf.

Above: An example of Aztec stone-carving. Temples and other important buildings were adorned with such figures.

Right: A bronze statue of one of the Aztec gods.

Above: An elaborately-adorned head-dress.

Below: A sacrificial knife with blade of volcanic stone and mosaic handle carved in the shape of a crouching warrior. The Aztecs knew nothing of steel and iron.

temples, while below were markets and administrative offices. On view also was a rack containing many thousands of skulls. We shall return to them in the section on religion.

As in ancient Egypt, schools were run by priests and again, like Egypt, the Aztecs used a picture writing, so they could keep accurate records. Aztec architecture was on the grand scale so, as well as skilled architects, a huge workforce was needed, along with fine craftsmen. The Aztecs worked in gold, bronze and copper as well as stone, their pottery and jewellery reflecting the influence of Mixtec culture. The Aztecs conquered the Mixtecs, a neighbouring Central American people, in the 15th century.

The Army

Naturally, in such an aggressive race, soldiers were admired above all. Like other Indians, the Aztecs fought with bows and arrows, though they also wielded jagged-edged swords to great effect.

Military service was compulsory. Soldiers were well enough protected until Europeans came with firearms, which made cane or cotton-padded armour utterly useless.

Once the Aztecs had conquered a tribe, the traders moved in. They were key figures in the Aztec Empire, carrying

Below: Scene from an ancient Mixtec manuscript, painted on deerskin, showing the creation of the Mixtec people.
Photo: Mansell Collection.

out a strenuous occupation as the wheel was unknown. No Indian tribe possessed the wheel.

Conquered peoples had to send goods to Tenochtitlan or its sister city, Tlatelolco, which meant that both cities, especially the capital, got richer and richer. Money was not used, which meant that taxes were paid for in goods.

The Aztecs were tough, proud, determined, yet kindly by nature, who loved laughter, but looked at life seriously. Unfortunately, their religion cast a giant shadow over them.

Human sacrifice

The shadow was human sacrifice on a colossal scale. Other Mexican peoples offered up sacrifices: the Aztecs finally made it a way of life.

Some of the gods were conventional enough. There was Tezcatlipoca, the wind-god, and Tlaloc, the rain-god. The greatly-revered Quetzalcoatl was the champion of learning and of the priests. According to legend, he had sailed away over the ocean but would one day return to his people. The Spaniards, as we shall see later, were to take advantage of this belief.

And there was the terrible Sun-god, who was also god of war, Huitzilopochtli, who fought daily against the dark night. The Aztecs came to believe that unless they made sacrifices to him of human blood and hearts, the Sun would not rise.

So it came about that the state needed daily victims — found from captives or slaves — to be fed to the ever-hungry god. Their hearts were torn out by the priests and their heads were then impaled on a nightmarish rack. The sacrificial priests dripped and reeked of blood.

As if these horrors were not enough, other captives were shot with arrows so that their blood might fertilise the earth, and still more burned alive to give thanks for the harvest.

Ordinary people, too, would buy a slave — man or woman — to sacrifice if they needed divine help. The need for sacrificial victims was unending. It was a black day when the god Quetzalcoatl, who had tried to ban sacrifices, had sailed away from his people.

The Fatal Flaw

The practical consequences of this constant slaughter — and it must be stressed that the Aztecs really believed that their salvation depended upon it — was that when the Spaniards arrived in 1519, they found it easy to get allies to side with them against their terrible persecutors.

It is a grim story and a tragic one, for the Aztecs created a remarkable civilisation and a majestic capital for their state. Yet because of their beliefs, they became brutal and cruel in the extreme and so sowed the seeds of their own destruction.

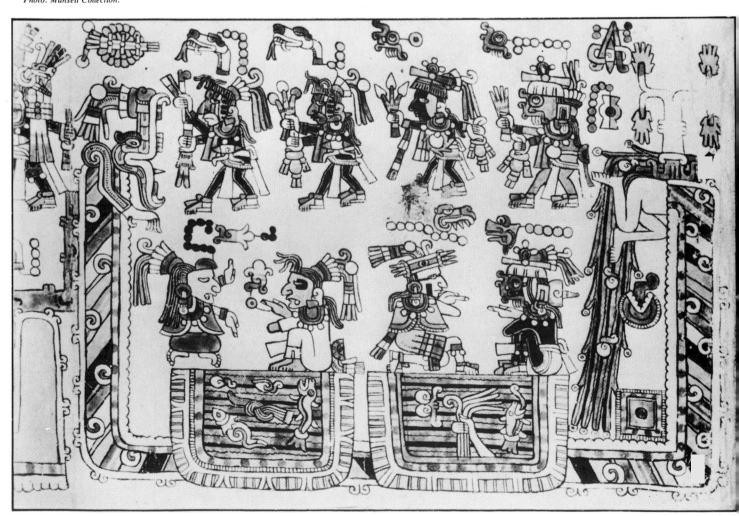

Seeking adventure and riches, a small army of Spanish conquistadors stumbled upon a mighty civilisation in Central America. It was a fateful encounter for it signalled . . .

The Fall of the Aztec Empire

THE Spanish fleet sailed from Cuba on November 18, 1518. Aboard the 11 ships were 508 soldiers, some 100 sailors, 16 horses and 14 cannon, not a particularly strong force, except against an enemy who had never seen horses or cannon.

It was just 26 years since Christopher Columbus had made his historic landfall on an island in the Bahamas, years that had seen the virtual destruction of the original inhabitants of the West Indies. They had been killed, enslaved, decimated by diseases unknown to them, or had died of despair.

Now the prize was a greater one — the exploration and conquest of the land we know as Mexico. The few Spaniards who had seen it had been amazed by the vast cities of stone of the Mayas, whose civilisation was now in decline. None had yet seen the Aztec Empire and its fabulous capital on Lake Tezcoco.

On the previous pages that empire was described, along with the advanced way of life of its people, who yet were cursed by a nightmare religion which demanded constant human sacrifices to ensure that the sun arose each morning.

None of this was known as yet to the Spanish commander, Hernando Cortés. He had been born in Spain in 1485 into a noble family, and had sailed to the West Indies in 1504 in search of adventure. Later, after an expedition to the mainland in 1516 had

Above: Hernando Cortés, the Spanish adventurer who led his conquistadors to the land of the Aztecs.

failed, the governor of Cuba, Diego Velázquez, gave Cortés command of a new expedition to explore Mexico.

The men that Cortés, and other Spanish commanders of that time, led were iron-hard adventurers known as *conquistadors,* meaning conquerors, or ruthless adventurers. Willing to follow only the most able leaders, their objectives were gold and other treasure, and the conversion of the heathens to Christianity.

In the Aztec capital Tenochtitlan, now Mexico City, the Emperor Moctezuma (Montezuma) heard of the bearded white intruders, who had landed down the coast in Cozumel. Unbeknown to Cortés and his men, the Spaniards had a striking piece of luck from the start. One of the great Aztec gods, the kindly Quetzalcoatl, bearded and light-skinned, had, as we saw last week, left his people and gone to the east. That meant over the ocean, or so many Aztecs believed. He had promised he would return, but it could only be in certain years — and 1519 was one of those years. So Moctezuma half believed that Quetzacoatl had returned as Cortés. Nothing else can explain his attitude to the strangers and his indecisiveness in dealing them when he could have wiped them out.

It is probable that Cortés knew something of this not long after

Left: Quetzalcoatl, the Aztec god of learning who was driven out of Mexico by the warlike god Huitzilopochtli. The Aztecs thought Cortés was Quetzalcoatl returning to claim his lost empire.

landing, for he was lucky enough to be given a slave girl who knew the Aztec language and traditions. 'The Lady Marina' the Spaniards were soon to be calling her, for she was invaluable to them and greatly honoured.

Yet how could a tiny army conquer a people of several million, perhaps as much as 15 million? Steel breastplates, horses and cannon cannot explain it. The answers must be the character of Cortés, his genius for diplomacy, and the Aztecs' half-belief that he was a god.

Cortés knew he must fight only when it was unavoidable. He must make alliances whenever possible among the Aztecs' subject peoples. And when emissaries from Moctezuma came, he must convince them that he was their friend. Added to all this, he had to cope with enemies in Cuba, where the Governor wanted all the glory for himself.

Such was Cortés's genius that only once on the march to the capital was he forced to fight. This was against the Tlaxcalans, who refused to be frightened of cannon and mounting casualties, and fought the Spaniards for many days, until deciding that such

Above: The central square of Tenochtitlan, the Aztec city described by the Spanish conquistadors as "the most beautiful city in the world". Likened to Venice, it had a system of canals around it, and among the many impressive buildings were the teocallis, or pyramids which were created as temples to the gods.

enemies would make good friends.

Nearer the Aztec capital, the Spaniards and their new allies camped at Cholula, where the Lady Marina heard of a plot to massacre Cortés and his men. Promptly, they massacred the Cholulans, Cortés diplomatically sending messages to Moctezuma saying that, of course, he knew the Emperor had nothing to do with the plot against him. Then he marched on.

The Spaniards marvelled greatly when they saw Tenochtitlan and the other cities around Lake Tezcoco. They admired everything except the terrible evidence of endless sacrifices. They were feasted, but life went on in the capital as before. Something had to be done, especially when news reached Cortés that his small garrison on the coast at Vera Cruz had been wiped out. So he decided to arrest the Emperor! His hostage was well treated

and allowed to govern his kingdom, but he was a prisoner.

Meanwhile the Spaniards busily melted down most of the golden ornaments they had been given by Moctezuma, putting aside a fifth for the King of Spain and a fifth for Cortés. They had conquered Mexico with an army reduced to 400, plus their allies, yet all Moctezuma had to do was order their destruction. Why did he not? Clearly, he was stunned and off-balance.

Early in 1520, a Spanish force landed at Vera Cruz. It was 1,400 strong and had been sent by the jealous governor of Cuba to depose Cortés. News came of the landing just as Cortés had risked an uprising by laying waste the Aztecs' main sacrificial temple and having Mass said there, but he did not hesitate. Leaving Pedro de Alvarado in charge in the city, he marched out with 250 Spaniards and 2,000 allied troops. They defeated the rival Spanish force, most of which promptly joined Cortés and marched back to the capital with him.

He was not a moment too soon, for Alvarado had lost control of the city. Cortés found that a rival emperor had been elected by the Aztecs' in place of Moctezuma. Cortés had him placed on the battlements of the Spaniards' stronghold to try and calm his people. Unfortunately a stone hit him, and three days later, the new emperor was dead.

Cortés ordered a night retreat, recalled by the Spaniards as the *Noche Triste* — the Night of Sorrow. The ordeal was made worse because the Spaniards took as much booty as they could carry with them, as they slowly fought their way along the causeways. More than 800 perished, from wounds, from drowning, or on sacrificial altars after being captured.

It was a full year before the Spaniards and their allies were able to mount an attack again on Tenochtitlan, complete with a specially built fleet. The siege lasted 85 days, the Aztecs only despairing when fresh water and food ran out.

Tenochtitlan fell on August 13, 1521, and with it fell the Aztec Empire, which for all the ferocity of its religion, was a great and glorious one. Cortés the conqueror was made governor of New Spain, as Mexico was now called, but his career steadily declined as lesser men gained power in Spain and the New World. He died in near obscurity near Seville in 1540.

The First Men Around the World

THE small fleet hoisted sail, fired its guns in farewell to the ctizens of Seville, and headed down the Guadalquivir River to the sea. It was August 10, 1519, and the five Spanish vessels, the *Trinidad, San Antonio, Victoria, Santiago* and *Concepcion,* were setting out on a voyage unequalled in history, which was to be both triumphant and tragic.

In command was a Portuguese soldier turned sailor, Ferdinand Magellan, whose mission was daring beyond belief. He was determined to triumph where Columbus had failed. He would find the sea route westwards to the Indies —

A portrait of Magellan from an old engraving.

Photo: The Mansell Collection

India, Malaysia and Indonesia in today's terms — that Columbus had wrongly thought he had found when he reached America.

Magellan, born in about 1480, had already sailed eastwards to the Indies and had proved a valiant fighter and leader of men. Surviving fierce battles and shipwreck, he came home to fame and fortune, only to be wrongly accused later of trading with Portugal's enemies in Morocco. Though cleared of the charge, he was not trusted by Portugal's vindictive king, who virtually told him to go and seek his fortune abroad. So, bitterly hurt, Magellan went to Spain and brooded on his great plan.

By now, the Pacific had been seen from Panama by the Spaniard Balgoa (1513). It was first called the South Sea and, so a mathematician friend told Magellan, could not be more than 2,000 miles across. In the event, it was found to be 13,000 miles.

Magellan was determined to find a passage to the new ocean and sail across it. The Spaniards were interested, not least because of a series of rulings by a Pope. To prevent great Catholic powers, Spain and Portugal, from quarrelling, he

The ruler of Mactan was a pagan whose name was Lapulapu. Because of his men's defeat of Magellan, a coin was struck (see above). It celebrates the first defeat of Europeans by Filipinos and so — in a sense — Magellan's death.

divided up the newly discovered lands between them, which basically gave the Indies and Brazil to Portugal and the rest of the Americas to Spain.

Magellan's mathematician reckoned, as he hopefully studied latitudes on his inaccurate maps, that the much coveted Spice Islands, or Moluccas (now part of Indonesia), were in the Spanish sphere of influence. Magellan was clearly the man to settle the matter.

He was given five ships which needed weeks of work to make them seaworthy, while the job of collecting crews proved just as hard. Apart from Spaniards, Greeks, Italians, Dutch, Africans, some Malays captured on previous expeditions, and an Englishman were signed up, along with too many Portuguese for the jealous Spaniards' liking. Three ships were commanded by Spaniards who resented Magellan's authority. It was a recipe for trouble.

Mutiny

All went well enough at first, but there was growing tension between Magellan and his Spanish captains. The fleet survived terrifying tempests in the Atlantic, then the first mutiny broke out aboard the *San Antonio.* Confronting her captain and grabbing his jacket, Magellan roared: "You are my prisoner." The captain, Juan de Cartagena, shouted for help but none came. Magellan had won the first round.

They reached the Brazil coast on November 29 and sailed south. Off southern Argentina another, more serious, mutiny erupted, many officers and men demanding to sail for home. Quick thinking by Magellan and the ruthless execution of ringleaders ended the crisis and, by pardoning the ordinary sailors who took part, he made them utterly loyal to him. It was just as well, for terrible times lay ahead.

The southern winter had now set in. Magellan made a camp at Port St. Julian and the *Santiago* was sent to explore southwards. She was shipwrecked with the loss of only one man, and the rest managed to rejoin the main fleet after an epic overland journey.

Spring came and they sailed south once again, reaching an inlet that was to be the start of their route to the Pacific. There was not the slightest proof that it was: it was a place of screaming gales and terrible snow-capped mountains.

Risking everything on a lie, Magellan made his men believe that this was indeed the passage they sought and sent two ships ahead. They came back with flags flying and guns firing. They had found the channel, the passage now known as Magellan's Strait. And after many false turns and dead ends, they reached the longed for South Sea, which Magellan was to call the Pacific because of its calmer waters and winds.

They sailed into the Pacific on November 28, 1520, beginning a 98-day epic across 13,000 miles, which nearly cost them all their lives. For not realising the ocean's width, Magellan failed to put in to South America for fresh water and food. The result was a nightmare journey when it seemed that all would perish of

On the island of Mactan a fierce battle took place in which Magellan was killed.

scurvy, starvation and sheer exhaustion. Biscuits turned to powder, the water was foul. They were reduced to eating sawdust and rats. They might so easily have come across islands which would have saved them, but found only a water-washed islet and another barren spot where sharks made fishing impossible.

At last, on March 6, 1521, they reached the Ladrones (the Marina Islands) and landed on one of them — Guam. They were reborn.

The great tragedy

Life became better still when they reached the Philippines, then disaster struck. Magellan had befriended the ruler of Cebu, Zula, who persuaded him to help conquer the nearby island of Mactan. His ships could not get near the island because of shallows, and Magellan led 49 men through them, only to be confronted by 1,500 natives. A fierce battle led to a retreat, Magellan refusing to leave his men, though they urged him to do so. Wounded first by a javelin, he was then set upon by men with bamboo and iron lances. He went down fighting.

His sailors were so heartbroken that for a time they sailed aimlessly from

island to island, at last reaching the Spice Islands and stocking up with cloves. There were now not enough sailors, so the *Concepcion* was stripped of everything useful, then burnt. The *Trinidad* then sailed back across the Pacific, but it turned again after near-starvation and storms, only to be destroyed by a Portuguese fleet. It was left to the *Victoria* under Juan Sebastian del Cano to give the expedition immortal fame.

He sailed westwards towards the Cape of Good Hope and into the South Atlantic in a leaking ship, and once again scurvy hit the crew.

The great voyage ended when they dropped anchor at Seville on September 8, 1522. Of the 60 who had sailed from the Indies in the *Victoria*, 18 Europeans and a handful of Asians were still alive — just. The citizens of Seville marvelled at the near-skeletons who tottered through the streets, each with a candle in his hand, towards the holy shrines where they gave thanks for their salvation.

A Spanish historian writing soon after the *Victoria* returned, claimed that the feat of navigation was the greatest since Noah's voyage. Certainly, it has never been eclipsed since.

Sharks stopped the men fishing. Antonio Pigafetta, a chronicler who actually travelled with Magellan, said of them, 'They have terrible teeth and eat men'.

The map below shows the main points of the first circumnavigation and the voyage as carried out by, first, Magellan and, later, by del Cano.

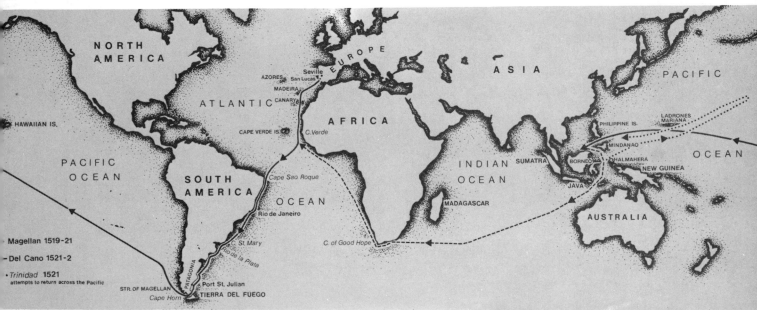

Here a cow is being taken on board. This could be used for milk but only for a very short time. It would then be killed and its carcass eaten as quickly as possible — before it rotted.

Fire Hazard

Wood was carried and used in the stoves on which the few hot meals were cooked. But, on wooden ships, there was always the danger of fire. Tossing on even a fairly calm sea would be considerable and, in a storm, would be alarming. Then, though, it would be impossible to cook anyway.

Each seaman would have his own chest in which he carried his very few personal belongings. He would sleep when and how he could and, in rare moments off duty when not sleeping, would play dice or, if lucky, be entertained by a tambourine player.

There were usually three masts — the foremast, the mainmast and the mizzen, and the sails were either square or lateen (triangular).

An anchor or two were obvious necessities as was ballast in the form of sandbags or similar and kept and moved about as needed in the bilges.

Unfortunately for the men, no fresh fruit or vegetables were carried, although ships could have carried lime-juice and some did. As a result, the men lacked vitamin C and scurvy frequently occurred. This was a painful and often deadly disease and was not helped by the filth, hunger and lack of ventilation which usually prevailed.

It seems surprising that any men went with Magellan. But many did and some actually survived!

C ONDITIONS at sea in Magellan's time (the early 16th century) were at best bad and at worst appalling.

The ships that he had were not in good repair even when work had been carried out on them. And during a voyage of such length and such dangers, repairs would have to be carried out again and again, often during terrible storms and under the most horrifying conditions.

Here we have an artist's impression of men loading one of the ship's before Magellan's departure from Seville in 1519.

Part of the side has been cut away, so showing the hold where barrels were stowed. These contained water, wine and probably many dry goods which needed to be kept dry in even moderate condition.

Also being loaded are goods for trading (carpets, glass beads, bells and bales of cloth), casks of food (biscuits and salt meat), and weapons for defence (swords, crossbows and assorted shot).

Ropes were needed, together with tools of various kinds — canvas for the repair of sails, nautical instruments, such as compasses and charts, all kept near the helmsman at the stern of the ship.

The Fight against Slavery

At long last the conscience of some nations had finally been stirred against the slave traders inhuman traffic in human flesh.

"**J**OHN BROWN's Body lies a-mouldering in the grave,"** sang the Northern soldiers during the American Civil War, "but his truth goes marching on."

The 'truth' — for which they were fighting — was that slavery should be abolished in the Southern States. John Brown, a fanatical opponent of slavery, had wanted to set up a refuge for escaped slaves in the mountains of Maryland and Virginia. To attract attention to his cause, he and his followers seized an arms-dump at Harper's Ferry in October, 1859. They were quickly captured and Brown was hanged for murder, treason and inciting slave rebellion. But he became a martyr, a symbol of the long struggle to free the black population from centuries of white oppression.

The fight began back in 1671. The Quakers, themselves a persecuted group and exiles from Europe, began to criticise the cruelty with which black Africans were being shipped to America. "It is a sin in the eyes of God," they said. Meanwhile, in France, enlightened thinkers like Voltaire condemned slavery for violating the natural rights of Man. In Britain, the 'Somerset Case' of 1772 decreed that slave-owners could not hold slaves in this country because slavery was against the law of the land. This early pressure had little effect, however, on the men who ran the slave-ships. The slave trade continued to grow unchecked.

The man who did more than anyone to stop the barbaric traffic in human beings was William Wilberforce. Himself a Quaker, Wilberforce formed the Abolition Society in 1787. With the help of his friend Thomas Clarkson, he continually urged the British Parliament to pass a bill outlawing the slave trade. He was rewarded in 1807 when such a bill became law. It was now a criminal offence to transport slaves to any British colony. In the same year, a law prohibiting the trade in America came into force. The slave trade was outlawed on both sides of the Atlantic — the first round of the battle had been won.

Opponents of slavery now turned their attention to the institution of slavery itself. Wilberforce and his followers formed another pressure-group called the Anti-Slavery Society in 1823. Ten years later, just a month after Wilberforce's death, a law was passed setting free all the slaves in British Colonies and paying compensation to their masters.

The effect in America was dramatic. The Southern States, terrified that Congress would pass a similar law, drew closer together to defend slavery as a harmless and valuable system. The Northern States did not agree. Having an industrial rather than an agricultural-based economy, they owned few slaves and had little or no financial interest in slavery. So they were free to dislike its cruelty. A rift began to appear between the two halves of the country.

At first the Northern public were not in favour of suddenly abolishing slavery in the South. It threatened the stability of the Union. But a number of factors caused them to change their mind. Anti-slavery campaigners like William Garrison became increasingly militant, denouncing the Southern slave-owners and demanding the end of slavery by law. At the same time, preachers like Theodore Welt and his 'Seventy Apostles' thundered against the sin of slavery from pulpits

John Brown, a fanatical opponent of slavery, led a disastrous attack on a government arsenal and paid for it with his life.
Left: Abraham Lincoln.
Bottom: William Wilberforce

all over the North. In 1852, Harriet Beecher Stowe published her famous book 'Uncle Tom's Cabin' in which the wrongs of slavery were clearly exposed. By the time John Brown stormed the military arsenal at Harper's Ferry, Northern feeling against slavery was running very high.

When Abraham Lincoln was elected President in 1860, the differences between the North and South flared into Civil War. The Southern

States wanted to introduce slavery into the new territories opening up in the West. Lincoln opposed this. So the South (11 states in all) pulled out of the Union and formed their own self-governing Confederacy. War broke out in April, 1861, and in 1863, Lincoln passed a law, freeing all the slaves in the rebellious Southern States. Two years later, when the war was over and the Confederacy defeated, the Thirteenth Amendment to the Constitution freed all other slaves in all other states. Slavery had finally been abolished.

Although free men, a great many slaves were no better off than before the act of abolition. They had to find work for very low wages. Those that

travelled North drifted into the great industrial towns, living together in poverty-stricken ghettos. Good jobs, houses and schools were kept for the whites. In the South, the resentful landowners openly persecuted the blacks, some forming the notorious Ku Klux Klan whose members wore terrifying white hoods and burned the homes of negroes trying to live a life of their own. But gradually black Americans demanded a fairer deal.

Speaking to a huge rally in Washington in 1963, civil rights leader Martin Luther King spoke of his "dream" of seeing black and white people living side by side in peace and equality. It was a dream that still has to come true.

In the bitter aftermath of defeat some Southerners formed an anti-Black movement, called the Ku Klux Klan, with bloody results.

Dr. Martin Luther King, a leading civil rights leader in U.S.A. King was awarded the Nobel Peace Prize in 1964.

Gettysburg

The turning point in the American Civil War between the Union of Northern States and the Confederacy of the South

To the north lay a dispirited Federal Army under Major General Joe Hooker. Only three weeks before, it had been brilliantly defeated by a Confederate army less than half its size. But Hooker was rallying his troops for a renewed attack.

To the south-west lay the great Confederate fortress of Vicksburg, the key to the Mississippi River, and in desperate need of help. It was surrounded by the Federal army of General U. S. Grant and it was likely to fall before long.

This was the position in which General Robert E. Lee, the Commander of the Southern Armies, found himself at the end of May, 1863. Lee, a fifty-six year old Virginian and one of the most skilful tacticians of the American Civil War, had to decide what to do.

Since the start of the war in 1861, Lee had fought hard and well for the South. But he did not agree with slavery which the industrialised Northern states of America wished to abolish and which the Southern states depended upon to supply labour for the cotton plantations. Nor did he agree with the 11 Southern states who wanted to break away from the Union with the 22 Northern states. It was in the defence of Virginia that Lee battled.

By 1863, Lee's troops had gained a reputation for being invincible. A series of victories, engineered by Lee and the legendary General Thomas 'Stonewall' Jackson, had boosted morale in the slowly-dwindling Confederate army, short of food and clothing. In early May, 1863, Lee's force of 60,000 men saved the South's capital, Richmond, from capture by brilliantly defeating a Federal army of 130,000 at Chancellorsville. Sadly, Jackson was mortally wounded and died days afterwards.

Not surprisingly, Lee was keen to follow up this victory by chasing the enemy out of Virginia and into Northern territory, before the initiative was lost. By invading Pennsylvania, he argued, they would compel the North to withdraw support from Grant's army at Vicksburg in order to defend its own soil.

President Jefferson Davis gave his consent to Lee's bold plan and the second invasion of the North began. A previous one, also under Lee's command, had failed in 1861. This one was to fare no better.

In Washington, the North's capital, President Abraham Lincoln, an astute leader, was quick to realise the importance of defeating Lee's army. With Grant triumphant in the south and Lee's 'invincibles' beaten in the north, the Civil War would be almost over.

At the end of May, 1863, Lee's army of 75,000 men was driving into Pennsylvania, aiming to cross the Potomac River and march on Baltimore, Philadelphia and Washington. On the other side of the river, moving in the same direction, was Joe Hooker's army of 90,000.

Unfortunately, Lee had lost touch with his cavalry corps, led by General 'Jeb' Stuart. Stuart had undertaken a lengthy detour around the Federal Army and Lee, without the cavalry's

By the middle of the 19th century, the anti-slavery movement was strong in the Northern states of America. But in the South, slavery was considered essential to the economy. It became a central issue in the Civil War which broke out in 1861. The Confederate states fought to preserve their traditional way of life and saw self-government as a way of achieving this. The North fought to keep the republic intact. The line which came to be regarded as the boundary between North and South was the border between Maryland and Pennsylvania. It was called the Mason and Dixon Line, after the two Englishmen who surveyed it in the 1760s. The far western states were still undeveloped and the settlers played little part in the Civil War.

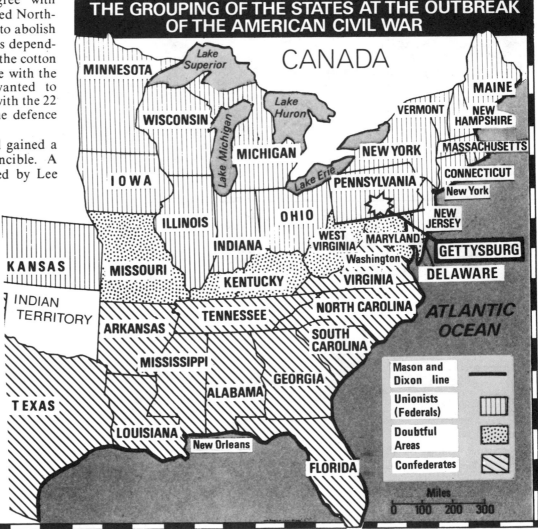

THE GROUPING OF THE STATES AT THE OUTBREAK OF THE AMERICAN CIVIL WAR

Mason and Dixon line	
Unionists (Federals)	
Doubtful Areas	
Confederates	

Miles
0   100   200   300

"...a new nation, conceived in liberty, and dedicated to the proposition that all men are created equal"

Abraham Lincoln, Address at Gettysburg 19 November 1863

reports on the enemy's position, had to march 'blind' for a whole week.

Suddenly, on June 28, Lee learned that the enemy was much nearer than he had expected. Hastily, he called his widely-scattered forces together at the nearby town of Gettysburg, partly to prepare for battle, but also to replenish supplies, including quantities of footwear which were rumoured to be stocked in that area.

Unknown to Lee, he would be without Stuart's cavalry until July 3, the final day of the ensuing battle.

Meanwhile, Lincoln had acted. Dissatisfied with the indecisive Joe Hooker, he replaced him with General George Meade, a reliable professional with nerves of steel. It proved a wise choice.

Meade believed that the forthcoming battle would take place at Pipe Creek, fifteen miles from Gettysburg. There, he waited with his army, blocking the route north, and unaware of Lee's exact position.

It took a chance encounter between a Federal scouting party and the Confederate 3rd Corps near Gettysburg to spark off the bloodiest battle of the American Civil War.

Once contact had been made, both sides marched towards Gettysburg and the crucial encounter which turned the whole war. Because Lee's army had a numerical advantage to begin with, things went well for him in the early stages of the battle. But slowly, Meade's troops arrived from Pipe Creek to aid their struggling comrades.

The Battle of Gettysburg, involving about 160,000 troops, began on 1st July, 1863, lasted for two and a half days, cost 51,000 men their lives and ended . . . in a draw.

The number of casualties was about the same for both sides. Lee's army lost 28,000 men (12,000 of them in the fatal

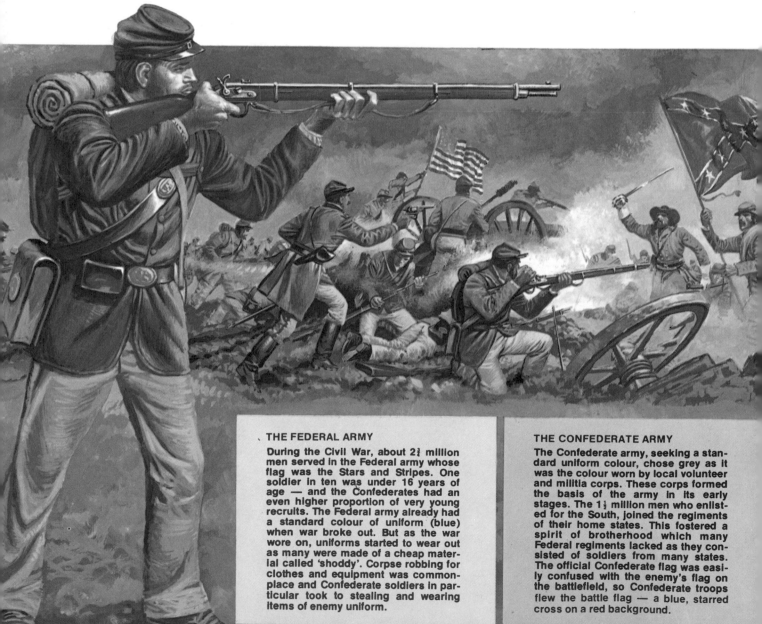

THE FEDERAL ARMY

During the Civil War, about 2½ million men served in the Federal army whose flag was the Stars and Stripes. One soldier in ten was under 16 years of age — and the Confederates had an even higher proportion of very young recruits. The Federal army already had a standard colour of uniform (blue) when war broke out. But as the war wore on, uniforms started to wear out as many were made of a cheap material called 'shoddy'. Corpse robbing for clothes and equipment was commonplace and Confederate soldiers in particular took to stealing and wearing items of enemy uniform.

THE CONFEDERATE ARMY

The Confederate army, seeking a standard uniform colour, chose grey as it was the colour worn by local volunteer and militia corps. These corps formed the basis of the army in its early stages. The 1½ million men who enlisted for the South, joined the regiments of their home states. This fostered a spirit of brotherhood which many Federal regiments lacked as they consisted of soldiers from many states. The official Confederate flag was easily confused with the enemy's flag on the battlefield, so Confederate troops flew the battle flag — a blue, starred cross on a red background.

ack on Cemetery Ridge, the decisive nt in the battle) but it managed to reat in good order. Meade's army s in no position to give chase. But a aw' was not good enough for the nfederates. Only a decisive victory uld have sufficed.

After Gettysburg the way north was sed. Vicksburg fell to Grant's army, ting the South in half. Thereafter, Confederate States were on the reat and Lee eventually surrendered Grant at Appomattox Courthouse in ril, 1865, signifying the end of the vil War.

Four months after the battle, Abra- m Lincoln delivered his famous eech, known as the Gettysburg dress, on the site of the battlefield. the address, widely regarded as a sterpiece of English prose, he nmed up the war as a triumph for mocracy which he defined, most morably, as "government of the ople, by the people and for the ople."

White

THE BATTLE OF GETTYSBURG

DAY 1

By the afternoon of July 1, the Federal forces were defending the high ground to the south of Gettysburg. Reynolds, the Federal general, was killed and Hancock took command. Lee, with 30,000 men in the field to the enemy's 20,000 and 90 guns to their 60, had a considerable advantage but Meade's main army was still arriving. Ewell, the Confeder- ate general, should have at- tacked Cemetery Hill from the north, as instructed, but chose to rest his men overnight. Nevertheless, at the end of the first day's fighting, the Confe- derate Army was well on top.

DAY 2

On July 2, Lee decided to at- tack the ends of the enemy's lines to get behind them. But he lacked the essential sup- port of Stuart's cavalry. Ewell battered the Federal positions at Culp's Hill, and Cemetery Hill and Cemetery Ridge were attacked with venom but, at the end of the day, they were still in Federal hands. A breakthrough was almost achieved when the Federal General Sickles unwisely moved his men from high ground to a more vulnerable position. Longstreet's 1st Corps inflicted heavy losses on them before Sickles retreated and was reinforced by Sykes's 5th Corps.

DAY 3

By July 3, Lee had failed to take the enemy on its flanks. Meade judged correctly that Lee would now attack the centre of his lines which Meade, therefore, reinforced. Against Longstreet's advice, Lee sent 10 brigades against the Union centre with disas- trous results. In the charge up Cemetery Ridge by 15,000 troops of General Pickett's division, the cream of Lee's army perished, mown down by the rifle-fire of Hancock's 2nd Corps. It was a high price to pay for a little over-confidence and Lee's willingness to place too much trust in his some- times stubborn commanders.

ORGANISATION IN THE ARMIES

Both sides organised their ar- mies along similar lines, as follows. In practice, units sel- dom fielded the maximum numbers of men.
ARTILLERY BATTERY — 4-6 guns, drawn by six horse team. 6-7 men plus reserves.
INFANTRY COMPANY — 100 men.
CAVALRY TROOP — 80-100 men.
INFANTRY REGIMENT — 10 companies.
CAVALRY REGIMENT — 12 troops.
BRIGADE — 2 or more regi- ments.
DIVISION — 2 or more brigades.
CORPS — 2 or more divisions.
ARMY — 2 or more corps.

CONFEDERATE ARMY AREA APPROX LINES	UNIONIST ARMY AREA APPROX LINES	SLOPES OF CEMETRY RIDGE NO-MAN'S LAND

THE SITUATION ON THE EVENING OF JULY 1

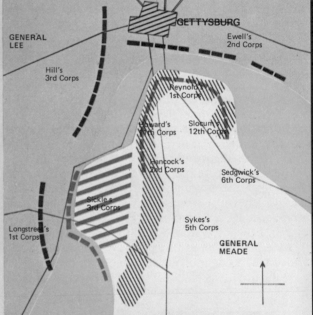

THE SITUATION ON JULY 2

THE SITUATION ON JULY 3

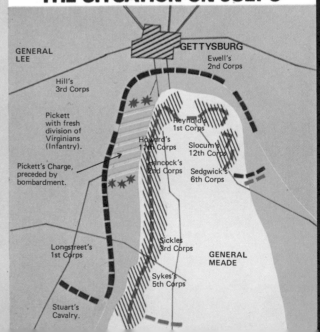

Twilight of an Empire

The Indian Mutiny left deep scars on both sides that were never completely healed until India was given its Independence . . .

IT all began quite simply, with a new gun and a new cartridge. The year was 1857 and it had been decided to issue the army in India with the new Enfield rifle, which had a much greater range and was much more accurate than the old 'Brown Bess' musket used up to that time. With the rifle went a greased cartridge which had to be bitten off before the gun was used. That fact sparked off the bitter series of events known as the Indian Mutiny.

It was the grease that caused the trouble. Hindus among the sepoys, as the native Indian troops were called, believed that the grease was based on the fat of cows, to them a sacred animal. Muslims among the sepoys believed it was based on the fat of pigs, to them an unclean animal. Not for the first time, supporters of these rival religions united in the face of what both saw as part of a long-standing British plot to undermine their sacred beliefs and impose Christianity upon them. They rebelled.

There was, of course, more to the Mutiny than that. The rebels had plenty of friends and sympathisers in high places. Britain's attempts to impose a more efficient administration upon a chaotic country, and to improve the lot of a peasantry who were little more than slaves, had alienated many hereditary princes and powerful landlords whose traditional powers had been cut down.

At the time, basically, India was ruled and administered

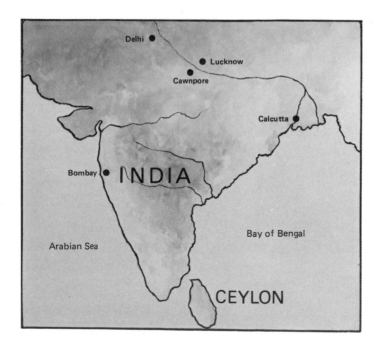

The Massacre at Cawnpore. British troops, believing they were to be attacked, opened fire on rebel troops who had been besieging them. The result was a mass killing of European women and children by the Indian troops.

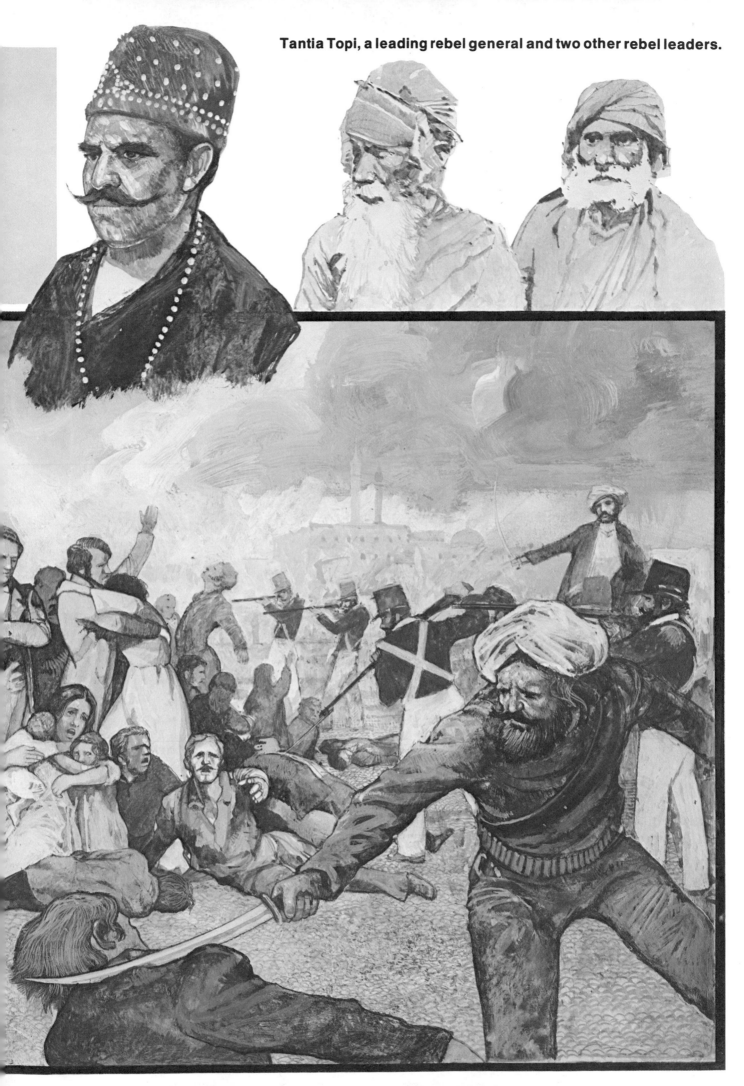

Tantia Topi, a leading rebel general and two other rebel leaders.

The new Enfield rifle which — with its greased cartridge — was to spark off the events later known as the Indian Mutiny.

by the East India Company. The Company had its own private army, backed up by hired regular troops from Britain, to protect its sprawling commercial interests. In that army, Indians (300,000) outnumbered Europeans (40,000) by nearly eight to one.

Fortunately for the British forces, which were not only thin on the ground but on the whole ill-led, by no means all of the sepoys rose in rebellion. Thousands not only remained loyal to the East India Company but fought against their own countrymen.

Indian Mutiny is, in fact, something of a false name. The whole of India was never involved. The rising began in the north and later spread to the six native States which made up Central India. But in both territories the struggle fragmented and there were thousands of hectares of countryside where the sound of battle was never heard.

More precisely, the Indian Mutiny was made up by a number of small mutinies, led by men who had no common strategy and little or no contact with each other.

There are three places which history remembers most clearly from the outbreak of the Mutiny in May, 1857, until it was finally quelled in April, 1859 — Delhi, Cawnpore and Lucknow.

On May 11, 1857, Delhi was taken over by the rebels. Many British officers and civilians were murdered and the Indian guards handed over the main military magazine to the mutineers. As a result, it took a siege of four months, by the British leader, John Nicholson and loyalist Sikhs from the Punjab, before the city was recaptured.

At Cawnpore, some 225 miles to the south-east, men of the 6th Native Infantry mutinied on June 4 after a parade and murdered several officers and cadets. Troops, civilians, women and children took refuge in the British fort while a mob burned the European quarter after looting anything of value.

The siege of the fort lasted until June 27 when the British surrendered under a guarantee of safe conduct. What precisely happened next is not clear. It appears that the combination of the sound of an accidental shot and frayed nerves led the British troops to believe that they were about to be attacked. They opened fire.

All but a handful were either killed in the subsequent shooting or executed. The women and children who survived were made captives until July 15 when news that a British relief force was drawing near resulted in their being murdered and their bodies thrown down a well.

News of this massacre escalated the brutality with which both sides had been pursuing their campaign.

Lucknow, just under 50 miles to the north-east of Cawnpore, came under siege at the end of June and was not reached by a relieving force until September 25. The relieving force, too, then found itself besieged in the three-storey residence of the chief commissioner. Not until November 17 did a second relieving force arrive.

This second relief of Lucknow resulted in the first award of a Victoria Cross to a civilian. Despite being tall and blond, a clerk named Thomas Kavanagh disguised himself with lampblack and oil as a native and made his way through the rebel lines with valuable information.

From the north the revolt had spread to Central India, but it petered out there after Tantia Topi, leading rebel general in the region, was betrayed on April 7, 1859, court-martialled, found guilty and hanged. In the meantime, Queen Victoria had signed an Act under which the British Crown became responsible for the government of India. At the same time she announced an amnesty which most rebel leaders accepted.

The Queen also made a proclamation designed to allay the religious fears of Hindus and Moslems. It disclaimed 'the right and desire alike to impose our (Christian) convictions on any other subjects . . .'

One good thing which came out of the Mutiny was greater concern — if for purely practical reasons — about the health of the men who fought Britain's battles. At the end of the campaign it was found that, while just over 2,000 white officers and men had been killed in action or died from wounds, nearly 9,000 had died from sunstroke or sickness, including the dreaded cholera.

The Indian Mutiny left deep scars on Britain and a legacy of distrust about its Indian Army. Fears of another Indian Mutiny certainly played a part in the decision to grant the country independence in 1947.

The day that shattered the World

THE Archduke Franz Ferdinand, heir to the throne of the Austro-Hungarian Empire was not happy. "A fine thing, Mr Mayor," he thundered, "I am invited to your city and I am greeted with bombs. This is a disgrace."

It was June 28, 1914. The day had dawned bright and clear in Sarajevo, the capital of Bosnia, a small outpost of the Austro-Hungarian Empire nestling in the mountains of Eastern Europe.

It was to be the last day of the Archduke's Bosnian tour. It was also to be the last day of his life — and the beginning of a war which would claim the lives of millions of others.

As the Archduke and his beloved wife Sophie had driven in state through Sarajevo that morning, a young man had burst out from the crowds lining the route and hurled a bomb at their car.

With an icy stare at his would-be assassin, Franz Ferdinand had contemptuously swept the fizzing object from the car. It had exploded in the street, injuring the occupants of the car behind.

Fatal Mistake

Now the furious Archduke stood fuming with rage in Sarajevo Town Hall, as the Mayor and other dignitaries frantically tried to appease his wrath. His wife begged him to go home, or at least change the proposed route. To this last suggestion, Franz agreed. No one, however, told the driver. It was a fatal mistake.

For only a few streets away, another youth was fidgeting nervously among the people who had come to see the Archduke pass. A young woman had already confided her suspicions to a nearby policeman — but he told her he was too busy to leave his post.

So it was that when the royal procession came down the street, there

The scene at Sarajevo June 28, 1914, after the shooting of the Archduke Franz Ferdinand of Austria. The murderer, Gavrilo Princip, is seen second right of the picture as he is being seized by a number of officials and onlookers. The 19-year-old Gavrilo was a member of a terrorist organisation called Young Bosnia, who claimed that they would liberate Bosnia from the rule of the Austro-Hungarian Empire. Nobody present in Sarajevo could have foreseen the world-wide consequences that would be sparked off by the assassination.

was no one to stop 19-year-old Gavrilo Princip leaping into the street and firing into the royal car from point blank range.

The first shot caught the Archduke in the throat. Sophie screamed and flung herself over her husband to protect him.

The second bullet pierced her heart. The third, fourth and fifth shots hit both of them. Half an hour later, they were both dead.

Six weeks later, the First World War broke out — and for four years

Europe was to be racked by the worst war it had ever known. Things would never be the same again. The repercussions of Gavrilo Princip's "shots that rang round Europe" still reverberate today.

Who was this young man? Why did those shots set Europe on the road to world war?

The son of an illiterate peasant farmer, Princip was a member of a terrorist organisation called Young Bosnia. Together with six other youths — most of whom were too

young to face the death penalty — he had been recruited to liberate Bosnia from the domination of the Austro-Hungarian Empire, ruled from Vienna by the enormously powerful Hapsburg family.

The people of Bosnia were Slavs — and fiercely proud of their race. For hundreds of years, Bosnia and her neighbouring countries of Serbia and Croatia had been fighting for independence from the oppression of the Turkish Empire.

In 1893, the people of Bosnia had won their freedom — but not for long. In 1908, Bosnia had been handed over to the Austro-Hungarian Empire.

But these new overlords were no more pleasing to the fiercely independent mountain warriors. Austria-Hungary did not provide hospitals or schools. There was no entertainment and the young people were bored. The conditions were perfect for revolution.

Gavrilo Princip saw no way out of the situation except through violent revolt. Young and hot-headed, he had eagerly read the works of Dostoervsky and Zola, in which downtrodden peasants conspired to overthrow their oppressors. He was ideal recruiting material for terrorist nationalist organisations.

And there were plenty of those. There was Young Bosnia, a group dedicated to the ousting of the Austro-Hungarian Empire. There was Narodna Odbrana ("Death or Unity") and the Russian-financed Black Hand a terrorist group whose crest of a skull, a poison bottle and a bomb left no doubt as to their intentions.

The Black Hand saw Princip's potential. Although he was only 19, he had studied bomb manufacture and pistol shooting. He was devoted to the idea of an independent Bosnia. Together with five other youths, some of whom were still at school, Princip was selected for the job of assassinating the Archduke Franz Ferdinand in Sarajevo.

The Road To War

At first, the European heads of state were slow to react to the news of Franz Ferdinand's assassination. It was mid-summer, and many of them had retired to the country.

But in Austria, the head of home affairs, Conrad von Hötzendorf seized his chance. The doddering old Emperor would be pleased if the rebellious Slavs could be quietened once and for all.

Von Hötzendorf therefore issued an ultimatum to the Serbian government, under whose jurisdiction Bosnia came — quell the rebels or face the consequences.

No independent nation could accept the terms of such an ultimatum and maintain its pride. However, Russia was not prepared to stand by and watch Austria-Hungary overrun a country so close to her southern border.

Only Russia and Austria-Hungary were directly involved in the situation. But for the previous four decades in Europe the political situation had been tense, and a network of rival military alliances had built up. The battle lines were drawn up and all that was needed was a spark to ignite the smouldering enmity between the rival alliances and turn them into open hostility and warfare.

The Germans sided with Austria-Hungary, while France and Britain supported the Russians.

In London, the last brilliant season moved onward in a swirl of top hats, boaters and parasols. It had been a glorious summer. Few people paid any heed to the storm clouds darkening the horizon, thinking that the affairs of a tiny province thousands of miles away could not possibly affect them.

Yet six weeks after the dramatic events in Sarajevo the First World War had started. The four years of fighting involved nearly every nation in the world, and claimed the lives of millions. Things would never be the same again.

Left: The fateful moment when Gavrilo Princip fired into the car carrying the Archduke Franz Ferdinand and set in motion the horror of the First World War.

The Arts

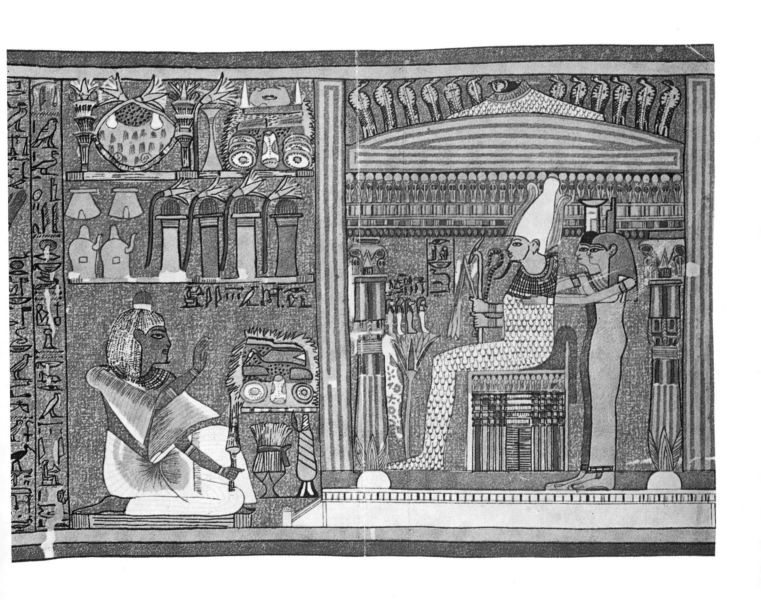

The inventiun of writing

HOW far away do you think a shout can be heard? More than a quarter of a mile away, perhaps , if the wind is in the right direction. But words carry distinctly only about a hundred metres. And that was the range of communication of a prehistoric man before he learnt how to write.

There are other methods of communicating besides the human voice, of course, and our remote ancestors used some of them. Drums, gongs and horns can be used to make sound carry a long way, though they will only convey the simplest messages, and smoke signals can be seen and understood a great distance on a still day.

Bugle calls, hunting horns, church bells and air-raid sirens all serve the same purpose. Yet before the invention of writing the great question was how to make a message transmitted by whatever method endure beyond hearing range, or to make it survive to a later time.

Picture Writing

Simple drawings — picture writing — provided some sort of solution at first, as some of the pictures show.

The ancient Egyptian conqueror you can see striding calmly forward and grasping an enemy by the hair (far left) is himself a form of writing, even though the scene is carved on a slate slab some 6,000 years ago. So is the Bayeux Tapestry (bottom), which commemorates in embroidery the successful invasion of England by William the Conqueror in 1066. And the wiping out of General Custer's entire command at the Battle of the Little Big Horn in Montana in 1876 later inspired Sioux Indians to 'write' an account of the fight, using only pictures — though they were very vivid ones.

Such straightforward events can easily be recorded by drawings, but, with the slow growth of civilisation, cleverer methods of writing were clearly needed, and part of mankind's early history was concerned with experiments to make a more serviceable way of recording events and communicating them to others.

The Incas of Peru, who ruled before the coming of the Spaniards in the 16th century, partly solved the problem by using the 'quipu'. These were knotted cords which acted as memory aids. Some North American Indian tribes used belts of shell beads called 'wampum'. These belts were used for gifts, money and as memory aids, with picture designs commemorating ceremonies.

Yet this was not writing as we know it.

Every picture tells a story. These are examples of communicating an idea by way of illustration. Left, a warrior from Egyptian time. Above, the Sioux Indians' account of the Battle of the Little Big Horn in 1876. Below, the Bayeux tapestry depicting the Norman invasion of England in 1066.

Early writing was often marked into clay while it was wet, and then the clay was baked hard in the sun. Signs were first scratched into clay with the pointed end of a stylus (picture immediately right). Later on the stylus was turned round in the hand and signs were made up of wedge shaped dabs (far right). This style was known as cuneiform which means wedge-shaped.

Below right, is a slab of clay recording details of the number of animals involved in a sale. It is, in effect, an ancient 'delivery note'.

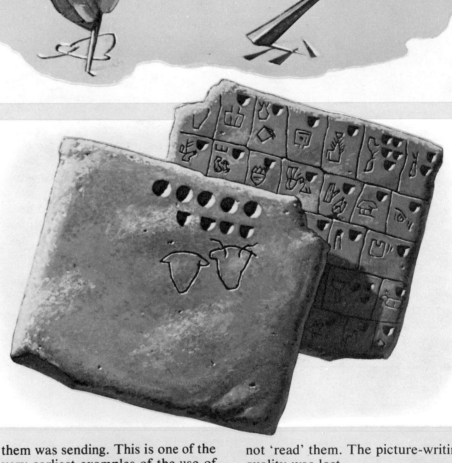

The first attempts at real writing, as far as it is known, were almost certainly made somewhere between the Black Sea and the Indian Ocean, where the twin rivers, Tigris and Euphrates, run southwards to the Persian Gulf.

It was there that the world's very first cities were founded and grew, and there also that true agriculture was developed from very early times.

Agriculture needs a calendar and town life spells trade: two reasons why records have — and had — to be kept.

In those distant days, if cattle were being sent to some far-off city, an official would take a slab of wet clay and scratch on it certain signs to represent the number of animals being sent away, and also to indicate the official's name.

Baked Hard

He would then put the slab of clay in the scorching sun and bake it hard so that nothing could rub out the marks. Next he would hand the slab to the drover as a form of delivery note, and the drover would be responsible for getting all the animals safely to their destination.

In the top right hand drawing can be seen such a 'delivery note' from ancient Sumeria, which, about 6,000 years ago, became the world's first true civilisation. One one side are scratched the head of an ox and a calf and two kinds of numerals giving the total number of animals — 54.

On the other side are the names of those contributing to the herd, with the number of animals that each of

them was sending. This is one of the very earliest examples of the use of numerals.

Baked clay was the main substance on which writing was done for many centuries in Mesopotamia, which included Sumeria and is now, roughly speaking, Iraq. At first the signs were drawings scratched on the clay with the pointed end of a 'stylus', but later the stylus was turned round in the hand, and the signs were made up of sets of wedge-shaped dabs, which could be made more quickly and clearly in the wet clay.

This kind of writing is known as 'cuneiform', which means 'wedge-shaped'. Inevitably, this system ceased to be drawings of objects and gradually became abstract symbols, unrecognisable to those who could

not 'read' them. The picture-writing quality was lost.

Meanwhile, in the Nile Valley in Egypt, where another, great civilisation was growing up at the same time, things were different. In ancient Egypt, unlike Mesopotamia, there was plenty of hard stone, and skilled masons carved inscriptions on the walls and columns of the temples dedicated to the Egyptian gods.

This laborious method produced carefully drawn signs which were used in Egyptian writing throughout Egypt's long history. The animals and the objects which made up most of these signs, called pictograms, remained clearly recognisable.

These carefully drawn Egyptian pictograms are known to those who study them as 'hieroglyphs'. In ancient Greek the word means 'sacred carvings'.

Besides having plenty of hard stone, the Egyptians had a vast number of reeds growing in the swamps along the banks of the Nile. From these reeds they made a kind of paper — the first ever made — which they called papyrus. Our modern word paper comes from it.

In the picture on the right an Egyptian scribe is seated writing on a scroll of papyrus with a reed brush. For official writings, the hieroglyphs continued to be carefully made little drawings of recognisable objects and animals. But when speed was more important than correct appearance, the use of the reed brush led to a more careless free-flowing (cursive) kind of writing called 'hieratic' (priestly).

In this style, the signs lost their resemblance to objects and animals and became mere artificial symbols, as the cuneiform signs were. Later still, in trading centres a commercial style of using the Egyptian method of writing was developed which was even more rapid and free-flowing. It was further removed still from the drawn hieroglyphs, and this new style was called demotic (popular).

Ideogram

In all these early forms of writing the signs did not continue to denote just those things represented. Only nouns can be represented in that way, and verbs and adjectives were needed, too.

So some signs were given extra meanings to signify those qualities associated with the nouns they had originally represented.

For instance, the sun no longer stood simply for the noun 'sun', but also for the adjectives 'bright' and 'white'. It even stood for a noun partly linked to it — 'day'.

So it became an 'idea' sign — an ideogram.

Even with the added ideograms, picture-writing was still not good

Above: In ancient Egypt the skilled masons carved inscriptions on the stone walls and columns of their temples. The inscriptions took the form of a series of signs, or pictograms, which today we know as hieroglyphics. The word hieroglyphics in ancient Greek means 'sacred carvings'.

Right: An ancient Egyptian using a reed brush to write on a scroll of papyrus. The map in the background shows the area where much of the early attempts at writing originated. The Mediterranean is the sea top left of the map, while the Arabian Ocean is bottom right corner. The Nile Delta is on the left and the twin rivers of Tigris and Euphrates are on the right.

enough. It was found that in every language certain sounds might have more than one meaning.

For instance, in ancient Sumeria 'ti' meant 'arrow', which could naturally be drawn. But it also meant 'life', which could not.

So it was that a drawing of an arrow came to stand for 'life' as well.

A sign used in this way is called a 'rebus'.

By using one sign to represent a single syllable, this sign could now represent the same syllable in many different words, thus greatly reducing the vast number of signs needed.

One drawback to rebus signs is that they are not understandable to people of other nations with different languages. Anyone can understand pictograms, and even ideograms to some extent, but with the rebus method it was necessary to know the language.

This meant that writing, though it had become more effective had also become localized.

The ancient Egyptians took the development of their writing even further, using certain signs as alphabetic letters to build up syllables, but, skilled as they were, they never perfected the alphabetic method of writing. The development of the true alphabet is another story.

The secret of Egyptian writing died with their civilisation and may have remained forgotten forever if a French army officer, whose name was either Boussard or Bouchard, had not found a slab of black basalt at Rosetta in Egypt in 1799.

On these two pages can be seen some ancient forms of writing. Above and right from Egypt, and below the Hebrew script still in use today.

THE HEBREW ALPHABET

This is one of the oldest alphabets in the world, remaining practically unchanged for more than 3000 years. It is often said to be the link between Egyptian hieroglyphics and the Greek alphabet. There are 22 characters, all consonants, and the language reads from right to left, with some characters having a special shape to denote they are the final letter in a sentence since there are no full stops.

Character									
Name approx. sound	'Aleph mute	Beth bh b	Gimel gh g	Daleth dh d	He h	Vov v	Zayim z	Heth h	Teth t
Character									
Name approx. sound	Yodh y	Kaph kh k	final letter	Lamdedh l	Mem m	final letter	Nun n	final	Samekh s	Ayin mute
Character									
Name approx. sound	Pe ph p	final letter	Cadhe soft C	final letter	Qoph q	Resh r	Sin s	Shin sh	Taw th t

Below: The first of the three examples shown below shows Egyptian hieroglyph-ics. The middle-band illustrates the free-flowing kind of writing known as hieratic. Below is an even more free-flowing style, removed still further from the drawing of hieroglyphics. This was known as demotic script.

A

B

G

D

F

H

K

M

N

P

Q

R

S

T

U

Y

Z

Ptolemy

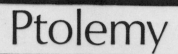

| 1 □ | 3 | 4 | 6 | 7 |
| 2 | | 5 | | |

| 1 P | 3 O | 4 L | 6 Y | 7 S |
| 2 T | | 5 M | | |

Cleopatra

| 1 | 3 | 4 | 6 | 7 | 9 | 10 |
| 2 | | 5 □ | | 8 | | 11 |

| 1 K | 3 I | 4 O | 6 A | 7 D | 9 A | 10 T |
| 2 L | | 5 P | | 8 R | | 11 ? |

It was by studying an inscription which contained the names of Ptolemy and Cleopatra that the relationship between hieroglyphics was discovered. Certain similar signs were noted. Right, Egyptian hieroglyphs in a wall painting.

Dr Thomas Young the English physicist whose research work was important in providing the key that was to finally solve the mysteries of the Rosetta Stone.

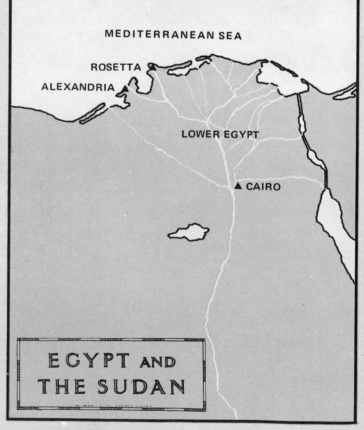

A map showing the position of Rosetta. The stone was moved to Alexandria before being shipped to England, where it was sent to the British Museum.

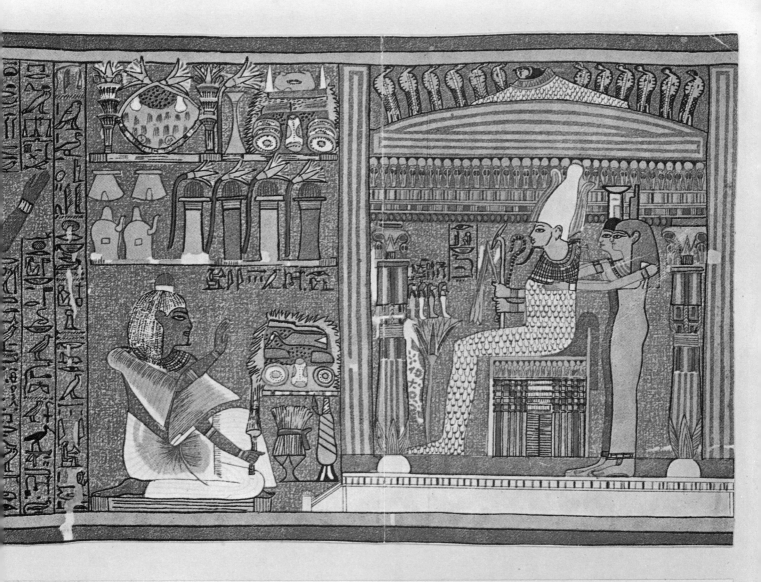

DIFFERENT TYPES OF HANDWRITING

Even today a study of different forms of handwriting can demonstrate just how difficult it was to decipher the ways of writing of long ago. A large part of the world today uses letters derived from the Roman alphabet. Thus we can all read Spanish — in the sense that we can recognise letter shapes — even if we can not understand what is being said.

However, there are still countries where forms of handwriting are quite different from our own. Below is an example of Persian, which is written from right to left.

Chinese writing began with little pictures such as the character that stands for 'man'. Later, characters were put together to stand for spoken words.

jen
MAN

nu-jen
WOMAN

英
國

ying-kuo
ENGLAND

中
國
人

chung-kuo-jen
CHINESE PEOPLE

An example of Japanese caligraphy or beautiful writing. The word comes from the Greek kallos, meaning 'beauty', and grapho, meaning 'I write'.

How we discovered the Egyptian Secrets

TO be able to record anything in writing, one must obviously have some sort of alphabet. These alphabets throughout the centuries have varied greatly, as we can see if we compare the Russian and Chinese alphabets to those of the European alphabets. Chinese, for instance, is notoriously hard to write and takes years to learn. But even this complex sign language cannot be compared to that of the sign language of the ancient Egyptians, whose alphabet so baffled scholars that the key that finally unlocked its secrets was not found until the 19th century.

It is possible that key might not have been discovered at all, if it had not been for a French engineer named Bouchard, who was with Napoleon's expeditionary force in Egypt. Stationed at Rosetta, some 43 miles east of Alexandria, he was wandering idly around the area one day when he came upon a large stone, half buried in the sand. Unearthing it, he found it to be a piece of black basalt, covered on its one flat surface with three kinds of writing.

This simple block of stone was to provide the key to the centuries-old puzzle of how to translate Egyptian hieroglyphics, a Greek work, meaning 'sacred carving' given to the ancient Egyptian pictorial symbols carved on their monuments and temples.

The stone was removed to Alexandria, where the scholars could study it, but before they could establish anything very much about it, Alexandria was forced to surrender to the British, and the Rosetta Stone was handed over to them.

It was shipped to England, and put in the British Museum, where it was immediately placed in the hands of the scholars to see what they could make of it. It soon became apparent to them that they were faced with a formidable task. The inscriptions were in Greek, Egyptian and the Demotic, the everyday language of Ancient Egypt. But because the scholars already knew Greek and Coptic — the Egyptian language as spoken by early Egyptian Christians — the scholars had, at least, a starting point for their investigations.

By reading the Greek, they were able to establish that the inscription told the story of the coronation and good works of Ptolemy V, who had ascended the throne in 197 B.C. And this was as far as the scholars were able to go — for the time being.

It was at this stage that English physicist, Dr Thomas Young, entered the scene. In 1814, after producing a paper on the nature of light, he decided to bring his scientific methods to the study of the Rosetta Stone.

Taking with him copies of the text, he retired to the quiet of Worthing, in Sussex, and set to work — with scissors and paste. He cut up text and arranged the words and letters of the three versions, one above the other. The comparison of the Greek and the Demotic script made sense, and he was able to establish firm links between them. But the hieroglyphs seemed to fail to obey any of the laws of language.

He looked again at the hieroglyphs and wondered. Perhaps this was not picture writing at all. Perhaps the actual objects pictured bore no relationship to the words they were meant to convey. Perhaps the pictures were merely signs to recall sounds, like ordinary writing.

Breakthrough

Scholars now know that Egyptian hieroglyphics did begin with crude pictures of natural things. Later, however, the same kind of symbols were used to express more complicated things. A symbol for a limb, for an instance, might represent, not only the limb, but also its activity, so that the symbol of legs might represent, not only the legs, but also walking. In turn, the sign of a man with upraised hands could mean, prayer, worship or praise.

To complicate matters even further, some symbols were chosen to represent sounds, while still remaining pictorial. The picture of a house, for instance, would indicate the sounds 'p-r' in any word, because the Egyptian word for house was 'pr'.

But having got this far, Dr Young could go no further, beyond identifying the name Ptolemy. But at least he had inserted the key into the lock. Now it was left to a Frenchman named Jean Francois Champollion to turn it and open the door.

Champollion had been a professor of history at Grenoble, but had fallen in disfavour owing to his deep involvement with Napoleon, for whom he had acted as secretary. Now banned from the University for his so-called traitorous activities, Champollion began to absorb himself with trying to decipher the hieroglyphs on the Rosetta Stone. Champollion turned his attention to a group of signs enclosed in an oval ring. It was this type of ring, which became known as a cartouche, that was to turn the key in

THE ROSETTA STONE

This slab of black rock was discovered near Rosetta in 1799. There was an inscription on the stone carved in three different kinds of writing — hieroglyphic, Demotic (or everyday) Egyptian and Greek.

← HIEROGLYPHIC

← DEMOTIC EGYPTIAN

← GREEK

The Rosetta Stone on show in the British Museum.

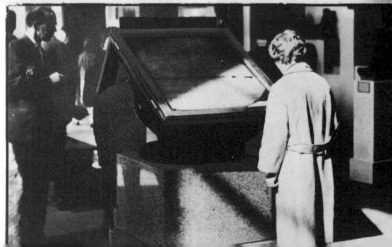

the lock of the puzzle which had baffled the scholars for so long.

Assuming by a piece of inspired guesswork, that the cartouche was set apart from the main body of hieroglyphs because it contained the king's name, Ptolemy, he assumed, also rightly, that a cartouche always contained a royal name. He was then able to confirm his theories by studying an inscription on an obelisk which contained the names of Ptolemy and Cleopatra.

By studying the two cartouches (shown on page 200) you will see that the second, fourth and fifth hieroglyphs for Cleopatra, match the fourth, third and first signs in the cartouche for Ptolemy.

The Word Borrowers

WHEN the Egyptians created a form of communicating their thoughts by word pictures more than 6,000 years ago, they laid down the cornerstone of our own alphabet which we can see taking shape almost from those earliest days.

The Egyptian word pictures, known as hieroglyphics, outwardly have no resemblance to our own alphabet, but we do see in the old Semitic word pictures some of our letters taking shape. The Semites, who came from Palestine, borrowed the Egyptian word pictures and adapted them to their own require-ments. For instance, we see among their word pictures the word *mayim*, meaning waters, which was represented by a wavy line. In this picture we see our own letter m already beginning to take shape.

The Phoenicians borrowed from the Semites and in due course the process of evolving our present alphabet was taken a stage further by yet another nation shaping the alphabet as it stood then to their own needs. In this instance, it was the Greeks who did the borrowing.

The Greeks, in a desire to evolve a more easy form of writing, began changing the words they had borrowed to such an extent that their word pictures no longer looked anything like the thing they were supposed to represent. This remodelled Greek alphabet, which is thought to have been created between the 11th and 9th centuries B.C., was passed on to the Etruscans and the Romans, whose Latin alphabet, altered in various ways, is the basis of all the alphabets of western, central and northern Europe.

The English alphabet can be traced back for about twenty three centuries to its home in central Italy. It is a member of the Latin family of alphabets and that is why some English printed letters (the upright ones as

A professor inspects a written and illuminated vellum scroll. Our modern alphabet was not built in a day. Its earliest ancestor first saw light in ancient Egypt. There the Phoenicians got it, in a form very strange to our eyes, and passed it on to Greece and Italy. Its family tree is shown here, from the alphabet the Phoenicians used down to the one fashioned by the practical Romans.

PHOENICIAN	Phonetic value	GREEK ALPHABETS			Phonetic value.	ITALIAN ALPHABETS			
		EASTERN	WESTERN	CHALCIDIAN		PELASGIAN	ETRUSCAN	EARLY LATIN	ROMAN
	A				A				A
	B				B				B
	GC				GC				CG
	D				D				D
	E				E				E
	FVU				W F				F
	Z				Z				
	CH				H				H
	th				th				
	I				I				I
	K				K				K
	L				L				L
	M				M				M
	N				N				N
	X				X				
	O				O				O
	P				P				P
	ts				S				
	Q				Q				Q
	R				R				R
	S				S				S
	T				T				T
	U				UV				V
	ph				ch				X
	ps				ph				
					ch				
					F				

opposed to the italic) are still called Roman type.

Naturally, the Latin letters had to be adapted to some extent to suit English sounds. The Anglo Saxons, who invented our own language, wrote on flat slabs of wood, generally beech, on which it is possible to carve more easily than on most other woods. It is interesting to note, incidentally, that our word 'book' comes from this source, as beech and book had the same meaning in those times.

Later, early books were written on rolls of parchment and rolled on two round sticks, one at either end. Whatever the form took for laying down words, all of it amounted to the one thing in the end — a desire to communicate (through time and space) to one's fellow men in the most easy and intelligible way possible.

There were periods in history, however, when this was not always the case. Although still using the Latin alphabet, various styles of highly ornate handwriting were developed. The results, seen particularly in illuminated manuscripts, were beautiful to look at, but hardly easy to read. This was a far cry indeed from man's original intention of creating an easily understood written language.

These fanciful essays in handwriting corresponded with the changes going on in the social background against which they took place. We have to remember, for instance, that most Saxon or Norman noblemen could not sign their own names, let alone write a letter, with the result that writing was in the hands of the professional scribes, or the clergy.

The general use of the alphabet in writing did not come until the 17th

1 **3rd Century B.C. Etruscan.**
2 **Roman capitals 1st century. Development of written letter begins with Roman square capitals, early script written on vellum with an edged needle or quill held parallel to the base line.**
3 **Miniscule-cursive, or flowing (later Roman cursive) Written for daily use quickly and with little care, using pointed pen, or stylus, on papyrus or wax.**
4 **Rustic capitals 5th century. They were produced with a square-edged pen held at a strong and constant slant.**
5 **Irish half-uncial, which comprised large rounded forms of letters 10th century. This owed its origin to the half-uncial brought by missionaries of the Norman Church in the 5th century. Written with more speed and slant of the pen.**

century, when the leisured classes began writing long diaries and private letters. A century later, the art of handwriting had become general — at which point it promptly began to degenerate! This degeneration has now become so complete that today many intelligent, educated people cannot write a legible letter. The desire for speed in putting down our language has led it to being almost unintelligible, so that in a way we have come in a full circle.

Sound problem

Today also, after all those centuries that have gone by since the Egyptians created their hieroglyphics, we have reached the strange situation in which our own English alphabet could now profit by being changed. In modern English we have 15 vowel sounds and only five letters with which to write them. In all, there are about forty sounds in English, but we have only 26 letters to indicate these sounds, though some of these could be omitted without affecting

pronunciation. The letter q is pronounced the same as kw. The letter x is either ks or z. The letter c can be k or s. One answer, of course, is shorthand, which uses single lines running in different directions, or small curves or hooks, as its letters. It is based on sounds, not upon the alphabet. Some shorthand writers can write as fast as any person can talk — although this is true only of the best shorthand writers.

Another alternative, of course, would be to write down our language in purely phonetic terms, such as the example below which was devised a number of years ago, by an organization known as International Phonetic Association. Somehow, though, one has the feeling that something would be lost if we abandoned the Latin alphabet.

meri hæd a litl læm
its fli:s wəz ʌait əz sno:
ænd ɛvriʌeɹ ðət meri wɛnt
ðə læm wəz ʃu:r tə go:

THE COLOURFUL KNIGHTS.

THE COLOURFUL KNIGHTS.

Friend or Foe?

With knights clad from head to toe in armour, the problem arose of identifying each other in battle. And so the art of heraldry was born.

TWO football teams run out on to the pitch and excited fans start to pick out their favourite players. "That's Joe Jordan, the number nine. I know his toothless grin." Someone else spots Terry MacDermott by his dark curly hair and the number ten on his back.

But what if these players were not so easily identified? If, for instance, their heads were covered and they didn't wear numbers, how would the fans know who was who from a distance?

Spectators and participants in mock battles, a popular form of entertainment around the 12th century, suffered from a similar problem. The 'sporting heroes' were knights clad from head to foot in armour. It was hard to tell one knight from another.

The problem became more acute for the knights on a real battlefield. It was often difficult to distinguish friend from foe.

The solution, it seemed, was sim-

ple. Each knight would bear a particular design, or pattern on his shield, picking him out from all the others.

The design was also embroidered on the knight's *coat of arms*, a sleeveless garment worn over a suit of armour (and not the six-sleeved jac-

ket often seen in joke books).

In the hundred years after the Norman Conquest of England in 1066, this idea became highly popular and it did not take long for a large number of these designs to spring into existence. But for the system to work properly, each knight had to have his own exclusive design.

What was needed was someone to control the whole system. Over the years, the people who came to know more about coats of arms than any others were the heralds who marshalled the nobles and knights at tournaments and ceremonies. Because the heralds developed an expertise in all matters governing arms borne by the leading families, it fell to them to control the granting of new arms and the registration of old ones.

Each coat of arms was meticulously recorded, and the various areas on a shield named so that the precise positioning of each part of a design could be noted.

Special terms were used to describe what went on the shield. The background colour was called the *field*, and devices set on it were *charges*.

A limited range of *tinctures* were used in colouring the shield. These are still known by their Anglo-French names and can be divided into three groups: *Colours, Metals* and *Furs*.

Colours were *sable* (black), *azure* (blue), *gules* (red), *vert* (green) and

Below: Heraldic creatures drawn from Nature and mythology. The Wyvern was a fabulous winged, two-legged dragon with barbed tail; the Griffin had an eagle's head and wings and a lion's body. Positions are described by special terms: *erased* **(nothing below the neck);** *affronte* **(body facing front);** *couchant* **(lying down);** *gardant* **(head facing us);** *salient* **(springing);** *displayed* **(wings, talons outspread);** *passant* **(walking on three legs);** *statant* **(standing still); and** *rampant* **(rearing, face in profile).**

The Royal Arms as borne by her Majesty the Queen

Leopards head erased and affronte

Lion couchant gardant

Griffin passant

Wolf salient

Eagle displayed

Antelope statant

Tyger rampant

Wyvern

THE ROYAL ARMS USED IN HER MAJESTY'S GREAT SEAL FOR SCOTLAND

- Motto
- Motto Ribbon
- Crest
- Banner
- Royal Crown
- Mantling
- Supporter (Lion)
- Helm (Royal)
- Supporter (Unicorn)
- Shield
- Collar (Order of the Thistle)
- Compartment

IN DEFENS

purpure (purple). Metals were *or* (gold) and *argent* (silver). It is a rule of heraldry that no colour should be placed upon another colour, or a metal upon a metal.

Some shields displayed patterns, derived from furs. One pattern, called *vair,* is based on the fur of the grey squirrel, which is grey on its back and white on its underside. The other pattern, *ermine,* is derived from the winter fur of the stoat, mainly white but with a black tail tip. The tips decorate the shield.

Kings often made *grants of arms* to loyal subjects and Richard III founded the College of Arms to control the 'science' of *heraldry.* The College still exists in London as the leading authority on arms. It isn't an outdated institution, either, as individuals, companies and even new countries register arms which will serve as symbols of their identities.

In its widest sense, the term *coat of arms* embraces a shield surrounded by an impressive array of adornments. The various embellishments have special names as you can see from the illustration of the Royal Arms of the Great Seal for Scotland, shown above.

The drawing of the Great Seal shows what is called an *achievement of arms.* An achievement when it is registered, is accompanied by a full

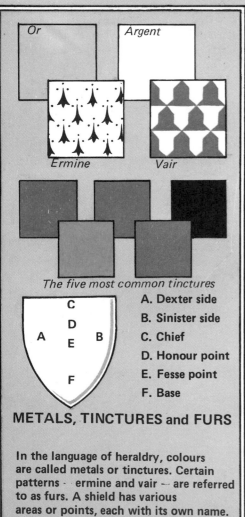

The five most common tinctures

A. Dexter side
B. Sinister side
C. Chief
D. Honour point
E. Fesse point
F. Base

METALS, TINCTURES and FURS

In the language of heraldry, colours are called metals or tinctures. Certain patterns - ermine and vair - are referred to as furs. A shield has various areas or points, each with its own name.

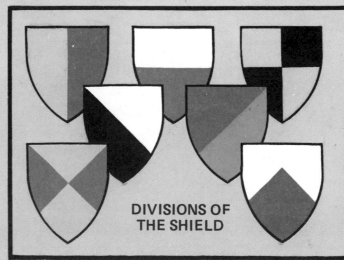

DIVISIONS OF THE SHIELD

The field of a shield is often divided into areas of contrasting tinctures. The dividing lines follow the directions of the *ordinaries,* which are geometric shapes, basic to all shields of arms. An *ordinary* is the simplest type of *charge,* or pattern. Although the shields shown here are all divided by straight lines, the lines used in heraldry need not always be straight.

THE CHARGES

A device used to decorate a shield is called a *charge*. Some of the most common ones are shown on the left, including the *fleur de lis* (lily) emblem of France (bottom left corner). Almost any object can be used as a heraldic charge.

Wales has borne the dragon symbol since Roman times, and Scotland has the unicorn as a supporter for its shield.

These creatures are shown in certain positions each of which has its own heraldic name.

As time went by and unwieldy suits of armour went out of fashion, arms no longer served their original purpose. They lived on, however, as status symbols of the families which had once sported them on the tournament field or battlefield.

The heralds scrutinized every application for arms very carefully before deciding whether to grant them.

Once granted, however, arms become hereditary. That is, they are handed down to the arms bearer's children. His sons add marks to the shield, indicating their position in the family. The eldest son places what looks like a blue 'M' on the arms while the second son is indicated by a black crescent, and so on.

A wife who has arms of her own might *impale* them with her husband's. This means splitting her shield in half down the middle and joining one half with half of her husband's shield.

The divisions and sub-divisions of a shield are almost countless but each one means something in particular which is the joy of studying heraldry. Once you have learned some basic points, you can start practising your newfound skills on the many fine examples of arms which still abound in modern-day life.

description in words, called the *blazon*.

Much can be learned about an arms bearer by the symbols on his shield, for instance. They tell us something about the life people led in the past.

If a shield bears a weapon of war, its owner was probably a soldier, but this is not always the case. William Shakespeare had a spear on his shield because it featured in his surname.

Different crowns and coronets indicate the ranks of the nobility and the lion, the 'king of beasts', features in the arms of many kings.

Beasts from myth and legend are associated with certain countries.

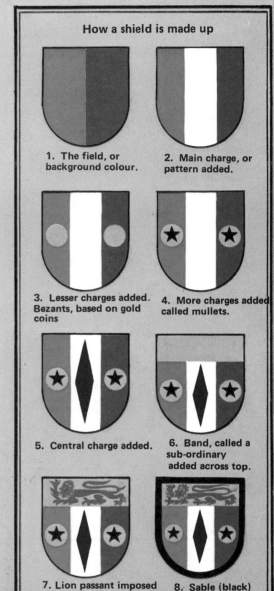

How a shield is made up

1. The field, or background colour.

2. Main charge, or pattern added.

3. Lesser charges added. Bezants, based on gold coins

4. More charges added called mullets.

5. Central charge added.

6. Band, called a sub-ordinary added across top.

7. Lion passant imposed on sub-ordinary.

8. Sable (black) border added.

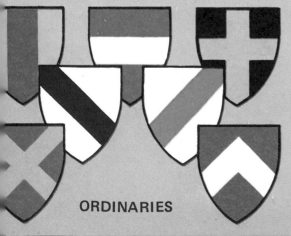

Each ordinary has a special name. The yellow cross on the black background is referred to simply as a *cross*. But the yellow cross on the blue background is called a *saltire*. An ordinary is often repeated on a shield so that, for instance, there might be several red stripes on the yellow shield (right). The ordinary assumes a more slender form and is called a *diminutive*.

ORDINARIES

DIMINUTIVES

MOSAIC: Painting in stone

MOSAICS are made of small, coloured pieces of stone, glass, pottery or other materials fitted together to make attractive and striking patterns and pictures. They can be used to decorate a floor, a wall inside or outside a building, or a ceiling. The pieces are called tesserae, which was their Roman name, and they are kept firmly in place by being pressed into wet plaster or cement.

The tesserae sometimes stick out at different angles, which makes them catch the light very effectively. Good mosaics are glittering works of art, while great ones can be breathtaking.

Mosaics have a very long history. They were made in ancient Babylon, where the Babylonians used inverted clay cones. The ancient Egyptians also made mosaics. In these and other early civilisations, pieces of glass, coloured stones and enamel were used as insets in jewellery, furniture and buildings.

It was in ancient Greece that the art of mosaic was truly developed. First, the Greeks made simple decorations of black and white pebbles but, later, stone pictures were created. As the artists' skill developed, so their mosaics became better and better. We have learned a lot about the appearance and lifestyle of the ancient Greeks and Romans from their mosaics.

Treasure trove

Every country which was occupied by the empire-building Romans has its share of these long-lasting treasures, which are continually being discovered. The cities of Pompeii and Herculaneum, which were buried when the volcano Vesuvius erupted in A.D. 79 proved a veritable treasure trove of mosaics when they were rediscovered in modern times. There are plenty to be seen still on their floors and walls, but some of the very finest — and biggest — can be marvelled at in the nearby National Museum of Naples.

By the fourth century A.D., the early Christians were using mosaics to even more spectacular effect. Unlike the Greeks and Romans, who had decorated floors and walls with mosaics, the Christian artists decorated only ceilings and walls with theirs. Naturally, this meant that constant wear by feet was avoided. The makers used glass, which is more colourful and shining than stone can be. A special hammer was used to cut the glass, and up to fifty different colours were available to the artists.

The centre of all this activity was Byzantium, better known now as Constantinople or Istanbul. The Byzantine Empire carried on Roman traditions when Rome fell to barbarians. Naturally, the great city's churches were superbly decorated, yet it was

Above (top) is a mosaic from the Church of St. Vitale, Ravenna, Italy. It depicts the court of Empress Theodora, wife of Justinian I, sixth-century ruler of the Byzantine Empire (eastern Roman Empire, centred at Byzantium, or Constantinople, now called Istanbul.) The artist is unknown. The portrait of a woman (above) and the cat stalking the parrots (right) are two mosaic pictures which survived the destruction of Pompeii after the eruptions of the volcano Mount Vesuvius in A.D. 63 and A.D. 79. Again the artists are unknown but the mosaics can be seen in the National Museum, Naples.

Photographs: Mansell Collection

OLD MASTERPIECE — NEW VERSION

Mosaic artist Brian Bull and his family undertook the task of copying the valuable Roman mosaic floor of the village church of Woodchester in Gloucestershire, using the same materials as the Romans used. Years of planning and studying were needed.

The drawings (above) took two years to prepare. The seven basic colours are the same as the Romans used: white — limestone; mid-tan — Cotswold stone; dark tan — Bristol sandstone; grey — blue limestone; light red — stock brick; dark red — brook clay; and brown — burnt brook clay.

Brian's labour of love, taking a year and a half to complete, taught him that the original artist must have had two assistants and he can tell, by studying the Roman mosaic, where each day's work began. One assistant, it would seem, took off in the middle of a day's work!

The mosaic tesserae — one and a half million of them — were cut by hand (above) before being pressed individually into the prepared wet stucco, or plaster. Slowly, painstakingly, the pattern developed.

The mosaic, covering an area of 23 sq. metres (29 sq. yards), features 12 animals, 12 birds, 7 fish, the gods Orpheus and Neptune, water nymphs and floral patterns. The irreplaceable original is uncovered for public viewing for only six weeks every ten years. Brian's reproduction mosaic, which can be lifted in sections and moved to another site if necessary, is intended for regular exhibition.

Photographs by John Drysdale, Camera Press, London

back in Italy that Byzantine mosaic work reached its highest peak of perfection.

This happened in Ravenna some 1500 years ago, where the most famous of all mosaics can still be seen in all their glory in the churches there. Perhaps the most famous of them all are to be found in the Church of St. Vitale.

Interest in mosaics was revived in Italy some 500 years later, and the results can be seen in the cathedral of St. Mark's in Venice, and in Rome, Sicily and elsewhere. Greek workmen were imported to make most of these superb examples of the mosaic art. Later, Italian artists became more interested in painting frescoes on walls. However, in Russia and other places in eastern Europe many beautiful mosaics were made.

Revival

For several centuries, interest in making mosaics declined. Then, in the nineteenth century, when architects began to look back to the Middle Ages for ideas and designs to copy, mosaics started to be made once more. They were put in public buildings in a number of European countries and this fashion has continued into modern times.

Nowadays, you can buy ready-to-make mosaic kits, which are paper squares with tessaerae already glued into position to be pressed straight on to a prepared mortar bed. It certainly saves a lot of time, but one could hardly indulge in such a method and claim to be a mosaic artist. Anyone wishing to follow this fascinating craft can start by borrowing books on the subject from most public libraries. It is a good way of entering a wonderful world.

Below is a pavement mosaic from St. John the Evangelist's Church, Ravenna. It depicts the fourth Crusade, or holy war, of the 13th century.

The mosaic above, from St. Mark's, Venice shows Salome bringing the head of John the Baptist to King Herod. Below, also from St. Mark's, is the baptism of Jesus Christ by John the Baptist.

The Artist and his colours

THE search for a reliable and convenient way of mixing coloured powders for painting began centuries before the birth of Christ. The ancient Greeks and Romans painted on plaster or chalk surfaces with powder colours mixed with yolk or white of egg but failed to produce durable paintings. Many other materials were tried but without any great success.

The earliest known paintings which were found in the caves of Lascaux in France, and Altamira, in Spain (see centre panel) date back as early as 15,000 B.C. and were painted with iron oxide. The Egyptians prepared colours from the soil and by 1500 B.C., were importing dyes such as indigo and madder to make blue and red pigments.

The art of painting as we understand it today did not begin until the early Italians began painting in fresco on walls and in tempera on panels of wood. Tempera is the name given to colours which are bound with an emulsion and then stabilised with an agent such as egg. Fresco is watercolour on freshly-laid plaster with no glue to hold it.

Up to and during the early Italian Renaissance period the fresco method of painting proved effective and lasting, except in northern countries where the moist air was harmful to fresco. It was not until the beginning of the 15th century, when a method of grinding coloured pigments with oil was invented, that a new approach to painting became possible.

Tradition credits the Van Eyck brothers, Hubert and Jan, with the invention of painting in oils. Almost certainly it originated in Flanders. The brothers not only made use of this new method, but also brought it close to perfection.

A bison painted in a cave in Altamira, Spain, after a tracing by H. Brevil.

Painting is one of the earliest pieces of evidence we have of man's artistic ability.

On the walls of caves in France, Spain and Italy are paintings of animals which are over 10,000 years old !

The artists made their outlines with sharp flint stones and used mineral oxides (earths) to make the colours: iron oxide for red and manganese oxide for dark blue, carbonate of iron for shades of yellow to orange.

Raw earths were pounded to powder and probably mixed with fat to make them stick to the rock.

Their paintings have withstood the ravages of time and climate better than a number of works painted centuries later.

Since then, variations on the methods laid down by the Van Eyck brothers have been attempted by other painters through the centuries — often with disastrous results. Sir Joshua Reynolds, the first President of the Royal Academy, used a paint containing bitumen because it gave a rich brown colour. Unfortunately it never dried properly and ruined parts of his paintings. Gainsborough used a lot of turpentine in his paint, and this may well be the reason why a number of his paintings eventually faded. Some even faded soon after he had painted them — a fact that did not seem unduly to worry his friends. "A faded portrait by Reynolds is better than a fresh one by anyone else," one of them airily commented.

Each age in painting has created its own way of laying down colour. The Venetian painters such as Titian and Tintoretto concentrated on rich and voluptuous colours on which transparent oil glazes were laid. In the 16th century, Caravaggio and his followers began painting directly on to the canvas solid colours **without** the addition of glazes. This technique, which rapidly spread to other countries, took a pride in displaying the bold sweep of the artist's brush, rather than trying to conceal it.

A major break-through in the painter's approach to his colours came with the Impressionists who realised just how complex colours can be in Nature, which gives one colour in light and a complementary colour in shadow. For instance, if sun on a wall gives yellow, violet may well be found in the shadows. Liberated from all the previous academic approaches to painting by this giant step forward, the artist in modern times has continued to experiment with colour, helped by factory-produced paints which have removed a great deal of the potential dangers that faced the old masters.

One of the early forms of painting was by mixing pigments with molten beeswax. When the picture was finished, it was 'burnt' into the clay, brick or chalk surface by passing a hot iron or some other implement over the paint.

The picture on the left shows some of the tools used for this technique, which were found in the graves of painters buried at St-Herne-Hubert and St-Médard-des-Prés, France.

Colours

that were supplied by the earth and by Nature…

From the earliest times painters have plundered the earth for materials to make their colours. Some of these materials have now been rejected by modern artists. Others are still being used today.

MALACHITE GREEN

A copper ore of a fine green colour. Besides being ground for use as a pigment, it is greatly valued as a mineral for the manufacture of vases and other ornamental objects. In ancient times it was worn as an amulet to preserve the owner from contagion and witchcraft.

CARBON BLACK

This is a form of soot taken from carbonised oils. And, as a pigment, is difficult to use when painting in oils. The problem lies in the fact that it needs a great deal of oil to bind it. This makes the drying process a very slow one.

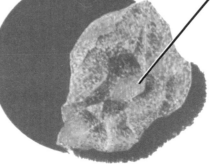

EARTH COLOURS —BROWN

REALGAR YELLOW

The crystals of this mineral conveniently crumble to a yellow powder when exposed to light. It is found mainly in Hungary.

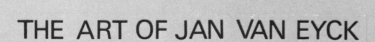

Several browns are derived from natural earth colours. These include Umber and Raw Sienna.

THE ART OF JAN VAN EYCK

Of all the great Flemish artists of the 15th century, Jan van Eyck is perhaps their finest representative. His painting, Jan Arnolfini and his Wife, which can be seen in the National Gallery in London, is a typical example of his work.

Unlike his brother, Hubert, who concentrated on religious subjects, Jan was very much a realist. He was also, as this painting indirectly shows, the father of modern portraiture. In it he makes concessions to his public's desire for detail by his infinitely painstaking treatment of the clothing and background, in which everything is rendered with infinite exactitude, down to the reflection of his subjects in the mirror.

But it is the Flemish burgher and his wife that hold the eye to the exclusion of almost everything else. Although their faces register nothing, we know that what Jan van Eyck has captured here for all time are two rather dull and humourless people whose lives are governed by the conventions of their society.

The picture is dated 1434.

Reproduction by courtesy of the National Gallery

ULTRAMARINE BL

Originally taken from lapis lazuli, semi-precious stone, its use as pigment in Europe goes back to t 16th century. It is valued for resistance to sunlight.

LEAD WHITE

This was manufactured in Roman times by suspending strips of lead in jars containing fumes from vinegar. A white crust of basic lead carbonate formed on the strips and was scraped off and used as pigment. Lead-white was the most important white pigment used in painting until about thirty years ago.

AZURITE BLUE

A vivid blue material which is a basic copper carbonate. It was known to the Roman writer, Pliny, under the name of caeruleum, and was given its modern name in 1824. It is a common mineral to be found in all copper mines.

LEAD TIN YELLOW

It had always been supposed that the pale and bright yellows in early paintings were lead oxide, but in about 1940 modern methods of chemical analysis proved that most of the samples examined consisted of a compound of lead and tin oxide.

LAKE PIGMENTS (DARK REDS)

The Lake pigments, which are of vegetable or animal origin, are now considered obsolete as they tend to dissolve. In Van Eyck's day red dyes were extracted from plant roots such as madder, lac resin, and Brazil wood, as well as the crushed cochineal insect.

VERMILION

This scarlet pigment is obtained direct from the native ore cinnabar. As a pigment, it has the merit of great durability, as well as being unaffected by acid fumes.

ORPIMENT YELLOW

This pigment, is chemically yellow sulphide of arsenic, and is not used by modern painters because of its poisonous nature. Orpiment Yellow was much used by 16th century Venetian painters.

VERDIGRIS

Like lead-white, Verdigris was known in Roman times and prepared in a similar way, using copper strips exposed to vinegar fumes. This copper compound is no longer used because it dissolves in the acid of linseed oil. The old masters overcame this problem by applying it with egg white between layers of varnish.

The Pre-Raphaelite Brotherhood

IT was the year of 1843, and art in England was in the doldrums. The great landscape painter, John Constable, was dead, and William Turner, once the pride and joy of the art world, was now considered well past his best. Behind them lagged a host of still living but lesser artists who were industrious and competent, but hardly likely to add anything to the country's rapidly fading reputation for breeding great painters as easily as it did grocers.

Even the august members of the Royal Academy, that bastion of mediocrity, were becoming depressed by the situation, as they spent one glum session after another, studying the latest crop of paintings by second rate artists, who seemed to specialise in painting historical pictures, generally executed in dark colours to make them look like Old Masters. The question they kept asking themselves was: "where are the new torch bearers for art?" The answer was, there were none in sight. Never before in the history of English painting had the future seemed so unpromising.

But within five years of that date, the whole art scene had been transformed by a group of painters who wanted to go back to the kind of art that flourished before Raphael, one of the great Italian painters of the Renaissance. Although admiring the quality of his paintings, they deplored the influence his cold, classical style had had on all the generations of painters that had followed after him. They wished, instead, to emulate the more literal approach of the early Italian painters, who had tried to paint Nature in its natural form.

The pre-Raphaelite Brotherhood, as they called themselves, insisted that every detail in their work should be completely lifelike, and that models, either living or inanimate, should be used for everything. This pursuit of realism was sometimes carried to an extreme. A typical case in point occurred during the painting of one of the most famous of all the Pre-Raphaelite paintings, *The Death Of Ophelia*, when the poor model was

For a while Holman Hunt specialised in painting religious subjects. Probably the most famous of all his pictures belonging to that period was *The Light of the World*.

made to lie in a large bath for hours on end, in order that the artist could paint exactly how her dress and hair appeared, immersed in water.

This quest for realism also sometimes affected the whole balance of a painting because the artist had filled his canvas with a jumble of carefully painted furniture and other details which tended to submerge the main subject matter.

Their great merit lay in the way they used colour. By painting large expanses of bright colours on a wet white ground, they were able to give their painting an arresting and startling luminosity that resembled stained glass with the sun shining through it. Ironically, this very technique gave their paintings an artificial look — the very thing the Brotherhood was trying to fight against.

The movement was started by William Holman Hunt and John Everett Millais. Friends before and after their student days, they suddenly found themselves in common agreement that art in England had become sterile, thanks mainly, in their opinion, to the pernicious influence of Raphael. As a result they began to evolve a technique that would, hopefully, break down the barriers that art had erected between the painter and the people. It was at this point that Dante Gabriel Rossetti came upon the scene.

Rossetti, who was the son of an Italian political exile, had fitfully attended the Academy schools, where he had met Hunt and Millais. After going on to study for a brief period under the famous Norwich painter, John Sell Cotman, he came to Hunt for lessons. The company now numbered three. Putting aside their talent as artists, they made an interesting trio.

William Holman Hunt had spent his early days hawking his paintings from house to house, returning in the evenings to a miserable garret, where he existed on a near starvation level. Later, when he had become a successful painter, he journeyed to the Holy Land, where he sat painting for hours on end in the wilderness, with a double barrelled rifle and a pistol near to hand, even though he had an Arab bodyguard. The irony of

Top left. *Bubbles*, by John Everett Millais. This highly sentimental picture was adored by the Victorians and was eventually used by Pears for one of their soap advertisements. **Left.** *The Death of Ophelia*, by Millais. The model for this painting was Rosetti's wife, who lay for hours on end in a bathtub of water, in order that Millais could study her.

Ophelia — reproduced by courtesy of the Tate Gallery, London.

it was that as most of the pictures he painted were allegorical, he might just as well have stayed at home and painted them in his studio in London. Like the rest of the Pre-Raphaelites, after his early work had been attacked, he ended up a respected figure. He died in 1910, and was buried in the crypt of St. Paul's Cathedral.

Tragic death

Rossetti, on the other hand, had no aspirations to respectability. An emotional and feckless man who was continually in debt, he was a familiar figure in the pawnshops, immediately recognisable by the plum coloured frock coat he wore for years. In 1850, he married a beautiful red haired young woman named Elizabeth Eleanor Siddal, who was to often act as a model for the Pre-Raphaelites. Theirs was an unhappy marriage from the beginning. She died from an overdose of laudanam at the age of 29, she was the one truly tragic figure in the Pre-Raphaelite group.

After her death, Rossetti was never quite the same again. The last vision we have of him in his later life, as described by various writers, is of a fat, pale faced man who had become a drug addict. He died at Birchington in 1882. He was only fifty four.

Millais was the most successful of them all. Unlike the others, he secretly yearned for academic distinction. Regretfully, for art's sake, if not for his bank balance, his subject matter became more and more sentimental, culminating in his cloying picture, *Bubbles*.

A genial, easy going man, he accepted with casual grace all the glittering prizes that were offered to him, including an invitation to become President of the Academy. But despite his position in the art world, he remained true to his friends to the end, which came in 1896. He, too, was buried in St. Paul's Cathedral.

The four remaining members of the Brotherhood were Rossetti's brother, Thomas Woolner, James Collinson, and Frederic George Stephens. In addition, they gathered around them a number of other talented artists, who either became friends or associates of the Brotherhood. Collectively, by breaking away from the old academic traditions, they influenced the whole development of English art for more than half a century.

Day Dream, by Dante Gabriel Rossetti, is a typical example of his work in which he often used a brooding sensuous figure.

`Old Crome´
and his companions

The painters who took a simple delight in their own countryside

IT has been said that the art of English landscape painting began as "a form of modest self-expression by provincials, a record by simple men of their own happiness in their fields and villages."

The truth of this can be seen, particularly, in the work of a 'school of painting' that came into being in 1803, in Norwich, the city and county borough of Norfolk.

The Norwich School, as it became known, was founded by John Crome, a self-taught painter who gathered around him some thirty artists of varying degrees of talent and who met in the

On the right is a detail from John Sell Cotman's watercolour, St. Luke's Chapel, Norwich Cathedral. Below. Yarmouth Jetty, painted in oils by 'Old Crome', as John Crome is often called.

John Sell Cotman spent a lot of time in Yorkshire before returning to Norwich. Whilst there, he painted this picture of Greta Bridge.

local taverns to discuss their work. Although influenced to some degree by the traditions of France and Italy, their work was distinguished by their unswerving devotion to their own locality.

Wooded lanes, quaint country cottages, old mills, forests and the narrow cobbled streets of Norwich itself were the subjects they painted in oils and watercolour with loving care.

Crome, whose work was often influenced by the Dutch painter, Ruisdael, nevertheless was sometimes able to achieve a style that was completely his own.

Wonderful simplicity

The son of a publican, Crome started earning his living at the age of twelve, acting as a general help for a local physician, who quickly dispensed with his services after he distinguished himself by bleeding one of the patients almost to death. Later, he became a coach, house, and sign painter, and thus learned how to lay on paint in a broad and simple manner. His later wonderful simplicity of technique was undoubtedly due to his early training in this type of work. He rarely painted outdoors, preferring instead to compose his oils from watercolour sketches and drawings made on the spot.

Incidentally, John Crome was usually referred to as "Old Crome", to distinguish him from his son John, also a painter. Crome was probably the most interesting character of the school. Although he seldom received more than £50 for one of his pictures, however large the work, he managed to live in comfort, keeping two horses and a carriage to enable him to drive him round to the great houses in the neighbourhood, where he gave lessons.

His jovial nature and lively conversation made him welcome everywhere, whether it was at one of the fine country houses or the local tavern. Even when famous, he was not averse to earning an honest penny by reverting to his old trade from time to time, painting and gilding signs.

Unhappily, Crome was perhaps a little too commercially minded for his own good. "Paint for fame," he told his son before he died, "and if you paint a pigsty, dignify it." It was this approach that led him to producing the occasional bad painting.

Unfortunately, for his reputation, his work had been obscured by bad copies or paintings by other artists which were attributed to him. This did not stop him, however, from being ranked in his time with those great landscape artists Joseph Turner and John Constable. Although this assessment gave him an international reputation for a while, latter-day critics see him, more correctly, as a major artist, rather than a great one.

Cotman and others

Although Crome founded the movement, John Sell Cotman was the most celebrated artist of the group, although he achieved neither fame nor fortune while he was alive, possibly because his techniques were often ahead of their time. His work consequently suffered a period of relative oblivion until near the end of the 19th century. Today, however, he is considered to be one of the most outstanding of our English watercolourists.

An art teacher by profession, Cotman travelled and painted in Wales and Yorkshire before he returned to his home town of Norwich, where he began painting the buildings and alleyways of

One of John Crome's pupils was George Vincent, who painted this picture of the Fish Auction at Great Yarmouth. Below is a detail from a watercolour by John Thirtle entitled Cottage by the River at Thorpe. *All reproductions by courtesy of the Norfolk Museums Service (Norwich Castle Museum).*

Norwich. But his work was not popular, and bowing finally to the popular taste of the times, he turned to seascapes and costume pieces in gaudily, melodramatic watercolours, probably under the influence of Turner, then at the height of his popularity. The year before his death Cotman found his true self again. Responding to a wet, dank autumn, he executed a series of monochrome pictures that rank as some of his very best work.

Both Cotman and Crome play an important part in the history of English painting for the way they extended the use of watercolour techniques.

The most tragic artist of the movement was George Vincent, one of Crome's pupils. After a short, unhappy life, which included a spell in the Fleet, the debtors' prison in London, he died at the early age of 36, leaving behind him a number of striking oil paintings, notably *The Dutch Fair at Yarmouth Beach*.

Others in the School included Joseph Stannard, whose pictures are full of lively observations of the life and scenery of Norfolk, James Stark, who concentrated on landscapes with brooding clouds, and John Thirtle, whose work is notable for his delicate use of colour.

The Norwich School lasted for three decades, and could be said to have officially gone out of existence after its last annual exhibition in 1833. Quarrels among themselves and a tendency for its members to die young were contributory factors. But perhaps more than anything it died because it had, by then, fulfilled its function of serving as a nursery school for a band of landscape painters who wished to express their simple pleasure in their own countryside. Their work is best represented in the Norwich Museum.

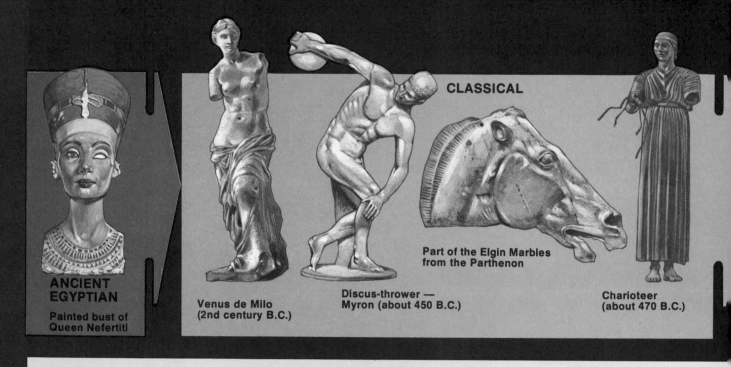

ANCIENT EGYPTIAN

Painted bust of Queen Nefertiti

CLASSICAL

Venus de Milo (2nd century B.C.)

Discus-thrower — Myron (about 450 B.C.)

Part of the Elgin Marbles from the Parthenon

Charioteer (about 470 B.C.)

Sculpture through the ages

WHEN primitive Man gave up his role as a hunter to become a farmer, he exposed himself to an entirely new situation in which his life was now governed by the seasons and the often terrifying forces of Nature. Always by nature superstitious and now in constant fear of the gods who controlled the sun, wind and rain, he began to make small figures out of clay as an offering to the evil spirits that might otherwise destroy his crops. In this manner, man the sculptor came into being.

Even so, historically speaking, it was not until the times of the Ancient Egyptians that man began producing sculptures of any major significance. These sculptures, which ranged from heads of the Pharaohs to gigantic sculptures such as the monolithic row of statues of the Pharaoh Rameses II, carved in the cliff of Abu

Simbel, were invariably set in rigid poses, with the eyes gazing forward out of expressionless faces. This convention was partially governed by the fact that the Egyptian sculptors worked only in hard stone which forced them to outline the subject in simple unbroken lines.

It is not until we come to the Classical worlds of Greece and Rome that we see sculptures being shaped in realistic forms. As the hard granite used by the Egyptians had produced a simplification of shapes, so the marble used by the Greeks led to softer forms of sculpture in which the artist was able to create perfect forms as befitted the gods he so often sought to portray. His figures also had one particular virtue. They were free-standing.

Roman sculpture, on the other hand, was mainly derivative, due mainly to the wholesale importing

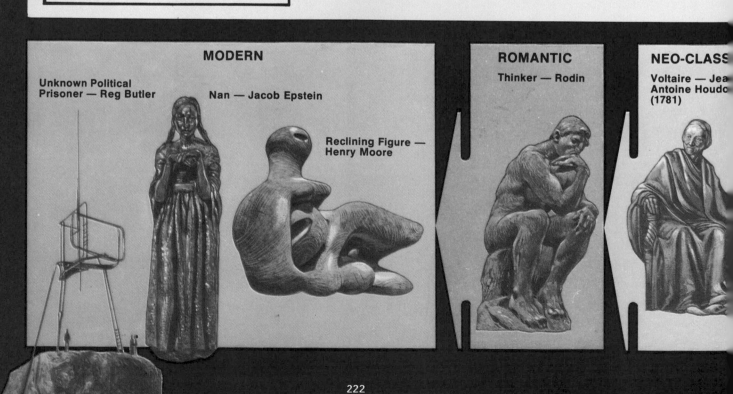

MODERN

Unknown Political Prisoner — Reg Butler

Nan — Jacob Epstein

Reclining Figure — Henry Moore

ROMANTIC

Thinker — Rodin

NEO-CLASS

Voltaire — Jea Antoine Houdo (1781)

ROMANESQUE

Christ in Majesty — Autun Cathedral, France (12th century A.D.)

GOTHIC

Three saints (Chartres Cathedral) and The Last Supper (part of the Altar of the Holy Blood, Church of St. James, Rothenburg-ob-der-Tauber, Germany) — Tilman Riemenschneider, 16th century

and copying of Greek originals. But for all that, the two forms were still worlds apart. Unlike the soft and graceful outlines commonly associated with Greek sculptures, the Roman sculptures were stern and rugged, in keeping with the Roman personality. Additionally, the Roman sculptor tried to reproduce people as realistically as possible, down to the last wrinkle on a senator's face.

Flowering

Sculpture, as we know, has formed an important part of the cultural development of almost every country in the world. But it is to Europe and the Middle Ages that we must turn to see a flowering in the world of sculpture which has never been surpassed, culminating as it did in the glorious achievements of the Renaissance.

This great age was signalled first by a new architectural style known as Romanesque, which incorporated a large variety of regional styles and was applied to many of the churches that were being built throughout the whole of Europe. This brought with it a revival of monumental stone sculpture in which figures were used as ornamentation in the churches, often illustrating some Biblical theme.

This form of church ornamentation lingered on when the Gothic style of architecture came into being around 1150, heralding the age of the great cathedrals. Animals, plants, birds and gargoyles, in particular, were used to decorate almost every nook and cranny of the cathedrals.

Gothic sculpture also now

HIGH RENAISSANCE

David — Michelangelo

St. George — Donatello

BAROQUE

Ecstasy of St. Theresa — Bernini

Perseus and Medusa — Cellini

Flying Mercury — Giovanni da Bologna (about 1570)

Pieta — Michelangelo

223

reflected medieval man's desire to endow the traditional themes of Christian art with a greater emotional appeal than before, which is why many of the great cathedrals built during this period contain narrative pictures carved out of stone, reflecting the intense religious fervour of the medieval sculptors.

With the arrival of that period in history we know as the Renaissance, which began soon after 1500, we enter into the truly great age of sculpture. It began in Italy, and as far as sculpture was concerned, its spiritual home was Florence, where its most distinguished representative was Donatello, one of the greatest figures of the Renaissance, who brought to his marble and bronze figures the same sense of anatomy which the Greeks had shown in their work, while at the same time revealing a sense of design and expression unknown to antiquity.

Michelangelo

The other famous son of Florence was Michelangelo, a truly great artist. Although he was a painter, architect, poet and master draughtsman, he nevertheless considered himself above all as a sculptor. Whether in carved stone or in fresco, his figures are of heroic dimensions, which still manage at the same time to express his profound religious faith. Nowhere is this more evident than in his famous *Pietà*, in St. Peter's, Rome. The impact of his genius on succeeding generations was tremendous.

In the late 16th century a new art style came into being which was notable for its richness of form and excessive decoration, which disregarded all the strict classical rules. Born in Rome, and known as Baroque, it was the final phase of the Renaissance.

Bernini

Its high priest was the sculptor Bernini, whose amazing mastery of technique allowed him to imitate in marble the textures of flesh and diaphanous fabrics. Throughout the whole of his working life, Bernini was obsessed with the idea of creating in marble something so realistic that people would ask, "Is this figure alive, or is it marble?"

How well he achieved this can be seen in Rome where his work can be seen, among other places, in St Peter's and in the Piazza Barberini, where his *Fountain of the Triton* is a constant source of pleasure to the tourists who flock there throughout the whole year.

In the first half of the 18th century, the solemn and often exaggerated forms of the Baroque began to be replaced by an art form known as Neo-Classic, which had come into being when the discovery of Pompeii and Herculaneum led to a revived interest in the classical world. The spirit of this particular era was very much reflected in the work of the French sculptor, Jean Houdon, who modelled in stone some of the men who had conspired to overthrow the monarchy, such as Voltaire and Rousseau.

Impressionism

When the age of the Impressionistic painters came in the 19th century, it revitalised sculpture no less than painting. The greatest of all the sculptors who became part of the new movement was undoubtedly Auguste Rodin, who, more than anyone else, rescued sculpture from being little more than a mechanical reproduction of the human form, just as the Impressionists had rescued painting from photographic realism.

Rodin's work is remarkable for the way he handles surfaces in an entirely new way, often deliberately giving them an unfinished look which imparts a tremendous vitality to his work. His famous pieces *The Burghers of Calais, The Kiss* and *The Thinker,* are typical examples.

Throughout the history of sculpture, we see the artist challenging all the traditional values, and perhaps never more so than in the 20th Century. Although many modern sculptors *do* still adhere to traditional techniques, the emphasis is now on more abstract forms.

Modern sculptors

The reclining or sitting sculptures of Henry Moore, for instance, reflect the artist's preoccupation with the weightiness and texture of his stone, which he considers more important than trying to achieve a naturalistic rendering of the human form. Reg Butler, whose prize-winning sculpture, *The Unknown Political Prisoner,* shown on the previous page, evolved many of his sculptures out of pieces of metal, wood and wire.

In some ways we have entered an age in which the blow-torch is almost as important to the sculptor as a chisel.

The Triton Fountain in the Piazza Barberini, Rome, by Bernini. This is one of the most famous of Bernini's fountains and, perhaps, his best. It represents the sea god, Triton, holding a shell to his lips, surrounded by other shells and with dolphins supporting him. Triton was also an emblem of 'Immortality acquired by literary study' and, as such, was probably a tribute to Pope Urban VIII, who was a skilled Latin poet.
Photo: Mansell Collection

Bringing stone to Life

A S with so many of the crafts, stone carving began as far back as the Stone Age, when primitive man first began to attack the walls of his cave with a flint tool. The end results of his carvings were crude, to say the least of it, but it says a great deal of his compelling desire to create something out of stone that man the sculptor was at work thousands of years before the first potter made his first bowl.

It was left to the Ancient Egyptians to acquire sufficient skill in stone carving to make relatively sophisticated stone images. With these stone carvings, generally representing the early pharaohs, sculpture as we understand it today really began.

There were, however, certain fundamental laws in Egyptian sculpture that would appal any latter day sculptor. One convention decreed that a standing figure must be quite vertical, with the feet resting flatly and firmly on the ground. The most extraordinary convention of all was the law of *frontality* — which meant that in all cases, the shoulders must squarely confront the spectator. Incredibly, this convention lasted for some 4,000 years.

The Egyptians, in addition, generally used limestone, which is fine grained and comparatively soft to work. It was left to the Greek and Roman sculptors to use marble, which, though difficult to cut, is ideal for obtaining precise outlines — something which was to be exploited to its

Above, left: The head of Canova's *Venus Victorieuse.* His style reached a peak in the early 19th century.

Left: Michelangelo's *Giant Awakening,* unfinished, but a vivid example of the sculptor's art.
Photos: The Mansell Collection

Above, right: Henry Moore's *Reclining Woman.* Moore's work falls somewhere between realistic and abstract.

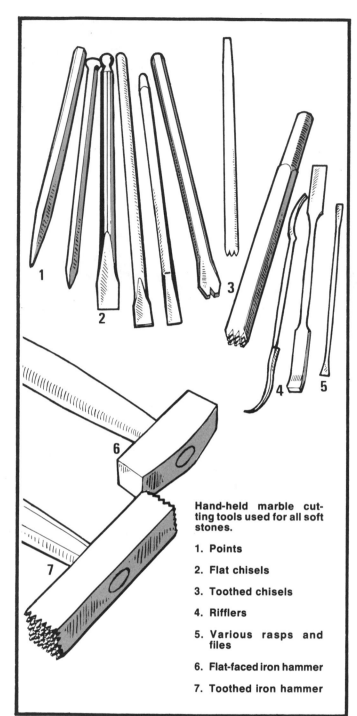

Hand-held marble cutting tools used for all soft stones.

1. Points
2. Flat chisels
3. Toothed chisels
4. Rifflers
5. Various rasps and files
6. Flat-faced iron hammer
7. Toothed iron hammer

fullest by the great Italian sculptors of the 13th century.

The sculptors of the Italian Renaissance, who strove always to achieve the ultimate in realism in stone, were still influencing the work of sculptors right up to the late 19th century, so much so, in fact, that even a master craftsman and innovator such as Auguste Rodin was accused of having taken one of his casts from life.

It is only when we come well into the 20th century that we see sculptors creating an entirely new language in stone, while still using many of the same tools used by the Greeks all those centuries ago.

This brings us to the question — how does the modern sculptor achieve his results? To understand the difficulties he faces and how he overcomes them, we must first look at his materials and then at the way he uses his tools.

To begin with, the modern sculptor works on a large variety of stones which range from soapstones and alabaster to hard granites. His choice of stone is obviously governed by his subject, so that, if he is intending to create, for instance, a really huge figure, he will, in all probability, use granite, which he carves by pulverising,

A master carver at renovation work on a gargoyle for the tower of Bristol Cathedral.

Photo: Press Association

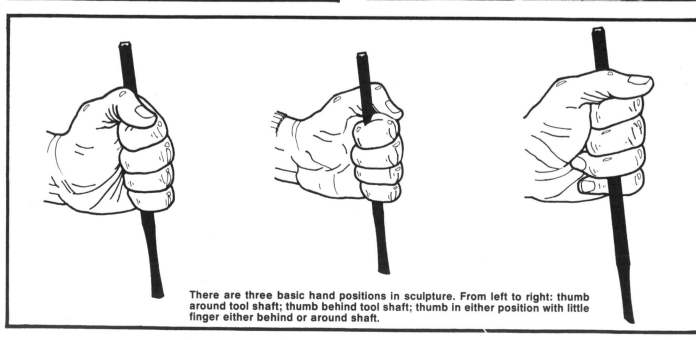

There are three basic hand positions in sculpture. From left to right: thumb around tool shaft; thumb behind tool shaft; thumb in either position with little finger either behind or around shaft.

rather than flaking off the stone with a chisel. His material, though, may come from the most unusual sources. An American sculptor used the pillar of a New York railroad terminal to make a large marble squirrel: others have used gravestones.

The sculptor, too, has to bear in mind the weather if his statue is to be placed outdoors. Moisture, freezing within a stone can cause it to rot and flake, quickly turning his masterpiece for posterity into a sorry ruin. Soot and smoke are particularly injurious, and the sun may change the colour of marble. The potential problems with any sort of stone are almost endless.

As to the actual working of the stone, this is achieved mostly by chipping away with a variety of tools after the first rough shaping of the block has been done by sawing off large pieces to make the stone more manageable. The major work on the outline is completed with a pointed chisel known as a 'pick'. The sculptor then sets to work in earnest with a whole battery of tools, including the boucharde, claw chisels, drills, rasps and gouges — all of them tools that were used by the ancient Greeks.

But not all modern sculptors restrict themselves to using only these basic tools. Pneumatic drills and electric hammers and saws are also employed, even though they have some obvious disadvantages, inasmuch as they are noisy to use and the sculptor has to wear a mask and special clothing to protect himself from dust and flying chips. No doubt the Renaissance sculptors would have looked down their noses at the very thought of using such equipment, but even so, some of the best examples of modern sculpture have been created with the help of such tools.

In more general terms, the modern-day sculptor still has to face the same problems that confronted the Renaissance sculptors. Any piece of stone has volume and mass which the sculptor has to turn ultimately into a finished piece of art, with all its planes flowing into one another. He has, too, the elementary problem of creating something that when it is finished will be perfectly balanced — which is to say that it will not topple over.

Once a sculptor knows how to solve these problems, the potential of the virgin block that faces him is limited only by his own vision.

Two contrasting statues by the French sculptor Auguste Rodin (1840-1917). Left: *The Kiss,* completed in 1898, is a smooth and even piece of work. Above: Rodin's most famous work, *The Thinker,* has a different feel about it. Not smooth and pretty, it is powerful and roughly modelled, giving the impression of a man concentrating intensely.

Photos: Mansell Collection

The Doll

The darling and delight of childhood

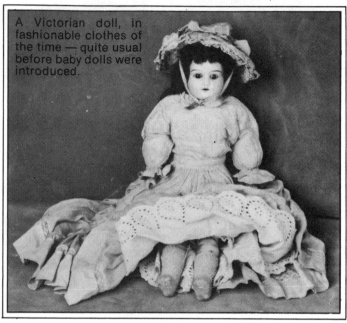

A Victorian doll, in fashionable clothes of the time — quite usual before baby dolls were introduced.

'I once had a sweet little doll, dears.
The prettiest doll in the world;
Her cheeks were so red and white, dears,
And her hair so charmingly curled.'

Those words, written by Charles Kinglsey in *The Water Babies*, published in 1863, must have struck a responsive chord in many a young girlish heart in England, where dolls had now become the rage since the Montanaris, a family of model doll manufacturers, had exhibited their range of wax dolls at the Great Exhibition of 1851.

The Montanari dolls were prohibitively expensive for those days, costing more than five pounds for an undressed model. There was, however, no shortage of buyers.

Almost as famous as a family of doll makers during that period was the Pierotti family, who supplied the London toyshop of Hamleys with dolls right up to 1930.

Papier mâché dolls

But although the Pierotti family had been making dolls in England since the 1780s, the baby doll as we understand it did not exist in England or any other country until 1825, when Germany began to export a new type of doll — made of flesh coloured papier mâché, dipped in a waxed solution to give an impression of human skin.

Previously, dolls had been made in the shape of a woman and were distinctly crude affairs, with the head moulded in papier mâché to which a stuffed body was attached.

That dolls existed at all during that period is rather surprising when one realises that a child unfortunate enough to have been born in the 18th century was expected to become an adult as soon as it was out of baby clothes, and was therefore encouraged to put away childish things as soon as possible.

The birth of the great Victorian middle class saw a change which paved the way to a new attitude to children. Instead of being treated with indifference, they were now

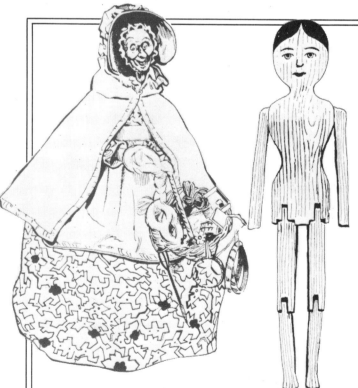

Above, left: A pedlar doll of about 1840. Her head is made from a pickled apple and her body of wood. She has glass beads for eyes. These dolls, not surprisingly, are sometimes known as 'Appleheads'. Right: A wooden, jointed 'Dutch' doll. The oldest known wooden dolls were made about 2000 B.C.

1. Wooden Egyptian doll with Negro head, c.500 B.C. Now in British Museum, London, numbered 6459.

2. British dolls of 17th C. (Lord and Lady Clapham). Dressed in typical aristocratic finery of that period. These dolls would have belonged only to the children of the rich. Now in Victoria and Albert Museum, London.

3. Victorian dolls — Rosa Mary, The Nurse, and Sandy — in period costume. The kilted Sandy reflects the Victorian vogue for all things Scottish, prompted by Queen Victoria's love of her Scottish retreat, Balmoral Castle. Again, these dolls would have been beyond the means of most children.

4. The highly-popular Sindy doll, introduced in the 1960s, fashionably dressed and with interchangeable costumes and accessories as extras.

Photograph: Palitoy

1

2

3

4

seen as 'little angels' who, in time, would grow up in the image of their mothers, and in turn would become mothers themselves. What better toy, then, for a little girl, than a baby doll on which she could indulge her maternal instinct?

Suddenly faced with an ever-increasing demand for dolls, the manufacturers began supplying them in large quantities.

The earlier dolls such as the German 'Biedermeir' dolls of the 1840s, with their rigid bodies and painted wooden limbs began to be replaced by dolls made of wax or china, and were not only well dressed, but also supplied with parasols, gloves, and sometimes a lace shawl.

Although England had now become the leader in their manufacture, Germany was also still making dolls in large numbers. They arrived in this country almost invariably with a hole in the crown, which was there for the very good reason that its reduced weight led to a lower tariff charge. On its arrival, the hole was generally closed up by some composition such as cardboard and hidden under a wig.

Fashion dolls

By the 1860s, the English doll makers were routed for a while by the appearance of the French 'Fashion Dolls', whose bodies were made from stitched kid then dressed in elaborate clothes that reflected the latest styles of the French fashion houses. Often supplied with furs and jewellery, they represented the ultimate in luxury toys for those who could afford them. But again, as in the case of the Montanari dolls, there was no lack of buyers.

At the other end of the scale in this country, there was the popular stuffed doll, the wooden Dutch doll, with its painted head and joints secured by tiny pegs, tiny dolls that cost only a farthing each, the indestructible rubber dolls made by Goodyear, and the black-faced golliwog.

All of them represented the various stages in the evolution of the doll whose origins go back to remote antiquity.

Dolls were known in ancient Egypt and were common in the days of early Greece and Rome. Cortez, the 16th-century Spanish conqueror of Mexico, is said to have found the Aztec leader Montezuma and his court playing with elaborate dolls dug up from prehistoric Peruvian graves; and the wife of the prophet Mahomet is known to have owned one.

They were to be found among all the African tribes, the Australian aborigines, the Red Indians, and the Eskimoes. More often than not they were made in the image of a man. Some of them were ancestor images, others acted as lucky charms, and a third group was supposed to possess magical powers.

It is not until we reach the medieval period in Europe that toy dolls made in wood or clay and shaped in the image of a woman, began to appear. Even then they were referred to as children's babies, rather than dolls, a word that came into being sometime after 1750, and was probably taken from the Norse word *daul* (woman).

The subsequent development of the doll from those early times to the highly-sophisticated mass product is one of constant change, with the manufacturers forever striving to produce a realistic-looking doll that could emulate many of a human being's actions.

The wooden head replaced by the china head, hair marked by modelling or painted on replaced by flax, mohair, and sometimes even real human hair, eyes that could open and close, the doll that could speak and walk, have all played their part in the evolution of the doll which today can dance, drink from a bottle, have a nappy rash, and hair that actually grows.

But despite all the tremendous expertise which has been put into the development of the modern doll, it is still highly debatable that they have more to offer to a child than those famous china dolls of the 19th century.

Left is a typical modern baby doll. Wide-eyed and appealing, she has her own milk bottle.

Left are a collection of dolls from all over the world. Nowadays, dolls show all races and all stages of development. They are dressable, undressable, movable, huggable, knockable, pullable — and usually unbreakable. The modern child, it would seem, has everything it wants — and more — in the way of dolls. But, as art forms, perhaps the modern doll does not equal her old sisters.

Theatre in the Round

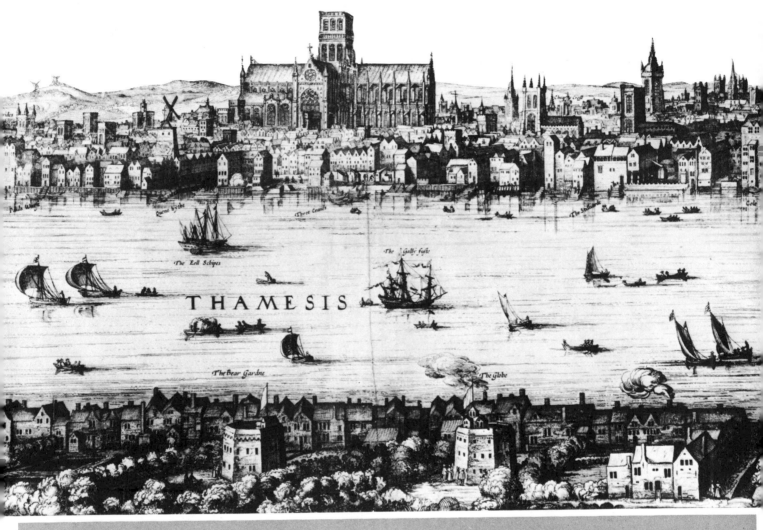

THAMESIS

Here is a glimpse of what 17th century London looked like, with Old St. Paul's dominating the sky-line, and the Elizabethan's love of the theatre emphasised by the presence of the Globe, bottom right. The first Globe was built in 1593 and was Shakespeare's playhouse. The Bear Garden, bottom left, was not a theatre as we understand it today but a centre for bear-baiting, a very cruel sport. Bears were kept just to be tied to a post and baited by dogs attacking and tormenting them. This was for the amusement of the men and women who crowded there to laugh and cheer. In fact, it was popular throughout Europe until 1835 — but it was then abolished in Great Britain.

A MODERN theatre audience would have been appalled. The theatre was partly open to the sky, leaving the audience at the mercy of the capricious weather, and that part of the roof that did exist was thatched, and therefore a fire hazard. The seats were hard and the scenery was of the most basic nature. As for the audience — who could be expected to enjoy a play sitting among a nut-cracking, orange-eating audience which seemed to take for granted the presence of wandering ladies of easy virtue and cut-purses?

It does not need much knowledge of the theatre to guess that we are at the Globe, watching a performance of one of the plays of William Shakespeare, who had shares in the theatre, which was built on the Bankside of Southwark, London, in 1593.

In 1613, it was destroyed by fire in which the only casualty seems to have been a man who had his breeches set on fire. This conflagration was happily put out by someone who happened to be carrying a bottle of ale, before any real damage was done. It was rebuilt in a year, only to be pulled down in 1664 because of a Puritan edict, by which time Shakespeare was in his grave, and England had become a very dreary place indeed in which to live.

The audience that attended the Globe may not have been the best behaved in the world, but they had a virtue sadly lacking in many theatre audiences. They all truly loved the theatre and their silence was total when the mind and the heart were gripped. They were certainly not slow to voice their disapproval, but, equally, they wept loudly when stirred.

This appreciation of the theatre, shared by all classes, was all part of the high summer of the Elizabethans, after the former mists of ignorance that had clouded the Middle Ages had given way to an extraordinary age which was to produce a gallery of immortals in all the fields of writing as can only by paralleled by Athens in the past, and once again by England herself early in the 19th century.

How did this miracle come into being? It was, to begin with, a time of awakening

The shining genius of the Elizabethan theatre was William Shakespeare, above. He understood perfectly how to play upon the emotions of his rowdy audience, and to make the best possible dramatic use of a stage that lacked props or scenery.

This could have been the scene as another audience began to gather for a play at the Globe theatre. They came on foot, or horseback, and from all walks of life; and they all truly loved the theatre. The Globe was built in 1593, and was destroyed by fire twenty years later. Fortunately the only casualty appears to have been a man whose breeches were set ablaze, and the theatre was rebuilt a year later. It was pulled down by the Puritans in 1664.

in England. The menace of Spain had been dispelled with the defeat of the Armada; the exploits of Elizabeth's sailors had stirred the most blasé English heart with pride and had greatly boosted the morale of England as a nation: most important of all, the tidal wave of the Renaissance had belatedly reached the shores of England, fortunately, at a time when there was a queen on the throne who had always encouraged the arts. In Italy, the Renaissance had expressed itself mainly in sculpture and painting. In England it was to express itself in literature.

The Elizabethan theatre itself was greatly influenced, strangely enough, by a book which had been published ten years before the first theatre had ever been built.

The book, a translation of some of the sonnets of Petrarch, by the Earl of Surrey, was published in 1557, and introduced blank verse to the English reading public. This new form of poetry, which consisted of the use of rhymeless verse, proved a perfect tool for playwrights such as Shakespeare, John Webster and Christopher Marlowe, who all found they were able to allow their imaginations to soar in a way which would never have been possible if they had been constricted by the need to rhyme each successive line. Not without cause has Surrey been called the first refiner of the English language.

But the band of Elizabethan playwrights, which also contained among its ranks the genial Ben Jonson, who lived on the fringe of dire poverty throughout his whole life,

represented only a small section of a noble array of writers which included poets, historians, clergymen and philosophers.

In the foreground of them were men like Edmund Spenser, whose long allegorical poem, *The Faerie Queene,* glorified his country and his queen, the tragic Sir Walter Raleigh, one of the most spectacular figures of his age, who spent thirteen years of his life writing his *History of the World,* in the Tower of London, before being led to the executioner's block, John Donne, the famous Dean of St. Paul's, whose fame rests mainly on his amorous poems, though only four of them were published in his lifetime, and Francis Bacon, whose sparkling prose style is seen at its best in his Essays.

In many ways they were a strange lot. Bacon despised English as a language, and was so convinced that it would not last that he had much of what he had written translated into Latin for posterity. Marlowe was suspected of being a secret agent for Queen Elizabeth, and was killed in a tavern brawl. Jonson killed a man in a duel, and after a spell in prison, was let off with the loss of all his goods and a brand on his left thumb. Raleigh beggared himself searching for El Dorado, the fabled city of gold, and Shakespeare, who always wrote in haste, thought so little of his work that he made no attempt to preserve it.

But in the end they all had one thing in common. Each, in his own way, enriched the English language, and in doing so laid down the foundations of English poetry and

The scene inside the Globe would have appalled a modern theatre audience. Below the players the "groundlings" — spectators who paid a penny, stood eating oranges, cracking nuts and drinking ale. The wealthier members of the audience sat in tiers around the yard. Cut-purses and ladies of easy virtue wandered through the throng, and occasionally the strains of the musicians triumphed over the noise from the audience. But they did follow the drama in their own way — and how they loved it! They could be deeply moved, and were not ashamed to weep as tragedy unfolded before them, nor to voice their disapproval in ribald fashion when the occasion deserved it.

In what was a Golden Age for the English language, Edmund Spenser, left, and Ben Jonson, were two of the eminent men of literature. Spenser's great work, The Faerie Queene, glorified his country and his Queen. Jonson, a genial although turbulent spirit, spent much of his life in poverty and killed a man in a duel. After being imprisoned he was let off with the loss of all his goods, and a brand on his left thumb.

prose for the generations that were to
come.

Many modern theatres are designed 'in
the round', that is with a circular stage and
the seating arrangements for the audience
also in a circular plan. The Elizabethan
theatre did not follow this plan exactly. The
stage itself would not be round and it would
jut out into the yard where the groundlings
stood. The wealthy in the covered galleries
would only be on three sides of the stage,
and not all the way round it. Sometimes,
stools would be placed on the stage itself, to
provide the best view — and most expensive
seats — in the house.

The roof of the covered stage was painted
to represent the heavens. In more
ambitious theatres a machine-room would
be housed over the stage and special effects,
such as gods falling from the heavens,
could be produced.

The Globe theatre itself was not
completely round, as can be seen from the
exterior view of it illustrated on the opposite
page.

Certainly, to be present at a theatre in the
round in Elizabethan times would be a very
different experience from a visit to the
theatre of today.

Putting on a play...

STAGE HANDS

SCENERY BUILDERS & PAINTERS

USHERETTES

BAR

MASTER CARPENTER

UNDERSTUDIES

BOX OFFICE

CHIEF ELECTRICIAN

COSTUME MAKERS

THEATRE MANAGER

PRESS REPS

DESIGNER

COMPANY STAGE MANAGER ASSISTANT AND DEPUTY

ANGELS

PLAYWRIGHT

PRODUCER

AGENT

DIRECTOR

CAST

LIGHTING DIRECTOR

When it comes to staging a new play professionally, the process is a very large scale one, involving all the people shown above.

Above and Right: Costume makers at work. Either men or women may do this. Technical skill is essential and patience and historical knowledge are both useful.

A play begins in a playwright's head. If he or she manages to get it accepted, the basic ingredients to its success are actors and an audience. You can do without a theatre in the last resort, without scenery, even without a stage, but you cannot do without players and an audience.

Once a play is decided upon, the producer decides how much it is likely to cost. Theatres that get money from the Stage can take risks: Ordinary managements have to be careful. Even a small-scale play with a single set can cost around £30,000 to stage nowadays, while a musical can cost £100,000 or more.

After the playwright has had his idea and got it down on paper, he must find a producer.

Men and women who enjoy a theatrical gamble are known as angels. They all put up varying sums of money, which they will lose if the play fails. But if it succeeds they will get their money back and make a profit.

Meanwhile, the producer has been looking for a director as well as angels. The director is the key figure in the production of a play. The play, or its stars, or both, may make the box office boom, but it is the director who shapes the play, interprets it, and rehearses the actors.

Either with the producer, or on his own, he will select the cast, though

picked, theatre lighting now having reached such a high standard that an expert is needed. But the director is in overall charge. He has to agree with the designs from sketches or small models until completion.

He has a team to work with him. His number two is the stage manager, who is responsible for the smooth running of the rehearsals and of the performances after the play has opened. The stage manager has his assistants, all of whom must take their turn "on the book".

The book is the actual play. Actors have to be prompted when they 'dry' - forget their lines - and 'moves' have to be written down.

The producer meanwhile will be deciding if the play will open in the capital or will first go on tour.

It is not always easy getting a theatre. Some producers own one.

Above: Rough colour sketch for a stage set.
Right: Ground plan showing exact positioning of furniture and props.
Below: Colour photograph of model stage design by Osbert Lancaster.

Reproduced by kind permission of Royal Opera House, Covent Garden.

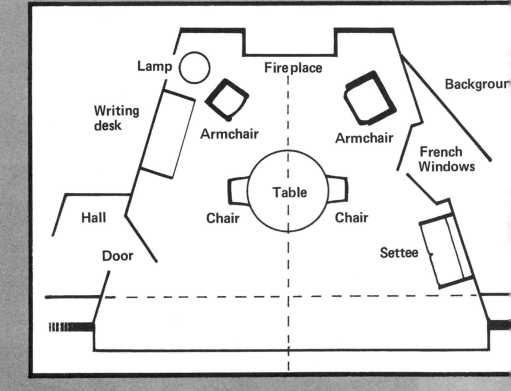

Lamp   Fireplace   Background

Writing desk   Armchair   Armchair   French Windows

Hall   Table

Chair   Chair   Settee

Door

the producer may have already chosen the stars.

Most actors are chosen at auditions, which are not at all pleasant affairs. The actor is handed a script and has to read it, often without a chance to glance through it, to a few invisible figures sitting in the dark in an almost empty theatre.

The director chooses his actors and also chooses the play's designer. He or she will design the settings and costumes, though there may be a separate costume designer.

A lighting designer also has to be

Others have to negotiate with theatre managers.

When the play opens, yet another section of the theatre world springs into action. It consists of the permanent staff of the theatre as well as the stage hands and key figures like chief electrician, property master and master carpenter.

There are also the 'front of house' staff - those who sell tickets, serve in bars or sell programmes.

The producer has other people in his own team, notably the press officer and the wardrobe mistress. She is in charge of the costumes while the play is running. The press officer is in charge of feeding advance

upstage right | upstage right centre | upstage centre | upstage left centre | upstage left
centre stage right | centre stage right centre | centre stage | centre stage left centre | centre stage left
down stage right | down stage right centre | down stage centre | down stage left centre | down stage left

forestage

apron stage

Above left: Diagram showing acting areas of stage.
Above: Lighting with lights overlapping to give even fall of light.
Left: Colour sketches of costume designs.
Below: Drawing of Chichester Festival Theatre stage.

Costume design labels:
Blue / Ostrich
organza cap frill longer at back
Velvet
Velvet
Velvet
Blue / Velveteen
Black Heel
Velvet recusion pleated in organza
Coat of Blue Shot Taffeta made Double

cloche hat
Imitation fur
Black Gloves
Imitation brown fur
Black 20's style button shoes

comes the official first night, complete with critics. There are plenty of backstage nerves, many people going on worrying until the reviews. Then, if they are good, they will relax but, if they are bad, they will worry even more.

Yet a play may survive despite bad reviews. That is all part of the magic of the theatre which has lasted now over 2,000 years. It applies to all forms of theatre but cannot exist without the audience that finally brings the theatre to life.

information to the papers and arranging interviews with stars and director.

All this time rehearsals are going on, scenery is being built and props are being obtained. At last, after several weeks, there are costume parades and lighting and dress rehearsals.

Amid all this, the stage manager will have had understudy rehearsals, for an actor may go ill any time.

Before a play opens officially, [the]re usually previews. Then

Giants of the New World

Writers of a country are a product of that country. Usually, they write about the world in which they have been raised and educated. Their points of view are coloured by the points of view of the society to which they belong and by the history which has preceded them.

The great American writers were no exception. They had the links of their common and varying backgrounds, the pioneering instincts shown in a practical way during the expansion westwards, and the belief in a new and worthwhile future which they were helping to create.

However, like all great artists, they were also individuals, with a unique and personal approach to their art form. Here we look at just a few of the famous names of American literature, men and women who were mainly writing before the turn of the century. They provide us with exciting and amusing stories as well as vivid pictures of life in those tumultuous days.

FENIMORE COOPER

(1789-1851)

Usually reckoned the first great American novelist and sometimes referred to as 'the American Scott', Fenimore Cooper was a Quaker whose father established a frontier settlement at the source of the River Susquehanna (now known as Cooperstown, New York). He is remembered mainly for the creation of Hawkeye, the pioneer scout and hero of a whole series of books.

The best known of these is *The Last of the Mohicans,* which appeared in 1826.

Cooper attended Yale from 1803 to 1805 but was expelled after a prank. He then served in the navy but resigned when he married in 1811. He had four children. The family lived in Europe from 1826 to 1833.

Unfortunately, his histories and political works were nowhere near so popular as his fiction, and even the fiction's popularity had declined by his death. Nonetheless, he was truly a literary 'pioneer'.

OTHER WORKS: The Pathfinder, The Deerslayer, History of the Navy of the United States of America, Home as Found.

NATHANIEL HAWTHORNE

(1804-1864)

At the age of 21, Nathaniel Hawthorne had a compulsion to become a writer, and applied himself to the task of learning his craft with a dedication typical of his Puritan upbringing. The form he decided on was the short story.

Twelve years of hard work passed before he published a collection of 18 stories under the title *Twice Told Tales.* But the book was scarcely noticed.

Married, he moved with his family to Boston. There he wrote several more books, including some tales for children. But his earnings were so small that he got a job in the customs.

At 45, he wrote a story called *The Scarlet Letter* which was an instant success. His great creative period had begun. *The House of the Seven Gables* and *The Blithedale Romance* followed.

He travelled Europe for seven years, extending the horizons of his mind. By the outbreak of the American Civil War, Hawthorne's health was breaking. His best work had been done.

OTHER WORKS: The New Adam and Eve, The Marble Faun, Doctor Grimshawe's Secret.

HENRY LONGFELLOW (1807-1882)

The creator of *Hiawatha* was a New Englander like Hawthorne — but a man of very different background and personality. Longfellow was highly educated and much travelled. He was one of the first of the modern Americans. Though proud of his country's pioneer past, he looked outwards to the world beyond.

The publication of several volumes of verse and prose brought him early celebrity.

He wrote *Hiawatha* in a style and metre suggested by a Finnish saga. This long poem is, in fact, a saga of the American Indians — an attempt by Longfellow to bring together the legends and customs of 'the original Americans'.

He was a good story-teller and this endeared him to children and those who had just discovered the joys of reading poetry.

His fame as a poet in his own lifetime was tremendous, for his works

EDGAR ALLAN POE (1809-1849)

The weird and uncanny tales of this strange and tortured genius reflect the mind of their creator. In his own words: "I became insane, with intervals of horrible sanity."

Poe had a tragic beginning. His mother, an English actress, died when he was only three, and he had to be adopted. He never saw eye-to-eye with his foster father — but took his name, Allan, as his middle name. Then, after a good education in England and America, he left home

and served in the U.S. army for three years.

Writing followed. He managed to have some of his poems published but lived in poverty and, after the death of his wife in 1847, friendless and alone. It was because of this, no doubt, that he turned to drink. The mental disturbances followed.

It was from the dark alleyways of his clouded mind that he drew the prose tales so familiar to all lovers of the bizarre and disturbing — such

LOUISA MAY ALCOTT (1832-1888)

"A philosopher," wrote Louisa May Alcott, "is a man in a balloon, with his family and friends holding the ropes which confine him to earth and trying to haul him down."

She obviously had her father in mind, for she and her mother were for ever trying to 'haul him down' and get the family out of debt.

She began writing short stories for magazines and at 22 her first book of

stories was published. She was 38 when she wrote what is probably the most popular girls' book published in America, *Little Women*.

To read *Little Women* is to read the story of Louisa's own life. It is virtually an autobiography told as fiction, and millions of girls have suffered with 'Jo', otherwise Louisa.

But despite her own problematic upbringing, her books are not depressing. On the contrary, they reflect an

MARK TWAIN (1835-1910)

Samuel Langhorne Clemens took the pen-name of 'Mark Twain' from a cry of the Mississippi river pilots ("By the mark twain" means two fathoms depth of water).

Young Sam had hardly any education. He learned all about life among the colourful characters of the Mississippi River where he was raised. Before he was 19, he had travelled widely around the country as an itinerant printer. During the Civil War, he went to the West and became an

unsuccessful gold miner — the wildly-funny story of which he recorded in his book *Roughing It*.

The publication of *The Celebrated Jumping Fog of Calaveras County* brought him instant fame.

Following *The Adventures of Tom Sawyer*, Twain visited Europe, and told of his adventures there in *A Tramp Abroad*.

He is best remembered as a humorist — but in *Huckleberry Finn*, at least, he showed himself as a writer of were read and enjoyed in his country and in Britain. He was given honorary degrees at Oxford and Cambridge Universities, and he was the first American poet to have a memorial to his name unveiled in Westminster Abbey.

OTHER WORKS:

Hyperion, Voices of the Night, Tales of a Wayside Inn, The Golden Legend.

---

tales as *The Fall of the House of Usher, The Black Cat, The Tell-Tale Heart* and *The Red Death*.

As so often happens with talented artists, Poe's genius was first recognised in Europe and America was slowly convinced of his greatness.

OTHER WORKS:

Morella, Man of the Crowd, The Murders in the Rue Morgue, The Raven.

---

optimism and a delight in the pleasures of growing up.

More family adventures followed in *Good Wives, Little Men, Jo's Boys* and *An Old-fashioned Girl.*

She wrote many books for adults, but it is *Little Women* that earned her a place in the Hall of Fame.

OTHER WORKS:

Hospital Sketches, Moods, Work, Flower Fables, Lulu's Library.

---

great poetic insight.

Eminently quotable, Twain once cabled the Associated Press who reported him to be dead, proclaiming, "The report of my death was an exageration!" And when asked to define cauliflower, he remarked, "Cauliflower is nothing but cabbage with a college education."

OTHER WORKS:

Life on the Mississippi, The Prince and the Pauper, A Connecticut Yankee at King Arthur's Court.

Through his legendary characters Huckleberry Finn and Tom Sawyer, Mark Twain portrayed the variety and excitement of life on the Mississippi.

Nature's Kingdom

The insect world's ugly duckling

Just as the swan grows out of the ugly duckling, so beautiful butterflies grow out of gobbling, creeping caterpillars.

NOT all insects are nasty creepy-crawlies that hide under stones or buzz round the dustbins on a hot day. One of the largest insect groups — the butterflies and moths — includes some of the most wistfully beautiful creatures on Earth.

There is very little difference between moths and butterflies. Moths have antennae (sense organs on the head) without a bulb or 'club' on the end, they usually fold their wings flat over their bodies when at rest, and they usually fly at night. Butterflies have 'clubbed' antennae, fold their wings tent-like when at rest, and fly — usually more slowly and gracefully

TRANSPARENT BURNET

SCARCE SWALLOW TAIL

RED ADMIRAL

PURPLE EMPEROR

SILVER-STUDDED BLUE

BRINTESIA CIRCE

PEACOCK

BRIMSTONE

ERI SILKMOTH

than moths — by day.

But although they look so beautiful when they are *adults,* butterflies and moths *are* creepy-crawlies — at least to start with. The magical butterfly grows out of a caterpillar feeding on leaves. This remarkable change is one of the most fascinating things in biology.

There are four quite separate stages in a butterfly's life. To begin with, it is laid as an egg by a female adult on a suitable piece of vegetation. Most caterpillars are very particular about what they eat and the female has to search to find the right kind of plant.

However, because there are so many different kinds of butterfly and moth, over 100,000 species, very few types of plant escape attack. Some non-plant materials are also eaten. The notorious clothes moth will attack fur, hair and wool. The wax moth eats the wax from beehives.

Caterpillars are very neat eaters. Starting from one point on a leaf, they will regularly nibble away little semi-circles of material until virtually the whole leaf is eaten. They then start on the next one. Little wonder then that millions of pounds of food are eaten annually by such common pests as the caterpillars of the

cabbage white butterfly, which eats cabbages and other green vegetables.

As it eats, a caterpillar grows. When it gets too big for its skin, it grows a new one inside the old, and then the old splits open and a fully formed, but bigger, caterpillar crawls out. Most caterpillars shed their old skins about five times before they turn into adults.

To change into an adult, the caterpillar undergoes a remarkable process called *metamorphosis.* Crawling to a suitably quiet spot, it suspends itself by a silk thread and changes into a *chrysalis* or *pupa.* (Moths also spin a cocoon of silk in which the pupa hides). Seemingly inactive, the pupa lives for between one week and several months — occasionally years in adverse conditions.

Complete change

Outside nothing seems to be happening. But inside the chrysalis, the body of the caterpillar is being completely changed. When at last the chrysalis splits open, it is not a caterpillar that crawls out, but a beautiful winged butterfly.

Just as the caterpillar is primarily an eating machine, so the adult butterfly is chiefly concerned with reproduction. In fact, some adult butterflies never eat at all, merely mating, laying eggs and dying. However, most have a long coiled 'tongue' which they insert into flowers to feed on nectar.

Often males perform a charming ritual to attract a mate. The grayling butterfly,

LARGE WHITE

CAMBERWELL BEAUTY

LARGE TORTOISESHELL

PERICALLIA MATRONULA

HUMMING BIRD HAWK MOTH

OAK EGGAR MOTH

Left: A few of the many thousands of beautiful butterflies and moths which can be seen in Britain. (Some are known only by their Latin names). The different parts of a butterfly's body can be seen clearly on the scarce swallow tail: 1. hindwing; 2. forewing; 3. thorax; 4. head; 5. legs; 6. abdomen.

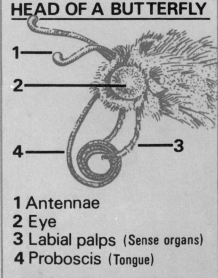

HEAD OF A BUTTERFLY

1 Antennae
2 Eye
3 Labial palps (Sense organs)
4 Proboscis (Tongue)

for example, will intercept a female in flight and entice her to land. Then he does a little dance, opening and closing his wings and waggling his antennae, before finally opening his wings fully and 'bowing' before her. Then he captures the female's antennae between his forewings and they mate.

The myriad beautiful colours and patterns of butterfly wings are not to cause admiration in people, or even to attract a butterfly mate. Instead they are a protection against predators.

Some patterns blend in with bark or plants, others draw attention to less important parts of the butterfly — like the edge of the hindwings — which if torn off allow the rest of the creature to escape.

Still other species have 'flash' coloration. The underside of the wings — or just the forewings — are brightly coloured. When the insect flies it is clearly visible, but when it stops the colour is hidden — causing confusion in the hunting predator.

Warning signs

Some of the brightest colours are warning signs, advertising the fact that the butterfly is poisonous or unpalatable to eat. For example, the brilliant metallic blue and red spotted burnet moth produces several poisons including histamine and prussic acid.

Other, quite edible, butterflies have similar markings to inedible varieties. This *mimicry* means that they too are left alone by predators, protected by the poisons of another species.

Nevertheless, millions and millions of butterflies and caterpillars get eaten every year. Even Man gobbles a few. The *gusanos de maguez* is a Mexican delicacy often tinned as an *hors d'oeuvres*. It is the larva of a skipper — a type of butterfly.

THE EMERGING ADULT

After the mystery of metamorphosis, a white admiral butterfly breaks out of the cocoon in which it has changed from a caterpillar. Some butterflies have a saw-toothed structure to cut their way out of the cocoon, others secrete alkali which dissolves the cocoon away.

THE FOUR STAGES OF A BUTTERFLY'S LIFE

Egg. Butterflies lay between 100 and 1000 eggs, usually on the plant which the caterpillar will eat.

Caterpillar (larva). This is the eating stage. As it grows, it sheds its skin several times to accommodate its increased size.

Chrysalis (pupa). Inside the chrysalis — sometimes supported by a silk 'girdle' round the middle — the larva changes into an adult.

Adult (imago). The adult's main function is to mate and lay eggs which will grow into the next generation.

The egg – symbol of new life

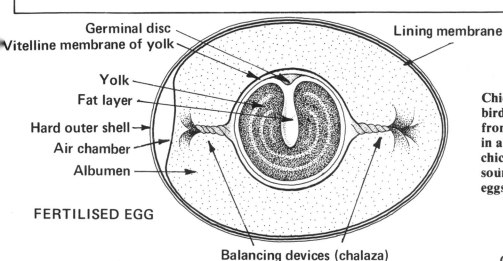

Germinal disc
Vitelline membrane of yolk
Lining membrane
Yolk
Fat layer
Hard outer shell
Air chamber
Albumen

FERTILISED EGG

Balancing devices (chalaza)

Chickens may seem very British birds, but they were developed from the wild jungle fowl in Asia, in about 2,000 B.C. The domestic chicken was a valuable, ready source of meat and, of course, eggs!

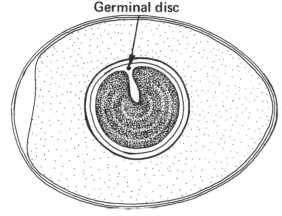

UNFERTILISED EGG

Germinal disc

The egg that reaches your table could never have become a chick. The germinal disc remains microscopic and does not divide because the egg is unfertilised. There is no difference in the nutritional content of the fertilised and unfertilised egg at the point of lay.

Which came first — the chicken or the egg? This is an old riddle, and one with no ready answer. We know that the egg is laid by a chicken, so without chickens there could be no eggs.

But wait . . . chickens hatch from eggs, and without eggs there could be no chickens!

An egg is a fascinating thing and yet one which we take almost completely for granted. To us, an egg is something we boil or fry, or make into an omelette. But that pale-coloured oval object, which we so casually break into a frying pan, is one of the great wonders of the world, containing some of the clues to the whole mystery of life. In fact, people of ancient times, who lived in close contact with Nature, saw the egg as the symbol of new life.

Amazing cell

The difference between life and non-life is the *cell*. All living things are comprised of cells, which continually grow and replace each other. An egg is simply a cell. When we think of a cell, we normally think of some minute thing which can only be seen with the aid of a microscope; yet an egg — even the enormous egg of an ostrich — is but a single cell, marvellously adapted to the task of producing a new creature.

There are two kinds of hen's egg: those produced for sale to the public which are unfertilised and cannot develop into a chick, and those produced for hatching out chicks. These have been fertilised by the male bird — called the cockerel.

From the outside both look alike but the diagram (above left) gives some idea of how complex an ordinary hen's egg

The nutritional value of eggs is always very high and they have been used as food from time immemorial. The yolk of the chicken egg contains 49 per cent water, 32 per cent fat, 17 per cent protein and 2 per cent minerals. The albumen, which is formed by alternate layers of dense and less dense material, contains approximately 87 per cent water, 12 per cent protein and 1 per cent minerals. The shell is composed almost entirely of calcium carbonate.

is. Just inside the hard but porous protective outer shell is a semi-transparent membrane which forms a kind of lining. Towards the 'big end' is an air chamber which is separated from the albumen or 'egg-white'. The albumen protects the central yellow yolk, the middle of which contains a layer of fat. Above the yolk is the germinal disc (proper name — cicratricle), the point from which the young chick will begin to grow.

At the time of being laid, the main difference in structure between the two types of egg is that in the fertilised egg, the germinal disc has started to divide. No

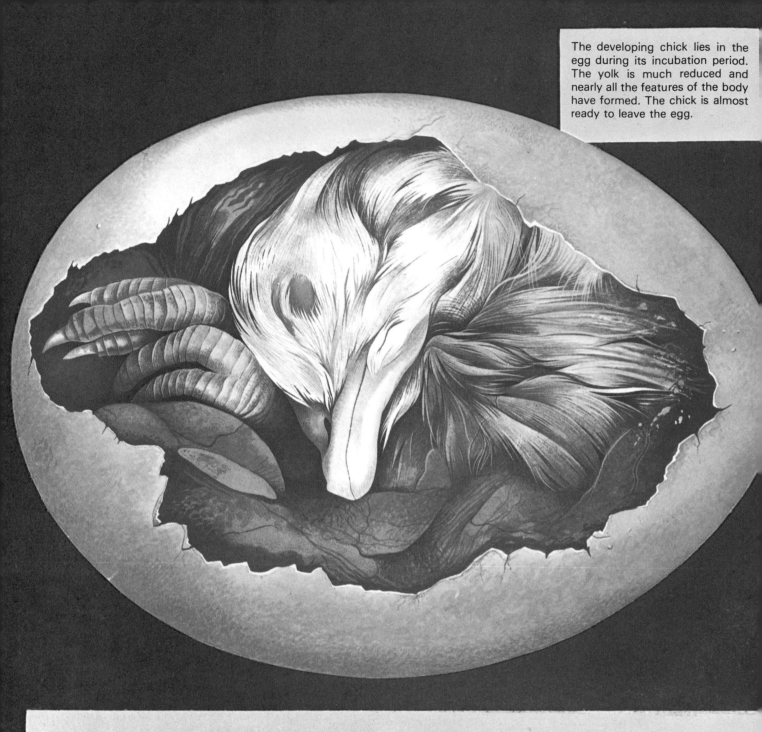

division occurs in the unfertilised egg.

After the egg has been laid, the hen *incubates* it simply by resting her body on it in the nest and keeping it warm. The sitting hen may roll the egg over but the vital germinal disc always remains uppermost, nearest the warmth of her body, due to the special balancing devices (chalaza) in the egg.

Cell division

The germinal disc from which the growing chick develops is where rapid cell division takes place. The one cell becomes two, then four, then eight, then sixteen and goes on doubling continuously as it grows away from the yolk. After about three days it has reached the embryo stage.

Over the next 18 days the features of the head and body are formed until the final embryo stage is reached — a small and bedraggled chick. The yolk it has been feeding on all the time has become very shrunken and lies beneath the chick like a cushion. Although its eyes are still closed, the chick is now ready to leave its efficient and protective shell.

The incubation period of 21 days is over. The yolk has nearly vanished and the albumen has been absorbed as the water needed by the chick. Much of the material of the shell (which contains a lot of calcium) has also been absorbed to help build the chick's bones, and is now very fragile.

The chick has a tiny beak, and growing on this is a bump which is sometimes known as the 'egg-tooth'. Using this it taps very weakly on the shell trying to break a way through. Sometimes it may take several hours to accomplish this, but in the end it manages to break a tiny hole. The cracks quickly enlarge and after several moments the young chick staggers weakly into the big world for the very first time.

Transformation

Its fluff is red and straggly, and sticks damply to its skin. In less than a day the fluff will have dried out and the chick will be round and healthy, a glowing yellow in colour. And in a few weeks the fluff will be replaced by adult feathers. The chick will become a chicken!

But the question still remains: which came first, the chicken or the egg?

The answer: neither!

All animals on Earth have evolved naturally. This process has taken hundreds of millions of years. Chickens as we know them today are distant descendants of those prehistoric species that no longer exist.

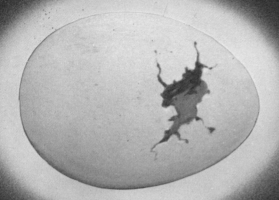

Using the 'egg-tooth', a tiny bump on its beak, the chick raps weakly on the shell, trying to break a way through. Sometimes this may take several hours, but eventually a small break is made in the shell.

Once the first break has been made the rest of the shell crumbles fairly easily, and the chick staggers weakly into the big world. Its fluff is red and straggly and sticks damply to its skin.

After several hours, the fluff has dried and the healthy, typically yellow chick is ready for the big world. In a few weeks the fluff will be replaced by adult feathers. But it would never have made it without the egg's superb efficiency.

America's Desert Creatures

LEEING from the law, the cowboy rides off into the desert to escape. Few posses will bother to follow him into this hot desolation, where there is nothing but sun, dust and rocks. You have got to be rough, tough and used to the terrain to survive.

Nearly every cowboy film has a desert scene. Most frequently, the films show the deserts of the south-western United States and of Mexico, with their stands of yuccas, agaves, giant cactus, and prickly pear cactus. Less often, the wind-eroded rock towers of Monument Valley, Utah, are favoured. But always the desert is simply used as a backdrop and the film gives little idea of what desert life is like.

The cowboys are just passing through, but what of the wild animals and plants which spend all their lives there?

Most American deserts are *rain-shadow deserts* — that is they lie in the lea of mountain ranges and, as the prevailing westerly winds rise up over the mountains, they drop their moisture before they reach the far side. Most of the rain which does fall in the desert does so in the winter and spring, but even this is quickly lost beneath the characteristically fast-draining, sandy desert soils.

Grasping water

Desert plants have to make the most of their opportunities, grasping water wherever they can. The roots of the sagebrush and the creosote bush, for example, lie just beneath the soil surface so that they can catch water as soon as it falls. Each plant's roots spread over a large area, and it is thought that it actually defends this area by producing chemicals which dissuade seeds from germinating on its 'patch'. In this way, the plants are spaced far apart and neighbouring plants do not compete for each other's water.

Cacti adopt a different strategy. They have a small surface root system but also deep roots able to extract water from depth. Moreover they are able to store water in their succulent stems. Up to ninety per cent of the cactus may consist of water.

Plants lose most of their water through their leaves, so the leaves of desert plants

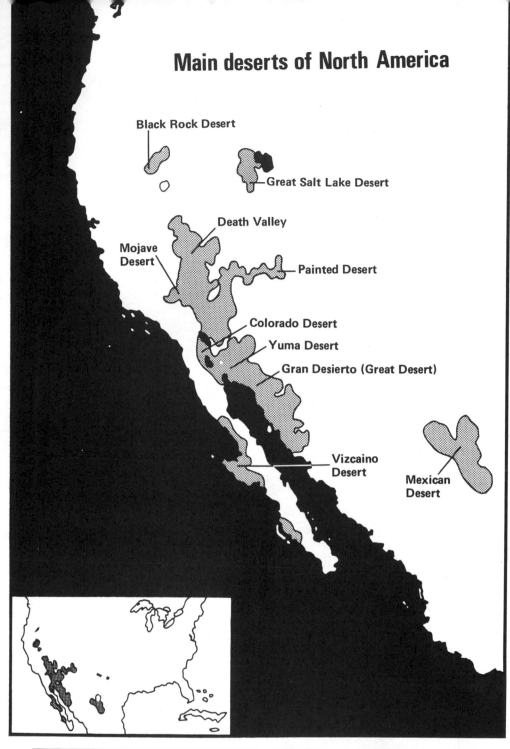

Main deserts of North America

- Black Rock Desert
- Great Salt Lake Desert
- Death Valley
- Mojave Desert
- Painted Desert
- Colorado Desert
- Yuma Desert
- Gran Desierto (Great Desert)
- Vizcaino Desert
- Mexican Desert

tend to be small. For example, the leaves of cacti are reduced to spines. The creosote bush goes a step further. This tough perennial drops its leaves during the summer, growing new leaves for the short, relatively moist winter and spring — the direct opposite of deciduous trees.

Other plants completely avoid the summer and autumn by surviving this period as seeds. These are annual plants, such as the Indian paintbrush and the desert primrose, which flower quickly and then die. Usually there is some special chemical in the seed coat which prevents germination and which must be washed out by a good spell of rain. But once this happens, growth and flower production both take place within a week or so. After rain, the desert becomes a blaze of colour — the 'desert bloom'.

Not only is it dry in the desert, it is also hot. In the height of summer, air temperatures regularly soar to 40°C and the temperature of the ground can reach an incredible 70°C — only 30 degrees off boiling point.

Water shortage

High temperatures and dry air mean that animals which sweat (or pant like dogs do) to keep cool can lose water very quickly and are in grave danger of dehydration. A man could last one, perhaps two, days without water. Most other animals can do no better. So how do they get by?

In winter and spring there is usually adequate water in temporary pools and heavy dews to supply most animals needs, but in summer the chance thunderstorm provides the only relief. Then most animals have to make do with whatever water is contained in their food.

Carnivores, such as the kit fox, have the least problem, as meat contains 60-70 per cent water. Birds, like the elf owl, can fly long distances to drink. The pack rat obtains water by eating the prickly pear cactus; for some reason, the cactus's spines don't harm the rat, which also seems to be immune to chemicals in the

Elf owl. The saguaro cactus is often inhabited by the elf owl, which, at 38 cm long, is one of the smallest in the world. By day it perches inside holes made by woodpeckers in the cactus, emerging at night to feed on insects, particularly grasshoppers and hawkmoths.

Gila monster. The Gila monster is a poisonous lizard with a bite which can cause loss of consciousness and palpitations, although it rarely proves fatal. The large tail contains food reserves, for the animal fasts for long periods between meals.

Gopher (or desert) tortoise. Spending the day in tunnels, this tortoise emerges at night to browse on succulent plants. During the mating season, the males fight for the females, each trying to overturn his opponent who is left helpless on his back.

cactus flesh, poisonous to most other animals.

But the most highly adapted of the desert animals, the kangaroo rat, eats dry seeds containing little water. Yet even this can be sufficient. Like all foods, the oils and fats in the seeds produce water as well as energy when they are digested. Thus, because the rat is careful not to lose water, it need never drink.

So desert animals do not so much make special efforts to find water, rather they conserve any they do have. In particular, as little water as possible must be lost in sweating (or panting) and in excretion. Urine, which must be formed to rid the body of harmful wastes, contains a large amount of water. This amount can be reduced by increasing the concentration of the urine or, better still, excreting a substance, called uric acid, which contains very little water. Insects, reptiles and birds excrete uric acid.

So that they don't have to sweat to keep cool, most desert animals shun the heat of the day and are only active at dusk and at night. Indeed, to stand in the middle of the desert at noon is a strange experience, for the overpowering sensation is silence — nothing moving, nothing singing — just silence.

Cool burrows

Smaller animals, such as the kangaroo rat, live in burrows about one metre beneath the surface. Although the surface temperature may fluctuate some 60 degrees between night and day, the burrow remains at an even 10°C. Other animals, such as the elf owl, find shade and relative cool in holes made by woodpeckers in larger cacti, while still others, such as reptiles, wait out the hottest part of the day beneath a rock or in the shade of a plant.

But despite all that animals can do, deserts remain harsh places in which to live. So perhaps they will forever remain out of Man's reach — cxccpt for the intrepid film producer attracted by their haunting beauty.

Bobcat. Like most desert animals, the bobcat is nocturnal. Sleeping during the day, usually in a hollow tree, it emerges at night to hunt. Although only one metre long, it is fearless, and will attack sheep and calves although its usual diet is mice and young birds. It is closely related to the European lynx, but has a shorter tail — hence its name.

Collared peccaries. These animals are close relatives of the domestic pig but are smaller, standing only 75 cm tall. They herd in groups of up to 15, often rolling in the sand to clean themselves. Their eyesight and hearing are poor, and they rely on smell to root our fruits and bulbs. When disturbed, they raise the hair on their necks so that it looks like a collar.

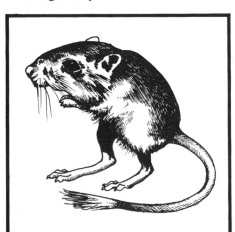

Kangaroo rat. 'Never drinking yet never thirsting' is a riddle solved by this desert rodent. It can live on water produced when it digests the seeds it eats. By day it hides in a complex burrow with many escape tunnels, appearing only at dusk and at night.

Kit fox. The large ears of this small (40 cm) nocturnal fox suggest that it has a very keen sense of hearing, especially important for detecting its enemies in the dark. When fleeing, it changes direction so quickly that it is difficult to see it, let alone catch it.

Spotted skunk. A cornered spotted skunk, like all skunks, can squirt a foul-smelling nauseating liquid with remarkable accuracy from glands at the base of its tail. This particular skunk is unusual, however, in that it performs this trick from a 'handstand' position.

251

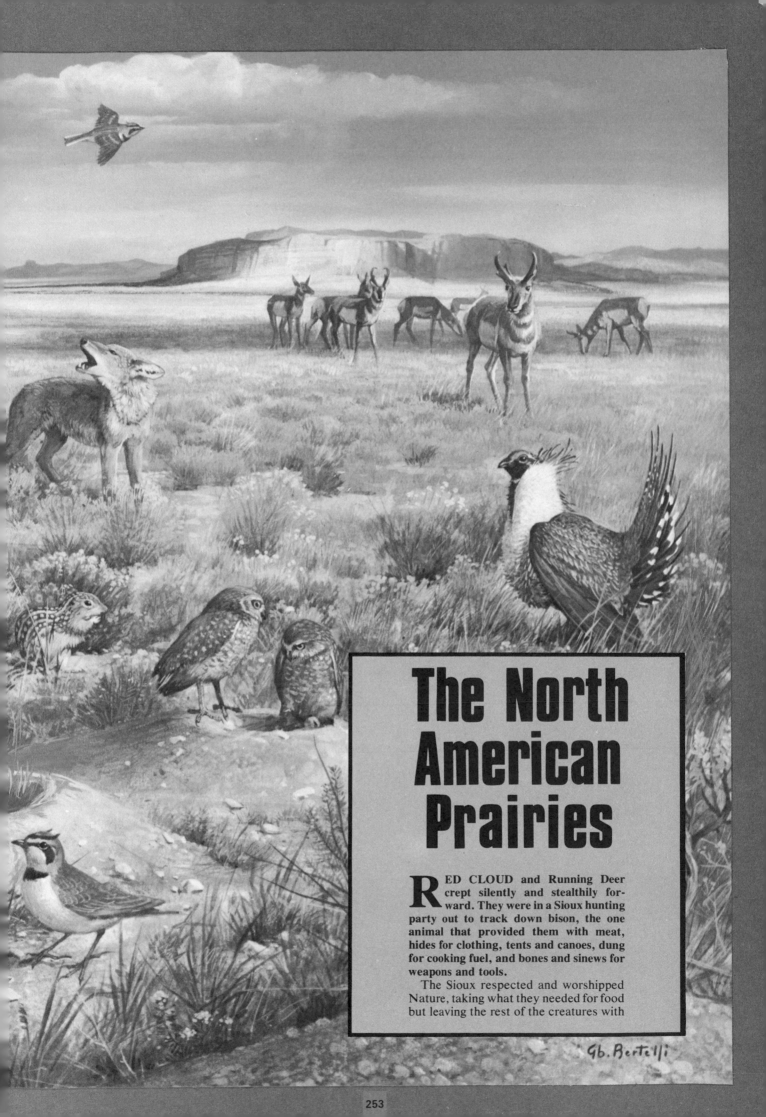

The North American Prairies

RED CLOUD and Running Deer crept silently and stealthily forward. They were in a Sioux hunting party out to track down bison, the one animal that provided them with meat, hides for clothing, tents and canoes, dung for cooking fuel, and bones and sinews for weapons and tools.

The Sioux respected and worshipped Nature, taking what they needed for food but leaving the rest of the creatures with

Gb. Bertelli

13-lined ground squirrel

Burrowing owl

American bison

which it shared the Great North American Prairie. The two braves stood motionless waiting for the right moment. Suddenly, there was a loud crack. A bison dropped to the ground. The rest of the herd stampeded in panic. European settlers had arrived.

Over 100 years ago enormous herds of American buffalo or bison migrated to and fro across the vast flat plains of central North America. In spring, as winter's browns turned to green, regimented formations of bison would move northwards, the youngsters in front and the older beasts to the rear. They would travel by day and rest at night. To ward off intruders huge guarding bulls, some as high as 1.8 metres at the shoulder, would pace around the herd in a wide circle.

But that was 150 years ago when an estimated 50 million bison roamed the plains. Such were the ravages of pioneers like Buffalo Bill, who would kill a hundred bison a day, that by 1889 there were only about 540 bison left on the entire continent. Today, conservation measures have ensured their survival at least in thousands if not in millions.

Each summer an uneasiness percolates through the small herds. The bison's thick winter wool falls away exposing his tender hides to the onslaught of other enemies — flies, mosquitoes, and, surprisingly, the seeds of spear-grass. Spear-grass seeds uncoil when in contact with the moist night air and coil up again during the dryer day. Turning eight times

in an hour the seeds can bore into hard parched ground, or into the soft hide of a bison unfortunate enough to rest beside the plant. The only answer to all these irritations is a cool, deep wallow in the mud beside a river.

Not far from the bison herds is often seen an antelope-like creature, the pronghorn. Standing one metre at the shoulder, these reddish-brown animals blend well into their surroundings. Their big eyes and large ears are constantly on the look-out for predators for which they reserve their perfect strategy — speed. The pronghorn is the fastest mammal in North America. It can cruise for eight kilometres at a constant 50 km/h, and burst for one kilometre at 80 km/h. Cartilage pads on the bottom of their hooves quieten their escape and if danger is really close they can leap six metres into the air in one bound.

Pronghorns are finely adapted for life on the prairie where temperatures can soar by day and drop to freezing by night. Muscles below the skin flatten the coarse hairs of their fur to exclude cold, and erect them to allow cooling. On the pronghorn's rump these moveable hairs form a white rosette like a powder-puff. If danger is near the hairs stand up and the patch seems to flash. The signal passes through the herd, and can be seen by a man three kilometres away.

The greatest danger comes in winter, when the snow covers the ground making it difficult to run. That is when pronghorns fall prey to the prairie wolf or coyote.

Coyotes and Prairie Dogs

The howling call of the coyote can be heard at dawn and dusk all year round, and in almost any part of North America, for the coyote has flourished where every other animal has been reduced. They have even moved into towns and cities like the urban fox, raiding trash-cans and litter-bins. Across the prairie they hunt in pairs, achieving speeds of 65 km/h over short distances and running in relays to tire their prey. They are also very cunning. A coyote will sometimes lay very still on its back shamming dead. An

Diamond-back prairie-dog

inquisitive carrion bird drops out of the sky to investigate the potential feast, and *wham!* the coyote leaps up and grabs it — an easy meal. The coyote's favourite food, though, is a small short-tailed ground squirrel, known as the prairie-dog or marmot.

Prairie-dogs live in vast underground cities, each with its own highly structured social organisation. According to geographical boundaries each town or city is divided into wards, and each ward is broken down into extended family groups. Harmony tends to exist between members of the same family, but territorial feuds develop between groups. The family retains its group identity by kissing. If two members of the same family meet they exchange kisses, nuzzle and groom each other. On the surface the prairie-dog city is marked by a series of small volcano-like craters which surround the entrances of each tunnel. The rim stops flood water from pouring into the underground complex and provides a vantage point on which the prairie-dog can watch for enemies. On spotting danger it barks and the warning sends all the others scampering for the safety of their subterranean homes.

Away from the open scrub of the plains, hidden amongst the rocks and thickets lives another type of ground squirrel. It has a bushier tail than the prairie-dog and striped fur. It often stretches up onto its hind legs in order to look around and has a twittering alarm call when danger threatens. The North American ground squirrel is active by day, gathering and hoarding nuts and seeds which it carries away in cheek pouches to be stored for use in winter.

They have to be constantly alert for the overhead shadow of their most feared predator, the burrowing owl. The burrowing owl is often seen in daytime bobbing up and down on its unusually long legs, on the ground or on fence posts. It nests in the burrows vacated by prairie-dogs, where it becomes infested with fleas. The young stay in the burrow until mature and will hiss, like a rattlesnake, at any intruder. The young need to be fed often, and the burrowing owl is very par-

tial to newly-fledged larks, the local variety being the horned lark. It is a brown bird, slightly larger than a sparrow, but with black whiskers, black horns and a black collar. On the ground it walks rather than hops and in the air it can be seen to fold its wings after each beat, and rises high into the sky singing as it goes.

A bird more reluctant to take to the air is the Californian quail, a small chicken-like bird with a black forward curving plume on the top of its head. Its defence against night-time predators is to roost in a circle with heads pointing outwards. If danger is near the quail-circle 'explodes' and the predator is confused by all the movement.

Perhaps the most spectacular of all the birds of the prairie is the sage grouse. The males come into their own during the courtship season. During display the black tail feathers are erected to form a spiky fan, and two bright orange air sacs on the throat are inflated. The male struts and bows, rattles its wings, and makes a loud booming and popping sound. At the climax of the display the head may disappear altogether in a ruff of black, yellow and white feathers and skin.

Another rattling sound coming from behind a flat prairie rock is more sinister. It is made by the highly venomous rattlesnake, out hunting for small rodents and rabbits. The rattle, bell, cloche, buzzer or whirrer of a rattlesnake is made up from a number of loosely interlocking scales. Each scale started out as the last scale at the tip of the snake's tail. During moulting, all the skin except this tail piece is sloughed off and the successive moults build up a small row of dried horny scales.

The purpose of the rattle is thought to be to ward off other animals that may accidentally tread on the snake and kill it. As a last resort the rattlesnake will strike at an approaching animal, including Man, its long-backward pointing fangs capable of injecting a dose of lethal poison into the victim. This *is,* however, a last ditch stand on the part of the rattler, for it would prefer to slide away and avoid confrontation. Unfortunately, for the rattler and all the other animals of the prairie there are fewer and fewer places in which to hide. As we spread our technological lifestyle further and further into the wilderness perhaps we should heed the rattlesnake's warning — "Please don't tread on me!"

Diamond-back rattlesnake

Horned lark

Sage grouse

Pronghorn

Coyote

Californian quail

Running away isn't the only way to stay alive. You can also shut the enemy out.

Animals in Armour

Crab

STAYING alive — that's the name of the game for all living things. If an animal hasn't some means by which to defend or protect itself, it won't last long in the struggle for survival.

There are many ways of staying alive. Some animals have long legs to escape their enemies, others live in trees or have learnt to fly or even take refuge underground. Yet others have developed armour, so that instead of fleeing they retreat within a shell, relying on the strength of their fortification. Others have less well-developed defences than shells but still have thickened skins to ward off the blows of attackers.

Shells

Shells are most common in the group of animals known as molluscs — snails, limpets, scallops, cockles and the like sit securely within their calcium carbonate bastions.

Only a few predators have developed ways of attacking them. Thrushes will crack open snail shells by 'hammering' them against stones, and dog whelks, themselves protected by a shell, have a boring rod in their mouths which they use to bore holes into winkles. The whelks can then suck out the contents of the shell. But one of the reasons why molluscs are one of the most abundant animals is because they are so well protected.

Crabs and lobsters (crustaceans) are also well armoured, but their mode of defence is rather different from that of snails. Instead of having a solid shell into which it can withdraw its whole body, a crab is covered with a jointed skeleton of calcium carbonate which moves and forms part of the body. Thus, the skeleton of the crab functions not only as armour but can also be used in offence, as anyone who has been pinched by a crab well knows.

Insects, as well, have a jointed exoskeleton but this is made of a material called chitin rather than of calcium carbonate, and is much lighter. Even so the armour does make flight difficult. Indeed the beetles, which are among the most heavily armoured insects, sometimes seem to have difficulty in manoeuvering. May bugs, (cockchafer beetles) are frequently found stunned, having flown into objects on still summer nights when flight would appear to be an easy matter.

Crab and insect armour, just like that of a medieval knight, is jointed to allow movement. The leg of a crab, for instance, has six joints and each moves at a slightly different angle, so that, in total, a wide range of movement is possible.

The problem of growth

But, despite the joints, this sort of armour is restrictive. Growth presents a problem, for the suit of armour can't grow as the animal inside grows. So it has to be shed for a larger size. Insects and crabs grow in spurts, then the old 'skin' is moulted just before the new armour, formed beneath the old one, has completely hardened.

Rhinoceros

Tortoise

The animals mentioned so far have what might be called 'plate armour'. This type of armour is also characteristic of many ancient fishes which inhabited the seas and lakes some 375 million years ago. But only rarely do modern fishes have armour, although the seahorses and boxfishes are examples.

Boxfishes, as their name implies, look like a swimming box. The body is rigid, armoured, and box-shaped, while the fins and tail project and thrash from the extremities of this suit of armour.

'Chain mail'

But, unlike the boxfishes, most modern armoured fishes have 'chain-mail' armour rather than plate armour. They have many small pieces of armour which can move relative to one another. This provides protection, yet still allows a considerable amount of flexibility.

Sticklebacks, for example, have solid head bones, but the body is encased in a flexible covering of enlarged scales. The fish also has spines along its back which provide the first line of defence.

Armadillos, which live in Central and South America, have a combination of 'plate' and 'chain-mail' armour. The head and shoulders are covered with an inflexible shield and there is a similar shield covering the rump and hind limbs. Both of these shields are composed of tiny hexagonal interlocking bony plates. Between these two shields there are semicircular hoops of armour (the number varies according to the species) which allow some degree of flexibility. The three-banded armadillo is able to roll up when threatened, but this ability is not shared by other species.

Large, horny epidermal scales cover the body and hind limbs of pangolins (scaly anteaters), while the modern-day giants of the land, the elephants, hippopotamuses and rhinoceroses, gain protection simply by having an extremely tough skin. The skin of an elephant is impregnable to almost everything, and that of an Indian rhinoceros is thrown into folds over the shoulders, back and rump so that in these vulnerable parts there is a double thickness of hide.

But surely the final word on armour must go to the tortoise. Like all reptiles, such as crocodiles, alligators, and lizards, the skin is covered with horny scales which themselves provide some degree of protection. The tortoise also has an underlying box-like bony shield, open at both ends, covering the back and belly. The part of the shell covering the underside is hinged fore and aft and when the head and legs are retracted the end flaps are raised so forming an impregnable box.

The price of armour

Armour is not without its price: it is heavy and the wearers are generally slow moving. But herein may lie a lesson. For among the armoured ranks are the longest living animals; 60-year-old elephants have been known and the greatest authenticated record for a tortoise is 152 years, which means that even if you do not get around very fast you've got a long time to do it in.

Armadillo

Alligator

Wonders of the Galapagos

THE Galapagos group of Islands lie straddled across the Equator, some 1600 kms west of the nearest land mass, Ecuador. There are 16 main islands though Darwin only knew of ten. Being mainly composed of volcanic soil, which, for the most part, supports no more vegetation than indifferent scrub, they have an inhospitable aspect. Perhaps this is why they were first settled as a place of exile for political dissidents by Ecuador only three years before Darwin arrived.

Then there were only 200 people living there. Today, no longer a penal colony, the islands have a population

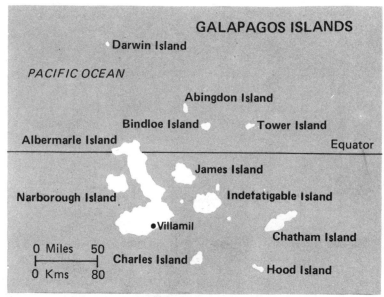

Galapagos Wild Life Key

1. Galapagos Albatross
2. Swallow tailed gulls
3. Marine Iguanas
4. Sally Lightfoot crabs
5. Flightless Cormorant
6. Sealions
7. Galapagos Hawk
8. Male Vermilion Flycatcher
9. Galapagos Woodpecker Hawk
10. Male Galapagos Tortoise
11. Blue Footed Booby
12. Female Vermilion Flycatcher
13. Land Iguana

GALAPAGOS ISLANDS

Darwin Island

PACIFIC OCEAN

Abingdon Island

Bindloe Island   Tower Island

Albermarle Island   Equator

James Island

Narborough Island   Indefatigable Island

•Villamil

Chatham Island

0 Miles 50

0 Kms 80   Charles Island   Hood Island

exceeding 4,000, most of whom scratch a sparse living as farmers or fishermen.

The word Galapagos derives from the old Spanish word for tortoise and it was the fantastic number of giant tortoises that roamed the islands that so impressed every caller there, including Darwin, who observed that they weigh as much as 2½ kg, walked at 302 metres an hour and needed six or eight men to lift one, though the males were much bigger than the females. The Galapagos tortoise is thought to be among the oldest living creatures on earth. Fossils reveal that on the continents they long ago died out. The shape and different markings on their shells make it possible to identify from which island each tortoise came.

Generally, there is a marked scarcity of animal life in relation to the area of the islands. Only 700 species have so far been listed. Compare this with 20,000 species in the British Isles. Mammals on the islands are represented by only seven types of rodents and two types of bats; snakes by only one non-poisonous variety.

However, the shortage of species is more than made up for by the exotic nature of many of them. After the tortoises perhaps the best example of this are the iguana lizards able to grow up to 5 metres long. The seagoing type is an excellent swimmer, having developed web feet, and can cling to rocks for hours on end feeding on seaweed. The land variety prefers a diet of cactus. Darwin thought them hideous and wrote that they looked like 'Imps of Darkness', but they are harmless vegetarians.

Red rock crabs, among them the Sally Lightfoot, also cling to the rocks in such masses that Darwin when he first saw them thought he was seeing red rocks suddenly come to life and move.

Unique

The Galapagos is the only place in the world where you can see penguins and sealions gliding together over the coral and living side by side with tropical animals. Like so many of the animal species on the islands the sealions exhibit no fear of predators or Man. They are usually most approachable but the dominant males can be dangerous as they jealously protect their territories, which may contain up to 30 cows, from other bulls and humans.

A unique animal life developed in the Galapagos because for so many centuries there was no interference from Man and the islands were divided from each other by very deep channels. Bird life, too, developed in the same way. Perhaps the flightless cormorant is the stangest bird to be seen there. Over the ages it has developed into the largest cormorant in the world. Presumably because it encountered no enemies on the islands and with plenty of fish to feed on close at hand along the shore it no longer needed to fly and the wings became stunted.

There are 25 kinds of land birds to be observed on the islands as well as swallow tailed gulls. Given the usually vagrant nature of gulls Darwin thought it odd to find them here.

He also thought the swallows smaller and duller than the American variety and that the hawk was not unlike the buzzard in structure. The justly named boobies are still apt to encounter man when they crash into masts of ships but are capable of an amazingly quick recovery.

Finches

Most of the land birds, though, are accounted for by Darwin's Finches and certainly these were most important to the great biologist's theories. There are 13 distinct species of this bird, some of which are peculiar to one island only. Each species has its own unique features mainly relating to the size and shape of their beaks which have evolved to fit their owners for specific diets.

The Mangrove Finch, has the ability to use twigs as tools, even breaking and trimming them to required shape, before using them to prise insects from cracks. Finches will also attack boobies to draw their blood and suck it.

Though the various species are closely related to each other they are separated by the shape of the beaks and geography and this it was, together with the tortoise's shells, that first led Darwin to the theory that was the basis of the 'Origin of Species'.

On the second largest island, Santa Cruz, there has been founded under the auspices of UNESCO the Charles Darwin Biological station which works in close co-operation with the Darwin Foundation in Brussels. It exists to promote scientific studies and to protect the indigenous vegetable and animal life of the islands.

Sadly, over the years this has become necessary because of the introduction of animals not indigenous to the islands. Goats, for instance, compete for all kinds of food. Moreover, dogs and cats as well as rats attack eggs of the various reptiles and lizards. Great advances have been made in restoring the tortoises which at one time looked like becoming a threatened species as they were taken away in their hundreds by ships that called.

Many of the islands now have the status of nature reserves which ensures they will repay fruitful study for years to come.

There doesn't seem much activity, but look closer. There's a lot happening on...

Sunny days in the meadows of Europe

IT is summer and a time for picnics, country walks and chasing games in and around the fields and hedgerows. But just stop for a moment. Stand still and look around. You are not alone. The meadow is alive with the frantic comings and goings of the natural world, for summer is a time of intense activity.

The busy honeybees must collect enough pollen and nectar to be stored as food for the winter. They visit the brightly coloured flowers that produce sweet nectar. While sucking out the sugary liquid the bee gets dusted with pollen which is stored in cleverly designed pollen baskets at the sides of the back legs.

The larger bumblebees also seek out the flower nectar. The problem is that some bumblebees have relatively short probosces, or tongues, and cannot reach down into the long tubular flowers. They pop around to the back of the flower and bite their way into the nectar store. They are known as 'nectar thieves'.

Another insect with yellow and black striped warning coloration is the hornet. The size of a large wasp, the hornet, like bees and wasps, is a social insect. It lives in a colony where the egg-laying queen, attended by loyal workers and a few lay-about males, is the centre of attention. Only the queen hibernates and survives the winter. She starts up a new colony, usually in the hollow of a tree, each spring. At the height of summer there may be as many as 20,000 individuals living in the nest.

Creatures which are more obvious to see — because of their colours and flittering flight — are the butterflies. The cabbage white and red admiral are common. They land on the flower heads, and uncoil a long tongue which sucks up the liquid food. The food gives the butterfly enough energy to survive its very short life. Male and female butterfly mate and the female lays eggs. The eggs hatch into larvae or caterpillars, the growing stage of the butterfly's life cycle.

Threat of Extinction

In our meadow overleaf, you can see the green caterpillar of the cabbage white, and the striped green of the swallowtail. Both are disguised in such a way that they blend in with the foliage. This is just as well, for the numbers of certain types of butterfly are fast decreasing. The swallowtail for example, is just holding on in the Norfolk Broads. The pressure of farming and expansion of towns has meant a loss of breeding sites, and many species of butterflies are threatened with extinction in this country.

One of the insects not native to the British Isles, but found elsewhere in Europe, is the praying mantis. It is disguised as a leaf, and sits motionless on a twig waiting for a meal to pass by. Then, its front feet shoot out at an amazing speed and snap tightly around the prey which is hastily devoured with the aid of immensely powerful jaws.

Also hidden in the grass is the great green grasshopper. You are more likely to hear it than see it, for grasshoppers locate one another by making sounds. The noise is produced by rubbing the 'file', usually on the leg, over a 'scraper' on the wing. You can imitate the action by running your fingers over a comb. The great green grasshopper's entire body quivers as it moves its legs 20 times a second to produce the familiar chirping sound.

The green rose chafer, seen landing on the ox-eye daisy, demonstrates another remarkable insect feat. When coming into land the beetle hits the flower head at a speed of 2 metres per second, its body comes to rest within half a centimetre in which it must slow down at about 400 metres per second and experience a force over twice that experienced by astronauts as they leave the launch pad.

Waiting patiently in the meadow for all these insects are a host of predators. The most numerous are the spiders, with their silk orb-web traps hanging invisibly between two stalks. The spider itself waits beneath a leaf with one foot resting on a thread from the web. When a flying insect blunders in, the spider feels the vibration of its struggle to get free, and races out to immobilise the prey by biting into it with poison fangs. The spider wraps up the prey and eats it at its leisure.

A bigger predator lying in wait is the green lizard, resident in the Channel Islands but absent from the British mainland. This beautiful brightly-coloured creature spends much of its time basking in the sun. It too is threatened in some areas of Europe because of over-collecting for the pet-trade.

The bird-life in the meadow is dominated by the ubiquitous sparrow. There are many varieties of the bird throughout Europe. Our picture overleaf shows the Italian sparrow, which has clear white cheeks. They are not at risk, and are abundant on farms, towns and villages, closely associated with and taking advantage of Man's activities.

Flying high above is the skylark. You will probably hear it before you see it. Instead of singing from a high branch or a post the skylark goes on a song-flight, flying up, singing all the way, until the bird becomes a small speck in the sky.

Back on the ground, the distinctive 'quicc, ic-ic' sound reveals the presence of a quail, a tiny, sandy-coloured game-bird that is seldom seen in open country. It prefers to hide away, occasionally skimming low over the meadow in short bursts of flying.

And while all this frantic summer activity is taking place, a snail, carrying its spiral-shelled home on its back, slowly slithers over a leaf. It leaves behind a tell-tale glistening trail.

The skylark, well-known for its high-pitched song, with the plump quail in the background.

Our picture illustrates a few of the many creatures to be found throughout the meadowlands of Europe. You would never actually find the creatures collected together as shown because some are native to only certain parts of Europe.

1 Bumblebee
2 Cabbage white butterfly
2a Caterpillar of cabbage white
3 Spider (shown enlarged in inset)
4 Red admiral
5 Swallowtail
5a Caterpillar of swallowtail
6 Green lizard
7 Praying mantis
8 Large tortoiseshell butterfly
9 Short-tailed blue
10 Snail
11 Great green grasshopper
12 Honeybee
13 Rose chaffer
14 Hornet
15 Italian sparrow

G.b. Bertelli

The Zoo Without Bars

THE Seminole Indians called it Pa-hay-okee, 'Grassy Waters', and it is hard to better that description of the Everglades, the great marshland at the southern tip of Florida in the United States of America. It covers an area of some 4,000 square miles (10,000 square kilometres), much of it overlaid with sharp-toothed saw grass growing to a height of over ten feet (three metres).

It is a subtropical zone and in its forests and 'hammocks' (the tree islands which dot the landscape) live a rich variety of wild life, including a host of wading birds, alligators, snakes, turtles as well as deer, wildcats and panthers.

As can well be imagined, such riches provided an irresistible temptation for hunters, and at one time there was a real danger that many of the species would disappear for ever.

For instance, in the early part of this century, the plumes of the American Egret were considered a highly desirable decoration on ladies' hats, and it was only the fierce action of the conservation groups of the day that prevented the bird from becoming totally extinct in that part of the world. In 1920, legislation was passed making these birds a protected species; it became a crime to catch or kill them.

The alligator was also in danger, for its hide had long been valued for handbags and shoes; and the Indians looked on its tail flesh as a tasty tit-bit - as well as claiming that it kept the mosquitoes away!

In 1947, however, in the southern and central parts of the area, the Everglades National Park was established to protect this unique patch of swampland and its inhabitants.

Once again the beautiful wading

White-tailed Deer

Bald Eagle

White Ibis

Brown Pelican

Green Heron

American Egret

Snakebird

Alligator

Limpkin

Common Snapper

birds like the Wood Ibis and the White Ibis could make it their home, sharing it with such other exotic birds as the Purple Gallinule - sometimes called the "water hen" - the Limpkin, the graceful Green Heron with its bright orange legs, the Roseate Spoonbill and the Snakebird.

Incidentally, the Snakebird is so called, not because it eats snakes, but because of the darting, snake-like movement of its head as it swims almost beneath the surface looking for fish to spear.

The Limpkin, on the other hand,

Wood Ibis

Roseate Spoonbill

feeds mainly on the green fresh-water snails found in abundance in this area. It carries a snail to its nest, holds it with one foot and repeatedly hits the shell with its beak until the shell breaks and it can get at the flesh. The Limpkin is also known as the "crying bird", because of its loud continuous wail.

The rare Roseate Spoonbill was another bird virtually exterminated in some areas by plume-hunters, but once again it flourishes in the Everglades Park. Its main diet is small fish or crustaceans which it scoops out of the mud or shallow water with its spatulate, or flattened, bill.

The Bald Eagle has a special place in the hearts of Americans. Not only is it the only eagle found solely in North

Water Moccasin

America, it is also the national emblem of the country. It is now protected, as its numbers are decreasing due, it is thought, to the use of pesticides.

The Brown Pelican, however, has multiplied in the region. It looks very ungainly on land but once it takes to the air, swooping low over the water or

soaring high into the sky, it seems veritably transformed. It catches fish by "dive-bombing" its prey, spearing downwards until it almost hits the water then folding back its wings and extending its neck.

In the Everglades, beauty and danger live continually side by side. For lurking in its waters is the vicious Garpike, with its long, pointed nose; the Common Snapper whose sharp teeth and powerful jaws can easily overcome water birds and young animals; and the deadly Water Moccasin, whose diet includes turtles, fish and birds.

The Water Moccasin is also known

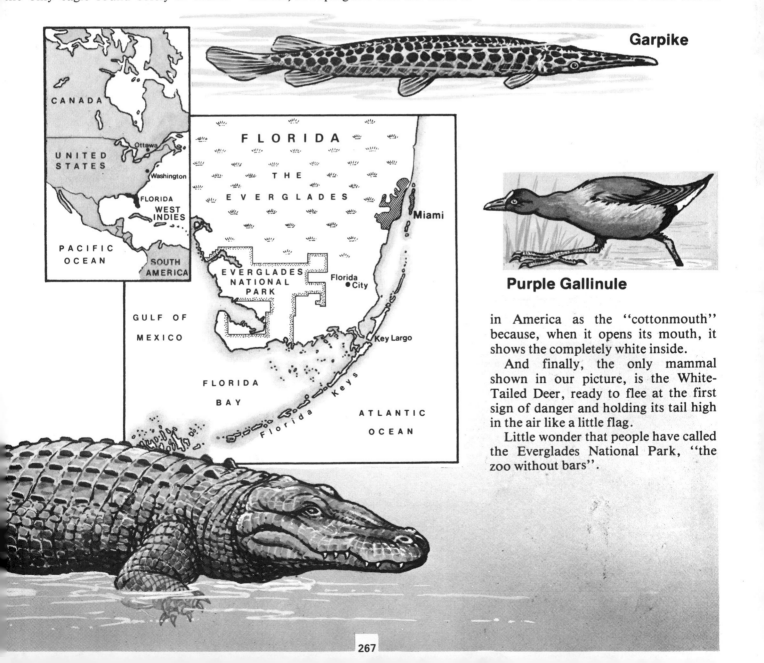

Garpike

Purple Gallinule

in America as the "cottonmouth" because, when it opens its mouth, it shows the completely white inside.

And finally, the only mammal shown in our picture, is the White-Tailed Deer, ready to flee at the first sign of danger and holding its tail high in the air like a little flag.

Little wonder that people have called the Everglades National Park, "the zoo without bars".

Believe it or not ...Sharks
are sensitive creatures

A shark accompanied by pilot fish. These small fish feed on scraps left by the sharks, but for some reason are never attacked themselves.

TO many people the word 'shark' conjures up images of unrivalled savagery and ceaseless quest for blood. The unseen presence, the menacing circling, the exploratory dash followed by the run in for the kill with feasome jaws agape is most people's idea of a shark attack. It is undeniably difficult to take a cool look at an animal which can, and has, ripped open bathers from limb to limb.

But what details do we know of this notoriety? What attracts sharks; are some species more dangerous than others; and what can we do to repel sharks? For many years details of shark attack have been analysed, fact has been sifted from the sometimes exaggerated claims of eye witnesses, and lucky survivors and some generalities have emerged.

Two principles have been established beyond reasonable doubt. First, all species of shark are unpredictable and therefore not to be trusted. Second, all species are dangerous if provoked — and provocation is the trigger for a high percentage of the 50 or so attacks each year which result in death.

There are some 250 species of shark, and most of these live in places rarely visited by man, such as the seabed or deep water. Clearly these species cannot be classed as dangerous. Equally, there are some species definitely known to be aggressive and to attack without provocation. Perhaps the most famous of these is the great white shark also known as the 'man-eater'. This shark lives a solitary life in open water and although encounters with man are rare they are usually fatal for the victim. Another proven aggressor is the blue shark.

Coastal sharks and those entering the lower reaches of rivers are potentially more dangerous. Among the top villians of the popular bathing beaches of Florida, South Africa, Australia and Japan are species of mako, tiger shark, lemon shark, dusky shark and the larger species of hammerheads. Locally, other species may be troublemakers but in such cases there is usually some evidence to suggest that only a few rogue individuals are concerned.

So what attracts sharks and how do they locate their prey? Noise and vibrations in the water are known to arouse their curiosity. Sharks can 'hear' these underwater pressure waves several hundred yards away.

They do this by means of their **lateral line**, a *sense organ* found in all fishes. It consists of a series of sensory cells sunk within a tube running along the body and over the head. These cells respond to vibrations, so the system is primarily for detecting movement. It is irregular vibrations, such as those caused by a fish or bather in difficulties, which produce the greatest response from the shark.

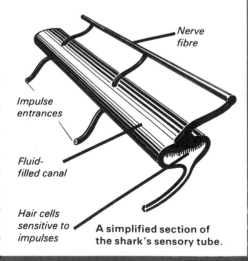

Nerve fibre

Impulse entrances

Fluid-filled canal

Hair cells sensitive to impulses

A simplified section of the shark's sensory tube.

It is not known whether all species of shark are man-eaters but here are four with which we certainly would not recommend you to go for a swim! Top left is the white shark, which will attack without provocation. It has been known to reach a length of up to eleven metres and is known as the 'man-eater'.

Top right is the whaler shark. Off the beaches of Australia it has attacked more people than any other kind of shark.

The curiously marked shark, above left, is the tiger shark, which is one of the marauding villains of the beaches of Florida and South Africa as well as Australia.

There's no mistaking the strange shape of the hammerhead shark, above, with the odd position of the eyes in its head. But it may be the way the eyes are set in the head which gives it a better ability to manouevre than any other species.

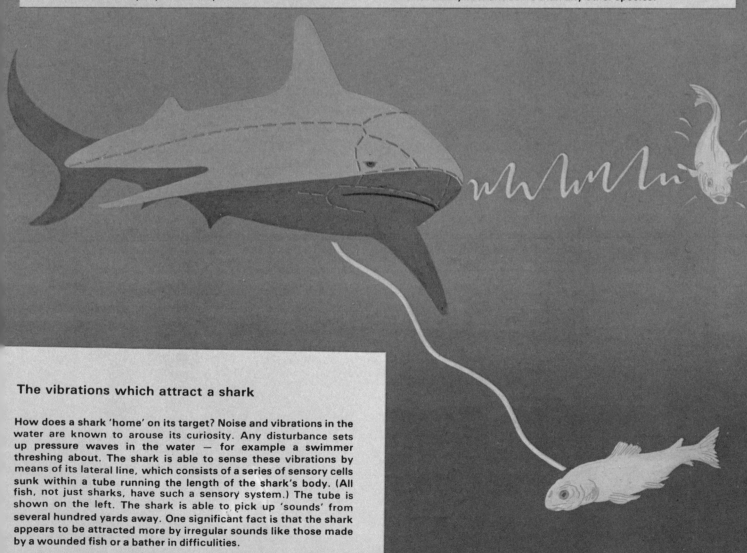

The vibrations which attract a shark

How does a shark 'home' on its target? Noise and vibrations in the water are known to arouse its curiosity. Any disturbance sets up pressure waves in the water — for example a swimmer threshing about. The shark is able to sense these vibrations by means of its lateral line, which consists of a series of sensory cells sunk within a tube running the length of the shark's body. (All fish, not just sharks, have such a sensory system.) The tube is shown on the left. The shark is able to pick up 'sounds' from several hundred yards away. One significant fact is that the shark appears to be attracted more by irregular sounds like those made by a wounded fish or a bather in difficulties.

Medium range sensing is by smell. The noses of all sharks are large and protrude beyond the upper jaw, shaping the very characteristic heads of these animals. That part of the brain concerned with smell is also large.

Some experiments suggest that sharks may detect blood at the astonishingly low concentration of 1 part in 10 million parts of seawater. Of course the smell has to be in the water already and so, unless a boat leaks, reports of sharks smelling sailors in boats are myths.

Short range detection is by sight. It is known that bright colours in particular attract sharks.

Once a shark has located its prey, it then makes a close-range exploration, which usually consists of 'bumping'; that is, it dashes past and noses the object of attention. This is when the trouble starts for the victim, since the shark's rough skin often cuts the prey.

Shark skin is very tough and is studded with tiny tooth-like scales (denticles), each of which points backwards. If rubbed the wrong way it feels like glasspaper and in fact was used as such by cabinet-makers. Shark skin has long been used in decorative leather work.

The final act of seizing and cutting the prey demands powerful jaws and ever-sharp teeth. The teeth are formed in rings (whorls) which run over the margin of the jaw. The youngest tooth of each whorl lies on the inner side and, as it grows, it moves around to become a functional tooth before dropping out. Since new teeth are constantly formed, there is a conveyor belt system of tooth replacement!

The shapes of the teeth varies considerably from species to species, and even between the male and female of the same species. Some shark teeth, such as those of the great white shark, are triangular with finely serrated knife-edges; others are awl-shaped as in the porbeagle; while the lower jaw teeth of the cow sharks are elongated and saw-like. But the specialised tooth form would count for nothing were it not backed up with the shark's ability to close on its prey.

The sight of a cruising shark makes man's efforts to move underwater pale into insignificance. Sharks are swimmers *par excellence*. Their streamlined bodies, pointed heads, and charateristically-shaped tails are designed to reduce water turbulence. The tail produces a powerful forward and slightly downward thrust, the latter being counteracted by the angled undersurface of the head and the hydrofoil-like pectoral fins.

The net result is a pattern of smooth, seemingly-effortless movement which can, in some species, reach high speeds. Very few speed trials have been made but a small blue shark, a mere 70 cm long has been clocked at 39kph rising to 71kph over short distances.

Although most sharks are the same shape, they do vary considerably in size: from the huge whale shark at 12m and 36,000kg, a harmless species which spends its day straining minute animals from the upper water layers, to the tiny midwater shark at only 20cm.

There are many aspects of shark behaviour which still remain a mystery, and considerably more needs to be known about their biology before advice on how to repel sharks can be given. Some divers have reported that a sudden burst of bubbles frightens the aggressor; others swear by copper acetate and other chemical 'shark chasers'. But even if we knew all the answers it is doubtful if the cloak of suspicion would be removed entirely from this most perfectly adapted of aquatic vertebrates.

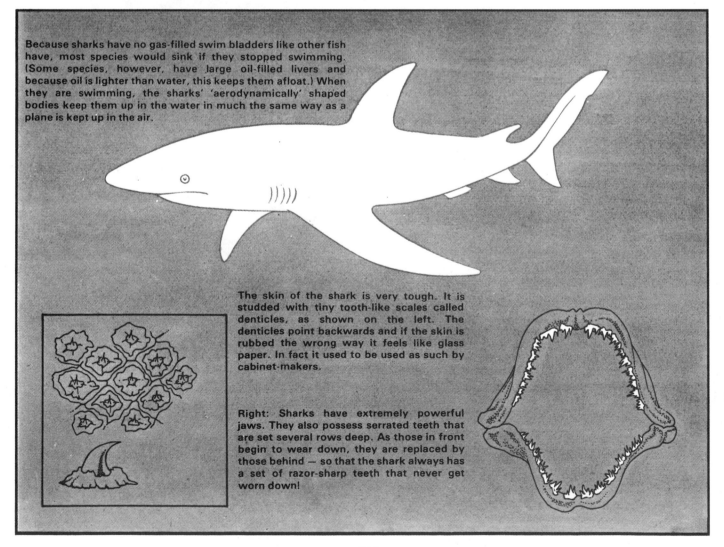

Because sharks have no gas-filled swim bladders like other fish have, most species would sink if they stopped swimming. (Some species, however, have large oil-filled livers and because oil is lighter than water, this keeps them afloat.) When they are swimming, the sharks' 'aerodynamically' shaped bodies keep them up in the water in much the same way as a plane is kept up in the air.

The skin of the shark is very tough. It is studded with tiny tooth-like scales called denticles, as shown on the left. The denticles point backwards and if the skin is rubbed the wrong way it feels like glass paper. In fact it used to be used as such by cabinet-makers.

Right: Sharks have extremely powerful jaws. They also possess serrated teeth that are set several rows deep. As those in front begin to wear down, they are replaced by those behind — so that the shark always has a set of razor-sharp teeth that never get worn down!

Creatures of the oceans

THE world's oceans are huge. So it is not surprising that they contain thousands upon thousands of different types of creatures. They come in all shapes and sizes, and the way in which they live is often very different too.

Man comes to the sea as a foreigner. He hunts some of its creatures, is fascinated by others, and regards others still with abject terror.

We expect fish to swim in the sea, but one family of fish travels quite effectively through the air as well. These are the so-called flying fishes. The question of whether they actually fly has puzzled Man ever since he took to sailing through tropical waters and observed schools of them scattering in all directions above the water in front of his ship.

Modern photographic techniques have shown that the flying fish does not fly but glides — without vibrating its wings — rather like the flying squirrels of North America. But its feats are none the less impressive.

Flying fishes glide at around 56 km/h and can cover up to 140 metres in about 10 seconds. There are two main types: the two-winged, which are about 25 cm long, and the four-winged, which are about 46 cm long. Both varieties become airborne by swimming rapidly forward and upwards to the surface. They then 'taxi' along the surface with the tail fin vibrating to provide power until the wings are spread wide enough to effect lift off — just like a plane takes off. Flying fish have been known to land on the decks of ships 11 metres above the sea level.

Another marine gymnast is the dolphin. It too often plays in schools alongside ships — even using the bow wave to surf on. The bottle-nosed dolphin is now a star performer in aquaria where its high intelligence and athleticism can be displayed profitably in front of appreciative crowds.

Extraordinarily, these lovable agile 'fish' are not fish at all. Instead they are a small variety of whale.

They are actually more closely related to Man than to fishes because, like him, they are *mammals*. Their ancestors probably walked on the land but then, many years ago, they returned to the water and became adapted to live in the sea. Nevertheless, whales still have their mammal characteristics. They are warm-blooded, have live young which are suckled by their mothers, and they breathe air through lungs — hence their need to rise to the surface every so often.

Tail power

A dolphin's (or whale's) tail spreads at its end to form two tail 'flukes'. These power the animal along as the tail waves through the water in just the same way as the tail fin of a fish does. But dolphin and whale tail flukes are always horizontal, while fish tail fins are vertical — this is the easiest way in which whales and dolphins can be distinquished from fishes.

As Man learns more and more about the intelligent dolphin it is becoming obvious that they are similar to us in many ways — including socially. Man probably feels friendlier to dolphins than to any other sea creature. Dolphins, too, seem to have a special regard for humans. There are many tales of dolphins helping drowning seamen to the shore.

No such special relationship exists between Man and jellyfish. These free-swimming relatives of the sea anemones and corals are 95% water. But that other 5% can be very nasty indeed!

There are many types of jelly fish, varying in size, number of tentacles and severity of sting. Those found in temperate water tend to be least dangerous and those in coral seas most venomous.

The purpose of the sting is to catch prey. Small fish and shrimps are paralysed by stinging cells in the tentacles and then transferred to the jelly fish's mouth situated under the 'umbrella'.

The Portuguese man-o'-war's sting is almost as powerful as a cobra's venom. These jelly fish usually live in mid-ocean, but occasionally thousands of them are washed up on the shore by a storm. Be careful if you find one because even in a dried-up specimen the stinging cells are still active and can produce a red weal on the skin.

The name of the Portuguese man-o'-war derives from the fact that it looks something like an eighteenth century Portuguese ship. The purplish bladder acts as a sail and is blown by the wind. It can be deflated during storms thus enabling the jelly fish to submerge away from the rough seas.

Some animals are almost immune

to the Portuguese man-o'-war's poison. For example, the loggerhead turtle can eat its way through a shoal with great relish even though its eyes may be swollen with stings.

Like the jelly fish, the sawfish has also inspired fear in Man. However, in this case, appearances have proved deceptive. The sawfish is a large ray — usually about six metres long — with a long double-edged 'saw' attached to its nose.

The saw is studded with 'teeth', although these are not the animal's true teeth which are in the mouth. At birth the saw is flexible with the teeth barely showing so that the mother is not injured.

The animal uses the saw to dig up shellfish and sea urchins from the sea-bed, and also to stun smaller fish. As it swims through a shoal of smaller fish it flails the saw from side to side stunning and wounding victims which it can pick up later.

Despite its ferocious appearance, however, divers have learnt not to fear the sawfish, for a swipe from the saw would probably do no more damage than puncture a diving suit.

The swordfish is armed with a similar weapon, only without the teeth. In some species the 'sword' is flattened — hence the name broadbill. Again the sword is used to stun and impale smaller fish, although it is also thought to assist the animal to cut through the water — it can swim up to 95 km/h.

Swordfish are usually 1.8 to 3.4 metres long and can be very terrifying. There are many reports of swordfish driving their swords through the wooden planking of boats. Indeed some scientists believe they occasionally go beserk and attack on purpose.

Even before the success of the film *Jaws*, sharks were the most feared of all marine creatures — although the number of actual attacks has always been surprisingly low. At the same time, blood in the water can induce a frenzied attack, and there are believed to be a number of renegade sharks who, unlike most sharks, attack people particularly. Despite the reassuring statistics these cold-eyed eating machines should always be treated with extreme caution!

The tiger shark has a striped (and sometimes spotted) skin. It eats any-

1. Flying Fishes
2. Common Dolphins
3. Bottle-nosed Dolphins
4. Portuguese Man-O'-War
5. Jelly Fish
6. Swordfish
7. Sawfish
8. Tiger Shark
9. Atlantic Salmon
10. Mackerel
11. Hammerhead Shark.

thing available, although turtles are a particular favourite.

Found in deep tropical waters, only occasionally pursuing prey into shallow water, it can grow to a maximum length of five and a half metres and has been fished commercially for its oil-rich liver.

More aggressive than the tiger shark is the distinctive hammerhead shark, although human remains have been found in both species.

Both the eyes and nostrils of the

hammerhead are located at the ends of curious lobes, making the animal hammer-like in shape: the length and shape of the lobes varies from species to species. It has been suggested that the hammer-shape evolved to assist balance, to make up for the lack of stabilizing fins.

The giant hammerhead grows as big as six metres. All species are found in tropical seas — although some may enter temperate waters during the summer.

The Atlantic salmon is, as its name

suggests, an ocean-living fish; although there are some landlocked populations found in lakes. The remarkable feature of this animal is that it feeds in the sea on plankton and shrimp-like creatures before returning to the same pool in the same river in which it was hatched. There it lays its eggs (spawns).

Because it may have travelled up to 1,500 km away from the river mouth while feeding in the sea, it is thought that the salmon navigates by the stars to find its way back. Once in the river an acute sense of smell leads it upstream to the right pool, sometimes leaping over three metres to overcome obstacles.

When going upstream the fish are in good condition, but after spawning they become thin and diseased from lack of feeding. They then return to the sea for one to six years before beginning their journey again.

Once salmon were plentiful, but now a combination of overfishing and river pollution is threatening them.

Mackerel are still very plentiful. They live in large shoals in the Atlantic, Pacific and Indian Oceans, and are second in importance only to herring as a commercial catch. They are caught in nets and on lines. And relying on their acute sense of smell, Breton fishermen lure them by pouring stale fish blood overboard.

Through commercial fishing and scientific study, Man has learnt much about many of the weird and wonderful animals of the sea. But others are scarcely known. It will take a long time yet to unravel all the mysteries of the creatures of the oceans.

Giants of the Oceans

EVER since primitive man could carve canoes and make spears, he has pitted his wits against the mighty whale. From the ninth century onwards, the Basques of Northern Spain built boats in order to hunt them throughout the North Atlantic — even reaching the coast of North America before Columbus — in their quest for whalemeat and oil.

By the 18th century many nations supported large whaling fleets. The Dutch, for example, had 400 ships manned by 20,000 men. These ships scoured the oceans for three and four years at a time, until their barrels were fully loaded with valuable oil melted down from the whales' blubber.

This relentless massacre gradually eliminated most of the slower, weaker whales; and then the invention of the steam ship and the devastating cannon harpoon with the exploding head enabled the whalers to catch the larger, faster species too.

In recent years many people have realised that whales are in danger of becoming extinct and so at last efforts are being made to protect them. Although they live in the sea, whales are much more closely related to man than they are to the fishes. In fact they are mammals — the same class as man — whose ancestors probably walked on land.

There are approximately 100 species of whale and all of them are immediately distinguishable from fish because their tails spread horizontally. But although they have successfully adapted to their watery environment, they have not lost the mammal characteristics they share with man. Whales are warm blooded, they breathe air through lungs, they have some hair, they give birth to live young and they are suckled by their mothers.

Their nostrils have moved from the more usual position near the mouth to the top of the head, forming the blowhole. When a whale surfaces its breath blows a spout through this hole — or holes — which was how whalers located their prey, giving rise to the famous cry, "Thar she blows!" Experts can identify the type and size of the whale from the shape and height of its spout.

Most whales migrate over vast distances to reach their mating grounds — some singly and some in groups — known as schools. But they can communicate effectively with each other on the way because they can hear sounds underwater. They make a sound which can be heard by another whale over three miles away — thus a mother knows exactly where her calf is even when they are far apart. Similarly a school can be alerted if an individual is in difficulty. Sonic echoes also provide whales with information on their immediate surroundings, to help find the way or detect prey.

Whales fall into two major categories — the toothed whales and

the baleen whales. The latter have no teeth in the accepted sense, but huge plates of whalebone (baleen) whose fringed edges act as a sieve filtering the small animals on which the whale feeds from the sea water. The spacing of these fringes decides the size of the animal a particular species eats.

Despite its enormous bulk, the blue whale (see drawing numbered 3) feeds mainly on a tiny shrimp-like creature called krill. And yet it is the largest animal *ever* to live on earth, growing to lengths of 24-30 metres and weighing as much as 135 tonnes (which is roughly equivalent to 30 elephants!)

These monster baleen whales are able to stay under water for periods of 10 to 20 minutes. They were the most avidly hunted species because they yield the greatest quantity of oil. It is estimated that there were about 200,000 blue whales and today there are as few as 6,000. They have been completely protected since 1966 but so far their numbers have not increased.

The toothed whales are flesh eaters of a more familiar appearance, although their number of teeth varies greatly among species. The most notorious of the toothed category must be the killer whale (7). They grow to an average length of 6 metres and weigh about a tonne. Killers prefer warm-blooded prey such as seals, dolphins and even baleen whales. A school will attack the giant blue whale, ferociously biting around the head and mouth until it is exhausted.

And yet in captivity 'the tiger of the sea' has proved surprisingly friendly to man and easy to train.

Because of its aggressive nature, the killer whale has few enemies — or friends. It was never seriously hunted by whalers although in recent

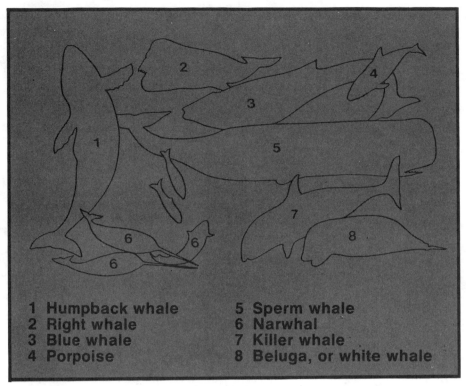

1 Humpback whale
2 Right whale
3 Blue whale
4 Porpoise
5 Sperm whale
6 Narwhal
7 Killer whale
8 Beluga, or white whale

worth its weight in gold.

The beluga (8) is a much smaller toothed whale, 3½ to 4 metres in length and weighing slightly less than a tonne. It travels in small groups in shallow water — feeding on fish and crustaceans. The name beluga derives from the Russian word *bieluha* meaning white.

The narwhal (6) is a close relative of the beluga. The male is noted for the long twisted horn on its forehead which was regarded as having magical powers.

Like the beluga, narwhals have not been commercially hunted — although the eskimos catch several hundred of each. There are said to be approximately 10,000 of both species.

Restrictions

The porpoise (4) is closely related to the dolphin and the killer whale. It is one of the smaller whales (1-2 metres and weighs about 72 kilogrammes) and had blade-like teeth. Porpoises travel in schools of a hundred or so and feed on small fishes that swim near the surface.

Professional whalers — alarmed at the decreasing numbers of whales worldwide — have been restricting their catches since 1931. The International Whaling Commission was formed by them in 1946 and has since set quotas controlling the numbers of particular species to be killed.

But it may be too late.

Only one species, the grey whale, has shown any increase in numbers so far. So man must do more to save his highly intelligent cousins of the deep.

years the numbers killed have started to go up.

The humpback (1) is another baleen whale whose name probably derives from the way it arches its back just before diving. It is recognisable by its large white flippers which can measure up to one third of its body. Its average length is 12 metres and it weighs nearly 30 tonnes. It lives in coastal waters and man was therefore able to learn its migratory patterns and kill it in large numbers — there are probably only 6,000 left today. Humpbacks are now completely protected

The slow, timid right whale (2) was almost extinct by the start of the twentieth century so they too are now fully protected. These whales grow 15-18 metres and are characterised by their enormous mouths that take up one third of their bodies. They used to live in large herds but are now mainly solitary or found in small groups. They feed on krill and have exceptionally long baleen plates. There are said to be only 4,000 right whales left.

Moby Dick, the giant whale featured in Herman Melville's famous book of the same name, was a sperm whale (5). These whales have long lower jaws studded with teeth 25 centimetres in length. Large males often measure 18 metres and weigh bet-

Fancy coming face to face with this? In fact the giant in our picture is no more than a replica of a blue whale which appeared in New York's American Museum of Natural History. The model was constructed of a steel skeleton, polyurethane flesh and a skin of fibreglass.

Photo: Associated Press

ween 35-50 tonnes. They live in family groups or harems, although there are occasional rogue males. The main food of the sperm whale is squid and cuttlefish and they are known for their deep dives and can submerge for up to an hour.

The whalers hunted the sperm whale not only for its blubber but for the valuable reservoir of spermaceti — a clear oily substance which man uses in manufacturing products such as candles. As much as 15 barrels could be tapped from one whale. The whale was also prized for a strange grey lump — called ambergris — which is found in the intestine and used in the finest perfumes and love potions. At one time this was literally

Life on the razor's edge

A giant razor guards the coast of north-east Australia. Over 2,000 km long, it can be seen clearly from the Moon. It looks like a huge string of sharp rocks, but in fact it is made up of the bodies of millions of small animals.

This is the Great Barrier Reef. The animals are corals. They are little marine animals that have a hard, chalky skeleton. They thrive in clear, salt water which never becomes much colder than 18°C. A few species are found in temperate or even polar waters but mostly corals live in the tropics where the sun can penetrate the crystal seas. Ideal conditions for them occur in the Great Barrier Reef.

Corals are nothing like land animals. Instead they live all the time in one place, feeding on the tiny animals and plants — the plankton — that float around in the sea. Lying in wait, they catch the plankton by sending out stinging tentacles, and then the prey is pushed into the coral's mouth.

Some corals live joined together in huge colonies of many thousands of individuals, but others live on their own. These solitary corals either sit in a chalky cup or on top of a chalky base. Even though each animal may be only a few millimetres across, many of them living close to each other can form huge coral structures.

Colonies start from just one individual, called a *polyp larva*, which unlike most corals is free swimming in the sea. Eventually, however, it gives up its wandering life and settles down on the sea-bed.

It develops a lump — a bud — which grows bigger and bigger and produces a mouth and tentacles. The bud is in fact a new animal, but it does not separate from the parent. So in the end there are thousands of animals all joined together in the colony.

Largest in the world

Each coral in the colony secretes a chalky skeleton at its base, so as the colony grows the new animals grow their skeletons on top of the older ones. Huge chalky formations are thus created, riddled with tiny cells in which the polyps once lived. The Great Barrier Reef is the biggest coral formation in the world.

Each type of coral has its own pattern of budding, so the shape and colour of the colonies varies immensely. Some form domes, others fans, antlers or intricate 'stony' flowers. There are sometimes enormous 'fields' of just one type. Alternatively, there may be a profusion of different types all living close together.

Although the sharp corals are a constant hazard to shipping, the Great Barrier Reef is a diver's paradise. During the day the coral makes a marvellous multi-coloured underwater forest, yet perhaps the most interesting scenes can be seen at night with a torch. Then the sharp outlines of the corals are softened by thousands of tiny tentacles stretched out to grope for food. For night is when the corals feed.

Colourful, plentiful life

Among the corals live an immense variety of other animals and plants. For the conditions on the reef are suitable for all types of sea life with plenty of oxygen, light, and warmth. Many of the animals are very colourful so that they blend successfully into the background of coral.

Two of the most beautiful fishes found on the reef are the butterfly and the angel fish. They come from the same family but the range of colour and patterns is astonishing. Some angel fish can grow up to 60 cm long whereas most of the butterflies are no longer than 20 cm. As a group they have small mouths with many small teeth and sometimes even sharper snouts which they use to pick food from the tiny crevices in the coral.

The parrot fish is also particularly well-adapted to life on the reef, for this colourful creature has a sharp, parrot-like beak which can remove food from the coral. In doing this it also bites off chunks of coral and too many fish can substantially erode the reef.

Silver scats also thrive around the reef, as do the beautiful batfishes which change their shape and colour as they grow bigger. Both fishes are said to eat offal, which is why the scat's family name is Scatophagidae — which means 'dung eater'.

As well as fishes, the coral also harbours shell creatures or *molluscs*. The cowrie is a single-shelled animal whose outer casing looks vaguely like a clenched fist with a highly polished, patterned surface. A muscular 'foot' protrudes through a slit in the shell, and the animals are able to move by rippling this foot.

Some molluscs, however, have two shells — or rather the shell is divided into two parts. These animals are much less mobile than cowries and use their 'feet' to pull themselves down into the sand until they are almost completely buried. Then they lie with the two halves open, sucking in water. From this they filter food

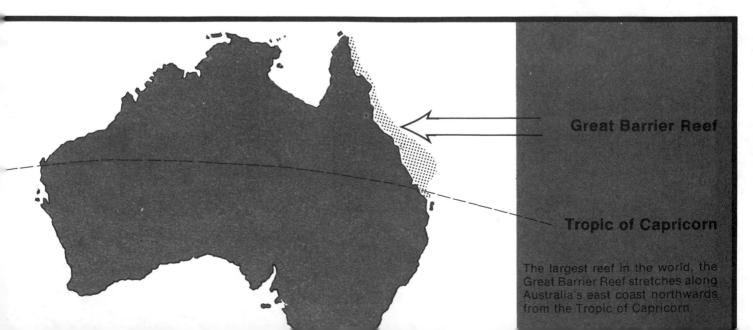

Great Barrier Reef

Tropic of Capricorn

The largest reef in the world, the Great Barrier Reef stretches along Australia's east coast northwards from the Tropic of Capricorn.

Our picture shows just a few of the many and varied kinds of life in the clear tropical seas around the Great Barrier Reef.

1. Two types of angel fish
2. Shark
3. Bat fish
4. Clown fish
5. Butterfly fish
6. Parrot fish
7. Silver scat
8. Prawn
9. Sea hare
10. Cowrie
11. Nassa
12. Sea urchin
13. Giant clam
14. Various corals
15. Various seaweeds

.before expelling the water again.

Because they don't even move, size is not a disadvantage to these animals. Some, therefore, are very big indeed.

Giant clams, for example, sometimes grow to a metre in length. They embed themselves in the coral and then lie in wait with the shells wide open and the brilliantly coloured flesh exposed in between.

Prickly sea urchins — or sea hedgehogs — slowly totter around among the corals. These curious creatures have practically no enemies once they are fully gròwn because their spines easily break off in the flesh of anything that gets too close. They are mainly vegetarians, feeding on seaweed.

Swimming about among the corals are prawns. These creatures provide a plentiful source of food for many of the other

animals there. The soft 'shell' of the prawn is in fact an external skeleton. In order to grow, the prawn must shed this old shell, revealing a new and eventually bigger one underneath.

Looking for bigger meat than prawns are the sharks, doubtless the most feared visitors to the Great Barrier Reef. Divers naturally treat thse animals with great caution, although attacks on Man are few. Nevertheless, a large, moving shadow *can* mean

danger to all.

As well as animals, the reef is also the home of many varieties of seaweeds, which also relish the clear warm water. The plants in turn provide nourishment for some of the animals.

But what makes the reef unique is that the landscape itself is animal-made.

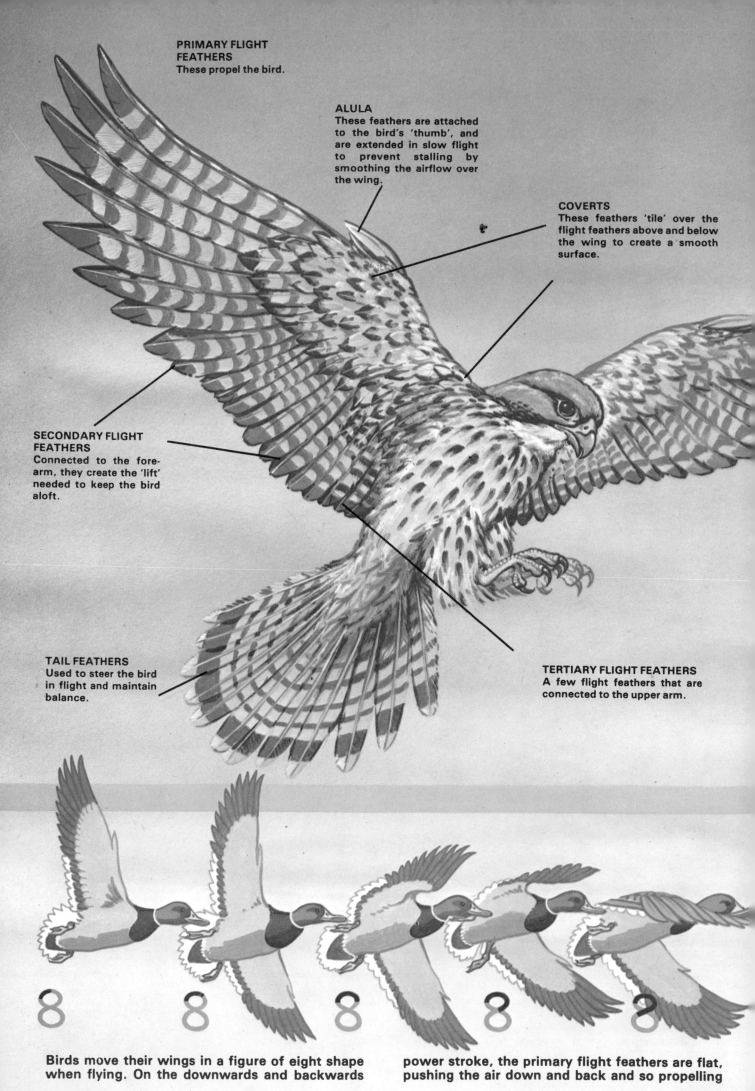

PRIMARY FLIGHT FEATHERS
These propel the bird.

ALULA
These feathers are attached to the bird's 'thumb', and are extended in slow flight to prevent stalling by smoothing the airflow over the wing.

COVERTS
These feathers 'tile' over the flight feathers above and below the wing to create a smooth surface.

SECONDARY FLIGHT FEATHERS
Connected to the forearm, they create the 'lift' needed to keep the bird aloft.

TAIL FEATHERS
Used to steer the bird in flight and maintain balance.

TERTIARY FLIGHT FEATHERS
A few flight feathers that are connected to the upper arm.

Birds move their wings in a figure of eight shape when flying. On the downwards and backwards power stroke, the primary flight feathers are flat, pushing the air down and back and so propelling

280

BUZZARD
Long broad wings for soaring flight

GANNET
Long narrow wings for long distance gliding.

SWIFT
Narrow, swept back wings for fast insect-chasing.

PHEASANT
Short, broad wings for rapid take-off when alarmed

The Marvel of Flight

NO one who has witnessed the seemingly effortless soaring of an albatross, the miraculous hovering of a humming-bird or the swift, erratic flight of a swallow can fail to be impressed by the birds' mastery of the air. But the apparent ease with which a bird flies conceals the enormous complexities and skills involved, as Man has discovered when he has tried to copy Nature.

Only four groups of animals — birds, insects, bats and pterosaurs (prehistoric flying reptiles, now extinct) — have acquired the power of true flight, that is, flight in which the wings are flapped to produce lift and thrust.

All fliers have to overcome similar problems. Air is such a thin medium — compared with water or earth, for instance — that travellers passing through it must have light bodies and aerofoils, or wings, if they are to exploit it fully. They must also have a high 'power/weight ratio'. That is, their flight muscles must be extremely powerful in relation to their body weight. A pigeon's heart muscles, which operate its wings, account for more than a third of its body weight.

Man has tried to compensate for the enormous weight of his aeroplanes by equipping them with huge engines which force the craft upwards. And he has further deviated from the birds in separating the power source from the flying surface. In other words, an aeroplane is not propelled by its wings, as a bird is, but by its engines. These modifications, or changes, have made Man's flying machines far less efficient than any of Nature's.

Birds have remarkably light skeletons. The skeleton of a blackbird, for instance, weighs only about 4 grams when dry. This lightness has been achieved without sacrificing strength. The skull bones of modern birds are very thin and heavy teeth have been replaced by lighter, horny beaks. Long bones, such as those in the wings, are hollow, supported by a criss-crossing system of internal struts. And the tail, which helps with steering, is formed entirely of that skin-covering unique to birds — feathers.

Feathers serve many purposes. They give buoyancy and lightness, aiding flight, they provide colourful adornment for courtship and camouflage and they retain body warmth.

This latter use was probably their main one when feathers began to evolve from the scales on prehistoric reptiles. Feathers served to keep up the body temperature of these reptiles as they slowly became warm-blooded. Most birds still have scales on their legs and feet, indicating, however unlikely it may seem, that they are distantly related to such reptiles as the lizard.

Extremely light, flexible and airproof, feathers are a miracle of flight technology. A 'primary' or flight feather consists of a *shaft*, or *quill*, hollow at its base for conveying nourishment, solid towards its tip, for strength, and a *vane* made up of side shafts called *barbs*. These barbs, in turn, support rows of *barbules*, equipped with interlocking hooks to form a fine mesh surface for the feather. If the barbules break apart, the bird can reset them by preening, an important task which occupies much of a bird's time.

the bird along. At the end of this stroke, the bird twists the primary feathers so that air will pass through them. It then moves its wings to begin another power stroke.

Near the base of the tail, a bird has oil glands, the oil being used during preening and cleaning to coat the feathers, keeping them waterproof and buoyant. This is especially important, of course, to waterbirds like ducks.

Birds usually moult twice a year, changing their small, covering feathers in spring and all their feathers in autumn.

Together with the skeleton and associated muscles, the primary feathers form a cambered wing which provides lift and thrust, or reverse thrust when landing.

Most of the lift is provided by the base of the wing which remains relatively still during flight, in contrast to the tip which provides most of the thrust. Viewed from the side, the tip of the wing describes a figure-of-eight during one complete wing beat and, as it moves through this cycle, the primary feathers flex to control the flight.

On the down stroke, they close to prevent air passing between them and so provide resistance and lift against airstreams — like a swimmer pulling back on water with his arms to propel himself forward. On the upstroke, the feathers slant open, like Venetian blinds, allowing air to pass between them.

Birds' wings can also rotate in a manner which produces only lift, enabling the bird to hover. Humming birds can turn round and even fly backwards, like helicopters, whilst hovering.

Birds' wings vary considerably in shape, from species to species, depending on flying habits. The albatross, for instance, the long-distance, high-speed glider of the Southern Hemisphere, has very long, narrow wings — a shape copied in high performance sailplanes. One species, the wandering albatross, has a wing-span of up to 4 metres. Such wings create a

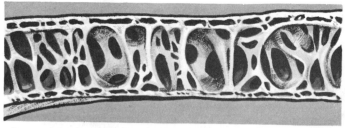

Some bones are honeycombed to give strength with lightness. This applies particularly to the upper arm bone (humerus) shown above.

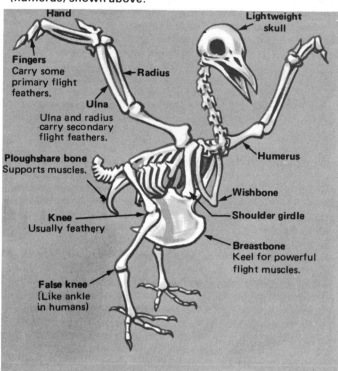

Hand

Fingers Carry some primary flight feathers.

Radius

Ulna Ulna and radius carry secondary flight feathers.

Ploughshare bone Supports muscles.

Knee Usually feathery

False knee (Like ankle in humans)

Lightweight skull

Humerus

Wishbone

Shoulder girdle

Breastbone Keel for powerful flight muscles.

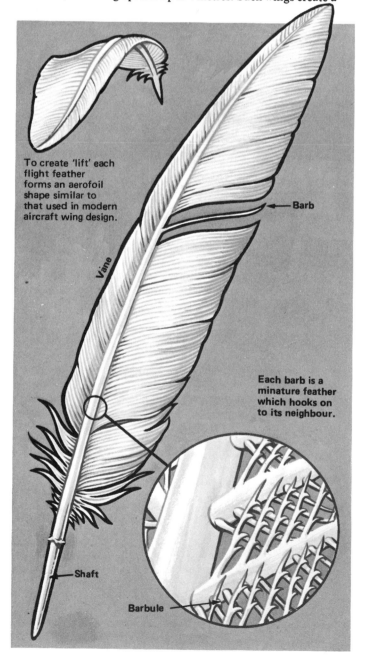

To create 'lift' each flight feather forms an aerofoil shape similar to that used in modern aircraft wing design.

Barb

Vane

Each barb is a minature feather which hooks on to its neighbour.

Shaft

Barbule

great deal of lift at high speed, but require enormous muscular effort to flap, hence the birds' preference for gliding. Coming in to land at relatively high speeds, these big-winged birds tend to stall, causing loss of control and awkward landings, often amusing to watch.

Another type of soaring is demonstrated by a buzzard or a vulture. In this case, the wing is relatively short and broad, designed to create plenty of lift at low speeds, and has splayed out, finger-like tip feathers to reduce the danger of stalling. Buzzards and vultures use thermals (upwardly spiralling currents of warm air) to soar high in their search for prey or carrion. Again, wing flapping is kept to a minimum.

Most birds, however, have to flap their wings throughout the time spent airborne, and wing shape is generally a compromise between that of the albatross and that of the buzzard.

The speed-merchants of the bird world, the swifts, have narrow wings which taper to a pointed tip, allowing some species to fly at speeds of 150 kph. They may also rise to a height of 1,800 metres and spend the night roosting on the wing.

Speeds of 100 kph have been claimed for a peregrine falcon diving for its prey and radar echoes from small migrating birds, possibly dunlin, have shown them to be flying at a height of 2,500 metres.

Birds are inherently unstable in flight in contrast to aeroplanes which are designed for stability. For birds, instability means that any slight deviation from straight and level flight will be quickly exaggerated if uncorrected. Inherent instability provides for high manoeuverability but it needs a sophisticated nervous system for effective control.

It is no surprise, then, to find that birds have relatively larger brains than mammals (higher primates, like apes, excepted) and that the 'cerebellum', the part of the brain which co-ordinates movement, is particularly well developed.

Flying uses up a lot of energy and, consequently, birds spend much of their time searching for food to fuel it. Oxygen is also

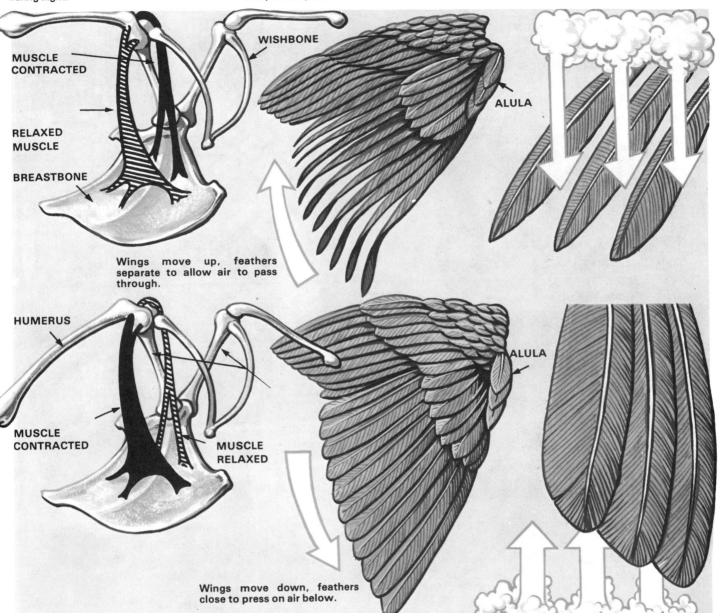

1. Muscles can only pull — not push, so two sets of muscles are needed to raise and lower the wings during flight.

2. When one of the flight muscles is relaxed, the other contracts and pulls the wing upwards ready for the power stroke.

3. Primary feathers twist to allow air to pass through them on the up stroke, thus offering no resistance.

MUSCLE CONTRACTED

RELAXED MUSCLE

BREASTBONE

WISHBONE

ALULA

Wings move up, feathers separate to allow air to pass through.

HUMERUS

MUSCLE CONTRACTED

MUSCLE RELAXED

ALULA

Wings move down, feathers close to press on air below.

4. The major flight muscle, which is firmly attached to the breastbone, contracts to pull the wing down for the power stroke.

5. The primary feathers flatten out on the down stroke to offer resistance to the air.

6. The closed feathers push air backwards and downwards — thus pushing the bird upwards and forwards.

needed in large amounts and birds have quite uniquely-designed lungs with special air sacs, which surround the vital organs of the body and even penetrate certain wing bones. Within these sacs, the air flows round a one-way system, enabling the bird to extract all the oxygen from one breath of air while, at the same time, expelling all carbon dioxide. The air sacs also allow the bird to lose the excessive heat produced during flight and, as a bonus, they reduce the density, or solidity, of its body.

Flight offers two considerable advantages to birds: it provides protection from predators and it enables them to be extra-ordinarily mobile. The latter is especially significant for the many migratory species, some of which fly thousands of kilometres to and from their winter and summer homes. The arctic tern flies approximately a 33,000 km round trip each year and British swallows winter in south Africa, navigating accurately even by night.

The amazing virtuosity of birds in flight and the technical perfections of the fliers themselves are miracles at which Man may marvel — but which he will never surpass.

The wing of a bird forms an aerofoil shape. The air moves faster over the curved top than under the flatter base, thus causing pressure beneath the wing, and producing the upward pull known as 'lift'.

The bird tilts its wing to gain height, but if it is tilted too far, turbulence is created in the airflow, and the bird 'stalls' as it loses flying speed.

If the bird begins to stall, then a tuft of feathers called the 'alula' is spread forward from the front of the wing causing air to pass through the slot it has created, and this reduces turbulence.

The Story of the Dog

Part 1

Alsatian

Spaniel Dog

Jackal

African Wild Dog

Wolf

WILD DOGS OF THE WORLD

AFRICA	African Wild Dog Somali Wild Dog Buansuah
ASIA	Indian Wild Dog Ceylon Wild Dog Malay Wild Dog Siberian Wild Dog Racoon-like Dog
AUSTRALIA	Dingo
NORTH AMERICA	Coyote Indian Territory Coyote Mexican Coyote
SOUTH AMERICA	Bush Dog Panaman Bush Dog Tyra Bush Dog Colpeo Tierra del Fuego Dog Falkland Islands Dog Aguarachay (Azara's Dog) Sclater's Dog Peruvian Wild Dog Chilla Crab Eating Dog Small Toothed Dog

Hunter — Shepherd — Soldier at war — Policeman — A Guide for the Blind — the dog has been all these to Man — and a lot more beside . . .

ALTHOUGH there is no reliable documented evidence as to the true origins of the dog, it is generally assumed that its early history goes back to some 35 to 40 million years ago, when all mammals were in a transitional state of development, being much smaller than their present day counterparts. Even then there was no such animal as the dog we know today, but there *was* a creature we know as *Miacis*, which was the forerunner of a number of different forms from which the true dog eventually evolved.

From *Miacis*, these other forms appeared over a period of some twenty million years, until, finally, about one million years ago, an animal known as *Canis* appeared, which, in its turn, appeared in a number of diversified forms, such as the wolf, jackal and coyote. Of these animals, the most likely ancestor of the dog appears to be the wolf.

Perhaps the most remarkable thing about the dog is how he became Man's faithful companion and assistant, long before there were any pictured records in stone of Man's history: his bones were even found with those of Stone Age Man.

Scientists are of the opinion that early Man developed dogs for hunting purposes from the wild wolves which scavenged around their camps. The very presence of these creatures would have proved beneficial to Man, not only as scavengers, but as a source of warning of threatened danger. Later, Man was to use these semi-domesticated dogs to herd and protect his flocks.

Despite their long association with Man, the dogs of today still retain many of their primitive instincts. The hunting dog bays — a reminder of the way that hunting wolves bay to keep the pack together. The dog howls at night, again an ancestral habit of calling the pack. He also turns round before lying down because his ancestors had to do so to make a flat sheltered bed in the grass.

He buries his bones, again as his ancestors did, in order to prevent his enemies from stealing them. The dog of today also has to thank his ancestors for his acute sense of smell, acute hearing, and sharp teeth.

The dog has followed Man all over the earth, adapting himself to every climate and to every use to which his master has chosen to put him.

In the First World War he acted as a rat killer in the trenches, and as a Red Cross dog, carrying vital medical supplies from one place to another. Some 10,000 of these four-footed soldiers were still working on the Western Front when the Armistice was signed in 1918. In World War II, he proved an invaluable aid in finding buried people and detecting mines. In the police force dogs are used extensively in combatting crime, and smelling out drug hoards. One could go on almost indefinitely.

A special mention must be made, however, of his use as a guide dog for the blind. The dogs used for this most important work have to be of a certain height, which enables them to be easily handled by their owners. Labradors are ideal for this work. In fact, some 80 per cent of all guide dogs belong to this breed. Alsatians and Golden Retrievers, too, are extensively used.

But despite his close association with Man, a surprisingly large number of wild dogs still roam the land. Most of them assemble in packs for hunting, which is mainly by scent. They live in burrows, caves and clefts in rocks, and most of them are nocturnal in their habits. They are found in most parts of the world, Madagascar and Sri Lanka being the notable exceptions. Of the various wild species (*see table*) the dingo of Australia is the best known. The Asiatic wild dogs are represented by the pariah dogs of India and the dholes, which are somewhat like jackals in appearance.

There are now 180 breeds of dog registered at The Kennel Club.

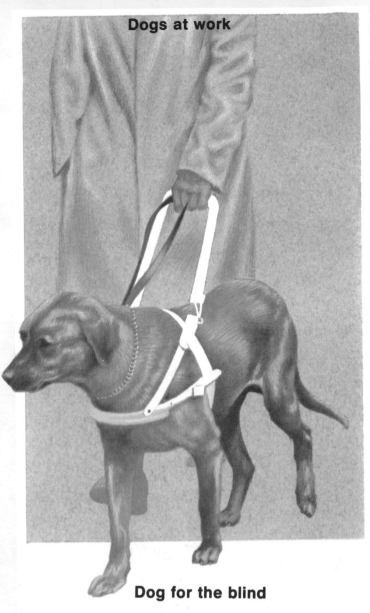

Dogs at work

Dog for the blind

Police tracker dog

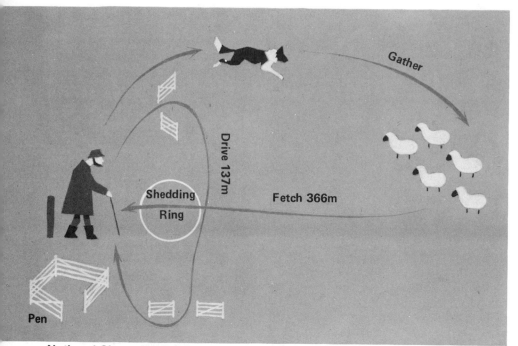

National Sheepdog Trials

Gather
Drive 137m
Fetch 366m
Shedding Ring
Pen

International Championship course

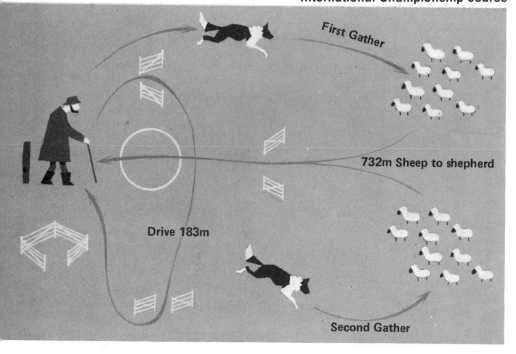

First Gather
732m Sheep to shepherd
Drive 183m
Second Gather

Sheepdogs

One of the best ways of seeing how the dog can be trained to serve Man is at the National and International Sheepdog Trials, where the sheepdogs from all over the world compete. At the National course, at each event a dog goes in with a handler and five sheep. The handler takes up his position from which he must not move more than a few metres. The sheep are then released for the dog to 'Gather' and bring to the handler. The dog then takes the sheep between two sets of hurdles, returning them to the handler. Dog and handler then move to the shedding ring. Two of the five sheep are marked, and the dog must now separate two of the unmarked sheep from the rest without moving out of the ring.

Once this has been accomplished all five are driven into the pen. The sheep are then released from the pen and the handler moves to the shedding ring. The dog must then 'shed' the two marked sheep and keep them separate from the others for a specified time.

In the International Championship twenty sheep are used in two groups of ten. These groups are released 1,000 m from each other and out of sight of the dog. The dog's task is to gather the first group of ten sheep, bringing them through two hurdles when they are abandoned at a marked place. He then fetches the other group through the same hurdles. All twenty sheep are then driven round a similar course to the first, and in this instance five sheep are separated and penned.

The Sporting Breeds

Although there are a number of sporting breeds of dogs, including a number of unlikely looking dogs such as the Saluki and the Afghan Hound, the Basset Hound is one of the most interesting of all of them, in as much as he is the most unlikeliest sporting dog of them all.

He was not known to British sportsmen before 1863, when he caused a great deal of curiosity and admiration among the English visitors to the first exhibition of dogs held in Paris.

With careful selection, a beautiful hound has now been produced which has a fine smooth coat and a head of noble character.

Basset Hound

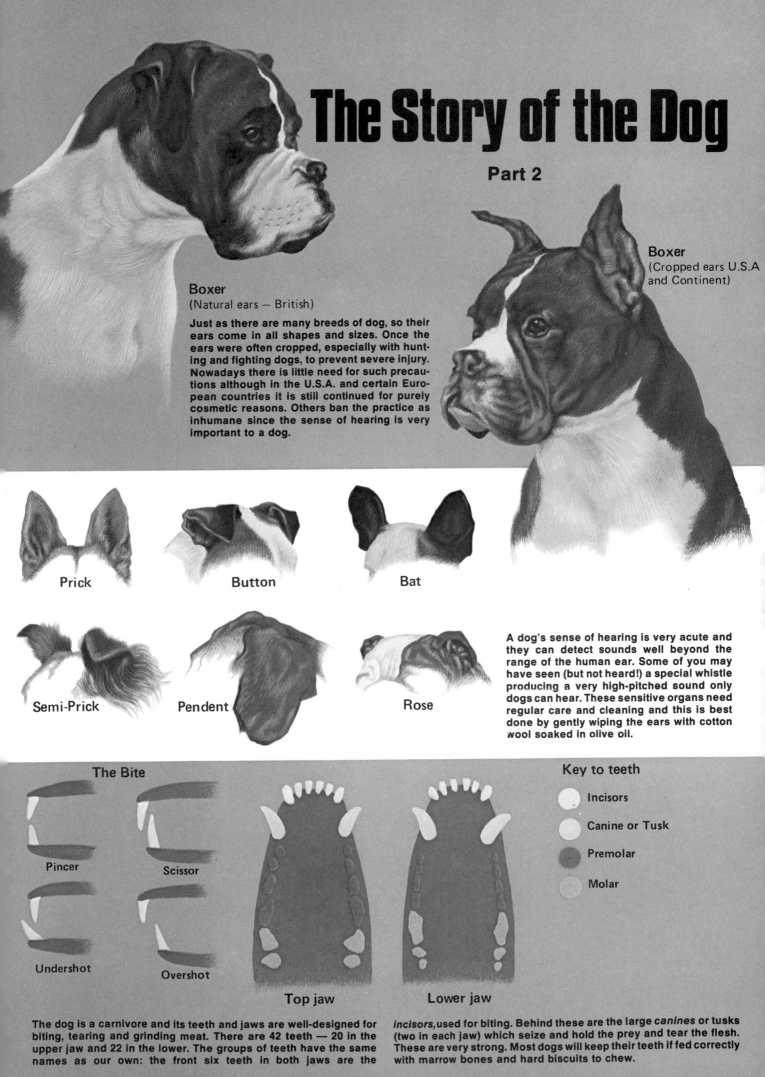

The Story of the Dog

Part 2

Boxer
(Natural ears — British)

Just as there are many breeds of dog, so their ears come in all shapes and sizes. Once the ears were often cropped, especially with hunting and fighting dogs, to prevent severe injury. Nowadays there is little need for such precautions although in the U.S.A. and certain European countries it is still continued for purely cosmetic reasons. Others ban the practice as inhumane since the sense of hearing is very important to a dog.

Boxer
(Cropped ears U.S.A and Continent)

Prick

Button

Bat

Semi-Prick

Pendent

Rose

A dog's sense of hearing is very acute and they can detect sounds well beyond the range of the human ear. Some of you may have seen (but not heard!) a special whistle producing a very high-pitched sound only dogs can hear. These sensitive organs need regular care and cleaning and this is best done by gently wiping the ears with cotton wool soaked in olive oil.

The Bite

Pincer

Scissor

Undershot

Overshot

Top jaw

Lower jaw

Key to teeth

- Incisors
- Canine or Tusk
- Premolar
- Molar

The dog is a carnivore and its teeth and jaws are well-designed for biting, tearing and grinding meat. There are 42 teeth — 20 in the upper jaw and 22 in the lower. The groups of teeth have the same names as our own: the front six teeth in both jaws are the *incisors,* used for biting. Behind these are the large *canines* or tusks (two in each jaw) which seize and hold the prey and tear the flesh. These are very strong. Most dogs will keep their teeth if fed correctly with marrow bones and hard biscuits to chew.

Tails

As with ears, there are different tails for different breeds of dog. There is a whole range going right through from the long, hanging type on a Great Dane, through the beautifully feathered appendage on a Setter to the short stump of the Fox Terrier. Several types are pictured below. Years ago tails were 'docked' (rather like ears were cropped) in order to avoid injury, and the operation is still considered desirable in some breeds. It should be performed as soon as possible after birth, ideally when the pups are three or four days old. Needless to say the operation should be carried out by a veterinary surgeon.

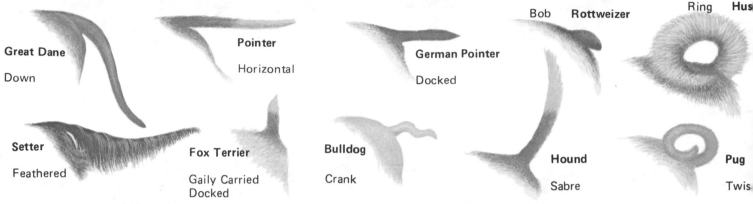

Great Dane
Down

Pointer
Horizontal

Setter
Feathered

Fox Terrier
Gaily Carried
Docked

German Pointer
Docked

Bulldog
Crank

Bob   **Rottweizer**

Ring   **Hus**

Hound
Sabre

Pug
Twis

The box on the right shows three of the world's most unusual breeds of dog. The *Komondor* is perhaps one of the strangest looking. This tremendously powerful herd dog originated in Hungary. It has been used for hundreds of years to protect herds of sheep or cattle roaming the Hungarian plains. Its appearance is due to a mass of matted hair which hangs down in felt-like cords. This gives the dog ideal protection against bad weather.

The *Mexican Hairless* looks something like a terrier and is bred mainly in Mexico. Hair grows only at the end of the tail and on the crown of the head. Obviously, it is only at home in a warm climate, away from the cold and damp.

A member of the greyhound family, the *Pharoah* dog closely resembles the hounds with large, erect ears depicted in ancient Egyptian drawings. It has an impressive turn of speed and combines a graceful agility with keen hunting instincts.

"**D**OG is Man's best friend." Nearly all of you will have heard that expression at some time and it is true that through his long association with Man, the dog has become a valuable servant and a loyal friend.

As already stated, although Man has been developing dogs to suit his needs throughout this time, there are still traces of the wild instincts of their ancestors. The pack instinct and the territorial instinct remain (in fact, Man has, for many dogs, become the pack leader) and such behaviour is important, for example in the training of guard dogs.

Man has also modified different breeds to bring out particular qualities: the greyhound has been developed for speed, the bulldog for strength and bloodhounds for their keen sense of smell. But although size and strength can be modified, other physical characteristics, such as the senses of sight and smell, retain their importance for all dogs.

The nose is a vital organ for dogs. Not only does it act as a cooling chamber, but the sense of smell is an essential source of information. For

Unusual Dogs

Komondor

Mexican Hairless

Pharoah
Hound

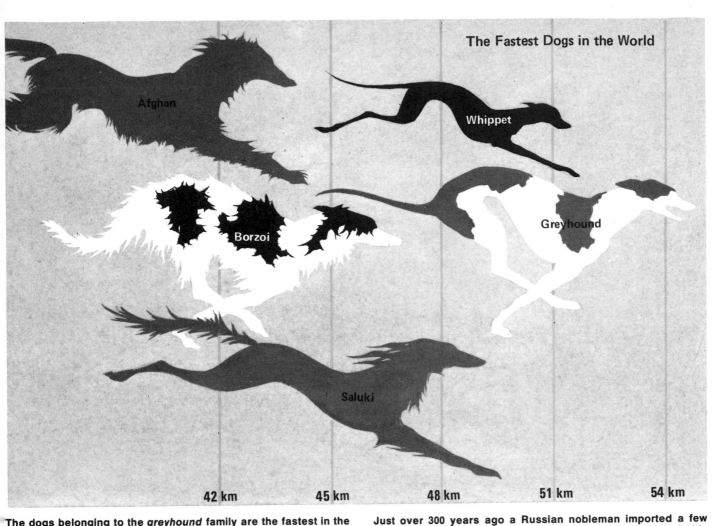

| 42 km | 45 km | 48 km | 51 km | 54 km |

The dogs belonging to the *greyhound* family are the fastest in the world and can reach speeds of over 50 kilometres per hour. They are perhaps the purest breed that has been developed. Bred for centuries to improve their speed these superbly agile and graceful animals have matched their swiftest prey. Today there is little need to use them in hunting but the sport of greyhound racing has become popular all over the world.

The *whippet* can be considered to be rather like a miniature greyhound. They have been bred as sporting dogs over the last 200 years, particularly in the North of England, and have remarkable powers of acceleration. With its friendly and affectionate nature the whippet makes an ideal house dog.

The oldest member of the greyhound family may well be the *Saluki* which was known in ancient Persia (Iran) thousands of years ago but was not introduced into England until around 1890. In its native land it has always been highly valued as a hunting dog. Throughout the rest of the world its obvious elegance has made it a prized show dog.

Just over 300 years ago a Russian nobleman imported a few Arabian greyhounds to act as sporting dogs. Although admirably fast for this purpose, they did not survive the severe Russian winter since they had been raised in a much warmer climate where a thick coat of hair was not needed. However, they had been cross-bred with native Russian collies and this established the *Borzoi* hound. This combined speed with protection against the weather and soon became very popular with the nobility who used them extensively for coursing. They were little seen outside Russia until 1842 when a pair were presented as gifts to Queen Victoria. The Borzoi is a fine example of successful cross-breeding.

A very popular dog is the *Afghan* hound, now considered as a native of Afghanistan but probably originating in the Middle East thousands of years ago. A formidable hunter, the Afghan is still highly prized by local tribesmen. It has all the grace of a greyhound and an unusually long and attractive coat. The tail is carried high and finishes in a characteristic curl. It is a fine greyhound type.

some dogs over 90 per cent of the information about their world comes to them through their noses. These scents are carried in the air and the moister the nose is, then the clearer the information. It is for this reason that you will see dogs often licking their noses to keep them moist. The use to Man is obvious and is perhaps best illustrated in the tracker dogs used by the police which can follow scents over many kilometres.

Hearing

The sense of hearing is very acute, even more so in dogs with larger ears which collect more sound. Dogs can detect very high-pitched sounds well outside the range of our ears. If you own a dog it is important to exercise great care when washing the ears.

Different breeds have a varying sense of vision. In some dogs the position of the eyes means that the dog does not have a wide field of vision but in a fast dog like the greyhound, once an important hunting dog, it is sight rather than smell that is important for following prey. Overall though, sight is not as important a sense as smell.

If you do own a dog or are thinking of getting a puppy then some useful and simple hints will help to ensure your pet has a successful life. Chewing is essential for the development of strong teeth and jaws. It is a good idea not to give the dog too much soft food. Buy indestructible toys such as imitation bones on which they can happily chew. Incidentally, in terms of biting averages it is believed that the German police dog is the dog

most likely to bite a person!

The correct lead and collar is important. Obviously it must not be too tight and the opening of the lead should not be at the point of greatest strain on the collar. And one point that is sometimes missed is that a dog's feeding bowls should be as clean as your own.

Training

Training your pet can be great fun but it is important to be patient and never train for too long a time. Always use the same name — even if it is only Rover or Spot! Firmness is needed at times if commands are to be understood but never forget to praise your dog whenever he responds properly. He will soon feel you are the best owner in the world!

This marmalade kitten is only a few weeks old but the story of the cat is a very ancient one. Its ancestors were wild and fierce, and even now the tabby is still . . .

The Hunter in your Home

A simplified family tree summarising the evolutionary descent of the domestic cat — in this case showing a Seal Point Siamese. Cats are part of the family Carnivora ('meat-eaters'). The ancestors of the modern carnivores were called *miacids* that flourished during the Miocene period about 30 million years ago. One of these ancestors was called *Dinictus* and it is thought that this was directly related to the present-day cat. Another evolutionary offshoot from this was the civet which shows strong resemblances to its ancestor while another branch is the hyena family.

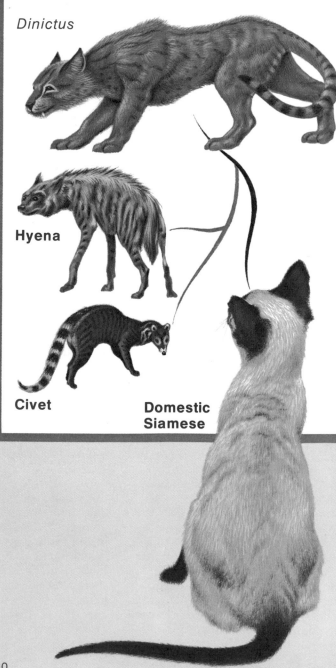

Dinictus

Hyena

Civet

Domestic Siamese

The cat was held in high regard by the ancient Egyptians who were probably the first people to domesticate it. The cat came to hold a special place in Egyptian everyday life: it was worshipped in their temples and owners had their cats embalmed when they died. Some even embalmed mice as food for the cats on their way to heaven! Anyone who killed a cat was liable to execution. Our picture shows a bronze statuette of the cat goddess Pasht (or Bastet) with four guardian cats.

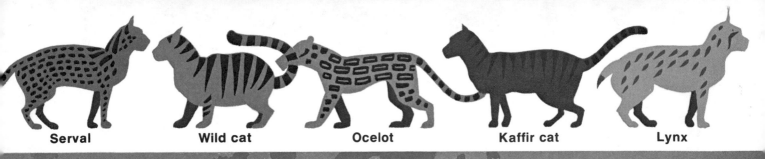

Serval   Wild cat   Ocelot   Kaffir cat   Lynx

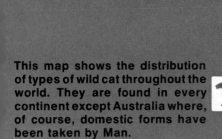

This map shows the distribution of types of wild cat throughout the world. They are found in every continent except Australia where, of course, domestic forms have been taken by Man.

ARE you an ailurophile? Well, many people are, others are not, for it simply means that you are a cat lover. But whatever your feelings there is no doubt that this very-ancient animal has fascinated Man for many centuries.

Much of this fascination is due to the fact that, just like its large and powerful cousins, the lions and tigers, the cat is a carnivore (meat-eater) and has retained over millions of years its ability for hunting prey. Even your house cat has changed little from its wild ancestors — it still has the stealth, speed and agility necessary for hunting. 'Hunter in your home' is not a misleading description!

Nature has designed cats very successfully because their evolutionary history goes back some 35 million years. Before this there were cat-like carnivores called *miacids* and these also gave rise to families like the mongoose, civets and hyenas. But 35 million years ago the cats were clearly distinguishable as a distinct type.

Within this cat group another division could be made into two types of cat differing in the design of their teeth and in their hunting patterns. One type became adapted for hunting active animals of similar size and had comparatively small teeth — this line eventually gave rise to all the cats we

know today, from domestic cat up to lion.

The other types were the sabre-tooth cats. Their upper teeth were much larger and the upper canine teeth had become long tusks. They were adapted to hunting large, slow-moving prey like mammoths and mastodens.

While these large creatures flourished, so did the sabre-tooths. But as they started to die out the sabre-tooths, being specialist creatures, were unable to adapt to other forms of hunting and followed them on the path to extinction. This left their cousins, the ancestors of the

All domestic cats are much the same size, but they are divided into two groups — short-haired cats shown here are the familiar tabby (left) thought to descend from the European wild cat, and the Siamese Blue Point (right) whose ancestry is uncertain but who illustrates the 'foreign' short-hair type. In the centre is the long-haired Blue-Cream Persian which may be descended from the wild cat of Eastern Asia which has a beautiful, thick coat.

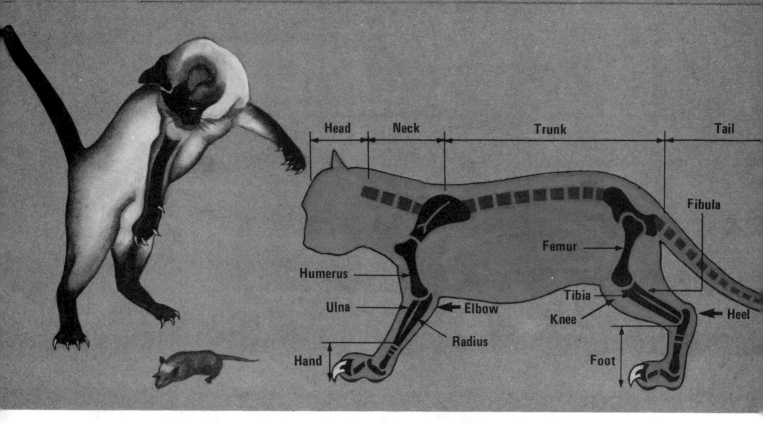

Cats have retained their hunting instincts over thousands of years so there has been little need for them to change their anatomy. Cat-style hunting needs a strong but flexible body. The backbone is very flexible while the leg bones are strong and connected to powerful muscles, enabling the animal to move agilely and spring quickly. Left: Cats often play with small prey like mice before killing them. Such behaviour teaches kittens how to hunt and kill.

modern cats, as the most successful adapters.

Today we still place cats in two groups. Large cats like lions, tigers and leopards come into the group called *Panthera* — basically this means that they can roar but cannot purr, as the domestic cat purrs. Small cats, such as the lynx, the wild cat and our own lovable pets belong to the second group, *Felix*.

As our map of the world shows, the small cats have flourished all over the world. They are found naturally in every continent except Australia and the Antarctic. And their characteristics mean they could adapt to hunting in almost any environment, be it mountains, desert or jungle.

Cats are perfectly designed for hunting. They have light, muscular bodies designed for speed and agility in stalking and catching their prey. Their teeth and claws are sharp and they have very keen senses of smell, hearing and sight.

In fact it was the cat's skill in hunting that gave Man the idea to domesticate it and led eventually to the popular house pet we have today (its scientific name is *Felis catus*).

Most experts now consider that the ancestor of the domestic cat was the caffre cat of North Africa. The ancient Egyptians certainly made use of the cat to keep their huge granaries free of rats and mice and there is evidence of domestication from about 1600 B.C.

The Egyptians were very dedicated ailurophiles! Cats became the most respected of all creatures and eventually a cat goddess came to be worshipped in their temples. Her name was Pasht (or Bastet) and it is from this that we get the word 'puss'. All cats were embalmed when they died and placed in ornate bronze mummy cases — often accompanied by mummified mice! The owners went into mourning and on the death of a temple cat the whole city mourned. To kill a cat was a terrible crime and was believed to bring a curse on the killer's family for several generations.

Breeds

The domestic cat was soon introduced to Europe and Asia, where it was interbred with the local wild cats to produce other breeds. It is thought that the Romans introduced the domestic cat to Britain.

Today there are about 40 breeds of house cat. Compared to most other animals that have been domesticated the cat has changed very little and our familiar 'tabby' still looks very much like its wild North African ancestor. The breeds differ mainly in the colour, pattern and length of hair on their coats. The two main groups are the *short-haired* like the tabby or the Siamese, and the long-haired of which the Persian is a beautiful example.

Many superstitions have grown up about cats over the years, possibly because they appear silent and mysterious. The black cat is a good example. During the Middle Ages it was thought that the Devil's favourite disguise was that of a black cat. The Chinese and Japanese believed that cats could talk when they reached the age of 10, and the expression 'nine lives of a cat' dates back to the days when cats were believed to have magical powers.

Several expressions involve the word 'cat'. "Letting the cat out of the bag" means that someone has given away a secret. "Waiting to see which way the cat jumps" is used by people to mean that they will wait to see what someone else does before taking action.

Much use has also been made of cats in stories and nursery rhymes. The legend of Dick Whittington and his cat is an old favourite.

So in many ways the cat has been a source of fascination to Man for many years. Sadly, wild cats have been considered our enemies and their numbers have been very much reduced. But even the cats we take to be pets can show us their untamed ways and we shall look at some of their many talents in detail on the following pages which concern the 'Cat about the house'.

The Talented Tabby

Here we take a closer look at the interesting life of the cat, its special abilities and behaviour

Top left: One of the similarities between the domestic cat and its wild cousins is their behaviour with kittens. When they are two or three weeks old, the mother's instinct is to move her young to a new 'nest' just as in the wild. She grasps each kitten in turn around the neck and carries them away. The mother will stay with the kittens for several weeks leaving only to obtain food if this is not provided.

Left: A cat will always fall on its feet! Cats have an amazing sense of balance due to the very sensitive balancing mechanism in the inner ear and the suppleness of their bodies. Should the cat fall in this way these abilities combine to turn the body into the landing position. The tail also helps to restore the balance. This move can be achieved over a surprisingly short distance or height.

Right: Another 'wild' instinct in the domestic cat. A wild cat will mark out and defend the territory that supports it. Similar behaviour can be seen in our own tabbies. In the open they tend to stay apart, keeping to favourite paths through gardens or along walls. Lines marking the extent of the territory can be marked out by spraying with urine or favourite objects can be rubbed with the scent of the animal. Should cats cross into another's territory the noise can be quite disturbing!

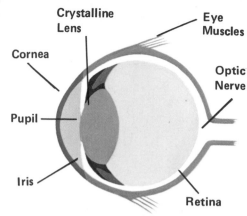

The eyes of the cat. Above: The major features of the cat's eye. Left: The eyes are adapted to make the most of available light. The most obvious adaptation is the vertical slit shape of the pupil. In bright light (large picture) this is a narrow slit. But in poor light (inset) this widens considerably to allow in more light. The eyes can work in a wide variety of light. Cats can also judge distance; important for jumping and hunting.

IT is sad to learn that wild cats are becoming scarcer, so rendering their movements and behaviour more difficult to observe. Fortunately, however, the domestic varieties have not greatly changed in their 3,000 years of domestication and can afford us a good idea of the unchanged 'wild' ways of the cat.

Cats are sometimes portrayed as pampered pets stretching out lazily in front of a warm fire. But while cats naturally deserve the same care as other pets, it is true that the cat is a solitary animal and has not become as dependent on Man as other domestic animals. Many farms keep cats which are given only milk so they do not become lazy about catching rats and mice. They are also kept in this way in dock warehouses where food is stored.

The hunting instinct of the cat is still important to Man and we have seen how superbly their bodies are designed for this task. Their movements are graceful and the sense of balance very acute — even though a cat may fall from a considerable height it can correct the position of its body while dropping and land safely on its feet.

A close-ups of the cat's paw. The toes are protected by pads. The retractile claws are shown extended (the mechanism is explained on the opposite page).

Adaptations

But while stealth is used to stalk the prey, there is also the power for the final sprint and pounce. And watch a cat when it is obstructed by a garden wall or fence. No problem! Using its strong hind and shoulder muscles the cat can jump to surprising heights even from a sitting position.

Evolution has given cats special and successful adaptations. If you look at their feet you will notice that cats actually stand and walk on their toes. The bend in a cat's leg which appears to be a knee is, in fact, an ankle. This is true throughout the cat family from tiger to tabby. It

The supple and freely-moving body of the cat gives it a graceful but powerful movement. When making a run a cat usually keeps a steady speed before breaking into a sprint as shown below. Both the strong back and shoulder muscles are needed. These also give the cat the ability to jump great heights from a sitting position.

The cat's sprint is like a series of bounding leaps. At the end of one leap the cat lands on one forepaw. Both forepaws then come together and the back legs are brought forward. These come into contact with the ground and thrust the cat forward once more.

means that the animal can run with long strides and also spring — very important in catching prey.

The paws are also adapted. The pads protect the toes and aid stealthy movement. The claws are kept in special openings while walking so they do not scrape or break on the ground. They are brought into the open to act as weapons or for climbing trees. Most cats are good climbers.

'Cat's eyes' is the name given to small glass reflectors set in the middle of a road to show in car headlights during the night. It is a fair comparison to make because cats do have exceptional eyesight in the dark and can detect objects almost invisible to the human eye. The pupils have a greater range of contraction and widening than those of Man and can adjust without effort in poor visibility. A cat's whiskers also give an added sense of touch.

Considering the size of a cat, its ears are comparatively large. They can detect very faint sounds and are able to swivel round into the direction the sound is coming from. In fact, the size of a cat's ear largely depends on the climate in which it lives. While domestic cats tend to have ears of similar size, those living in warmer places have larger ears than the Snow Leopard, for example, which lives in the cold mountains of central Asia. There, long ears would be a disadvantage because they would lose too much heat.

Feelings

Cats do not have as good a sense of smell as dogs. They find their prey by sound, sight or smell but stalk it only by sight whereas dogs can trace scent over quite long distances.

A domestic cat will show 'wild' instinctive behaviour. It will often mark out a favourite 'territory' as wild cats do. Should other individuals cross into this, especially at night, a fearful racket may develop as the cats cry at each other. This 'caterwauling' isn't too welcome if you are trying to get some sleep!

Cats have a number of ways of expressing their feelings. The familiar "miaow" usually means that the cat is hungry or wants to be stroked. When given attention or when content a cat may purr with pleasure, which is something its big cousins like the lion cannot do. On the other hand, and perhaps fortunately for us, a cat cannot roar!

When cats are angry they wave the tips of their tails from side to side. If they are frightened, by a dog for instance, they will arch their backs and hiss and spit.

Most cats live to ages between 12 and 14 years (usually shorter in the wild) though some have been known to live up to 25 years. When fully-grown, females give birth to litters of between four and six kittens. As with their wild counterparts they make good mothers and rarely leave the young until they have learned to fend for themselves. Often the mother will carry the kittens to a new 'nest' as wild cats do to protect them from predators.

Today the cat has come to rival the dog as a pet and show animal. It was during the last century that people became interested in maintaining breeds of cat and keeping lists of pedigree breeds. The first Cat Show in Britain was held in 1871.

There is a National Cat Club to which all cat lovers can belong but it is the grandly-named Governing Council of the Cat Fancy that deals with all important matters concerning breeds of cat. It keeps a register of all pedigrees and formulates the rules governing all major shows. Combining long-haired and short-haired types over 35 varieties are recognised.

Perhaps one of the most interesting and worthy of special mention is the famous Manx cat. Completely tailless, it is named after the Isle of Man in the Irish Sea but it is not known how it got there. Some people have suggested that it first appeared in Cornwall while others maintain that it is descended from the mascots of ships from the Spanish Armada which may have been wrecked on the island. Whatever the origin, it is a very popular show cat.

The cat has fascinated Man for many years: loved as a pet, admired on display and still used as a working animal. The British government, incidentally, officially employs a large number of cats and provides them with a weekly 'wage'!

But for whatever reason, long may our fascination with the impressive cat continue.

The structure of the cat's paw and lower leg. This has evolved so that the cat walks on its toes enabling it to run with long strides and to spring. Cats have five toes on the front feet and four on the hind feet. The claws are retractile and normally hidden in special openings so they do not scrape on the ground and hinder stealthy movement. They are unsheathed by contracting a leg muscle which causes a tendon to pull on the third phalange of each toe. This extends the claws. When the muscle is relaxed, ligaments draw the claws back in.

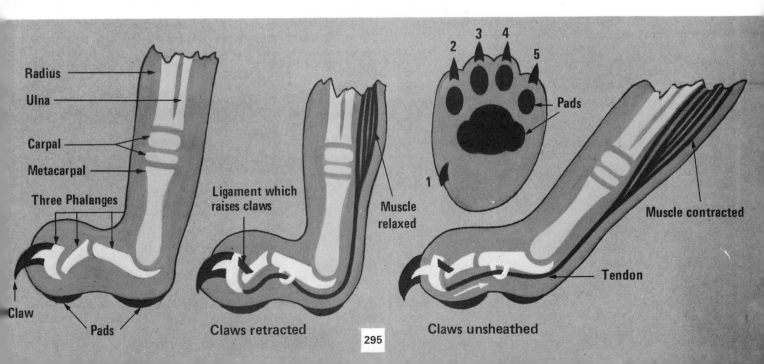

Radius
Ulna
Carpal
Metacarpal
Three Phalanges
Ligament which raises claws
Claw
Pads
Claws retracted
Muscle relaxed
Pads
Muscle contracted
Tendon
Claws unsheathed

Big Cousins of the Tabby

THE dozing tabby cat, sunning itself on a garden wall, is one of the smallest members of the cat family. In many respects, our domestic tabby resembles all its cousins including the largest, the magnificent Siberian tiger. It is a meat-eater (carnivore), an efficient killer, and its claws are retractable and can be withdrawn into sheaths in the paws.

In so many ways our pet tabby is a scaled-down replica of the planet's most beautiful and graceful creatures — the five members of the family Felidae (from the Latin word meaning cat) that can be grouped together as 'big' cats. These are the tiger, the leopard (including the snow leopard), the lion, the cheetah and the jaguar and, apart from their size, they share one other feature in common. If you watch a domestic cat crouching, you will notice that it tucks its feet under its body. The big cats, however, extend their paws in front of them when at rest.

The cheetah is the world's fastest land animal over a short distance, with probably a top speed of about 100 kph over flat ground. However, the cheetah cannot sustain this rate for more than about 500 metres. It tires quickly and if it has not brought down its quarry it will retire to the shade to rest.

Cheetahs differ from most of the cat family in having claws that cannot be fully retracted. They are also the smallest of the big cats weighing about 45 kg, with an overall length (including tail) of about two metres. They are, however, perfectly designed for speedy chases, having exceptionally long legs, blunt claws that act like the spikes on running shoes and a supple, springlike body.

They hunt the smaller antelopes which they often panic into wild flight, making a kill possible. Once it has killed its prey, a cheetah will frequently haul it up to a tree-branch 'larder' safe from lions and other large meat-eaters.

Nowadays, cheetahs are most abundant in East Africa but once they ranged through North Africa, Arabia and India. The Indian cheetah is almost certainly extinct due to hunting for its prized fur.

Sadly this most elegant and stream-lined of big cats is still under pressure in the world and is perhaps the most difficult of all to breed in captivity.

The jaguar is the largest of the New World cats. There, it ranges from the southern United States through South America. It looks rather like the leopard. The spotted coats of the two are similar but the jaguar's is marked by a spot in the centre of a black circle.

The coat is a camouflage in the dense jungles where most jaguars live. It is hard to see among the tangled vegetation. Nevertheless, both pure black and albino animals are not uncommon.

The jaguar is the least studied of all the big cats due to the near impenetrability of the jungles where it lives. It is known to be an excellent hunter, however, and will take animals as big as cattle and even alligators. Its favourite food, though, is the peccary, a South American type of wild pig and it is also fond of fish, as it does not share most cats' hatred of water and is a strong swimmer. It is said that the jaguar flicks its tail on the surface, to attract fish and then scoops them out of the river with its paw.

There are many accounts of 'rogue' jaguars which have turned to man-eating but though instances of man-killing have occurred — especially when an animal has been wounded or cornered — few reports of human flesh being eaten by jaguars have been verified. Indeed, the jaguar prefers to shrink from man by blending into its surroundings. Nevertheless it is highly territorial, and some human

A male lion, distinguished by its mane — although there are, in fact, mane-less lions in some areas of Africa.

intruders have reported jaguars shadowing them through the jungle as if they were being escorted out of the animal's patch.

The leopard is close in length to the jaguar but only about half its weight. It is probably the best-known of all the spotted cats but its beautiful coat has been used for many years in the fur trade and indiscriminate hunting has reduced its numbers drastically. Indeed several types are now so rare that they are listed by the World Wildlife Fund as 'critically endangered'. These include the Anatolian and Amur leopards and the Sinai — from Egypt — which was thought to be extinct in 1970. In zoos you may see 'black panthers' — these are leopards whose colour is predominantly black but, in the right light, spots are still distinguishable. They occur most frequently in South-East Asia.

Leopards are to be found in most parts of Africa, as far north as Turkey (where they are very rare) and eastwards into China. In the Himalayas, too, there is a close relative of the familiar spotted leopard called the snow leopard. This has a far thicker coat of a lighter colour.

Solitary animal

Like the cheetah, the leopard is a solitary animal which spends much of its time in trees. Lacking the cheetah's speed, though, it has a different way of hunting. It lurks on a branch, over a well-worn track and waits until prey passes beneath. Then it drops on the unsuspecting animal, delivering killing bites to the throat. Favourite food includes many types of antelopes, young zebras, wildebeests, and creatures as small as rats, birds, hares and even beetles.

In the past, African leopards have been slaughtered in great numbers — not just for their valuable skins but also because

leopards were supposed to attack both humans and cattle. In fact, leopards are probably more beneficial than destructive as they keep down the numbers of crop-eaters like rats and hares.

The lion is the most common of all the big cats. It differs from the four others in that it is highly social, living in groups — called prides — of up to twenty animals. These comprise, typically, one or two adult males, several lionesses and a number of adolescents and cubs. Whereas the other big cats are solitary hunters, lions will cooperate in catching and killing their prey. A hunting pride has been seen to split into three groups which stealthily approach a herd of wildebeests from down wind (so the potential victims do not pick up their scent). Two groups break off to right and left in a circling movement until they are behind the wildebeests. Then they make their charge, driving the animals towards the third group that is lying in wait.

Although a wildebeest is large, a lion has little trouble in bringing one down. Lions (and lionesses which usually do the hunting) are extremely powerful. An adult male may measure nearly three metres in length and stand over a metre tall at the shoulder. It may weigh over 230 kg and can reach a top speed of 64 kph in short spurts.

It was always thought that lions were primarily hunters and that other animals, particularly hyenas, stole their kill. But recently it has been discovered that hyenas are very effective killers and that lions — essentially lazy beasts — will take the hyenas' kill.

Although they live in groups, lions do not get along very harmoniously. They are extremely aggressive and quarrelsome (fights between rival males are common and sometimes bloody). Although the lionesses do most of the hunting, the males always feed first and the rest of the pride takes turns in order of age, sex and

A group of female impala in danger from a hunting lioness.

A female lion (a lioness) with cubs. Two or three cubs are usual in each litter but up to six have been known.

seniority. The cubs are last and frequently have to risk a hefty clout from an adult paw to get some pickings.

Wildebeests (also known as gnus) form the main part of the lion's diet but lions also feed on other animals that share the open plains of Africa south of the Sahara — zebras, impalas, buffaloes, porcupines and even giraffes. Occasionally lions will become man-eaters, the most notorious example being at Tsavo, Kenya in 1898. Two lions terrorised the country through which a railway was being built. Construction was halted for three weeks as a result of their attacks and, in all, 28 railway workers and an unknown number of natives — perhaps dozens — were killed.

Although the lion's territory in Africa has been much reduced, there is little danger of extinction there. In earlier times, however, lions were common in India, but by the end of the last century, they were restricted to just one area — the Gir forest in the north-west corner of the country. Despite strict protection, the numbers dwindled and by 1968 there were less than two hundred.

Although sometimes called the 'mountain lion', the puma is not closely related to the lion at all. A full-grown adult may weigh 100kg, may be three metres long, and is quite capable of killing large prey such as moose and deer (pumas have even been known to attack bears) but it doesn't rest its forepaws in front of itself and it yowls rather than growls. In fact, zoologists usually consider this fierce American hunter to be an overgrown 'small cat' rather than a 'big cat'.

The tiger, the largest of all the big cats, has suffered a catastrophic decline in numbers. There are seven races of this most noble animal, of which four — the Caspian, the superb Siberian, the Javan and the one from Bali — were listed as being 'critically endangered' by the World Wildlife Fund in 1970. The Sumatran and Chinese races were acknowledged as endangered and the Bengal tiger — the most familiar and at one time probably the most numerous — was also severely threatened.

Unlike other big cats, the tiger seldom ventures into trees. Its coloration is beautifully adapted to the vegetation of the jungle floor where it merges perfectly. It also has a marked liking for water — unusual in a cat — and has been known to plunge into a pool during the heat of the day.

The tiger is a lone hunter that seeks out its prey — mostly deer, occasionally buffaloes and sometimes smaller creatures like monkeys — using its keen hearing. It steals up on them and pounces, its weight alone often being enough to break a victim's back. After the kill it likes to drag the carcase to dense cover where it feels safe.

Bad reputation

Males and females are together only for the brief mating season. The rest of the year is spent in solitary splendour and any strange male tiger that wanders into another's territory — stretching between 8 and 80 square kilometres — is fought off furiously.

Of all the big cats the tiger has the worst reputation for preying on humans. Perhaps one reason for this is that man has persistently encroached into tigers' strongholds. Generally, it is old or injured animals which have turned to the easy, usually unprotected and slow target of man.

It is easy to feel sympathy for the tiger. It has been hunted to near extermination and one must wonder why man has persisted in trying to wipe this and the other big cats from the face of the Earth.

The lioness does most of the hunting, approaching her prey from down-wind.

Animals of the Antipodes

THE wildlife of the Australian continent includes many rare and exotic creatures.

The koala bear and the Tasmanian devil are both marsupials — that is to say, they carry their young in their pouch. The koala bear eats nothing but the leaves of the eucalyptus tree, from which it also gets most of the water it needs.

The duck-billed platypus has a beak like a duck and lays eggs in a nest of dried leaves. The echidna (spiny anteater) also lays eggs and feeds entirely on ants.

The squirrel glider and the pygmy possum are both found in the forests of south-west Australia. The possum is mouse-like and eats nectar, berries and small insects. The squirrel glider has its front and hind legs joined by a flap of skin which enables it to glide from branch to branch.

The tree frog really does climb trees, looking for the insects on which it feeds.

Among birds, the kookaburra or laughing jackass is probably the best known. Its call sounds like laughter — hence its name. It feeds on snakes.

Another forest dweller is the diamond bird which builds a nest from strips of bark at the end of a 61 centimetre long tunnel on the ground.

Perhaps the most extraordinary and exotic of the Australian birds, however, is the lyrebird. The male has a wonderful display of tail feathers and is a marvellous mimic. As well as copying the calls of other birds, it can imitate the barking of a dog, the neighing of a horse and even the sound of a motor horn — so you have to see one to be able to assure anyone that you really have heard it.

KOALA BEARS

DUCK-BILLED PLATYPUS

TREE FROG

KOOKABURRA

DIAMOND
BIRD

TASMANIAN DEVIL

PYGMY
POSSUM

ECHIDNA

LYREBIRD

SQUIRREL
GLIDER

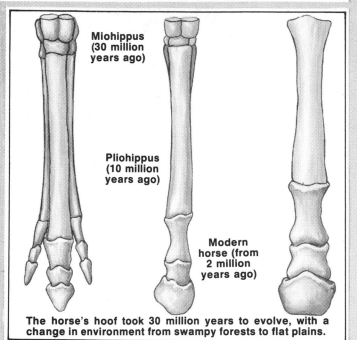

This prehistoric cave painting at Altamira in Spain is over 10,000 years old. The horse depicted is similar to the tarpan, a wild horse that became extinct in 1851.
Photo: The Mansell Collection

Miohippus
(30 million
years ago)

Pliohippus
(10 million
years ago)

Modern
horse (from
2 million
years ago)

The horse's hoof took 30 million years to evolve, with a change in environment from swampy forests to flat plains.

The Story of the Horse

OVER 50 million years ago a small mammal, about the size of a poodle dog, ran easily through the swampy undergrowth feeding off the succulent plant life. The creature could outrun and hide from its enemies in these conditions and so it flourished and increased in numbers. This was *Eohippus*, the Dawn Horse, the ancestor of all the horses we know today.

We know this because the rocks of North America have yielded a very detailed fossil record of the evolution of the horse from 60 million years ago until recent times. *Eohippus* looked very different from present-day horses. Apart from size it had four toes on the front feet and three on the hind or back feet, a short jaw and small teeth.

These features were suitable for life in the forests but the horse evolved as its environment slowly changed from forests to prairies. The diagram on the left illustrates a major evolutionary development — the hoof.

The horses which could escape most easily from their enemies were those which could run fastest. This meant an increase in size and in the length of the legs, together with a lengthening of stride by running on the tips of the toes. So *Miohippus*, who lived around 30 million years ago, had three toes on each foot, of which the central toe was the largest.

Przewalski's horse

The wild horse, whose sole survivor is Przewalski's horse, is the ancient ancestor of about 60 breeds of horse — from ponies to work horses and show horses.

Pit pony

Shire horse

302

As horses moved on to the plains they had to become long-distance runners and so the extra toes disappeared to reduce weight. This is seen in the *Pliohippus* of 10 million years ago.

Eventually the hoof became slightly wider for stability as in the modern horse, *Equus,* which has only one toe on each foot. In fact the hoof is actually the toenail. *Equus* first appeared about two million years ago.

Another change which had taken place during those millions of years was that the eyes had moved from the front to the sides of the head. This arrangement meant that predators could be detected easily. Horses have a very wide field of vision, and the eye is not round, which means that light from nearby objects (like the grass on which the horse grazes) is focused on one part of the eye. At the same time, another part of the eye focuses the light from distant objects. This is an important safety factor, because it means the horse does not have to refocus in order to detect predators while it is grazing.

As well as the hoof and eyes, the teeth also changed to enable the horse to grind down the tough grass, and the brain increased in size. As a result of all these changes the horse therefore looked very much as we see it now but was somewhat smaller, being about the size of a donkey.

Man and the horse

Man's first relationship with the horse was not as a friend, but as a hunter. Cave paintings like those at Altamira in northern Spain, over 10,000 years old, excitingly depict the hunting of animals, including the horse. And at the horse hunters' camp at Solutré in southern France nearly 10,000 horse skeletons lie among the debris of food remains.

The first horse to be domesticated was probably the tarpan, which roamed the Russian steppes, by nomadic tribesmen in about 4350 B.C. They were useful because of their docility, strength and speed although at this time individual horses were still too small to carry a rider. The Ancient Egyptians used horses to pull their war chariots and began to breed larger riding horses. The uses of horses in war is recorded on the elaborate friezes of the Egyptians, Assyrians and other ancient civilisations.

Due to Man's intervention, different types of horses were developed for agriculture, war and transport, and domesticated horses played an important part in everyday life. Sadly nearly all of the true wild horses have been exterminated as men wanted to prevent interbreeding with domestic horses. The tarpan became extinct in 1851, and only one species of wild horse still exists, Przewalski's horse of Mongolia, which is now a protected species.

But although wild horses are few, Man has taken his horses all over the world and in some places these have escaped and flourished. These are known as feral animals. Thus the 'wild' horses of America and Australia, and the ponies of the remoter parts of Britain, still enjoy the freedom that their very ancient ancestors once knew.

All domestic horses and ponies of the present day are descended from different forms of the European and Asiatic wild horse. Domestication and selection for size, strength and colour has produced breeds from ponies to Thoroughbreds and Shire horses. Man uses these for several purposes including shows, heavy work and racing. Domestic true horses differ from their wild ancestors in size and shape, and noticeably in the form of the mane, which is erect in wild horses (as the photograph of a Przewalski's horse shows), but falls over the neck in domestic breeds.

Some of the most famous breeds are pictured on these pages. The beautiful Arab is the most ancient of all domesticated horses and is the purest in blood. It is the ideal breed for speed, strength and good looks, and has been used to improve many other types of horse. Every grey horse seen on a racecourse is descended from one Arab called the Alcock Arabian. From Arab stallions (male horses) and native English mares (female horses) comes the most famous British breed — the Thoroughbred. Bred for centuries to win races, these are the fastest horses the world has ever known.

Working horses have served us faithfully for centuries but have now largely been replaced by machines. The Shire horse is the largest British horse and can reach up to 17 hands in height (one hand measures four inches) and weigh more than a ton. Often used for ploughing our fields, in the Middle Ages they carried knights wearing full armour and were usually armoured themselves. The Shire is very good tempered. The Clydesdale is Scotland's own breed. It is not as big as the Shire but is more active, and like the Shire has lots of white on its legs. Hackney 'cabs' used to be a familiar sight in our towns and cities but today you are more likely to see these energetic horses in shows or trotting races although Hackneys are still used to pull carriages on ceremonial occasions.

Several breeds belong especially to North America as descendants of horses taken there when America was first settled in the 16th century. Of these, the Palomino is the most magnificent with its golden body and pure white mane and tail. It is known as the 'golden horse of the West'.

Ponies

Ponies are often mistaken for young horses but in fact they are a distinct type. The main difference between ponies and horses is in size. Ponies must be smaller, and 15 hands is usually taken as the limit for a full-grown pony. Ponies are hardy and sure-footed creatures. They can live on small amounts of poor food and appear to be slightly more intelligent than horses.

Some of the best known ponies are found in the British Isles. The New Forest pony is found in the New Forest in Hampshire and is very sturdy and manageable. They are great favourites with people learning to ride. Welsh Mountain ponies are popular with children as they are very handsome. Officially they cannot be taller than 12 hands which makes them the smallest pony except for the world-famous Shetland pony. Although tiny, it is almost the strongest type of pony, and can carry incredible weights for its size. The Shetland was once used in coal mines to draw trucks underground but today it is often used as a riding pony for small children. In the wild state, on the Shetland Islands, it is the toughest of all ponies.

Hackney

Shire

New Forest Pony

Arab

Shetland Pony

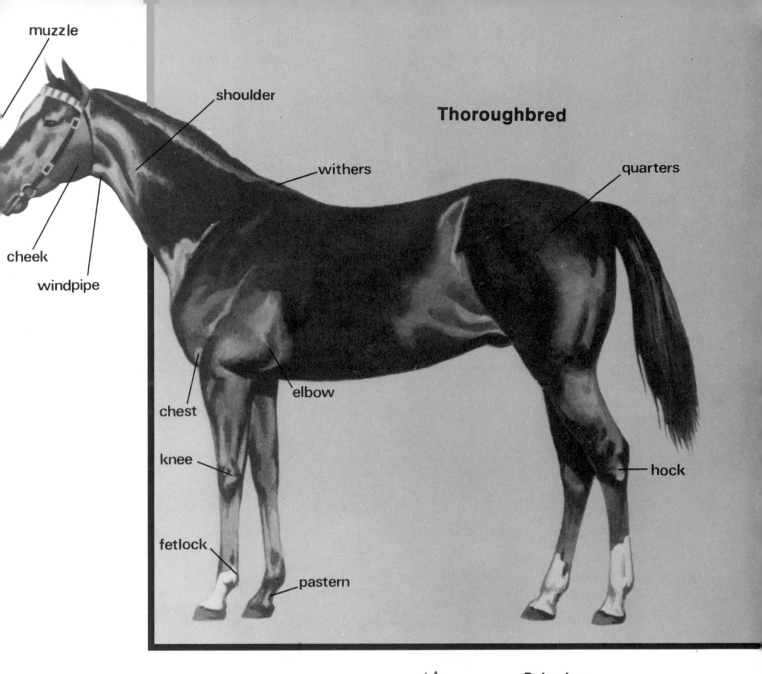

muzzle

shoulder

Thoroughbred

cheek

withers

quarters

windpipe

elbow

chest

knee

hock

fetlock

pastern

The only truly wild horse now in existence is named Przewalski's horse (below), after the Russian explorer who rediscovered It In 1879. Found only in western Mongolia, in Asia, it lives in small herds of usually no more than 15, each under the leadership of an old stallion (male). The average height is only about 1.2m. An expedition in 1902 managed to capture 32 foals, and from these a good many specimens have been bred. Several zoos around the world now exhibit this very ancient horse.

Palomino

Clydesdale

Welsh Pony

Plants with a taste for meat

THERE'S something particularly sinister about a meat-eating plant. Perhaps we've all had nightmares of some fiendish monster slowly strangling us within its leafy embrace. Luckily such man-eating plants do not exist.

But things are different if you are an insect or equally small animal. There are many types of seemingly innocent-looking plants that are just waiting to gobble you up for dinner.

Anyone who has walked in the peat marsh areas of Britain, on the tops of the Pennines for instance, may have noticed an attractive little plant growing with its leaves pressed close to the ground. All over the leaves there are sticky hairs covered with droplets of liquid. These droplets shine like dew and give the plant its name — the sundew.

Beware the unwary

However, the innocent appearance of the plant belies its life style — for the leaves form highly effective snares for the unwary insect attracted by the shining droplets. An insect which lands on the hairs is trapped by the sticky liquid and soon the hairs bend over and enclose it. It is then digested.

Butterworts are similar in both appearance and life style to the sundews. They too are found in marshy areas. They are, in some ways, even more innocent looking than the sundews. At least sundews have large sticky hairs which give some hint of danger. But the hairs on the leaf of the butterwort are tiny.

The trap of the butterwort is sprung by an insect landing on the hairs — which are sticky. The entire leaf margin then rolls inwards and entombs the insect.

Sundews and butterworts are familiar enough plants to the rambler and nature enthusiast, but another meat-eating plant, the bladderwort, is rarely seen. That is because it lives underwater in lakes, ponds and

Venus's flytraps are undemanding pets — this sausage should keep this one going for months.

ditches.

The plant looks normal enough, with finely divided leaves, so common in water plants. But if the leaves are examined closely, numerous small 'bladders' can be seen. Each bladder is a highly ingenious trap.

The entrance to the bladder is closed by a little 'trap door', and special cells pump out most of the water inside the bladder. The trap door is kept tightly closed by the pressure of the outside water trying to get in.

Sucked in

Around the edge of the trap door are 'trigger' hairs. If an animal — often a little water flea — touches one of these hairs, the trap door opens and the unfortunate victim is sucked in to its death. Once it is inside, the trap door closes and it is slowly digested and absorbed.

Just as nasty as the bladderwort, but not found in Britain, is Venus's

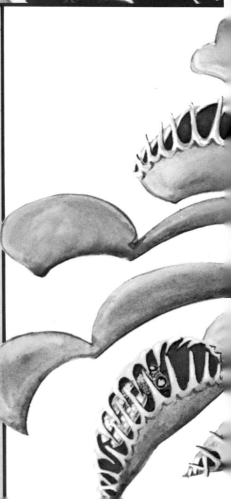

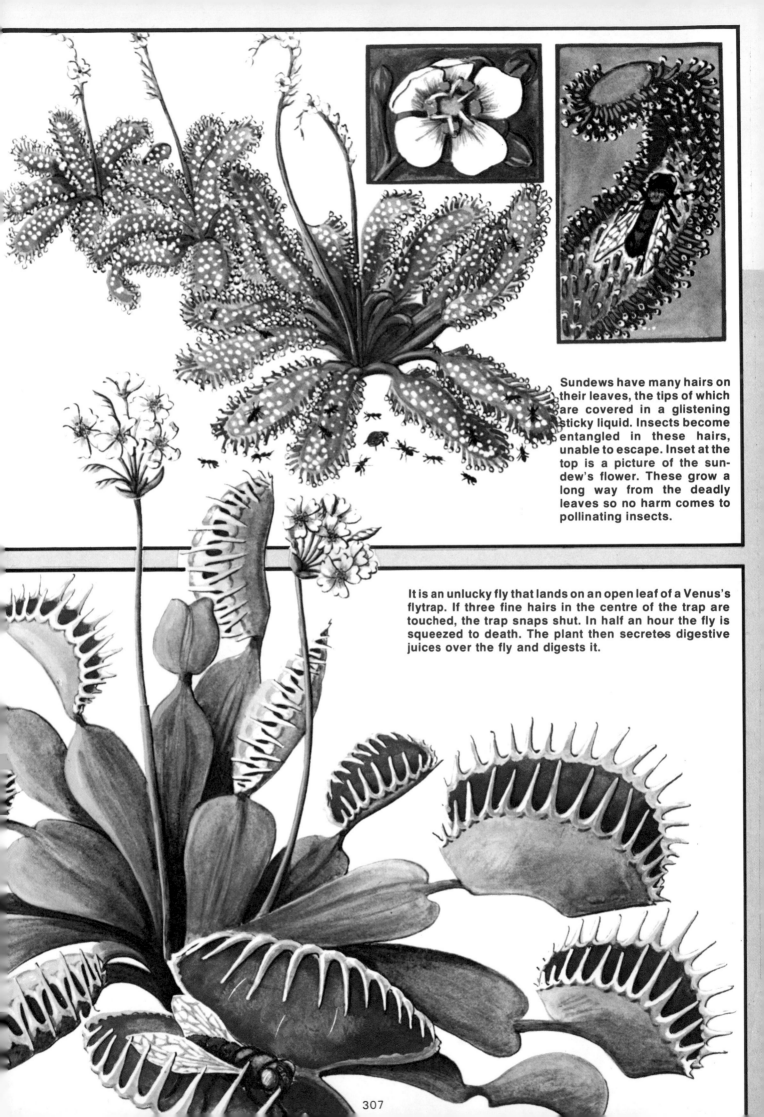

Sundews have many hairs on their leaves, the tips of which are covered in a glistening sticky liquid. Insects become entangled in these hairs, unable to escape. Inset at the top is a picture of the sundew's flower. These grow a long way from the deadly leaves so no harm comes to pollinating insects.

It is an unlucky fly that lands on an open leaf of a Venus's flytrap. If three fine hairs in the centre of the trap are touched, the trap snaps shut. In half an hour the fly is squeezed to death. The plant then secretes digestive juices over the fly and digests it.

flytrap — a native of the Carolinas in the United States. In this plant, the leaves are hinged like the pages of a book and edged with stiff hairs. When an insect lands on one of these leaves the trap springs shut and encloses the prey, which is digested by juices secreted from tiny hairs on the inside of the leaf. Once digested, the luckless animal is absorbed.

Perhaps the most impressive, and certainly the most numerous meat-eating plants, are the pitcher plants.

They are found in warm moist areas of the world from Asia and Africa to California and Australia, and they are particularly common in rainforests. The largest of them all is the Californian pitcher plant, the pitcher of which can reach up to 60 cm in length. Other species are climbers and may be found growing among the upper branches of tall forest trees in the forests of Asia.

Pitcher plants have special leaves which form a large hanging pitcher often brightly coloured in shades of reds and purples, yellows and greens. The colours mimic those of the surrounding flowers and insects are attracted to their deaths.

In some, the pitchers are open and so rainwater collects in the bottom of the pitcher. Usually this type of pitcher plant relies on small creeping insects accidentally stumbling over the lip. Once inside the pitcher the insect cannot get a footing on the slippery surface and slips down to drown in the liquid at the bottom. Then it is digested.

Death trap

In other, more sophisticated, pitcher plants the pitchers are closed and they form a highly effective death trap. In one, the yellow pitcher plant from the U.S.A., the pitcher produces nectar, and flies, seeking this food, land on a specially provided platform. From here they are invited to crawl through inwardly projecting hairs to reach the nectar.

But once inside, the insects cannot crawl back through the hairs and so continue on into the interior of the pitcher where they are trapped. For the fly this is a one-way journey, for potent digestive juices are produced at the base of the pitcher and the exhausted insect finally falls into a pool of digestive juice in which it is consumed.

So with ingenuity it is quite possible for a stationary plant to trap and eat small animals, just like many stationary animals, such as corals, do. But seeing that *some* plants are meat-eating, why haven't more taken up the habit? Why aren't there thousands of different species lying in wait to gobble up every moving thing that comes their way?

Terrifying

It is a terrifying thought. Luckily most plants can get all the nourishment they need from sunlight, carbon dioxide in the air, water and salts in the soil. They simply don't need to eat meat.

But in some places, such as mountain bogs, the soil is poor — particularly in the vital element nitrogen. Animal flesh is rich in nitrogen. And so to supplement the nitrogen they get from the soil, meat-eating plants also devour animals — sometimes in bizarre and gruesome ways.

The insects among you are warned!

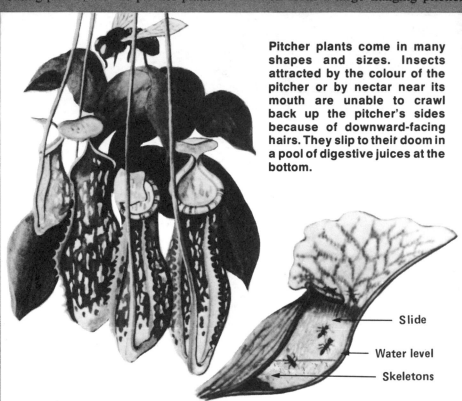

Pitcher plants come in many shapes and sizes. Insects attracted by the colour of the pitcher or by nectar near its mouth are unable to crawl back up the pitcher's sides because of downward-facing hairs. They slip to their doom in a pool of digestive juices at the bottom.

Slide

Water level

Skeletons

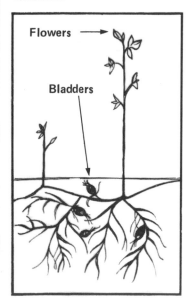

Bladderworts flower above water. But beneath the surface are bladder traps which suck small animals in to their deaths when trigger hairs near the trap entrances are touched.

Flowers

Bladders

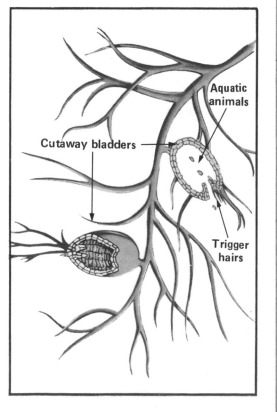

Aquatic animals

Cutaway bladders

Trigger hairs

The Magnificent Birds of Paradise

BIRDS of the world range impressively from the huge ostrich to the tiny bee hummingbird; from the fierce grandeur of the golden eagle to the twittering charm of the budgerigar. Amid all this wonderful diversity of bird life, the birds of paradise stand alone in magnificence. They are the most elaborately ornamented, brilliantly coloured birds on Earth.

The very name — birds of paradise — indicates the beauty and exotic nature of their feathering. There are over 40 species and many have been given individual names that reflect their gorgeous plumes names like the 'superb', the 'king', the 'magnificent', the 'Prince Rudolph's' and the 'King of Saxony' birds of paradise.

Many birds boast glorious feathers but those of the birds of paradise stand above all others. Not only are they breathtaking in their colouration, they also sport plumes of extraordinary length and com-

plex shape, in addition, some of them perform the most elaborate and lengthy rituals or dances to court their drab female mates.

True birds of paradise live only in New Guinea and its surrounding islands. Since the beginning of history New Guinea tribesmen — many of whom were fierce warriors who only recently gave up their head-hunting habits — have prized the feathers of the birds of paradise as adornments. Impressive head-dresses, some as high as five metres, were constructed from the plumes. The warriors wore the feathers for the same reason as the male birds of paradise — to attract females. A New Guinea tribesman is more likely to win a wife if he has a vivid display of plumes; precisely the reason why the male bird of paradise has developed such a gaudy ornamentation.

Birds of paradise are solitary creatures inhabiting the dense and isolated jungles, each keeping to their own parcel of territory. The males and females are only drawn together during the breeding season when the males show the dowdy females that they are suitable mates by displaying their finery. Some spread their already magnificent feathers in huge fans, others inflate them into ruffs. One species, Raggiana's bird of paradise, climaxes his display by leaning his whole body forward from a branch — and arches his red back feathers in a cascade above his head. Other species use their tail or head feathers like banners, allow-

The plumes in the head-dress of this New Guinea chief include those of the lesser bird of paradise (centre) and a variety of the greater bird of paradise (top). Through his nose are plumes of the King of Saxony species.

Also pictured is the twelve-wired bird of paradise, remarkable for the fact that 12 of its plumes develop into wire-like bristles almost 300 cm long.

ing them to stream out in long ribbons which can assume a fantastic variety of shapes.

The magnificent bird of paradise shows off his breast feathers, forming them into a shield and pulsing them in his intended mate's direction, turning to keep his best feature always in view. If the female is impressed, they mate, after which she flies off to her own territory to lay her eggs and bring up the chicks alone.

Although the fabulous birds of New Guinea have been known to exist for many centuries and their feathers have been much valued in Europe since the 16th century, it is only recently that much hard scientific data has been unearthed. This is mainly because of the nature of the island. Much of it is inaccessible, covered by nearly impenetrable jungle. For example, it was only in 1933 that a plane managed to fly over a portion of the interior. To the crew's astonishment, they saw a huge valley, previously unsuspected, spreading beneath them. Living in it were 100,000 natives, totally isolated from the outside world and living a Stone Age existence. Similarly, new species of bird of paradise have been found intermittently over the years.

Exports to Europe

At one time the birds were much sought-after by traders from Europe. Ladies of fashion in London and Paris recognised their beauty as much as the Stone Age natives and skins were exported from New Guinea in a steady flow from the 16th century onwards that became a flood by Victorian times. At first little was known of these near-mythical creatures and scientists evolved elaborate theories about them.

The skins that reached Europe had no feet attached and it was assumed that the birds were naturally legless because they spent all their life in the air, borne by their spreading tail and wing feathers. This was one of the reasons for the name 'birds of paradise'; they were not of this world at all but had wandered down from some heavenly realm. Another theory is that the New Guinea natives — who made their living selling the feathered-skins to merchants — did not want their buyers to know the exact location of the birds' nesting sites in case they went out to hunt them themselves. When asked where the birds dwelt they said, "Paradise!"

It is easy to see that anyone could believe that these gorgeous birds were from another, more serene, world. Even as recently as 1894 there was disbelief when a King of Saxony bird of paradise was shown in Paris. Many thought it was a fake — the feathers of one bird attached to the body of another — because no one could imagine a small, 18 cm bird sprouting two immense 45 cm plumes of shimmering blue fron its head!

The demand for bird of paradise feathers to adorn ladies' hats was immense. Tens of thousands of males were killed and exported every year. Even 100 years ago the finest specimens could fetch £40 apiece on the dockside in New Guinea. What price when they reached the milliners in London?

This unceasing slaughter was slackened only by the outbreak of the First World War in 1914. Nobody knows the exact effect it had on numbers, indeed, whether any species were hunted to extinction. Fortunately, after the war there was an outcry against wanton des-

truction and in the 1920s a ban was imposed on the export of bird of paradise feathers from New Guinea. Hunting continued, however. The natives had not lost their love of feathered finery and even today men are willing to pay £100 or more for a single plume.

Thankfully, the export ban has diminished the numbers being killed and saved those species under the greatest pressure. Long may the world's most bizarre and magnificent birds continue their outrageous posturings in the safety of their remote jungle home.

1. White-Billed Sickle Bill
2. Long-Tailed Bird of Paradise
3. Lesser Bird of Paradise
4. Most Splendid Longtail
5. Magnificent Bird of Paradise
6. Standard Wing Bird of Paradise
7. Red Bird of Paradise
8. King Bird of Paradise
9. Crested Golden Bird
10. Goldie's Bird of Paradise
11. Blue Bird of Paradise

The island of New Guinea is divided from west to east between Indonesia and the independent state of Papua New Guinea. Much of the land is rugged mountain country with dense tropical jungle, and it is here that the birds of paradise are found.

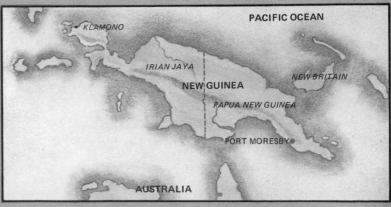

Have compasses

BOBOLINK

ARCTIC WARBLER

ARCTIC SKUA

GOLDEN PLOVER

WHITE STORK

SWALLOW

RUFF

ARCTIC TERN

O N the radar scanners at Heathrow Airport the air-traffic controllers watch a large bright patch move slowly across their screens. It is not one of the many hundreds of aircraft that pass through Heathrow every day, and it is not a U.F.O. from another planet. The controllers are watching a huge cloud of starlings.

It is autumn and the starlings, in flocks containing twenty to thirty thousand individuals, are moving westwards to escape the early snows of Eastern Russia and Poland. In spring they will all fly back across Europe again.

Food shortages

They are said to be *migrating*. They are flying from place to place to escape shortages of food, and to seek out those places where there is a temporary abundance.

During the winter, for example, most British insects are either dead or hibernating. It is too cold for them. So, the insect-eating swallows must fly south in order to survive. They go to Africa where insects abound all the year round.

Restless hordes

Thousands of them may be seen to line up on telegraph wires. There is an urgency in their twitterings and chatterings. Then suddenly, at some invisible signal, the restless hordes take to the sky, circle in a great cloud, orientate themselves, and set off across Europe and the Mediterranean Sea, across the Sahara Desert, down the coast of West Africa, until they finally land exhausted and hungry in South Africa. They have travelled 8,000 kilometres non-stop. But this feat is nothing compared

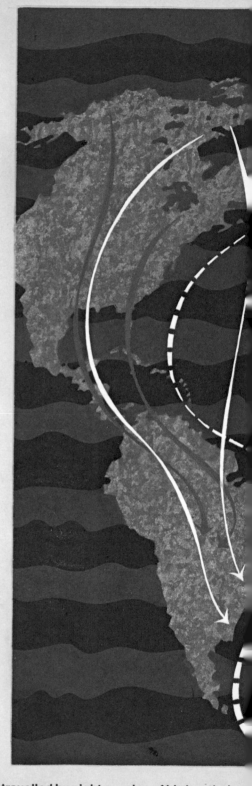

Our map shows the incredible distances travelled by eight species of bird on their annual migrations. What makes them undertake these vast journeys? The main answer is food. In winter, edible plants and insects become increasingly hard to find. Moreover, short winter days mean that birds — most of which hunt by eyesight — have less time in which to find their scarce prey. Those birds that live in the most northerly areas tend to travel farthest. For each species of bird is adapted to live in a particular type of *habitat* and must fly on until it finds it. So the Arctic tern, adapted to live near the poles, must fly all the way to the Antarctic to find a suitable home. The journey from pole to pole is 18,000 kilometres — and remember that is only one way.

will travel

How do migrating birds fly halfway across the world but never lose their way? And why do they do it?

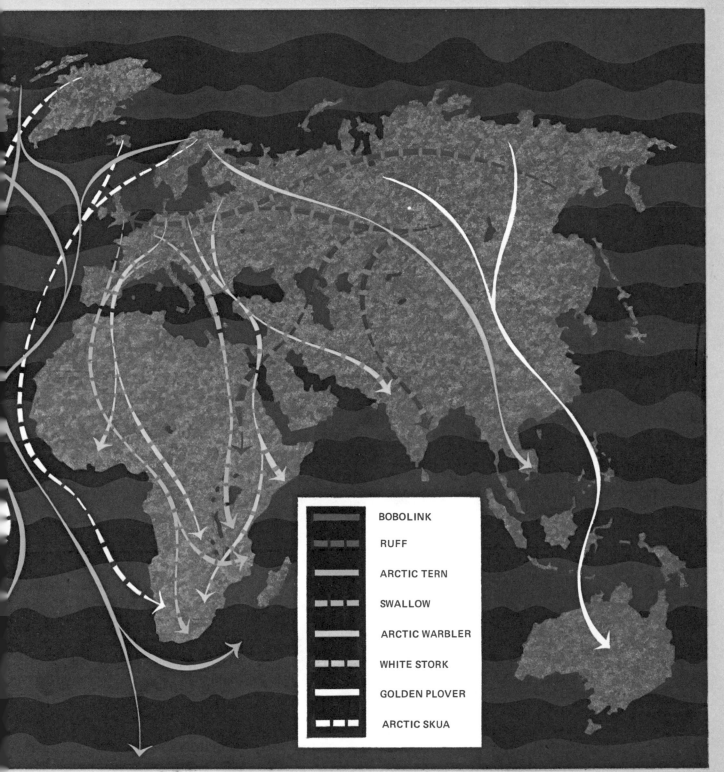

Legend:
- BOBOLINK
- RUFF
- ARCTIC TERN
- SWALLOW
- ARCTIC WARBLER
- WHITE STORK
- GOLDEN PLOVER
- ARCTIC SKUA

SPECIES	LENGTH IN cm	DISTANCE TRAVELLED IN km (APPROX)
BOBOLINK	16·5 – 20	8,000
RUFF	22 – 30·5	5,000 – 9,500
ARCTIC TERN	35 – 38	18,000
SWALLOW	18 – 19	8,000 – 11,250

SPECIES	LENGTH IN cm	DISTANCE TRAVELLED IN km (APPROX)
ARCTIC WARBLER	12	6,500 – 11·250
WHITE STORK	102	6,500 – 11·250
GOLDEN PLOVER	25·5 – 28	9,750 – 13,000
ARCTIC SKUA	42	6,500 – 13·000

with that of the Arctic tern. This little bird, no bigger than a pigeon, flies as much as 18,000 km across the world, nesting within the Arctic Circle in summer, and spending the winter along the edge of Antarctica.

But despite the thousands of birds that desert Britain and Europe during the autumn, there are still plenty of birds about in the winter. As the terns, swallows and others fly away, other birds fly in from the north.

Barnacle geese

In their easily recognised V-formations, barnacle geese descend from widely spread regions of the Arctic Circle to spend the winter in Britain. One batch from Greenland end up in north-west Ireland and Scotland. Another group from Spitzbergen finish their journey in the Solway on the Scottish borders, and yet another distinct flock from Novaya Zemlya off the north coast of Russia pass Britain by to finish up in the Netherlands.

Whooper swans, having bred in the Siberian tundra of Arctic Russia, arrive in the winter to browse on the grassy fields beside some of Britain's larger river estuaries.

Surprisingly, it is only relatively recently that people have realised that birds make these incredible journeys. In the 18th century it was thought that swallows spent the winter at the bottom of ponds. But today, by placing a numbered identity ring on its leg, a bird can be tracked from country to country, and its travels plotted and followed. The migration might be the short distance from the bottom of a valley to the top of a nearby mountain, or the tern's incredibly long journey from the North to the South Pole.

Complete mystery

How does a bird travel these distances, through storms, across featureless deserts and oceans, and unerringly find, not only its approximate destination, but the exact nesting place from where it hatched as a chick in a previous year? Perhaps it remembers the route from the outward journey. But then how does a Manx shearwater, taken from its nesting place on the Welsh coast, and flown by aeroplane to Boston, U.S.A., find its way back home in only 12½ days — a remarkable feat?

Complex answer

For many years, migration remained a complete mystery. But now scientists are beginning to understand it.

Visiting sea birds include:
Manx Shearwaters
Arctic Terns
Sandwich Terns
Common Terns
Fulmars
Kittiwakes

1,600km
3,200km
4,800km
6,400km
8,000km

⬡ Breeding areas of British winter visitors

+ Wintering areas of British summer visitors

〰 Areas in which migrating sea birds disperse outside breeding season

→ Probable migration routes

Britain's bird population contains three types of birds — those that stay in Britain all year round (the *residents*), those that migrate to Britain for the winter (*winter visitors*), and those that migrate to Britain for the summer (*summer visitors*). In April all three may be in Britain at the same time.

Summer visitors (and residents, of course) breed in Britain, but winter visitors, escaping from harsher lands to the north, usually breed in those lands. Sea birds are a special case. They may breed in Britain usually along marshy estuaries or on rocky coasts in summer but spend the rest of the year feeding at sea.

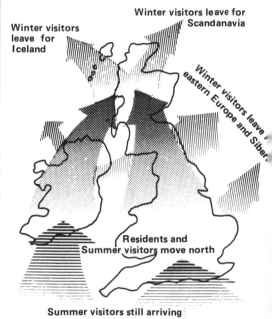

THE MOVEMENT OF BIRDS IN GREAT BRITAIN IN APRIL

Winter visitors leave for Iceland

Winter visitors leave for Scandanavia

Winter visitors leave for eastern Europe and Siberia

Residents and Summer visitors move north

Summer visitors still arriving

Residents include:	Winter visitors include:	Summer visitors include:
Blue Tits	Barnacle Geese	Blackcaps
Woodpeckers	Blackbirds	House Martins
Doves	Knots	Red-backed Shrikes
Canada Geese	Mallards	Sand Martins
Jays	Meadow Pipits	Sedge Warblers
Raven	Pink-footed Geese	Swallows
Tawny Owls	Redpoll	Swifts
Wrens	Snow Buntings	Willow Warblers
Robins	Chaffinches	Cuckoos
Song Thrushes	Starlings	Nightingales
Buzzards	Arctic Skuas	Lapwing

FINDING OUT HOW THEY DO IT

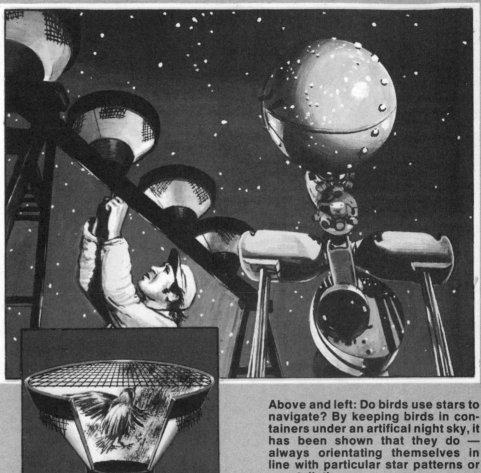

Above and left: Do birds use stars to navigate? By keeping birds in containers under an artifical night sky, it has been shown that they do — always orientating themselves in line with particular star patterns or constellations.

How do migrating birds find their way across thousands of kilometres? Research — particularly in America — has gradually unravelled some of the mysteries. Sight, sound, smell, and several 'senses' unknown to Man are all involved.

Pigeons have been used in many experiments. Their ability to find their way home is well known by pigeon racers. It seems they have a 'celestial radar' that is able to locate the position of the Moon even in the middle of the day. They can also recognise the position of the Sun even if it is obscured by clouds.

The stars, too, are used as guides. Birds placed under an artificial night sky (a *planetarium*) always fly in line with a particular pattern of stars no matter which way the artificial sky is turned.

In addition, birds can hear low frequency sounds, so crashing waves against a sea-cliff might give them a clue as to the direction in which they should fly, and if their smelling ability is removed they have difficulty finding their way, so this too is involved.

To cap it all, material within a pigeon's skull acts like a magnet and can detect the Earth's magnetic field. What better way to navigate than with your own built-in compass?

Above, right: This experiment was to see if a pigeon could see ultra-violet light. This light was randomly beamed to the pigeon through a hole in the top of the box and soon afterwards the bird was given a small electric shock which made its heart beat faster. When the shocks were stopped, the bird's heart still beat faster every time the light was switched on — anticipating the shock and so showing that the bird could see the light.

Left: Rings like this identify birds so that their journeys can be followed.

---

1. Britain 2. Czechoslovakia 3. Denmark
4. Sweden 5. Germany 6. Hungary 7. Holland
• • • • • Swallows' paths

Above: Swallows travel together when migrating, so where birds set out from can have an effect on where they finally end up. Swallows from several European countries were ringed and traced to their winter homes in Africa. Birds from the same starting point tended to keep together, separate from birds that had set out from a different place.

The answer is turning out to be very complex. The positions of the Sun and Moon, the patterns of the stars, the Earth's gravitational pull, characteristic odours and visual landmarks associated with the home destination, changes in atmospheric temperature and pressure, prevailing winds and weather systems, sources of ultra-violet and polarised light (light in which the lightwaves are all vibrating in the same direction, such as that produced when sunlight shines through clouds) have all been identified as playing a part in this intriguing story.

Built-in magnet

But perhaps most fascinating of all is the discovery that pigeon's have a material in their heads that acts like a magnet and can detect the Earth's magnetic field. They have their very own built-in magnet.

Migrating birds not only have a 'sixth sense', but a seventh, eighth, ninth and tenth as well.

Jewel-box of the seashore

FOLLOWING the outgoing tide can be fun. Clambering down over slippery rocks, you may see strange creatures scuttle or dart from view as your shadow passes over the scattered rock pools the sea has left behind.

At the low tide mark you must stop. You can go no further. You're standing on the brink of an alien world that you may only enter with mask, snorkel, and flippers.

This is the shallow coastal zone. Permanently covered by the sea, it's brightly lit and full of life. Our picture shows a section of Mediterranean shore, but many of the animals and plants can also be found around the coast of south-west England.

On your way over the rocks, you may have noticed little red blobs of jelly attached firmly in cracks and crevices in the rock pools. Now they are curled up

Shallow waters and rock pools around the coast teem with life. Not all of it can be seen with the naked eye, of course, yet the jerky movements of the prawn (1) and its smaller relation the shrimp (2) can be spotted almost everywhere. You may also see the strangely pointed *Streetsia* (3).

Lying on the sea-bed and occassionally on the beach may be different kinds of starfish (4), some brightly coloured like the red star (5).

There are many kinds of crab (6), among them the many-legged spider (7) and the

hermit (8), which makes itself a home from the abandoned shell of a whelk or similar creature. Far too big to fit a shell is the rock lobster (9) or crawfish; it is not found in pools, of course, and it does not have claws, as do other lobsters.

Looking so much like flower heads nestling among rocks are the sea urchins (10), while other plant-like animals, with 'plant' names, too, are the anemones — dahlia (11), opelet (12) and beadlet (13). In water a little deeper there is to be found the soft coral with the weird name of 'dead-man's fingers' (14).

protectively, but when the sea covers them they slowly unfold to reveal a central circular mouth surrounded by a ring of brightly coloured tentacles.

They are beadlet sea anemones, and each tentacle is lined with hundreds of stinging cells with which the anemone catches its prey. If disturbed, the anemone can contract and draw in its tentacles to form a defensive blob, and this is how it stays when left high and dry by the tide.

Waving tentacles

Another even more striking anemone, the snakelocks or opelet, is, however, unable to draw in its long wavy tentacles. So, unlike the beadlet, it only lives below the low-tide mark. It chooses the brightest lit areas, spreading its tentacles towards the light.

Microscopic algae (plants) live in the tentacle tissue. The algae, protected by the sea anemone, use the light, carbon dioxide and salts dissolved in the water to grow, and the anemone uses the algae's waste products to do the same. The algae give the otherwise pale anemone a general brown or green colour with mauve tips to the tentacles.

In deeper water, white or red-lobed masses of jelly may attract your attention. Waving in the current, like tree branches in a breeze, they could be plants, but closer inspection shows them to be colonies of animals — soft coral known as 'dead-man's fingers'. Hundreds of miniature eight-armed *polyps* are imbedded in a jelly-like material stiffened with tiny needle-like pieces of lime. Inside they are all joined together by a continuous canal.

Dead-man's fingers used to be used in medicine. Roasted, it was offered as a cure for goiter (iodine deficiency) for the creature has a high iodine content.

Covering soft chalk or limestone rocks are often groups of rock urchins. They may be so close together they form a black spiny carpet. They're known as 'diggers', for by gnawing at the rock with teeth on their undersides, and by rotating their spines, they are able to burrow into stone.

With its spiky coat, the sea urchin is safe from most undersea predators — with the exception of a close relative, the spiny starfish. Starfish have a remarkable way of feeding. They eject their stomachs over their prey, such as the sea urchin. The stomach can infiltrate down between the sea urchin's spines, slowly digesting the urchin's body *outside* the starfish. In the end, all that is left behind of the urchin is an empty shell.

On the rocky walls and under cliffs lives another starfish, the red star, which has long slender brick-red arms. It too has little spines buried in the skin.

Another spiky creature you may encounter along the coast is the spiny spider crab. Sometimes they are found in large conical heaps on the sea-bed with 50 to 80 individuals clustered together. They do this for protection when the young are ready to shed too-small skins and the adults are about to mate. Each heap has the large males on the top and sides as guards, with the more vulnerable crabs inside.

The hermit crab has developed another form of protection. It places its soft naked tail into a discarded shell, for instance that of a whelk, leaving only the business-end sticking out. Notice how it has one big and one small pincer.

Winkling out hermits

Hermit crabs are often caught by the box crab. This rounded crab sits buried in the sand with just the mouthparts protruding. It seizes a passing hermit crab and progressively chips away at its shell until the occupant is reached. Then it inserts a small peg on one of its legs to

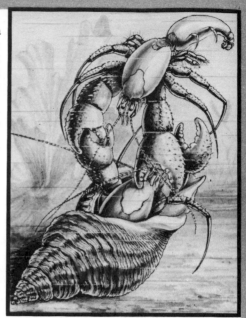

Hermit crabs live in the discarded shells of other animals. When they grow bigger, they find another one. But if suitable homes are scarce, two crabs may fight for possession of a likely shell.

winkle the hermit out. Once out, the hermit is grabbed and devoured.

The yellow crab scuttles about in the evening in search of food. It's commonly found in shallow waters, particularly in holes and crevices and under stones. It has coarse hairy pincers.

The spiny rock lobster or crawfish is one of the larger shore creatures. The North-American variety, caught mainly off the coast of Florida and the Bahamas, has a strange migration ritual which takes it from shallow to deeper waters.

The crawfish link up and march across the sea-bed, one behind the other, with each crawfish hooking its front legs on to the tail of the one in front. There may be as many as 50 males and females in a line.

The myriads of small transparent creatures you may see darting across rock pools, and swimming in and around the rocky coast, are common prawns. Prawns only become pink when they are boiled. They are found virtually everywhere.

The young prawns scavenge throughout the day, but the larger, older adults hide in crevices until night.

At certain times of the year, the females can be seen 'in berry', with clusters of tiny pink eggs tucked under the tail.

Prawns are widely netted for food. So too are shrimps, not only transparent types but also the yellow-brown shrimp which is sold all over the world as 'crabtails', and the rose pink shrimp, which turns a bright fleshy colour when cooked before being sold in the fish markets of Spain and Portugal.

The curious shrimp-like creature with the long snout in our picture is another type of crustacean with the name *Streetsia*. Its head and eye are elongated into a narrow pointed cylinder.

It is just one of the many animals in the jewel-box of strange and beautiful creatures that is the seashore.

Every scoopful of a net can bring up another fascinating creature along the seashore. For the biggest selection rock pools are best, as many normally sea-dwelling animals become stranded in them as the tide retreats.

One for All

No animal is as selfless as the honeybee. From birth to death her one thought is the good of the hive. On this and the next two pages we pry into her closely regulated life.

Eye
The 'compound' eye of the bee is made up of 6,000 simple lenses.

Abdomen

Thorax

Intestine

Gullet

Head

Antenna

Mouth

Jaws

Tongue

Honey sac

Stomach

Sting
The sting is rarely used — when it is the bee dies.

Pollen sac
Pollen is carried on hairs on the bee's legs.

A BEE-HIVE is both 60,000 individuals and just one huge organism. Each of the individuals has no life outside the hive and lives entirely for the benefit of the community as a whole. A worker bee born in the busy period of high summer works herself to death in just six short weeks. Yet a hive may 'live' for tens of years.

The picture on the left shows the anatomy of the honeybee. Like all insects, it has a three-part body — a head, a thorax and an abdomen. Honey is nectar regurgitated from the honey sac.

A bee is a marvellous animal — and her role in pollinating flowers and trees is far more important than the value of the honey she produces.

Pictures: Oxford Scientific Films Ltd.

All in a bee's life!

Right: A swarm hanging on a tree. Far right: A worker covered in pollen. Below, right: Two bees (left) feed nectar to a newly born worker. Below: Each to its own cell, worker pupae (the stage between larva and adult) are exposed by removing the wax cap that normally seals them in.

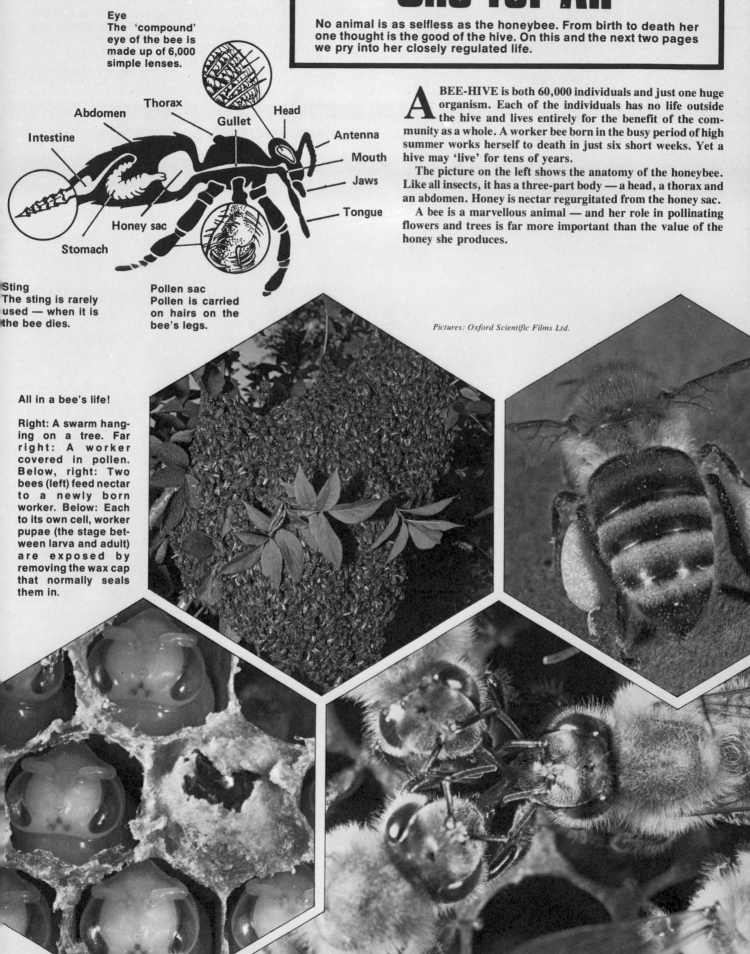

Being queen is just a matter of diet

IT'S easy to become queen — provided you're a bee of course. All you need do is eat *royal jelly* for two extra days. Then when you hatch out you'll be queen and the centre of attraction — unless another queen emerges before you. If that happens, she'll destroy all the other rival queen larvae, including you, before beginning her royal duties.

There is just one queen in every hive. Her only job is to lay eggs, and she is tended and fed by *worker* bees, who also do all the other work in the hive.

She lays one egg in each hexagonal (six-sided) cell in the hive. Most of the eggs develop into workers. These are females too, but do not normally lay eggs.

A few of the cells are larger than the others. Into these the queen lays an unfertilised egg which develops into a *drone*. The drone is male. Its only function is to mate with a queen, if one appears.

To develop into these three different sorts of bees, the larvae when they hatch are fed different diets. Royal jelly is a very rich food produced by worker bees. It is fed to all the larvae for the first three days, but after that workers and drones are fed pollen and nectar (for another two days in the case of workers, three and a half days in the case of drones.)

But future queens are not fed pollen and nectar. Instead, they are fed royal jelly for another two days — five gluttonous days in all.

No one is quite sure why royal jelly has its almost magical effect — but it seems to be all that is needed to make a queen. But it doesn't have the same effect on people, although some claim it as a cure for all kinds of ailments.

After feeding, all the larvae are sealed into their cells with beeswax and left to develop into adults. Queens emerge 16 days after sealing, workers after 21 days, drones after 24 days.

Queens are usually only produced when the old queen is about to die. But sometimes — particularly when a hive is overcrowded — a queen is reared while the original queen is still active. Before the new queen emerges, the old queen sets off with several thousand workers and a few drones to found a new colony. This huge horde of bees — called a *swarm* — usually alights on a tree or branch while scouts find a suitable site for a new hive.

And so a new city of bees is founded.

The centre of attraction, a queen lays eggs in the hive.

Two-day-old larvae of worker bees.

Worker larvae after eight days.

Four stages in the development of a queen bee.

DRONE

The sole purpose of a drone is to mate with new queens if they appear. While waiting for this to happen, it does no work and is fed and tended by the workers. There are something like two to four hundred drones in an average hive of 60,000 bees.

The numbered squares show how the larvae are fed to make the three sorts of bees.

| 1 | 2 | 3 | 4 | 5 | 6 | 7 | 8 | 9 | 10 | 11 | 12 | 13 | 14 | 15 | 16 | 17 | 18 | 19 | 20 | 21 | 22 | 23 | 24 | days |

QUEEN

There is only one queen in a hive — but she is more of an egg-laying machine than a regal lady. At the beginning of her life she makes one or two flights, during which she is mated by a drone. After that, she does nothing but lay eggs. She lives for three to five years before being superseded by a new queen.

| 1 | 2 | 3 | 4 | 5 | 6 | 7 | 8 | 9 | 10 | 11 | 12 | 13 | 14 | 15 | 16 | days |

WORKER

Workers are the backbone of the hive. In their short lives — about six weeks in summer — they nurse the larvae, drones and queen, build the cells of the hive, forage for food, and act as sentries before dying of sheer exhaustion.

| 1 | 2 | 3 | 4 | 5 | 6 | 7 | 8 | 9 | 10 | 11 | 12 | 13 | 14 | 15 | 16 | 17 | 18 | 19 | 20 | 21 | days |

1 Development of egg	**2** Fed on royal jelly	**3** Fed on pollen and nectar	**4** Development of adult in sealed cell

60,000 workers and never a strike!

JUST as Man stores food from harvest to harvest, so too do bees. The food the bees store is honey, and is made from the nectar produced by flowers.

Bees travel from flower to flower collecting nectar. The nectar is usually produced by the plant at the base of the flower, so that as the bee collects the nectar it becomes covered in pollen. When the bee goes to the next plant, it carries the pollen with it and so fertilises the plant.

All the beautiful variety of flowers, their scents and their nectar are produced solely to attract bees and other insects.

To make it easier to collect the honey, bee-keepers construct artificial hives. In one of the commonest types of hives, the hive is split into two parts, the brood chamber, in which the queen lives and new bees are raised, and the super-frames, from which the honey is collected. The queen is prevented from laying eggs in the super-frames by a wire screen.

Bees sting. To collect the honey, bee-keepers use smoke to drive the bees into the brood chamber. They also usually wear a hat surrounded by a fine string mesh which prevents the bees from reaching the face.

To obtain the honey, the wax cover on the super-frames is cut off with a knife and the honey driven out by spinning the frames in a drum. The frames are then cleaned and returned to the hive.

The flavour of honey depends on the flowers which the bees have visited. Clover is said to produce a particularly tasty honey.

An average colony produces about 25 kg of delicious honey in a year — or about 0.4 g for each of those 60,000 workers.

Above: Inspecting a super-frame. The honey made on these frames is collected by the bee-keeper.

Super-frames

Bees' entrance

Brood chamber

Bees' landing place

Left: The 'smoker' makes smoke to keep the bees away from the bee-keeper.

Above: The 'telescopic' type of hive. It has double walls, as insulation against the cold, and two main parts — the brood chamber and the super-frames. The queen lives in the brood chamber and is prevented from laying eggs in the super-frames by a metal mesh.

Left: The usual way of obtaining honey from the super-frames is first to cut off the wax cover, or 'capping', and then to drive out the honey using centrifugal force. This is done by spinning the frames in a drum. The frames are then washed and returned to the hives.

Above: Using the smoker, the bee-keeper drives the bees into the bottom of the brood chamber. He can then remove the super-frames in relative safety.

Right: If their store of honey runs out, bees can be fed artificially by placing a can containing sugar water in the hive. The can has holes in its base allowing the sugar water to seep out.

321

Science And Technology

The Harrier brings a new dimension to the Royal Navy

The Jump-Jet goes to sea

CLAD in an immersion suit zipped tight and with waterproof seals at neck, wrists and ankles, the pilot of the *Sea Harrier* strides across the flight deck of the aircraft carrier to make his pre-flight checks on the little plane. He examines the engine nozzles. There are four of them situated in pairs under the wings instead of at the tail, and they make an important contribution to the aircraft's unique performance.

As the pilot pulls down the simple steps from the fuselage the cockpit canopy slides open automatically. He climbs up, settles himself in the cockpit, straps himself to the ejection seat, puts on helmet and oxygen mask, connects oxygen and radio leads and goes quickly through a cockpit check. He is trained to know every switch in the cockpit blindfold. As he closes the canopy the steps duly retract into the fuselage.

Now he brings the engine to life and soon it is roaring, ready to go. When he opens the throttle the engine will come up to full power in four seconds. Next to the throttle is a small lever which controls those four nozzles — they are all linked and move together. He sets the angle he wants and pushes the throttle open.

Turbofan

With a teeth-rattling roar the *Sea Harrier* lifts straight up into the sky. The pilot punches controls to raise the wheels and wing flaps, pushes the nozzle lever forward and the aircraft accelerates rapidly — quickly reaching over 1100 km/h low over the sea.

The *Sea Harrier* is built by British Aerospace and powered by a Roll-Royce Pegasus Turbofan engine. This is the secret of its ability to sit in the air stationary — or even fly backwards. The aircraft has a very high power-to-weight ratio — meaning that its engine is very powerful for the weight of the aircraft — so it can accelerate rapidly and is very agile in the sky.

A 'Turbofan' is the modern type of jet engine with a much bigger set of compressors or front fans (see diagrams) than previous engines. In older engines all the air sucked in was compressed, accelerated and burnt with fuel in th combustion chambers

before leaving as a single hot jet of gas. In a Turbofan much of the air is compressed and accelerated *cold* to produce thrust and the remainder used to produce hot gas. The chief advantage of the Turbofan is fuel saving and, particularly in big airliners, much less noise.

The four nozzles of the Pegasus can be set at any angle from horizontal (for forward flight) down to vertical — and even slightly forwards to enable the plane to fly backwards!

Although it is very spectacular, the vertical take-off is only used when the aircraft is operating from a confined space or must get airborne in the shortest possible time. A vertical take-off

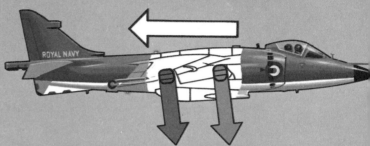

FLYING BACKWARDS! Another ability of the remarkable Sea Harrier. The swivelling nozzles can be rotated just past the vertical so that the thrust is directed slightly forward and the aircraft does indeed fly backwards. This means the aircraft can slow down very quickly to a precise landing.

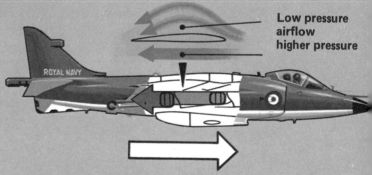

Low pressure airflow
higher pressure

FORWARD FLIGHT is the same as in normal aircraft. The nozzles thrust directly backwards and the aircraft's wings are producing lift. The top surface of the wing is more curved than the underside so that the air passing over has to travel faster to rejoin the air going underneath. The faster-moving air 'sucks' the wing up and creates lift.

ENGINE CONTROLS — the conventional throttle increases or decreases engine power and a lever alters the angle of the nozzles. The basic idea is simple: push forward to go faster (more power, nozzles pointing backwards), push back to slow down (less power, nozzles downwards).

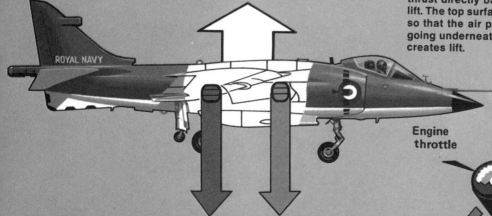

Engine throttle

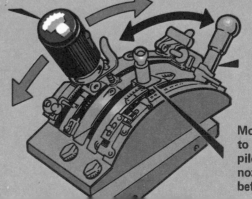

Nozzle lever

VERTICAL TAKE-OFF is made with engine nozzles pointing downwards to direct the engine's thrust straight down at 90°. As it ascends the aircraft's entire weight is being supported by its engine power alone; the wings add no lift. The same applies when a vertical landing is made. In practice, a forward 'rolling' short take-off is used so that the wings are supplying some lift. When operating from a ship a vertical landing is always made.

Movable stop to allow the pilot to set a nozzle angle before take-off

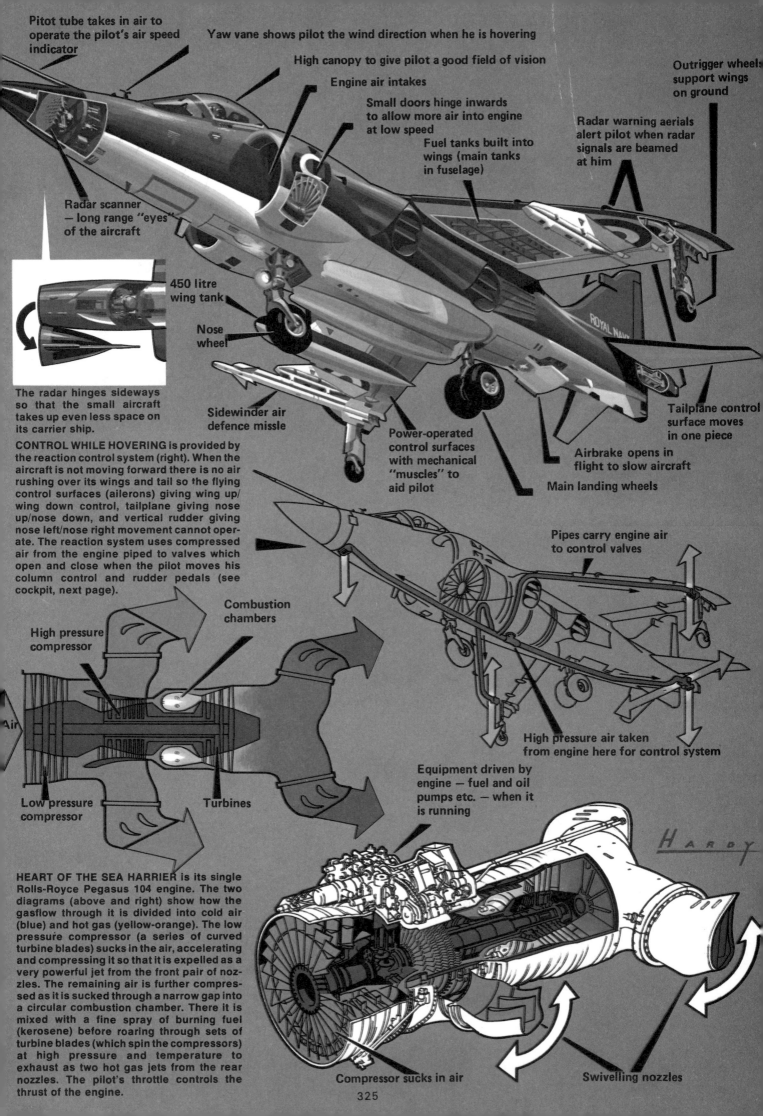

Pitot tube takes in air to operate the pilot's air speed indicator

Yaw vane shows pilot the wind direction when he is hovering

High canopy to give pilot a good field of vision

Engine air intakes

Outrigger wheels support wings on ground

Small doors hinge inwards to allow more air into engine at low speed

Fuel tanks built into wings (main tanks in fuselage)

Radar warning aerials alert pilot when radar signals are beamed at him

Radar scanner — long range "eyes" of the aircraft

450 litre wing tank

Nose wheel

The radar hinges sideways so that the small aircraft takes up even less space on its carrier ship.

Sidewinder air defence missle

Power-operated control surfaces with mechanical "muscles" to aid pilot

Tailplane control surface moves in one piece

Airbrake opens in flight to slow aircraft

Main landing wheels

CONTROL WHILE HOVERING is provided by the reaction control system (right). When the aircraft is not moving forward there is no air rushing over its wings and tail so the flying control surfaces (ailerons) giving wing up/wing down control, tailplane giving nose up/nose down, and vertical rudder giving nose left/nose right movement cannot operate. The reaction system uses compressed air from the engine piped to valves which open and close when the pilot moves his column control and rudder pedals (see cockpit, next page).

Combustion chambers

High pressure compressor

Pipes carry engine air to control valves

Air

Low pressure compressor

Turbines

High pressure air taken from engine here for control system

Equipment driven by engine — fuel and oil pumps etc. — when it is running

HARDY

HEART OF THE SEA HARRIER is its single Rolls-Royce Pegasus 104 engine. The two diagrams (above and right) show how the gasflow through it is divided into cold air (blue) and hot gas (yellow-orange). The low pressure compressor (a series of curved turbine blades) sucks in the air, accelerating and compressing it so that it is expelled as a very powerful jet from the front pair of nozzles. The remaining air is further compressed as it is sucked through a narrow gap into a circular combustion chamber. There it is mixed with a fine spray of burning fuel (kerosene) before roaring through sets of turbine blades (which spin the compressors) at high pressure and temperature to exhaust as two hot gas jets from the rear nozzles. The pilot's throttle controls the thrust of the engine.

Compressor sucks in air

Swivelling nozzles

325

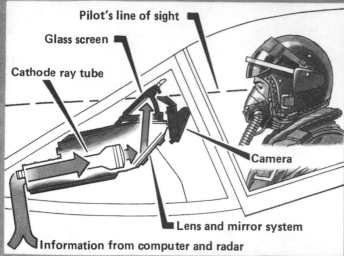

Pilot's line of sight
Glass screen
Cathode ray tube
Camera
Lens and mirror system
Information from computer and radar

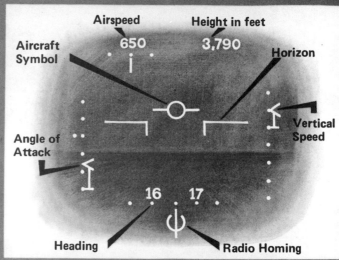

Airspeed
Height in feet
Aircraft Symbol
650
3,790
Horizon
Vertical Speed
Angle of Attack
16
17
Heading
Radio Homing

Like many modern aircraft the Sea Harrier's cockpit is fitted with a HUD (head-up display). This projects onto a glass screen in the pilot's line of vision, the most important information he needs at any point in a flight. The purpose of the HUD is to stop the pilot having to look down at instruments in the cockpit at difficult times (e.g. when flying low at high speed). The display takes information from the aircraft's computer and presents it on the face of a small cathode ray tube (similar to a mini TV screen). From there it is reflected upwards onto the glass by a lens and mirror system. An automatic sensor adjusts the brightness of the display to the correct level.

Above: General flying information on the HUD screen. The aircraft symbol shows the aircraft's nose above the horizon (climbing); the indicated airspeed is 650 knots (1128 km/h). The height is 3,790 feet (1155 metres). The vertical speed symbol shows the rate at which the aircraft is moving upwards. The radio homing symbol shows the pilot he is flying accurately towards a radio homing beacon. The heading is a compass direction of 165°. The angle of attack indication shows the angle of the wings to the horizontal. The HUD control (below) allows the pilot to set up many different displays for other stages of a mission.

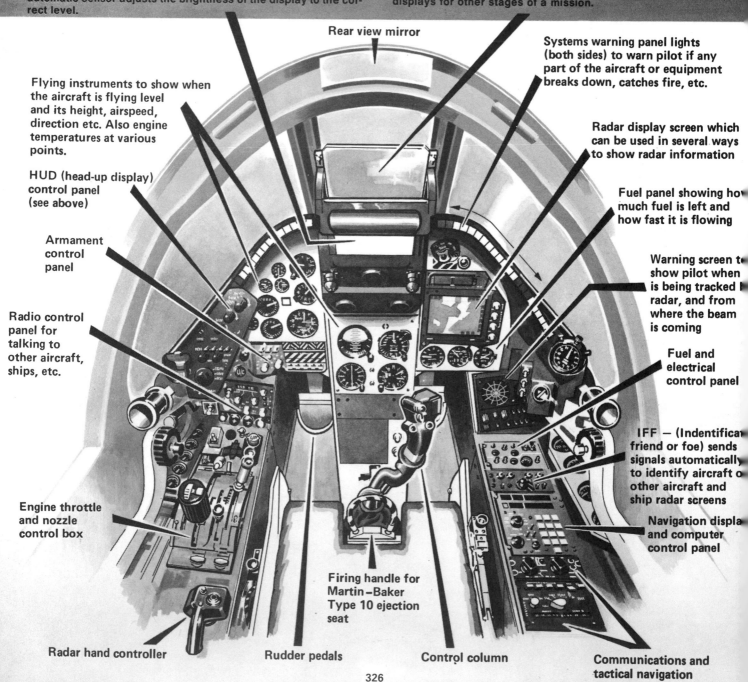

Rear view mirror

Flying instruments to show when the aircraft is flying level and its height, airspeed, direction etc. Also engine temperatures at various points.

HUD (head-up display) control panel (see above)

Armament control panel

Radio control panel for talking to other aircraft, ships, etc.

Engine throttle and nozzle control box

Radar hand controller

Rudder pedals

Systems warning panel lights (both sides) to warn pilot if any part of the aircraft or equipment breaks down, catches fire, etc.

Radar display screen which can be used in several ways to show radar information

Fuel panel showing how much fuel is left and how fast it is flowing

Warning screen to show pilot when is being tracked radar, and from where the beam is coming

Fuel and electrical control panel

IFF — (Indentifica friend or foe) sends signals automatically to identify aircraft o other aircraft and ship radar screens

Navigation displa and computer control panel

Firing handle for Martin—Baker Type 10 ejection seat

Control column

Communications and tactical navigation control panels

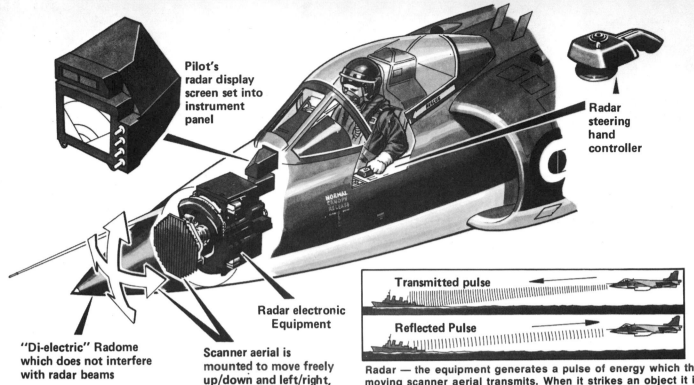

Pilot's radar display screen set into instrument panel

Radar steering hand controller

Radar electronic Equipment

"Di-electric" Radome which does not interfere with radar beams

Scanner aerial is mounted to move freely up/down and left/right, automatically or controlled by pilot

Transmitted pulse

Reflected Pulse

Radar — the equipment generates a pulse of energy which the moving scanner aerial transmits. When it strikes an object it is reflected back to the aerial and is shown on the cockpit screen. The pulse is repeated many times every second.

The Sea Harrier's radar, code-named 'Blue Fox', is adapted from the type carried in the Westland Lynx anti-submarine helicopter. The radar electronic equipment is fully tied in with the aircraft's computer to enable the pilot to use it in many different ways according to his task. It can be used, for instance, for airborne search and interception or for searching the sea ahead of the aircraft at long range. Flying low over land it can provide the pilot with a clear picture of the safest path ahead.

from engine start to wingborne forward flight can be made in two minutes.

To obtain some lift from the wings and carry a greater load, a 'rolling' take-off is usually made with the aircraft moving forwards a short distance before leaving the ground.

A British invention which dramatically increases the take-off performance of the *Harrier* is the 'ski-jump' launching ramp that has been fitted to British warships.

When the *Sea Harrier* is in forward flight it is designed to be controlled like any other modern aircraft. To assist the pilot in moving the control surfaces at high speed they are power-operated. When the pilot moves his control column and rudder pedals (see cockpit illustration) electrical and mechanical linkages cause hydraulic fluid to flow at high pressure into small power units which move the flying control surfaces on wings and tail.

Another device fitted to assist the pilot flying for long periods over the sea is an *automatic pilot* which will keep the aircraft at the speed and height, and the course (compass direction) set by the pilot.

On returning to its ship the *Sea Harrier* will always land vertically. It requires a clear square of deck only 24 m. in size and can be positioned for landing with great accuracy using its reaction control system (see diagram).

Should the *Harrier* be called on to defend its ship or other task force, it is a tricky opponent for any ordinary fighter to deal with. Its pilots have developed ways of using to full advantage their ability to direct or 'vector' their engine's thrust in the air.

The technique is called VIFF (Vectored Thrust In Forward Flight) or 'Viffing'. They can throw the aircraft around the sky and speed up or slow down very suddenly in a way impossible to a conventional aircraft, and easily out-manoeuvre their opponent.

Sea Harriers are also in service with the US Marine Corps. There are two other jump jets similar to the *Sea Harrier* — the US Grumman *Type 698*, which has rotating engines, and the Russian *Yak-36 Forger*, which is supersonic and has a computer-controlled flight system.

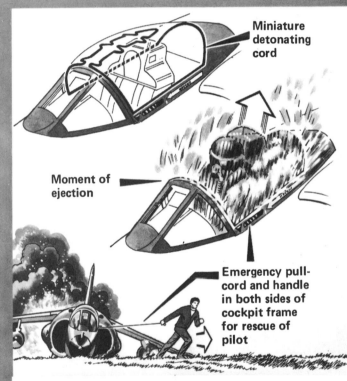

Miniature detonating cord

Moment of ejection

Emergency pull-cord and handle in both sides of cockpit frame for rescue of pilot

The Harrier has a very rapid escape system to save the pilot if something goes wrong. The Martin-Baker Type 10 ejection seat takes only 1½ seconds from firing to parachute opening! An explosive cord is built into the canopy to shatter it automatically just before the pilot and seat eject.

The Sea Harrier's pilot can alter his speed and flight path very suddenly by altering the angle of the engine's nozzle. This makes the Sea Harrier a formidable 'dogfighter' in close-in fighting with conventional aircraft.

The Monorail dream

Air-conditioned passenger compartment

Electromagnets

Shoe collecting electricity from live rail.

For 150 years, railways designers have cherished an ideal — high speed trains which zoom along on single rails. But dreaming up a monorail system is easier than building one.

The greatest problem when designing a monorail system has always been balancing the train and making it stable.

In 1821, H. R. Palmer built what is believed to be the first mono railway — powered by horses! It was used in the London Docks. It was not fast but it was cheap to build and maintain.

Palmer's Mono Railway

H.R. Palmer's mono railway was extremely simple — a plank on its edge supported on top of stakes set in the ground. The wagons were in two halves, one half on either side to balance them and the wheels (probably ships' pulley wheels originally) in a suitable supporting framework. It was designed initially to transport goods from the dockside to the warehouses nearby. At first, the wagons were man handled, but soon horses were introduced. Palmer patented the system in 1821 and later proposed fitting it with a sail but this proposal does not seem to have been followed up.

Lartigue's Mono Railway

Frenchman Charles Lartigue patented a strange monorail system, originally intended to provide a light, cheap railway across a plantation. It could be lifted and relaid in a new area quickly and easily. In this form, it was horse-drawn. Lartigue developed it for steam haulage and used it on the Listowel and Ballybunion Railway, built in Ireland in 1902. The track ran on an 'A' frame, the weight being taken by the top rail with the vehicles being balanced by a light rail on either side. The railway was closed in 1924 and dismantled shortly afterwards.

The Brennan Mono Railway

Brennan's system was the only true mono railway ever devised. The vehicle's top speed was 35 kph (22 mph). It was propelled by one petrol motor and balanced by two heavy gyroscopes driven by another motor. It was intended originally as a quick, convenient system with a very light track which the Army could lay from its supply bases to the battlefront. Demonstrated at Gravesend in Kent in 1909, it was hailed as an invention with a great future but interest in it disappeared thereafter and so did the system. Shortly afterwards, similar systems were invented in Germany and Russia.

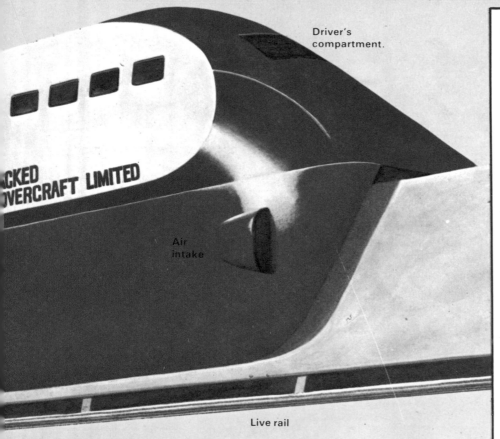

Driver's compartment.

Air intake

CKED
OVERCRAFT LIMITED

Live rail

The train which floats

The most exciting monorail projects for the future are not monorails in the ordinary sense because the carriages have no wheels and they do not run on a track. Instead they float above the track and travel along it without friction at speeds that would be impossible using wheels.

The first of these 'flying trains' was designed by Eric Laithwaite, Professor of Heavy Electrical Engineering at London's Imperial College of Science and Technology. The train was to be 'supported' by magnetism. Everyone knows that two bar magnets will fly apart if placed north pole to north pole or south pole to south pole, and Professor Laithwaite's plans were based on the use of this magnetic force to lift a train above a track. Electromagnets are used, which develop a strong magnetic field when supplied with electric current. Experiments have also been made into the use of air to make a train float above the track like a hovercraft, but these were abandoned.

No moving parts

The main advantage of such a system of transport is that it can move large amounts of people at great speed without causing the wear and tear of moving parts like wheels on rails. The trains would not only be magnetically levitated above the track but would be forced along by a linear induction motor — a magnetic motor which also has no moving parts. The motor contains an electromagnet situated on the train producing a magnetic field which pushes against magnetic fields formed by more electromagnets in the track.

The principle used by Palmer was to balance the load by designing the wagons along the lines of the panniers slung across a packhorse's back.

This worked quite well when the wagon was horse-drawn and slow, but when horses were replaced by engines and movement was speeded up, difficulties arose. Inventors began to put steadying tracks on either side of the monorail. This worked well on a number of light railways, the most famous of which was the Listowel and Ballybunion Railway in Ireland. But, of course, once the

The Kearney High-Speed Railway

Kearney's monorail car was designed to run on a single weight-bearing rail while being kept in an upright position by an overhead guide rail. Great plans were suggested to use the system above, on and under the ground. An almost-full-size model was built and exhibited but no investment money was forthcoming so the idea died and with it went Kearney's plans for a massive commuter system for London.

The Wuppertal Mono Railway

Started in 1901 and running profitably until quite recently, the Wuppertal monorail (right) was probably the most successful system built to date. The line, which straddled the River Wuppertal in Germany, provided a steady and reliable passenger service between two towns. The coaches, suspended from electrically-driven trolleys, travelled at an average speed of 24 kph (15 mph).

The Tokyo Mono Railway (above)

This suspended monorail was set up, as an experiment, in a park in Tokyo in 1957. Difficulties were experienced with the suspension and when later, it was decided to build a mono railway from the airport to Tokyo, the Alweg System (see right) was chosen. The Alweg railway runs from Haneda Airport to Hamamatsucho station, a distance of about 16 km, taking 15-20 minutes.

The Bennie Railplane and the Alweg System

The Bennie Railplane (above, left) was designed for high-speed travel. Electrically powered airscrews drove the cars which hung from an overhead line and picked up current from a guide-rail below. An experimental track was built in Glasgow in 1930. Dr.

Axel Wenne Gren's Alweg system (above, right), although classified as a monorail, runs on a massive concrete beam. The cars are fitted with pneumatic-tyred wheels which run on top of the beam.

The Safege System and the Bertin Aerotrain

The French Safege system (above, left) uses a tube with a slot along the bottom. The car hangs from this tube by means of wheels which run along inside it on pneumatic tyres. The idea is to protect the track and machinery from the weather, but the running gear tends

to overheat. The Bertin Aerotrain (above, right) was an air-cushioned hovertrain, running on an inverted T-shaped track. The cars were powered by an airscrew. High costs caused the project to be abandoned.

steadying rails were introduced, the lines ceased to be true monorail systems.

The simplest way to keep vehicles steady when they run on a single line is to hang them *below* the track. A number of inventors have designed railways of this kind. The outstanding example is the Barmen and Elberfeld Railway in Germany, invented by Eugen Langen, and which is today the classic example of a successful public mono railway.

But the most exciting kind of mono railway consists of a single line along which streak streamlined, gyroscopically-stabilised coaches. A space age idea for the future you might say. But you would be wrong. A gyro-car was patented in 1903 by Louis Brennan, an Irish engineer from County Mayo, who built a remarkable vehicle which ran on two

two-wheeled bogies. Although it was shown in Europe and America, it came to nothing.

Despite its long history and all the apparent advantages it offers today's world, the monorail has literally never 'got off the ground'. Monorails are so utterly different from conventional railways that few people will take the risk of investing money in them. They cannot, for instance, be integrated into normal railway systems, but can only supplement them. They can carry only passengers and lightweight freight — and, in the past, much more money has been made on heavy freight. At present,

for economy's sake, they are really suitable only for straight runs without sidings or branch lines.

However, monorail trains using magnetic levitation and linear induction motors are being developed in the United States, Canada and Japan. Speeds of 500 kilometres an hour have already been achieved in test runs. Another kind of monorail driven by air pressure is being tested in Brazil. It can reach only 70 kilometres an hour, but is completely silent.

So the monorail still remains an exciting and challenging possibility to the railway designers of the world.

The British and French Hovertrains – two non-starters!

Claimed to be the world's first electric hovertrain, the British monorail, or beam-rail, was made to hover magnetically and was propelled by a linear induction motor. After several years of encouraging development, including test runs on a demonstration track at Earith, Huntingdonshire (above, left), the project was abandoned because of increasing costs, and limited prospects.

However, further research has proved more successful and pilot maglev systems are under development in several countries. The French hovertrain (above, right) was developed to use jet engines to increase its speed. On a concrete circuit, the car achieved 375 kph but the performance was not sufficient to ensure its development and this particular monorail project died.

From the storm-tossed seas comes the international cry for help, Mayday, the signal that means instant action—and danger—for the

Part-time heroes

IT is four o'clock on a pitch-black winter's morning in the town of Tenmouth on the rugged North Sea coast. The townsfolk are all snugly asleep, oblivious of the sleet driving against their window panes and the icy wind whipping the sea into a frothing frenzy and sending huge waves crashing on to the quayside at the harbour. All, that is, except for the coastguard whose job it is to keep a lonely vigil for any emergencies which might arise along his stretch of coastline.

Suddenly, an urgent call crackles over the radio telephone. "Mayday! Mayday! Mayday!" (from the French 'M'aidez' - Help me!) The thrice-repeated distress call is from a trawler driven on to the rocks.

Quickly but calmly, in an orderly routine, the coastguard determines the trawler's position before starting a chain of events which will involve at least five men, possibly seven, being roused from their warm beds to dash out into the violence of the storm to risk their lives aboard a bobbing life-boat. What is more, most of these men will do so freely. They will receive no pay for their troubles, only the satisfaction of knowing that they are helping fellow seamen.

For most of the crews of Britain's life-boats are part-timers. Some are seamen in their normal daily occupations. Some, however, do other jobs and will have already done a hard day's work in a factory or at a coal-yard or driving a bus before being called upon in the middle of the night to perform their heroics. But none of them will complain. It is all part of the job of manning a life-boat and they accept it.

As a rule, there is only one professional full-time employee of the Royal National Life-boat Institution at a life-boat station, of which there are about 200 scattered around Britain's coasts. He may be the coxswain, the person in charge of the boat and her crew. Or he may be the mechanic whose job it is to ensure that the boat is always ready to put to sea at a minute's notice, day or night, summer or winter. Or he may be both.

Summoned by phone on this rough January morning, the life-boat's crew arrive within minutes of each other on the quayside, some dashing from their hastily-parked cars, others arriving breathless on foot. Soon, they are aboard their Waveney life-boat, one of several kinds of life-boat used by the R.N.L.I. and among the most modern. Because it is relatively large, the Waveney remains permanently afloat by the life-boat station and is not launched down a slipway as are smaller life-boats.

The coxwain, who may steer, knows the call came from the Blackstone Rocks, the graveyard of many a ship, but visibility is poor, radio contact with the trawler has been lost and she may well have drifted from her earlier position.

Then, a red flare, the accepted distress signal for inshore use, goes up in the near distance. "There she is!" shouts a life-boatman, heartened by the sight. At least they are not too late to be of assistance.

Ten minutes later, the listing silhouette of the trawler can be made out. Torchlights flash from on board as the crew wave with relief to the approaching life-boat. They are miserably cold and wet. A few hours more and they would have had to take to the rocks, for their ship was slowly sinking into deeper water.

One by one, they transfer to the life-boat. But the danger is not yet over. The life-boat herself, despite being self-righting and fully stocked with life-saving equipment, is not immune to being dashed against the rocks. The helmsman's skilful handling is all that stands between the life-boat and her own shipwreck.

But the ordeal passes and, at last, every man is aboard the Waveney. She signals ashore that all is well, turns and starts the hazardous journey back to safety.

When a ship is wrecked, members of its crew are sometimes transferred to another vessel or to the shore in a **breeches-buoy.** This is a circular lifebuoy fitted with canvas breeches in which the person being rescued sits. A rocket gun (see left) fires one end of a cable to the stranded vessel where it is secured before the buoy is hauled along it on a pulley. Should the cable slacken and drop the person in the breeches-buoy into the sea, he will float until the cable tightens again.

How the Waveney life-boat rights itself

Nowadays, most life-boats are designed so that they right themselves if they capsize. The secret lies in trapping air within the cabins below deck so that the vessel becomes a kind of bubble with a heavy base. Older-style life-boats used tanks between which quantities of water poured to right the boat but these boats are gradually being phased out.

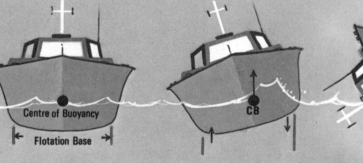

Centre of Buoyancy — Flotation Base

CB

CB

Direction of wind and breaker

In calm water, the life-boat rests level with most of its weight low in the hull, the force of gravity pulling it downwards being equalled by the buoyancy of the water pushing it upwards. Small waves will cause the boat to tilt, in which case the force of gravity, acting against the bouyancy of the water, pulls the raised side down again.

On a very rough sea, a large wave may throw the boat over and capsize it. But watertight doors keep the cabins full of air.

Jackstaff: Jack is the nautical term for the flag of any country flown at the bows of a ship. A staff is a flagpole, hence the term jackstaff. When a ship is riding at anchor at night, it carries a white light at the front. In the case of the Waveney life-boat, the most convenient position for this light is on top of the jackstaff.

Fairleads are guides for mooring ropes or other ropes being led across the deck or over the side. They may be used for ropes holding fenders, or buffers, in position to prevent damage to the ship when berthing.

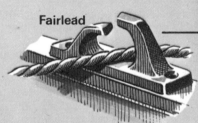

Fairlead

Bollards and **mooring bitts** are small stanchions around which ropes can be secured when the ship is anchoring or attaching itself to another vessel. Bollards are usually set up in pairs on ships and are normally made of iron.

Mooring Bitt

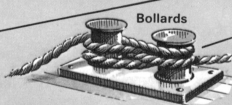

Bollards

8

Echo Sounder

Radar

Ship's Compass

Because they work close to the shore, life-boats use small magnetic compasses, rather than the larger gyro compasses carried by big ships. The magnetic compass has a needle, or needles, and a card marked with directional points. This card floats on oil contained in a bowl mounted in gimbals - a swivelling fitting which keeps the compass level at all times, despite the rocking of the ship. A binnacle, or case, protects the compass from the elements.

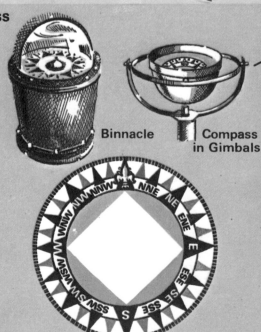

Binnacle

Compass in Gimbals

Compass Card

The echo sounder measures the depth of the water beneath the ship by bouncing sound waves off the seabed. The time taken for the sound signal to return indicates the depth of water, which is shown on the echo sounder's dial. Radar (Radio Direction and Range) works on a similar principle, bouncing radio waves off objects to detect their presence.

Radar Screen

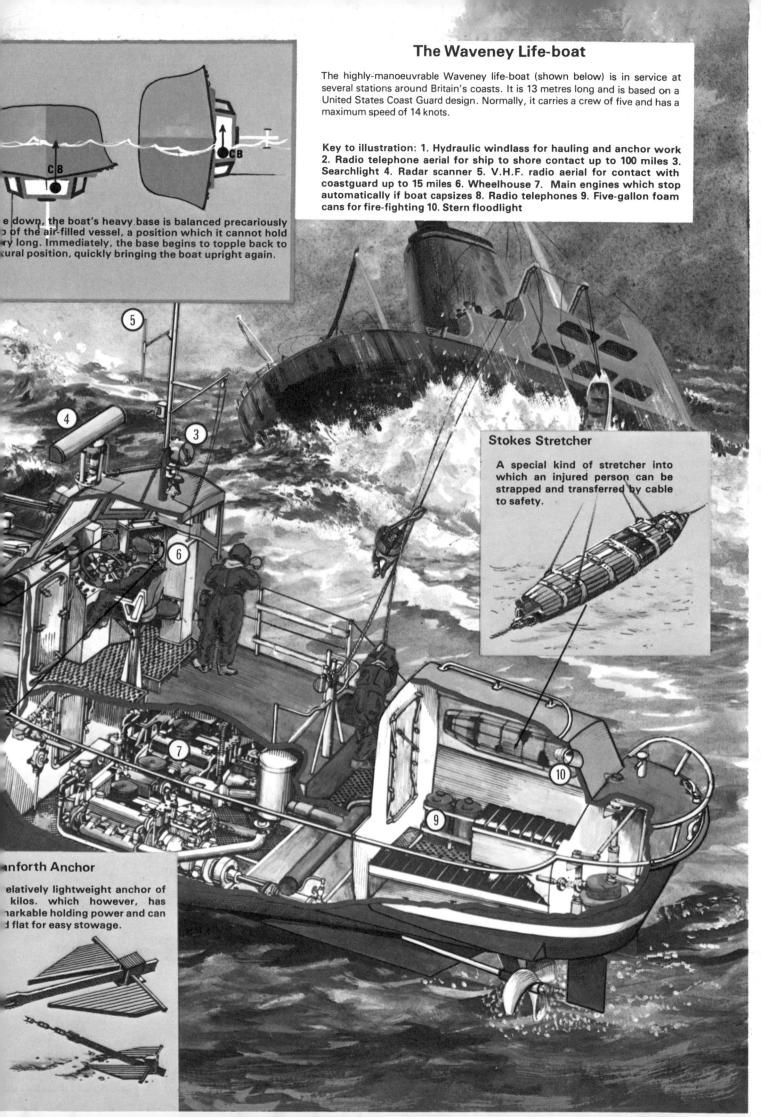

The Waveney Life-boat

The highly-manoeuvrable Waveney life-boat (shown below) is in service at several stations around Britain's coasts. It is 13 metres long and is based on a United States Coast Guard design. Normally, it carries a crew of five and has a maximum speed of 14 knots.

Key to illustration: 1. Hydraulic windlass for hauling and anchor work 2. Radio telephone aerial for ship to shore contact up to 100 miles 3. Searchlight 4. Radar scanner 5. V.H.F. radio aerial for contact with coastguard up to 15 miles 6. Wheelhouse 7. Main engines which stop automatically if boat capsizes 8. Radio telephones 9. Five-gallon foam cans for fire-fighting 10. Stern floodlight

e down, the boat's heavy base is balanced precariously of the air-filled vessel, a position which it cannot hold ry long. Immediately, the base begins to topple back to ...ural position, quickly bringing the boat upright again.

Stokes Stretcher

A special kind of stretcher into which an injured person can be strapped and transferred by cable to safety.

...nforth Anchor

...elatively lightweight anchor of ... kilos. which however, has ...narkable holding power and can ...d flat for easy stowage.

Probing the Ocean Depths

MAN'S ability to explore the world under the seas has increased dramatically in the last 20 years or so, and has answered an urgent need. Most of the world lies underwater, but it is impossible to live and work there normally. We need air or oxygen to breathe, we need protection against the cold, and we need sources of artificial light, because hardly any natural light penetrates deeper than 15 metres from the surface.

In addition, the pressure of the water at depths of more than 20 or 30 metres causes problems when a diver has to return to the surface.

For all these reasons, man explored the most difficult, inaccessible and dangerous parts of the land above sea level

before attempting any serious exploration underwater.

But now we have to go there. We need to prospect underwater for oil and other minerals — some valuable minerals even lie on the sea-bed. We need also to study the sea-bed and the plant and animal life of the deep oceans to extend our knowledge of the world we live in. Finally, the deep sea has become a possible battleground in future wars. We need ways of finding and hunting enemy craft underwater.

The first problem for any underwater explorer is air. It seems simple: the man swims below, holding the one end of a tube in his mouth, and the other end sticks up above the surface of the water.

Unfortunately, this doesn't work. The pressure of water is so enormous that no one can suck in air if he is more than a few metres under water. The air must be delivered at pressure. The simplest way of doing this is to fit the diver with a helmet, with glass panels so that he can look out, and then pump air down to him.

The diver needs weighted boots, otherwise he may be turned upside down by the weight of his helmet, and he needs a protective suit to keep out the cold. He is lowered from a ship and pulled back up with a lifeline.

This is the old-fashioned hard-hat diving that was invented about 150 years ago and first used in 1840 by divers who had to clear a wreck obstructing a shipping lane.

Left: *Star III* is one of a series of observation submarines built in the United States for underwater exploration. It carries a crew of two, and is designed to reach a depth of almost 600 metres. *Star III* has often been used in archaeological investigations of the sea-bed using the monitoring camera and mechanical 'grabbers' which can be seen at the front end.

Below: *Trieste* was designed by the Swiss physicist Auguste Piccard. It reached the deepest known part of the ocean where its powerful searchlights enabled some valuable deep-water photographs to be taken.

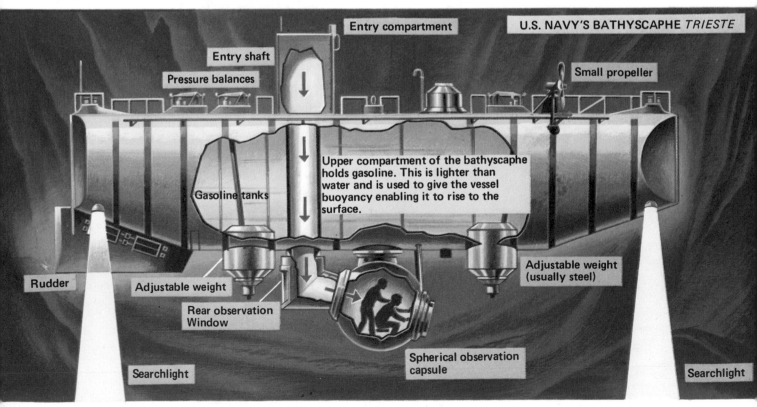

U.S. NAVY'S BATHYSCAPHE *TRIESTE*

Entry compartment

Entry shaft

Pressure balances

Small propeller

Upper compartment of the bathyscaphe holds gasoline. This is lighter than water and is used to give the vessel buoyancy enabling it to rise to the surface.

Gasoline tanks

Rudder

Adjustable weight

Rear observation Window

Adjustable weight (usually steel)

Spherical observation capsule

Searchlight

Searchlight

Scuba diver no deeper than 120 metres (m)

SEA-LEVEL

Continental Shelf — average 183 m

Porpoise — 400 m

shark 20 m

Submarines no deeper than 500 m

Sperm whale — 900 m

d — 670 m

Viper fish — 1,000 m

Gulper — 1,000 - 2,100 m

Swallower fish — 2,000 m

Continental Slope

erage Ocean th — 3,660m

Lowest level where fish generally observed — 7,000m (have been sightings at greater depths)

January 23, 1960. *Trieste* reaches bottom of Marianas Trench — 10,900m

Above: Jacques Cousteau's "Diving Saucer" — a small, highly manoeuvrable two-man submarine. It is launched from a mother ship and powered from a two-speed motor. Commander Cousteau has been responsible for many such undersea equipment innovations, including the Aqualung and sea-bed laboratories.

Left: This diagrammatic illustration shows that while Man has now developed sophisticated equipment to explore the depths of the ocean, this is more than matched by the adaptations of various living creatures which can survive and exist at different depth ranges. Even large submarines would crack under the great pressure at depths greater than 400m, and it is doubtful if large deep sea vessels will ever be built.

Below: A cut-away section of Jacques Cousteau's "Conshelf" — a sea-bed laboratory. Such structures may make it possible for Man to farm and mine the óceans successfully.

Hard-hat divers have great problems. They have to keep their lifelines and air-lines clear of all obstructions and this makes it difficult for them to go through holes in wrecks or investigate underwater caves, for example.

A diver using a self-contained 'Aqualung' has much more freedom. The Aqualung was invented by Jacques-Yves Cousteau and his colleague Emile Gagnan in wartime France in 1942. It is fairly easy for a diver to carry a cylinder of compressed air with him. Their invention, which made free diving possible, was what is called a 'demand-regulator valve'. This delivers the air to the diver at the same pressure as the water around him.

If the diver is to go deep, he has other problems. One is the cold, but there are much greater difficulties caused by the effects of pressure on the air that he breathes. (It is possible to dive short distances under water breathing pure oxygen, but it is very risky with prolonged exposure.) Some of the air dissolves in the diver's blood, and the deeper he dives, the more air dissolves, because the pressure is higher.

If he comes to the surface quickly, the air will bubble out, just as gas bubbles from cola when the lid of a cola bottle is

Power and communication cables to surface

Crewmember talking to surface by phone

Cut-away diagram of crew's compartments

T.V. Camera

Deep-freeze food store

Emergency lifeboat for crew

Lifting cable

Test and communication bench

Store for canned foods

Bunks

Supporting 'legs' with broad pads

Ballast tanks (on both sides)

Spiral staircase

Diver leaving vessel through sea-hatch

Water container (9 tonnes)

taken off. These bubbles of air cause the diver great pain, and they can cause Caisson disease — an affliction commonly known as 'the bends' (or compressed-air sickness) — which, in turn can cause permanent harm or even death. To avoid the bends, a diver must come to the surface very slowly, and if he wishes to work at great depths, he may need a few hours of decompression after working for only ten or twenty minutes.

The other problem is called 'nitrogen narcosis'. Four-fifths of atmospheric air is nitrogen, and only about one-fifth oxygen. If a diver goes below about 40 metres, the nitrogen dissolved in his blood makes him behave as if he were drunk — divers have drowned because they offered their mouthpieces to a passing fish. Divers nowadays avoid this problem by breathing a mixture of oxygen and helium.

This avoids nitrogen narcosis but leads to another difficulty. Working divers communicate with the surface by telephone or some underwater speaking device: if they breathe a helium mixture the vocal chords are affected and their voices become squeaky and cannot be understood without electronic gadgets.

An underwater explorer who stays in a closed, protected vessel avoids these problems. One of the first of the underwater exploration vessels was William Beebe's 'Bathysphere'. As the name suggests, this was a sphere, and it was lowered into the water on the end of a steel cable. The sphere was strongly made of steel and was one and a half metres in diameter. William Beebe breathed air. The carbon dioxide that he breathed out was absorbed by chemicals and the oxygen he used up was replaced from oxygen cylinders. Eventually he descended to the depth of 924 metres.

The problem with the Bathysphere was that it could not move about. Also, if anything went wrong with the cable, Beebe was doomed.

The problems of the cable were solved by Auguste Piccard, a Swiss physicist who had already made record-breaking high-altitude flights in balloons. He used, in a very original way, the same principle for diving. In his 'Bathyscaphe', the two-man crew stayed in a strong spherical gondola. This was attached to a large float filled with petrol. Petrol is less dense than water, so the float acts as an underwater balloon.

The Bathyscaphe carried ballast and in any emergency, the ballast was to be dropped so that the Bathyscaphe floated up. It had two electric motors and electric searchlights for observation and photography.

Early versions of the Bathyscaphe reached depths of 4,160 metres, but a later version, the *Trieste,* built for the U.S. Navy and launched in August 1953, reached the deepest known part of the ocean. It descended to 10,900 metres — roughly seven miles — in the Marianas Trench off the island of Guam, in the Pacific Ocean. Jacques Piccard, Auguste's son, was one of the crew in the record-breaking descent. He observed life, even at this astonishing depth: he saw a shrimp and what looked like a flatfish.

The Bathyscaphe was an observation vessel only and has been succeeded by the submersible, a vessel powered by electric motors. This has an observation window and underwater floodlights, and is fitted with 'manipulators' — tools like grips and spanners, operated from inside.

Nowadays, the crew of a submersible work together with divers. The divers travel down in a special compartment and when the craft reaches the working area, the divers swim out.

When the task is finished, the divers return to the submersible. The water is pumped out of their compartment, but the pressure is kept up, so that there is no risk of the bends. Eventually, the pressure is

Right: The diving bell and research vessel *Purisima*. Such vessels are useful at depths down to about 1,500m. The spherical gasoline container which gives the vessel buoyancy can be seen above the observation capsule.

lowered in the safety of dry land.

If the divers stay long enough at high pressure, their blood becomes 'saturated' with air. No more can be dissolved. It takes a long while for them to decompress, but the time does not increase if they go on working, as their blood can take up no more air. They work for days on end, living under pressure in a dry compartment when they are not working, and decompressing only when the task is finished. The divers who work with their blood saturated — 'sat divers' as they are called — are brave, skilled and essential. An elite group among underwater workers! They are given enormous amounts of pay, but they earn every penny of it.

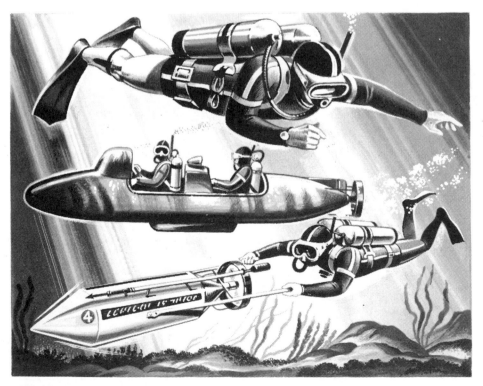

Left: A scuba diver with an Aqualung. The Aqualung was developed during the Second World War. Scuba stands for — 'Self-Contained Underwater Breathing Apparatus. Scuba divers cannot descend more than about 120m, but by using equipment as shown — the fibreglass, two-man underwater propelled vehicle and the one-man, hand-held version; both with motor-driven propellers — they can be very mobile.

It'll never fly

And for many years it looked as if the helicopter never would. But slowly, early ill-conceived contraptions of string and wire gave way to less ridiculous machines. And the idea of going straight up finally got off the ground.

FLY like a bird — that has been Man's dream through the ages. Aeroplanes fly but they have to have long runways to land and take-off. But helicopters go straight up and down with no runway at all, they can hover — something few birds can do — and they can even fly backwards, which is something no bird can do.

The manoeuvrability of helicopters in the air is unsurpassed.

First helicopters

But the first helicopters were anything but manoeuvreable. Although the idea of using a propeller to force an aircraft vertically into the air is not new — Leonardo da Vinci put the idea on paper in 1500 — no practical helicopter was built until the 1930s, when aeroplanes were already almost commonplace. Why?

The answer is simple. Because, at the same speed, the rotors of a helicopter cannot produce the same amount of lift as the much larger wings of an aeroplane. So a helicopter needs a very powerful motor relative to its weight.

Steam engines, of course, are far too heavy. Men's muscles are just not powerful enough. So it was not until the twentieth century, when the light and powerful petrol engine was developed, that some early helicopters, admittedly strange-looking, did leave the ground.

The performance of these early machines was unpredictable, and in many cases uncontrollable. But they did prove that the principle, at least, was sound.

Then, in the 1930s, the French aircraft pioneer, Louis Breguet, built a small helicopter he called the *Gyroplane Laboratoire*. On test it flew over 43 km in 62 minutes at a height of just over 150 metres, although compared with a modern chopper its manoeuvrability was very limited.

Nazi 'copters

In Germany, the Focke Achgelis company became interested in helicopters and they began to build them seriously. Some were shown at Nazi rallies and indeed Germany had a few flying during World War II, although they were considered unsuitable for combat duties and were used only for ferrying messengers and similar duties.

Yet the Germans lost the war, and

THE AUTOGYRO

The first really practical step in the development of an aircraft able to take-off and land without having to use long runways was the *autogyro*. Sometimes called the 'flying windmill', the autogyro was invented by Juan de la Cierva Corfonia, a Spanish aero-engineer. The first autogyro took to the air in 1920, and its principles were the basis of many later models.

Like the helicopter, the autogyro had a two-, three- or four-bladed rotor mounted above the fuselage. But unlike a helicopter's rotor, the autogyro's rotor was not driven by an engine, but instead rotated freely. There was an ordinary aeroplane propeller in the nose of the fuselage driven by a petrol engine. When the propeller in the nose turned, the airstream set up caused the rotor blades to revolve and eventually lift the machine off the ground. Once the autogyro was airborne, it was driven forwards by the propeller in its nose. At the same time, the rotor blades continued to revolve in the slipstream from the propeller and acted as wings to keep the machine airborne.

Although the autogyro partially solved the problem of vertical take-off and landing, it still needed some runway space and could not operate from a helicopter's postage-stamp pad. But before helicopters proper had been developed, the autogyro was a useful compromise. If flying into a breeze, it could even hover over the ground. However, there was little further development of the autogyro after Cierva's death in a flying accident in 1936. Thereafter aero-engineers concentrated on helicopters, compared with which the autogyro was slow, clumsy and inefficient.

NON-FLIERS — EARLY IDEAS THAT DIDN'T QUITE MAKE IT

Probably the first man to think of helicopters was Leonardo da Vinci (1542-1519). Da Vinci is one of the world's greatest artists. But he was also a distinguished scientist and engineer. Da Vinci kept elaborate notes of all his many ideas and activities and in 1500 he sketched the design for a helicopter-like machine. It consisted of a spiral-shaped vane which when rotated would screw itself vertically off the ground into the air. Da Vinci's helicopter was never more than an idea sketched on paper. Even if the machine had been built, at that time there was no engine suitable for rotating the vane.

Since da Vinci's day, scores of inventors have been tantalised by the idea of helicopters. Many machines were built with primitive rotors which their optimistic designers hoped to get off the ground by using legs and pedals. None managed to rise so much as a centimetre.

An additional power source — other than muscle power — was obviously needed. One of the first attempts to build such a helicopter was made about 1885 by W. O. Ayre, an American doctor. More like a bedstead than an aircraft, Ayre's helicopter had several small propellers mounted horizontally. Some of the propellers were driven by compressed air fed from steel cylinders, while others were turned by chains and pedals operated by the pilot. There was a hand-operated rudder.

But despite its additional power, Ayre's helicopter, too, never moved off the ground just like so many other of those flying machines.

Leonardo's flying machine

W. O. Ayre's 'flying bedstead'

The Royal Navy's *Lynx* helicopter

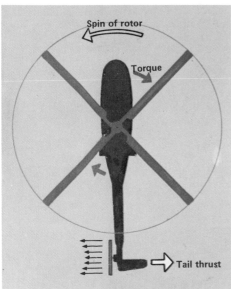

Spin of rotor

Torque

Tail thrust

TORQUE COMPENSATION

One of the major problems to be overcome in helicopter design is the tendency of the fuselage to spin round beneath the rotor. This spin is known as *torque*. In the diagram, the blades spinning in the direction of the yellow arrow tend to spin the body in the direction of the red arrows. This is where the tail rotor come in. It creates thrust (white arrow) in the opposite direction to that caused by the main rotor.

A helicopter is turned to the right or to the left by the pilot using one or other of two control pedals. To turn right, he pushes on the right pedal. This decreases the thrust from the anti-torque propeller. The natural torque created by the rotor blades then swings the fuselage to the right. If the pilot wants to turn left, he applies the left pedal. This increases the thrust of the anti-torque propeller and slightly reduces the speed of the rotor arms, so swinging the helicopter to the left.

the name that is most connected with helicopters is that of a Russian, Igor Sikorsky. Working in the U.S.A., Sikorsky was given an immense research budget which he put to good use. During the Forties he ironed out most of the problems bugging helicopter development. Since then, choppers have been put to more and more uses — many of them impossible by any other means.

Life saver

Helicopters have saved thousands of lives which would have been lost without them. Hovering over stricken ships, they have plucked the crews to safety by cable and winch. Similarly, alongside towering mountains and cliffs they can pick up the victims of falls.

When floods prevent rescue by road or rail transport, helicopters can lower food and medical supplies to any spot required. They can also lower feedstuffs to starving sheep and cattle when snow has blocked roads.

Without helicopters, undersea oil wells like these in the North Sea would be many times more difficult to operate than they are. Choppers ferry the crews to and from the rigs in a fraction of the time that it would take by ship. Urgent supplies can be sent to the rigs with the minimum of delay. And all the helicopter needs for landing is a small platform.

Because helicopters can carry loads slung beneath them, and do not need to stow them in the fuselage as aeroplanes have to, they can act as combined freighters and flying cranes. When building oil pipelines across desolate and roadless country, for example, they have carried in sections of piping and then lowered them accurately into position.

In war, the manoeuvrability of helicopters has allowed them to be used as 'gunships', capable of harrying ground forces while safely in the air.

But despite its many advantages over the aeroplane, the helicopter is slower and more expensive to fly. Many designers have tried to combine the advantages of both plane and 'copter. In these designs the aircraft has both wings and rotor(s). The rotors lift the aircraft and are then swivelled once it is airborne to propel it along.

Convertiplanes

But these 'convertiplanes', as they are called, have never been successful. The rotors tend to be too small to be efficient helicopter rotors yet too large to be efficient aeroplane propellers. Only recently have the problems of vertical take-off plus normal flight been fully solved. And it took a jet — the Harrier 'Jump jet' — rather than a propeller-driven aircraft to do so.

MANOEUVRING

A helicopter is manoeuvred by using the force generated by the spinning rotor to drive it in the required direction as well as keep it up in the air. This is done by tilting the rotor.

In (1) the blades are horizontal and the helicopter will move up and down vertically — or hover. In (2) the rotor is tilted forwards. This means that some of the rotor thrust is directed backwards, pushing the helicopter forwards.

Tilting the rotor right or left will also move the helicopter right or left.

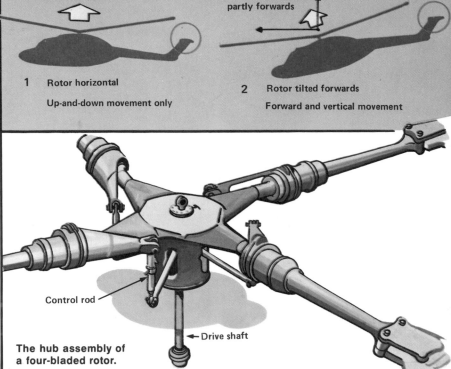

All force upwards

1 Rotor horizontal

Up-and-down movement only

Force partly upwards, partly forwards

2 Rotor tilted forwards

Forward and vertical movement

STAYING UP

Although they look completely different, helicopters, aeroplanes, and birds are kept up in the air in much the same way. This is the aerofoil effect described on page 283 in the *Marvel of Flight* story. The rotor blades of a helicopter are aerofoils and keep the aircraft up.

To increase the lift, the blades are tilted upwards along their front edge. This forces more air downwards and makes the helicopter climb. The angle at which the blades are tilted is called the *angle of attack (A)*. The greater the angle of attack, the greater the lift.

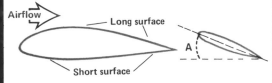

Airflow

Long surface

Short surface

A

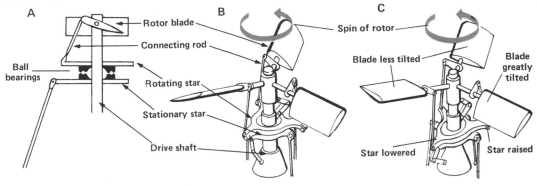

Control rod

Drive shaft

The hub assembly of a four-bladed rotor.

CONTROLS

Complex controls are necessary to alter the angle of tilt of the rotor blades while they are spinning. The close-up (A) shows the hub to which the blades are attached. Two metal plates, the *rotating star* and the *stationary star*, are fixed round the central rotating shaft which drives the blades. The rotating star spins with the shaft, but the stationary star does not rotate. Ball bearings reduce the friction between the two plates.

Rods which are connected to the pilot's controls are used to tilt the stationary star. When the stationary star is tilted, the rotating star tilts also. When the rotating star tilts, it tilts the rotor blade by means of a connecting rod.

Diagram B shows the hub assem-

A — Rotor blade, Connecting rod, Ball bearings, Rotating star, Stationary star, Drive shaft

B — Spin of rotor

C — Spin of rotor, Blade less tilted, Blade greatly tilted, Star lowered, Star raised

bly set up so that all the blades are tilted to give the maximum angle of attack. With such a setting the helicopter would rise straight up into the air.

Diagram C shows the assembly arranged so that each blade is tilted a

different amount. This is achieved by pushing the star assembly up in one place only, and is possible because the three (or four in the case of a four-bladed rotor) rods which tilt the star can be moved independently of each other.

As the rotor spins, the tilt of each blade continually changes.

In the diagram the star is arranged so that the helicopter would fly forwards out of the page. Other settings of the star can move the helicopter backwards or sideways.

The largest helicopter in the world is the Russian Mil *Mi-12*. It weighs 105 tonnes and its rotors span 67 metres.

Ordinary light, such as that given off by a light bulb, is like a raggledy crowd leaving a football match. It is out of step and going in all directions.

Light reflected from a concave mirror — like the light from a searchlight — is all going in the same direction. But it is still out of step.

Laser light is like a troop of marching soldiers. Not only are the soldiers all going in the same direction, they are also marching in step. Because laser light is like this, it is extremely powerful. It can cut cloth, weld metal — and also make incredible three-dimensional images called holograms.

Light is all around us. We see with it and it is our major link with the outside world. Lasers are terrifying beams that will blast a spaceship to eternity or vaporise rock. But lasers too are only light. So what is so special about

The amazing laser

WHAT can be used to cut out a pair of jeans, to weld metal, to perform delicate eye operations, to draw a straight line to the Moon, or to create three-dimensional 'objects' out of thin air? The answer: a laser.

Light is made up from lots of small bundles of energy called *photons*. These photons travel along a regular wave-like path at the fastest speed possible in the Universe — the speed of light, 299,793 km per second.

Lasers are lamps in which all the photons are neatly sorted out so that they are of the same wavelength and are exactly in step with each other, like soldiers on parade.

Light from other lamps and from the Sun itself is a great jumble of waves, all of different wavelengths. It is like a raggledy crowd at a football match, containing small children taking short quick steps, and big men with enormous slow strides, all moving in different directions and all walking out of step.

Football crowd

If we imagine white light as that football crowd, then the short quick-stepping children are the light we see as blue light. The big-striding men are red light. The mixture of blue and red and all the different-sized waves in between we see as white.

To get waves marching in step with one another, they must all have the same length of stride. There are some sorts of lamp, like the yellow ones used in street lamps, or the red neon lamps used in advertisements, which do produce light in which the waves are all the same length.

To make a laser we have to find some way of getting the waves of a lamp like this in step with one another. The text and illustrations on the opposite page tell how this is done.

When light is in step, like that troop of marching soldiers, it becomes far more powerful than disorganised normal light. The beam is so powerful that it can be used to cut cloth or plastic, or melt metal to weld it. It can be used to make very fine incisions in surgery when a knife would be far too clumsy. Also, because lasers are absolutely straight, they can be used like rulers for surveying.

Accurate measure

Another use of lasers is to measure distances not much larger than atoms. The way this is done is to split a laser beam in two and then rejoin the two parts. If one part of the beam travels half a stride (wavelength) farther than the other part, the two parts become exactly out of step and when they join together again they cancel each other out and the beam disappears.

If the two parts travel the same distance, or one part travels exactly one or any other whole number of wavelengths farther, when the parts join together again they are in step and the beam is as bright as ever.

It is this effect of two halves of a beam adding together to make brightness of darkness which is the basis of the *hologram,* probably the most fascinating of all the uses of lasers.

The laser is used to make an image on a photographic plate. When illuminated by another light, the image *looks* three-dimensional. In other words, exactly the same sort of light comes from the image as comes from the solid object in reality. The effect is stunning — a 'solid' object you can put your hand through.

HOW A LASER IS FORMED

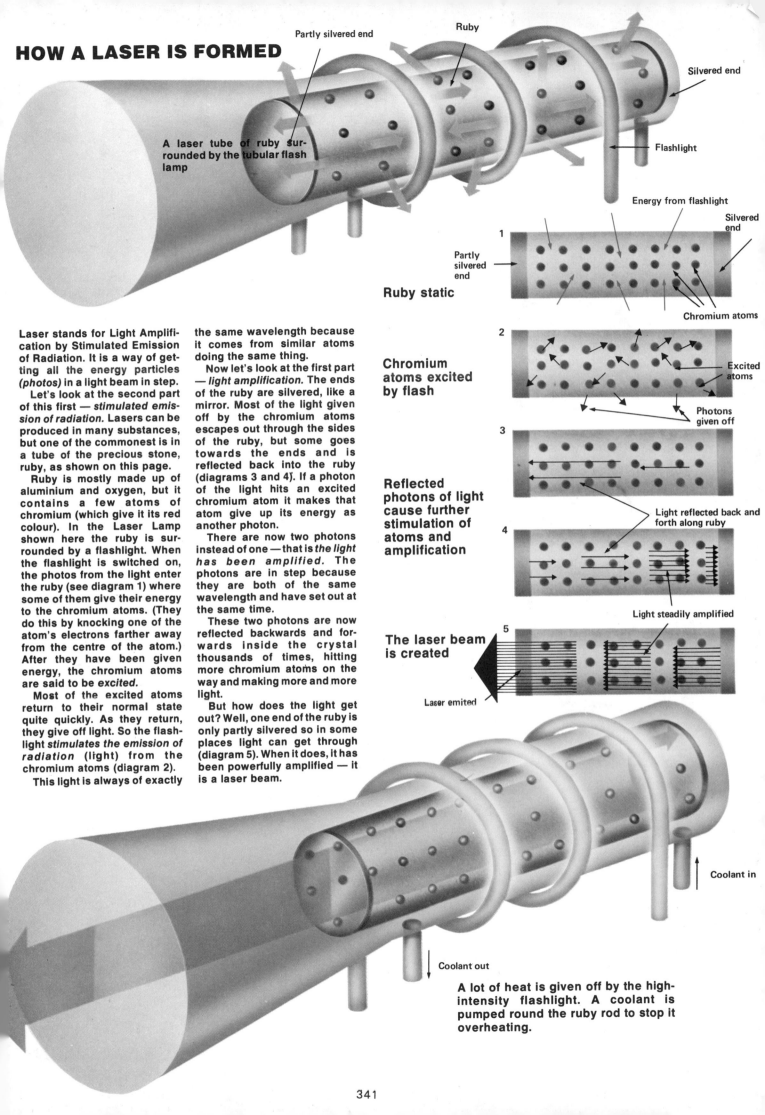

Partly silvered end

Ruby

Silvered end

A laser tube of ruby surrounded by the tubular flash lamp

Flashlight

Energy from flashlight

1

Partly silvered end

Silvered end

Ruby static

Chromium atoms

2

Excited atoms

Chromium atoms excited by flash

Photons given off

3

Reflected photons of light cause further stimulation of atoms and amplification

Light reflected back and forth along ruby

4

Light steadily amplified

The laser beam is created

5

Laser emitted

Laser stands for Light Amplification by Stimulated Emission of Radiation. It is a way of getting all the energy particles *(photos)* in a light beam in step.

Let's look at the second part of this first — *stimulated emission of radiation.* Lasers can be produced in many substances, but one of the commonest is in a tube of the precious stone, ruby, as shown on this page.

Ruby is mostly made up of aluminium and oxygen, but it contains a few atoms of chromium (which give it its red colour). In the Laser Lamp shown here the ruby is surrounded by a flashlight. When the flashlight is switched on, the photos from the light enter the ruby (see diagram 1) where some of them give their energy to the chromium atoms. (They do this by knocking one of the atom's electrons farther away from the centre of the atom.) After they have been given energy, the chromium atoms are said to be *excited.*

Most of the excited atoms return to their normal state quite quickly. As they return, they give off light. So the flashlight *stimulates the emission of radiation* (light) from the chromium atoms (diagram 2).

This light is always of exactly the same wavelength because it comes from similar atoms doing the same thing.

Now let's look at the first part — *light amplification.* The ends of the ruby are silvered, like a mirror. Most of the light given off by the chromium atoms escapes out through the sides of the ruby, but some goes towards the ends and is reflected back into the ruby (diagrams 3 and 4). If a photon of the light hits an excited chromium atom it makes that atom give up its energy as another photon.

There are now two photons instead of one — that is *the light has been amplified.* The photons are in step because they are both of the same wavelength and have set out at the same time.

These two photons are now reflected backwards and forwards inside the crystal thousands of times, hitting more chromium atoms on the way and making more and more light.

But how does the light get out? Well, one end of the ruby is only partly silvered so in some places light can get through (diagram 5). When it does, it has been powerfully amplified — it is a laser beam.

Coolant in

Coolant out

A lot of heat is given off by the high-intensity flashlight. A coolant is pumped round the ruby rod to stop it overheating.

How an airport

TODAY millions of people travel by air. Businessmen and holiday-makers think no more of stepping on to an aircraft than of getting into a bus.

Yet it is only 61 years since Imperial Airways, the forerunner of British Airways, inaugurated the first British national airline. At what was little more than a large flat field in Croydon, south of London, a few single-engined aircraft, the slip-streams from their propellers setting the grass waving, landed with their dozen or so travellers.

The growth of air travel has shrunk the world so much that now you can travel by Concorde to arrive in New York two hours before leaving London Heathrow!

The 3,000-mile flight takes just over three hours, but New York time is five hours behind that of London.

To keep pace with this increased traffic airports, too, have had to expand and become increasingly complex. Croydon airport would have fitted into Heathrow over nine times.

Heathrow is one of the world's busiest airports, and can handle more than 100,000 passengers and nearly 1,000 flights in a day — more international traffic than any other airport.

The airport at Chicago, for example,

It is generally acknowledged that London's Heathrow is the busiest international airport in the world.
In one day 112,880 passengers have been recorded. The total per year is in excess of 27 millions.
The peak rate of landings and take-offs is 78 per hour and statistics show that these figures are being increased all the time.

is the busiest in the world with aircraft taking off or landing in an average time of less than a minute. Atlanta airport handles almost 50 million passengers a year, nearly twice as many as Heathrow, and has the capacity to handle half as many passengers again! However in America, there is of course a much greater amount of domestic flying than elsewhere.

All this means an aircraft is arriving or leaving less than every minute. Many are giant Jumbos, carrying more than 500 passengers.

The job of an international airport is to guide aircraft safely to the runways, to disembark passengers as speedily as possible, unload hundreds of tons of baggage — and carry out the same functions for passengers and aircraft taking off.

The passengers and their baggage are dealt with by airport ground staff. After 'checking-in', passengers make their way to the departure lounge, undergoing security checks and passport controls on their way. Metal detectors and X-ray machines scan their hand luggage for weapons or explosive devices.

Meanwhile, suitcases are travelling on conveyor belts to the baggage handling area from the check-in desks where a receptionist has tagged them with a destination code.

The take-off weight of an aircraft has to be carefully controlled and each item of baggage weighed. To discourage passengers from taking too much baggage with them, an excess charge is made for luggage weighing more than the allowance.

A Jumbo can carry 30 tons of cargo, including passengers' bags, in specially-shaped containers which make loading and unloading speedier.

The organisation of air traffic in and

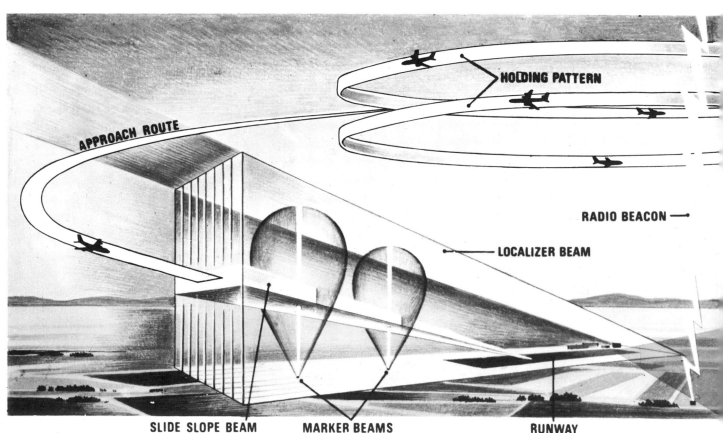

APPROACH ROUTE · HOLDING PATTERN · RADIO BEACON → · LOCALIZER BEAM · SLIDE SLOPE BEAM · MARKER BEAMS · RUNWAY

works

The destination of travellers from all parts of the globe, a modern airport like London's Heathrow is used by over seventy airline companies and employs 45,000 people.

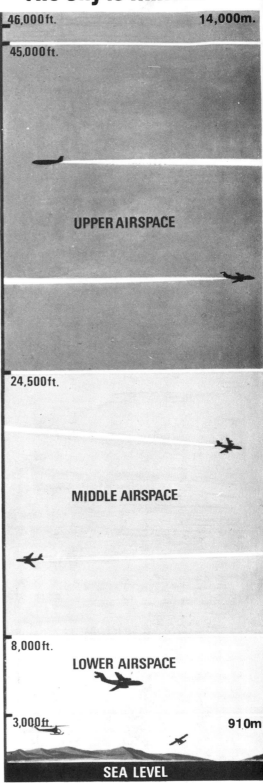

The sky is limited

46,000 ft.	14,000m.
45,000 ft.	

UPPER AIRSPACE

24,500 ft.

MIDDLE AIRSPACE

8,000 ft.

LOWER AIRSPACE

3,000 ft. — 910m

SEA LEVEL

The sky is divided into layers with clearly defined airways along which aircraft going in one direction must fly at the same height and speed. Generally, the smaller the aircraft, the lower it flies. Small, less powerful craft fly in Lower Airspace, larger craft in Middle Airspace, Jumbo jets in Upper Airspace and, topping them all, Concorde zooms along at 15,000m. (50,000 ft.). Its size belies its power!

---

around the airport is the responsibility of the Control Tower, the nerve centre. There, various controllers, aided by computers in busy areas, take charge of different flight stages.

The Ground Controller organises the movements of all aircraft once they have landed. Without his permission, no aircraft may move. In poor visibility, he can see the whole airport on a radar screen.

The Approach Controller ensures that aircraft have room to land. The runway must be clear before a flight arrives — usually within minutes of the previous one at busy airports. Allowance must be made for the turbulence left in the wake of larger aircraft and also for wet conditions which demand gentler braking and, therefore, more time on the runway.

Near the airport, the Control Tower is linked to aircraft by radio. But beyond that area, pilots establish radio contact with Area Traffic Controllers along their routes.

After a flight, an aircraft is cleaned, aired and restocked with pre-packed meals, water and provisions, in preparation for its next one. Baggage is unloaded and new baggage put in its place. Maintenance engineers check the landing gear and tyres and do minor repairs. The fuel tanks have to be reloaded, taking up to 920,000 litres (203,750 gals.) for a big aircraft.

An hour before departure, the new flight crew boards to carry out routine checks on the aircraft's instruments, systems and controls, which are run by a ground power unit while the aircraft's auxiliary power unit is off.

A small jet, such as Concorde, can be 'turned round' for another flight in about an hour, but a Jumbo jet takes three hours.

Much of the work of an airport is done behind the scenes. But it is no less important because of that.

The airport police station always has officers on patrol, available to deal with any problems.

The fire-fighting crews must also be on constant alert for any emergency. Fortunately, accidents are very rare, and accidents involving fires are even rarer; but there is always a slight risk from fuel leaks or minor damage which could lead to a fire. In such an event the fire-fighters would spring into immediate action in their vehicles, which are loaded with water and a special chemical which produces a thick foam. This foam smothers the fire

---

When an airport is particularly busy, aircraft may have to 'queue' while awaiting their turn to come in to land. The Air Traffic Controller 'stacks' the waiting aircraft in a holding pattern, as shown in our illustration on the left.

Guided by radio beacons, the aircraft in a stack fly around in circles. Each circle is separated by 300m. (1,000ft.) of airspace. The Approach Controller calls in the bottom plane in the stack and aircraft above it all descend 300m.

Invisible radio beams guide the aircraft to the runway. The *Slide Slope Beam* ensures that the pilot knows precisely what height he should fly at on his descent towards the runway.

Another beam, the *Localizer*, indicates the position of the centre of the runway, and *Marker Beams* show the distance between the aircraft and the runway.

At night, or in poor visibility, the pilot is also aided by ground lights around the runway. Visual Approach Slope Indicator (VASI) lights at both sides of the runway help to guide the aircraft in at a correct angle. If they appear red to the pilot he is coming in too high. If white, too low. Both red and white lights show if the angle is correct.

Once down on the runway the pilot is told which taxi-ing track to follow to the parking bay allocated to him.

While the plane is being unloaded and reloaded it is refuelled and flight-serviced.

If the plane is not being "turned round" that is, if it is not taking off immediately, it will then be directed to a parking area.

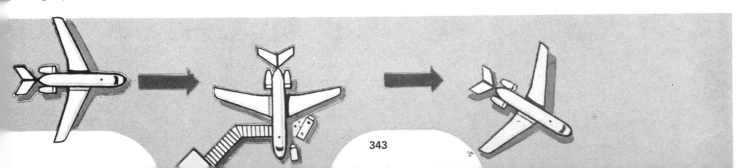

The air lanes which lead across Britain to London and are used by aircraft 'en route' to both Heathrow and Gatwick airports.

AIRWAYS IN UK AIRSPACE

West Scottish Control Area
Scottish Terminal Control Area
White 9
Blue 2
Belfast Terminal Control Area
Blue 2
Isle of Man Terminal Control Area
Red 4
Amber 1
Amber 25
Scottish Flight Information Region
London Flight Information Region
Halifax Control Area
Blue 1
Manchester Terminal Control Area
Daventry Control Area
White 39
Red 14
Birmingham Control Zone
Amber 1 West
Red 3
A1
Red 1 North
Green 1
London Terminal Control Area
B3
Red 1 South
Amber 25
W17
White 12
A34W
Amber 1
Amber 34
Worthing Control Area
Channel Islands Control Zone
White 8

The traffic control of aircraft but also the conveying them t

AIRLINES

INTERNATIONAL CARGO AREA IMPORT & EXPORT CUSTOMS

AIRCRAFT PARKING

← AIRCRAFT TAXI-ING TO TAKE-OFF POSITION

Once the plane is on the ground, the controllers direct it to the unloading bay. Later, if the plane is not to take off again immediately, it will be directed into a service bay to await its next assignment.

Air traffic over Britain and at most of her major airports is controlled by a special organisation which is responsible to the Civil Aviation Authority and the Ministry of Defence. Its job is to guide both civil and military aircraft through British airspace.

Apart from flowing safely and in an orderly manner, air traffic has to be organised in such a way as to reduce delays, fuel consumption and the amount of aircraft noise inflicted on people on the ground. Aircraft are, therefore, restricted to flying along certain routes, or airways.

Airways, which could be described as motorways in the skies, are ten miles wide and from 1,500 m. (5,000 ft.) to 7,400 m. (24,500 ft) high. They pass over the Control Zones surrounding and protecting major airports and the Terminal Control Areas which supervise the inter-sections, or 'crossroads'. Each airway is identified by being allocated a colour and a number. High-flying aircraft fly above the airways in Upper Air Routes above 7,600 m. (25,000 ft.).

by cutting off its supply of oxygen.

The works maintenance depots also have an important part to play in keeping the runways in perfect condition. When you remember that a fully laden Jumbo jet can weigh up to 370 tonnes and that that weight is landing at a speed of about 135 knots (250 km/h) you can see how vital it is that the runways are never allowed to deteriorate. Inspectors regularly examine the runways for cracks or damage

Forty minutes before departure of aircraft, computer generates flight progress strips.

After passengers have embarked, pilot requests permission to taxi.

Taxi-ing to point of take-off.

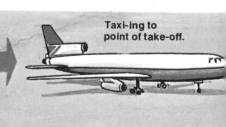

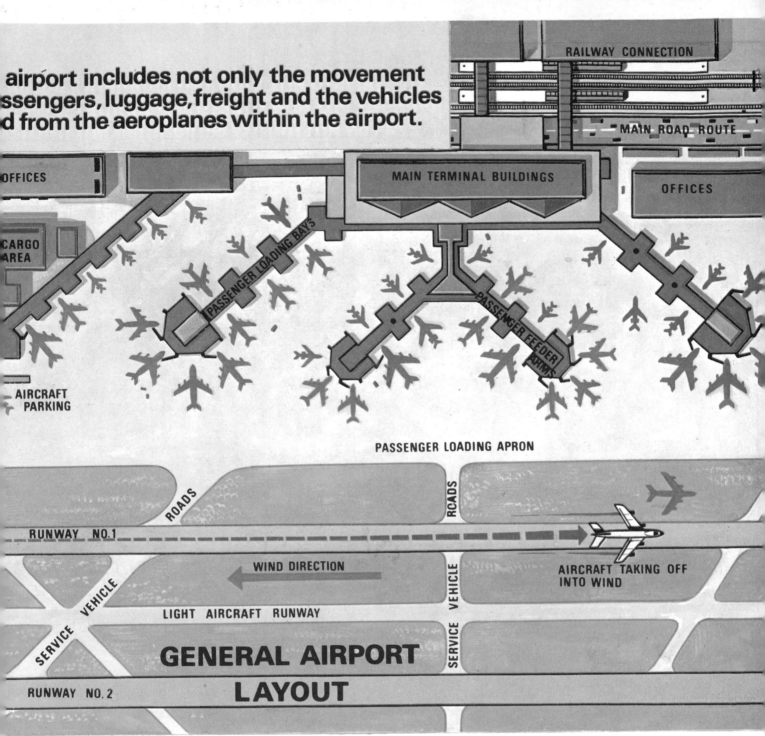

airport includes not only the movement ...ssengers, luggage, freight and the vehicles ...d from the aeroplanes within the airport.

RAILWAY CONNECTION

MAIN ROAD ROUTE

OFFICES

MAIN TERMINAL BUILDINGS

OFFICES

CARGO AREA

PASSENGER LOADING BAYS

PASSENGER FEEDER ARMS

AIRCRAFT PARKING

PASSENGER LOADING APRON

ROADS

ROADS

RUNWAY NO.1

AIRCRAFT TAKING OFF INTO WIND

WIND DIRECTION

SERVICE VEHICLE

SERVICE VEHICLE

LIGHT AIRCRAFT RUNWAY

GENERAL AIRPORT LAYOUT

RUNWAY NO. 2

or to seek any pieces of debris that might be on them.

Then there are the motor transport depot which garages and services the ground vehicles needed around the airport; the catering service building where companies prepare meals for consumption aboard the aircraft; the maintenance hangars to which aircraft are taken once a year for structural checks; the cargo areas which sometimes have to handle a wide variety of items, from livestock to refrigerated goods; and the fuel store and its tankers which are indispensable.

All these services play their parts in the smooth running of an airport. But the chances are that the only service noticed by passengers as they disembark is the one provided by H.M. Customs Officers.

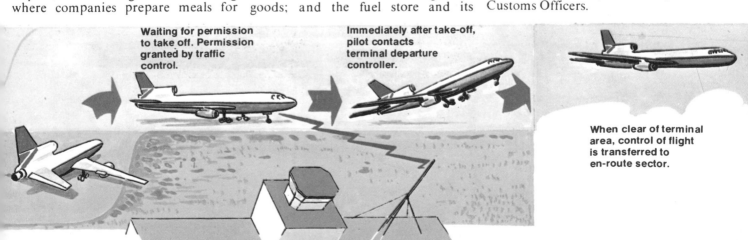

Waiting for permission to take off. Permission granted by traffic control.

Immediately after take-off, pilot contacts terminal departure controller.

When clear of terminal area, control of flight is transferred to en-route sector.

Up, up and away: and nothing to keep you there but
A lot of hot air-or hydrogen

On the first manned balloon flight, the two aeronauts were kept busy putting out the fires caused by sparks coming from the fire that produced the 'electric smoke' (hot air).

September 19, 1783 and the first to fly by balloon were a sheep, a cockerel and a duck. They survived — despite a rough landing in a forest close to Paris.

Watched by 200,000 people, Professor Charles and M. N. Roberts made the first manned flight by hydrogen balloon in December, 1783 from the Tuileries in Paris.

The first channel crossing by balloon took place on January 7, 1785 in a hydrogen balloon.

FLOATING gracefully about the sky by balloon is a fascinating sport that really started almost 200 years ago, when the first hot-air balloons were invented by Joseph Montgolfier and his younger brother Etienne.

They were paper-makers in Vidalon-les-Annonay, in the South of France. They began experimenting with small paper parachutes and realised that a lighter-than-air gas could keep their parachutes afloat for longer.

After studying cloud formations, the Montgolfiers tested small paper balloons filled with steam, but these collapsed almost as fast as they were launched — the moist steam ruined the paper. Then they noticed how smoke and sparks rose up from fires, mistakenly believing that this was due to some kind of gas made by burning. Of course the sparks were rising because hot air expands so becoming lighter than normal air. Nevertheless, the idea of hot-air balloons had been born.

In December, 1782, the two brothers sent a 20 cubic metre balloon 300 metres into the air. It was fuelled by what they called 'electric smoke', produced by burning a mixture of wool and moist straw. It was so successful that the French Academy des Sciences asked them to give a demonstration in Paris.

Yet before they could do so, Professor J. A. C. Charles succeeded in launching a hydrogen balloon in Paris on August 27, 1783. Nevertheless, the Montgolfiers went ahead with their plans and built a beautifully decorated 22-metre tall balloon; but it was wrecked in a sudden storm at Faubourg Saint-Antoine on September 14 during a trial run.

Quickly they built another balloon. But King Louis XVI, before whom the demonstration was to be made, refused permission for any of his subjects to risk their lives in it. So the first land animals to travel through the air were a sheep, a cockerel and a duck.

Still, it was a successful test flight which opened the way for the first manned flight. But the king was still cautious and suggested that such a risky journey should be made by a convict, who would be rewarded with his freedom.

Then a young scientist, Jean-Francoise de Rozier, pointed out that such a mission was too great an honour to be given to a criminal and volunteered himself. The Montgolfiers made a 23-metre tall, 1,600 cubic metre balloon for the flight.

The fire to provide the hot air was in an iron basket suspended beneath the balloon's open mouth and there was an iron

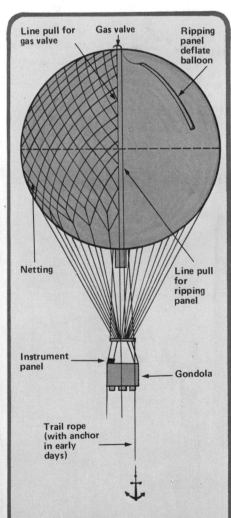

Line pull for gas valve
Gas valve
Ripping panel deflate balloon
Netting
Line pull for ripping panel
Instrument panel
Gondola
Trail rope (with anchor in early days)

Invented at about the same time as hot-air balloons, hydrogen balloons proved more practical and safer than hot-air balloons. This is a modern balloon but it differs little from those flown 200 years ago. These were made from silk impregnated with rubber, with valves to release hydrogen during descent, or if the gas expanded at great height threatening to burst the balloon.

gallery on which the first aeronauts could stand to stoke the fire. Several tests were made to raise the balloon while it was held captive by ropes.

Then on November 21, 1783, from a garden in the Bois de Boulogne, the first manned voyage in a balloon began. The Marquis d'Arlandes went with de Rozier and their flight lasted 25 minutes, during which they drifted across the Seine to land in the Place d'Italie. Throughout the voyage, there was such an obvious danger of sparks from the fire setting the balloon alight that hydrogen balloons eventually became far more popular.

The early hydrogen balloons were called 'Charlières' after Professor Charles. They were used for many exciting feats. The first balloon ascent from British soil took place in Edinburgh on August 27, 1784. On January 7, the next year, Jean-Pierre Blanchard and Dr. John Jeffries succeeded with a very hazardous flight from Dover to Calais. And the first parachute jump from a balloon was made on October 22, 1797.

With modern techniques hot-air balloons are becoming popular again. This modern balloon shows how the sport has come full circle since 1783. It has a willow cane gondola with leather upholstered edging, a propane gas burner placed at the top of the frame to provide the hot air, and a navigational instrument pack. Its design is practically traditional.

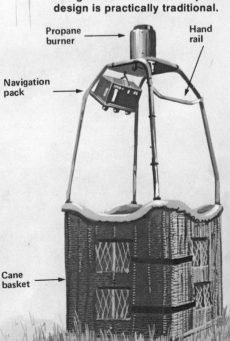

Propane burner
Hand rail
Navigation pack
Cane basket

Captive balloons like the *Intrepid* were used during the American Civil War to help the Federal armies against the Confederates. Observers relayed information about enemy activities back to the ground by telegraph. No effort was made to camouflage the balloons, which were brightly decorated with insignia.

Four balloon corps were formed by the Royal Engineers during the Boer War in 1899. The balloons were transported (while inflated) across the rough South African countryside by special waggons pulled by oxen or horses. Called 'bottle cars', each group of six cars, specially built to withstand rough ground, carried nine hydrogen bottles, which were linked by rubber hoses and held enough hydrogen to inflate two 368 cubic metre balloons if necessary.

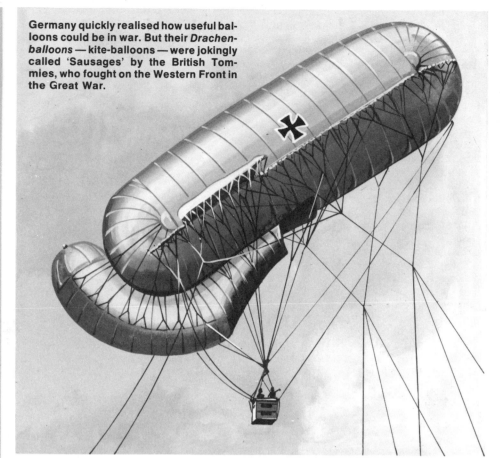

Germany quickly realised how useful balloons could be in war. But their *Drachenballoons* — kite-balloons — were jokingly called 'Sausages' by the British Tommies, who fought on the Western Front in the Great War.

It was quickly realised, too, that captive balloons — anchored by ropes — could prove useful in warfare as observation platforms to spy on enemy activities and movements. During the first Battle of Bull Run, on July 21, 1861, in the American Civil War, for example, the balloon *Enterprise* was used by the Federal forces to spy on Confederate troop movements. It proved so useful that the Federal army soon had six others in service.

But captive observation balloons had one disadvantage. They were so unsteady in the slightest breeze that the observers suffered air-sickness. By 1893, however, German army officers Major August von Parseval and Captain Bartsch von Sigsfeld overcame this problem by designing the more stable *Drachenballoon,* which was a mixture of a balloon and a kite. Within a few years it was widely used by European armies.

Kite-balloons proved invaluable during the First World War. Naval cruisers used them to spot submarines, and they were used both by the Germans and the Allies on the Western Front to direct artillery. They were often attacked by planes, but the balloonists had one advantage over these early fighter pilots: they could easily escape by parachute and few pilots were issued with these. At this time, too, the large passenger and bomb-carrying Zeppelins were filling the skies, bringing tragedy as well as benefit.

By the 1930s, ballooning had become an exciting sporting pastime and balloons and gondolas had been so improved that they could reach 5,000 metres — higher than any aeroplanes could fly at that time.

One of the leading balloonists then was Auguste Piccard — a Swiss-born physicist. Piccard had a special, high-altitude

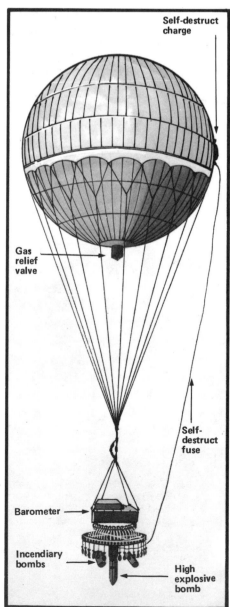

Self-destruct charge

Gas relief valve

Self-destruct fuse

Barometer

Incendiary bombs

High explosive bomb

gondola made. It was constructed from aluminium, was airtight, with its own oxygen-supply, and was shaped just like a diving-bell. On May 27, 1931, Piccard's balloon soared to 15,781 metres in 30 minutes above Augusburg, in Bavaria. It drifted south across the Tyrolean Alps and landed on a remote snow-covered mountainside. Piccard and his assistant made their way to safety, but had to leave their balloon and equipment behind until almost a year later.

Epic voyage

It was certainly an epic voyage, but Piccard was disappointed that he failed to reach 16,000 metres. So he started designing a new and improved balloon and on August 18, 1932, he set off from Dübendorf airport near Brussels accompanied by Dr. Max Cosyns.

On board, they carried sufficient oxygen for 32 hours and provisions for two days. And when their balloon landed at Lake Garda, in Italy, late the following afternoon, their altimeter proved that Piccard had set a new world altitude record of 16,700 metres.

Surprisingly, Auguste Piccard appeared to lose interest in the stratosphere after that and took to deep-sea diving instead. But on October 3, 1934, his brother Jean made the next record of 17,385 metres from Detroit in America. Jean's wife was with him on that trip and she became the first woman to enter the stratosphere.

Her record stood until 1963, when Russian woman astronaut Valentina Tereshkova went into space in a *Vostok 6* spacecraft.

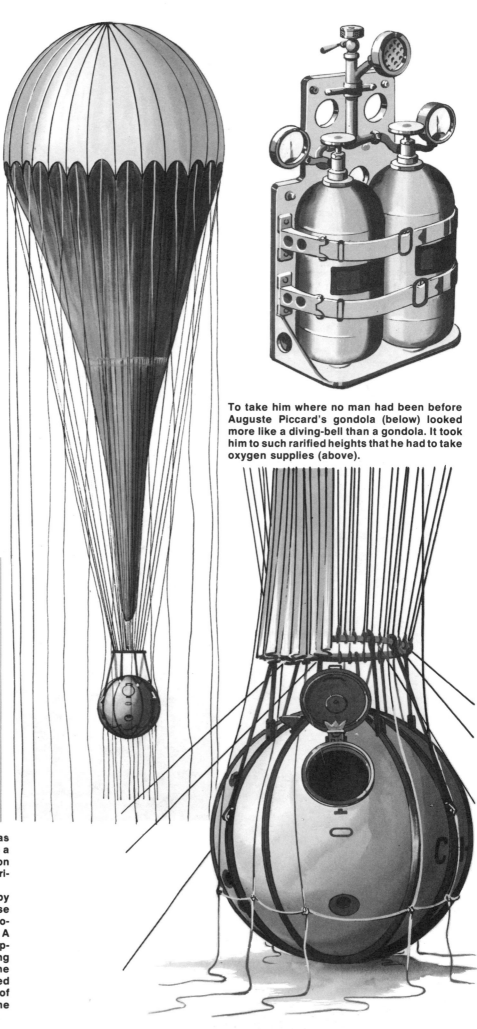

To take him where no man had been before Auguste Piccard's gondola (below) looked more like a diving-bell than a gondola. It took him to such rarified heights that he had to take oxygen supplies (above).

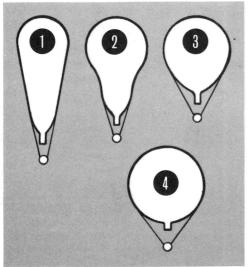

One of the most celebrated balloon ascents was made by Auguste Piccard in 1930. He climbed to a record 16,700 metres. As it rose, the balloon changed from an elongated pear shape to spherical (above).
Left: 'Death balloons' like this were released by Japan in the last years of World War II to terrorise America. Cheaply made from paper, they were floated across the Pacific on the prevailing winds. A barometer monitored the balloon's height, dropping sandbags if the balloon sank too low, letting out gas if it rose too high. Finally, when all the sandbags were used up, the balloon destroyed itself. American secrecy about the effectiveness of the balloons led to their abandonment by the Japanese in April 1945.

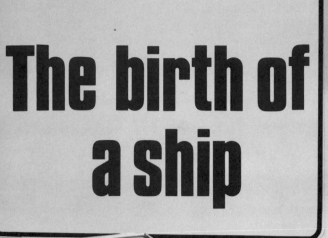

The birth of a ship

WHEN a ship is launched, a bottle of wine or champagne is smashed against its bows to send it on its way — but this is only the end of a very long industrial process.

It may already have taken several months or even years to get the ship to the stage where it is ready for launching. At this point it is complete except for its engines, boilers, funnels, radar installations, navigational instruments and other fittings and machinery. A great deal of pride and effort has gone into the work, as well as a great deal of money.

It is no wonder, then, that such care is taken to transfer the ship to the water without serious damage, especially with huge weights of tens of thousands or even hundreds of thousands of tonnes in the case of modern cargo ships and oil tankers.

In fact, the ship is built with the stern facing the water so that it is launched 'backwards'. This is done because the rounded end of the stern gives better support and stability during the launching. The sharper-ended bow, on the other hand, is better at dealing with the twisting stresses which the ship's framework experiences at its launch.

The ship must, of course, be constructed on a firmly founded *shipway*. This is supported by piles which may be driven down to

Heavily-greased slipways

Launching cradle

Control drag chains

Above: An artist's impression of the actual launching of a ship. Just before the launch the wooden supporting props have been knocked away so the ship rests only on the launching cradles. The ceremonial smashing of a wine bottle is the signal for the release of the hydraulic triggers (above right) and the ship starts to move down the heavily-greased slipways. To stop the ship 'running away', drag chains are used. The ship's stern enters the water, at first floating low in the water and thus reducing the pressure on the ship's bottom. Eventually the launching cradle lifts off the groundways, the stern rises and the bow reaches the end of the slipway. Soon the ship is level and afloat!

depths of over 15 metres. Piling can be very extensive, because the presence of water would make the ground itself too soft to support the great bulk of the ship. It is not unusual for a shipway to have as many as 6,000 piles spaced beneath the *groundways*.

When a ship slides down to the water at its launching, it normally does so on two parallel groundways. The tops of these groundways are very thoroughly greased and sometimes huge amounts may be needed. For instance *Yorktown*, an American aircraft carrier in the Second World War, required nearly 20 tonnes of launching grease to help it slide into the water.

Actually the ship does not slide down the groundways. It travels on sliding ways which run about four-fifths of the ship's length and are placed on top of the grease. These sliding ways are prevented from moving until the right moment by special blocks and by two hydraulic triggers, one on each groundway. After the shoring- and keel-blocks have been removed, the smashing of the 'christening' wine on the ship's bow is the signal for the hydraulic triggers to be released.

The slideways and ship begin to move. After a few moments, the ends of the sliding ways approach the end of the groundways, and the vessel tips in the water, with the bow rising. Because of this, great pressure is put on the groundway ends and on the bottom of ship. Fortunately, the stern of the vessel, by now floating low in the water, usually counteracts this 'tipping' and so

Wooden supporting props

Ship's bottom

Hydraulic triggers

Wooden supporting pillar

Just prior to the launch, when the props have been removed, the ship rests on the launching cradle, held back only by these enormous hydraulic triggers. At the moment of launch the supporting pillars are knocked away by sledgehammers and the triggers released. The ship then slowly starts down the greased slipway.

Partly-built bridge and funnel

lway

Floating wooden props

Ship's rudder

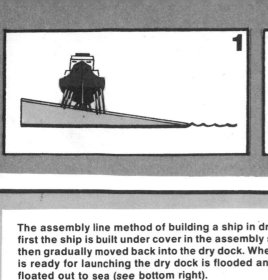
1

2

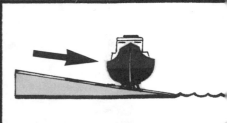

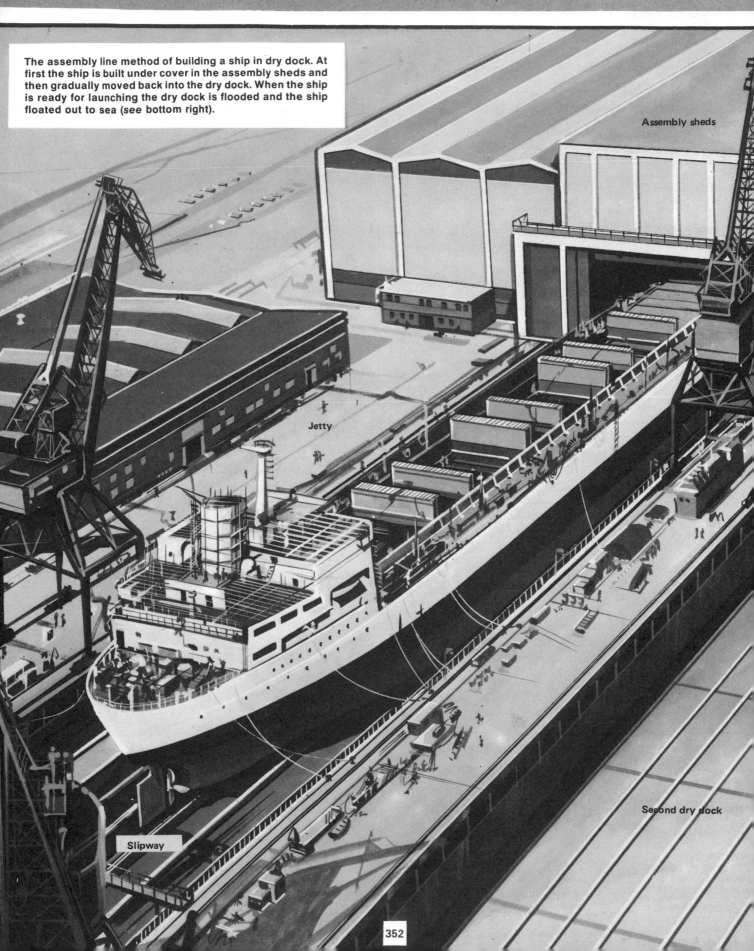

The assembly line method of building a ship in dry dock. At first the ship is built under cover in the assembly sheds and then gradually moved back into the dry dock. When the ship is ready for launching the dry dock is flooded and the ship floated out to sea (*see* bottom right).

Assembly sheds

Jetty

Slipway

Second dry dock

352

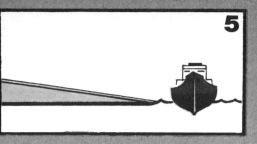

reduces the pressure and any buckling of the ship's bottom that pressure may cause.

Soon, the ship becomes buoyant enough for the stern to rise in the water, although the whole of the launching cradle is not yet free of the groundways. When the cradle finally lifts from the groundways, the part of the vessel not supported by the water is thrown onto a set of sturdy wooden blocks known as the fore poppet at the end of the groundways. At this stage, the ship is said to be 'pivoting', while continuing to slip down into the water. Eventually, the fore poppet drops off the groundways, or it floats off, and the ship is afloat, and upright in the water.

At least that is what is supposed to happen when a ship is launched. It may appear relatively simple but in actual fact, launching a ship is a considerable feat of engineering and mechanics. The remarkable thing is that most ship launches are perfectly smooth and are completed without any trouble.

Risk

Nevertheless, the risk factor is great enough for things to go disastrously wrong. Over the years some serious, and even fatal accidents, have occurred. This has often happened because the ship itself was unstable. One spectacular incident occurred in 1907, when the 150 m long S.S. *Principessa Jolanda* was launched at La Spezia, in Italy. Because the Mediterranean is tideless, it is possible, in countries like Italy, to launch a ship virtually complete. In fact, the *Principessa Jolanda* was almost ready for her sea trials. Her machinery had been installed, but the trouble was that she carried insufficient ballast (stabilising weight). A few moments after the launch, the *Principessa Jolanda* keeled sideways and capsized. Within 15 minutes she had sunk, and all that could be salvaged was some of her boilers!

Bad luck, rather than bad judgement, can also play its part in bedevilling ship launches. In 1857, the side-on launching of Isambard Kingdom Brunel's *Great Britain*, five times the size of any vessel then built, was marred by an accident with the gearing drum which killed one man and injured another four. In 1898, 40 spectators were drowned by the backwash caused by the battleship H.M.S. *Albion* at her launching on the Thames.

Of course, fear of bad luck and superstition has always surrounded the sea and launchings have several of their own — some very gruesome! As a matter of fact, the bottle of wine which sends ships on their way today is a modern substitute for the blood which used to be liberally smeared on a ship's bows to ensure good luck.

The bloodshed at launchings could be even more grisly than this. When Europeans first began extensive explorations in South America, in the 16th century, and Africa in the 19th century, they were horrified to discover that tribesmen launched their war canoes on shipways consisting of human bodies. In fact, in the past, more than one slave or prisoner of war had his throat cut for the sake of sending a new vessel to sea with the blessing of the gods. Making sacrifices — human or animal — was the custom in ancient Rome whenever a ship was launched, and centuries later, the splendid Viking longships and the trading 'knorrs' were introduced to the sea in the same way.

Although the superstitions which made seafaring peoples strive to ensure good luck for their ships, even in such brutal fashion, still persist today, the launching ceremonies are more civilised now. The Japanese will make a ship launch a thing of artistic beauty. At Japanese shipyards a red and white striped cloth cage with birds inside might be suspended over the bow of a ship. As the ship starts to move down the slipway, the cage is ripped open, releasing the birds: they, in gratitude for their freedom, are supposed to make it their business to guide the ship to safety on its voyages.

It is as true today as it ever was, despite our modern technical efficiency, that the launching of a ship is an impressive ceremony, to send the ship safely on its way with those famous words, "God bless all who sail in her."

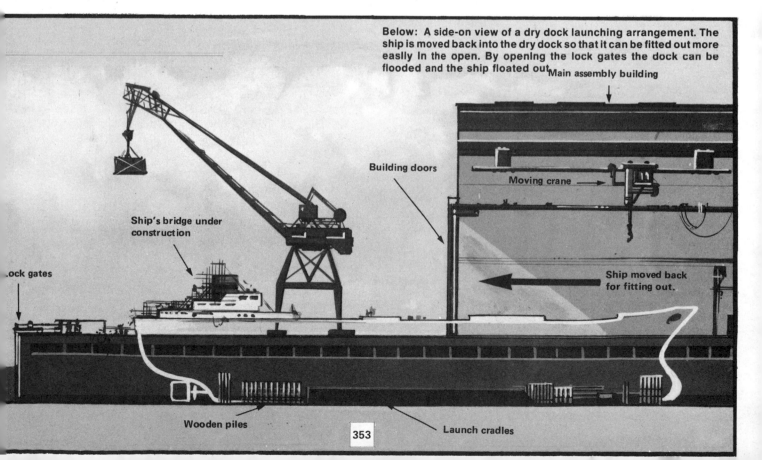

Below: A side-on view of a dry dock launching arrangement. The ship is moved back into the dry dock so that it can be fitted out more easily in the open. By opening the lock gates the dock can be flooded and the ship floated out. Main assembly building

Building doors

Moving crane

Ship's bridge under construction

Lock gates

Ship moved back for fitting out.

Wooden piles

Launch cradles

It's not a boat, it's not a plane, it's...
The ship that flies

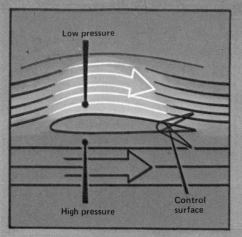

The diagram above shows the effect of water flow on a hydrofoil section, creating lift.

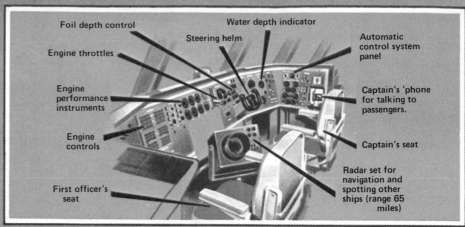

This view of the flight deck shows some of the main controls and instruments. The radar display set is mounted on a swivel so that it can be turned towards either seat.

ALTHOUGH boats float on water, it is also an obstacle. It sets up so much resistance that only by lifting the greater part of the hull clear, as with speedboats and powerboats, can really high speeds be achieved. This is the principle used by hydrofoils — the ships that fly!

They 'fly' on wings which raise the hull completely clear of the water as speed increases. These wings (or hydrofoils, which give the craft its name) are shaped like aircraft wings. They are, however, very much smaller and stronger: as water is several hundred times as dense as air, a relatively small lifting surface operating beneath the sea can provide support equal to that of a large wing in the air. Foils are normally made of such materials as high-strength steel or titanium and hulls of light alloys to reduce the amount of power needed to raise them clear of the sea.

An Italian inventor, Enrico Forlanini, is generally believed to have built the first true hydrofoil in 1898. Although it operated for several years, no details of its performance appear to survive.

It is known, however, that speeds of 80 kph (50 mph) were reached by a rival craft of the same type produced in Italy at around the same time.

Great excitement greeted the news at the end of the First World War that Alexander Graham Bell, inventor of the telephone, and a partner had set a new world water-speed record of 60 knots (109 kph - 68 mph) in a hydrofoil, the HD4, powered by two aircraft engines providing a total of 700 horse-power.

The efficiency of the HD4 was rather low, however, and while a number of new models were later produced in various parts of the world during the 1930s, it took the

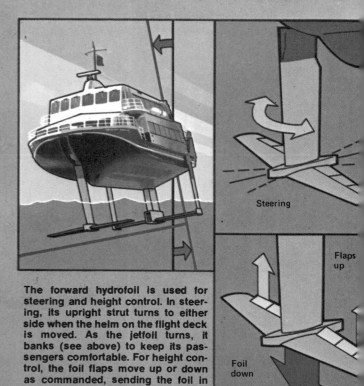

The forward hydrofoil is used for steering and height control. In steering, its upright strut turns to either side when the helm on the flight deck is moved. As the jetfoil turns, it banks (see above) to keep its passengers comfortable. For height control, the foil flaps move up or down as commanded, sending the foil in the opposite direction.

Steering

Flaps up

Foil down

For docking, the hydro are retracted. With the in the water, speeds of 24 kph (15 mph) ca reached.

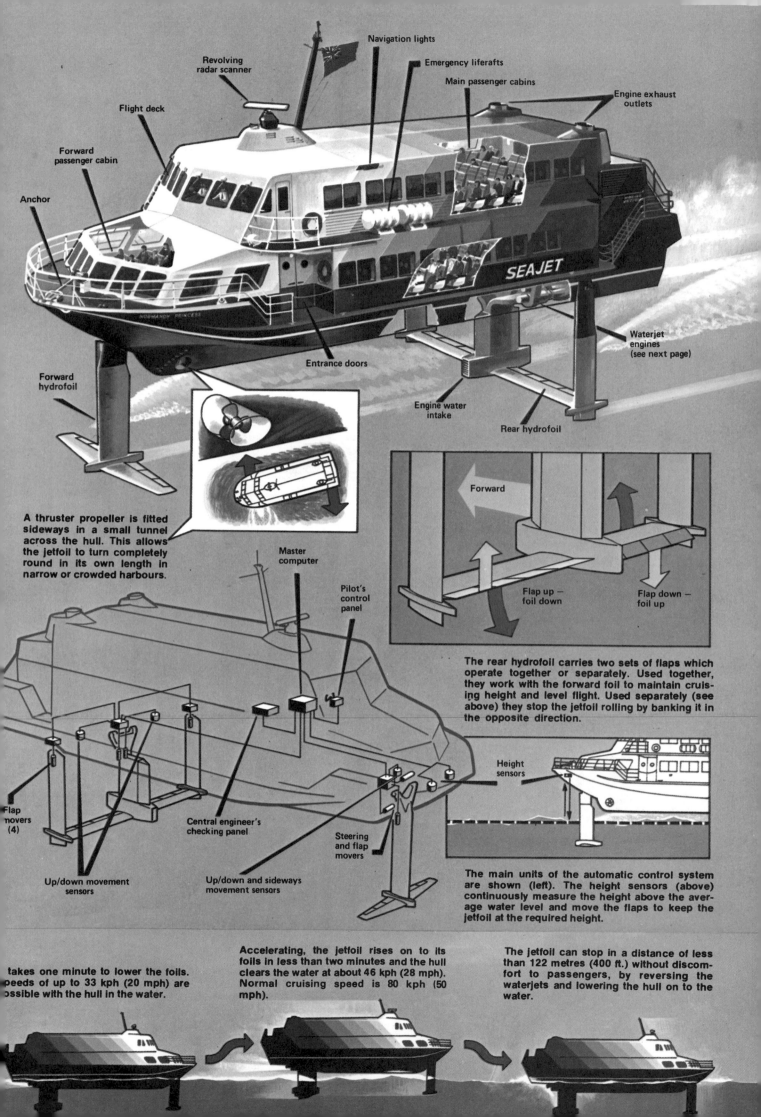

Navigation lights

Revolving radar scanner

Emergency liferafts

Main passenger cabins

Engine exhaust outlets

Flight deck

Forward passenger cabin

Anchor

SEAJET

Waterjet engines (see next page)

Forward hydrofoil

Entrance doors

Engine water intake

Rear hydrofoil

A thruster propeller is fitted sideways in a small tunnel across the hull. This allows the jetfoil to turn completely round in its own length in narrow or crowded harbours.

Master computer

Pilot's control panel

Forward

Flap up — foil down

Flap down — foil up

The rear hydrofoil carries two sets of flaps which operate together or separately. Used together, they work with the forward foil to maintain cruising height and level flight. Used separately (see above) they stop the jetfoil rolling by banking it in the opposite direction.

Flap movers (4)

Central engineer's checking panel

Steering and flap movers

Height sensors

Up/down movement sensors

Up/down and sideways movement sensors

The main units of the automatic control system are shown (left). The height sensors (above) continuously measure the height above the average water level and move the flaps to keep the jetfoil at the required height.

takes one minute to lower the foils. peeds of up to 33 kph (20 mph) are ossible with the hull in the water.

Accelerating, the jetfoil rises on to its foils in less than two minutes and the hull clears the water at about 46 kph (28 mph). Normal cruising speed is 80 kph (50 mph).

The jetfoil can stop in a distance of less than 122 metres (400 ft.) without discomfort to passengers, by reversing the waterjets and lowering the hull on to the water.

HOW THE JETFOIL HAS GROWN IN SIZE AND

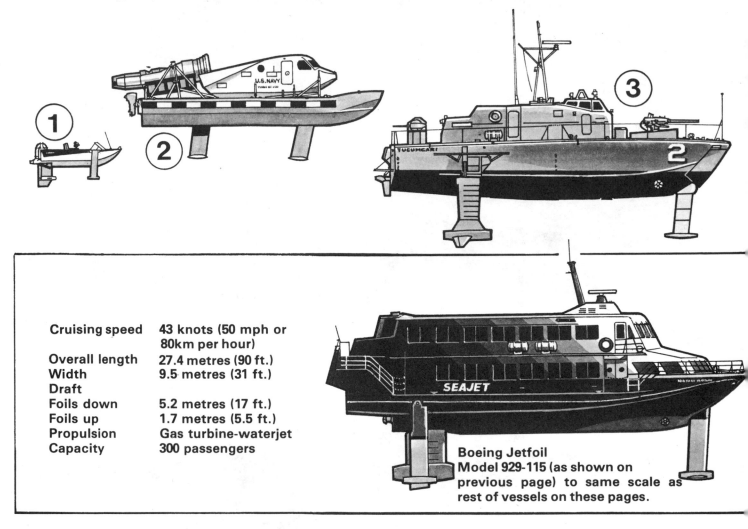

Cruising speed	43 knots (50 mph or 80km per hour)
Overall length	27.4 metres (90 ft.)
Width	9.5 metres (31 ft.)
Draft	
Foils down	5.2 metres (17 ft.)
Foils up	1.7 metres (5.5 ft.)
Propulsion	Gas turbine-waterjet
Capacity	300 passengers

Boeing Jetfoil Model 929-115 (as shown on previous page) to same scale as rest of vessels on these pages.

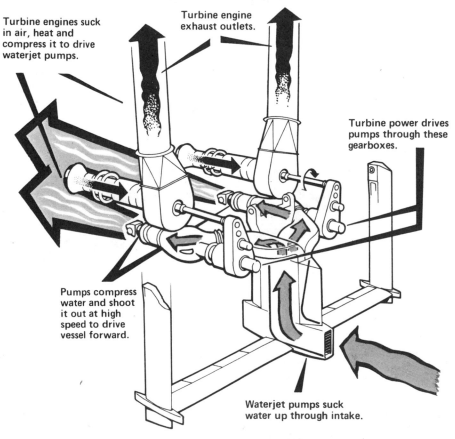

Turbine engines suck in air, heat and compress it to drive waterjet pumps.

Turbine engine exhaust outlets.

Turbine power drives pumps through these gearboxes.

Pumps compress water and shoot it out at high speed to drive vessel forward.

Waterjet pumps suck water up through intake.

The waterjet propulsion system in operation. Two identical waterjet units use a single water intake. The system works with the hull in or out of the water. It does not trail a turbulent wake behind it and produces no visible exhaust.

Below, we show how the jetfoil can move forwards or backwards by changing the direction of the waterjets.

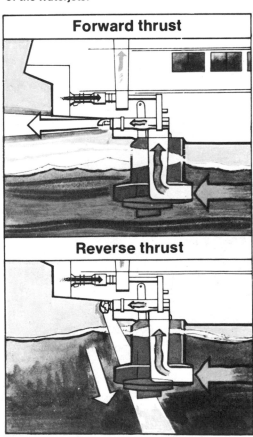

Forward thrust

Reverse thrust

RANGE OF USES

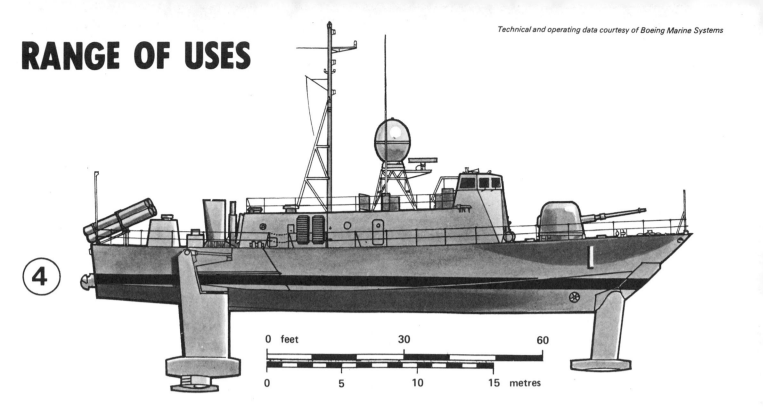

④

Some research, military and commercial members of the Boeing hydrofoil family drawn to the same scale. 1. Little Squirt was built in 1962 and gave a sensational performance for its size and power, compared with previous hydrofoils. 2. This was followed by Fresh 1 the following year. This was still a research and development vessel but from this point on, the jetfoils began to grow in size. 3. Inevitably, a naval capacity was seen in this fast stable hull and in 1968 Tucumcari appeared, armed with light automatic weapons. 4. Now NATO has a patrol hydrofoil carrying a heavier, quick-firing gun and missile projectors, supplied in 1975.

Second World War really to revive interest in the hydrofoil as a means of high-speed transport over water. Germany developed craft of up to 80 tons capable of 60 knots, but severe Allied bombing delayed experiments and production to such an extent that the craft never became operational.

One of the criticisms of hydrofoils at this stage was that they provided a bumpy ride. A surge of post-war interest in the craft, however, with experiments taking place all over the world, resulted in the early 1950s in the patenting of a sonic device to measure the distance from the bow of the ship to the water.

This information was used to control the depth of the actual foils beneath the surface. The result of this ability to 'read' the waves was a much faster and smoother ride when conditions were not ideal. Far more sensitive electronic controls have today replaced the earlier sonic devices. The Boeing Jetfoil, for instance, now in service all over the world, uses a fully-automatic, computer-controlled system to smooth its path through the waves.

Two-man operation

The jetfoil can be operated by two men, the captain and the first officer. The controls are simple. A height command lever sets the cruising height above the water, a helm (looking like an airliner's centre wheel) controls the steering and sets the course of travel, and engine throttles control the speed.

Once the crew has set all these control requirements, the automatic system's computer will keep them exactly the same as long as required.

The computer also automatically 'flies' the vessel to give the passengers a smooth ride. Precise, rapid control of movement is obtained in exactly the same way as in an aircraft, by fitting control surfaces or 'flaps' on the trailing (back) edge of the hydrofoils. If these flaps are raised, they reduce the lift of the foil and it goes down. If they are lowered, the lift is increased and the foil rises.

All movements, rolling or pitching, are detected instantly by sensitive devices called accelerometers. A message passes to the computer and at lightning speed it in turn signals the "mechanical muscles" which move the flaps to bring the jetfoil back to level flight.

If a wave begins to lift the bow (front) up, the flaps move the hydrofoils to send it down. If the side of a wave causes the vessel to begin to roll, the flaps on the rear hydrofoil move independently — up on one side to push the foil down, down on the other side to lift the foil up.

All these adjustments happen so quickly and smoothly that the result is level flight.

To turn the jetfoil or change course, the captain turns the helm which causes two control movements. The bow hydrofoil's upright strut moves to steer like a rudder and the rear hydrofoil flaps cause the vessel to bank or lean over in the same direction, as in a turning aircraft.

The twin-engine propulsion system moves the jetfoil at 80 kph (50 mph) about 3 metres (9 feet) above the waves. It works like a jet engine but uses water instead of air, sucking in water, speeding it up and putting it under great pressure so that it shoots out of the small nozzle at the stern at great speed. The power of the jet of water rushing out backwards pushes the vessel forwards. The throttles on the flight deck control the speed by changing the amount of air and fuel being used by the jet engines.

If the crew need to stop the jetfoil quickly, they pull the throttles down and automatically a cap swings down over each water jet, turning it to thrust forwards and down. This 'reverse thrust' can also be used, like backing a car out of a garage, to move the vessel backwards in a narrow harbour.

Floating on Air

Hovercraft are used for much more than just ferrying holiday-makers across the English Channel

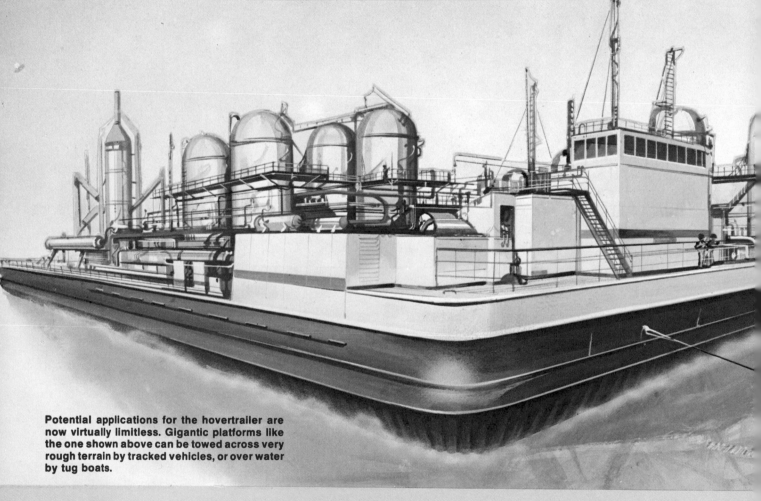

Potential applications for the hovertrailer are now virtually limitless. Gigantic platforms like the one shown above can be towed across very rough terrain by tracked vehicles, or over water by tug boats.

I N 1959, Sir Christopher Cockerell demonstrated his brainchild, the hovercraft, to the general public for the first time. With its unique ability to ride on a cushion of air just above the ground or the surface of water, the hovercraft soon proved itself to be a totally practical form of transport.

In early 1969, ten years after this momentous demonstration, a British company led by an ex-member of Cockerell's pioneering team exhibited the ACE-7, a 'hovertrailer' with a lifting capacity of seven tonnes.

The hovertrailer was a new concept, born of the realisation that a conventional hovercraft, when its pilot/passenger compartment and propulsion system have been removed, becomes an ideal vehicle for carrying heavy loads across inhospitable terrain.

Where a normal wheeled vehicle would soon become bogged down trying to cross marshland or very rocky territory, a hovertrailer merely 'floats' just above the ground with its load safely secured on top. Hovertrailers have an additional superiority over wheeled vehicles in that they can pass over meadows and farm land without making deep tracks and causing damage to crops.

Hovertrailers are of fairly straightforward construction. They usually consist of a rigid, rectangular steel platform with a sturdy sub-frame bolted beneath, to which the all-important segmented rubber 'skirt' is attached. This skirt is a feature common to all types of hovercraft and hangs below the main structure. It provides a seal between the hovercraft and the ground, preventing all but a small amount of air from the vertical lift fans from escaping.

Much larger hovertrailers are now being developed. Even huge airliners that have crash-landed can be shifted by using a number of hovertrailers simultaneously.

As can be easily imagined, towing a hovertrailer down a steep gradient by tractor or some similar vehicle could lead to problems if the hovertrailer suddenly swung to right or left. To combat this potentially dangerous situation many hovertrailers are now fitted with special wheels mounted on swinging arms attached to the rear of the platform. These pivoting wheels also assist reversing manoeuvres.

Often as unconventional as the hovertrailers themselves are the 'tugs' used to pull them. Small agricultural hovertrailers in Poland, for example, are frequently towed by horse or even by a farm labourer; while the National Research Council of Canada, anxious not to cause undue damage to vulnerable farmland, employ a Sikorsky S-55 Skycrane helicopter as a tug! The S-55 can pull the fully-laden hovertrailer along at speeds of up to 32 km/h.

Another original application for the

The wheels mounted on swinging arms attached to the rear of this hovertrailer help keep the hovertrailer under control whilst it is being towed downhill. Without them, the hovertrailer might well swing to the left or right and drag its tractor 'tug' with it. The wheels also assist reversing manoeuvres.

Hover-rigs like the one illustrated below are a very ingenious solution to the problems of establishing oil drilling facilities in geographically inhospitable territory. Power from the engines that drive the lift fans when the hover-rig is being towed is diverted to the drilling shaft when operations commence.

hovercraft principle, and one that is being used more and more in difficult territory, is the hoverborne oil rig. In the Tyumen area of Siberia in the Soviet Union are rich deposits of oil, but nearly 80 per cent of it lies beneath treacherous swamps, salt marshes and lakes. Almost impossible terrain for any kind of vehicle — except hovercraft. By 1968, the Russians had designed and built the BU-75-VP, a hovering platform weighing over 200 tonnes. It was capable of carrying a complete oil rig and supporting equipment across virtually any obstacle and proved to be the perfect solution to the problem of getting oil out of the vast Tyumen field. The power needed to lift this gigantic machine off the ground was provided by two mighty diesel engines. When the craft had been towed to a suitable drilling site, the power from these engines was diverted from the vertical lift fans to the drill-shaft in the oil derrick.

Another variation on the hovertrailer

The air-cushion goes over the ice . . .
. . . and into the sky

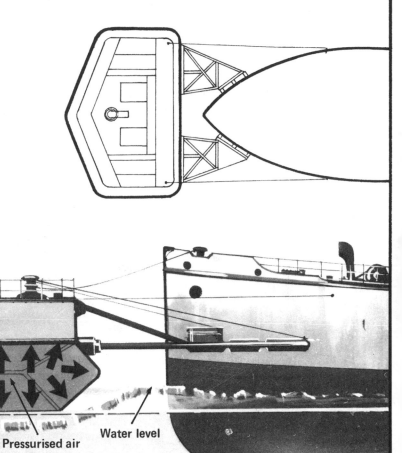

Ice sheet at water level

Depressed water level
(within skirt)

Plough blade
(vertical to disperse ice)

Pressurised air

Water level

VIBAC . . .

VIBAC (Vehicle, Ice-Breaking, Air-Cushion) is one of the most ingenious applications so far found for the air-cushion principle. Attached to the bow of a conventional ship by a sturdy metal framework, it is positioned to skim just above the water's surface. When a layer of ice is encountered, the segmented rubber skirt pushes up over the edge of the ice layer. Once inside the unit, the edge of ice is no longer supported by the water, as the powerful force of air from the VIBAC's fans have depressed the water inside the unit to a level below that of the water outside. The unsupported section of ice then breaks off and is pushed away from the ship's bow by the VIBAC's vertical plough blade.

and STOL!

The air-cushion principle may revolutionize STOL (Short Take-Off and Landing) aircraft of the future. A tubelike arrangement encircles the underside of the fuselage and emits a constant flow of air through hundreds of tiny perforations in its lower surface. The aircraft literally lands on a cushion of air which means that aircraft with such landing gear will be able to work in areas and on ground that were, up to now, totally unsuitable.

Bottom of fuselage

Fan

Trunk

Jet holes

Pressurised air

Tank

Winch

Skirt

Engine/Fan Unit

Petrol goes up again — on air!

Moving gas or petroleum storage tanks from one location to another has proved to be a relatively straightforward task when air-cushion techniques are applied. A hovercraft-style segmented rubber skirt is wrapped around the entire circumference of the storage tank at ground level. Air from a portable engine/fan unit is pumped into the skirt via flexible rubber pipes and in no time at all the storage tank is hovering just above the ground. In this state it requires very little effort to move it to its new location by means of a winch.

theme is the relatively simple technique of attaching a segmented rubber skirt around the entire circumference of large gas or petroleum storage tanks and pumping air into the skirt by means of a portable engine. When 'airborne' the storage tank can be moved to a new location.

Far out at sea, too, air-cushion technology comes into its own. Large vessels voyaging in the Polar regions frequently encounter a thick layer of ice floating on the surface of the water. Special ice-breaking ships often have to be called in to help, and this can make a voyage even more expensive than usual.

Some ships are now fitted with an incredible device known as VIBAC. These initials stand for Vehicle, Ice-Breaking, Air-Cushion, and the idea behind its operation is very simple, yet highly effective.

It operates on the same basic principle as a normal hovercraft, but because it is held firmly in position by the framework fixed to the ship's bow, it cannot ride up out of the water on a cushion of air. When the ship is not travelling through ice, the VIBAC skims just above the water's surface, so that the water immediately beneath the VIBAC unit is pushed down

below the level of the surrounding water by the powerful flow of air from its fans.

When a VIBAC-equipped vessel approaches an area of water covered with a thick layer of ice, its crew need not worry. The VIBAC's rubber skirt rides up above the edge of the ice-floe, forcing the edge down. The section of ice breaks off, to be pushed aside by a vertical deflector plough before it can come into contact with the ship's bows. At a steady speed, the ship just sails on through the ice, leaving a trail of clear water behind it.

Having made itself at home on both land and water, the air-cushion principle is now the subject of intensive study in aviation. A joint US/Canadian test programme is currently evaluating a de Havilland Buffalo STOL (Short Take-Off and Landing) aircraft modified to take-off and land on a layer of air rather than a conventional wheeled undercarriage.

This extraordinary-looking aircraft (it is known as the CC-115) has a large rubber tube resembling an inflatable life-raft encircling the underside of its fuselage. The underside of this tube is perforated with hundreds of vent holes, through which air from a compressor unit housed in the fuselage is allowed to escape.

When the CC-115 lands, it literally floats on a cushion of air, so there is no danger of conventional wheeled undercarriage units becoming bogged down in soft ground. It is thought that aircraft fitted with air-cushion landing gear will be able to operate from areas previously considered totally unsuitable for aircraft.

Medical science too is enjoying the benefits of air-cushion technology. For the treatment of patients suffering from severe burns, several hospitals are now equipped with 'hoverbeds'. In the same way that the hovercraft's rubber skirts form a seal with whatever surface is beneath it, the hoverbed has two rows of pockets which fit closely around the patient's body. A steady flow of air is then pumped into the hoverbed and leaves the patient supported solely on a cushion of air. The patient's body cannot be further injured by contact with blankets, as is normally the case, and the pocket seals automatically conform to the patient's shape if his position on the hoverbed is altered.

One wonders if Sir Christopher Cockerell ever imagined that his brainchild, the hovercraft, would yield so many offspring.

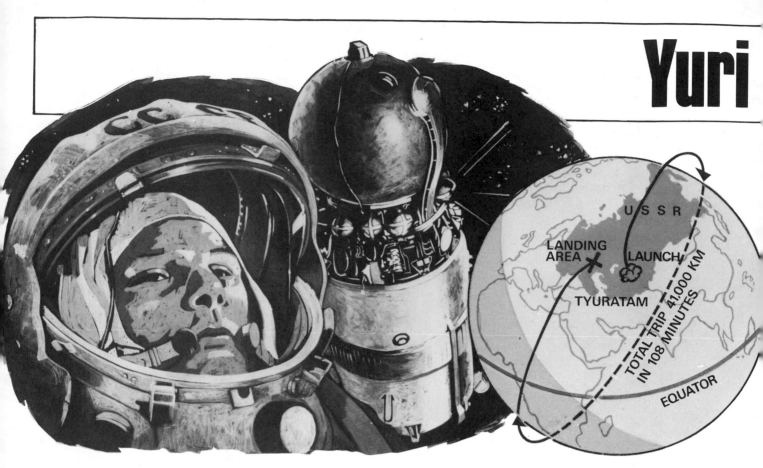

Yuri

HURTLING in orbit around Earth at 29,000 km/h was the Russian space-capsule *Vostok 1*. Inside it was a young Soviet Air Force pilot, Major Yuri Gagarin. It was April 12th, 1961, and Gagarin was about to become one of the world's most famous people. No one else could claim his special place in history — the first man to successfully orbit the planet.

Gagarin was a brave man. Nowadays, when space travel is almost commonplace, almost safe, it is difficult to appreciate the daring of those first flights.

Gagarin's flight was Russia's greatest triumph in what was known as the 'space race'. Both the U.S.S.R. and the U.S.A. vied with each other to gain the prestige which went with space pioneering. In 1961, the Russians were well ahead. And now Gagarin had successfully orbited the globe.

Gagarin was a farmer's son. He was born on, March 9th, 1934. Appropriately his favourite books when a boy had been Jules Verne's science-fiction novels. He qualified as an air force pilot in 1957, the year in which the first satellites — the *Sputniks* — were launched. And he was among the first to volunteer for training as a cosmonaut.

His great moment came on April 12th, 1961, at 7.58 a.m. (British Summer Time) when he was rocketed into space inside the *Vostok* space-capsule. *Vostok* weighed 4,725

kg. At its greatest height, it was 327 km above the Earth. The flight lasted just 108 minutes.

But although Gagarin only completed one orbit of Earth, it was an unforgettable experience. He enjoyed the weightlessness of space, sitting suspended about a metre above his seat in the capsule's cabin and watching the Earth far below through the portholes.

As *Vostok* left the Earth's shadow, Gagarin saw a breathtakingly beautiful sight. As the Earth began to be lit by the Sun, it changed from deep blue to violet, and then into all the colours of the rainbow.

Gagarin remembered that "large mountain areas, large rivers and forests, the coastlines and islands, were all easily distinguishable.

"The clouds covering the surface of the Earth could also be seen, and also the shadows of these clouds on the Earth."

At 8.25 that morning, *Vostok* started its descent back to Earth. Gagarin had been less than one hour travelling through space, but he had gone where no man had been before.

Half-an-hour later, *Vostok* parachuted back down on to Russian soil, almost precisely on its pre-arranged

He had plenty of reason to smile! Gagarin returning from visiting Britain's Prime Minister in 1961.

Gagarin – Conqueror of Space

It lasted only 108 minutes, but it was one of the most epic voyages in the history of mankind. Only the landing of American astronauts Neil Armstrong and Edwin Aldrin on the Moon's surface in July 1969, or Columbus's voyage to America, equal it. One man, Yuri Gagarin, had been flung out into Space. He was looking at the world from 300 kilometres above it — and yet he was to come back safely, one orbit later, to near where he had set off. When he landed, Space had been conquered.

landing spot. A few minutes later, Gagarin stepped out to be greeted by a peasant woman, with her small grand-daughter. They had watched the space-capsule coming down. They were the first people on Earth to greet the first man from Space.

Few men have ever received such worldwide adulation as Gagarin did after his space triumph. The Russian government awarded him many honours, including Hero of The Soviet Union, the Order of Lenin and also the newly-minted medal of Pilot Cosmonaut of the Soviet Union.

Wherever he went, Yuri Gagarin received a hero's welcome. Crowds surrounded him, everybody wishing to speak to him, to shake his hand, to hug him. He was invited to visit Britain, where he dined with the Queen at Buckingham Palace. Many other countries also wanted to honour the modest young man who had become one of the truly great pioneers of the 20th century.

Later, he became Commander of the Soviet Cosmonauts' Detachment and played a key role in training and preparing other pilots for space projects. But he never travelled in space again.

On March 28, 1968, Russia's hero of heroes died a heroic death at the controls of a MIG-15 fighter plane.

Both Gagarin and his co-pilot, Colonel Vladimir Seryogin, could have saved themselves by ejecting

A hero's welcome. Soviet Premier Kruschev greets Gagarin at Moscow airport after his epic-making orbit of the world.

from the crippled plane. But it was hurtling down from the skies towards a group of Russian villages. Both pilots remained with the fighter, wrestling with the controls so that it swept clear of the houses and schools before crashing into open country.

A hero's welcome. Part of the huge banner-carrying crowd that also turned out at Moscow airport to welcome Gagarin.

Gagarin landed in a field in the Saratov region of Russia. A simple pole was erected to mark the exact spot where *Vostok* parachuted down.

How the first man was . . .

Launched into Orbit

Nose cone (protects Salyut during flight through atmosphere)

Transfer compartment

Escape system hatch

Third stage mounting

Vernier engines

Nozzle of upper stage engine

Liquid oxygen tank

Command module Soyuz spaceship

Liquid oxygen tank

Escape system

Cruciform booster link

Adjustable fin (for auxiliary course correction in the atmosphere)

Third stage

Second stage

First stage

Exhaust RD-108 engine (second, central, stage)

Vernier engine

RD-107 first stage rocket (four of these, which together form the first stage)

The Vostok Rocket

The Russian engineers adapted the same basic design of their *Vostok* and *Soyuz* launcher to produce a whole family of booster rockets for launching their manned and unmanned spacecraft.

The basic launching vehicle is a central core booster with four conical boosters strapped to it. To produce the added power needed for the *Vostok* space programme, the central sustainer booster was lengthened to give greater fuel capacity. The third stage was attached by a light but strong interstage tubular framework.

In operation, *Vostok* lifts off with all of its lower booster motors and vernier steering motors firing. A total of 32 in all; every one of which must fire at the same time. When the strap-on boosters are exhausted they are jettisoned, leaving the sustainer core to carry on. This is in turn jettisoned, when exhausted, leaving the third stage to inject the spacecraft into orbit. Steering corrections on the spacecraft are then made by four small vernier engines.

Vostok 1 had a total thrust power of all its stages of over 600,000kg.

IT can be said that the Space Age began in 1957, when the Russians sent their satellite, *Sputnik 1*, into Space, putting them decisively ahead in the 'Space Race' with the Americans.

It was a race which had begun as far back as the years immediately preceding World War II, when the Russians had started working in the field of rocketry, which led to the creation of their famous Stalin Organ, a mobile rocket battery which caused havoc among the German lines.

Already far ahead of anyone in this field (including the Germans) the Russians, nevertheless, did not make any further major advancements in the field of rocketry until after the war, when, like the Americans, they began using German scientists and technicians to assist them in their work.

However, the work which the Germans did for them did not play a decisive part in the Russian Space programme. Eventually sending the Germans home, the Russians began working alone, developing a series of rockets of fairly low capacity. Realising that they would need more powerful engines in their rockets if they were to use them on a larger scale, they began developing mammoth engines which would give them the necessary thrust to take them into hitherto unexplored areas of Space.

The turning point came in 1957, when the Russians announced they were about to launch into Space a satellite, much to the dismay of the Americans, whose own Space programme was now running far behind that of the Russians.

On October 4, 1957, the Russians launched their satellite, *Sputnik 1*. The era of Space exploration had begun.

Within a month, the Russians had launched their *Sputnik 2*, an event which created a sensation around the world, for emotional, rather than technical reasons. The reason for the furore was that enclosed within *Sputnik 2* was a dog named Laika, whose survival in Space became a matter for concern to all animal lovers, the world over. As it happened, there was no chance of Laika surviving the trip, and after 10 days, she died from lack of oxygen. Scientifically, the loss had been justified, for she proved for the first time that a living vertebrate could survive, at least for a while, in Space.

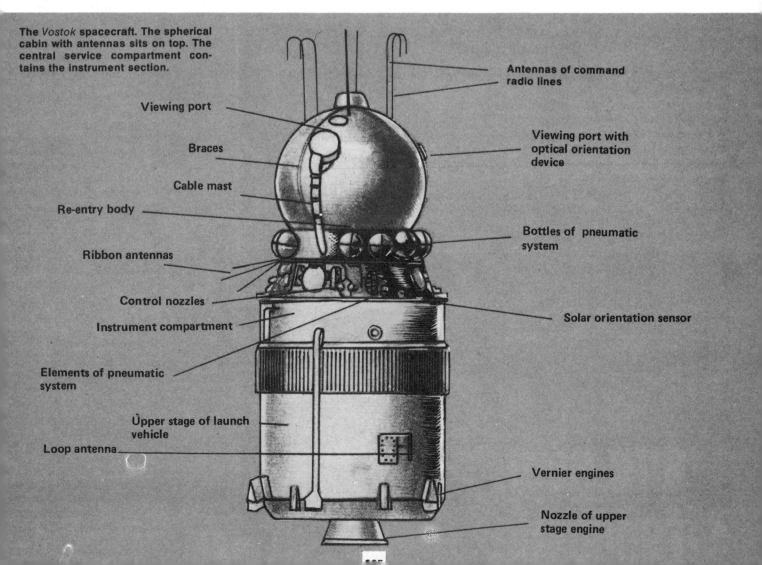

The *Vostok* spacecraft. The spherical cabin with antennas sits on top. The central service compartment contains the instrument section.

Viewing port

Braces

Cable mast

Re-entry body

Ribbon antennas

Control nozzles

Instrument compartment

Elements of pneumatic system

Upper stage of launch vehicle

Loop antenna

Antennas of command radio lines

Viewing port with optical orientation device

Bottles of pneumatic system

Solar orientation sensor

Vernier engines

Nozzle of upper stage engine

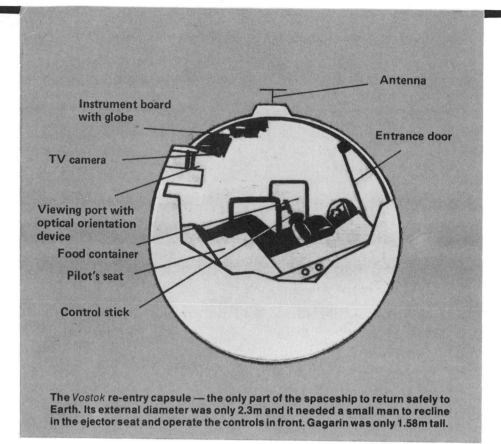

The *Vostok* re-entry capsule — the only part of the spaceship to return safely to Earth. Its external diameter was only 2.3m and it needed a small man to recline in the ejector seat and operate the controls in front. Gagarin was only 1.58m tall.

Labels: Antenna · Instrument board with globe · TV camera · Entrance door · Viewing port with optical orientation device · Food container · Pilot's seat · Control stick

Now thoroughly in their stride, the Russians launched their *Sputnik 3*, which stayed in Space for 691 days, before it burned up on April 6, 1960 on its re-entry into the atmosphere, after having circled the Earth 10,037 times.

The following month, the *Sputnik-Spacecraft 1* was launched. This had a recovereable capsule, containing a dummy astronaut. To the Russians' disappointment, it burned up after 844 days in Space.

The *Sputnik-Spaceship 2*, which was launched the same year, with two dogs, Belka and Strelka, as well as a number of rats and mice, survived, and its living cargo emerged in a satisfactory state of health, after being in Space for 25 hours.

Now, as far as the Russians were concerned, the time had come to take a giant step into Space, by launching a rocket containing a man.

The rocket the Russians had designed for Man to conquer Space was the *Vostok 1*, a 4.75 tonne spacecraft, which had an automatic guidance system as well as manual control. It was the ultimate spacecraft to date in the Soviet space marathon.

The story of the first *Vostok* flight began at dawn on April 12, 1961, when a young air force pilot named Yuri Gagarin (see page 362 of this book), was awakened by the physician who had monitored his health from the time he had been chosen to make the flight. After a breakfast of meat paste, marmalade and coffee, he was given a series of medical examinations, while the technicians were busy checking out the instruments that would transmit information about his bodily condition throughout the flight.

Finally, at 7 a.m. Moscow time, Gagarin made his way up to the assembly platform, where he took a brief farewell of all those who had come to see him. With a final wave, he disappeared into the capsule.

The spaceship was hermetically sealed, and a few minutes later, Gagarin's voice was heard in control centre, as he checked out his instrument panels. Finally, he announced he was ready for take-off.

Would the *Vostok* launch occur without mishap? And, if it did, would Gagarin be able to withstand the weightlessness to which he would be subjected once he had gone into orbit?

Both these questions were soon answered. The *Vostok* rose effortlessly and soared steadily into the upper atmosphere. Inside the capsule, in the head of the rocket, Gagarin has already adjusted himself to his feeling of weightlessness. He recalled afterwards that he had the feeling he was hanging somewhere in the air, while such unsecured objects as his atlas, pencil and notebook floated around him.

Gagarin's flight lasted only 108 minutes while he made a single orbit around the Earth. Finally, at 10.25 a.m. the Vostok's retro rockets were fired over Africa. Half an hour later, the capsule landed with the aid of a large parachute, near Saratov, on the banks of the Volga.

FACTS ABOUT THE FIRST FIVE SPACE FLIGHTS

DATE	CRAFT	COUNTRY	SPACEMAN	NUMBER OF ORBITS AND TIME	POINTS OF INTEREST
12th April, 1961	Vostok 1	USSR	Yuri Gagarin	1; 108 minutes	First man in space
5th May, 1961	Freedom 7	USA	Alan Shepard	Sub-orbital; 15 minutes 22 seconds	First to 'fly' his craft
21st July, 1961	Liberty Bell 7	USA	Virgil Grissom	Sub-orbital; 15 minutes 31 seconds	Rescued after capsule sank
6th August, 1961	Vostok 2	USSR	Gherman Titov	17; 25 hours 18 minutes	First to spend a day in space
20th February, 1962	Friendship 7	USA	John Glenn	3; 4 hours 55 minutes 23 seconds	First American in full orbit

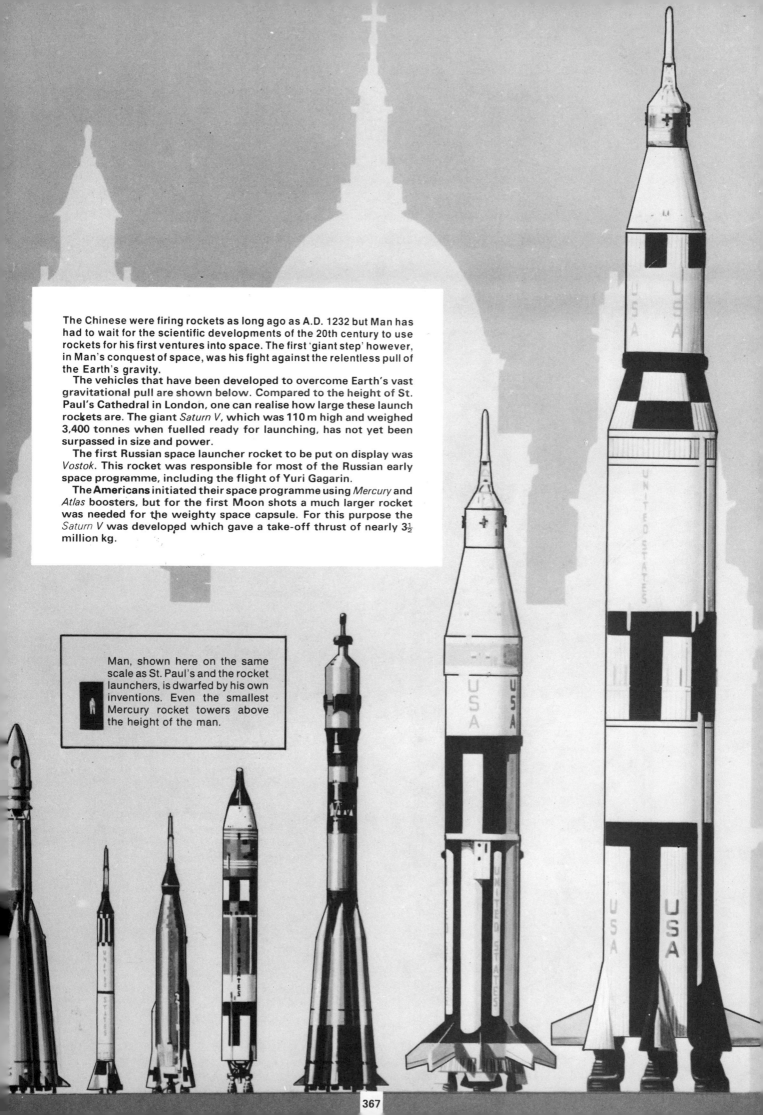

The Chinese were firing rockets as long ago as A.D. 1232 but Man has had to wait for the scientific developments of the 20th century to use rockets for his first ventures into space. The first 'giant step' however, in Man's conquest of space, was his fight against the relentless pull of the Earth's gravity.

The vehicles that have been developed to overcome Earth's vast gravitational pull are shown below. Compared to the height of St. Paul's Cathedral in London, one can realise how large these launch rockets are. The giant *Saturn V*, which was 110 m high and weighed 3,400 tonnes when fuelled ready for launching, has not yet been surpassed in size and power.

The first Russian space launcher rocket to be put on display was *Vostok*. This rocket was responsible for most of the Russian early space programme, including the flight of Yuri Gagarin.

The **Americans** initiated their space programme using *Mercury* and *Atlas* boosters, but for the first Moon shots a much larger rocket was needed for the weighty space capsule. For this purpose the *Saturn V* was developed which gave a take-off thrust of nearly $3\frac{1}{2}$ million kg.

Man, shown here on the same scale as St. Paul's and the rocket launchers, is dwarfed by his own inventions. Even the smallest Mercury rocket towers above the height of the man.

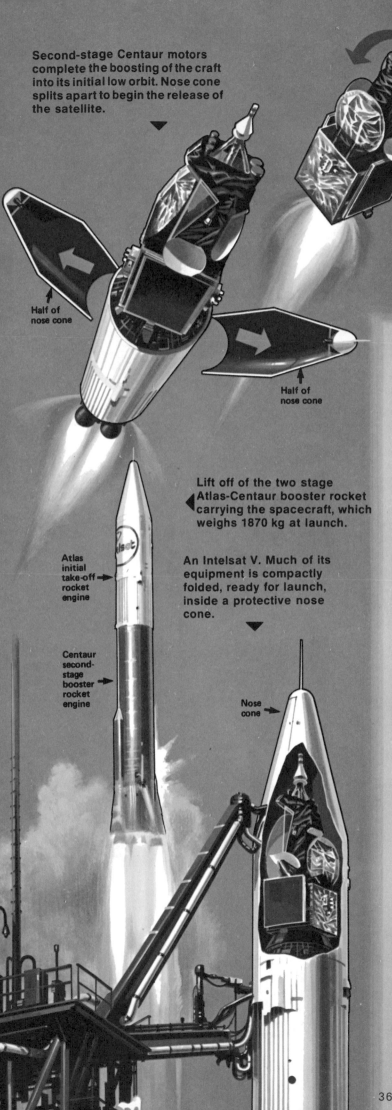

Second-stage Centaur motors complete the boosting of the craft into its initial low orbit. Nose cone splits apart to begin the release of the satellite.

Half of nose cone

Half of nose cone

Spacecraft is spun in order to stabilise it and its own rocket motor is fired to put it into orbit.

In final orbit, spacecraft is despun and its solar panels are extended, followed by its antennas.

Lift off of the two stage Atlas-Centaur booster rocket carrying the spacecraft, which weighs 1870 kg at launch.

Atlas initial take-off rocket engine

An Intelsat V. Much of its equipment is compactly folded, ready for launch, inside a protective nose cone.

Centaur second-stage booster rocket engine

Nose cone

"LIVE VIA SATELLITE" — when you see the winning goal in a football match in South America, it comes to you from a complex robot nearly 36,000 kilometres out in space

Voices

WITH three blinding sheets of white flame flashing from its main engines, the Atlas-Centaur booster rocket thrusts upwards from its launching pad at Cape Canaveral in Florida, U.S.A. Inside the pointed nose cone is a very special satellite — one of the new Intelsat V series designed to meet the ever-growing demand for telephone and television communications between nations thousands of kilometres apart.

As the Atlas rocket burns out high above the Atlantic Ocean, it separates automatically from the Centaur second stage whose engines ignite to continue the precisely programmed path into orbit. 55 km above the Earth the nose cone splits off and, as the vehicle drifts over Africa, powerful springs are released to push the Intelsat V clear of the dead rocket. The satellite is now "parked" in transfer orbit: it has only just begun the journey to its final position. The controllers on the ground start a long series of tests to ensure that, despite months of testing on the ground beforehand, the satellite is ready for its task. When they are satisfied, the controllers send a series of instructions. First, to stabilise the craft, they fire tiny thrusters on its side to set it spinning at high speed, so that, like a top, it will remain upright. Next, they fire the rocket motor built into its base for placing it in a high circular orbit precisely 35,780 km above the equator. At this very special distance, the movement of the satellite will exactly match the rotation of the Earth and so it will be in effect stationary over one spot. This 'geostationary' orbit is the one from which most communications satellites (comsats) operate.

When the final motor is fired, the spinning craft curves far out into outer space and, having reached its desired position, is commanded to 'despin' (stop spinning) and to unfold its dish-shaped antennas and the long solar panels which will provide its own electrical power supply.

The Intelsat V design is the latest group of spacecraft developed for Intelsat (The International Telecommunications Satellite Organisation), which was created on

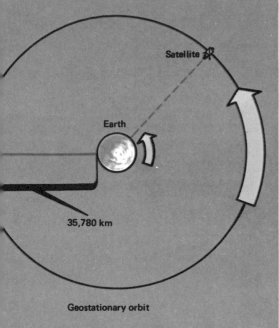

Geostationary orbit

Satellite

Earth

35,780 km

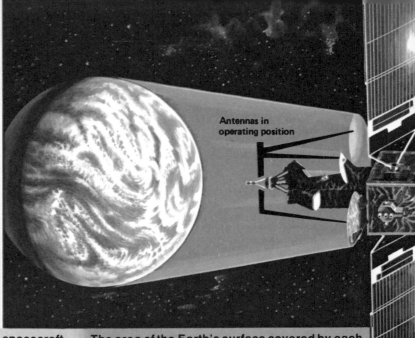

Antennas in operating position

Above: The geostationary orbit in which a spacecraft matches the rotation of the Earth and remains over the same point. Above right: an Intelsat V in orbit, with its antennas folded down to receive and re-transmit telephone, telex and TV signals.

The area of the Earth's surface covered by each of three Intelsat Vs is shown below. Placed over the great oceans, they link the continents on either side. The antennas and internal electronic equipment are arranged to provide the three types of signal shown below.

rom space

August 20, 1964, following an agreement by 11 nations to establish a global commercial satellite system. Today, this organisation has grown to a vast network comprising 224 Earth stations with 274 ground antennas in 125 countries, territories and possessions. Intelsat Vs will join the existing orbiting comsats throughout the early 1980s. Later ones are to be launched by the European space rocket Ariane and by the American Space Shuttle system.

From its position out in space the Intelsat V can 'see' and 'be seen' by about one third of the world's surface and can receive and transmit from and to anywhere that has a ground station. The shapes of its antennas are designed to collect and focus each signal as it comes in. The signal passes into the electronic systems on board and is beamed out again to the correct ground station, so that you can sit at home and watch, as it happens, say, an Olympic event or the flag-raising ceremony as a new African nation gains its independence.

The signals received by the spacecraft are amplified by its own electrical power supply and retransmitted using a different frequency. The array of antennas and the frequencies (narrow wavebands of energy) in which they operate have been designed to make maximum use of the spacecraft's equipment so that it can handle a total of 12,000 circuits (that is 12,000 separate communications of any kind, for example, telephone calls) *and* two separate

Intelsat V over Indian Ocean

Intelsat V over Atlantic Ocean

Intelsat V over Pacific Ocean

ANTENNA COVERAGE PATTERNS

Steerable spot beams (TV)

Zone antenna coverage

Hemisphere antenna coverage

Diagrams above show where communications satellites' radio signals provide coverage for most of the well-populated continents. Zone coverage concentrates on smaller areas, mainly in north. TV services are used by a few well-populated areas.

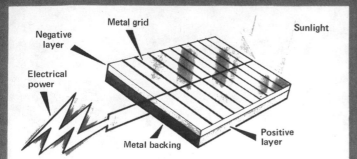

Power from sunlight is generated by the craft using thousands of tiny solar cells like the one shown above. The current is collected into the satellites' batteries through the metal grid fixed to the surface.

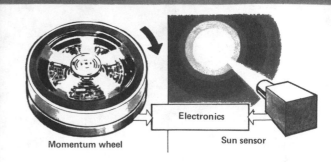

Stability in orbit is obtained using momentum wheels and sensors. Sensors designed to fix on the Sun and the infra-red heat from the Earth combine with the wheels to sense change in position and correct it.

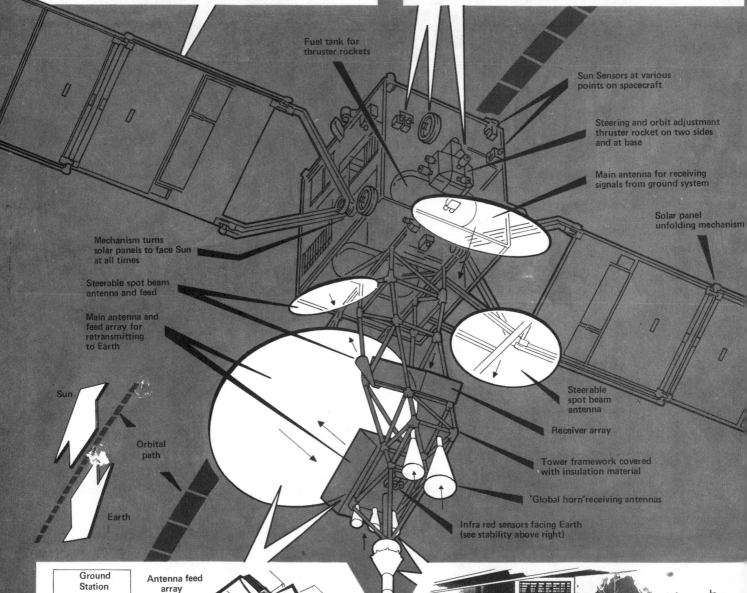

Fuel tank for thruster rockets

Sun Sensors at various points on spacecraft

Steering and orbit adjustment thruster rocket on two sides and at base

Main antenna for receiving signals from ground system

Solar panel unfolding mechanism

Mechanism turns solar panels to face Sun at all times

Steerable spot beam antenna and feed

Main antenna and feed array for retransmitting to Earth

Steerable spot beam antenna

Receiver array

Sun

Orbital path

Tower framework covered with insulation material

"Global horn" receiving antennas

Earth

Infra red sensors facing Earth (see stability above right)

Ground Station

Antenna feed array

Antenna

The antennas are shaped like shallow car headlamp reflectors. Headlamps focus light into strong, narrow beams and the antennas do the same with signals. The antennas of the ground stations in the Intelsat network, though much bigger, work in exactly the same way.

Command and control of the spacecraft is maintained from centres and smaller ground stations manned 24 hours a day. Their task is to carry out the complex switching operations necessary to keep communications "traffic" flowing smoothly and to sort out problems.

television link-ups at the same time. The electronic equipment built into the satellite can be commanded from Intelsat's control centre to connect itself internally in nearly 600 different combinations to produce this massive capacity, and because the antennas are so accurate, signals on the same frequency can be beamed at different ground stations without any danger of their being mixed.

Yet such is the constant increase in the demand for this global communications service, that work has been going on for some time on the next generation — Intelsat VI, which will join the eight Intelsat Vs already scheduled for launching throughout the early 1980s.

The remarkable man who foresaw this possibility back in 1945 was Arthur C. Clarke, the science fiction writer, who, with uncanny accuracy, wrote down and drew in diagrams almost exactly the way in which communications satellites could operate.

In 1960, two scientists at the Hughes Aircraft Company in America proposed a way to build a comsat. This idea grew into Syncom, the first experimental craft to be put into geostationary orbit. In 1965, the technology was put into Intelsat I, known as "Early Bird", and in April of that year it began carrying telephone "traffic" between Europe and North America. From then on the system grew and the scientists and engineers keep on producing bigger and better satellites to match it.

Intelsat V represents many improvements on its predecessors. One interesting difference is that all the previous craft, including those still working hard in space, are stabilised in orbit by constant spinning at high speed (hence their drum shape) with only the centre section and antennas facing Earth, whereas Intelsat Vs use the other methods described to control their positions.

Produced with the co-operation of Intelsat

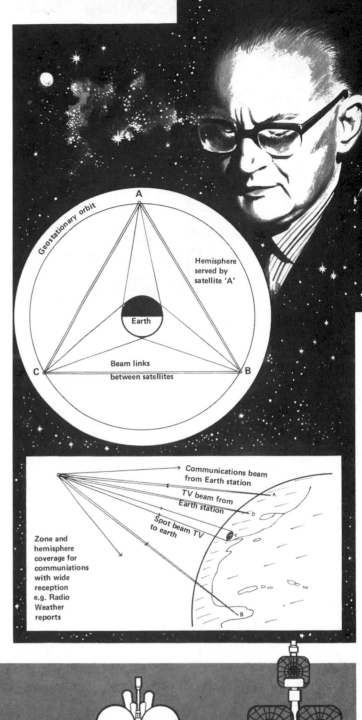

Above right: The scientist and science fiction writer, Arthur C. Clarke, with one of his diagrams (annotated by us for clarity). This shows beam links between three satellites A, B and C. The lower diagram shows coverage patterns. Below: The Intelsat family spacecraft, drawn to the same scale and shown in size relation to an average man.

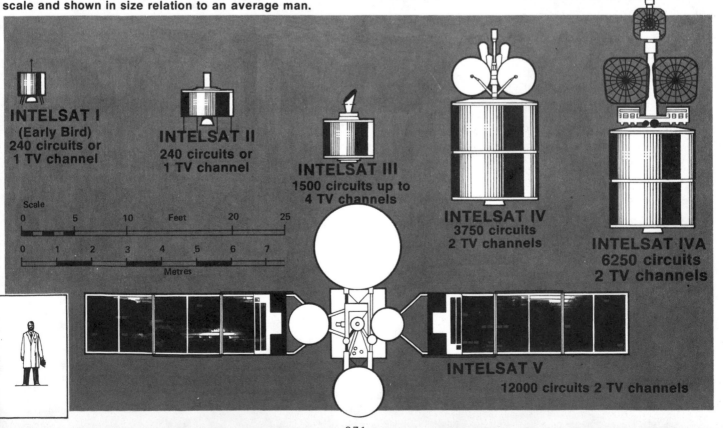

Messages from Outer Space

The *Voyager 2* spacecraft is away out in space beyond Saturn, but scientists and engineers know where it is, and can control it — How?

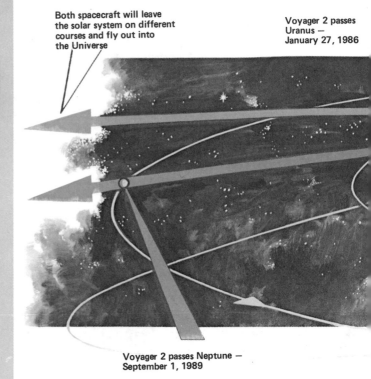

Both spacecraft will leave the solar system on different courses and fly out into the Universe

Voyager 2 passes Uranus — January 27, 1986

Voyager 2 passes Neptune — September 1, 1989

The diagram above shows past, present and future events in the *Voyager* programme, as the two craft use the pull of planet gravity to power themselves across the solar system.

70 Metre antenna

64 Metre antenna

34 Metre antenna

Signals combined and processed

Better pictures and information

Deep space tracking station

ON March 9, 1979 a young lady engineer called Linda Morabito was at work in the Jet Propulsion Laboratory in California — America's headquarters for deep space exploration. Four days before, the *Voyager 1* probe had encountered the giant planet Jupiter, and she was conducting a routine check of navigational accuracy.

Punching the computer keys she put on the TV screen *Voyager's* film of one of Jupiter's moons. Suddenly she stiffened with excitement — the film showed a great hump of brightness exploding from the surface, an active volcano shooting its plume 280 km into black space. The first active volcano ever found on another body in the Solar system!

A new Jupiter

This is just one of the discoveries that have made scientists throw out most of their theories about Jupiter and start again. The *Voyagers* show Jupiter to be a violent giant with an atmosphere constantly swirling in massive, banded storms some bigger than our planet. Its atmosphere contains particles which are hotter than the interior of the Sun, its immensely powerful radiation belt and magnetic field affect space for vast distances around it. Jupiter also has a ring around it — like the famous rings of Saturn but much fainter.

The stream of information and clear detailed colour pictures of distant planets, rings and moons was repeated as the two robots flew past Saturn. *Voyager 1* arrived in November 1980 and *Voyager 2* in August 1981. Both spacecraft sent back spectacular pictures of the giant planet and its rings as well as several hitherto unknown moons.

Left: 'Arraying', the method used to increase the power and quality of signal gathering by the giant antennas at great distances. The *Voyagers* (right, above) are sending back streams of information and spectacular pictures like the one of Jupiter illustrated.

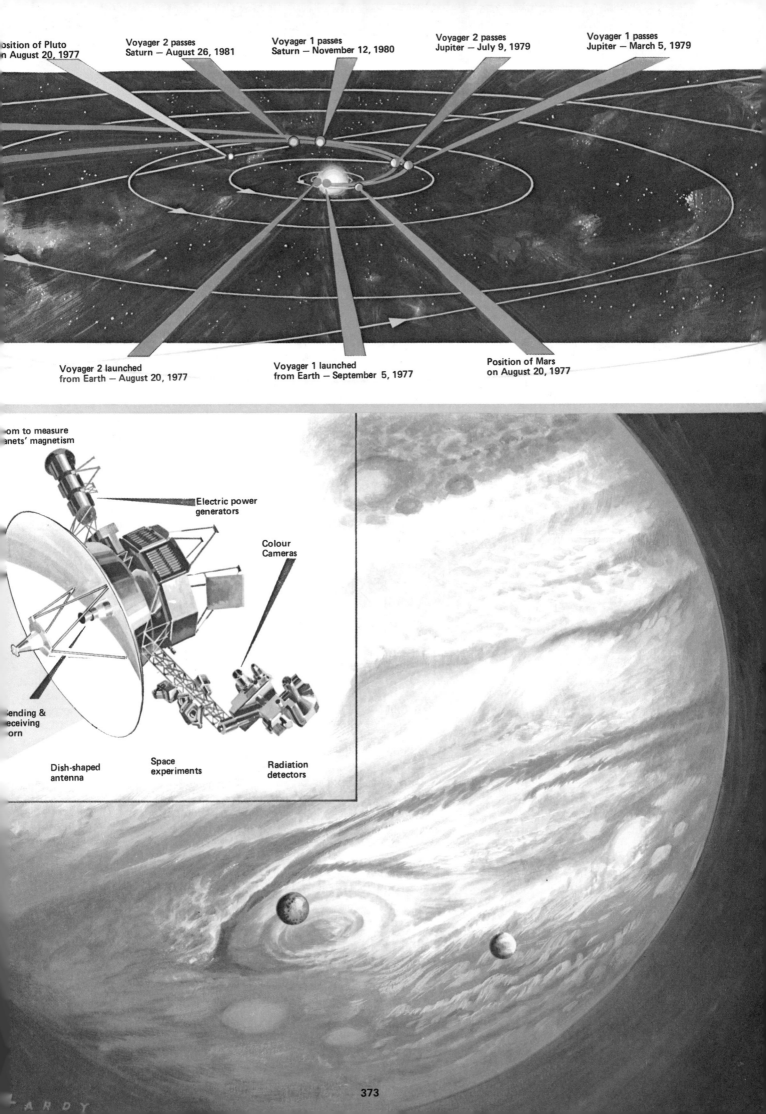

Position of Pluto on August 20, 1977

Voyager 2 passes Saturn — August 26, 1981

Voyager 1 passes Saturn — November 12, 1980

Voyager 2 passes Jupiter — July 9, 1979

Voyager 1 passes Jupiter — March 5, 1979

Voyager 2 launched from Earth — August 20, 1977

Voyager 1 launched from Earth — September 5, 1977

Position of Mars on August 20, 1977

Boom to measure planets' magnetism

Electric power generators

Colour Cameras

Sending & receiving horn

Dish-shaped antenna

Space experiments

Radiation detectors

373

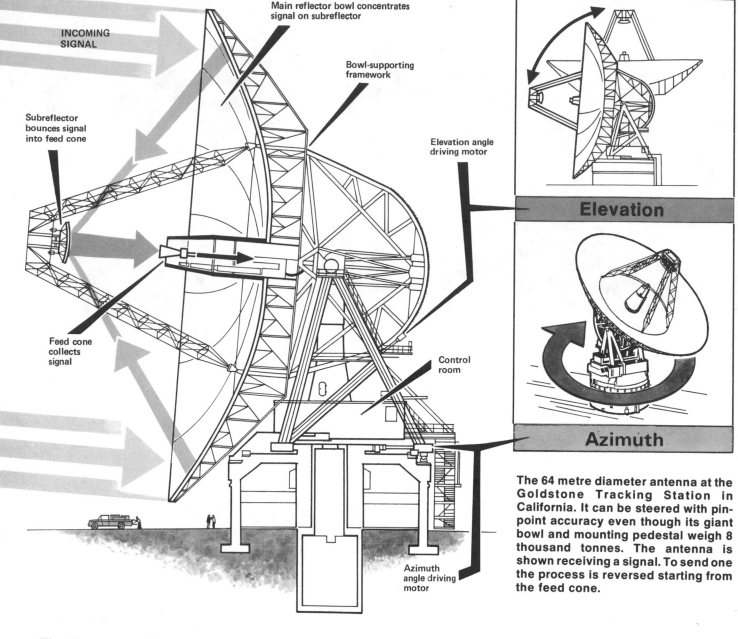

INCOMING SIGNAL

Main reflector bowl concentrates signal on subreflector

Bowl-supporting framework

Subreflector bounces signal into feed cone

Elevation angle driving motor

Elevation

Feed cone collects signal

Control room

Azimuth

Azimuth angle driving motor

The 64 metre diameter antenna at the Goldstone Tracking Station in California. It can be steered with pinpoint accuracy even though its giant bowl and mounting pedestal weigh 8 thousand tonnes. The antenna is shown receiving a signal. To send one the process is reversed starting from the feed cone.

The *Voyagers* are identical craft, weighing less than a tonne each, which were launched by rocket into space 16 days apart in 1977. *Voyager 2* was in fact launched first because its slower course would allow No. 1 to overtake it en route. Their journey across the solar system is by courtesy of gravity — the scientists set and adjust the course by allowing the pull of each planet they pass to hurl them onwards to the next destination. This is known popularly as the 'slingshot' method.

Both are equipped not only with colour cameras which

The problems for a team controlling deep space exploration probes are shown below. The further away the craft flies the longer it takes to signal a command to it and for confirmation to come back that it has been obeyed. The times shown are for the complete double journey.

produce exciting pictures but with equally important scientific instruments which measure and analyse many different aspects of the space around them and the planets they pass.

All the information we are gathering, teaching us more and more surprising things about our solar system, is transmitted back to Earth as a stream of coded signals to be interpreted by Earth-based computers. This applies also to the colour pictures which are built up from thousands of tiny pieces of colour mosaic signalled in sequence from the spacecraft's camera equipment then 'enhanced' by the computer in the same way you might adjust your TV set to get a stronger, clearer picture.

But all these signals are coming from far away in space — and the strength of the spacecraft's transmission at the 1,400 million kms distance from Saturn to Earth is about the same as the energy from a flashing light on top of an

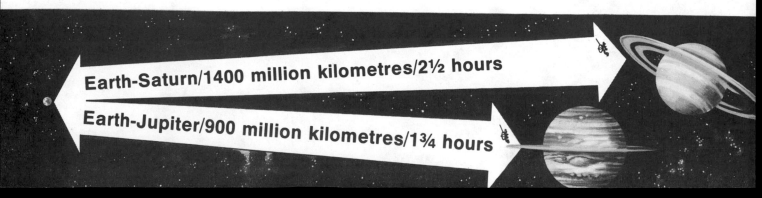

Earth-Saturn/1400 million kilometres/2½ hours

Earth-Jupiter/900 million kilometres/1¾ hours

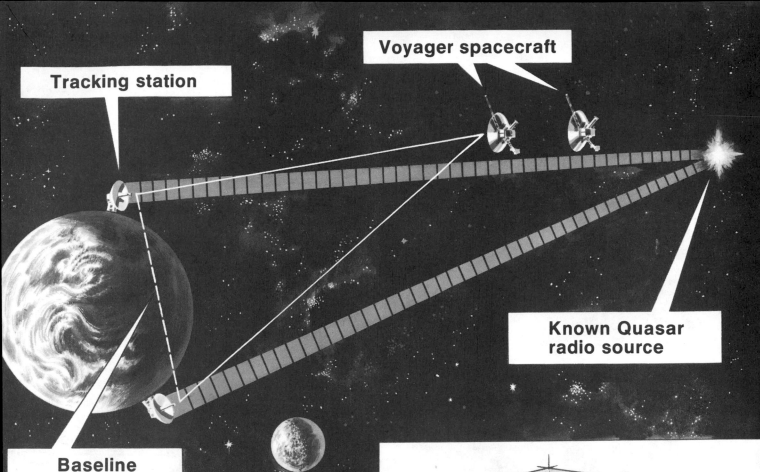

Tracking station

Voyager spacecraft

Known Quasar radio source

Baseline

60 kms

60 kms

5 kms x 5 kms

ambulance!

It's the task of the Deep Space Network of America's N.A.S.A. (National Aeronautics and Space Administration) to gather in these tiny, distant whispers from across the solar system. The giant ears which pick up the signals are the saucer-shaped antennas which, while weighing hundreds of thousands of tonnes, can be positioned at the angle required with incredible accuracy. They have also the task of transmitting from Earth the instructions necessary to operate the spacecraft.

It must be commanded, for instance, to switch its equipment on and off at the right time, to turn its cameras and instruments to face in the right direction, to fire its thrusters to make alterations to its course which are small but vital to the outcome of the mission.

Arraying

As the distance of the craft from Earth increases, more power to listen or transmit is needed so 'arraying' is used — two antennas working together to produce, in effect, a single larger one when the signals they receive are combined by computer.

To carry out the years-long 'slingshot' flights and set the spacecraft's course accurately at each stage, requires, naturally, the best possible information as to exactly where it is at any time. The system used is shown in a diagram on these pages. The astonishing accuracy achieved can be compared to fixing the position of an object over the city of Los Angeles to within 20 cm from Washington — nearly 3,700 kilometres away!

The next big probe to make the journey of discovery will be Galileo, which is due to be launched in 1986. It will carry and release on command a capsule to parachute down into the boiling cauldron of Jupiter's atmosphere — as it does so the giant antennas of the Deep Space Network will be waiting to hear, from 900 million kilometres away, what it has to tell us!

The method used to find a spacecraft's position is shown in the top illustration. Two tracking stations measure signals from the spacecraft against emissions from a radio source far out in space. Its position and distance are exactly known and from the difference in the signals and the known distance between the stations (baseline) the position is fixed within a 'box'. By 1985 the engineers hope to refine the system to improve accuracy to the dramatic extent shown above.

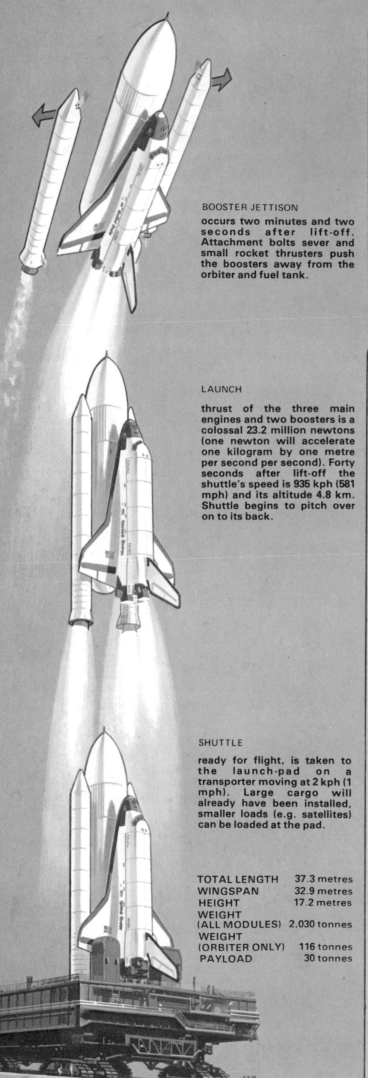

BOOSTER JETTISON

occurs two minutes and two seconds after lift-off. Attachment bolts sever and small rocket thrusters push the boosters away from the orbiter and fuel tank.

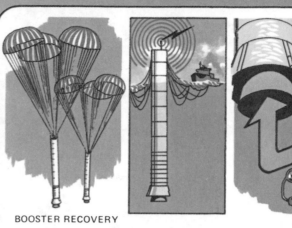

BOOSTER RECOVERY

— three 35-metre diameter parachutes lower each unit into the sea and a radio beacon then guides in the recovery ship. A remote-control plug is guided into the booster nozzle to seal it. Air is then pumped into the body and it is towed back to base for cleaning and re-filling.

LAUNCH

thrust of the three main engines and two boosters is a colossal 23.2 million newtons (one newton will accelerate one kilogram by one metre per second per second). Forty seconds after lift-off the shuttle's speed is 935 kph (581 mph) and its altitude 4.8 km. Shuttle begins to pitch over on to its back.

The Spac

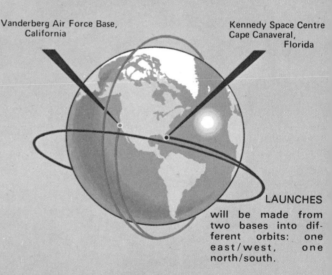

Vanderberg Air Force Base, California

Kennedy Space Centre Cape Canaveral, Florida

LAUNCHES

will be made from two bases into different orbits: one east/west, one north/south.

SHUTTLE

ready for flight, is taken to the launch-pad on a transporter moving at 2 kph (1 mph). Large cargo will already have been installed, smaller loads (e.g. satellites) can be loaded at the pad.

TOTAL LENGTH	37.3 metres
WINGSPAN	32.9 metres
HEIGHT	17.2 metres
WEIGHT (ALL MODULES)	2,030 tonnes
WEIGHT (ORBITER ONLY)	116 tonnes
PAYLOAD	30 tonnes

I t is Friday, 17th September, 1976. At United States Air force plant 42 in Palmdale, California, the crowds have gathered and the band is ready to play for a most important ceremony — the first public appearance of what could be the most significant vehicle ever seen on, or above, the face of the Earth.

Slowly the hangar doors grind back and the squat, blunt-nosed shape of the craft is trundled into the fierce Californian sunlight. And then the band strikes up and surprises the crowd. For on this day so important to the American nation, they had expected to hear the rousing patriotism of *The Star Spangled Banner*. Instead, they are treated to the lyrical chords of the theme of television's *Star Trek* science-fiction series.

Afterwards, everyone agreed that the Star Trek theme was far more appropriate, for the craft they had come to watch was the Space Shuttle, named 'Enterprise' in honour of Captain Kirk's fictional star-cruiser.

But the Shuttle programme has more in common with Star Trek then a mere name. It is a bold step into "Space — the final frontier". To understand exactly how bold it really is, we must look at the spacecraft which have preceded Shuttle — the Geminis, Apollos and Vostoks — and compare them with what was presented on that September day in California.

Previously, all ventures into Space were achieved with giant rockets which, after a certain amount of time, were directed back into the Earth's atmosphere to be reduced to a cinder by the enormous heat of re-entry — after the crew and their capsule had

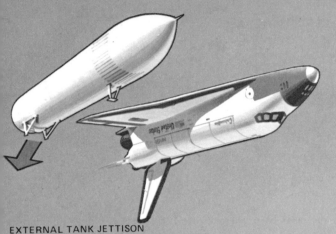

EXTERNAL TANK JETTISON
is performed at a height of 115 km, 30 seconds after the main engines have been shut down. The tank, now empty, was filled with 715 tonnes of liquid oxygen and liquid hydrogen at lift-off.

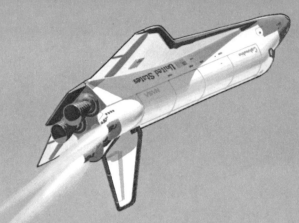

FINAL ORBIT
is achieved 9.5 minutes after lift-off using a burn of 65 seconds from two small motors. The orbitor is now over 2,000 km downrange from Cape Canaveral and moving at 26,000 kph (16,000 mph) at an altitude of 116 km.

huttle
Bold step towards the final frontier.

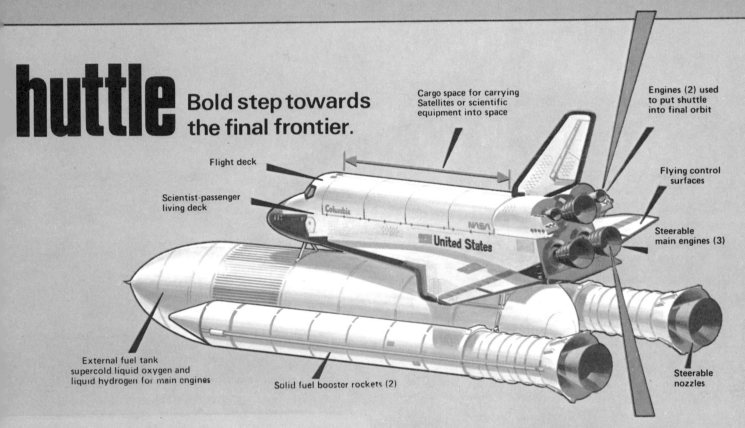

Cargo space for carrying Satellites or scientific equipment into space

Engines (2) used to put shuttle into final orbit

Flight deck

Scientist-passenger living deck

Flying control surfaces

Steerable main engines (3)

External fuel tank supercold liquid oxygen and liquid hydrogen for main engines

Solid fuel booster rockets (2)

Steerable nozzles

been ejected. Virtually all of that tremendously expensive equipment was destroyed after only one use.

The shuttle, however, to quote a National Aeronautics and Space Administration official, "Is the first craft to be launched like a rocket, haul like a truck and land like an aeroplane."

It goes into orbit round the Earth taking into Space scientists, artificial satellites, complete laboratories and equipment, then returns to its base ready to repeat the exercise time and time again.

Even the booster rockets are parachuted back to Earth for re-use. In fact, the only part of the Shuttle's system which is wasted is the external fuel tank — and there are plans under consideration to use even these as base-modules for space stations.

New manufacturing processes

But the development of such a bold new project has not come cheaply. The programme has already cost many billions of dollars and whole new manufacturing processes have had to be pioneered.

New systems in aviation electronics — *Avionics* — have been developed: Shuttle's computers can handle all her manoeuvres without human assistance, even the most hazardous re-entry. For this, the craft is rotated to present her tail towards the direction of orbit, her engines are fired to slow her speed by 440 km per hour and then, as she falls back towards the atmosphere, she is rotated back into the correct direction and attitude for re-entry.

All this is done automatically, the Shuttle's crew merely watching while the computers fly their ship for them.

MAIN ENGINES
are of a unique design, being re-usable and throttleable (power can be varied in flight). Liquid oxygen and liquid hydrogen are pumped at high pressure into partial burners and then into the main combustion chamber where they are burnt to provide thrust. The freezing hydrogen is first pumped round the hollow bell-shaped nozzle to cool it.

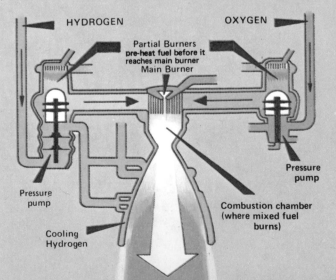

HYDROGEN OXYGEN

Partial Burners pre-heat fuel before it reaches main burner
Main Burner

Pressure pump

Pressure pump

Cooling Hydrogen

Combustion chamber (where mixed fuel burns)

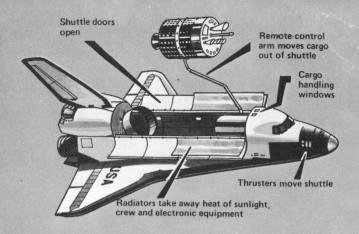

Shuttle doors open

Remote-control arm moves cargo out of shuttle

Cargo handling windows

Thrusters move shuttle

Radiators take away heat of sunlight, crew and electronic equipment

Airlock tunnel to living quarters

Scientists' working quarters

Instruments and experiments

Oxygen and power

OPERATIONS IN ORBIT

are controlled by the Mission and Payload Specialists. Above, we see a large communications satellite being placed in orbit using the mechanical arm controlled from inside the flight-deck. A satellite can be brought on board in the same way.

SPACELAB

is one of the payloads designed to fit into the Shuttle. It has been built by a group of European countries and the pallets holding the scientific experiments are designed and built in Britain. Spacelab is designed so that complete sets of instruments can be quickly changed for different flights.

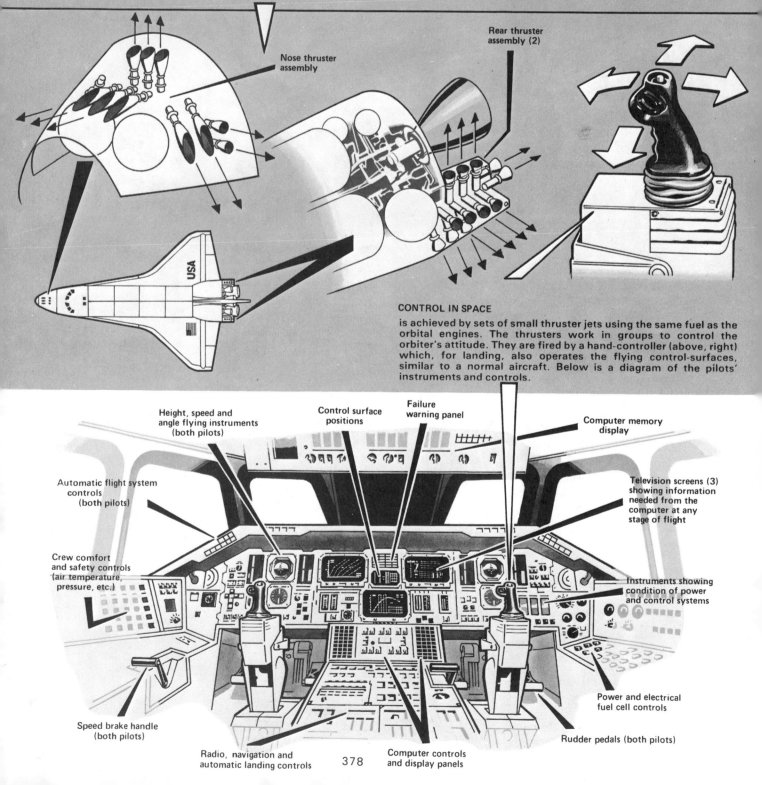

Nose thruster assembly

Rear thruster assembly (2)

USA

CONTROL IN SPACE

is achieved by sets of small thruster jets using the same fuel as the orbital engines. The thrusters work in groups to control the orbiter's attitude. They are fired by a hand-controller (above, right) which, for landing, also operates the flying control-surfaces, similar to a normal aircraft. Below is a diagram of the pilots' instruments and controls.

Height, speed and angle flying instruments (both pilots)

Control surface positions

Failure warning panel

Computer memory display

Automatic flight system controls (both pilots)

Television screens (3) showing information needed from the computer at any stage of flight

Crew comfort and safety controls (air temperature, pressure, etc.)

Instruments showing condition of power and control systems

Speed brake handle (both pilots)

Power and electrical fuel cell controls

Radio, navigation and automatic landing controls

Computer controls and display panels

Rudder pedals (both pilots)

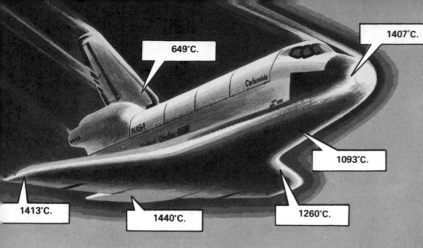

649°C.   1407°C.   1093°C.   1413°C.   1440°C.   1260°C.

RE-ENTRY

is a critical part of each mission. The orbiter enters the Earth's atmosphere at a nose-up angle of about 40°. The nose and leading edges of the wing have to endure the highest temperatures and have extra protection. The thruster jets (see below, left) are used to keep the angle exactly right.

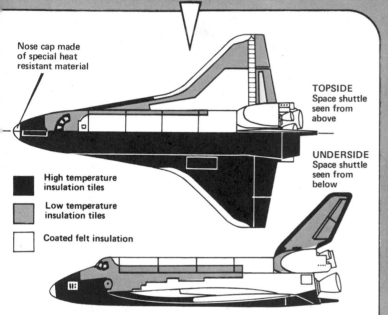

Nose cap made of special heat resistant material

TOPSIDE Space shuttle seen from above

UNDERSIDE Space shuttle seen from below

■ High temperature insulation tiles

■ Low temperature insulation tiles

□ Coated felt insulation

RE-ENTRY PROTECTION

is given by 34,000 tiles, shaped where necessary to match the craft's curved surfaces. The tiles are made from silica fibre (other materials are being studied) which can absorb intense heat without burning, melting, or allowing any heat to pass through to the surface which it protects.

The Space Shuttle Main Engine (SSME) has also been a very expensive project in itself, for it has had to be designed from scratch with capabilities never before used in a rocket motor (see illustration). There have been enormous technical problems to overcome, and it was those problems which largely contributed to the postponement of the first launch date. Initially planned for March 1979, the Space Shuttle made its first flight in April 1981 and second flight in November 1981.

Is it worthwhile?

So, have all those years of effort and billions of dollars been worth it? Some would say not, claiming that there are more pressing projects, such as the energy crisis, demanding Man's attention. But others argue that it is unwise to think only of the present and ignore the future. The Shuttle, they say, is just a tool — a tool which Man will use to make it easier, cheaper and safer than ever before to get into Space. And once in Space, he has a whole new frontier to explore — a frontier which will stimulate engineering, medicine, astronomy, almost every field of human endeavour.

One day Man may build a star-ship similar to Captain Kirk's *Enterprise.* That day lies a long, long time in the future and the Shuttle programme is the first small step towards it. We cannot tell what the first real star-ship will look like, but we'd like to hazard a guess at the tune they will play when she is rolled out of the orbital factory for the first time!

Rudder also splits open to act as speed brake

Nose and mainwheels locked down

Body flap moves to help raise or lower nose

Elevons move together to raise or lower nose, move separately each side to bank shuttle

Elevons up = nose up

LANDING

can be made automatically, monitored by the pilots. Eight minutes after re-entry, the orbiter is at a height of 77 km and its speed is 28,000 kph (17,000 mph). Its altitude and speed are gently and carefully decreased as it approaches the runway. Final approach is made at a steep angle and wheels are lowered 2 km from touchdown. Landing speed is 350 kph (217 mph).

PREPARATION

for the next flight begins immediately. Both the Cape Canaveral and Vandenberg bases are equipped with all the hardware needed to receive a shuttle, overhaul and load it, and then launch it again. The diagram below shows Canaveral's main features with the newly-built runway and overhaul buildings.

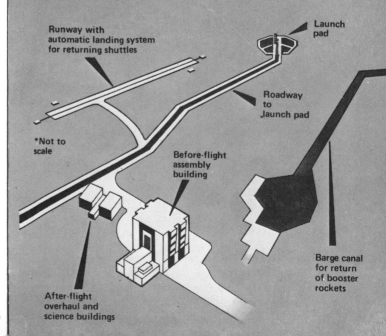

Runway with automatic landing system for returning shuttles

Launch pad

Roadway to launch pad

*Not to scale

Before-flight assembly building

Barge canal for return of booster rockets

After-flight overhaul and science buildings

Benz motor car 1889

Engines - power

MILLIONS of years ago, Nature began to store energy by creating petroleum from the decaying remains of prehistoric life. Now we have tapped this energy and put it to work in heat engines. These machines turn the heat produced by burning fuel into mechanical energy, which then produces motion. One of the best known heat engines is the *internal combustion engine* which has been driving (with few changes) all types of motor car for nearly a century.

The internal combustion engine was one of the most important inventions of the 19th century. It has had far-reaching effects ever since — revolutionising transport, and developing new industries and other types of engineering.

It's development was made possible by the earlier development of the steam engine. However, the steam engine is an *external* combustion engine because the fuel (wood, coal or petroleum) is burned outside the engine in a boiler. This produces steam which expands in a closed space (the cylinder) and pushes the engine piston.

In the internal combustion engine the fuel is burned *inside* the engine, in the combustion chamber at the top of the cylinder. The combustion is very sudden, producing an explosion which pushes the piston and very little energy is wasted.

At first inventors met with little success in designing such an engine. There were two main reasons for this: it was difficult to find a fuel which would burn without leaving ash or soot to clog the cylinder; and it was just as difficult to devise a system to set light to the fuel in a completely enclosed space.

The first reasonable successful engine was built by the French engineer J. J. Lenoir in 1859. Basically it was a modified steam engine with coal gas as fuel, but the engine suffered from high fuel consumption and low power output. Over the next few years many attempts were made to produce a more efficient design. However, it was not until 1876 that two German inventors (working separately), Nikolaus Otto and Gottlieb Daimler, came up with a solution to overcome the major design problems.

Their brilliant idea was to use a fuel that would burn very easily as a fine spray or vapour which they could ignite inside the closed cylinder by means of an electric spark. The fuel would burn without leaving soot that could

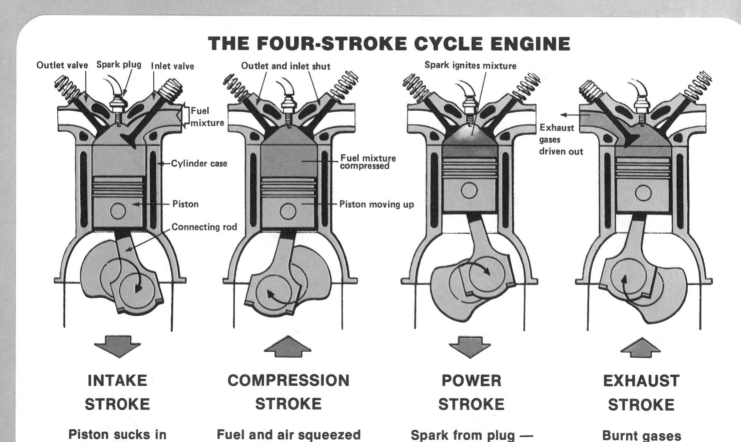

THE FOUR-STROKE CYCLE ENGINE

Outlet valve · Spark plug · Inlet valve · Fuel mixture · Cylinder case · Piston · Connecting rod

Outlet and inlet shut · Fuel mixture compressed · Piston moving up

Spark ignites mixture · Exhaust gases driven out

INTAKE STROKE
Piston sucks in fuel and air

COMPRESSION STROKE
Fuel and air squeezed to a high pressure

POWER STROKE
Spark from plug — air/fuel mixture burns

EXHAUST STROKE
Burnt gases driven off

clog the cylinder. At first they used alcohol but by 1883 had switched to petrol which was much cheaper. How your parents would wish that were the case now!

The four-stroke engine

The heart of the engine is the *piston* and *cylinder* combination. The piston slides up and down inside the cylinder which is closed at one end to form the combustion chamber. The cylinder has two valves to allow petrol and air to leave.

The piston is joined by a hinged connecting rod to the crankshaft which can only make a circular movement. As the piston moves up and down it produces a turning motion of the crankshaft and it is this spinning that turns the wheels of a car.

Most internal combustion engines, such as those in motor cars, operate on a four-stroke cycle. This is sometimes called the *Otto cycle* in honour of the German inventor. The pistons move to turn the crankshaft in a sequence of *four* operations.

Intake Stroke. During this stroke the inlet valve is open. As the piston moves downwards from the top to the bottom of the cylinder a mixture of petrol and air (rather like a fine mist) is sucked into the cylinder.

Compression Stroke. When the piston starts to move up again both valves are closed. The petrol and air mixture cannot escape so it is squeezed and compressed. The pressure of the mixture is raised.

Power Stroke. As the piston nears the top of the cylinder, a spark is generated between the points of the spark plug. This ignites the mixture which burns very quickly and the hot gases formed push the piston down like a powerful hand. This movement rotates the crankshaft.

Exhaust Stroke. As the piston starts to move back up the space above it is filled with burned gas. The exhaust valve opens and the burned gas is forced out by the moving piston.

The crankshaft turns twice to complete a cycle. Only one stroke of the cycle helps to turn the crank. The rest of the time, the crank is making the piston go up and down.

The two-stroke engine

The four-stroke cyle engine powered the first motor cars (one designed by Daimler) which ran on the road in 1886. However, the four-stroke bothered some engineers because it needed two turns of the crankshaft to produce one power stroke from the piston. This led to the design of a two-stroke cycle engine.

The two-stroke engine is quite cheap and relatively simple in design. Lightweight motor cycles, motor scooters and lawnmowers are generally powered by this type of engine. It has no valves and the induction inlet and exhaust outlet are opened and closed by the piston.

As the piston moves upwards it compresses the fuel mixture already in the cylinder and also closes the inlet

and outlet. On nearing the top of the cylinder, fuel is sucked into the vacuum created by the moving piston.

The mixture is ignited by the spark from the spark plug and the piston is pushed down by the rapidly expanding gases. This compresses the new charge of mixture into the crankcase. As the piston nears the end of its downward movement, the outlet opens and the burned gases rush

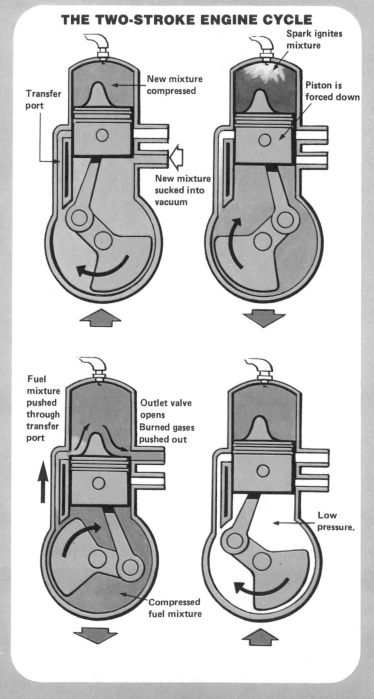

THE TWO-STROKE ENGINE CYCLE

Transfer port — New mixture compressed — New mixture sucked into vacuum

Spark ignites mixture — Piston is forced down

Fuel mixture pushed through transfer port — Compressed fuel mixture

Outlet valve opens Burned gases pushed out — Low pressure.

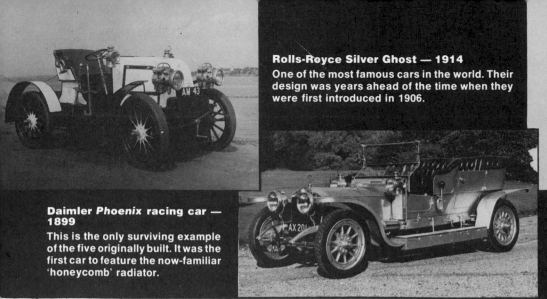

Rolls-Royce Silver Ghost — 1914
One of the most famous cars in the world. Their design was years ahead of the time when they were first introduced in 1906.

Daimler *Phoenix* racing car — 1899
This is the only surviving example of the five originally built. It was the first car to feature the now-familiar 'honeycomb' radiator.

Model T Ford — 1908
The first car to be mass-produced in a factory. Designed by Henry Ford, it was tough, easy to drive and simple to repair. It's moving assembly line was Ford's idea.

out. More fuel mixture is then pushed into the combustion chamber through the transfer port. The piston then moves up to compress the fresh mixture and begin the cycle again.

Because it delivers one power stroke for each turn of the crankshaft, the two-stroke engine will give more power than a four-stroke of the same size. However, the design is wasteful since unburned fuel is exhausted with the burned gases. This makes it only really efficient for small machines.

Internal combustion engines can have different numbers of cylinders. If there is only one cyclinder then a

flywheel is fixed to the crankshaft and as this rotates it moves the piston through all the strokes of the engine cycle except the power stroke.

But usually large engines have four cylinders or more. The four strokes (exhaust, intake, compression and power) take place after each other in each different cylinder. For instance, when the intake stroke takes place in the first cylinder, compression is taking place in the second, the exhaust in the third, and the power stroke in the fourth cylinder. In this way there is always a power stroke in one cylinder to rotate the crankshaft and keep the pistons in the other cylinders moving.

The carburettor — vital part of the internal combustion engine

One of the most important parts of the internal combustion engine is the *carburettor*. It is this piece of equipment which mixes the air and petrol vapour before it passes through the inlet valve and into the engine. The mixing must be very efficient to give a smooth ignition.

The carburettor is attached to a float chamber which controls the supply of petrol from the main fuel tank. It works by means of the suction produced by the pistons moving downwards in the cylinders.

The petrol is fed through the air intake or the carburettor and this helps to atomize the fuel (break it up into very small droplets). To get the correct petrol-air mixture, the amount of fuel fed into the airstream is controlled through

a narrow neck called a *venturi* or choke.

How much mixture is allowed into the engine is controlled by a *butterfly valve* (also known as a throttle). When this is opened by pressing down on the car's accelerator pedal a large amount of mixture is sucked into the cylinder. With less pressure on the accelerator less mixture gets through, so effectively the valve controls the speed at which the engine runs.

The carburettor was invented by the English engineer Edward Butler in 1884. A simple but very efficient device, it ensures that fuel reaches the engine and power is obtained even when the car has to defy cold winter mornings to start.

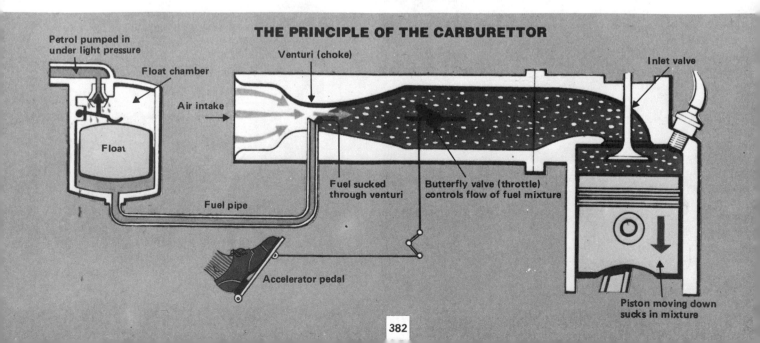

THE PRINCIPLE OF THE CARBURETTOR

Petrol pumped in under light pressure

Float chamber

Venturi (choke)

Inlet valve

Air intake

Float

Fuel pipe

Fuel sucked through venturi

Butterfly valve (throttle) controls flow of fuel mixture

Accelerator pedal

Piston moving down sucks in mixture

Morris Oxford — 1920
With its familiar bullnosed shape, perhaps the most famous Morris car. William Morris introduced Ford's mass-production ideas to Britain in 1912.

Austin Mini Cooper — 1960
Better known as the 'Mini' and designed by Alec Issigonis in 1959. With the engine across the car, rather than pointing ahead, it was spacious but not lengthly.

Rolls-Royce Silver Ghost II — 1978
Continuing the tradition of superb quality in Rolls-Royce motor cars, their great expense is understandable in view of the high workmanship involved.

THE WANKEL ENGINE

After the four-stoke cycle engine came the two-stroke cycle engine. This first took to the road in 1888 but it was not until 1957 that there was a really new development in petrol engine design.

This came about with the *Wankel rotary engine* invented by Dr. Felix Wankel in Germany. He noticed that there was a loss of power in converting the up-and-down movements of the piston into the rotary movement of the crankshaft. He designed a triangular rotor to fit inside a combustion chamber. This rotates around a fixed gear joined to an output shaft which is linked to the craft.

The idea of a rotary engine was not new but Wankel's proposal of combining the triangular rotor with the surrounding casing was very original. It meant that the arrangement could be used to produce the normal four-stroke cycle of intake, compression, power and exhaust.

As the rotor moves round this causes fuel mixture to be sucked from the carburettor and through the inlet valve. The rotor continues to turn and the space between the rotor and the wall of the combustion chamber gets smaller. This compresses the fuel mixture.

Ignition occurs when the spark plug fires and the expanding gases drive the rotor round. The final phase of one sequence occurs with the exhaust of the burned gases through the exhaust valve.

The Wankel engine reduces power loss, has fewer moving parts than other engines and because it rotates it runs more smoothly. However, the engine has had pollution control problems and the combustion chamber has proved hard to seal.

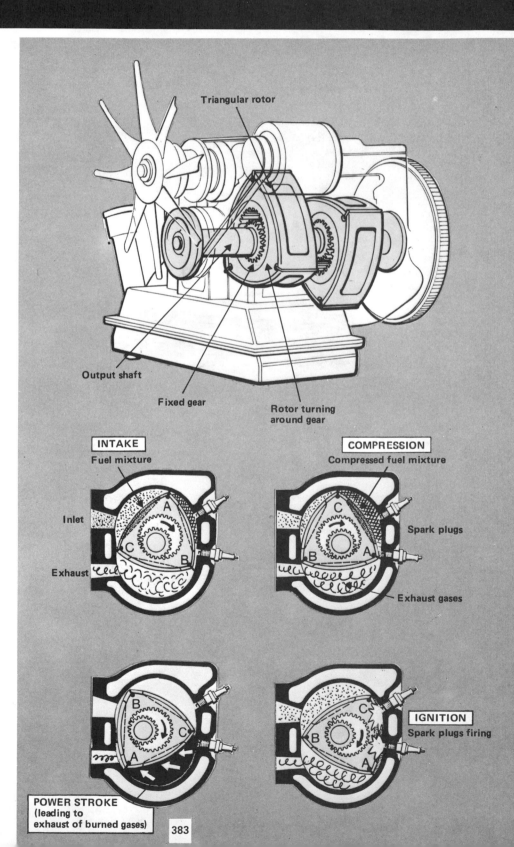

Triangular rotor

Output shaft

Fixed gear

Rotor turning around gear

INTAKE
Fuel mixture
Inlet
Exhaust

COMPRESSION
Compressed fuel mixture
Spark plugs
Exhaust gases

POWER STROKE
(leading to exhaust of burned gases)

IGNITION
Spark plugs firing

He gave us the motor cycle

On two wheels or four, on land or on water, the name of Gottleib Daimler was never far from the fore in those early pioneering days of transport.

THE petrol-powered motor car, motor boat and motor cycle were all invented just under a century ago. As with most inventions, no one man can be given complete credit for them, yet this astonishing sequence of engineering advances was more due to one extraordinary pioneer than any other. His name was Gottlieb Daimler.

Before the 1880s, there had been powered transport on the roads, the power being steam. As long ago as 1769 a

French engineer named Nicolas Cugnot had developed a self-propelled artillery tractor that had a steam engine. Steamers, as they were sometimes called, were widely used throughout Europe in the early 19th century.

In 1863 Etienne Lenoir, a French engineer, built an engine which ran not on steam but on gas. Another important change was that the burning or combustion took place inside the engine unlike the steam engine where it took place out-

Gottlieb Daimler

Daimler and his friend Wilhelm Maybech worked together to develop the first petrol-fuelled motor cycle.

side. Lenoir was working on the prototype of the internal combustion engine, which is far and away the most usual form of car propulsion today. It was left to a German, Nickolaus Otto, to build the first practical internal combustion engine in 1876, Daimler was to continue work on this project.

Daimler had been born near Stuttgart in Germany in 1834. He went to a technical school then became a gunsmith's apprentice. After more study and a spell in a steam engine factory, he visited Britain and France to study new engineering methods. He grasped the need for a small low-powered engine and when he was in France he saw the one designed by Etienne Lenoir.

Chief Engineer

Daimler returned home and, in 1872, he became chief engineer of Garmotoren-Fabrik in Deutz and, with Otto and another German, Eugen Langen, worked on Otto's famous engine and other projects. Then, in 1882, he started his own works in Stuttgart with his friend Wilhelm Maybach, their great objective being a petrol-powered internal combustion engine which was both high speed and lightweight. Held back at first by ignition problems the pair at last achieved a good self-firing ignition system. Daimler was on the brink of fame.

It came first with the original motor cycle, patented on August 29, 1885, and powered by a single-cylinder, 4-stroke engine which could produce 700rpm. Features included fan-cooling, internal

flywheels, an inlet valve which was operated automatically and a mechanically operated exhaust valve. The first rider was Daimler's son Paul, who took it out on a six mile trip on November 10, 1885.

The first car

In fact, Daimler was more interested in experimenting with his motor cycle's engine than in developing his invention commercially. That was left to others. The same year saw him putting another engine on a carriage, a more powerful water-cooled one. In 1886, his four-wheeled petrol-driven car — the first ever produced — was shown in public for the first time.

In the same year Karl Benz constructed a light three-wheeled petrol-engined car. The two men had worked on similar projects at the same period of time in the same country, but they were unknown to each other.

Breakthrough

Daimler's next breakthrough was the Stahlradwagen (steel-wheeled carriage) of 1889. Benz's first car had been designed as an entirely new vehicle, whereas in Daimler's 1886 model the engine had been placed on what was really a carriage made for horse transport.

Daimler realised that the future of motoring lay with special cars and the 1889 car was designed to be just that. Another notable feature was its 2-cylinder V-engine capable of high-

revving. It was far ahead of its time and had a top speed of 17.5kph.

The new car was displayed at the Paris Exhibition. Only the experts realised how good it was and two of them, the Frenchmen, Panhard and Lavassor, began manufacturing cars in France in 1891 using an advanced form of the engine.

Daimler had another decade to live — he died in 1900 — and during that decade his fame increased. He and Maybach never ceased experimenting and they entered their cars for races and endurance trials which showed the growing band of motorists just how reliable the word Daimler was in the booming world of cars.

It was a word to be reckoned with in the world of motor boats as well. Back in 1886, Daimler and his team had built the first motor boat using a petrol engine, which was launched on the River Neckar in August. At that time there was a rumour that petrol engines were liable to explode, so the great inventor decided to disguise his new boat's engine. He covered the vessel with wires and insulators, which made everyone who saw it imagine that it ran on electricity. All went well and four years later the new motor boats went into commercial production. Some of the first customers were the Hamburg Harbour Police.

Royal Transport

Daimler lived to see his motor cars cross the Channel to Britain when in January, 1896, the Daimler Company was registered there. It never looked back, production being continuous except during the two world wars, and Daimler limousines became the most popular form of transport of the Royal Family.

Daimler had not founded the motor manufacturing industry as such. His rival Benz can be said to have done this in 1888. Benz did not die until 1929, three years after a historic amalgamation had taken place when the firm of Benz and Cie amalgamated with Daimler Moteren-Gesellschaft. The new title was Daimler-Benz AG. Strangely enough, Daimler and Benz, who names were to be linked in one of the greatest partnerships in all motoring history, never actually met.

Photos: Mansell Collection

Above: The first car built by the Daimler Company at Coventry. Left: The only surviving example of the 1899 Daimler 'Phoenix' racing car. Five were originally built.

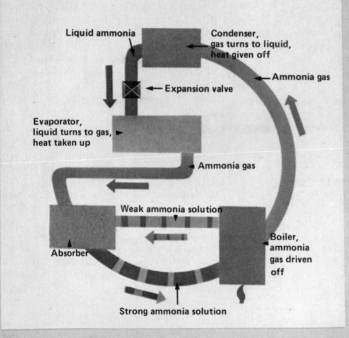

Compressor compresses the vapour

Vapour at high pressure

Vapour at low pressure

Condenser, gas turns to liquid, heat given off

Evaporator, liquid turns to gas, heat taken up

Liquid under high pressure

Liquid under low pressure

Expansion valve

HOW THE REFRIGERANT IS CIRCULATED
Compression (above) and absorption (below) fridges

Liquid ammonia

Condenser, gas turns to liquid, heat given off

Ammonia gas

Expansion valve

Evaporator, liquid turns to gas, heat taken up

Ammonia gas

Weak ammonia solution

Absorber

Boiler, ammonia gas driven off

Strong ammonia solution

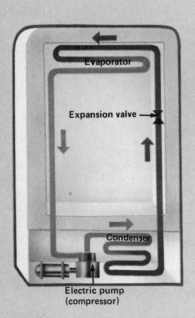

Evaporator

Expansion valve

Condenser

Electric pump (compressor)

The compression fridge is the commoner simpler form of fridge. An electric pump drives the refrigerant round the pipes.

Keeping it cool!

Why a refrigerator has to have heat to make things cold!

FRESH meat from the other side of the world. Ready-to-cook meals prepared three months ago. Precious medical supplies brought to the middle of the desert as cool as when they left the laboratory. These are just some of the ways in which the refrigerator and the freezer have transformed our daily lives.

Imagine how different things used to be. Meat would quickly decay unless it was salted — making it tough and unpalatable — while medicines and vaccines would soon lose their power to com-

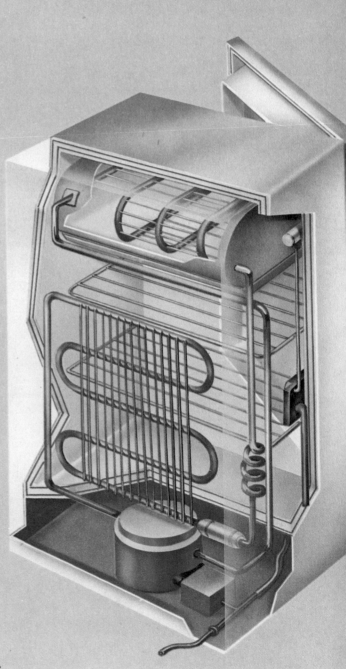

bat disease once exposed to heat. Refrigeration has made our lives more comfortable and played a vital part in public health.

Yet few people know how a refrigerator works. In fact at first sight it seems like a mystery. If you feel the back of a fridge it is hot, yet inside is cold.

How can heat be necessary for cold?

A simple experiment will help to explain. If some water is put into a pan and heated, steam will be given off while the water level gradually goes down. The water is *evaporating* — it is changing from a liquid into a vapour.

Then if a metal saucepan lid is held over the pan, water collects on it and drips back down. The water vapour has *condensed* back to its liquid state because the lid is colder than the boiling point of water. When the water drips back down into the pan, it can be turned back into steam all over again. Something very similar occurs within a refrigerator.

There are two sorts of refrigerator — *compression* refrigerators and *absorption* refrigerators.

Compression fridges are the more common and are often known simply as 'electric fridges'. They have an electric pump or *compressor*. This pumps a liquid called a *refrigerant* round a series of pipes. Usually the refrigerant is a substance called Freon — which contains carbon and flourine, and has a very low boiling point. In other words, it is normally a gas.

As we have seen heat is needed to change a liquid into vapour. In a refrigerator, the Freon changes into vapour inside a series of

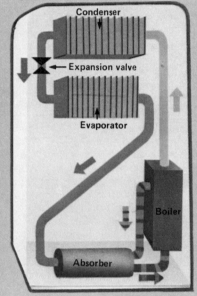

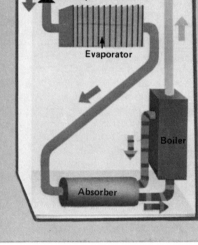

The absorption fridge has the advantage that it has no moving parts. It can run on any fuel, but gas is commonly used.

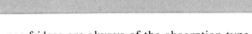

pipes called an *evaporator*. In a domestic fridge, the evaporator pipes are usually part of the ice-making compartment — which is why this is the coldest part of the fridge.

The heat needed to make the Freon evaporate is taken from the ice-making compartment and hence from the whole fridge.

From the evaporator, the Freon is pumped into another series of pipes called a *condensor*. This is the row of pipes at the back of the fridge, and these pipes eventually lead back into the evaporator. But a valve separates the compressor and evaporator. This valve keeps the pressure high in the condensor, low in the evaporator.

As the Freon is pumped into the condensor, it is compressed. If a gas or vapour is compressed enough it will turn into a liquid. This is what happens in the condensor. Just as heat is needed to turn a liquid into a gas, so heat is given off when a gas turns into a liquid. So as the Freon condenses in the condensor, it gives off heat.

That is why the pipes at the back of the fridge are hot. It is here that the heat originally taken from the ice-making compartment is given off into the outside world.

The absorption fridge works a little differently — although the basic principle is the same. The exact way it works is complicated, so a simplified account is given here.

Instead of Freon, a mixture of ammonia gas dissolved in water is used. This mixture is heated in a *boiler*. The boiler can be heated electrically, but it can also by a gas flame, which is why

gas fridges are always of the absorption type.

As the mixture in the boiler is heated, the ammonia boils off and travels up into a condensor. The condensor is outside the fridge and in it the ammonia turns into liquid — giving up heat.

The liquid ammonia then passes through a valve on the other side of which the pressure is much lower. Because the pressure is lower, the liquid is able to turn into gas in the next part of the fridge — the evaporator.

The evaporator is part of the ice-making compartment, and as the liquid ammonia turns into gas it takes heat from the compartment just as in a compression fridge.

The ammonia gas now passes to an *absorber*. This is a tank in which the gas is mixed with some of the weak (mostly water) ammonia solution produced by heating the strong ammonia solution in the boiler. The ammonia dissolves in the weak solution, turning it back into a strong solution. This strong solution passes to the boiler to start the cycle all over again. No pump is necessary. The pressure produced by the evaporating ammonia in the boiler is sufficient to power the fridge.

Both absorption and compression fridges have a device called a *thermostat*. This keeps the fridge at the required temperature. In a gas fridge, the thermostat controls the amount of gas burnt and hence the amount of cooling. In a compression fridge the thermostat switches the pump on when the temperature rises and off when it falls. If you listen to an electric fridge, you will hear the noise the pump makes as it switches off and on.

Quick as a flash
Measuring the speed of light

DID you know that every time you look at the stars shining in the night sky you are gazing into the past? For that light from the stars is light that began its journey across the vastness of Space years before.

Although the speed of light has now been very accurately measured — and is fantastically quick — the stars are so far away that it takes *four years* for the light of the *nearest* star to reach us.

In fact, scientists have been trying to measure the speed of light for centuries. Galileo, the famous 17th century Italian astronomer, tried a very simple experiment involving a lantern placed on a hilltop nearly two kilometres from where he stood. However, his timing instruments were so primitive that the error in timing must have been much greater than the time he was attempting to measure which was less than one hundred-thousandth of a second!

It was in 1675 that Olaus Röemer, a Danish astronomer, made the first reasonably accurate measurement and also suggested that light had a maximum speed which it could not exceed.

By observing and making measurements concerning the eclipses of one of the 11 moons of the planet Jupiter, he came to the conclusion that the speed of light was around 186,000 miles per second (299,274 kilometres per second).

There were no real improvements over Röemer's method and result until the mid-19th century.

In 1849 a French scientist, Armand Fizeau, set about confirming Röemer's figure. But he did not use distant stars or planets to measure the speed of light. His arrangement (pictured opposite) involved a system of mirrors, lenses and a toothed wheel placed at measured distances *on Earth.*

His method was to direct a beam of light through the teeth of a rotating disc on to a mirror five kilometres away. The light was then reflected back another five kilometres.

Since the disc was rotating, the light going outwards through one space between the teeth came back through another space because the disc had moved on. Knowing the speed of the disc's rotation Fizeau was able to calculate how long the light had taken to cover the 10 kilometres.

The result he obtained was close to Röemer's figure but scientists went on researching into even more accurate methods for finding the speed of light.

The next important individual was another Frenchman, Leon Foucault. He was already a well-known scientist when he published the results of his research into the speed of light in 1862.

Foucault's equipment was much simpler than Fizeau's and the light was timed over a much shorter distance; in fact, the whole arrangement was contained in Foucault's laboratory and the distance travelled by the light ray was only 20 metres.

He shone an image on a rapidly rotating mirror, which reflected it to another mirror 10 metres away. By the time the light was reflected back to the first mirror, this had rotated slightly. Foucault could then measure the angle of displacement of the light and, knowing exactly the distances involved, could calculate the speed of light.

He arrived at a value of 298,000 kms for the speed of light in air. But Foucault's method had another advantage. Because it only took up a small space, Foucault could withdraw the air to produce a vacuum or add tubes of water. In different experiments he found light travelled fastest in a vacuum, travelled more slowly in air and travelled through water with only three-quarters of its speed in air.

These discoveries greatly interested a young American researcher, Albert Michelson. He was able to show that not only water affected the speed of light but other denser substances such as different types of glass. And he decided to adapt Foucault's method to obtain a really accurate value for the speed of light.

Michelson spent many years designing high-precision instruments to help him obtain really accurate measurements. His final arrangement, used in 1924, is illustrated below.

Instead of a rotating flat mirror, Michelson used a finely-polished eight-sided rotating mirror to reflect the light. The light source was a powerful arc lamp. The light was reflected from the octagonal mirror to other reflectors over an exact distance of 44 miles (70.81 km). However, by adjusting the speed of rotation of the octagonal mirror, in the time take for the light to return to the rotating mirror it had made exactly one-eighth of a revolution.

Michelson was able to calculate the speed of light as 299,771 kms. Since he

RÖEMER'S METHOD (1675)

Earth's orbit around Sun

Earth

Sun

Earth on far side of Sun

Io

Jupiter

Light path from Io to Earth

Jupiter

Io

Extra distance light has to travel from Io

Röemer knew that Jupiter had several moons and from time to time these passed behind the planet and were eclipsed. But these eclipses did not take place at regular intervals. By observing Io, one of these moons, he realised these irregularities were caused by the Earth changing its position — sometimes it was much nearer to Jupiter. Röemer's inspired guess was that the time-lag was caused by the varying distances travelled by light. Knowing this and the approximate distances involved he produced a figure that was surprisingly accurate for the time.

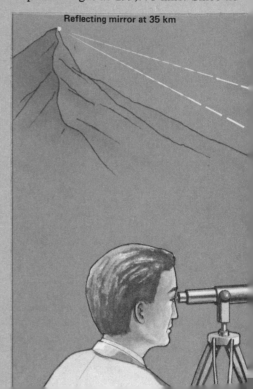

Reflecting mirror at 35 km

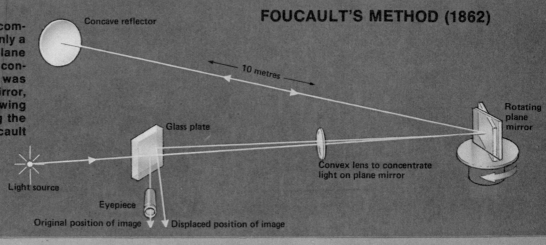

FOUCAULT'S METHOD (1862)

Foucault's apparatus was compact and the light travelled only a short distance. A rotating plane mirror reflected the light to a concave mirror so that when it was reflected back to the plane mirror, it was slightly displaced. Knowing the distances, by measuring the angle of displacement Foucault could estimate the speed of light. Further experiments with this equipment showed that light travelled fastest in a vacuum.

Concave reflector

10 metres

Rotating plane mirror

Glass plate

Convex lens to concentrate light on plane mirror

Light source

Eyepiece

Original position of image   Displaced position of image

FIZEAU'S METHOD (1849)

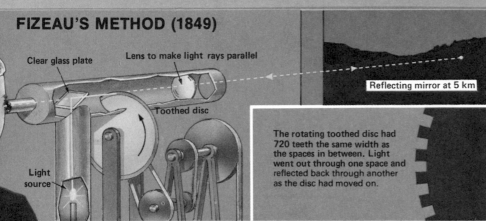

Clear glass plate

Lens to make light rays parallel

Toothed disc

Light source

Reflecting mirror at 5 km

The rotating toothed disc had 720 teeth the same width as the spaces in between. Light went out through one space and reflected back through another as the disc had moved on.

Fizeau had a disc very carefully cut so that it had 720 teeth spaced equally around its rim. This was arranged to rotate and a beam of light was directed through the disc to a distant mirror (at 5 kilometres) and back again to the observer. As he knew the speed of rotation of the disc Fizeau could calculate how long it took the light to travel from the mirror through a space in the disc.

had removed nearly all sources of possible error this was, at that time, the most accurate value ever produced. Comparison with Röemer's result over 200 years before shows how well the Danish astronomer did, with relatively primitive equipment and having to estimate the great distances involved.

Light years

Since then scientists have been able to produce even more experiments to get a more accurate value. These include bouncing a laser beam off a reflector left on the Moon by Apollo astronauts. At present, the speed of light has been most accurately measured as 299,792 kms.

Consideration of how fast light travels give us some idea of the enormous distances involved in our Universe. Light from the Sun takes over eight minutes to reach the Earth over a distance of 150 million kilometres. A space ship travelling at this speed would take one second to reach the Moon!

In fact, scientists now use the measure of *light-years* when talking about the distances of stars and galaxies from the Earth. One light-year is the distance light travels in a single year — nearly ten million, *million* kilometres.

Unlike sound, light does not need any medium, such as air or water, to travel in. It travels fastest through a vacuum like outer Space. There the speed of light never changes.

When you see lightning during a thunderstorm, count the seconds between the flash and its thunder. Both occur at the same time, but because light is so much faster than sound, we see the flash of lightning before we hear the sound of thunder.

MICHELSON'S METHOD (1924)

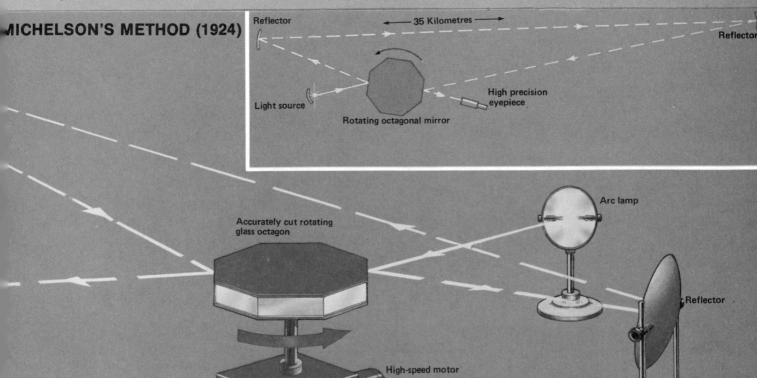

Reflector

35 Kilometres

Reflector

Light source

High precision eyepiece

Rotating octagonal mirror

Accurately cut rotating glass octagon

Arc lamp

Reflector

High-speed motor

Full Speed Ahead

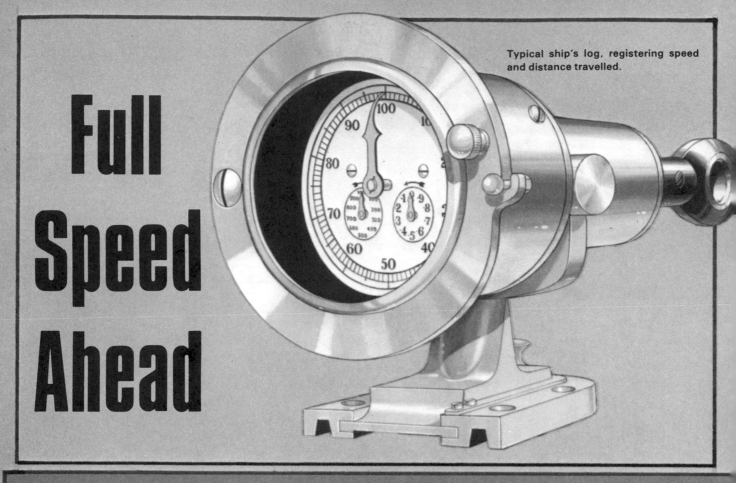

Typical ship's log, registering speed and distance travelled.

Don't call this instrument a speedometer — it's a log

WHEN early mariners first began to understand how to navigate by science rather than guesswork, there used to be an hourly ritual aboard sailing ships. Two seamen would throw a log of wood over the stern and carefully watch a length of cord attached to it.

At intervals along the cord, knots had been tied and, as the cord was paid out over the ship's rail, the knots would pass at a certain rate. Nearby would be an hour-glass which the seamen consulted and, with its help, they could estimate the speed of their vessel by counting the number of knots that passed over the rail in a given time.

It was from this simple method of calculation that we have two nautical terms which survive to this day. *Knots* came to denote a ship's speed — a knot meaning the number of nautical miles a ship travels in one hour. A nautical mile used to be 6,082 feet (1,854m), but this has recently been internationally revised to 6,080 feet, (1,852m), compared to 5,280 feet for a land mile. The term *log* also remains to describe a ship's speedometer, although it is normally referred to as a speed log to distinguish it from the captain's 'log', the written daily account of a voyage.

Mechanical log

There are now much more sophisticated ways of measuring the speed of a ship, and the most familiar of these is the mechanical log illustrated at the top of this page. A torpedo-shaped float is towed at a distance behind the ship to keep it well clear of turbulence caused by the propeller. Movement of the float through the water causes it to turn in a clockwise direction. The cable to which it is attached revolves and, in turn, makes a pointer travel across a recording dial calibrated in knots.

Other speed logs have no moving parts at all, so are instruments not machines. One of these, the venturi, is designed to allow water to pass through it, causing a change in pressure which is proportional to the speed and which can be measured and displayed on a meter.

Magnetic logs, usually fitted to large vessels, have an almost flush skin-fitting which houses a coil and two probes. The coil produces a magnetic field, and the probes sense changes in the field which are amplified electronically and displayed as speed and distance.

Doppler system

Lastly, there is the doppler system which is a form of underwater radar and works in the same was as the radar 'speed traps' used by the police to catch unwary motorists exceeding the speed limit by measuring a frequency shift in a transmitted signal. The shift is caused by the relative movement of a reflecting surface (in this case water) and can be measured electronically.

One of the problems associated with non-mechanical speed logs is that of turbulence close to the ship's hull where this type of device is fitted, and the earlier mechanical logs are still frequently used as a reliable check, even on large modern vessels. The mechanical logs are occasionally trailed in the water from the end of a boom projecting out from the side of a ship in preference to trailing from the stern.

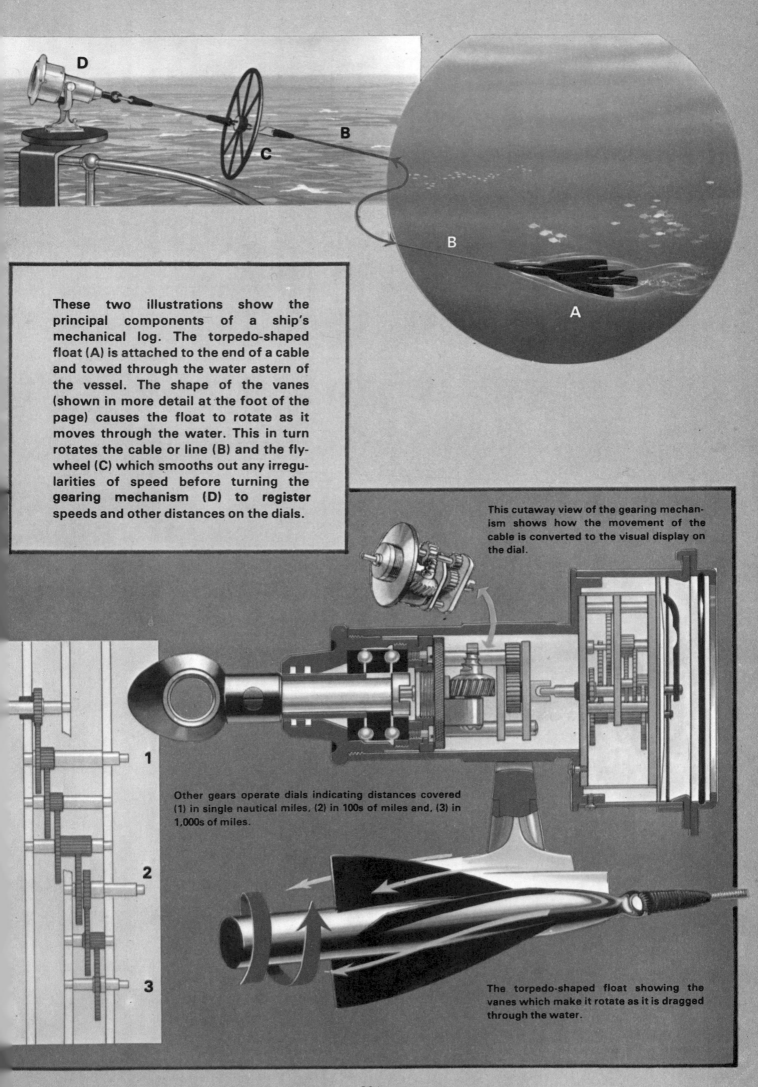

These two illustrations show the principal components of a ship's mechanical log. The torpedo-shaped float (A) is attached to the end of a cable and towed through the water astern of the vessel. The shape of the vanes (shown in more detail at the foot of the page) causes the float to rotate as it moves through the water. This in turn rotates the cable or line (B) and the flywheel (C) which smooths out any irregularities of speed before turning the gearing mechanism (D) to register speeds and other distances on the dials.

This cutaway view of the gearing mechanism shows how the movement of the cable is converted to the visual display on the dial.

Other gears operate dials indicating distances covered (1) in single nautical miles, (2) in 100s of miles and, (3) in 1,000s of miles.

The torpedo-shaped float showing the vanes which make it rotate as it is dragged through the water.

HMS *Invincible* has revolutionized the aircraft carrier.

The Ski-Jump Ship

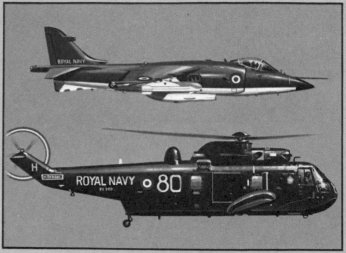

UNDER a stormy sky, a great grey ship ploughs through the seas, white foam smashing against its bows and whipping back across the open expanse of the deck as it patrols in search of submarines. Its navigation officer has fixed his position with minute accuracy using navigation satellites orbiting overhead far out in space.

From the appearance of its big, flat deck and slim island superstructure, masts and funnels set to one side, it is obvious that the ship is an aircraft carrier with as much space as possible left clear for flying operations.

The order is given to launch a Sea Harrier. A large oblong hole suddenly appears as part of the flight deck drops away. One of the lifts is descending to bring the aircraft from the hangar to deck level. The Harrier is quickly checked, the pilot, already briefed (given his instructions), starts the engine and is given permission to take off by the flying control officer perched in his office high above the flight deck.

The roar of the Harrier's engine is audible even above the wind and waves as it rolls forward with its jet exhaust turning the water on the deck to spray and steam.

At the forward end of the flight deck is an upward-sloping ramp — the Sea Harrier swoops up it and instead of levelling off continues upward in a graceful curve until it is in level flight 60 metres above the sea. This sloping ramp is the now famous invention popularly called the 'Ski-jump'.

The aircraft picks up speed and roars away to the position its pilot has fed into his computer. Once there he wheels round and begins releasing small tubes into the water from containers mounted under his wings. The tubes are 'Sonobuoys' — underwater listening devices which can pick up noises from a submarine and sense their direction. A string of them placed by an aircraft will, of course, give a series of 'bearings', or directions for the noise, and where those bearing cross each other — there will be the submarine! Behind the Harrier the ship has launched her big Sea King helicopters with weapons to deal with the submarine . . . . exercises like this keep the ship and her crew at a high pitch of training and readiness.

HMS Invincible (The sixth naval ship to bear that name since 1747) was launched by Her Majesty the Queen on May 3, 1977, and spent until early 1980 being completed and undergoing series of tests of her engines and equipment, starting on March 26, 1979. Then on March 19, 1980 she was officially accepted into

HMS Invincible and her sister ships will operate the two types of aircraft shown above to the same scale. Top, the Sea Harrier jump-jet, length 14.5m, featured on page 324, and the Sea King anti-submarine helicopter, length 17.01m. Both aircraft are, of course, capable of vertical take-off and landing (VTOL).

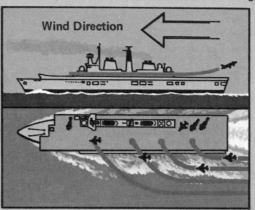

Above, top — The ship does not need to turn into the wind for launching as an ordinary carrier must. Similarly, because they land vertically, a number of aircraft can land at the same time (above) and regardless of wind direction.

Winches and cab for raising/dropp ship's anchors

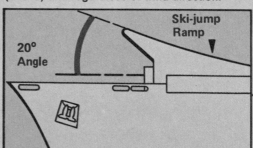

HMS Invincible is fitted with a 7° angle ski-jump launching ramp, but the best ski-jump angle is 20°. Later ships may have ramps as shown above. The diagrams below show the difference between a flat deck launch and a ski-jump take-off.

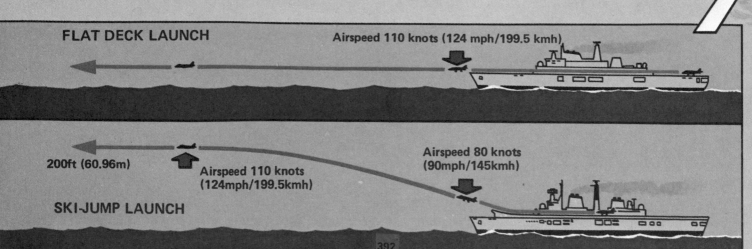

FLAT DECK LAUNCH Airspeed 110 knots (124 mph/199.5 kmh)

200ft (60.96m) Airspeed 110 knots (124mph/199.5kmh) Airspeed 80 knots (90mph/145kmh)

SKI-JUMP LAUNCH

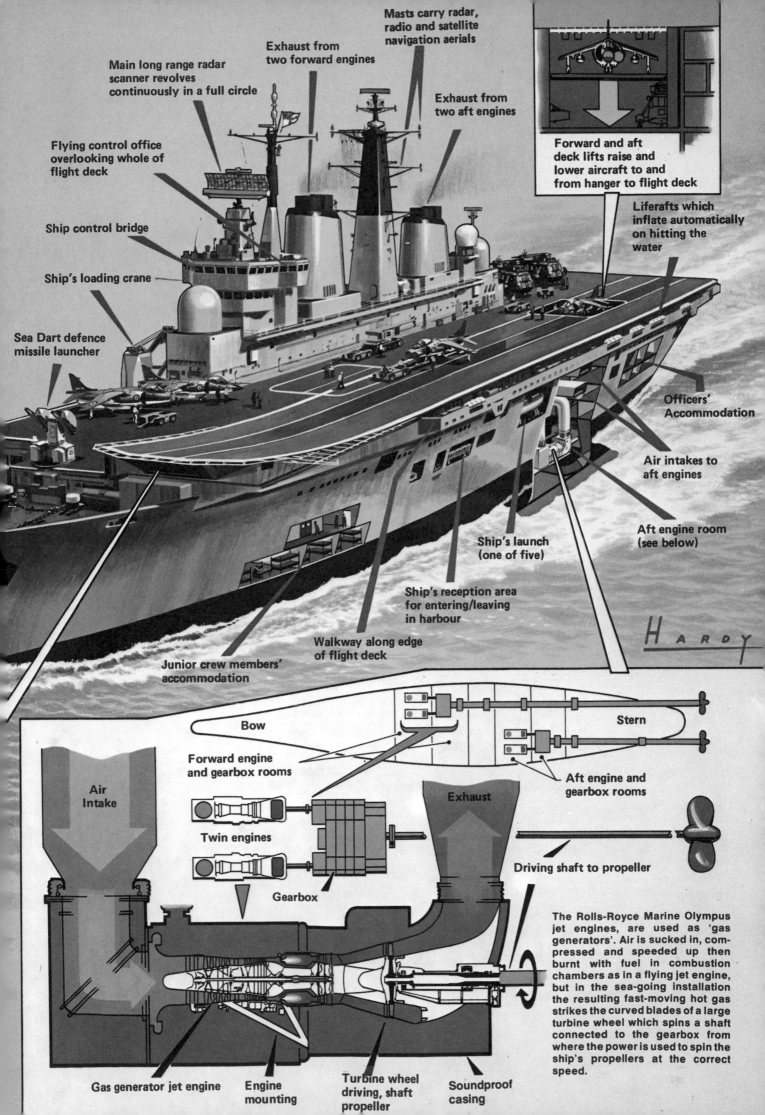

Masts carry radar, radio and satellite navigation aerials

Exhaust from two forward engines

Main long range radar scanner revolves continuously in a full circle

Exhaust from two aft engines

Flying control office overlooking whole of flight deck

Forward and aft deck lifts raise and lower aircraft to and from hanger to flight deck

Ship control bridge

Liferafts which inflate automatically on hitting the water

Ship's loading crane

Sea Dart defence missile launcher

Officers' Accommodation

Air intakes to aft engines

Aft engine room (see below)

Ship's launch (one of five)

Ship's reception area for entering/leaving in harbour

HARDY

Junior crew members' accommodation

Walkway along edge of flight deck

Bow

Stern

Forward engine and gearbox rooms

Aft engine and gearbox rooms

Air Intake

Exhaust

Twin engines

Driving shaft to propeller

Gearbox

The Rolls-Royce Marine Olympus jet engines, are used as 'gas generators'. Air is sucked in, compressed and speeded up then burnt with fuel in combustion chambers as in a flying jet engine, but in the sea-going installation the resulting fast-moving hot gas strikes the curved blades of a large turbine wheel which spins a shaft connected to the gearbox from where the power is used to spin the ship's propellers at the correct speed.

Gas generator jet engine

Engine mounting

Turbine wheel driving, shaft propeller

Soundproof casing

How the Aircraft Carrier developed

H.M.S. Furious
completed, as carrier, 1917

H.M.S. Ark Royal
Launched 1937

Feet								
0	100	200	300	400	500	600	700	8

0	30	60	90		180	210

Metres

U.S.S. Enterprise
Launched 1961

H.M.S. Invincible
Launched May 3rd, 1977
accepted into service March 19th 1980

service by the Royal Navy. She is the largest warship built for the navy in 25 years and the largest in the western world powered solely by gas turbines (jet engines). *Invincible* saw action in the Falklands War in 1982.

She is 209.6m long overall, 192.8m long at the waterline and her draught (depth below the water surface) is 6.5m. Her flight deck is 31.9m wide and she displaces 19,810 tonnes.

Four Rolls-Royce Marine Olympus engines (see diagrams) give her a maximum speed of 28 knots (31.5mph, 50.66kmh) and a range (maximum sailing distance without refuelling) of over 8,000kms (roughly 5,000 miles) at 18 knots (20.25mph, 32.5kmh). High standard accommodation is provided for over 1,000 officers and men, including an Admiral and his staff and the ship's air squadron.

She carries five British Aerospace Sea Harriers and nine Westland Sea King helicopters. The ski-jump ramp at the bow is used only by the Harriers and was specifically designed to take advantage of the unique way in which the aircraft can support itself in the air on engine power alone without lift from its wings.

Using the ski-jump the aircraft can take off at a lower speed

The four scale views of aircraft carriers, above, and the other illustrations on these pages, show how different and much more easy the task of operating aircraft at sea has been made by the use of V/STOL Sea Harriers. *HMS Furious,* the first of all carriers, was converted from her original design as a cruiser and had separate landing and take-off decks behind and in front of her superstructure. *HMS Ark Royal* was a typical World War II carrier with a straight flight deck. The 1960's brought the first of America's enormous super-carriers, the mighty nuclear-powered *U.S.S. Enterprise,* fitted with an angled deck (see opposite page, top right). *HMS Invincible* does not need an enormous flight deck or any of the equipment shown opposite.

with a shorter run along the deck and carry a much greater load into the air. What the ramp does is to launch the Harrier on an upward flight path. As it leaves the ramp at low speed it is not flying — that is to say is is not being supported by lift from its wings — so the continuation upwards is maintained by the thrust of the engine alone. After about 10 seconds the Harrier has increased speed to the point where it can start to level out into normal wingborne flight.

Arrester Hook

Arrester Wires

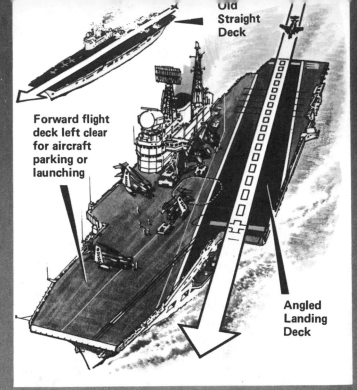

Old Straight Deck

Forward flight deck left clear for aircraft parking or launching

Angled Landing Deck

The first major problem to be overcome in carriers was that of stopping the aircraft quickly and safely on landing. The solution eventually adopted was the arrester system. This used, and still uses, on conventional carriers, a retractable hook at the rear of the aircraft which catches one of a series of thick wires stretched across the flight deck. There are usually five wires and the ideal to hook is number three. The wires are fitted with a hydraulic system which makes them extend to stop the aircraft quickly but smoothly. They must be set correctly for each type of aircraft before it lands.

The angled deck, a simple yet ingenious British invention revolutionised carrier flying in the 1950's. As high-speed jets came into use it became more and more dangerous to land them on the straight flight deck. Other aircraft parked at the bow might be hit by a landing aircraft. The angled deck gave a separate landing area pointing away from the forward flight deck where other aircraft could be safely parked and launched.

As her other aircraft are helicopters *Invincible* needs none of the complicated equipment used by conventional aircraft carriers. For example, a giant American super-carrier launching her aircraft needs to turn into the wind and steam at high speed to create a WOD (Wind Over The Deck) of about 48kmh (30mph). Although a WOD eases the take-off of a heavily-loaded Sea Harrier it is not necessary for *Invincible* to even alter course into the wind or increase speed for launching, thus saving much time and fuel.

Our supercarrier must next create queues of aircraft at her catapults to launch them. The steam catapults, a British invention, use steam from the ship's engines (plus the help of the aircraft's own engine/s at maximum power) to hurl them off the deck with enough acceleration for the wings to support the aircraft as it leaves the ship and climbs away. The launch rate achieved is about one plane a minute.

To land her aircraft the supercarrier must create WOD again and bring them in one by one, clearing them from the landing area angled deck as quickly as possible (The landing area must be sufficiently large to cope with heavy jets landing at high speed). The aircraft come in at relatively high speed so that if they miss the wires they have enough speed in hand to open the throttles wide and climb away safely to join the queue again. Any mishap closes the landing area to other aircraft until it is cleared, so they must have enough extra fuel to "wait" in the sky if necessary.

Invincible's V/STOL (Vertical/Short Take-Off and Landing) aircraft need only their own deck spot to land on and can come aboard (Or recover to use the correct expression) without the ship altering course or speed. Four Sea Harriers, for example, returning to the ship can arrive in formation, reduce speed, gradually transferring from wing lift to hovering on engine power, come alongside the flight deck and land vertically aboard at the same moment.

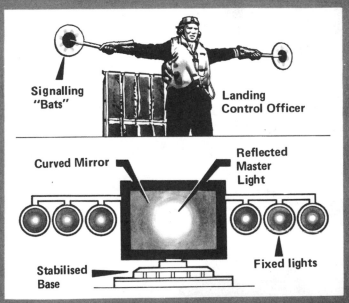

Signalling "Bats"

Landing Control Officer

Curved Mirror

Reflected Master Light

Stabilised Base

Fixed lights

Above:— At one time a control officer would be stationed on the edge of the flight deck to guide pilots down using hand signals and signalling 'bats'. As landing speeds increased hand signals were no longer fast enough and the human was replaced by the mirror sight. The landing pilot has to fly so as to keep the fixed and reflected lights in line. Another British invention was the steam catapult (below) which provided enough power to launch big, heavy jets safely.

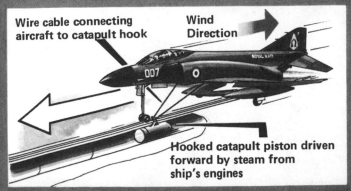

Wire cable connecting aircraft to catapult hook

Wind Direction

Hooked catapult piston driven forward by steam from ship's engines

The thin end of the wedge

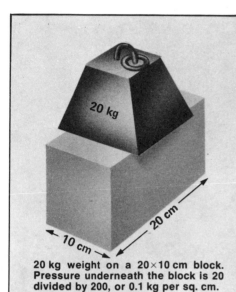

20 kg weight on a 20×10 cm block. Pressure underneath the block is 20 divided by 200, or 0.1 kg per sq. cm.

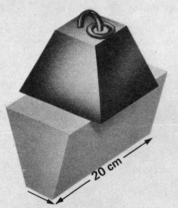

If the block is narrowed at its base so that its area is only 20×5 cm, pressure is 20 divided by 100, or 0.2 kg per sq. cm.

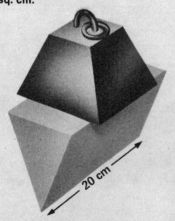

If the block is narrowed to a wedge, the area is 20×0 cm. Pressure is 20 divided by 0 or infinitely large.

How a wedge works. Because the area of cutting edge is so small (in theory it is zero) the pressure on the edge is very large (in theory infinite). The great pressure forces the wedge in, cutting into even the hardest materials.

MANY thousands of years ago lived one of Man's remote ancestors called *Homo habilis*, or 'Handyman' to give him his non-scientific name. He was a toolmaker, as we know from uncovering some of the beautifully shaped flints that he used as knives, axes and general-purpose tools for hunting and homemaking.

These flint blades were cut in wedge shapes, because Handyman had learned from experience that the wedge enabled him both to cut the skins off a hunted animal and to split a length of wood — perhaps to make a spit to roast his dinner on.

So the wedge is probably the first tool that Man ever had.

It is also the simplest of tools. It works on the principle that it is easier to get an object into a small or tight space when the front of the object is narrow.

Perhaps the most common example is the knife. If you look at a sharp knife, you will see that the metal of the body of the blade is really quite thick. Yet the cutting edge is ground very fine. Sharpening is really wedge-making; the sharp edge slips into the thing we are cutting while the rest of the blade follows on behind.

Let's look more closely at this. The wedge is a kind of machine. That is, it is a method of using a force more efficiently. It enables the force to be applied gently rather than energetically, yet still get the desired effect.

The diagrams on the left show how this is done. Because one edge of the wedge is blunt, one sharp, the force originally applied to a large area is concentrated into a very small area.

Pressure is calculated by dividing a force by the area over which it acts, so when the force is concentrated onto a very small area, the pressure is very great. It is this very high pressure that enables the wedge to cut into even hard objects.

After the edge of the wedge has entered a body, how much force is then needed to push it in? That depends on the thickness of the wedge. A broad wedge pushes a body apart more rapidly so it needs a greater force to push it in. A thin wedge, on the other hand, needs less force to push in, but because it is thinner it has to be pushed in farther to open the body up as far as a thick wedge pushed a short distance.

Compare the wedge to a hill. The steeper the slope, the harder the walk to get to the top. The more gradual the slope, the longer the distance but the easier the climb. So too with a wedge.

There is another factor to bear in mind as well. What material are you going to try to split or cut with your wedge? A surgeon's knife wouldn't be appropriate for chopping wood, nor would an axe be of much use to a doctor! But there is nothing that can't be cut once the thin end of the wedge has been forced home.

The sloping sides of the wedge are used to split wood. As the wedge is forced in, the tissues of the wood are slowly spread apart.

If you look at the cutting edge of a knife, a scalpel, a chisel or any other blade, you will see that it is quite sharply tapered as in the diagram above left. Very fine edges, like that above right, although they cut easily also break easily.

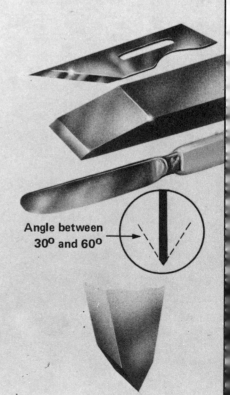

Angle between 30° and 60°

Index

This edition first published 1985 by
Deans International Publishing
Bridge House, 69 London Road, Twickenham, Middlesex, TW1 3SB
A Division of The Hamlyn Publishing Group Limited
London · New York · Sydney · Toronto
Reprinted 1986
Copyright © IPC Magazines Ltd., 1979, 1980, 1981, 1982, 1985
Copyright this arrangement © The Hamlyn Publishing Group Limited 1982, 1985
ISBN 0 603 00447 4

Printed in Yugoslavia